# OXFORD MONOGRAPHS ON
# CLASSICAL ARCHAEOLOGY

*Edited by*

J. D. BEAZLEY

BERNARD ASHMOLE

*Oxford University Press, Amen House, London E.C.4*

GLASGOW   NEW YORK   TORONTO   MELBOURNE   WELLINGTON
BOMBAY   CALCUTTA   MADRAS   KARACHI   KUALA LUMPUR
CAPE TOWN   IBADAN   NAIROBI   ACCRA

# THE
# LOCAL SCRIPTS OF
# ARCHAIC GREECE

A STUDY OF
THE ORIGIN OF THE GREEK ALPHABET
AND ITS DEVELOPMENT FROM THE
EIGHTH TO THE FIFTH CENTURIES B.C.

BY

## L. H. JEFFERY

OXFORD
AT THE CLARENDON PRESS
1961

© *Oxford University Press 1961*

PRINTED IN GREAT BRITAIN
AT THE UNIVERSITY PRESS, OXFORD
BY VIVIAN RIDLER
PRINTER TO THE UNIVERSITY

† T. T. J.

*patri dilecto*

# PREFACE

THIS book was begun in 1937 as a study of the *boustrophedon* system in early Greek inscriptions, and was cut short, like many other studies of the kind, by the war of 1939–45. In 1947 it was begun again on a larger scale and accepted as a thesis for the degree of Doctor of Philosophy at Oxford in 1951. The material of Parts I and II has undergone little alteration between thesis and book; the views remain substantially as they were first presented, though many have lost any novelty that they had when they were first written. In Part III the Catalogues of inscriptions have been expanded to include material published since 1951, and parts of the text have been modified or rewritten.

The aim of this work has been to produce a chronological framework for the study of archaic Greek inscriptions, based on the twenty-five year period which is now in standard use for the studies of Greek sculpture and pottery. Inevitably, I have reared much of my framework on the enduring foundations laid by the great epigraphists Kirchhoff, Roehl, Roberts, and Larfeld two generations ago; but many more early inscriptions have been published in the intervening years, so that it is now possible to essay a closer dating of the known examples. It may be a long time, however, not merely before the absolute dating of early Greek lettering can be securely achieved, but even before the relative dating of the inscriptions can be as soundly established as are those of the sculpture and pottery. In the analysis of letter-forms one is conscious all too often of resorting to general impressions, with the attendant risk that what goes in at one door as a hypothesis may come out at another as a fact. But the analysis of letter-forms must remain in most cases the chief aid for dating any archaic inscription, since comparatively few of these records refer to known people or events.

I have tried throughout to remember that, particularly where archaic inscriptions are concerned, epigraphy is a branch of archaeology; the letters are written on objects of varying type and material, and inscription and object must be considered in relation to each other. The epigraphist may not agree with the absolute date assigned by the experts concerned to a vase or figurine, but he cannot afford to ignore it. He can afford, perhaps, to be more dogmatic when dispute arises over an inscribed object's place of origin, for the differences between Greek local scripts, though sometimes small, are usually identifiable. Like a wine-taster, the epigraphist may go wrong over the year, but not over the district.

Basically, then, the approach of this book is archaeological. I have not attempted to discuss philological points except when essaying a new reading; and historical problems have, in many cases, had only summary treatment. Even on the epigraphic side there are, unavoidably, many gaps. The size of the subject forced me to omit any fifth-century material from Attica, while elsewhere lack of material has hampered any attempt to date the end of a local script in any but the vaguest terms. I have made use of coin legends wherever possible, but have had very reluctantly to omit any coins from the plates, mainly for reasons of space. The bibliographies in Part III are selective, and I cannot hope that my principles of selection will square with those of everyone else. In the spelling of Greek names the intention has been, for place-names, to keep only such long-established English or Latin forms as Athens, Corinth, Mycenae, and to spell the rest as in Greek, including any modern places where ancient Greek words are retained (e.g. Hagios Georgios, not Ayios Yeoryios; but Tourkovrysi, Vourva); and, for personal names, to reduce all to the Attic form; but inconsistencies have crept in despite all efforts at uniformity.

Later generations will count fortunate those of us who studied archaeology in Oxford in the years following the end of the war. Among the many people who helped me to write this book, I wish to record my debt of gratitude above all to five Oxford scholars. Dr. M. N. Tod, *archegetes* of present British epigraphists, was my first guide and teacher in this field, and his wise counsel and never-failing assistance have been an inspiration throughout the work. Sir John Beazley, in addition to many other kindnesses, read all the proofs, gently curing blemishes of style or content on almost every page. Professor H. T. Wade-Gery discussed many points and threw new light on all of them, especially on the part played in early Greek history by the settlement at Al Mina. Mr. R. Meiggs has given most generous help throughout, and has also read, and greatly improved, the proofs. Finally, all who knew the late Mr. T. J. Dunbabin will recognize how much this book owes to the unrivalled archaeological knowledge which he placed ungrudgingly at the service of his friends.

I also owe especial gratitude to Professor Rhys Carpenter, whose work on the origin of the Greek alphabet proved a starting-point for a whole generation of historians and epigraphists, and who read this text in 1952, and contributed many stimulating suggestions and well-justified corrections: to Dr. E. S. G. Robinson and Dr. C. M. Kraay, for valuable help in all numismatic problems: to Professor G. R. Driver, for similar help on the Semitic side: and to the late Mr. S. G. Campbell, to whom I owe my first introduction to Greek philology and epigraphy at Cambridge over twenty years ago. At the time of his death in 1956 he was working on a projected revision of E. S. Roberts's *Introduction to Greek Epigraphy*, and when I was preparing this book for the Clarendon Press I had the great privilege, through the generosity of his widow, of receiving all the notes and references which he had collected, which provided a most valuable check, particularly for the catalogues.

Many other scholars have helped me generously in other ways, among them notably: Professor E. Akurgal, Professor J. K. Anderson, Mr. J. Boardman, Mr. R. M. Cook, Mr. P. E. Corbett, Professor G. Daux, Mr. P. M. Fraser, Mr. D. E. L. Haynes, Mr. B. G. Kallipolitis, Dr. and Mme C. Karouzos, Miss I. K. Konstantinou, Mr. I. D. Kontes, Dr. N. M. Kontoleon, Dr. E. Kunze, Mr. D. I. Lazarides, Mr. E. I. Mastrokostas, Professor B. D. Meritt, Dr. M. Th. Mitsos, Mr. R. V. Nicholls, Dr. I. Papademetriou, Dr. B. Philippaki, Dr. N. E. Platon, Dr. J. Pouilloux, Miss L. Talcott, Dr. I. Threpsiades, Mr. E. Vanderpool, Mr. N. M. Verdelis, Dr. C. C. Vermeule, and, most recently, that anonymous team of guides well known to the world of scholars, the readers and other technical experts of the Clarendon Press, whose combination of meticulous scholarship and resourceful skill brings every author placed in their care over the crevasses of his own errors, and safely to the summit. I wish also to record my deep gratitude to Sir John

Beazley and the late Professor P. Jacobsthal for accepting this work for inclusion in the Oxford Monographs on Classical Archaeology, to the Delegates of the University Press for undertaking the onerous task of publishing it, and, for generous grants to help to meet the high cost of publication, to the British Academy, the Committee for Advanced Studies and the Craven Committee (Oxford University), the Jowett Copyright Trustees (Balliol College), and the Trustees of the Eleanor Lodge and Elizabeth Levett memorial funds (Lady Margaret Hall). I owe long-standing debts of thanks to Newnham College, the British School of Archaeology at Athens, the Institute for Advanced Studies at Princeton, and Lady Margaret Hall, for the scholarships, studentships, and research fellowships which, between 1937 and 1951, gave me the means and leisure to collect the material and write this book. Lastly, I record here my thanks to my sister Mrs. J. Neufville Taylor, *unanima soror*, but for whose continual help at all stages of the work I should never have managed to complete it.

*Lady Margaret Hall, Oxford*                                                          L. H. JEFFERY
*June 1960*

# NOTES TO THE READER

(i) The 'blue' and 'red' of Kirchhoff's original colour-chart are retained here purely as conventional terms to denote the different forms of *xi, chi,* and *psi:* that is, *chi* X and *psi* Ψ are 'blue', *xi* X and *chi* Ψ are 'red'. It has long been recognized that (contrary to Kirchhoff's belief) neither racial nor geographic factors account always for this distinction; thus the Ionic neighbours Attica and Euboia differ over *chi,* and the Doric neighbours Rhodes and Knidos over both *xi* and *chi.* It is possible that, in some similarities at least, early trade-routes between states may be reflected. (ii) It is assumed without discussion that the letter M which appears in some inscriptions, and in archaic abecedaria between *pi* and *qoppa* (i.e. in the place of *ṣāḏê* in the Phoenician), is the sibilant letter which the Greeks called *san.* (iii) Since our word 'alphabet' has two shades of meaning—the general concept of letters, and the actual written row of signs—the word 'abecedarium' is here used for the written row, for which the Greeks perhaps used the term στοῖχος. (iv) In the transliteration of epigraphic texts the lengthened ē and ō are used only for those vowels which would be spelt with η and ω in the standard (i.e. post-Euclidic) Attic script and dialect. (v) *Figures in the text.* Since majuscule type can give a misleading idea of an epichoric letter-form, I have adopted the method—cumbersome, but, I hope, more accurate—of prefacing the sections on the letters in Part I (pp. 23 ff.) and on each local script in Part III by a text-figure showing the various forms of each letter, numbered (α1, α2, &c.), and of then referring in the text to these forms. The conventions used in the text-figures are as follows (see, for example, p. 109, Fig. 32, Aigina): the vertical order 1, 2, &c., normally shows the chronological development; but a comma linking (e.g.) α2 and α3 means that these are merely variants, α3 not necessarily later than α2. A dash (—) at the top means that this letter was not used. A blank space at the top means that, though existing inscriptions give no example, the early form may well have been used; the inscriptions either are all too late in date to show it, or else are early, but chance not to need that letter.

# ACKNOWLEDGEMENTS FOR ILLUSTRATIONS

I DESIRE to offer my thanks for those photographs, and the permission to publish them, which are due to the kind courtesy of the following: the Trustees of the British Museum (Plates 15, **4**; 19, **9**; 27, **14, 18**; 38, **53**; 42, **6**; 45, **5**; 46, **10**; 47, **3**; 50, **8**; 51, **7**; 64, **29**; 67, **8**; 69, **41, 47**; 72, **75**); Metropolitan Museum of Art, New York (Plates 3, **20**; 4, **32, 34**; 6, **24**; 29, **26**; 40, **11**; 48, **22**; 51, **15**; 53, **1**; 60, **18**; 68, **30**); Deutsches Archäologisches Institut, Athen (Plates 3, **21**; 17, **21**; 21, 29, **38**; 36, **15, 19**; 43, **21**; 46, **13**; 49, **19**; 63, **21**; 71, **35**); American School of Classical Studies at Athens (Plates 1, **4**; 2, **9c**; 4, **33**; 21, 35, **37**; 22, **1**; 66, **61**); Museum of Fine Arts, Boston (Department of Classical Art) (Plates 6, **22**; 7, **1**; 15, **17**; 19, **13**; 39, **64, 67**; 53, **4**); National Museum, Athens (Plates 10, **20**; 11, **10**; 14, **2**; 31, **2**; 41, **27**; 55, **2**); Staatliche Museen zu Berlin (Antiken-Abteilung) (Plates 37, **29**; 62, **23**; 64, **33**); École française d'Athènes (Plates 12, **4**; 33, **7**; 58, **61, 76**); Musée du Louvre, Paris (Plates 9, **18**; 19, **14b**); Archäologisches Institut der Universität Bonn (Plate 10, **22**); Barber Institute of Fine Arts, University of Birmingham (Plate 44, **6**); Deutsches Archäologisches Institut, Rom (Plate 47, **1**); Greek Archaeological Society (Plate 22, **2**); Kunsthistorisches Museum (Antikensammlung), Wien (Plate 53, **51**); Musées Royaux du Cinquantenaire, Brussels (Plate 36, **25**); Museum of Art, Rhode Island School of Design, Providence (Plate 9, **16**); La Soprintendenza alle Antichità, Firenze (Plate 48, **18**); the Syndics of the Fitzwilliam Museum, Cambridge (Plate 42, **1**); Dr. Adamesteanu (Plate 53, **50**); Professor E. Akurgal (Plate 72, **73**); Professor G. E. Bean (Plate 71, **50**); Mr. J. Boardman (Plate 65, **42e**); Dr. H. Cahn (Plate 68, **32a**); Mr. I. D. Kontes (Plate 67, **13**).

Thanks are due also to the following for permission to reproduce illustrations: American School of Classical Studies at Athens, for Plates 2, **9e**; 4, **44**; 29, **30**, from *Hesperia*; Archaeological Institute of America, for Plates 1, **3a–c**; 25, **11**, from *American Journal of Archaeology*, and Plate 4, **43**, from A. E. Raubitschek, *Dedications from the Athenian Akropolis*; the Council of the Society for the Promotion of Hellenic Studies, for Plates 16, **2**; 22, **6**; 37, **49**; 40, **38**; 54, **1**; 66, **69**, from *Journal of Hellenic Studies*; Istituto di Archeologia e Storia dell'Arte, Roma, for Plates 59, **12**; 60, **15, 19a, 29a**, from *Inscriptiones Creticae*; the Managing Committee of the British School of Archaeology at Athens, for Plates 16, **1**; 45, **1, 2**; 65, **41**; 71, **41**, from *Annual of the British School of Archaeology at Athens*; Oxford University Press, for Plate 3, **29**, from R. P. Austin, *The Stoichedon Style in Greek Inscriptions*, and Plates 18, **7**; 19, **12**; 20, **17**, from H. Payne, *Perachora* i; Verlag Gebr. Mann, Berlin, for Plates 2, **17**, from Kirchner, *Imagines Inscriptionum Atticarum*; 23, **8**; 66, **63**, from *Athenische Mitteilungen*; the Trustees of the British Museum, for Plate 66, **53**, from D. G. Hogarth, *Excavations at Ephesus: the Archaic Artemisia*.

# CONTENTS

# LIST OF PLATES

*(at end)*

# ABBREVIATIONS

| | |
|---|---|
| *AA* | *Archäologischer Anzeiger* (in *JdI*). |
| *AAG* | G. M. A. Richter, *Archaic Attic Gravestones*, 1944. |
| *Abh. Ak. Berlin (Wien, &c.)* | *Abhandlungen der Akademie der Wissenschaft zu Berlin (Wien, &c.).* |
| *ABV* | J. D. Beazley, *Attic Black-Figure Vase-painters*, 1956. |
| *AD* | *Antike Denkmaeler.* |
| *A. Delt.* | Ἀρχαιολογικὸν Δελτίον. |
| *AE* | Ἀρχαιολογικὴ Ἐφημερίς (1910–; previously Ἐφημερὶς Ἀρχαιολογική). |
| *AGA* | G. M. A. Richter, *Archaic Greek Art*, 1949. |
| *AH* | C. Waldstein, *The Argive Heraeum* i–ii, 1902–5. |
| *AJ* | *Antiquaries' Journal.* |
| *AJA* | *American Journal of Archaeology.* |
| *AJP* | *American Journal of Philology.* |
| *AM* | *Mitteilungen des deutschen archäologischen Instituts: Athenische Abteilung.* |
| *Ann.* | *Annuario della Scuola Archeologica di Atene e delle Missioni italiane in Oriente.* |
| *AO* | *The Sanctuary of Artemis Orthia at Sparta*, 1929, ed. R. M. Dawkins. |
| Arangio-Ruiz | V. Arangio-Ruiz and A. Olivieri, *Inscriptiones Graecae Siciliae et infimae Italiae ad ius pertinentes*, 1925. |
| *Arch. Class.* | *Archeologia Classica.* |
| *ARV* | J. D. Beazley, *Attic Red-Figure Vase-painters*, 1942. |
| *ATL* | B. D. Meritt, H. T. Wade-Gery, M. F. Macgregor, *Athenian Tribute Lists* i–iv, 1939–53. |
| *AZ* | *Archäologische Zeitung.* |
| B | E. Babelon, *Traité des monnaies grecques et romaines*, i–iii, 1901–32. |
| *BCH* | *Bulletin de correspondance hellénique.* |
| Bérard² | J. Bérard, *La Colonisation grecque de l'Italie méridionale et de la Sicile dans l'antiquité*, ed. 2, 1956. |
| *BMC* | *British Museum Catalogue of . . .* |
| *BMI* | *The Collection of Ancient Greek Inscriptions in the British Museum* i–iv, 1876–1916. |
| *BSA* | *Annual of the British School at Athens.* |
| *BSR* | *Papers of the British School at Rome.* |
| Buck | C. D. Buck, *The Greek Dialects*, 1955. |
| *Bull. Metr. Mus.* | *Bulletin of the Metropolitan Museum of Art, New York.* |
| *CAH* | *Cambridge Ancient History.* |
| *CIG* | *Corpus Inscriptionum Graecarum* i–iv. |
| Conze | A. Conze, *Die attischen Grabreliefs* i–ii, 1890–4. |
| *CP* | *Classical Philology.* |
| *CQ* | *Classical Quarterly.* |
| *CR* | *Classical Review.* |
| *CRAI* | *Comptes rendus de l'Académie des Inscriptions et Belles-Lettres.* |
| *CVA* | *Corpus Vasorum Antiquorum.* |
| *DAA* | A. E. Raubitschek, *Dedications from the Athenian Akropolis*, 1949. |
| *DABF* | J. D. Beazley, *The Development of Attic Black-figure*, 1951. |
| *DGE* | E. Schwyzer, *Dialectorum Graecarum exempla epigraphica potiora*, 1923. |
| *DLZ* | *Deutsche Litteraturzeitung.* |

DM                            *Mitteilungen des deutschen archäologischen Instituts*, i–vi.
Driver                        G. R. Driver, *Semitic Writing*, ed. 2, 1954.
Dunbabin                      T. J. Dunbabin, *The Western Greeks*, 1948.

*FA*                          *Fasti Archaeologici.*
*FD*                          *Fouilles de Delphes.*
*FGB*                         E. Langlotz, *Frühgriechische Bildhauerschulen* i–ii, 1927.
*FGH*                         F. Jacoby, *Die Fragmente der griechischen Historiker*, 1922–.
*FHG*                         C. and T. Müller and V. Langlois, *Fragmenta Historicorum Graecorum* i–v,
                              1848–70.
Fick-Bechtel                  A. Fick and F. Bechtel, *Die griechischen Personennamen*, ed. 2, 1894.
FR                            A. Furtwaengler and K. Reichhold, *Griechische Vasenmalerei*, 1904–32.
Friedlaender                  P. Friedlaender and H. B. Hoffleit, *Epigrammata*, 1948.

*GHI²*                        M. N. Tod, *A Selection of Greek Historical Inscriptions to the end of the Fifth
                              Century B.C.*, ed. 2, 1946.
GL                            B. Graef and E. Langlotz, *Die antiken Vasen von der Akropolis zu Athen* i–ii,
                              1909–33.

*HN²*                         B. V. Head, *Historia Numorum*, ed. 2, 1911.

*IAOSPE*                      B. Latyschev, *Inscriptiones antiquae orae septentrionalis Ponti Euxini Graecae et
                              Latinae* i–iv, 1885–1916.
*IC*                          M. Guarducci, *Inscriptiones Creticae* i–iv, 1935–50.
*ID*                          A. Plassart, *Inscriptions de Délos* (nos. 1–88), 1950.
*IG*; *IG* i², &c.            *Inscriptiones Graecae*; i², &c., ed. minor (1924–).
*IGA*                         H. Roehl, *Inscriptiones Graecae antiquissimae*, 1882.
*IGB*                         E. Loewy, *Inschriften griechischer Bildhauer*, 1885.
*IIA²*                        J. Kirchner, *Imagines Inscriptionum Atticarum*, ed. 2, 1948.

*JdI*                         *Jahrbuch des deutschen archäologischen Instituts.*
*JHS*                         *Journal of Hellenic Studies.*

*K. Ch.*                      Κρητικὰ Χρονικά.
Kern                          O. Kern, *Inscriptiones Graecae*, 1913.
Kirchhoff⁴                    A. Kirchhoff, *Studien zur Geschichte des griechischen Alphabets*, ed. 4, 1887.
*Kouroi*                      G. M. A. Richter, *Kouroi*, 1942.
*KZ*                          A. Kuhn, *Zeitschrift für vergleichende Sprachforschung.*

Larfeld³                      W. Larfeld, *Griechische Epigraphik*, ed. 3, 1914.
Lindian Chronicle             Chr. Blinkenberg, *Lindos* ii. 1 (1941), Inscriptions, no. 2.
Lippold, *Griech. Plastik*    G. Lippold, *Die griechische Plastik* (Handbuch d. Archäologie, Otto and
                              Herbig, iii. 1), 1950.
LSJ                           Liddell and Scott, Greek Lexicon, ed. 9 (Stuart Jones and McKenzie), 1940.

*MA*                          *Monumenti Antichi pubblicati per cura dell'Accademia Nazionale dei Lincei.*
Marcadé i, ii                 J. Marcadé, *Recueil des signatures des sculpteurs grecs* i, 1953; ii, 1957.
Mihailov i                    G. Mihailov, *Inscriptiones Graecae in Bulgaria repertae* i, 1956.
*MMNYC*                       *Metropolitan Museum, New York, Catalogue of . . .*
Mon. Piot                     *Monuments et Mémoires publiés par l'Académie des Inscriptions et Belles-Lettres,
                              Fondation Eugène Piot.*
Moretti                       L. Moretti, *Iscrizioni agonistiche greche*, 1953.
*MuZ*                         E. Pfuhl, *Malerei und Zeichnung der Griechen* i–iii, 1923.

*NC*                          H. G. G. Payne, *Necrocorinthia*, 1933.
*NS*                          *Notizie degli scavi di Antichità.*
*Num. Chron.*                 *Numismatic Chronicle.*

| | |
|---|---|
| *Ö.Jh.* | *Jahreshefte des österreichischen archäologischen Institutes in Wien.* |
| *Ol.* | *Olympia* i–v, 1890–97. |
| *Op. Arch.* | *Opuscula Archaeologica.* |
| *PAE* | Πρακτικὰ τῆς Ἀρχαιολογικῆς Ἑταιρείας. |
| Pape-Benseler | W. Pape and G. Benseler, *Wörterbuch der griechischen Eigennamen*, 1884–1911. |
| Peek i | W. Peek, *Griechische Versinschriften* i (*Grab-Epigramme*), 1955. |
| *Ph. W.* | *Berliner Philologische Wochenschrift.* |
| *RA* | *Revue Archéologique.* |
| *RE* | *Paulys Real-Encyclopädie der classischen Altertumswissenschaft*, ed. G. Wissowa. |
| *REA* | *Revue des études anciennes.* |
| *REG* | *Revue des études grecques.* |
| *Rend. Acc. Pont.* | *Rendiconti della Pontificia Accademia Romana di Archeologia.* |
| *Rend. Linc.* | *Rendiconti dell'Accademia Nazionale dei Lincei.* |
| *Rev. Num.* | *Revue numismatique.* |
| *Rev. Phil.* | *Revue de philologie.* |
| *Rh. Mus.* | *Rheinisches Museum für Philologie.* |
| Richter[3] | G. M. A. Richter, *The Sculpture and Sculptors of the Greeks*, new revised edition, 1950. |
| *RIGI* | *Rivista Indo-greco-italica.* |
| *Riv. Fil.* | *Rivista di filologia classica.* |
| *RM* | *Mitteilungen des deutschen archäologischen Instituts: Römische Abteilung.* |
| Roberts i | E. S. Roberts, *An Introduction to Greek Epigraphy*, Part i, 1887. |
| Robertson[2] | D. S. Robertson, *A Handbook of Greek and Roman Architecture*, ed. 2, 1945. |
| Roehl[3] | H. Roehl, *Imagines Inscriptionum Graecarum antiquissimarum*, ed. 3, 1907. |
| *Sb. Ak. Berlin* (*Wien*, &c.) | *Sitzungsberichte der Akademie der Wissenschaft zu Berlin* (*Wien*, &c.). |
| *SCE* | *The Swedish Cyprus Expedition.* |
| Schwyzer | E. Schwyzer, *Griechische Grammatik* i (Handbuch d. Archäologie, ed. Otto, iii. 1, 1), 1939. |
| *SEG* | *Supplementum Epigraphicum Graecum.* |
| *SGDI* | H. Collitz and F. Bechtel, *Sammlung der griechischen Dialekt-Inschriften*, i–iv, 1884–1915. |
| *SIG*[3] | H. Dittenberger, *Sylloge Inscriptionum Graecarum*, ed. 3, i–iv, 1915–24. |
| *SMG* | *Atti e memorie della Società Magna Grecia.* |
| *TAPA* | *Transactions and Proceedings of the American Philological Association.* |
| *VS* | K. Friis Johansen, *Les Vases sicyoniens*, 1923. |
| Wilhelm | A. Wilhelm, *Beiträge zur griechischen Inschriftenkunde*, 1909. |
| *ZDMG* | *Zeitschrift der deutschen morgenländischen Gesellschaft.* |

| MUSEUMS: BM | British Museum, London. |
|---|---|
| EM | Epigraphical Museum, Athens. |
| MFA | Museum of Fine Arts, Boston. |
| MM | Metropolitan Museum, New York. |
| NM | National Museum, Athens. |

EPIGRAPHICAL SYMBOLS:  α = α (&c.) uncertain or incomplete.
⟨ ⟩ = letter omitted in error.
{ } = letter included in error.
[ ] = letter restored by editor.
[. .] = two (&c.) letters lost.
[- - -] = unknown number of letters lost.
| = start of a new line on the stone (metal, clay, &c.).

# PART I

# THE ORIGIN AND TRANSMISSION OF THE GREEK ALPHABET

Τίς γὰρ ἂν ἄξιον ἐγκώμιον διάθοιτο τῆς τῶν γραμμάτων μαθήσεως;
διὰ γὰρ τούτων μόνων οἱ τετελευτηκότες τοῖς 3ῶσι διαμνημονεύονται. (DIOD. xii. 13. 2.)

## I. THE ORIGIN

THE Greeks learnt many inventions from their eastern neighbours, and the greatest of these was the art of alphabetic writing. It is known beyond any doubt that the North Semitic script was the model for the Greek, and there are existing examples —all too few, it is true—both of the model and of the copy in their early stages. Yet the full history of the birth and first growth of the Greek alphabet is still a matter of uncertainty and dispute. The ancient literary tradition offers a series of contradictory statements concerning the origin and date, only one of which has stood firmly the test of time: οἱ δὲ Φοίνικες . . . ἐσήγαγον διδασκάλια ἐς τοὺς ῞Ελληνας, καὶ δὴ καὶ γράμματα (Hdt. v. 58). The archaeological evidence is still incomplete, especially outside mainland Greece; and the bare epigraphical evidence, as derived from the lettering of the earliest extant inscriptions, illustrates the growth, but cannot by itself explain whether these illustrations depict the primary or secondary stages of that growth.

There are thus four questions which must be answered before the history of the early Greek alphabet can be written. All have been already propounded in various forms, and answered in differing ways, by past generations of epigraphists and philologists; their views are cited in the discussions which follow, and it will be evident how much is owed to them by the present writer and all other students of this generation who approach the problem afresh.

The questions are: first, where in the Greek or Semitic area did the first transmission to Greek from Semite take place? second, when did it take place? third, by what routes was it then transmitted throughout Greece? and fourth, when and whence did those additions and divergences appear which distinguish (*a*) the Greek alphabetic system as a whole from the North Semitic (i.e. the creation of the vowel-system, the alteration of certain letter-forms, the addition of the letters following *tau* in the alphabet and the use of the *boustrophedon* style), and (*b*) the local Greek scripts from each other?

Before attempting to answer these questions, we should first consider briefly what are the natural reactions of an illiterate people when learning a method of writing from another people. This point is important, both as a general preliminary and because it has a particular bearing on the fourth and most complicated of our questions.

How does an illiterate people *A* normally achieve literacy? It may be in sufficiently close contact with a literate civilization *B* to acquire the knowledge inevitably from mutual intercourse, particularly if there are intermarriages which produce bilingual speakers; this may be either because literate members of *B* are scattered throughout *A* or because in one particular area people of both *A* and *B* are in contact, whence the knowledge is spread to the rest of *A*. The diffusion of the Roman alphabet country by country throughout the Roman Empire illustrates the former method on a large scale; the spread of the alphabet through archaic Etruria from the original contact of the Greeks of Kyme with the Etruscans illustrates the latter. Alternatively, a script may be deliberately introduced into the illiterate country *A* by an individual or small group of persons, as happened in the cases of the Gothic, Armenian, and Cyrillic (or Glagolitic) scripts.[1] A member of *A* or *B*, outstanding in position and personality, and with a thorough knowledge of the *B* script, creates a script for *A* by synthesis, basing it upon the existing *B* script and adding any extra signs felt to be necessary for the *A* language, either by borrowing from other scripts or by newly invented signs. The underlying motives for this may be either political or religious, or a mixture of both, but in either case they imply a more deliberate connexion between the two countries than is indicated by the more haphazard method of commercial contact, such as the contact between the Etruscans and the Greeks of Kyme.

Was the North Semitic alphabet then brought to the Greeks in the first way, by close contact between Greeks and Phoenicians at some meeting-place in one territory or the other, or was it deliberately introduced by a gifted individual (Greek or Phoenician), who had resided in both territories, realized the advantages of the North Semitic alphabet, and adapted it to the Greek language? The Greek literary tradition, being mostly from authors who followed the popular convention of tracing every amenity of civilization back to a named εὑρετής, naturally spoke of individuals; but these were frankly divine (as Hermes), or otherwise superhuman (Prometheus), or heroes of saga (as Danaos, Palamedes, Kadmos).[2] Some modern scholars, while wisely declining to assign the event to any of these names, nevertheless believe that it was indeed the work of one man, from internal evidence; they hold that the creation of the Greek vowels α, ε, ι, ο, υ from the North Semitic *’ālep*, *hē’*, *yôd*, *‘ayin*, and *wāw* suggests the deliberate, brilliant innovation of a single creator (pp. 21 f.). But the vowel-system can no longer be cited as good evidence for this belief. It has been pointed out that the *wāw* and *yôd* were on occasion given their vocalic values in Semitic also, and that the initial sounds of the words "*’ālep*', '*hē*", and "*‘ayin*' would have also, to the Greek ear, their nearest equivalents in the vowels *ă*, *ĕ*, and *ŏ* (pp. 21 f.). A εὑρετής, in a sense, there must have been, in that there must have existed once a Greek who was in point of time the first to repeat the North Semitic alphabet, including the names of these five letters, and who, pronouncing them in the way most natural to his own tongue, gave them in fact a true vocalic value. That is to say, in a place where Greeks were in contact with Phoenicians this contact and intercourse,

---

[1] The Gothic was invented by Ulfilas in the 4th c. A.D. for his translation of the Bible into Gothic speech; the Armenian by Mesrop *c.* 400 A.D. for the propagation of Christianity through the Armenian church; the Cyrillic for the conversion of the southern Slavs by Cyril in the 9th c.; cf. Peeters, *Rev. des études arméniennes* ix (1929), 203 ff.; Diringer, *The Alphabet* (1948), 320 ff., 473 f., 475 ff.

[2] The Greeks' own views on the invention of writing form an interesting historical study by themselves; I hope to deal with them in detail elsewhere. Cf. meanwhile Franz, *Elementa Epigraphices Graecae* (1840), 12 ff.; Roberts i. 2 f.; Larfeld³, 212 ff.; Schmid, *Philologus* lii (1893), 212 ff.; Driver, 128 f.

limited though it may have been, in time produced a Greek, or a number of Greeks, who, knowing a certain amount of the Phoenicians' language, learnt their alphabet too, and proceeded to try to write Greek in this alphabet.

Will he (or they) at once realize its limitations, and start consciously to improve on it? Let us consider the case of the illiterate Greek, faced with the twenty-two signs, sounds, and names of the North Semitic alphabet. He may know that other nations with which he has had some kind of contact—the Egyptians, or the Assyrians, or the Late Hittite cities of Cilicia—possess systems of writing, but they are technical mysteries, not understood in fact by the ordinary people of those lands, but confined to a class of trained writers. He may himself have the tradition of a system of σήματα (the Mycenean 'Linear B' system) whereby certain of his own ancestral heroes could write. But he has nothing similar in his own experience to make him critical of the details of the North Semitic system; he is simply aware that he is now learning twenty-two signs which will enable him to put his own language into writing. It is, I think, legitimate to postulate that an individual, or a people, learning for the first time a wholly new technical device, is apt to learn it without rejecting or even disputing details, since to try to correct them at this stage implies a previous notion as to what that detail ought to imply; it presupposes a background, a familiarity with the subject, which as yet he is not in a position to have. Thus the illiterate learner may be expected to absorb the letters of the alphabet withou deliberate alteration or rejection. He will learn the names and copy the letter-shapes as well as he can. He will accept the sound-value attributed by his teacher to each letter, and will equate it with a familiar sound which occurs in his own language and which seems to him to be more or less the same, though it is in fact, to a modern philologist's ear, produced by a totally different method of manipulating the breath. Even if there is a sound among the series which is plainly alien to his own speech-system, or else redundant because its sound is for him already expressed by another letter, he will learn it none the less with the rest, because his teacher writes and repeats the series as a whole, and he learns it as a whole; he will not at once omit this sign as useless from his alphabet, although he may never use it in practice.[1] Nor will he, when taught that a certain sign represents a certain sound, nevertheless employ that sign to express a totally different sound, because the latter is absent from the model, and he wishes to include it in his alphabet; nor, again, will he deliberately invent new shapes straightway to fill what he feels to be omissions in his model. Only in cases of similarity between letters will he perhaps depart from conservatism; if two are sufficiently alike in his version (not necessarily in the original model) to cause confusion, the shape of one may be deliberately altered. Otherwise, in this first stage he accepts as complete the system presented to him, and all the sounds of his own language which are not expressed by existing letters he will express either by two letters combined, or by the single letter which (to his ear) comes

---

[1] Cf. Carpenter, *AJA* xlix (1945), 456 ff. A good example of this has been pointed out to me by Dr. Meinrad Scheller. The Sogdian script was taken almost entirely from the Aramaic alphabet at a date perhaps shortly before the Christian era; the twenty-two letters and their order are the same, with three additional non-Aramaic signs at the end, presumably to express Sogdian sounds. The recorded Sogdian alphabet shows twenty-five letters; but the Sogdians actually used only eighteen of them. Some (not all, apparently) of the remaining signs may have been used as ideograms. Cf. Ross and Gauthiot, *Journal asiatique* 1913, 521 ff.

nearest to the required sound. The letter which does duty for two 'kindred' sounds may be written in a variant form to denote the second sound (cf. *j* and *v*, made from the capitals of *i* and *u*); and then the 'doublet' form becomes a letter in its own right.

The force of convention shows strongly in the history of an alphabet learnt by one people from another (as distinct from a synthetic creation by an individual), mainly for this reason, that it is the natural instinct of the learner to accept it *en bloc* and fit the separate letter-signs to his own language, not demanding additional signs for certain sounds; such additions as do arise come later, either in the form of doublets of existing letters, or by loans from another script to express a particular sound. Thus the existing Etruscan abecedaria show that the Etruscans retained in their formal alphabet the three Greek letters *beta, delta, omikron* (useless to them) for some time before abandoning them, and to that alphabet added only the sign 8 = *f*, perhaps an adaptation or loan borrowed from elsewhere.[1] The Romans likewise retained *zeta*, in the *Carmen Saliorum*, when they no longer had a practical use for it in ordinary speech, and in the abecedarium until Sp. Carvilius replaced it by the G *c.* 234 B.C.;[2] the only additions which they made were this doublet G (from C) in the third century B.C., and the loans Y and Z, re-taken from the contemporary Greek script in the first century, to express those sounds in words which were themselves loans from the Greek.[3] The English alphabet has achieved only three permanent additions to the Roman version, again by doublets (J from I, U and W from V); all additional sounds are expressed approximately, by combinations of letters. The same convention which held past users of the alphabet still holds us today, secure in the conviction that, as long as the language is living, the true pronunciation of the written word will be understood by the reader.

On general grounds therefore it may be argued that the same instincts for convention which held the Etruscan learners of the Greek alphabet, the Roman learners of the Etruscan, and the later inheritors of the Roman, held also the Greek learners of the Phoenician; and that the additions which appeared were not the results of any immediate and deliberate intentions to repair omissions in the original alphabet by the creation of new signs, but arose from similar causes, either from doublets (as *upsilon* is admitted to have come from *vau*, and possibly *omega* from *omikron*), or else because they were loan-letters, borrowed from the script of a people with whom the Greeks were in contact (as the Ionic letter '*sampi*' may be derived from a non-Greek script of Asia Minor; cf. pp. 38 f.). To evolve a new symbol from an existing letter which itself has a quite different sound-value (in contrast with the doublet method, in which one sound is obviously close to the other), or deliberately to give a quite different sound-value to a 'disused' letter, are feats for which the alphabets cited offer no parallel. Yet some explanations often accepted today maintain that the signs Φ and X are artificially derived from other existing letters (*theta* and *tau*), that the Ionians gave new sound-values *ps* and *ks* to the 'useless' signs Ψ and Ξ, and that other Greek alphabet-users in the same way employed the (to them) 'useless' sign X to express the sound *ks*.

---

[1] Buonamici, *Epigrafia Etrusca* (1932), 160 ff.; Pallottino, *The Etruscans* (1955, English ed.), ch. 12.

[2] Sandys and Campbell, *Latin Epigraphy*[2] (1927), 35 f.

[3] Ibid. The three new letters added by the Emperor Claudius did not survive his own reign (ibid.; cf. also Oliver, *AJA* liii (1949), 249 ff.).

The theories of the origins of the supplementary letters will be discussed in more detail below, pp. 35 ff.; for it is time now to turn to the specific problems of the date and place of introduction of the Greek alphabet, returning to this general question of its conservatism when we have to consider the problem of its transmission (pp. 22 ff.). But meanwhile, in this general preliminary consideration of probabilities, it may be objected that, whatever other alphabet-users have done, the deliberate rejection or alteration of useless signs, and creation of new ones, is far more typical of the alert Greek mentality than mere passive acceptance of whatever signs were offered to them by the Semitic or any other script. To this I would reply that, in accepting a borrowed framework without seeking deliberately to recast it, the earliest Greek writers were only following the same instinct as that which prevented vase-painters for about two hundred years from advancing beyond the profile rendering of the human face, or sculptors for over one hundred from altering the traditional stance of the kouros. This is not to depreciate the peculiar quality of the Greek mind, but merely to stress its practical side. The framework in each case, economical though it was, served well enough to hold what the Greek genius built on it. As has been said already by many writers in many ways, the essence of that genius lay not in the transformation of its borrowed instruments, but in the results which flowered from their imperfect help.

## A. *Place of Introduction*

The Greek letters from *alpha* to *tau* are derived from those of the North Semitic alphabet. This fact has long been established so firmly that to repeat the evidence in detail here is unnecessary.[1] It may be summarized briefly as follows:

(1) In the early fifth century B.C. (there is no earlier direct evidence), the Ionians already called the letters of the alphabet 'Phoenician' (φοινικήϊα γράμματα or φοινικήϊα). This is attested by Herodotos, and confirmed by a fifth-century inscription from Teos.[2] (2) The names of the letters in both alphabets are basically the same, although the Greek tongue could not reproduce the correct sound of any but the simplest North Semitic name, such as *tāw*. (3) The order of the letters is the same, both visually in the written abecedarium and orally in the recited list, except that in the recited list where the sibilants occurred (*zayin*, *sāmek̠*, *ṣādê*, *šîn*) the Greeks appear to have applied in each case a wrong name + sound-value to the written sign (for the detailed discussion of this confusion, see below, pp. 25 ff.). (4) The shapes of the letters are basically the same, although in the various Greek local versions they have been reversed, inverted, elaborated, simplified, or even stood on end; in fact they have suffered all the unintentional maltreatment likely to befall a meaningless shape with an unintelligible name, transmitted as a stereotyped symbol to a quick-witted but illiterate people; and further they have undergone occasional deliberate alteration if accidental resemblance threatened confusion (as, for example,

---

[1] Cf. Kirchhoff⁴, 1; Roberts i. 4 ff.; Hiller von Gaertringen, *ap.* Gercke-Norden, *Einleitung* i. 9 (1924), 6 ff.; and Ebert, *Reallexikon* xi (1927–8), 357 ff.; Schwyzer, 139 ff.; Klaffenbach, *Griechische Epigraphik* (1957), 32.

[2] Hdt. v. 58; *SIG*³ 38, l. 37 (Teos). At Mytilene there was an official called the φοινικογράφος (as well as a γραμματεύς) employed in the cult of Hermes: *IG* xii. 2. 96 and 97. The title is known only from these two inscriptions.

crooked *iota* probably became I to avoid confusion with *sigma*; pp. 30, 41). (5) The North Semitic script ran consistently from right to left, and this method, unnatural for any right-handed person, was faithfully reproduced, at least as far as the first line of writing was concerned, in the earliest Greek inscriptions (pp. 43 ff.). (6) Finally, I think that a further proof of the connexion may be suggested by the material employed. The advantages of dried clay tablets as a cheap, easy, and durable medium for writing are obvious, and were usually fully realized in countries where the clay was good, as in Babylonia and in Greece herself during the Minoan–Mycenean period; yet it is plain that the early alphabetic-writing Greeks took little or no advantage of this simple and indestructible type of writing material in which their country was prolific. It is true that, long before its name assumed a political significance, the ostrakon was used for the casual graffiti of everyday life, but this was merely making use of the existing surface of a broken pot; normally the Greeks used for their material leather, wood, metal (bronze, tin, and lead; very rarely gold or silver), stone, and imported papyrus (pp. 50 ff.). Professor Driver has pointed out that in the home area of the North Semitic alphabet a suitable clay was hard to find, and therefore it was only employed for writing in a few exceptional cases; the general medium used was wood, leather, papyrus, or stone, the surface of stone being plastered to take the letters in areas where it was of poor quality.[1] It is possible therefore that the curious neglect by the Greeks of the clay plaque as writing material should be regarded as a direct inheritance from their first teachers of the alphabet.

It is plain, then, that the Greek alphabet must have had its birth either in a part of the Greek area where the people whom they called Φοίνικες were active, or in a part of the North Semitic area where Greeks were active. Before reviewing the places in both regions where such mutual intercourse is attested, either by literary record or from the evidence of excavation, it is important that three points should be borne in mind, which will assist in limiting the boundaries of the search. Firstly, as is generally agreed, the Greek alphabet appears to have originated in a limited area; it was not created independently at a number of different points where Greeks and Phoenicians had intercourse.[2] This is suggested by certain striking divergences from the North Semitic model which, as far back as we can trace them, are the common property of all the Greek local alphabets, whatever may be the variations of those alphabets in other respects: namely:

(*a*) the use of the North Semitic sounds *'ālep̱, hē', 'ayin* to express the Greek vowels α, ε, o; (*b*) the misapplication of the names and sound-values of the North Semitic sibilants *zayin, sāmek̠, ṣādê, šîn* (pp. 25 ff.); (*c*) the use of the *boustrophedon* system of writing, which was not used in the North Semitic script (pp. 43 ff.); (*d*) the doubling of the North Semitic semi-vowel *wāw* into two forms, a semi-vowel *vau* (= later *digamma*) and a pure vowel *u*(*psilon*) (pp. 24 f.); (*e*) and, apparently, the taking of certain Greek letters, the *vau* and *iota*, for example, from the cursive Phoenician script (p. 18). Different centres evolving each its own alphabet from the North Semitic might hit independently on the same values *a, e, o* for *'ālep̱, hē', 'ayin,* if the average Greek ear heard

---

[1] Driver, 78 ff.
[2] This was suggested by Taylor, *The Alphabet* ii (1883), 68; E. Meyer, *Gesch. d. Alt.* iii². 349. See Addenda.

those vowels in the start of the Semitic names; but it is unlikely that all would independently get, for example, *zeta* (*ds*) out of *zayin* (voiced *s*), the same sign for the pure
vowel *u* out of the semi-vowel *wāw*, the *boustrophedon* system out of the consistent retrograde of the North Semitic, and the cursive forms of the same Semitic letters in each case.

The second point was well brought out by Professor Carpenter:[1] that only in an
established bilingual settlement of the two peoples, not merely in a casual North Semitic
trading-post somewhere in the Greek area, will the alphabet of one be taken over by the
other. The barrier of an alien language must be surmounted by one party or the other
before one can learn the art of writing from the other. It is not likely that the Greeks
could have picked up a system of writing merely from Phoenician traders who came
periodically from overseas to Greek ports with their wares for barter, a proceeding for
which a few words of the alien language and much gesture are sufficient. Nevertheless,
it is still true to say that the Greeks owed their alphabet to their traders; for such a settlement must have owed its existence to the commercial enterprise of one or both sides,
and the people who composed it would be the trading elements of Greek and Phoenician
society; whence it may be guessed that the Phoenicians from whom the Greeks learnt
had no pretensions to being professional scribes. The internal evidence of the earliest
Greek inscriptions may offer some support here, for certain points hint that the Semitic
teachers were in no sense literary experts, but merely had a working knowledge of the
alphabet sufficient for simple practical purposes. These points are treated in detail later,
but may be mentioned here in advance: (*a*) that, although the Greeks learnt faithfully
the retrograde line of the Phoenician abecedarium, and the obvious precept arising therefrom that an inscription should begin from right to left, they did not adopt (and therefore,
it may be suggested, were not aware of) the North Semitic system of consistent retrograde
writing for inscriptions of more than one line (pp. 43 ff.); (*b*) that none of the earliest
inscriptions shows the useful device of punctuation by a single dot or a short vertical
stroke, which forms an integral part of the North Semitic script; (*c*) that in the oral
repetition of the abecedarium the Greek confusion of the sibilants passed uncorrected
(pp. 26 ff.); (*d*) that, as was said above, certain Greek letters appear to be derived from
Phoenician cursive script. These points suggest that the first Greek learners (from whom
came the subsequent dissemination of the alphabet to the rest of Greece) were not properly
trained in the usage of the North Semitic model as represented, for example, in the
monumental stone inscriptions of Byblos or Zinjîrlû,[2] but that they learnt the alphabet,
and how to put it to practical use, from Phoenicians who themselves wrote briefly in
a cursive script.

The third clue is the obvious conclusion that this birthplace of the Greek alphabet
must have been itself on a fairly well-frequented trade-route, or must at least have had
good connexion with some of the main trading centres of Greece in the early period, to
bring about the subsequent rapid dissemination of the script by the Greeks.

Having attempted thus to define the boundaries of our search, we may review the
places which have been suggested by ancient or modern authors. The island of Cyprus,
which had the obvious qualifications of a population of both Greeks and Phoenicians,

[1] *AJA* xlix (1945), 456.          [2] For these see Driver, 105 ff., 121.

and a good position on the east–west trade-route, has to be excluded from the search, for the well-known reason that the Cypriot Greeks possessed a syllabic script of their own. This syllabary is generally held to be a variety of the Linear script current in the Aegean during the late Bronze Age, which survived in this remote area, and therefore was in use when the Phoenicians arrived on the island.[1] The cumbersome syllabary, as nobody discussing it has failed to remark, was wholly unsuited to the Greek language; nevertheless, the Cypriot Greeks persisted in using it as late as the Hellenistic period.[2] The syllabary fulfilled what was evidently the only important requirement—bare intelligibility; and this was apparently enough. When once it had been learnt, the power of convention maintained it against all the superior attractions of later arrivals, the Phoenician and the Greek alphabets.

If we are seeking a settled bilingual community, the prospects of finding it anywhere in Greek territory are not encouraging, since the theory, once popular, of Phoenician dominance in early Greek history is now discredited by modern historians. Nor do the majority of the places to which the ancient authors ascribed a Phoenician settlement seem to be suitable places from which an alphabet, once acquired, would be disseminated. Thasos[3] can be excluded at once, for her alphabet is generally agreed to have been taken from her mother-city Paros. The case for Thebes breaks down because, even if we should hesitate to reject Herodotos' statement of the Phoenician dynasty here (which few would now maintain),[4] there still remain the objections that the Palace of Kadmos itself showed no traces of Phoenician occupation:[5] that Thebes was not a focus for outside trade, but an inland state:[6] and finally that the Boiotian alphabet is obviously closely connected with the Euboic, and, from the internal evidence, the transmission seems to have been from Euboia to Boiotia, not the converse (pp. 82, 90). In Kythera, the undoubted existence of an Astarte-cult and a murex-fishing industry supports the case for a Phoenician settlement (Hdt. i. 105); but she, again, was on no trade-route except that established later from Lakonia to Egypt or Kyrene in Libya (Thuc. iv. 53). The only archaic inscription found there, as far as I know, is Lakonian of the end of the sixth or the fifth century.[7]

As is well known, the alphabets of the Doric islands Crete, Thera (with Anaphe), Melos, and Sikinos, form a particular group known as the 'Primitives' (Kirchhoff's 'green' alphabet), whose common type is the nearest to the North Semitic of all the local Greek alphabets. It is plain that one member of the group first received this 'primitive' alphabet and passed it on to the rest; was it received from other Greeks, or directly from resident Phoenicians? Sikinos and Anaphe may be discounted. Melos has a certain claim by virtue of a late literary tradition of a Phoenician element (Steph. Byz., *s.v.* Melos), but no supporting claim as yet for this from archaeology. No inscriptions have yet been found there

---

[1] The date of the Phoenician arrival is disputed. A Phoenician inscription in the Nicosia Museum is dated in the 9th c. by Semitic epigraphists (Honeyman, *Iraq* vi (1939), 106 ff.; Albright, *Studies in the History of Culture* (1942), 41; Dupont-Sommer, *Rev. d'Assyriologie* xli (1947), 201 ff.). The opposing theory maintains that the Phoenicians did not arrive before the eighth century (Hill, *History of Cyprus* i. 52; Gjerstad, *SCE* iv.

2. 436 ff.).

[2] Mitford, *CQ* xliv (1950), 97 ff.

[3] Hdt. ii. 44–46; vi. 47; cf. Paus. v. 25. 12.

[4] Hdt. v. 57–58; cf. Mentz, *Rh. Mus.* lxxxv (1936), 365.

[5] Keramopoullos, *A. Delt.* iii (1917), 5.

[6] E. Meyer, op. cit. ii. 2². 115.

[7] *IG* v. 1. 945; see below Lakonia, p. 194, n. 4.

which are earlier than the second half of the sixth century. Thera has a more serious claim;[1] not only does Herodotos (iv. 147–8) attest the presence there of an early dynasty of 'Kadmeians', whom he equates with Phoenicians, but some of the rock-inscriptions of Thera appear to be among the oldest Greek writing yet known. But Herodotos' 'eight generations of Phoenicians', if indeed they lived here, left no trace of any Phoenician artefacts;[2] moreover, the local pottery, with its persistent geometric tradition lasting into the seventh century, supports the inference which might also be drawn from Thera's inhospitable geographical features: that she was not a port which many traders frequented, but made her one colonial venture in Kyrene, and for the rest derived her outside contacts mainly from Crete and in a lesser degree from Corinth.

The Cretan alphabet is the closest of all to the Semitic,[3] and Crete had external connexions in the eighth century, possibly with Cyprus,[4] more certainly with Athens and Corinth.[5] Phoenician ivories have been found in Crete;[6] moreover the series of bronze shields from the Idaian cave appear to some scholars to show a connexion, direct or indirect, with the coast of North Syria, whether the actual technique was native to Syria or to the Urartian culture near Lake Van.[7] But here the literary tradition is discouragingly weak. It is true that the Hellenistic Cretan historian Dosiadas maintained that the alphabet had originated in Crete (*FGH* iii, no. 458, F 6), but nothing is known of the reasons on which he based his claim; it may well have been on the scattered examples of Minoan script which must have been found occasionally in the soil. The Phoenicians (or Sidonians) are mentioned, as craftsmen and as pirates, in both the *Iliad* and *Odyssey*; but when the poet is listing in some detail the peoples whose languages intermingled in ninety-citied Crete (*Od.* xix. 175 ff.)—Achaians, Eteocretans, Kydonians, three-tribed Dorians, Pelasgians—he makes no mention of any Phoenicians (or Sidonians) among them.

Rhodes, on the other hand, can show a literary tradition of unknown date, mentioning a Phoenician settlement, which is defined more precisely by Diodoros (v. 58) as a settlement of Kadmos' followers at Ialysos, with a dedication by Kadmos himself in Athena's temple at Lindos (p. 347). As a junction for traffic going east and west through the Greek islands to Cyprus and the coast of North Syria, or going north to the Greek cities of Asia Minor, she was in an excellent position for the dissemination of the alphabet, and may indeed have been the source, direct or indirect, whence the majority of Greeks received their letters. The influence of the Near East has been detected in Rhodian ivory-work,[8] and Eastern connexions in the many small Phoenician artefacts found on the island; but it is impossible to say how they came to Rhodes.

The conflict between the literary and archaeological evidence will continue until it can be decided once and for all who were in fact these Kadmeians whom the literary tradition

[1] Cf. Taylor, op. cit. ii. 286; Hiller von Gaertringen, Ebert's *Reallexikon* xi (1927–8), 358; Arvanitopoullos, *Epigraphike* i (1937), 133 f. All suggest that Thera was the birthplace of the Greek alphabet.

[2] *Thera* i. 141 ff.; ii. 235.

[3] A Cretan origin for the Greek alphabet is maintained by Hiller von Gaertringen, *IG* i². 267 f. and Guarducci, Ἑταιρεία Μακεδονικῶν Σπουδῶν ix (1953), 342 ff.

[4] Demargne, *La Crète dédalique* (1947), 328 ff.

[5] *NC*, 53. On the connexion with Athens especially, see J. K. Brock, *Fortetsa* (1957), 218.

[6] Demargne, op. cit. 208 ff.

[7] Kunze, *Kretische Bronzereliefs* (1931), *passim*.

[8] Poulsen, *Der Orient* (1912), 83 ff.; Barnett, *JHS* lxviii (1948), 16 f.

records as present once in Thebes, Thera, and Rhodes. If they prove to have been no Semites, but an element of the Late Helladic stock, and if the equations 'Kadmos = a Phoenician, therefore Kadmeians = Phoenicians' is proved to be founded on the original misconception of a Greek historian,[1] then the archaeological argument will triumph. Meanwhile, in the matter of the alphabet's origin, the archaeological evidence is enough for us to admit that, if the birthplace of the Greek alphabet was in the Greek area at all, then Rhodes and Crete have the strongest claims. But here there seems to be an awkwardness concerning the scripts themselves. Rhodes and Crete, with only Karpathos between them, are close links in the Doric chain which stretched from the south-eastern Peloponnese to the south-western corner of Asia Minor. They must have had fairly close dealing with each other from an early period,[2] and one would expect that, if Crete received the alphabet originally, Rhodes would have been one of the earliest places to benefit, and vice versa; in other words, if ever two local scripts ought to be similar, it might be expected of Cretan and Rhodian. But actually they are consistently different from each other as far back as can be traced, which for Crete is the second half of the seventh century, and for Rhodes earlier, perhaps the very end of the eighth. It is true that this difficulty can be abolished if we fall back on the statement, impossible to disprove, that there was a 'lost period' during which the Rhodian alphabet slowly altered from an original 'primitive' type like the Cretan (with crooked *iota*, five-stroked *mu*, and *san*) to her own forms; but, as I try to show elsewhere (pp. 14 ff.), this argument, universal panacea though it is, is founded rather on negative than on positive evidence. Hence it seems to me to be more likely on the whole that Crete and Rhodes each drew its alphabet separately from some earlier source than that Rhodes, for example, was the originator.[3]

This brings us to the final hypothesis, which in recent years has been growing in favour, namely, that the birthplace which we are seeking was not in Greek territory, but was a settlement of Greeks resident for purposes of trade on the Syrian coast, and that from this common source the alphabet was carried to certain trading places independently—Crete and Rhodes, perhaps other islands such as Euboia[4]—and thence in stages to the rest of Greece (pp. 40 ff.).

In the period before the late eighth century B.C. (the latter being the latest date that has been suggested as yet for the introduction of the alphabet), the North Semitic alphabet was current over an area which extended from the 'Late Hittite' states of the North Syrian and East Cilician borders[5] down through North Syria and Phoenicia to Palestine

---

[1] Gomme, *JHS* xxxiii (1913), 66 f., 71 f., 223.

[2] Demargne, op. cit. 331 ff. The late T. J. Dunbabin informed me, however, that there is 'surprisingly little positive evidence'.

[3] I have not discussed here the theory of a Rhodian-Cypriot origin suggested by Rhys Carpenter in *AJA* 1933, 23 and 1938, 68, as Professor Carpenter informs me that, since the publication of the Greek site at Al Mina (p. 11 below) he no longer holds this view. The claim of Rhodes was upheld by M. Falkner, *Frühgeschichte u. Sprachwissenschaft* (ed. Brandenstein, 1948), 110 ff.; see also Klaffenbach, op. cit. 34.

[4] See J. Boardman, *BSA* lii (1957), 24 ff., who argues

strongly for direct contact between Euboia and Al Mina (Posideion) in Syria on the evidence of the pottery from Al Mina hitherto classed as Cycladic; he suggests that Euboia may have been the first transmitter of the alphabet to the rest of Greece.

[5] Examples of the 9th and 8th c. B.C. have been found at Zinjîrlû, Arslan Taš, and Sûjîn (Driver, 107, 119 ff.); Karatepe (8th c.?; Bossert and others, *Karatepe Kazıları* (1950), 60 ff.; Barnett, *Iraq* x (1948), 1 ff.; Dupont-Sommer and Bossert, *CRAI* 1948, 76 ff., 250 ff., 534 ff.; Obermann, *Trans. Connecticut Acad.* xxxviii (1949), 1 ff.; Albright, *AJA* liv (1950), 164); Bossert, *Belleten (Türk Tarih Kurumu)* xvii (1953), 143 ff.

and Moab.[1] How far, in this long coastline, did the area extend which the Greeks themselves called ἡ Φοινίκη? The proper domain of the Phoenicians was from Mount Carmel northward to Arvad; south of Carmel lay Palestine, and north of Arvad were the Aramaic-speaking Semites of North Syria. But Herodotos, describing this coastline, makes it clear that in his day the part north of Arvad as far as the Cilician border was included in ἡ Φοινίκη by the Greeks; for, speaking of the geographical νομοί from which the Great King exacted tribute, he describes the fifth νομός as extending from Posideion, the Greek colony on the Cilician–Syrian border, southward as far as Egypt, and consisting (from north to south) of (a) Phoenicia, (b) Palestinian Syria, and (c) Cyprus (iii. 91); and again, he says that the southern coast of Asia Minor runs westward as far as the Triopian headland from the Myriandic gulf, which lies πρὸς Φοινίκη (iv. 38). From this it is evident that the Greeks regarded the whole area between Posideion and Palestinian Syria as 'Phoenician', and therefore Greeks settled anywhere in this region, from the Orontes to Mount Carmel, would call the script which they learnt 'Phoenician'.

In recent years our knowledge of Greek activity on the North Syrian coast has widened greatly, first and foremost from Sir Leonard Woolley's excavations in 1936–7 at Al Mina on the south side of the Orontes, a site which he identifies tentatively with Posideion itself.[2] Here there was a settlement of Greeks at least as early as the eighth century and probably earlier,[3] whose connexions appear from the oldest pottery found there to have been first with some part of the Cyclades, Rhodes, and Cyprus, and later with Corinth.[4] It is true that no archaic inscriptions, Greek or Phoenician, were found in these excavations, but Woolley believes Al Mina itself to have been the port area only; the residential area he identifies provisionally with Sabouni, a site not far inland, which is still unexcavated. At the Aramaic site of Hamath, lying inland on the south bank of the Orontes, H. Ingholt[5] reports graffiti of the eighth century (?) (Phoenician script, Aramaic dialect) and also a clumsy scrawl in letters which resemble Greek rather than Phoenician, as well as Greek pottery. In addition, there are reports of early Greek ware from other sites down the coast.[6] Most of this material may be only stray imports; but Al Mina at least was certainly a Greek settlement, and would satisfy the requirements mentioned on pp. 6 ff.: here were Greek traders settled in a limited area where the Phoenician alphabet was current—at least until the second half of the eighth century, when the Aramaic varieties in the letter-forms may have begun to show.[7]

More than this cannot be said. Although for convenience I call the birthplace 'Posideion (?)' henceforth, it is obvious that the identification is quite uncertain. The alphabet

[1] Inscriptions of the 8th c. have been found at Hamath in Syria (Driver, 121, 231; Ingholt, *Rapport préliminaire* (1940), 115 ff.); at Byblos, Phoenicia (dated from the 10th (?) c. onwards; Driver, 104 ff.; Dunand, *Byblia Grammata* (1945); Albright, *JAOS* lxvii (1947), 153 ff.); at Gezer and Samaria in Palestine (10th to 8th c.?; Driver, 109 f.); in Moab (9th c.; Driver, 108 f.).

[2] Woolley, *JHS* lviii (1938), 1 ff.; S. Smith, *AJ* xxii (1942), 87 ff.

[3] The earliest Greek sherds found were of the 8th c., but there had been earlier strata, now eroded by the river; Woolley, op. cit. 7 f.

[4] M. Robertson, *JHS* lx (1940), 2 ff. But cf. p. 10, n. 4.

[5] See n. 1 above.

[6] Cf. Hanfmann, *The Ægean and the Near East* (*Studies presented to H. Goldman*, 1956) 167; Desborough, *PG Pottery* (1952), 181 ff., 328; Clairmont, *Berytus* xi (1955), 85 ff.

[7] These divergences are summarized by Lidzbarski, *Hdb. d. nordsem. Epig.* i (1898), 186 ff.; Driver, 119, n. 2; Rosenthal, *Die aramäistische Forschung* (1939), 270 ff.

may have been adopted in some Greek settlement in Phoenicia proper. It has been pointed out[1] that the presence of the products of a centre (e.g. 'Rhodian' pottery) does not prove direct contact by that centre with Al Mina—i.e. the settlement and its trade connexions may not have been as mixed as I have implied. Nevertheless, the bare facts of the Al Mina site—an early Greek settlement with mixed Greek island pottery in a part which was called by the Greeks in general terms 'Phoenicia', and where the Aramaic alphabet was only differentiated from the Phoenician during the course of the eighth century—seem suggestive.[2] The possible importance of this settlement as a disseminator of Eastern art to the Greeks has been recently stressed;[3] and with the art the alphabet may have gone too.

## B. *Date of Introduction*

The dispute concerning this date has ranged over seven centuries—from the fourteenth to the late eighth.[4]

It is now known beyond all doubt that the 'Linear B' syllabic script was in use on the Greek mainland in the period Late Helladic III (*c.* 1425–1100).[5] Any theory which sets the date of the Greek alphabet before the eleventh century must therefore hold that, for a certain time, the two forms of writing were actually current in Greece together, as cuneiform and Aramaic were in the later Assyrian Empire, and that the syllabic script disappeared with the rest of the Mycenean culture under the Dorian Invasion, leaving the simpler Phoenician derivative to hold the field—or, possibly, survived the Invasion, but faded in process of time before its more practical rival.[6] Such an argument can only float in a vacuum as long as there are no examples of Mycenean script occurring as late

[1] M. Robertson *ap.* Smith, op. cit. 99.

[2] If the Aramaic form of the North Semitic alphabet had already diverged from the Phoenician by the start of the 8th c., that might rule out Al Mina, for her Greeks would then learn the Aramaic, not the Phoenician version; but as far as I know, so early a date has not yet been suggested.

[3] Barnett, *JHS* lxviii (1948), 1 ff. and *The Ægean and the Near East*, 234 ff. See now also T. J. Dunbabin, *The Greeks and their Eastern Neighbours* (1957), 24 ff., who suggests as birthplace Al Mina or Tarsus (p. 61).

[4] *c.* 1400: A. Mentz, *Rh. Mus.* lxxxv (1936), 347 ff.

*c.* 1200–1100: B. L. Ullman, *AJA* xxxi (1927), 326; 1934, 359 ff.; *Studies presented to E. Capps* (1936), 333 ff.; J. Boüüaert, *L'Antiquité classique* xiv (1945), 344 ff.

*c.* 1100: Larfeld[3], 208.

*c.* 1000: Szanto, *RE* (1894), s.v. Alphabet, 1613; J. B. Bury, *CAH* iv (1926), 470; A. Sigalas, Ἱστορία τῆς Ἑλληνικῆς γραφῆς (1934), 72; Schwyzer, 141.

*c.* 1000–900: A. Rehm, *Handbuch d. Archäologie* (ed. Otto), i (1939), 193 f.; J. P. Harland, *Stud. Phil.* xlii (1945), 426; C. Wendel, *Das griechisch-römische Buchbeschreibung* (1949), 80 and n. 449; F. P. Johnson, *AJP* lxxvii (1956), 36.

*c.* 900: E. Drerup, *Musée Belge* v (1901), 137; E.

Meyer, *Gesch. d. Alt.* iii[2] (1937), 347; P. Demargne, *La Crète dédalique* (1947), 148; G. Glotz and R. Cohen, *Histoire grecque* i⁴ (1948) (= i, 1926), 146; M. Falkner, *Frühgeschichte u. Sprachwissenschaft* (ed. Brandenstein, 1948), 110 ff.; F. G. Kenyon, *Books and Readers in Ancient Greece and Rome*² (1951), 15; Driver, 171 ff.; M. Guarducci, Ἑταιρεία Μακεδονικῶν Σπουδῶν ix (1953), 342 ff.; Buck, 348; G. Klaffenbach, *Griech. Epigraphik* (1957), 35.

*c.* 900–750: Beloch, *Griech. Geschichte* i. i² (1913), 228; W. F. Albright, *BASOR* lxxxiii (1941), 21 n. 28; *Studies in the History of Culture* (1942), 49; *AJA* liv (1950), 164; *The Ægean and the Near East* (1956), 162; R. Harder, *Die Antike* xix (1943), 95; H. L. Lorimer, *Homer and the Monuments* (1950), 128 (not later than the middle of the 8th c.). Cf. also Dunbabin, op. cit. 60.

*c.* 750–700: R. Carpenter, *AJA* xxxvii (1933), 8 ff.; 1938, 58 ff.

[5] See the excellent discussion by Dow, *AJA* lviii (1954), 78 ff. For the detailed publication on the transliteration of Linear B, see Ventris and Chadwick, *Documents in Mycenaean Greek* (1956).

[6] Cf. Mentz, op. cit. 365; Harland, op. cit. 419 f.; Albright, *AJA* liv (1950), 164 f.

as the Protogeometric period (11th–10th c.), nor of alphabetic writing earlier than the late eighth century. The alternative and simpler theory, accepted by most scholars, is that the Mycenean script died with Late Helladic civilization, and Greece knew a Dark Age of illiteracy again until the Phoenician alphabet was introduced. The Mycenean script contained at least eighty-eight complicated signs, as well as ideograms. Like hieroglyphic and cuneiform, it must have been a highly skilled craft, practised only by a small section of the community who were trained scribes, priestly or secular, attached to the local ruling classes. Had its use been widespread it might well have survived an invasion; but a craft so restricted would disappear with the deaths of the wealthy and their households.

It is generally agreed that there is no surviving example of the Greek alphabet which can be dated earlier than the late eighth century (pp. 16 f.). What then are the arguments of the scholars who set the introduction earlier by half a century or even several centuries? Nearly all of them were cited, and rebutted, by Carpenter in the course of his vigorous article in *AJA* 1933, 8 ff. Acknowledging the acumen which enabled him so often to set his finger directly on the weak points, I discuss the reasons again here only because in some cases either modification or expansion may be suggested.

The arguments that have been adduced in favour of an early date are as follows: needless to say, they are not all supported by every writer; but all have been reiterated since Carpenter's article, by one authority or another:

(1) The alphabet was obviously introduced at a time when the Phoenicians and Greeks were in contact; that contact occurred (according to these writers) in the *floruit* of Phoenician power from the twelfth to ninth centuries.[1] (2) If the earliest extant examples are of the eighth century, and show already a marked divergence both from each other and from the parent Phoenician, we must allow time for a period of development during which this divergence took place.[2] (3) The absence of surviving inscriptions before the late eighth century can be explained by assuming (i) that they may be yet found, (ii) that they were on perishable material, according to the ancient testimony—wood, skin, papyrus, bark, even leaves—and so have naturally left no trace.[3] (4) The early Greek letter-forms resemble those of Phoenician inscriptions of the eleventh to ninth centuries rather than those of the eighth.[4] (5) Colonies founded before the end of the eighth century used the alphabet of their mother-city, which must therefore have been brought out by the original colonists.[5] (6) The existence (i) of the *Iliad* and *Odyssey*, (ii) of written records of events whose start was ascribed to the eighth century (i.e. the Olympic register and the Spartan ephor list) show that the art of writing must have been already familiar before the middle of the eighth century.[6]

The arguments may be discussed in the same order:

(1) Though we may reject the extreme theory[7] which denies any Phoenician expansion

[1] Boüüaert, op. cit. 347.

[2] Larfeld[3], 210; Buck, *CP* xxi (1926), 15; Hiller von Gaertringen in Ebert, *Reallexikon* xi. 358; Guarducci, op. cit. 292; Demargne, op. cit. 148; Klaffenbach, op. cit. 34 f.

[3] Kenyon, op. cit. 8 f.; Buck, loc. cit.

[4] Ullman, *AJA* xxxviii (1934), 366 ff.; Klaffenbach, loc. cit.

[5] Rehm, op. cit. 173; Klaffenbach, op. cit. 34.

[6] Busolt, *Griech. Staatskunde*[3] (1920–6), 44 f.; Harder, op. cit. 105.

[7] Carpenter, *AJA* xxxvii (1933), 18. Albright holds that the expansion lasted from the 10th to the 8th c. (*Archaeology of Palestine* (1949), 112 ff., esp. 122).

westwards at all until the end of the eighth century, modern historians have repeatedly denied that the Phoenicians' connexion with Greece during the period of their expansion was anything more than the tenuous links of small trading-posts, established tentatively when circumstances were favourable, and abandoned without traces when they were adverse;[1] there are no signs of the settled intercourse which Dr. Carpenter rightly maintained to be essential for the transplanting of an alphabet (p. 7). But by the eighth century at least one Greek settlement had been made on North Semitic territory, at Al Mina, and by the end of the century (perhaps earlier) the Greeks had made themselves known at Hamath on the Orontes, and possibly elsewhere in this area.

(2) This argument has been reiterated more often, perhaps, than any of the others. It is generally stated as accepted and obvious: the earliest extant Greek examples already agree with each other in certain variations from the Phoenician letter-forms, and, on the other hand, already differ from each other in certain locally used forms; all but the 'Primitives' of the south Aegean use the supplementary letters, Φ, Χ, Ψ; we must therefore allow a considerable period of time (illustrated by one famous example, the Dipylon oinochoe; cf. p. 16) during which these developments occurred. The brief history of this process would be that an original alphabet ('Uralphabet') was evolved, very close to the Phoenician, and proceeded to spread, and from this common model which they had originally received more or less intact the local states, hedged off from close intercourse with each other, in process of time developed their own local alphabets, which we find already established by the early seventh century; and at the same time (in contradiction to the isolation that bred local forms) certain general developments also took place. For example, the earliest Rhodian inscription uses only the vertical *alpha* and straight *iota*, the earliest Theran only the four-stroked *mu*, the earliest Ionic shows no *vau*; but it is inferred that the Rhodian (and all others) originally used the horizontal *alpha* and crooked *iota* because the writer on the Dipylon oinochoe did: that the Theran (and all others) originally used the five-stroked *mu* because Cretan, Eretrian, and Melian did; that Ionic originally used the *vau* as (e.g.) Cretan did, because the sign is proved by the Milesian numeral system to have existed in the eastern Ionic abecedarium (pp. 326 f.).

Before discussing this theory it is as well to remember that the changes in the letter-forms are not all of the same kind. There are a few which appear to be merely mistakes, of the easy kind typified in English by the и and ꙅ; i.e. *lambda* with its crook at the top or base, *mu* with five or four strokes; these mistakes might well occur independently, and they are widely spread. Others are far less obvious, and hardly likely to have been achieved independently by different states; i.e. upright *alpha* from sidelong, straight *iota* from crooked. It is difficult to believe that the states were in close enough contact with each other in the eighth century (or even earlier) for the upright form to spread from one to the other and oust an earlier sidelong form. The simpler inference is that the original mistake or alteration was made in the very earliest stages of transmission, from Posideion (?) to, for example, Rhodes and Crete, and thus it was passed on to the rest (p. 23). The differences among the Greek local alphabets, both from the Phoenician and from each other, are, I think, due fundamentally to this cause; some of the changes were brought

---

[1] E. Meyer, op. cit. ii. 2². 117; Glotz-Cohen, op. cit. 145 f.; Albright, op. cit. 40 f.

about by the first receivers, so that the majority of receivers never knew the original Phoenician letter-form; and others (including the peculiar local forms) occurred in the subsequent process of transmission from one centre to another. The easy mistakes may have been made again and again independently by various transmitters or receivers. If the modern English alphabet were an archetype which was being transmitted by degrees through a large area, now by able writers and now by barely literate traders, would not И and Ƨ be found occasionally in places as accepted forms? Would it be necessary to postulate that these places had once received the correct forms N and S, and in process of time evolved the incorrect? An involuntary mistake made by either the person who teaches or the first person who learns the new script stands a good chance of being perpetuated as the correct form, in the primitive conditions of which we are speaking. In Thera, for example, the first transmitter or the first receiver may have made the initial mistake of omitting the last stroke of *mu*, and then any state which took its script from Thera would take the four-stroked form; whereas Melos received the five-stroked correctly, and retained it. We are thus spared an obvious awkwardness which besets the theory of the gradual development: namely, that peculiar local letter-forms and the 'undeveloped', near-Phoenician crooked *iota* and five-stroked *mu* occur most noticeably in such states as Corinth, Eretria, and Crete, which had far more external connexions in the eighth century than, for example, Boiotia, which in the early seventh century used straight *iota* and four-stroked *mu*. I have stressed elsewhere (pp. 3 ff.) that users of an alphabet tend to be conventional in their retention of forms; and I conclude that, if a mixed collection of states was using the straight *iota* in the early seventh century, it does not mean that they had all evolved (independently or by borrowing) this way of distinguishing the original crooked *iota* from *sigma*, but that one early transmitter (Rhodes?) had made the original alteration, and this altered form was handed thence, directly or indirectly, to a large part of Greece. This argument is further developed in the discussion of the individual letter-forms and the stages of transmission (p. 41); and I hope that sufficient grounds are there shown for the inference that most of the apparent 'development away from the Phoenician' actually occurred in the process of transmission, primary or subsequent, and that the changes actually seen in process in the local scripts during the seventh and sixth centuries, before the start of standardization in the fifth, are remarkably local and limited if compared with the widespread developments envisaged for the 'lost period'. The problem of the supplementary letters is also discussed below (pp. 35 ff.), where it is argued that some may have been known in Posideion (?), although apparently they did not reach the 'Primitives'. But the case of the Dipylon oinochoe (Attica 1, p. 68) must be discussed here, because it apparently offers valuable support to the belief in a 'lost' period of general development. On this oinochoe, of Attic fabric and found in an Attic grave, is a scratched retrograde inscription which shows crooked *iota*, *lambda* with its hook at the top, and (unique among Greek inscriptions[1]) *alpha* sidelong; whereas later Attic inscriptions—and the earliest of these may be not far in date from the Dipylon vase—show different forms (Fig. 26). Is not this a clear case of an alphabet

---

[1] Among the unpublished sherds from Hymettos, two are reported to have *alpha* 'almost on its side' (*AJA* xlvi (1942), 124).

which started in an 'Urform' very close to the Phoenician, and gradually developed its own local peculiarities? And if this is proved for the Attic, why should it not be inferred for every local alphabet? To this I can only reply that I do not believe this inscription to be Attic, because it seems incredible that, had the alphabet thus taken root in Attica by the period *c.* 725, there should not be other inscriptions among all the mass of Late Geometric pottery and bronzes now extant: not one owner's name on any of the innumerable Geometric cups and bowls, not one dead person's name on any of the funeral amphorae which stood as σήματα above the graves, not one deity's nor dedicator's name on any of the pottery and small bronzes offered in the sanctuaries; whereas in the succeeding periods (the end of the Geometric, the Subgeometric, and Protoattic) there is a number of inscribed examples in which *alpha* is completely vertical, *iota* straight (a change more easy to understand, although in fact the *sigma* and *iota* on the Dipylon oinochoe are so different in shape that there is no danger of their confusion) and *lambda* the near-Phoenician type with hook at the base. Although it is no longer maintained that the oinochoe should be brought down as low as *c.* 700 B.C. or even the first quarter of the seventh century,[1] the difference in time between it and the earliest of the Hymettos cups (Attica **3**) does not seem to me to be sufficient in itself to account for the absence of inscriptions on anything else as early as the oinochoe; and so, siding with others[2] who have suggested that the inscription is non-Attic, I conjecture that a literate person came to Athens in the late eighth century from Posideion (?), where these forms were in use, and the supplementary *chi* X was by this time known (p. 37), and inscribed the oinochoe on request, to demonstrate his ability; but the alphabet was not established in Attica until the end of the Geometric period, when the trading cities of Euboia and Aigina may have been responsible between them for introducing the type which took root and became the standard Attic which we know (pp. 42, 67).

(3) A few more very early inscriptions have been published since Carpenter's articles were written, but the Dipylon oinochoe still remains the only one which can be ascribed with any confidence to a date before the last years of the eighth century. The list of these inscriptions may be mentioned here, its members being discussed in detail under the relevant sections in Part III:

*Attica*: the Dipylon oinochoe (pp. 68 f.), and uncertain single signs on Geometric ware (p. 69); one painted inscription on a vase-fragment disputed as Geometric or Protoattic (p. 69); the Subgeometric ware from Hymettos (p. 69).

*Rhodes*: Subgeometric cup with graffito inscription (p. 347).

*Argolid* (Heraion): Subgeometric cup with graffito inscription (p. 149).

*Boiotia*: bronze statuette, early Orientalizing period (?), inscription cut with the bronze-worker's instruments (pp. 90 f.).

*Etruria*: abecedarium (written in the alphabet of Euboia, which was transmitted to Etruria via the Euboic colony Kyme), found at Marsiliana d'Albegna in early Orientalizing context (pp. 236 f.).

---

[1] Cf. Carpenter, *AJA* xxxvii (1933), 24 f.; Young, *Hesperia*, suppl. ii (1939), 228. Dr. Carpenter tells me (by letter, 1952) that he would now prefer a date *c.* 725–700, and that Young would suggest 'end of 8th c.'

[2] e.g. Young, op. cit. 229; Carpenter: 'possibly an early form of an Attic-Central Ægean type?'

*Corinth*: sherds of disputed date (late eighth century, early seventh, or even late sixth), with graffiti inscriptions (pp. 120 ff.); inscribed stone stelai bearing spits, possibly from beginning of seventh century (pp. 122 ff.).

*Ithake*: conical oinochoe, early Orientalizing style, with painted inscription (p. 230).

*Kalymna*: sherds bearing painted inscriptions and graffiti, Geometric (?) to early Orientalizing period (pp. 154, 353 ff.).

*Aigina*: plaque with painted inscription, Late Geometric style (? *c.* 720–700; pp. 68 f., 110).

*Pithekoussai* (Ischia): cup with incised verse, possibly eighth century (pp. 235 f.).

Nothing need be added to Carpenter's succinct comment (*AJA* 1933, 27): 'the argument *ex silentio* grows every year more formidable, and more conclusive. A negative argument is not valueless if the negative is universal.' As for the argument of lost inscriptions on perishable material, nobody doubts that there must indeed have been losses of this kind, but they do not affect the evidence of clay and bronze, two of the most durable writing materials known. Must we believe that the inhabitants of Greece in the ninth and first half of the eighth centuries, in flat contradiction to the habits of their descendants, forbore to inscribe their pottery with graffiti in any circumstances? Or that the Geometric potters and painters themselves either were all illiterates until the end of the Geometric period or had a convention (quite unshared by their descendants who produced the Orientalizing ware) against introducing any inscriptions, though the geometric shapes of the letters might have served admirably as additional decoration? Nor is pottery the only witness; none of the many Geometric bronzes dedicated in the sanctuaries at Olympia, Delphi, Delos, Dodona, Athens, and many lesser shrines, bears even the shortest dedication.[1] The earliest example of this kind is the Boiotian statuette mentioned above. If writing was indeed known in Greece from the early eighth century or earlier, it is extraordinary that the practical instinct for marking certain types of object, whether dedications which were to be the property of a deity, or utensils which were the property of individuals, or the σῆμα over a tomb, should have lain dormant for so long.

(4) Comparison between the appearance of the letter-forms used in archaic North Semitic inscriptions and in the earliest extant Greek is one of the most obvious methods of determining the date of the introduction. The letter-forms used in all the known archaic Semitic examples are arranged alphabetically in a chronological table, and a representative Greek alphabet, formed by synthesis from the earliest Greek inscriptions, is then matched against the successive columns, and where the general similarity seems greatest, there the date of the introduction is set. The theoretical value of this method is plain; so are the actual drawbacks. In any argument about likenesses, a subjective element is bound to enter; moreover, in using these facsimile tables it is easy to forget differences of place and material, so that a Semitic official inscription cut on stone in an unusual (relief) technique from Zinjîrlû would then be judged by the same standards as one written cursively in ink on a sherd from Samaria. Moreover, the dates proposed for the

---

[1] It has been suggested that a bronze Geometric horse in the collection of the late C. T. Seltman (who most kindly allowed me to examine it) has an inscription κα incised on the neck (Chittenden and Seltman, *Greek Art* (1947), 26, no. 43); but the letters bear no resemblance to the Phoenician or early Greek forms, and appear to me to be untidy incisions meant to represent the mane (*pace* C. Picard, *RA* 1958 i, 248).

Semitic inscriptions by the Semitic experts, on whom the Greek archaeologist must rely, are naturally subject to revision, as the scanty number of these inscriptions slowly increases; so that a table drawn up in 1934 and still cited in 1950[1] will inevitably be unreliable in its Semitic dates at several points, and often at those particular points where the Greek archaeologist has finally matched his list.

At the present time, the work of the Semitic experts has established a *terminus post quem* for the Greek alphabet somewhere in the ninth century,[2] using, as well as the general appearance of the other letters, the particular evidence of the *kap* and *dālet*. Both these Semitic letters grew a tail in course of time; the Greeks evidently knew only a *kap* already tailed, and a *dālet* still tailless. This tailed *kap*, from which the Greeks must have taken their *kappa*, cannot be attested with certainty earlier than the Meša inscription from Moab (*c.* 850 B.C.),[3] but is regular thereafter; while the tailless *dalēt*, the model for the Greek *delta*, occurs still at Byblos in the ninth century, but not in the Zinjîrlû inscriptions of the late ninth and the eighth century, nor normally anywhere later; but it does appear (sometimes, it is true, with an embryo tail) in the cursive painted script of the Samaritan sherds (? Jeroboam II, *c.* 774–766),[4] and again in the incised Phoenician dedication on some bronze bowl-fragments from Cyprus, dated in the second half of the eighth century, or possibly the early seventh. The upright lettering of these bowls, as has been pointed out,[5] is very like the earliest extant Greek forms; and the evidence of the Samaritan sherds is perhaps even more important, because they show also that in the middle of the eighth century—if this date is finally accepted—there existed, as well as tailless *dālet*, cursive forms of three other letters, *wāw*, *yôd*, and *ṣādê*, which look very like the prototypes of the Greek forms of *vau*, crooked *iota*, and *san* (pp. 24, 29, 33, Figs. 6, 10, 17),[6] though the signs on the sherds for *zayin*, *sāmek̲*, and *qôp* sometimes also show more cursive forms, which are not like the earliest Greek forms. Obviously, more examples of eighth-century cursive script and examples from farther north than Samaria are needed before any safe conclusions can be drawn concerning the date of the birth of the Greek alphabet; but the absence of these cursive forms of *wāw*, *yôd*, and *ṣādê* on any known Phoenician stone inscriptions of the eighth century supports the theory (p. 7) that the Greeks learnt the art of writing from the cursive script of Phoenician merchants more than from the more orthodox forms of monumental inscriptions. Indeed, it may be that the 'upright stance' of Greek *alpha* and *sigma* was not a Greek alteration from the Semitic, but was taken from ink-written, i.e. cursive, versions of *'ālep* and *šîn*, which might tend through speed to tilt the left part of the letter down from the horizontal (as p. 23, Fig. 1, no. 2).

(5) In general, the arts and industries of the Greek colonies suggest that ties with the mother-city remained strong at least for the first few generations; and this weakens the argument concerning the colonial alphabets. It is justifiable to conclude that if (for example) Kyme, founded in the middle of the eighth century, used the script of Euboia,

[1] Ullman, *AJA* xxxviii (1934), 364, table 1 (= M. Falkner, op. cit. 112 f.; Lorimer, op. cit. 130 f.).

[2] Driver, 178.

[3] For the list (with bibliography) of the archaic North Semitic inscriptions from which analyses are made, cf. Driver, 104 ff. and figs. 96–97. The table drawn up by Ullman (n. 1) is also very helpful, but the dates there suggested are now subject to revision in many cases.

[4] Driver, 109 ff.

[5] Carpenter, *AJA* xxxvii (1933), 13.

[6] Falkner rightly points out the likeness of the *wāw* and *ṣādê* to Greek *vau* and *san*, op. cit. 115.

then Euboic colonists must have brought that script with them; but it is not justifiable to conclude that these must have been the first colonists. The script might equally well have come with any later ἐποικία. If two adjacent colonies planted by different states use each the script of its mother-city, then it could be inferred that the later of the two brought its script with it (as, for example, Taras and the nearest Achaian colonies in south Italy); but even this is not certain, for bad relations may have kept both parties from even limited intercourse with each other.

(6) The problem of the composition of the *Iliad* and *Odyssey* ranges far beyond the scope of the epigraphist. With the arguments for simple or multiple authorship he is not directly concerned; he may start from the general conclusion that at some time during the Geometric period the poems were composed substantially in the form in which we have them now. It has never been denied that the trained memory, particularly among illiterate people, can both construct poems of this length and retain them for recitation without the aid of writing; and it has been pointed out in great detail by the late Milman Parry and others[1] that the repetitive element in the Homeric poems is characteristic of oral, not literary, composition. It is when the quality of such poetry is under consideration that the problem arises as to whether the human brain can in fact compose, without the aid of writing, a work of this length which is not merely a rambling, continuous narrative, but a unity of interrelated parts;[2] and such a point seems so subjective as to be incapable of proof on either side. Thus, if it is agreed that these poems could be retained in the memory, and undemonstrable whether they could or could not be constructed by memory alone, they offer no secure contribution *qua* poems as to the date of the birth of the Greek alphabet; nor do they offer internal evidence, for I take the σήματα λυγρά of Bellerophon's saga to be a traditional part of the Lykian story.[3] On the reverse side, all that the epigraphist can offer towards the solution of the Homeric problem is the observation that the Greeks may well have learnt the use of leather as a writing material when they first learnt their letters from the Phoenicians (p. 58). Papyrus was a foreign import, and was expensive even in the fifth century B.C.; but leather was a native product, and, were it felt to be necessary, poems of great length could be written on a leather roll as soon as the alphabet had established itself in Ionia. The circumstances which would cause such a procedure can only be guessed. An early rhapsode probably did not feel the need to aid his memory by writing down his stock of poems any more than the early musician felt it necessary to create a system of notation for recording his tunes; but when once contemporary poets committed their own poetry to writing, it could not be long[4] before somebody, either a wealthy patron of the arts or perhaps one of the Homeridai, undertook to have a written text made of these familiar epics, used as they were in the education of

[1] Cf. Lord, *AJA* lii (1948), 34 ff., and Dodds, *Fifty Years of Classical Scholarship* (ed. Platnauer, 1954), 13 ff.; Page, *The Homeric Odyssey* (1955), 138 ff.

[2] Cf. Wade-Gery, *The Poet of the Iliad* (1952), 37 ff.

[3] *Il.* vi. 168 ff. The diptych with its 'baneful signs' is an essential part of the story, which is set in Lykia. This suggests that writing was known in Lykia when the story took shape, but when Homer described the object he may have had **no** more intimate knowledge of the art of writing than he had of the Lykian monster— also an essential part of the story—which in Greek legend became the Chimaira. For a recent discussion of the passage cf. Lorimer, op. cit. 473 ff.; Miss Lorimer considers that the art of writing was in fact known to Homer at the time.

[4] The middle of the 7th c. is suggested on internal evidence by Miss Lorimer, op. cit. 526.

the young, the celebration of festivals, and even in arbitration over territorial disputes. Little can be said of the later tradition[1] which assigned such a role to Lykourgos of Sparta, alleging that he brought a copy to Sparta from the descendants of Homer's son-in-law Kreophylos in Samos; for the date and very existence of Lykourgos himself is still disputed. Hipparchos the Peisistratid, who made a poets' circle in Athens, introducing Simonides of Keos and Anakreon of Teos among others, was said to have first brought Homer to Athens and ordained that in the competitions at the Panathenaia the rhapsodes should take up the recitation one from another, so that the epics were delivered as a whole, in their proper continuity.[2] Obviously such a rule could not be enforced unless a definitive version of the text existed. Did Hipparchos bring to Athens an existing text, or did he himself first create it from scattered, orally transmitted lays? In spite of the views expressed by late authors that Hipparchos, or even his father Peisistratos, was the first editor of the Homeric poems,[3] it is hard to believe that the first texts of Homer came from anywhere but Ionia. The Peisistratidai possessed a collection of oracles collected for them by Onomakritos (Hdt. v. 90; vii. 6), and a tradition of unknown date (Athen. i. 4) related that they had a library of literary texts; but according to the same tradition Polykrates of Samos also made a collection of texts, among which we might well expect the poems of Homer to be included. From such a source Hipparchos might have brought a copy to Athens and atticized it in various ways.

The second line of argument in (6), it will be recalled, suggests that the practice of inscribing certain kinds of records—i.e. name-lists—must be older than the middle of the eighth century, because the Olympic list of victors in the stadion could be traced back to a beginning in 776, and that of the ephors at Sparta to 756; and such lists are manifestly official records, not to be regarded in the same light as genealogies, royal or heroic, which might be preserved unwritten in the family or the popular mind in various ways for various reasons. There can be no doubt that in the early Greek state there were holders of offices whose duties consisted, in part or in whole, of being recorders of events or decisions in both sacred and secular matters; their names reveal it: μνήμονες, ἱερομνή-μονες, the council of ἀ⟨να⟩μνήμονες at Knidos, and possibly the αἰσιμνᾶται (αἰσυμνῆται) at Megara and in eastern Greece, whose title seems to have meant originally a judge or umpire.[4] Plato describes in the *Hippias Maior* (285e)[5] how a similarly trained mind (that of the learned Hippias himself) could memorize fifty names upon hearing them once only. Obviously, the old name of 'remembrancer' was not affected by the later practice of recording such matters in writing; the Athenian θεσμοθέται were never called θεσμογράφοι, although Aristotle defines their duties as being 'to write up the laws, and keep charge of them' (*Ath. Pol.* 3. 4). But how are we able to define the point in time when records ceased to be carried only in the memory of those whose business it was to know them,

[1] Plut. *Lycurg.* 4; Herakl. Lembos, Πολ. ii. 3 = *FHG* ii. 210.

[2] Ps.-Plat. *Hipparchus* 228b. On the whole question of the part played by Peisistratos or the Peisistratidai, cf. T. W. Allen, *Homer: the Origins and the Transmission* (1924), 225 ff. Wade-Gery suggests (op. cit. 30 f.) that it was not Hipparchos but Perikles who invented the rule about continuity in recitation, in his

enactment which, according to Plutarch (*Per.* 13), first established musical events in the competitions at the Panathenaia. See further Page, op. cit. 129, 143 ff.

[3] Cicero, *De Orat.* iii. 34; Paus. vii. 26. 13; Aelian, *VH* xiii. 14; *Anth. Pal.* xi. 142.

[4] Cf. Busolt, *Griech. Staatsk.* i. 362, 372 ff., 488 f.

[5] Cf. Meritt, *Hesperia* viii (1939), 65.

and the memorized lists were inscribed in public? How can we divine whether it was a written or a memorized list that began in 776? Here again we touch upon a wide-stretching problem, that of the written sources which were available to Greek authors when they first became interested in composing prose accounts of past historical events. The absence in archaic Greece of such records of public events as those which were erected in Egypt or Assyria or Persia is a fact too well known to need enlargement here. The military deeds of whole nations were recorded for the reverence of their countless subjects by Rameses III on his temple of Amon, Shalmaneser on the Black Obelisk, and Darius on the Rock of Behistun. The kind of record which a Greek writer would find if he wished to narrate how Kleoboulos of Lindos led his army into Lykia (Lind. Chron., c. 23), or how the aristocracy of Chalkis and Eretria struggled over the Lelantine plain (Strabo 448), or how Kedon rose against the ruling power in Athens (*Ath. Pol.* 20. 5), was more obscure: a dedication from the spoils, a treaty banning the use of long-range missiles, a snatch from a drinking-song. No early chronicles of events, even in briefest form, have yet been found in any Greek state.[1] Fragmentary epigraphic evidence for the inscribing of name-lists exists for the sixth century, but not as yet earlier; it is given below, pp. 59 f.

The positive conclusions which may be drawn from the present evidence for the date of birth of the Greek alphabet are very few. The alphabet can be traced back to the end of the Geometric, the Subgeometric, and the early Orientalizing periods at many points; the most westerly are the colonies of Pithekoussai and Kyme, which must have been the source of the abecedarium found at Marsiliana d'Albegna (pp. 236 f.); the most easterly is Rhodes, with the Subgeometric skyphos of Korakos (p. 347). The contention remains true that the only certain inscription before the last years of the Geometric period is that on the Dipylon oinochoe from Athens, which shows a script unlike the normal Attic in the three letters *alpha, iota, lambda*; the first two are in near-Phoenician forms, but the third is not. We are not justified in inferring that, though no other local alphabet shows the 'Phoenician' sidelong *alpha*, they all nevertheless possessed it once, and all either evolved or borrowed the prevailing form (vertical *alpha*) during a period of development as yet unrepresented by any examples. If one of the earliest receivers received *alpha* in the latter form, then the majority of Greek states would never know any other form. The date for the establishment of the alphabet in the trading cities of the Aegean islands and mainland Greece should lie late in the Late Geometric period, according to our present evidence; it must therefore have been already in use at Posideion (?) in the Late Geometric period, and, if commerce between Posideion (?) and the nearest trading cities was active, the interval between the invention of the alphabet and its early transmission will not have been very long. On the present evidence we might infer that the date of birth was somewhere about the middle of the eighth century. See also Addenda.

## II. THE TRANSMISSION

A. *Primary Transmission from Semitic to Greek*

It seems a reasonable hypothesis, then, that a settlement of trading Greeks from certain

[1] Cf. Jacoby, *Atthis* (1949), 176 ff.

of the Aegean islands, established on the Syro-Phoenician coast, learnt the twenty-two-letter alphabet from the local Φοίνικες during the Late Geometric period, perhaps about the middle of the eighth century. I have already (pp. 2 ff.) argued against a particular view of this event which is still often expressed;[1] it is that of an individual inventor, who, observing the weaknesses of the Semitic alphabet as a vehicle for Greek speech, improved it straightway by converting the useless sounds of 'ālep, hē', and 'ayin and the semivowels wāw and yôd into vowels; and subsequently some inventor deliberately created extra symbols for the aspirated letters *phi* and *chi*, and (in the Ionic area) for *psi* and long *o*. As was said above, this suggests a desire for improvement for which the history of later alphabet-learners, even to our own day, offers little warrant. The reactions of the Etruscans, the Romans, and later inheritors from the Roman indicate that, unless the Greeks were exceptions from the usual rule, they too accepted their alphabet in the beginning uncritically from their teachers, making changes, indeed, from their very inability to pronounce exactly the Semitic names, but with no conscious desire to improve the set of letters by deliberate removals, alterations, and additions, except on the rare occasions when two letters seemed to them to be indistinguishable. The vital fact to which they held was the acrophonic principle—i.e. that the initial sound of each barbarous name which they had to repeat was the actual sound which the sign represented: 'ā-lep, b-êt, g-īmel, and so on. In this way, the usage of 'ālep, hē', and 'ayin to express *a*, *e*, and *o*, means that for the Greek, listening to the Semitic repetition of the alphabet, those vowels were the approximate Greek equivalents of the initial sounds in the names of the Semitic letters.[2] He did not consciously realize that the sounds which he made were, to a philologist's ear, in a different category from those of the Semite; the Semitic initial sound in 'ālep, hē', and 'ayin resembled his own sounds *a*, *e*, and *o* more than they resembled anything else to him, and so he used them as those vowels. As for the semi-vowels wāw and yôd, it has long been pointed out[3] that the Phoenicians themselves pronounced them on occasions almost as vowels, so that the alteration here was barely an alteration at all. The case of Cypriot Greek may be cited as a further parallel. The syllabary had no signs for the voiced sounds *b*, *d*, and *g*, essential parts of the Greek language, nor for the aspirated *th* and *ph*. But the early users accepted this lack, and did without the signs; and such was the power of convention that they remained unrepresented (as far as we know) as long as the syllabary was used.

It is now time to try to reconstruct the signs and sounds of the letters in the first Greek alphabet, including further such secondary changes as occurred, through error or other causes, when the alphabet spread among the rest of the Greeks. As a reminder of their Phoenician models, the Greek letters are here written in their earliest form, i.e. from right to left;[4] the Phoenician (=Ph) precede them, in square brackets.

---

[1] Roberts i. 6 f.; Hiller von Gaertringen, *IG* i². 267 f.; Bury, *CAH* iv. 469 f.; E. Meyer, op. cit. ii. 2². 118; Rehm, *Handbuch d. Archäologie* (ed. Otto, 1939), 192; Harder, *Das neue Bild* (ed. Berve), 95; Klaffenbach, op. cit. 33 f.

[2] Praetorius, *ZDMG* lxii (1908), 283 ff.; Schwyzer, *KZ* lviii (1929), 180, n. 1; Driver, 154 f. Cf. Boüüaert,

*L'Antiquité classique* xiv (1945), 344 f.; Schmitt, *Der Buchstabe H im Griechischen* (1952), 11 and 14.

[3] Larfeld³, 214; Driver, 154; Lorimer, op. cit. 129, n. 3.

[4] For general discussions of the Greek letter-names, see Hammarström, *Arctos* i (1932), 1 ff.; Schwyzer, 140 f.

ἄλφα (*'ālep̲*)

Ph  1  2  3  4  5  6  7  8  9  10

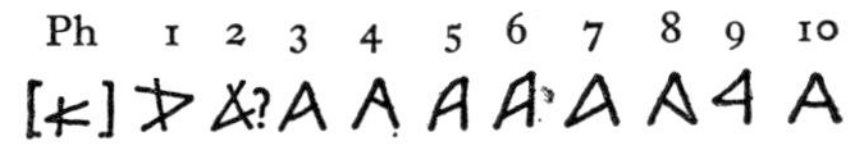

FIG. 1

One Greek example (Attica **1**) shows the sidelong type 1, reversed from the Phoenician; (cf. also p. 15, n. 1). Otherwise an upright form is used. This latter is not so obvious a simplification that we can dismiss it as a development made independently by all who used it. Hence I should guess that in Posideion (?) the Greeks learnt the sign 1 (reversed or otherwise), but that a variation such as 2 (which is quicker to write) became the form most generally used in cursive script, and this was the one which was spread to the 'first receivers' and thence onward. According to this theory, the use of 1 in Athens is isolated, a 'formal' letter written by a Greek from Posideion (?) or Athenian(s) who had visited there. In the local scripts, certain variations of *alpha* are characteristic: 3 in early Attic, and the majority of places; 4 in earliest Rhodian and Corinthian, and persistently in Megara and Aigina; 10 in Lakonian; 5–6 in Boiotian and occasionally elsewhere; 6 in the Achaian colonies *c.* 500–450. During the fifth century the symmetrical form 10 gradually became general.

βῆτα (*bêt̲*)

Ph  1  2  3  4  5  6  7  8  9  10  11  12

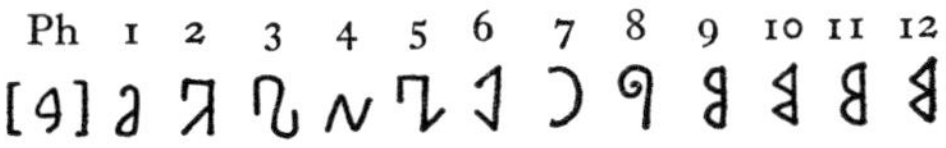

FIG. 2

*Beta* has more local variations than any other letter: Theran, 1–2; Corinthian, 3; Melian and Selinountine, 4; Byzantine (= Megarian), 5; Argive, 6; Cycladic, 7; Cretan, 8 (Gortyn); elsewhere, 9–12.

It has been maintained[1] that the allegedly alien forms such as 3, 7 are deliberate formations from *pi* to avoid confusion perhaps with *rho* or (in Corinthian, Megarian) with the freak *epsilon* (see below). I suggest rather that the original *beta* was envisaged as a vertical stem with curled ends, and in transmission the form was inadvertently altered in divers ways, the curls being exaggerated by one transmitter, minimized by another, and twisted by another. Phoenician *bêt̲* could be twisted also; cf. p. 114, n. 2.

γάμμα, Ionic γέμμα (*gīmel*)

Ph  1  2  3  4  5  6

FIG. 3

The earliest form in most places is 1, with variations 2 or 3. As the stem was sometimes written sloping, this could easily be confused with *lambda* (cf. the early Rhodian inscriptions); hence in most mainland states, and Rhodes, *gamma* was modified early to 4 or 5. In Lakonia, Euboia, Boiotia, Thessaly, and the Ionic of the Cyclades and Ionia it remained as 1 (in Melos reversed). In Attic (where *lambda* could not be confused) the isosceles form 6 prevailed.

[1] Kirchhoff[4], 102; Carpenter, *AJA* xxxvii (1933), 20, 22; xlii (1938), 67 f.

δέλτα (*dāleṯ*)

FIG. 4

Rarely (in early Eretrian, and spasmodically elsewhere), a slightly-tilted 'Phoenician' form 1 may be found; but the majority exaggerated it either to 2 or to 3 (variant 4). 3–4 are essentially mainland forms (Argos, Elis, Lakonia, Euboia (modified at first, see above), Boiotia, Phokis, Lokris, Achaia); they are not normal in the Aegean islands or Asia Minor, but occur once in Aiolis, in graffiti from Larisa (Aiolis **1**, p. 359). A shorthand form 5 was used at Eltynia in Crete (with *gamma* 3; p. 308).

εἶ, later ἒ ψιλόν (*hē'*)

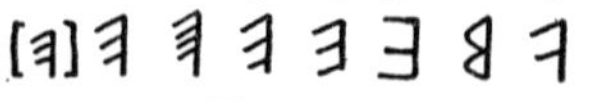

FIG. 5

This letter represented in Phoenician an aspirate *h*, with a potential vowel-sound *ē'* following it (p. 2). Phoenician possessed also the more emphatic-sounding aspirate *ḥêṯ*, which was naturally therefore the one to be used for the aspirate ⊢ (*hēta*) by the Greeks (p. 28). Hence it is not surprising that in the less emphatic Phoenician aspirate *hē'* the initial aspirate was passed over and the inherent vowel-sound was the one fastened on by the Greeks to express their own 'equivalent' sound, the vowel ε. For the use of this letter as a vowel (whether ε, ē, or the false diphthong ει) is universal in the Greek scripts; in Corinth and her neighbours, it was used for the false diphthong ει only, the curious *beta*-like form 6 being employed for normal ε and η. This 6 has been interpreted as a cursive type of 1,[1] but I follow Gercke's view[2] that it is a variant or doublet of closed *heta*: cf. pp. 28 and 114 f. A shorthand form 7 was used at Eleutherna in Crete (p. 308). The letter is occasionally found (as 2) with four or even more bars, e.g. in Gela, Boiotia, Delphi, Smyrna; but there is no good support for the theory that the four-barred *epsilon* was deliberately used as a local form at Gela (pp. 266 f.).

Ϝαῦ (*wāw*); see also ὔ ψιλόν.

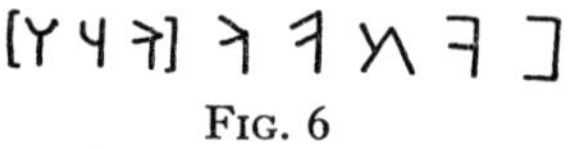

FIG. 6

The adoption of the Semitic *wāw* (semi-vocalic *u̯*) into the Greek alphabet was not a straightforward process. All Greek dialects used the pure vowel *u*, a sound which existed potentially in the Semitic letter (p. 22); but only certain dialects used the semivowel as well. The letter appears as (*a*) in Phoenician inscriptions, (*b*) in Aramaic (Zinjîrlû), and (*c*) in the cursive script of the Samaritan sherds (p. 18). In the earliest Greek inscriptions from all the states the Aramaic or Phoenician forms of the letter appear at the end of the alphabet, serving as the vowel *u*; while divers forms resembling the cursive Samaritan

[1] Larfeld, *Handbuch* i. 395; Falkner, op. cit. 125.   [2] *Hermes* xli (1906), 547 f.

type appear in the alphabet in the proper place of *wāw*, and were used by those states whose dialects employed the semi-vocalic sound as well. Hence it seems probable that the first Greek receivers formed a doublet from the Semitic letter, using the more cursive form for the true (semi-vocalic) value, and adding the other form, (*a*) or (*b*), at the end of the row, for the vowel. The Cretan types 1, 3 in particular seem to preserve a distorted form of the Semitic cursive type; elsewhere the letter may have been helped into its prevailing form 2 by the proximity of the like-shaped *epsilon* in the abecedarium. In the Peloponnese, northern and central Greece (except Attica), Crete, Euboia (through Boiotian influence?), *vau* was normal in the dialect. In Attica and Naxos it is attested in poetry only. In Rhodes, Thera, Melos, and Ionia it is not attested, nor in the Cyclades except for Naxos. But the early abecedaria of Attica and Amorgos, and the archaic Ionic abecedarium preserved in the so-called 'Milesian' alphabetic numeral system, all show that *vau* remained in its place in the row, as *san* and *qoppa* also appear to have done (pp. 66, 289, 326 f.). In its development the letter followed *epsilon*; the bars became horizontal, the tail was lost (5) or shortened (4). 4 is the most common form, but 5 is used in Euboia and her colonies, and in Boiotia and Thessaly; also in Korkyra in the fifth century.

ζῆτα (*zayin*; ζῆτα actually from *ṣādê*?); see also ξεῖ, σάν, σίγμα.

Ph   1   2   3

[I] I I ⊥

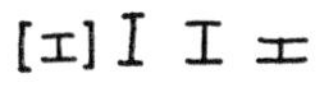

FIG. 7

With Phoenician *zayin* we reach the most complicated part of the alphabet for the Greek tongue—the pronunciation of the four Phoenician sibilants *zayin* (voiced *s*, i.e. *z*), *sāmek* (unvoiced *s*), *ṣādê* (*ts*), *šîn* (*sh*); and here it will be necessary to pause and consider what are the actual processes involved in learning an alphabet.

To learn an alphabet implies a triple feat of memory, two parts aural and one part visual. The pupil must learn by ear (1) the name of each letter, which, on the acrophonic principle, will give him in its initial sound the sound represented by the letter; *alpha, beta*, and so on, (2) the solitary sound itself, divorced from the complete name; and by eye (3) the visual sign of the letter. His aural memory will hold the names of the letters in their fixed order in the alphabetic recital, and his visual memory will hold the position of their shapes in the same sequence; and since in this particular case (in which a people of Indo-European speech is learning an alphabet developed for the Semitic tongue) exact accuracy of sound can hardly be expected, we might expect that there will be a few involuntary inaccuracies likewise in the order of the signs and their names. Whether the inaccuracies occur chiefly in the seen sign-list or in the heard sound-list depends in great part on the way in which the alphabet is taught by the master to the pupil. There is no direct evidence of the method by which the Greeks were taught. The method followed by the Romans is described by Dionysios of Halikarnassos and Quintilian.[1] It is evident from their descriptions that the children were taught first aurally, i.e. with the repetition of the names, and second visually, by writing the sign, repeating at the same time the

[1] Dion. Hal. *Demosthenes*, 52; Quintilian, *De Orat.* i. 1. 24; cf. Schwyzer, 140; Marrou, *Histoire de l'éducation dans l'antiquité*, 210 ff.

sound. Quintilian objected to this method, saying that the names and their shapes were thereby dissociated too much from each other: that children, having learnt the abecedarium as a patter, readily associated a name with the following name, but grew confused when they had to take each sound from its alphabetic context and associate it with other sounds to spell out words. M. Nilsson has rightly observed[1] that this is the obvious primitive method—to learn first to recite the name-list as a whole, and then to draw the sign-list; and he concluded that the Greeks learnt it in this way. This theory is certainly confirmed by the early Hebrew practice, whereby the master recited the names, the children repeating them, and so the Semitic name for the alphabet came from *higgāyôn* (= alphabetic poem), an onomatopoeic word formed from the root meaning 'to mutter or hum continuously'.[2] It would therefore be expected that, if the Greeks also learnt it by this method, in which continual repetition takes first place, this perpetual repetition would render mistakes in the order of the sounds less likely than mistakes in the order of the signs. But the earliest Greek abecedarium which we have, the Marsiliana tablet (pp. 236 f.), shows that visually the Greeks received the Phoenician alphabet-signs in the correct order (though the actual Phoenician shapes were not always accurately reproduced). Yet the names which they gave to these signs show that in certain cases they did not learn the correct aural order of the names. This brings us back to the case of *zayin*, for it was in the sibilants that this confusion arose.

In the places of the acrophonic names *zayin* (= voiced sibilant, *z*), *sāmek* (= unvoiced sibilant, *s*), *ṣādê* (= *ts*) and *šîn* (= *sh*), the Greek alphabet placed the acrophonic names *zeta* (= *ds* or by metathesis -*sd*-), *xi* (= guttural *k* or *ch*,+ sibilant), *san* (= Doric sibilant) and *sigma* (= unvoiced sibilant, *s*). Much has been written as to which Greek name represents which Phoenician, or, alternatively, whether any of them are not Phoenician at all, but Greek substitutes; for it is of course obvious that Greek *zeta* cannot be derived directly from Phoenician *zayin*, nor *xi* from *sāmek*, nor *san* from *ṣādê*, nor *sigma* from *šîn*. *Zeta* might certainly have been brought about by assimilation with the following *eta, theta*;[3] but the other three Phoenician names have unquestionably suffered either transplanting or total abolition.

If, in studying these names, we bear in mind our previous hypothesis, namely, that the first Greek learners were following the Semitic alphabet to the best of their ability, not consciously trying to alter it by addition or subtraction, we should conclude that, though neither the sign nor the sound was reproduced with complete accuracy, nevertheless the four Phoenician names with their sounds are all represented in the Greek, and therefore must be out of order. Which then are the names which should be equated? I think there can be little doubt that *ṣādê/zeta* must be paired, and likewise *sāmek/sigma*; in both cases the names are very similar, and (even more important) the acrophonic principle holds good, i.e. the sound-values which the Phoenicians gave to *ṣādê* (*ts*) and *sāmek* (*s*) are the sounds given by the Greeks to *zeta* (*ds, sd*) and *sigma* (*s*). *Zayin* and *san* are equally close in name; if we equate them, the acrophonic principle should hold here also, and I therefore infer that this was indeed the case, and that (originally at least) the sound of *san* was

[1] *Die Übernahme u. Entwicklung d. Alphabets durch die Griechen* (1918), 6 ff.  [2] Driver, 90.

[3] Cf. Larfeld[3], 205. For the existence of a variant Semitic form *zayit*, see Schwyzer, 140, n. 4.

not an unvoiced sibilant like *sigma*, but a voiced sibilant, as English *z* (see further, pp. 33, 41). This leaves *šin/xi* for the final pair; and if the final *n* of *šin* is dropped on the analogy of the surrounding letters (*mēm, nûn, šin, 'ayin* becoming *mu, nu, ?shi, ou*), we should then have *šî(n)/xi*. At this point it must be recalled that the sound which went under the general name of *xi* was in fact pronounced in varying ways in the different dialects of Greece, and only certain of the local scripts in fact used the letter Ξ, namely, the majority of the Ionic states, and the Corinth–Argos group on the mainland. The Naxians, for example, used the combination *heta+sigma*, i.e. -*hs*- (pp. 289, 291); the Athenians, and most other Greeks, the guttural aspirate *ch+s* (ΧΣ, sometimes becoming Χ; see further under ξεῖ). It is difficult to believe that these states had never known of the existence of the sign Ξ; we are not dealing here with a supplementary letter-sign, but with one embedded right in the centre of the Phoenician abecedarium. I suggest therefore that the first Greek learners, confusing the pair, gave to the Semitic *šin*-sign the name and value of *sāmek*, *s*, and to the Semitic *sāmek*-sign the name and value of *šin*, *sh*, as near as their tongue could get to it, which may have been something like *ksh*: that for most Greek dialects this sound was useless, and the letter was accordingly left 'frozen' in the formal abecedarium (as in the Marsiliana tablet, where it appears in a curious 'closed' form (Fig. 15), while the Greeks proceeded, quite naturally, to express their own compound sound by the combination of whichever two other signs, *ks* or *chs* or *hs*, best expressed the sound in their dialect. But the majority of the Ionic and the Corinth–Argos group of alphabets did use the (Semitic) sign Ξ to express the sound, and this I take to mean that in their dialects (or, if one got it from the other, in the dialect of the first) the pronunciation of the compound did approximate, originally at least, to the *?kshi* (*šin*) sound (see further under ξεῖ).

Thus the first Greek learners passed on to their immediate receivers an alphabet in which the four sibilants were visually in their correct places in the row, but aurally had been transposed in pairs—a transposition easy to understand, for the sounds of the sibilants *z* and *ds* (*ts*) are not dissimilar, nor the sounds of *s* and *sh*. Yet the mere fact that mistakes could be made in this way suggests that the first Greeks learnt their alphabet more from concentrating on the written row and applying the names than from continuous oral repetition; and the same dissociation deplored by Quintilian (produced by not learning each unit separately as a comprehensive whole—name, sound, and sign)—caused them, in the case of these somewhat similar pairs of sibilants, to apply the wrong name (and therefore the wrong sound) to the correctly placed sign. A further point may endorse this. The Semites called the alphabet *higgāyôn*, 'the muttering', and the Romans called it 'abecedarium', after the first four names;[1] in both cases the general name is derived from the aural sound. But the early Greek names for it—τὰ γράμματα, τὰ φοι-νικήϊα (γράμματα), τὰ στοιχεῖα—suggest that for Greeks learning it its most salient factor was not the spoken sound, but the written sign—the 'drawing' (γράμμα), the 'unit in the row' (στοῖχος); p. 40). *Zeta*, then, has the correct Semitic sign which followed that of *wāw*, but the name+sound of another sibilant, *ṣādê*. Its fundamental value in Greek appears

---

[1] Cf. Hammarström, *Beiträge z. Gesch. d. etrusk., lat. u. griech. Alphabets* (1920), 15 ff.

to have been that of *ds*, although it was also used, by metathesis, for *sd*.[1] In archaic Elean and Arkadian it appears for the dental δ or τ. The form remained close to the Phoenician; archaic examples tend to be tall; the squat 3 appears sometimes in the fifth century (Corinth, p. 115).

ἦτα (*hêt̯*)[2]

Ph  1   2   3   4   5   6   7

[ꓧ] ⊟ ⧠ ⊟ H H H ⌐

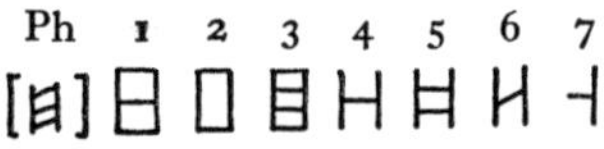

FIG. 8

As Phoenician *hē'* had for the Greeks on hearing it a syllabic value *he*, which became in Greek '*e*, so *hêt̯* seems to have been learnt originally by the Greeks as *hēta = hē*, the whole, both aspirate and following vowel, being a more vigorous sound than that of *hē'*. In dialects which used the aspirate, i.e. those of the Greek mainland (except Elis and Arkadia), the Doric Pentapolis, the central and southern Aegean islands (except Crete), and which needed therefore to express it in their script, the initial sound, the aspirate, naturally predominated over that of the following vowel; but in the eastern Ionic dialect and Cretan, which were both psilotic, the name was pronounced '*ēta*, and the value *ē* naturally attached to it. If this view is right, it is inaccurate to speak of the Ionians as employing a 'useless' letter to mean η; η was the value which their psilotic dialect naturally gave to it. Some of the early receivers whose dialects possessed the *h* managed to retain the double value inherent in '*hē*' either simply by using the same letter for both ⊦ and η (Rhodian, Parian), or by evolving some form of doublet. Thus in Naxian 1 (or 4) stands for ⊦, and also for the η which came from an original *ā̄, while a doublet 2, used only in combination with *sigma*, has the value of a medial aspirate verging on a guttural (Ναⷭσιος= Ναξιος). In Knidian, 2 stands for η and 1 (or 4) for ⊦; and in Corinthian 1 (or 4) for ⊦ and (if Gercke's theory is right; see εῖ above) a doublet formed from 1 for ε and η. In a few archaic inscriptions 1 seems to be used with the full syllabic value: cf. Naxos **2**, where it stands for the initial ⊦ε in ⊦εκηβολοι: Metapontion **16** (⊦ερακλῆς). The sign 1 seems to have been simplified to the 'open' 4 in Ionia and the Aegean islands by about the mid-sixth century, in Attica shortly after, and in the rest of central Greece and the northern Peloponnese by about the end of the sixth century; in the rest of the Peloponnese and in Crete 1 was still used in the fifth century. 6, the open *heta* with sloping bar, occurs spasmodically in various places, rarely before the fifth century; though common in the scripts of the Italic peninsula, it seems to have been only an occasional form in Greek. The 'open' form 4 was perhaps evolved for cursive, ink-written script (p. 64). The form 5

[1] Wackernagel *ap.* Nilsson, op. cit. 24.

[2] For a detailed study of this letter, see A. Schmitt, op. cit. (p. **22**, n. 2). His thesis is that the 'Erfinder' of the Greek alphabet used only the sign E for the sounds of ε, ἔ, η, ἤ; but the sign of *heta* (= *he*) was preserved by convention in the abecedarium. Later it was realized that the *heta*-sign could be used to express the aspirated ἔ and ἤ, and thence came the further development, the use of *heta* for ⊦ only. I am not convinced by this argument, because I cannot accept its epigraphic premiss,

namely, that the 5th-c. Gortyn Code (Crete **7**), which uses E for ε and η alike, shows in this an archaism representing the Cretan script in its earliest form, i.e., earlier than the known 7th-c. and 6th-c. inscriptions of Crete, which certainly use the *heta*-sign for η. If this premiss is rejected, there is no other evidence to disprove that this sign was (as one would expect) used as an aspirate from the start by those dialects which contained the aspirate. For the syllabic use of *heta*, see Schwyzer, 145 f.; Lejeune, *REA* li (1949), 6 f.

occurs regularly at Eleutherna in Crete, spasmodically elsewhere. 3 is also attested spasmodically, chiefly in Euboic and Boiotian (pp. 89, 190 n. 4, 237). I do not think that the occurrence of this form is frequent enough to suggest that it was ever a regularly used variety. The type 7 is attested mainly on south Italian vases, after the fifth century; the earliest example that I know is that on a 'phlyax' vase in New York, *c.* 400: εγω παρⱶεξω.[1] It occurs also in the fourth century in the inscriptions from Herakleia *DGE* 62–64, and in a local decree from Olympia[2] in the word αδεαλτωⱶαι, itself a *hapax legomenon*. An earlier example apparently occurs on a bronze fragment from the Asklepieion at Epidauros, which can hardly be much later than *c.* 500 (p. 181). The subsequent palaeographical history of type 7, the *spiritus asper*, is well known; its place of origin may have been Taras (p. 183), for most of the early examples are from that area.[3]

θῆτα (*ṭêṭ*)

FIG. 9

The approximate sound of the Phoenician letter found its equivalent in all the Greek dialects. In early inscriptions the forms 1 or 2 appear to be used indifferently; by the late sixth century 2 is the more regularly used. The crossed form lasted to the second half of the fifth century in the Peloponnese, but in most places elsewhere it was replaced before the middle of the fifth century by 3. 3 sometimes appears in inscriptions of the third quarter of the sixth century or even earlier (e.g. Eretria **9**, Boiotia **1**, Attica **30**). When a cutting-compass has been used, it is possible to explain an early example of dotted *theta* as due only to the mason's forgetting to add the cross; but obviously this cannot be always the reason. The dotted *theta* was probably first evolved by those writing rapid script with a brush; it is normal on Attic vases from *c.* 560 onwards (see further pp. 66, 74).

ἰῶτα (*yôḏ*)

FIG. 10

The local scripts of Greece are divided into those which used a crooked form of *iota* (1–4), and those which used a straight (5). There can be no doubt that the crooked is the original form, and I have mentioned above (p. 18) the possibility that it came from a cursive rendering (*b*) of the Phoenician letter (*a*), which was written as (*b*) in order to achieve the letter by a single stroke of the brush (as on the Samaritan sherds, p. 18 above). The first Greek receivers apparently learnt this merely as a zigzag line with an indefinite number of strokes, for local variants are many: 1 (Corinth), 3 (Crete), 2 (Achaia), 4 (Ithake); crooked *iota* 2 is also attested in Phleious and northern Arkadia, perhaps by contamination with Achaian (see p. 209), and in the solitary graffito Attica **1**. Except for

[1] Beazley, *AJA* lvi (1952), 193 ff.     [2] Szanto, *Ö.Jh.* i (1898), 197 ff.     [3] Roberts i. 271.

Attica and Arkadia (in neither of which was crooked *iota* normal), the sibilant-letter used in all these places was not the (unvoiced) *sigma*, but voiced (?) *san*, whose sign was quite distinct from the crooked *iota*. The straight *iota* is an obvious simplification for any state to adopt whose dialect used *sigma* for the sibilant. It is generally maintained that originally the crooked *iota* was used by all the local scripts, and was gradually replaced by the straight form 5. I find this hard to accept, because of the great discrepancies in the dates which it involves; for instance, Rhodes, Attica, Boiotia, Euboic Kyme and Pithekoussai, Amorgos, and the Argive area already used 5 by the early seventh century (the last-named district being, moreover, a *san*-user), while Corinth used the crooked form until at least *c.* 500. Hence one may guess that the alteration from crooked to straight was made by one of the first receivers, whose dialect required the use of (unvoiced) *sigma* (e.g. Rhodes, Euboia, Ionia?), and straight *iota* was thus passed on to the numerous places which ultimately derived their script by this channel, and which, according to this view, never had the chance of using crooked *iota*. But the latter, the original form retained by the southern Aegean Doric islands and an area round Corinth and Achaia, was the form used in Posideion (?), and made a single appearance in a graffito as far afield as Athens (on the Dipylon oinochoe, Attica **1**).

κάππα (*kap̲*)

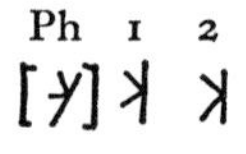

Ph  1  2

FIG. 11

In archaic examples the transverse bars do not always join the vertical at the same point. 2 is normal by the fifth century.

λάμβδα, λάβδα¹ (*lāme̲d*)

Ph   1  2  3  4  5  6

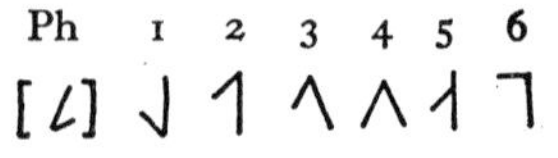

FIG. 12

The Phoenician sign was reversed (1) and further inverted (2) in the local scripts of Greece. The reversal was perhaps natural, for the Semitic letter appears to face against the current of the retrograde abecedarium; but the further inversion seems to have been an involuntary mistake (perhaps because the following two letters *mu* and *nu* also carried their 'crooks' at the top), made by some at least of the first Greek receivers and perpetuated in the majority of Greek scripts. Those which used the form closest to the Semitic were the group Euboia, Attica, Boiotia, and Opountian Lokris, and certain scattered places in Crete—Dreros, Knossos, Eltynia, and Praisos. Inversion from 1 to 2 is a simple mistake that could be made independently, and it would be rash therefore to ascribe all local examples of 2 to a single archetype in one of the earliest transmitters; the case of Crete, with her variety, is sufficient warning (pp. 308 f.). *Lambda* 2 tended

---

¹ λάβδα is the earlier form; Schwyzer, 140, n. 2.

to become 3–4 in the course of the late archaic period, except in places where *gamma* already had these forms. The only notable variation is 5, the Argive, presumably a deliberate alteration to avoid confusion with Argive *gamma*. 6 appears in the fifth century occasionally (e.g. in Paros (with Thasos), and Afrati in Crete).

μῦ, Ionic μῶ (*mēm*)

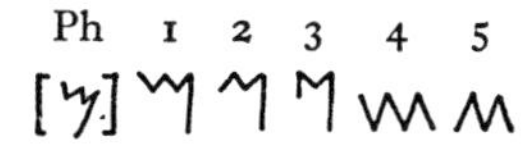

Ph   1   2   3   4   5

FIG. 13

As the number of strokes in the crooked *iota* varied among the local scripts, so in *mu* the original five strokes were in many places shortened to four. The original form 1 was transmitted to Crete, whence it appears in the scripts of Melos and Sikinos also; but Thera, the other Doric island which presumably also took her alphabet from Crete, shows 2 even in her earliest inscriptions; so also does Corinth, and all her neighbours which likewise used an alphabet akin to the Cretan. In Euboia Eretria certainly (Chalkis possibly, p. 81) used the original 1; but (unlike *lambda* 1) 1 is not found in Boiotian or Attic, even in the earliest examples before the middle of the seventh century. Since there is otherwise a close connexion of Euboic with Boiotian, Cretan with Theran, I infer that these examples show that 1 could be altered (in error?) to 2 during the process of transmission, and 2 need not be explained invariably as a later development from a 1 in previous use; it is not necessary to postulate that 1 was once used in Thera and Boiotia in an early period of which we chance to have no examples. 1 was retained in Eretrian until the late archaic period, developing to 4 as the parallel form 2 developed elsewhere to 5; in Cretan and Melian 4 was retained with all the other local forms into the second half of the fifth century. Apart from the general development of the four-stroked *mu* from 2 to 5 during the late sixth and early fifth century, two minor local variations may be noted: in certain Peloponnesian states (Argos, Kleonai, Phleious, Tiryns) the outer strokes of the archaic form were parallel, 3 (in contrast with the more splayed 2); in Lakonian and eastern Ionic the fourth stroke is lengthened (5) even in the earliest examples. It will be noted from the above illustrations that the use of 1 has no particular connexion (as has been sometimes inferred) with the use of *san* in the same alphabet.

νῦ, Ionic νῶ (*nûn*)

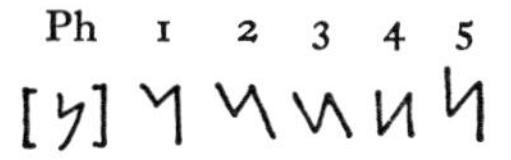

Ph   1   2   3   4   5

FIG. 14

There are no marked local variations of *nu*. It developed steadily from early 1 to the more cursive 2, the outer strokes becoming vertical finally during the fifth century (4). As far as can be judged, the form 5 occurs first in Ionic some years before the middle of the fifth century, and elsewhere (Attica, the Western colonies) during the third quarter.

ξεῖ (*sāmek̲*; ξεῖ actually from *šīn*?); see also ζῆτα, σάν, σίγμα.

Ph   1   2   3   4   5   6   7   8   9

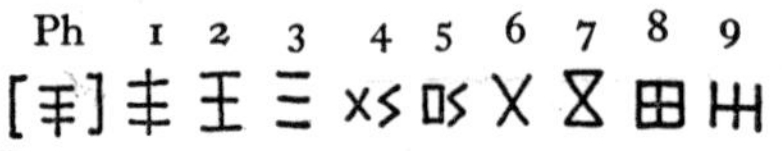

FIG. 15

A possible origin for the Greek name *xi* has been outlined above under *zeta*, where it was suggested that the Phoenician sibilants *sāmek̲* (*s*) and *šīn* (*sh*) were endowed with each other's names + sounds in error by the Greeks. If the letter Ξ was thus held to represent a sound something like *sh* by the Greeks, this would at least explain why it was used only in certain local scripts, notably the eastern Ionic; the sibilant *sh* was alien to the purer Greek dialects, but may have been less so among those of Ionia (which, it will be recalled, differed perceptibly among themselves (see further p. 327), and must in some cases, e.g. Miletos, have owed something to their contact with the non-Greek races of Caria and Lydia). The letter Ξ ('blue' *xi*) was used in eastern Ionic, and in the Argive–Corinthian circle; among the Cyclades it is attested at Keos in the late archaic period, and in Crete in the Eteocretan language of Praisos, and in Thera, where it is used for the initial consonant of the name Zeus (p. 317). I would suggest therefore that the original abecedarium ran '*mu = m, nu = n, xei = sh*'; the earliest receivers learnt it thus, and of these the Ionians found a use for it; the Cretans did not (except in Eteocretan), but passed the abecedarium containing it to Thera and Corinth, which each used it, the Corinthian usage being mainly due not to their dialect, but to influence from Ionia, whence (perhaps) they had also taken the complementary letters Φ, Χ, and Ψ = *ps*. Among the other Greeks, the sound was spelt as 4 (= *chs*?) by Paros, Attica, Boiotia, Rhodes; 5 (= *hs*?) by Naxos; 6, 'red' *xi* (originally as 4?) by Euboia, most of the Peloponnese, Phokis, Lokris, Thessaly; 7 by Knidos; and quite simply as *k+s* by Doric Crete, Thera, Melos. 'Blue' *xi* was retained in the early abecedarium of Euboia in the 'fossilized' form 8 (see p. 80), though the later abecedaria of 'red' *xi*-writers (i.e. Χ-users) have apparently dropped it (e.g. Boiotia **20**, Metapontion **19**). Its earliest shape in Greece seems to have been 1, becoming 2 in some places as early as the end of the seventh century; 3, an Ionic development from 2, occurs in the sixth century and later (pp. 290, 325, 369). 9 was apparently the practice of Argive masons during the fifth century (p. 152).

οὖ, later ὂ μικρόν ('*ayin*)

This sound became in Greek pronunciation the vowel *o* (see p. 22), and the sign was used for both the pure vowel and the improper diphthong ου (except in Corinthian; see p. 116). The loss of the final consonant in its name may have come by analogy from the preceding *mu, nu, xi* (*mēm, nûn, ?šīn*). In the earliest inscriptions the letter is very small in proportion to the others; otherwise it has little scope for any idiosyncrasy, compared with that of its colleague *omega* (see below). In the first half of the fifth century an exaggeratedly small *omikron* was sometimes used in the Argos–Corinth area and occasionally elsewhere.

πεῖ (*pē'*)

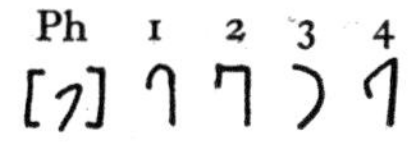

Ph   1   2   3   4

[7] ٦ ٦ ) ٩

FIG. 16

The sign and sound of this letter were both simple for the Greeks and little need be said of it. The earliest form is sometimes rounded, 1 (Crete, becoming 3 at Gortyn, Lyttos, Eltynia, Afrati, in the fifth century); Boiotian frequently shows 4.

σάν (*ṣāḏê*; 'σάν' actually from '*zayin*'?); see also ζῆτα, ξεῖ, σίγμα.

(a) (b)   1   2

[ᛗ ᛉ] Μ Ϻ

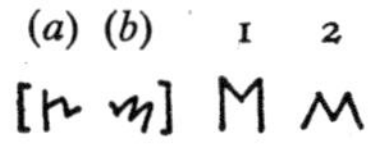

FIG. 17

It has been suggested above (under ζῆτα) that the names + sounds of the Phoenician *zayin*-sign and *ṣāḏê*-sign were exchanged in error by the Greeks, so that the *zayin*-sign was called '*ṣāḏê*', *ts*, and the *ṣāḏê*-sign '*zayin*', *z*. Perhaps this latter sound, the voiced sibilant, was used in the Doric dialect of Crete and Corinth (which used *san*), but not in the Ionic (which therefore used the sign of the harder sibilant, *sigma*), nor in the Doric of Rhodes and Lakonia. Hence (like *vau* and *xi*) the letter was used by some, left unused by others; by the sixth century, the abecedaria of *san*-users had lost the sign *sigma* (Corinth **16**, Metapontion **19**) and, perhaps, those of *sigma*-users the sign *san*. By the second half of the fifth century, the sign of *san* was no longer in use, except in conservative Crete, and as an emblem on the coins of Sikyon, and also as a brand for the breed of horses called σαμφόραι;[1] but, though it was now written as ξ, the name *san* for the letter still persisted among the Doric states (Hdt. i. 139). It was also used widely as a poetical name for the sibilant (even in places where the *sigma* was always used), partly perhaps for metrical reasons.[2] The Greek form of the letter, 1, has no particular resemblance to the *ṣāḏê* (a) of Phoenician formal lettering on stone, but might well be derived from the cursive form (b) as used on the painted sherds from Samaria, which have been dated near the middle of the eighth century (p. 18). Like *mu*, *san* develops to 2 in cursive writing by the late archaic period, occasionally earlier.

ϙόππα (*qôp*)

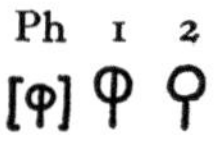

Ph   1   2

[ϙ] Ϙ Ϙ

FIG. 18

The use of *qoppa* (i.e. the guttural *k* before the vowels *o* and *u*) was widespread among the local scripts; only Lakonia and Phokis apparently lacked it altogether (pp. 100, 183).

[1] Böttiger suggested (*Kleine Schriften* ii. 162) that, as both Corinth and her neighbour Sikyon had horse-breeding plains, the horses branded with the *qoppa*-sign (the κοππατίαι) may have been a notable Corinthian breed, and those with the *san* Sikyonian. If this were so, it would add point to Ar. *Eq.* 603; the Athenian cavalry chargers, having drawn their iron rations and issue mugs and embarked in horse-transports for their attack on the Corinthian coast, reproach the *samphoras* for not pulling his weight: οὐκ ἐλᾷς, ὦ σαμφόρα;

[2] Cf. the citations in Athen. 454f (Neoptolemos of Parion), 455c, 467b (Pindar), 466f (Achaios of Eretria).

After the middle of the sixth century it gradually fell out of use, lingering in some of the Doric dialects until well into the fifth century (Argos, Corinth, Crete, Rhodes). The earliest Greek form (1) resembled the Phoenician; 2 seems to be established everywhere by the middle of the sixth century, perhaps earlier.

ρ̃ῶ (*rêš, rôš*)

Ph   1   2   3   4   5   6
[4]  ٩   ٩   ۹   ۹   ◁   ▽

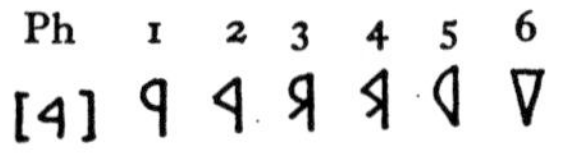

FIG. 19

1 or 2 is the normal form everywhere in the early period. 3–4, variants of the tailed form which was developed probably to distinguish *rho* from *delta* 3–4, are well attested from the late archaic period (*c.* 520–480) onwards; earlier examples are very rare (Lakonia **1**, Argos **14**, Naxos **3**?). 5, the legless *rho*, occurs in eastern Ionic (Samos, Miletos) and spasmodically elsewhere; 6 is characteristic of Megara, and occasionally Corinth.

σίγμα (*šin*; 'σίγμα' actually from *sāmek̠*?); see also ζῆτα, ξεῖ, σάν.

Ph   1   2   3   4   5
[w]  ٤   ٢   ٤   ٢   ٤

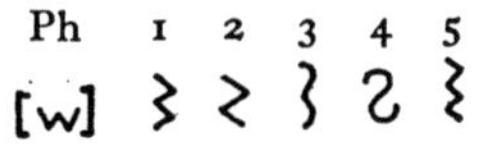

FIG. 20

It was suggested above (ζῆτα, ξεῖ, σάν) that the Greeks confused the names + sounds of *sāmek̠* and *šin*, calling the Phoenician *sāmek̠*-sign *ši(n)* (ξεῖ) and the *šin*-sign *sāmek̠* (σίγμα). The letter was stood on end by the Greeks; and the earliest writers apparently had not a fixed idea of how many strokes it should contain. The four-stroked 1 is normal in early Samian and Milesian (often also 3), Rhodian, Parian, Arkadian, Boiotian; the three-stroked 2 in Naxian, Euboic (4 in Rhegion), Attic, Thessalian, Elean, in the Ionic of Kolophon and Smyrna: but the use of one form or of the other is never invariable. The only notable local variation is the Lakonian 5, first attested in the early sixth century (pp. 184 f.); it ceased to be the normal form during the first half of the fifth century, but makes a last appearance in a state document of the years 403–399 (Lakonia **62**). 5 also appears on an early sherd from Smyrna (p. 341), and apparently in a very early Attic graffito (Attica **2**).

ταῦ (*tāw*)

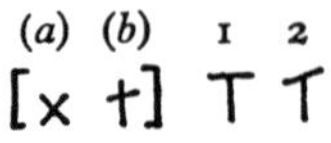

(a) (b)   1   2
[× †]   Τ   Τ̆

FIG. 21

The type 1, universal in Greek except for variations like 2 in badly-written graffiti, has its nearest equivalent in Semitic in the form (b) on the bronze bowls from Cyprus which are dated perhaps *c.* 700.[1] No marked changes in the shape took place; evidently the

---

[1] Carpenter, *AJA* xxxvii (1933), 12 f.; Driver, 107 (whose date is here followed).

Greek instinct for symmetry was satisfied with it from the start. In Etruscan, however, the form 2 is often found, and we can trace this back to the Etruscans' early model abecedaria (pp. 236 f.).

ὔ (later ὔ ψιλόν)

(a) (b) (c)  1  2  3  4  5

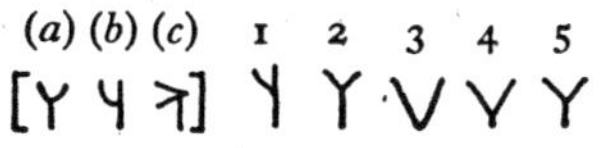

FIG. 22

The early history of this letter has been discussed under Ϝαῦ, the generally accepted view being that the actual sign is that of the Phoenician letter *wāw* (above, (a); (b) is Aramaic, (c) cursive as on the Samaritan sherds). The cursive equivalent (c) was apparently employed as a doublet by the Greeks to express the semi-vowel. The usual early form is 1; 2 occurs in, for example, Theran, Corinthian, Amorgan. The simplification to 3 (occasionally 4) appears first in painted vase-inscriptions (Corinth **9**, *c.* 625, Athens **14**, *c.* 575–550) and graffiti, becoming common on stone in the second half of the sixth century. During the fifth century the form 5 came into favour, in most places *c.* 450 or later.

φεῖ, χεῖ, ψεῖ

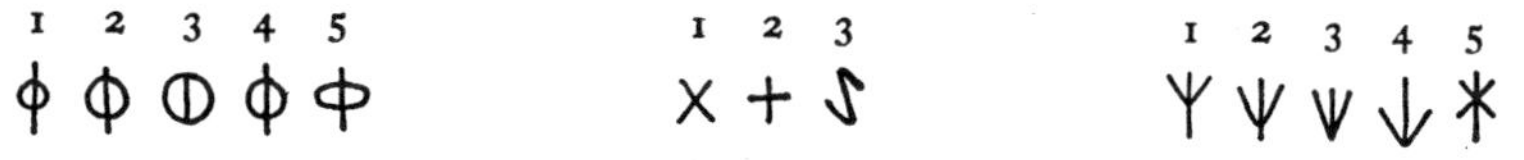

1  2  3  4  5         1  2  3         1  2  3  4  5

FIG. 23

The origins and sound-values of these supplementary letters have not yet been satisfactorily explained, though many solutions have been offered. For the signs we are reduced to speculation. More is known, happily, about the sound-values. It is known that Φ stood for *p+h*, and was used in all the local scripts except those of the 'Primitives' Crete, Thera, Melos. Whether this letter ever came to Crete 'fixed' in the abecedarium is not known, because the dialect was psilotic and so might not use it in any case, and we have as yet no abecedaria from Crete; the general view is that it was not known in Crete because the alphabet had been transmitted to these parts before these supplementary signs had been added to it (whence arose the practice in epigraphical works of calling these islands the 'Primitives'). Apparently Crete did not transmit any Φ—even if she ever did receive it in an abecedarium—to Thera and Melos; in these dialects, which were not psilotic, the sound was simply rendered by *pi+heta* in the early inscriptions (as *xi*, *chi*, and *psi* were also rendered by the two appropriate letters in each case). But before we deny any knowledge of the signs Φ, X, Ψ to the 'Primitives' it is well to remember that we should have said this also of the Ξ (for they all rendered *xi* by *kappa+san*), were it not that in Crete the sound represented by Ξ, and hence the sign itself, chanced to be used in Eteocretan (cf. Praisos, p. 309), and in Thera it chanced to be suitable for their pronunciation of 'Zeus' (p. 317); and thus the letter was actually used, though in rare instances only.

It is known also that X stood for an aspirated guttural (*ch*?), was used as such ('blue' *chi*) by the Greeks of Asia Minor, Attica, Corinth and her circle, and the Aegean islands (except Euboia, Rhodes, and the 'Primitives'), and also was used, with or without *sigma*, for the guttural+sibilant (i.e. ξ) by all the scripts except the Ionic and Corinthian circle (which used Ξ), that of the 'Primitives' (which used *kappa*+sibilant), Knidian, and Naxian; whence it has been inferred[1] that those places which show X without a following sibilant for ξ had simply dropped the sibilant-letter because it was redundant in their view, inasmuch as they used Ψ for χ, and so the single sign X was enough to denote the *xi* ('red' *xi*).

Lastly, it is known also that Ψ stood for an aspirated guttural (*kh*?), and was used by all the Greeks of the mainland except Attica and Corinth and her circle, and by Euboia and Rhodes ('red' *chi*); that it was used for a totally different sound in the scripts of Ionia and the Argive–Corinthian group, viz. the *ps*; and that it was used by the 'Primitives', apparently only from the late archaic period onwards, for the *ks* (p. 309); whence it has been inferred[2] that the true values of Ψ and X were two kinds of aspirated guttural, perhaps *kh* and *ch*, and the usage of one or the other depended upon the variations in the dialects (at least in the early stages of the transmission).

Concerning the origin of the signs themselves, most scholars have argued that they belong, in a sense, to the Graeco-Phoenician alphabet, in that they have been formed from existing signs in Greek or Phoenician: Ψ (= χ) being a doublet from a long-tailed *kappa*; X being also a doublet from *kappa*, or a re-use of the Phoenician form of *tāw*, ×; Ψ (= ψ) being from *phi* halved; Φ itself being from *theta*, or from a curved *pi*, or even from one *upsilon* inverted on another.[3] The alternative explanation which has been given[4] is to class them all as non-Greek symbols, which came into the Greek alphabet from a version of the Aegean syllabary, which persisted, for example, in Cyprus and apparently in parts of the opposite Anatolian mainland also; for many syllabic signs resembling Cypriot occur, with other signs taken from the Greek, in the archaic script of Caria. I hold this explanation to be the true one, in the belief that the Greeks were receptive and economical rather than experimental in their adoption of their alphabet. It is one thing to create as doublets the signs for *u* from *u̯* and *ō* from *ŏ*; it is quite another to feel the lack of a special single sign for *ph* or *kh* or *ps* so keenly as to invent Φ *ph* from *theta* or *pi* or *qoppa* or some other existing letter, and to alter the meaning of the 'useless' Ψ to supply the others. It is true that none of the Greek signs Φ, X, Ψ has an exact replica in the Cypriot syllabary; but we have to remember that (*a*) very little about the syllabary and

---

[1] Kretschmer, *AM* xxi (1896), 420.

[2] Gercke, *Hermes* xli (1906), 549 ff.; cf. Hammarström, *Stud. Orientalia* ii (1928), 186 ff.

[3] The details of these hypotheses are given in Larfeld³, 232 ff.; cf. further Schwyzer, 144 f.; Ullman, *CP* xxii (1927), 136 ff.; Boüüaert, op. cit. 348 ff.; Carpenter, *AJA* xxxvii (1933), 21; F. P. Johnson (*AJP* 77 (1956), 29 ff.) suggests that the letters were evolved by a man who chose the two symbols O and X, and modified them by a vertical line drawn through. The

second was simplified in one way by the 'red' scripts, in another by the 'blue'. The *psi* of the latter, he concludes, may have been borrowed from a non-Greek Anatolian script, which had itself got the sign from some early 'red' Greek state in these parts. This does not seem to me very convincing, particularly as he has to assume that Greek *tau* at that time resembled a cross X—or the original symbol selected need never have been modified.

[4] Deecke, *Baumeisters Denkmäler* i (1885), 51.

its variants in the eighth century is known to us,[1] (*b*) our knowledge of the signs in the existing classical syllabary is still incomplete, and (*c*) some of the Carian signs do not correspond closely with any classical Cypriot characters; yet presumably they also are from the syllabary or its archetype. If these signs occurred among the Aegean syllabic letters which survived in Cyprus and the area round, and were used in the names of people and places with which the earliest Greek settlers in the Levant were familiar, they might be added to the earliest Greek alphabet, and pass thence to Crete—where they were useless for the dialect—Rhodes and the Greek colonies in Caria. The Rhodians found a use for Φ, for X = *ch* (?) (i.e. used with *sigma* to express ξ) and for Ψ = *kh* (?). The Ionians in Caria used Φ and X = *ch* (?), but not Ψ = *kh* (?). It is often argued that 'red' Ψ (*chi*) and Ψ = *psi* are the same letter, the Ionians having decided, because they already had X for *chi*, to use Ψ to express a quite different sound, *psi*. I should prefer to guess that the Ionians independently acquired a sign Ψ = *ps* from Carian, like their sibilant 'sampi', which is also held to be from a local native letter (p. 39); and that they never acquired Ψ = *chi* as well as X, precisely because they already had a very similar sign in their alphabet (for *psi*), and held the extra guttural sign to be unnecessary.

As for the shapes: the tailed *phi* 1 is the normal form in the seventh century and for most of the sixth; but in Naxian the tailless 3 appears already in the earliest (7th c.) example. In the course of the sixth century the circle enlarges and the tails dwindle, till the form 3 becomes the normal for the period *c.* 525–450. After that the tailed form (4, flattening out to 5) returns, just as in the case of *upsilon*. *Chi* has only two normal types; 1 is on the whole the earlier; 2 is common in Attic in the late archaic period, but 1 returns in the fifth century. The Knidian *xi* (p. 351) may be from this letter. For type 3, see pp. 39 f. *Psi* follows the course of *upsilon*: a tail at first (1), then the letter tends to become 3 by the last quarter of the sixth century. 4, with a tall central stroke, is found especially in Chalkidic and Boiotian (on 'Chalkidic' vases from the second half of the sixth century onwards, and in formal inscriptions from the late archaic period). The sign 5 for ψ, attested in Arkadia and Ozolian Lokris, appears to be an elaboration of Υ; see pp. 212 ff.

There is one last significant point about these enigmatic letters: their order in the abecedarium. In the Ionic alphabets, the order is that with which we are of course familiar: Φ X Ψ. But in the abecedaria of Euboic origin found in Etruria (pp. 236 f.), and in Boiotia (p. 94), the order is X Φ Ψ. In an Achaian fifth-century abecedarium from Metapontion (p. 256) it is Φ Ψ X X—i.e. 'blue' *chi* and 'red' *xi* together.

ὦ (later ὦ μέγα)

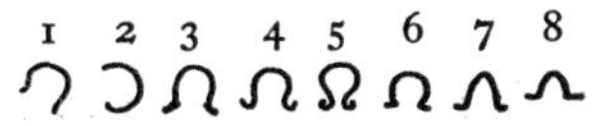

FIG. 24

Ionia (with her colonies), Knidos, Paros (with Thasos), and Melos all marked the difference between the short and long *o* by the use of Ω, a new sign which appears to be

[1] The evidence for the Bronze Age script is increasing (cf. Daniel, *AJA* xlv (1941), 249 ff.; Dikaios, *Antiquity* xxvii (1953), 103 ff.; and Schaeffer, ibid. (1954), 38 f.); and from the 6th c. onwards the syllabary is well attested (cf. in general Dikaios, *Guide to the Cyprus Museum*[2] (1953), 183). For scattered signs perhaps of the 7th c., see Myres, *Handbook of the Cesnola Collection* (1914), 474, 480–1.

a doublet formed from O by breaking the circle. The earliest examples of the letter in Ionic show it with a marked tilt and only very small, undeveloped struts at the ends (1); this may explain the shape of the letter in Knidian, which has the break at the side, 2. It will be recalled that, whereas Ionic used this broken letter for *ō*, Knidian used it for *ŏ*; Parian also used the broken version for *ŏ*, but in the Ionic shape (not the Knidian), perhaps because Parian *beta* already had a curved form like 2. The Melian practice was the same as the Knidian; it may, indeed, have been introduced from Knidos, because it first appears in Melian during the late archaic period (p. 321). It is possible that Kos also used the same form as the Knidian (p. 352), and others likewise of the Sporades whose archaic scripts are unknown. The Parian source may have been Miletos (the signs being confused in transmission), or Knidos before the (presumed) original shape had settled into 2.

So few archaic inscriptions have been found in Asia Minor that examples from the seventh century are almost unknown. *Omega* is the last letter of the row, and was presumably then the latest addition; but the invention can hardly have taken place later than *c.* 600, for it appears in a Samian inscription (2) with closed *eta* (which had already become open H in Samos by the second quarter of the sixth century; p. 328), and in a graffito from Smyrna which is earlier than the sack of the city *c.* 585 B.C. (p. 341). It is not used for *ō* in the signature of the Kolophonian mercenary at Abou Simbel (594–589), nor in the main inscription there. The latter fact might be easily explained, since we know of its writers only that they spoke the Doric dialect and did not (from their script) come from Rhodes, Knidos, or Kos (?); see further pp. 354 f. But the Kolophonian's use of O for ω is difficult to explain now that Ω is attested in early Smyrna.

Occasional examples of the tilted *omega* 1 occur as late as the fourth quarter of the sixth century (cf. Thasos **50**); but on the whole it seems to have settled down to 3 in formal inscriptions during the third quarter, and at the same time to have adopted an embellishment already practised by vase-painters before the middle of the century (cf. p. 338), the curling of the struts (4). In the first years of the fifth century its shape was often hook-like, 5 (Chios **46**, Kos **38**), but thereafter it was steadily simplified to 7 by about the middle of the century (Halikarnassos **42**, Chios **48**); whence it grew smaller during the second half (8).

It appears likely that the letter was first evolved in some place in south-west Asia Minor, whence its spread was at first very limited. It does not appear even in Rhodes until the late archaic period; but thereafter its orbit steadily expanded.

### *Other Non-Phoenician Letters Used in the Local Scripts*

(i) 'sampi'

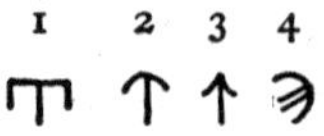

FIG. 25

This letter, used for a compound sibilant later spelt by *xi* or double *sigma*, has been attested in the following places: Ephesos, Erythrai, Teos, Halikarnassos, Kyzikos, and

Pontic Mesambria. It has been attributed[1] also to Apollonia Pontica (a colony of Miletos, like Kyzikos), in order to explain how Mesambria, a colony of Doric Megara and Kalchedon, came to possess a letter otherwise confined to users of the Ionic script; but this hypothesis is unnecessary, for Kalchedon herself used the Ionic script at least as early as the sixth century (p. 366). It is to Kalchedon therefore that the use should be conjecturally assigned. It has also been tentatively restored in the poetry of Hipponax of Chios, to explain the apparent Atticism θαλατ[της] of the papyrus;[2] but in the earliest Chian inscription (41: c. 575–550?) φυλασσων is spelt with double *sigma*. Finally, it has been identified[3] with the letter called by much later grammarians 'like *pi*' (σὰν πῖ, σάμπι: Fig. 25, 2–4), which was the last sign, following *omega*, in the so-called 'Milesian' numeral system, a system whose use can be traced back to the sixth century in vase-graffiti, but, as yet, no earlier (p. 327). Like its true name, the origin of this letter-form is still unknown; it has been derived from ṣāḏē/san,[4] but in that case one would expect to find it in *san*'s place between *pi* and *qoppa*, since *vau*, which likewise was a 'dead' letter in the Ionic dialect and script, retained its proper place (no. 6 in the numeral system). Since a somewhat similar letter exists in Carian, the Greek letter may have been originally borrowed from the Carian to express the Carian sibilant, when used (e.g.) in native names.[5] Its usage was evidently inconsistent among the Greeks, for, though it is attested in Milesian colonies, in Miletos itself there is as yet no example; instead we find single or double *sigma*, e.g. Τειχιοσης (29, c. 550–540?) and κηρυσσεται (33, c. 525–500?). Its known period of activity, according to the inscriptions, ranges from c. 550 to c. 450; it was apparently given up during the second half of the fifth century (except, of course, in the numeral system), in favour of σσ or ξ.[6]

## (ii) (Fig. 23, Χ3)

I have discussed elsewhere[7] this rare zigzag letter-form (as yet attested in Greek only among the 'Primitives'), and therefore only repeat briefly here what is known of it. It occurs (1) in Crete, (a) Dreros 1, in an Eteocretan text, (b) Praisos 19, in an Eteocretan text; value unknown; in both cases it is translated by editors as *iota*, but it differs plainly from the shape of the *iotas* in these texts; (2) in Sikinos, where the alphabet is of the same type as the Cretan; value that of *chi* (κεχαρισμένον; p. 322); (3) in the non-Greek inscriptions of the Pelasgians of Lemnos;[8] value unknown; (4) in the archaic inscriptions of Phrygia (script similar to (3) above; value translated usually as *z*); (5) in a graffito on a vase-handle at Delphi[9] (catalogued among the Corinthian ware; perhaps from a Phrygian dedication?).

[1] Gercke, op. cit. 542.

[2] Latte, *Philologus* xcvii (1948), 46. I owe my knowledge of this article to Zuntz, *Museum Helveticum* viii (1951), 21. I cannot agree, however, with Zuntz's thesis that this letter was used by Sappho in Aiolic (cf. p. 361); nor with the suggestion by Froehner (*Rev. Num.* 1907, 100 f.) that it was used at Selinous, because certain Selinountine coins appear to show the letter instead of *psi* for the normal Ⱶυψας (p. 271). Inversion of letters is common in coin legends, and this letter is surely an inverted *psi*.

[3] Cf. Roberts i. 10; Schwyzer, 149.

[4] Larfeld³, 225 ff.  [5] Schwyzer, 149, n. 3.

[6] Cf. *SGDI* 5515 (Iasos, 4th c.): Βρυασσις corrected to Βρυαξις.  [7] *K.Ch.* iii (1949), 143 ff.

[8] *BCH* x (1886), 1 ff.; Della Seta, *Scritti in onore di B. Nogara* (1937), 119 ff.

[9] *FD* v. 144, no. 137, fig. 597.

It may be inferred from these examples that this letter, with the value of a guttural aspirate (?), was known in Crete in the archaic period (though the sound suited only the Eteocretan language), whence it passed to Sikinos; what may be the connexion here between the Cretan and Phrygian examples, I cannot say.

## (iii) И

This letter was used in Arkadian Mantinea in the fifth century for the dental $\tau < *q^u$, with several other abnormal letter-forms; and I should guess it to be a short-lived local invention (pp. 212 f.). It does not occur elsewhere in Greek, apart from a like sign used for *sigma* in an inscription from Brentesion, which might be a Messapic letter (p. 282).

The name τὸ ἀλφάβητον for the alphabet itself is not attested before the Hellenistic period, although Nikochares, an Athenian comic poet of the fourth century B.C., spoke of an illiterate man as ἀναλφάβητος (F2 Demiańczuk).[1] We know that in the fifth century in Ionia—perhaps elsewhere also?—the alphabet was called 'the Phoenician letters', τὰ Φοινικήια γράμματα or simply τὰ Φοινικήια (p. 5). At least as early as the fourth century the letters were also called τὰ στοιχεῖα, στοιχεῖον being used alike for the letter itself and for the element of sound which it represented.[2] As στοῖχος means a row or rank of units (| | | | | | | |), so στοιχεῖον must mean a single unit (|) in the row; thus Aristophanes called the shadow of the sundial's gnomon στοιχεῖον (*Eccl.* 652). Presumably then, if the Greeks called the letters στοιχεῖα, they called the abecedarium itself ὁ στοῖχος, though for this last there is no direct evidence.[3]

### B. *Secondary Transmission throughout Greece*

The alphabet had now become the possession of the Greeks in Phoenicia. Henceforward it was to be carried by Greeks in stages to the rest of Greece.

The earliest beneficiaries were likely to be Rhodes and Crete, the two islands nearest (after Cyprus) to the source, and perhaps also the Cyclades, if the earliest Greek pottery in Al Mina is Cycladic (though cf. p. 10, n. 4). Rhodes' commercial contacts with the near East were close (pp. 9, 346 f.). Crete's connexion may have been of a more piratical nature, according to her early reputation,[4] but her products also show the influence of the East. The marked dissimilarity between the Rhodian and Cretan scripts suggests that they were taken independently of each other from the original source, and offers a good example of the way in which the local character of the various scripts was formed. The Cretan, it will be recalled, is much closer than Rhodian is to the Phoenician, and I have already said

---

[1] Cf. in general Schwyzer, 141, n. 3 and *KZ* lviii. 199 ff.; Arvanitopoullos, *Epigraphike* i. (1937), 47 ff.

[2] Plato, *Crat.* 424a–b; *Theaet.* 202e; Aen. Tact. 31. 21; Xen. *Mem.* ii. 1. 1; Arist. *Poet.* 20 (bracketed by some edd.).

[3] Wade-Gery has drawn my attention to the lines in Aesch. *Pers.* 429–30: οὐδ' ἂν εἰ δέκ' ἤματα | στοιχηγοροίην, οὐκ ἂν ἐκπλήσαιμί σοι, and Schol. ad loc.: στοιχηγοροίην· ἐφεξῆς λέγοιμι, στοιχομυθοίην. He suggests that the meaning may be: 'I speak the στοῖχος', i.e. 'reel off the list by rote'.

[4] *Hom. Hymn.* ii. 123 ff.; Hdt. i. 2. T. J. Dunbabin pointed out to me that there was no Cretan pottery found at Al Mina.

above (p. 10) that I find it difficult to accept the theory that Rhodian originally resembled the Cretan, but evolved thence to the stage in which we first meet it on the Subgeometric skyphos of Korakos (Rhodes **1**). There are, in my view, three main reasons for the creation of those variations which distinguish one local script from another, and none of them requires of necessity a long period of evolution. In the first place, mistakes may arise in the actual process of transmission. The agents who spread the art of writing from one state to another may sometimes have been travelled Greeks who made their wealth in a literate area and returned to end their days in their own state; but much of the spreading may have been done by professional teachers, γραμματισταί. Writing was a craft, though a simple one, and had to be taught like any other new craft; Herodotos calls it a διδασκάλιον (v. 58). The γραμματιστής probably settled in the nearest illiterate area, and there undertook to be a scribe to the unlearned, or to teach them for a fee (p. 63). Thus, when the transmitting lay in the hands of a single person, any error which existed in his version of the alphabet (as the omission of *mu*'s fifth stroke, or *lambda* inverted) would stand a good chance of being perpetuated in the script of an area; on this hypothesis, Rhodian *lambda* and *mu* are errors, and parts of Crete also used the incorrect *lambda* (p. 308). In the second place, local differences in pronunciation undoubtedly played a part in the creation of the local scripts. We are familiar with various differences in grammar and syntax among the local Greek dialects, and also with certain of the differences in pronunciation, but only with those for which the Greek alphabet happened to possess a suitable sign; as, for example, the Elean broadening of *e* to *a* (Buck, 23 f.), or Lakonian and Argive intervocalic aspirate for *s* (op. cit. 55 f.) in the fifth century. Obviously there must have been many more differences in pronunciation of which we have no knowledge, because the Greek alphabet possessed no equivalent sign; for instance, the extant inscriptions from the Ionic Dodekapolis preserve very few traces of the four different dialects into which their common Ionic was in fact subdivided (Hdt. i. 142), just as today the existing English alphabet can give only a rough idea of the shades of differences in pronunciation between the dialects of the English counties. It may therefore have been differences in local pronunciation which from the start caused Crete to use the (voiced?) sibilant *san* of the early Greek alphabet, and Rhodes the (unvoiced?) *sigma*; or, again, which led Rhodes to use Ψ (= *kh*?) for *chi* and ΧΣ (= ?*ch*+*s*) for *xi*, while the Ionic states used Χ (= *ch*?) for *chi* and Ξ (= *ks*(*h*)?) for *xi* (see above, pp. 32, 35 ff.). In the third place, a few letters appear to have been deliberately altered by some states because they were too similar to other letters; *lambda* in Argive, for example, was written as it was apparently to avoid confusion with *gamma* (p. 152). It seems likely that the straight form of the *iota* was created to avoid confusion with *sigma*, and perhaps this alteration had its origin in Rhodes. Any state, therefore, which received its alphabet directly or indirectly from Rhodes would use the straight *iota* from the beginning. It would receive an abecedarium which contained fossil letters unused in the Rhodian dialect (as *vau*, *san*), and these might or might not be of use in its own dialect.

It is a reasonable assumption that the spread of the local scripts should correspond with what we know of inter-state trade-connexions in the late eighth and early seventh centuries; but in our present state of knowledge it is risky to press conclusions of this kind.

Political hostility did not stop state A from using the products of state B,[1] and Samos may have got her script from Miletos (or *vice versa*) even though they belonged to rival 'Trade Leagues'.[2] The possible sources from which the script of each state came are discussed in each case in Part III; but the broad outline may be briefly traced here, the points being stated as facts for the sake of brevity, though the uncertainty of such reconstruction needs no emphasis. The alphabet spread rapidly to Rhodes and the rest of the Doric Hexapolis, and to the Cyclades and Ionia; the chief differences made by the Ionians were the alteration of the aspirate letter from *hēta* h(e) to '*ēta ē*, through their inability to pronounce an initial aspirate; the use of Ξ for *xi* and a non-Greek (?) sign Χ for *chi*; and the subsequent addition of the non-Greek (?) signs Ψ and '*sampi*', and the doublet Ω. This eastern Ionic version is like that of the Cyclades, but not in all details: Naxian used an open form of *beta*, *eta* for a special vowel *ā, Χ for χ, and its own peculiar rendering of *xi*; Parian was nearer to the Ionic version, but had open *beta* and used the doublet Ω not for ω, but for o (as happened also at Knidos). Crete meanwhile had spread her script to the Doric islands to her north, notably Thera and Melos; but perhaps even before this the chief trading states of central Greece—Corinth, Aigina, Euboic Chalkis and Eretria—had formed their versions. That of Corinth appears to have come chiefly from the Cretan, but with the addition of the Φ, Χ, Ψ (from an Ionic source such as Samos? cf. p. 116); that of Eretria and Chalkis resembles the Rhodian, but with *heta* for the aspirate only, and the near-Phoenician *lambda* and *mu*, as in Cretan; it may even have come direct from Euboians settled in Al Mina (p. 10, n. 4). That of Aigina resembles the Cycladic, except in the Aiginetan use of *heta* as aspirate only, and lack of *omega*. The script of Argos bears a general resemblance to the Corinthian, but finds in Kalymna connect the Argive with the area of the Doric Hexapolis also: see pp. 153 f., 353 f. Corinth's script spread (with minor variants) to the smaller states round her, and along the northern coast of the Peloponnese through Sikyon and Achaia. Achaia in turn spread it farther to the Ionian islands and to her own western colonies, and influenced the script of Aitolia on the other side of the Gulf. Meanwhile the rest of the Peloponnese—the eastern Argolid, Lakonia, Messenia, Arkadia, Elis—used a script like the Rhodian; if this was indeed its source, Lakonia may have been the receiver which spread it to the rest, for she had good trade relations with the eastern Greeks in the eighth and seventh centuries B.C.[3] Euboia passed on her version to Boiotia and Opountian Lokris; a modified form (with *lambda* inverted) was used in Phokis, Thessaly, and Ozolian Lokris; and, more important than any of these, a version of combined elements from Euboia and Aigina had early taken root in Attica.

---

[1] e.g. Aigina imported Attic pottery despite her ἔχθρη παλαιή with Athens; Dunbabin, *BSA* xxxvii (1936–7), 83 ff.

[2] Cf. Drerup, *Musée Belge* v (1901), 136 ff.; but his reconstruction sought to prove that Corinth belonged originally to the 'red' alphabet-users, equating the 'blue' with the 'Trade League' Miletos, Eretria, Megara, Athens, the 'red' with the rival group Corinth, Chalkis, Rhodes, Samos; see further p. 115, n. 2.

[3] *CAH* iii. 559; Michell, *Sparta* (1952), 12 ff.; but see pp. 184 f.

# PART II

# WRITING IN ARCHAIC GREECE

Τίς κεν αἰνήσειε νόῳ πίσυνος Λίνδου ναέταν Κλεόβουλον
ἀενάοις ποταμοῖσιν ἄνθεσί τ' εἰαρινοῖς
ἀελίου τε φλογὶ χρυσέας τε σελάνας
καὶ θαλασσαίαισι δίναις ἀντία θέντα μένος στάλας;
ἅπαντα γάρ ἐστι θεῶν ἥσσω· λίθον δὲ
καὶ βρότεοι παλάμαι θραύοντι· μωροῦ φωτὸς ἅδε βουλά.

SIMONIDES, F 57 Bgk.

## 1. *Direction of the Script and Methods of Inscribing*

NORTH Semitic inscriptions were written continuously from right to left; this has been amply demonstrated, at least from the time of our earliest surviving examples in the second millennium B.C. It is also evident from the earliest surviving Greek inscriptions that, in adopting the Semitic alphabet, the Greeks naturally accepted with it the basic principles (*a*) that the correct direction of the letters, following each other in the abecedarium, was from right to left, and (*b*) that therefore any writing ought to begin in this retrograde way. As illustrations of this may be cited the Dipylon oinochoe and the earliest sherds from Hymettos (pp. 68 f., Attica **1, 3**), the cups from Rhodes (p. 347, **1**) and the Argive Heraion (p. 149, **11**), the Marsiliana abecedarium (pp. 237 f., **18**), the earliest rock-inscriptions from Thera (pp. 318 f., **1**) and Amorgos (p. 293, **15**), and the graffito from Pithekoussai (p. 236, **1**). But is there in fact any evidence to suggest that the Greeks originally adopted the Semitic practice of writing continuously from right to left, before they evolved the method of writing *boustrophedon*? This is the assumption stated or implied by the standard treatises on Greek epigraphy. An example may be given from such a work: 'Die Schriftrichtung: erst linksläufig (wie das semitische Alphabet), dann βουστροφηδόν . . . (in Gortyn noch im 5 Jhdt.), dann rechtsläufig (in Athen seit 550 v. Chr.).'[1] Hence it has naturally been used as a criterion for dating an early inscription: 'The alphabet [on the Mantiklos Apollo, Boiotia **1**] is, however, relatively late. The writing is boustrophedon, not retrograde.'[2]

It cannot be too strongly emphasized that the earliest surviving Greek inscriptions give no warrant for this assumption of an initial stage of continuous retrograde script, followed after a time by the adoption of the *boustrophedon* system. It is certainly an obvious assumption, in view of the North Semitic evidence, and future excavation on Greek sites may lead to the discovery of inscriptions which do in fact support it; but the existing material which we have at present on which to base our conclusions consists of

[1] Schwyzer, 141. Cf. also Franz, *Elementa Epigraphikes Graecae* (1840), 35; Roberts i. 5 and 11; Hicks and Hill, *Manual of Greek Historical Inscriptions* (1901), p. xxxii; Maunde Thompson, *Introduction to Greek and Latin Palaeography*[2] (1912), 4 f.; Larfeld[3], 131 f.; Bury, *CAH* iv. 470; Arvanitopoullos, *Epigraphike* i (1937), 70; Diringer, *The Alphabet* (1948), 453.

[2] Ullman, *Studies Presented to Edward Capps* (1936), 34.

(*a*) single lines written retrograde, among which are the very early inscriptions mentioned above (except for the Pithekoussan; see below), (*b*) *boustrophedon* texts which may begin either from right to left, or from left to right, some of which are demonstrably very early, (*c*) single lines written from left to right, some of which are also very early, and (*d*) scattered examples of two or more lines written in continuous retrograde, which are by no means confined to the earliest period. Since two methods of writing may persist side by side for some time before the older is finally abandoned, the lateness of some examples of (*d*) would be of little significance, provided that we could point also to a reasonable quantity of evidence among the earliest inscriptions; but as the examples of the sixth century and later were convincingly explained by Wilhelm[1] on technical grounds, so the few earlier examples are likewise capable of explanation on grounds other than chronological. Wilhelm pointed out that on public monuments which stood on the right-hand side of the path for a visitor approaching his goal (e.g. temple or city-gate) the inscriptions were sometimes cut retrograde simply to balance the effect of those which stood on the opposite side, inscribed in the normal way from left to right. This hypothesis, providing as it does a satisfactory explanation for several retrograde inscriptions of the sixth and fifth centuries which are otherwise inexplicable, is now generally accepted; and there are various factors to account for other examples, or apparent examples, of continuously retrograde script. For instance, there are examples from Crete: the inscribed wall-blocks from the temple of Apollo Pythios at Gortyn (pp. 311 f., **2**). They are described further in Part III; here it is enough to say only that in Crete a system of paragraphing appears to have been established already in the seventh century—at Dreros, for example—in the long inscriptions which adorned the walls of temples. These inscriptions (legal codes, sacred and secular) were written *boustrophedon*, beginning from right to left, and it was the practice to begin each new clause afresh from right to left. Thus the final line of clause A might chance to run from right to left; and the first line of clause B would follow it, producing two lines of continuously retrograde script. Again, the available wall-space might be long, or the clauses short, so that a complete clause was contained in a single line. Thus isolated blocks from a wall inscribed in this manner might contain parts of lines which ran *boustrophedon* throughout, or partly *boustrophedon* and partly retrograde, or retrograde throughout. The current explanation which reduces these fragments on blocks to a chronological sequence by regarding all the retrograde examples as 'first period' and all the *boustrophedon* as 'second period' has to ignore the fact that occasionally the letter-forms on a retrograde fragment look distinctly later than those on one cut *boustrophedon*. Other cases of what appears to be continuous retrograde script may be mentioned briefly here; they also are described more fully in the relevant sections of Part III. Among the earliest sherds from Hymettos (*c.* 700?) is a small fragment (p. 69, and n. 7) containing part of an abecedarium written from right to left, with a second copied immediately under it, and therefore naturally written from right to left also. The same thing occurs slightly later on a vase from Kyme (p. 237, **2**), but in this case both run from left to right. The earliest inscribed grave-stele from Attica (p. 71, **8**) bears a single statement cut in two straggling lines which are both retrograde, but they appear

[1] Wilhelm, 31 ff.

to have been placed in this way so that the actual names of the deceased Keramo and her father (?) Enialos might abut on their figures depicted on the stele, like the names of figures on vases, or those of Dermys and Kittylos on a Boiotian stele (p. 92, **8**). An early offering of spits in the Heraion at Perachora (p. 123, Corinth **17**), inscribed vertically on a stone support of which less than one-half (cut longitudinally) survives, contains the opening part of the first line written vertically upwards retrograde, and three letters from another line also retrograde just below its start. It seems likely that a writer who had included in a single line all his hexameter but three letters would not return right to the bottom again to add them, but would rather crowd them in somewhere immediately below the end of the line; so I infer that the second part of the hexameter was cut vertically down the lost half of the stone, still retrograde, and curled across to finish just below its start (see p. 123). Again, early vase-fragments might be found bearing parts of several lines apparently written continuously from right to left (or, as in the case of Corinth **1** (p. 121) and Ithake **1** (p. 230), from left to right). But to interpret them thus would be to ignore the circular shape of the vase; for what the sherds show are far more likely to be parts of a single line written round and round the vase in a spiral. An excellent illustration of this is the little Protocorinthian aryballos found at Kyme, which bears an incised inscription describing the vase as 'Tataie's lekythos', and threatening blindness to any thief (p. 238, **3**). It happens to be complete, so that there is no doubt that the inscription is in a single line spiralling round the vase; but if a particular sherd from it chanced to be alone preserved, it would present the appearance of three lines from an inscription written continuously retrograde. In fact, Tataie's aryballos has already proved a trap for the unwary; for the standard facsimile of the inscription separates it into three lines, owing to the great length of its spiral when unwound for purposes of reproduction; and so editors in the past, who have not seen the vase itself nor a reproduction, have described the inscription as being in three lines continuously retrograde.[1]

I know of only one early inscription showing more than one line retrograde which does not belong to one of the above categories. It is the graffito from Pithekoussai (pp. 235 f.), and here the use seems to be deliberate, in order to separate the three lines of the verse. Of the numerous archaic inscriptions written *boustrophedon* some—as Thera **1***a* (p. 318), Attica **2** (pp. 69 f.), Boiotia **1** (pp. 90 f.), Naxos **2** (p. 291)—are obviously exceedingly early in date, as early as any of the single-line inscriptions written retrograde (except for the Dipylon oinochoe). It is therefore concluded here that the Greeks who adopted the North Semitic alphabet were never really well-grounded in the process of writing continuously retrograde, and so from the beginning, when more than one line was required, they used instinctively the *boustrophedon* system, regarding the signs as reversible profiles.[2] We may therefore infer that neither the Semites who taught, nor the first Greeks who learnt, were concerned with much more than the basic elements of instruction in the art of writing. The Greeks accepted a set of ideograms which represented nothing intelligible—let alone beautiful—to the eye, a list of names which to their ears were pure barbarism, and the rule, highly inconvenient for a right-handed person, that any writing should start from right to left, as the abecedarium itself was written; and therefore it seems reasonable to

---

[1] Kirchhoff[4], 121; Larfeld[3], 134; Arvanitopoullos, loc. cit.          [2] See p. 50, n. 1.

assume that, if they had been instructed in the process of continuous retrograde writing, they would at first have accepted that also as part and parcel of the new art. But, as I have said, there is nothing to show that in Greek hands it ever preceded the *boustrophedon* system as a normal method.

For an unlettered people who had no accepted tradition of continuous retrograde writing, the *boustrophedon* system was a natural one to adopt; for thus the inscription ran continuously for the eye (and, if necessary, for the finger) from beginning to end. When the inscription could be included in one line on the available space, it was naturally written so—a single retrograde line, on walls sometimes a very long one, on vases a spiral. But if sufficient space was not available, the writer turned at the end and retraced his path, as the plough is turned at the end of a furrow, or the shuttle sent back in weaving. The earliest inscriptions would tend mostly to be short, perhaps just spilling over into a second line; and thus the *boustrophedon* system would naturally suggest itself to the un-practised writer. Even in the last quarter of the sixth century Attic masons, for whom the system of continuous left-to-right had long been the established convention, still used the *boustrophedon* system for the last few letters of an inscription, in preference to isolating them at the head of a new line (p. 75).

There is no reason to suppose that the Greeks borrowed the idea from any other system of writing. The *boustrophedon* method occurs in the Middle Minoan hieroglyphic system,[1] in Hittite hieroglyphs,[2] and, rarely, in the South Semitic alphabet.[3] Its adoption simply implies a pictorial conception of the letters as outlined figures which can be turned in either direction according to need. This notion was evidently present in the minds of the first Greek writers, and it was the easier for them to carry it out because twelve of the twenty-six shapes were symmetrical (δ, З, Ͱ, θ, ξ, o, *san*, Ϙ, τ; later φ, χ, ψ), six required very little change (α, γ, crooked *iota*, λ, σ, υ), and only eight looked markedly different in reverse (β, ε, Ϝ, κ, μ, ν, π, ρ).

Thus the Greek writer and reader was from the beginning familiar with the practice of writing or reading the letters from left to right upon occasion; and from his being aware that the letters could be used in this way the next step for him was only natural: namely, that, when circumstances required it, an inscription might be begun also from left to right. Much of the earliest Greek writing consisted of explanatory inscriptions on existing objects—dedications on offerings, personal names on property, epitaphs on tombs, names of figures in drawings—and therefore was not done upon a blank piece of prepared writing-material such as a tablet or a scroll, but upon the best surface offered by the object itself: the flank of a statuette, the narrow face of a rough stone stele, the vacant spaces between the decorations on a vase. In these cramped circumstances practical reasons will decide whether the serpentine course of the letters shall begin from right to left, or from left to right, the essential factor being that the start of the inscription shall be obvious to the spectator. Sometimes the practical reason is no longer obvious to us; for example, we have to infer that the bronze statuette dedicated by Mantiklos (Boiotia **1**) was a warrior,

---

[1] Evans, *Scripta Minoa* i. 250 f.; von Bissing, *Hand-buch d. Archäologie* (ed. Otto) i (1939), 155; J. L. Myres, *BSA* xliv (1949), 326 f.

[2] Sayce, *Antiquity* i (1927), 208; von Bissing, op. cit. 159.

[3] Driver, 124, 146.

wearing a helmet and carrying a spear in the right hand and a shield on the bent left arm, before we can understand why the bronze-worker chose the right (unshielded) thigh on which to start his lettering; having chosen it, he had to begin from left to right, to make the best use of his limited space. In the case of Nikandra's statue on Delos (Naxos **2**), we can realize that the flat front of the dress, now blank, was once painted elaborately with zones of little patterns, so that the dedication had to be inscribed on the flank; we can see why the starting line should hug the edge nearest to the (frontal) spectator, and therefore, being on the left flank, begin from left to right; but we do not know now what reason, strong or trivial, the sculptor had for choosing the left flank rather than the other. It may have had some connexion with the statue's position in the precinct, as Wilhelm's thesis showed to be the case with certain retrograde inscriptions (p. 44). The reasons underlying the direction of the names of figures on vases are more obvious. The name will naturally be written as close as possible to its owner, as it were issuing out from him; and in a pair of opposed figures there will be an equally natural tendency to set their names also in antithesis, to match the figures. Thus on vases the direction of the writing is governed both practically, by the amount of space available beside the figure to be named, and stylistically, by the position of the figure itself.

When the practice of beginning an inscription from left to right was once admitted, the result, among right-handed people, was inevitable. The initial situation was gradually reversed, and inscriptions were begun from left to right with increasing frequency, while those which were begun from right to left became in their turn the exceptions, in most cases owing their existence to the practical or stylistic reasons mentioned above. The convention of writing the names of figures in a decorative antithesis lasted late. It was evidently used in sculptural groups also: in a fifth-century group by Onatas, seen by Pausanias at Olympia (v. 25. 9), the name of Agamemnon was written retrograde; and the practice is followed on a late fifth-century relief showing Orpheus and Eurydike, now known only from Roman copies.[1] The extension of this practice from early times to include whole inscriptions written retrograde if their positions required it has been already mentioned (p. 44). In addition to these cases, there are the legal texts of Crete, which even in the fifth century still began from right to left; a practice which is evidently part of that insular conservatism which made the Cretans retain the *boustrophedon* system also through the fifth century. In Lakonia likewise a large number of inscriptions retained the convention of a retrograde start throughout the archaic period (e.g. pp. 193 ff., **26–27, 29, 31, 34**). Lastly, the left-handed writer must not be forgotten. The prevailing style will naturally be that of the right-handed majority; but it is, I understand, the natural instinct of many left-handed persons to write retrograde (the most famous example of this being the script of Leonardo da Vinci), and therefore, as long as the *boustrophedon* system itself lasted, a left-handed writer might start his inscription retrograde, or write a brief line from right to left. I cannot think of any other explanation for the graffiti names which are occasionally written retrograde even in the fifth century.[2] By the time of

---

[1] For the bibliography see H. Thompson (*Hesperia* xxi (1952), 47 ff.), who attributes the original to the Altar of Pity in Athens, erected towards the end of the 5th c., perhaps to commemorate the Sicilian disaster of 413.

[2] Cf. the Attic ostrakon cast against Hippokrates in the decade 490–480, *Hesperia*, suppl. iv. 38, fig. 30.

the New Comedy, however, 'to write backwards' had become a standard joke: ἐπαρίστερ' ἔμαθες, ὦ πόνηρε, γράμματα (Theognetos *ap.* Athen. 671b–c).

The right-handed majority, then, had established the convention that an inscription should start in the way easiest to write, i.e. from left to right; but, owing to all the qualifying circumstances mentioned above, it is impossible to estimate the exact period when the original practice of the retrograde start ceased to be normal; for instance, is the retrograde line on Chairion's altar in the early sixth century (p. 71, Attica **12**) an example of normal writing, or was it written thus because of the position of the altar on the Akropolis? Though generalization here is obviously unsafe, it may be hazarded that by the early sixth century the practice was becoming abnormal (cf. further p. 117). A possible clue may be derived from the surviving abecedaria; for of the six known early Etruscan examples, which are close copies of a Euboic model perhaps from Kyme, only the earliest (that of Marsiliana) runs retrograde; the rest, of which the earliest belongs apparently to the late seventh century, are written from left to right (Pl. 48), as is the Corinthian example **16** (p. 117; early sixth century?).

All this time, it must be recalled, the *boustrophedon* system of writing was in use; but when the abecedarium itself thus represented the correct position of the letters as being from left to right, the decline of *boustrophedon* writing was bound to follow ultimately; for now, with over a hundred years of usage behind them, the letters were no longer a novel series of shapes which could be turned either way equally well, like figures in profile, but a set of fixed, familiar symbols (as they are to us today), whose proper direction was from left to right. Convention could, and did, play a large part in extending the life of the *boustrophedon* system in various ways, even in the fifth century; but it could not hold out for ever against the admitted fact that to write continuously from left to right is the most practical method for the writer in ink on leather or papyrus. Had we now any such cursive documents surviving from the early sixth century, we should almost certainly see in them the germ and early growth of continuous left-to-right script; for it is significant that our earliest datable examples of this system are painted inscriptions on vases, and inscriptions from the eastern side of the Aegean, where the use of leather and papyrus may have been known earlier, and more widely developed, than in the rest of early Greece (pp. 56 ff., 327). In the first quarter of the sixth century the Corinthian painter Timonidas wrote his signature in two lines from left to right (p. 118, **15**), and so did the Athenian Nearchos *c.* 550 (p. 72, **24**); an unknown Lakonian pot-painter used the method for a dedication on a plate (p. 188, **2a**). The earliest example on stone is the main inscription at Abou Simbel, *c.* 594–589 (pp. 348, 355), which has five lines written from left to right. It was the work of two Doric Greek mercenaries perhaps born in Egypt, and would rank as a graffito were it not hacked out with some military weapon in letters over a foot high. It may be presumed that this pair were not pioneers in the development of a simpler writing system, but merely reflect the informal script of their time, as distinct from the work of the craftsmen who cut the formal stone inscriptions (pp. 63 ff.). In the second quarter of the sixth century a sculptor of Samos cut a dedication of two lines from left to right (p. 329, **5**), and another, named Geneleos, wrote two lines retrograde at the right-hand end of a long row of statues on the spectator's right (**6**). By the middle of the century or slightly later, we find dedicatory or funeral inscriptions written continuously from left to right in Rhodes (p. 349, **11, 15**), Athens (p. 72, **21–23**), and Delos (pp. 294 f., **30**); in all these instances the masons were careful to end each line with a complete word, a practice which could not be retained after the introduction of the *stoichedon* system during the second half of the century.[1]

During this half-century the new system continued to spread in informal and formal inscriptions alike; but the *boustrophedon* system took its time to die, continuing in some parts of Greece long after it had ceased as a normal practice in others. Even in Attica the last half-line of an inscription might still be written thus for convenience in the last quarter of the sixth century (**34**), and the *leges sacrae* in the Eleusinion at Athens were written *boustrophedon* in the early fifth century, perhaps through religious conservatism (**44**). In Crete the long legal codes were written thus even in the fourth century (p. 313). Crete is an extreme case; but in Miletos also several dedications and sacral texts of the last quarter of the sixth century, and even later, were written *boustrophedon* (pp. 334 f., **32–39**). In the latter part of the sixth century texts were still written thus in the islands of Naxos (pp. 292 f., **13**) and Thera (p. 319, **14**), in Ozolian Lokris (p. 105, **2**), Elis (p. 219, **2**), in the Sicilian colonies Leontinoi (p. 242, **2**), Zankle (**5**), Megara Hyblaia or Selinous (p. 271, **36**), and in Lakonia in the fifth century (pp. 195 f., **50**). Not only conservatism but stylistic considerations also aided its survival on occasion, particularly in the case of inscriptions on coins. The legend was inscribed in the field round the device which served as the city's badge at the time, and which naturally had the place of honour in the centre of the flan. If the legend contained more than two or three letters, the die-cutter sometimes needed all the available field-space, and therefore had to write half the letters either upside down or *boustrophedon*. Examples of types with *boustrophedon* legends in the early fifth century may be cited from Kyme, Metapontion, Rhegion, Akragas, Thessaly (Pharsalos, Trikka, Pherai), Phokis, Erythrai, Melos, Skione.[2]

Such were the systems of writing employed during the archaic period. The arrangement of the inscription, particularly in *boustrophedon* examples, calls for further comment. References are sometimes made to inscriptions written *boustrophedon* in which every now and then the mason cut some of the letters, or a whole line, 'upside down'.[3] It is true that such a lapse does occasionally happen, but examples are very rare (cf. pp. 107, 127, 175 f.: Opountian Lokris **7**, Corinth **6**, E. Argolid **1**). In most cases which are quoted as examples of inversion, it will be found that the quoter is reading as horizontal a text which was in fact cut vertically up and down a stele or similar object. Much early *boustrophedon* writing was vertical, and sometimes the lines were deliberately written so that the letters actually faced in the same direction throughout: that is to say, at the top of the first line (e.g. written upwards from left to right), instead of proceeding down again with reversed letters, the mason would simply turn the line over like a hairpin and continue down again,

---

[1] Cf. Austin, *The Stoichedon Style in Greek Inscriptions* (1938), 11 f.

[2] *BM Guide to the Principal Coins of the Greeks*, pl. 7. 18–19 (Rhegion, Akragas); 8. 26 (Erythrai); 11. 20 (Skione); 13. 3 (Kyme); *HN²*, 76 (Metapontion); B ii. 4, pl. 288. 26; 291. 11; 294. 1 (Thessaly, various);

ii. 3, pl. 205. 7 (Phokis); *Rev. Num.* xiii (1909), pls. 5–6, nos. 20, 30 (Melos). Dunbabin pointed out to me also the tondo-inscriptions of vase-painters, Beazley, *AJA* xlv (1941), 593.

[3] e.g. Larfeld³, 135; Bizard, *BCH* xliv (1920), 241; Kirsten, *Neue Jahrb.* (1940), 304 and *AA* 1941, 102.

still from left to right; this I call 'false *boustrophedon*',[1] because this is not the true turn of the ploughing ox, but an ingenious simplification which was only possible when the course pursued was vertical. Examples are Boiotia **10**, Lakonia **31** (pp. 92, 193 f.). Sometimes, while cutting true *boustrophedon* vertically, the mason would lay an odd letter here and there on the wrong side (e.g. pp. 84, 249 f., 97: Eretria **9B**, Metapontion **16**, Thessaly **1, 2**); he might even do this in a single vertical line (Aigina **18**, p. 109). In vertical inscriptions of any length a line of false *boustrophedon* might be introduced at the start, to mark the beginning; for an inexperienced reader, faced with the four sides of a stone stele inscribed continuously in vertical *boustrophedon*, might well require to have the start marked as clearly as possible; cf. pp. 313, 72: Crete (Prinias) **12**, Attica **18**. Clauses in vertical inscriptions were often separated from each other by the system of paragraphing described above as especially common in Crete (p. 44); the first line of the new clause would run in the same direction as the final line of the old above it; cf. Thessaly **2**, Chios **41** (p. 337), Metapontion **16**. Nor must it be forgotten that some *boustrophedon* texts were written horizontally, but began at the bottom line and read upwards to the top, as Wilhelm has pointed out;[2] to his examples (Phokis **1**, Samos **2**) may be added the legal text Crete (Dreros) **1e**, and probably Chios **41**. A last refinement which deserves mention is the practice of writing at once *boustrophedon* and *stoichedon*, a rare technique which belongs to the last days of the *boustrophedon* system; to the examples of Attic and Ionic noted by Austin[3] and Raubitschek[4] may be added the grave-stele Samos **10**, the Alkmeonid dedication **25** from Athens, a legal fragment from Miletos (**37**), and a brief graffito dedication on a sherd from Naukratis.[5]

The *boustrophedon* system was not used in name-lists. This is understandable, for the style implies a textual continuity such as does not exist in a bare list of names. When the names formed an integral part of the inscription (as in the Attic dedication **18**, mentioned above) they are written *boustrophedon* with the rest; but in any separate list they are written from left to right, one below the other in the usual way; cf. Argos **7–8**, Attica **28**, and the Attic stele *SEG* x. 326.

I have commented on the technical details of punctuation and the use of guide-lines in the *Notes on letter-forms* in Part III. Here it may be noted only that punctuation does not appear in any of the earliest inscriptions except that from Pithekoussai (p. 235, **1**); it seems to have taken root in the course of the seventh century, and thereafter to have been used in some states often (Crete, Attica, Argos, Lakonia), and hardly at all in others (Corinth, Elis). The common types used are: two or more dots in a vertical row (e.g. Attica, Boiotia, Argos, Euboia, Miletos); a vertical line (Crete); a half-circle (Lakonia); a single dot (Achaian colonies). Guide-lines, shallow or deep, are used by many states throughout the sixth and fifth centuries, but, as far as I know, not earlier (e.g. Attica, Lakonia, Corinth, Argos, Melos, the Achaian colonies, Miletos).

## II. *Materials Used*

The various prepared materials on which Greek inscriptions were written have been often listed already by modern scholars.[6] They are: stone, wood, metal (bronze, tin, lead,

---

[1] See Addenda.
[2] Wilhelm, 3 ff.
[3] Op. cit. 21 f.
[4] *DAA* 195, 230 f.
[5] Petrie, *Naukratis* ii, pl. 21. 716.
[6] Cf. Birt, *Kritik u. Hermeneutik nebst Abriss d.*

and—rarely—gold and silver), papyrus, leather, waxed tablets, and (according to the traditions of the Greeks themselves) linden-bark and palm or other leaves.[1] Clay tablets were not used; the reason for this neglect of a cheap and abundant medium is not known, but may perhaps have been due at least in part to the force of convention, since the Phoenicians, the Greeks' first teachers of writing, did not use them either (p. 6). 'To read' was expressed by ἀναγιγνώσκειν (to recognize, i.e. decipher) or, less commonly, ἐπιλέγεσθαι (to say over to oneself, repeat).[2] Γράφειν was used alike for 'to draw' and 'to write'. Since its primary meaning was 'to scratch lines', it has been suggested that the first Greek inscriptions must accordingly have been incised on clay or wood or stone, rather than written in ink on papyrus or leather.[3] But it must be recalled that γράφειν was, as far as we know, the only specific word used for drawing of any kind, whether scratched or painted;[4] and the art of drawing was far older than that of writing in Greece. By the time that the alphabet was introduced, the meaning of γράφειν may have long ceased to refer only to incising, as far as the drawing of shapes was concerned; and the same verb would naturally be used for the drawing of letter-shapes, whether the latter were incised or painted. Thus, though it may well be correct to say that the earliest Greek writing was scratched, not painted, I do not think that we should quote the use of the word γράφειν in support of this, because its original limited meaning of 'drawing lines by incision' had already been widened to mean simply 'drawing lines'. In Cyprus the same process apparently took place in reverse; that is, εἰσαλίνειν could be used to express the cutting of syllabic signs in metal (*SGDI* 60, l. 26), although its meaning, according to Hesychios, was that of ἀλείφειν (= to smear), which should refer to painted letters only; whence it has been concluded that in Cyprus the earliest inscriptions were painted rather than scratched.[5] The technical terms for 'inscribe' and 'delete' were κολάπτειν, ἐκκολάπτειν.[6]

As wood was the material from which the Greeks of the eighth and early seventh centuries made their cult-statues and the structural parts of their buildings, before they mastered the art of carving in stone on a monumental scale, so it was one of the earliest materials used for public inscriptions of any length. The most famous example of this practice, the set of wooden 'axones' on which Solon's law-code was inscribed at Athens, has been so well discussed already that little need be said here.[7] Fragments of them were still shown in the Prytaneion in the time of Pausanias (i. 18. 3) and Plutarch (*Solon* 25); the latter described them as wooden axles turning within the frames (πλαίσια) which surrounded

---

*antiken Buchwesens* (1913), 247 ff.; Maunde Thompson, *Greek and Latin Palaeography*[2] (1912), 27 ff.; Larfeld[3], 109 ff.; Schubart, *Die Antike* xiv (1938), 175 ff.; cf. also Wendel, *Die griechisch-römische Buchbeschreibung verglichen mit der des Vorderen Orients* (1949), *passim*.

[1] Leaves were certainly used for lovers' praises; cf. Kallimachos, fr. 73, and Pfeiffer ad loc.; but the alleged use of palm-leaves seems to spring from the confusion of the term φοινικήια both for 'letters' and 'palms'. For ostracism by 'petalism' at Syracuse in the 5th c., see Diod. xi. 87.

[2] P. Chantraine (*Mélanges . . . H. Grégoire* ii (1950), 121 f.) derives ἐπιλέγεσθαι = to read from λέγειν in its primary sense: 'il s'agit d'assembler, de recueillir pour comprendre.'

[3] Birt, op. cit. 248; Carpenter, *AJA* xlii (1938), 67.

[4] Cf. Lorimer, *Homer and the Monuments* (1950), 527.

[5] Lorimer, loc. cit. I note that διφθεράλοιφος (= γραμματοδιδάσκαλος) is translated by Wendel, op. cit. 89, as one who rubs the leather to prepare it for writing, or to clean it for reuse; not as a 'writer on leather', the more convincing rendering supported by Miss Lorimer.

[6] Cf. LSJ, s.vv. and Wilhelm, 265.

[7] Cf. the discussions listed below, p. 53, nn. 3–5, especially that of Oliver (n. 4).

them, while Polemon, who apparently saw them himself over two centuries earlier, said that they were squared and inscribed on all sides (Harpokration s.v. ἄξονι). Neither described them as resembling pinakes in any way, nor as being mounted vertically, though these are parts of the final picture produced by the combined efforts of later grammarians; but if the simplest interpretation is given to the ἄξονες, i.e. long logs of wood squared and well trimmed, they were probably inscribed lengthways like the earliest stone stelai (below); and, if so, they may have been set horizontally in their frames like rollers, which would be the easiest way to read and turn them. It may be noted also that wood was used for the early laws of Mytilene under Pittakos, at least according to a saying of Pittakos, preserved by Diodoros (ix. 27. 4), that the strongest rule was that of 'the painted wood' (τοῦ ποικίλου ξύλου), that is, the Laws. In early Rome also (Dion. Hal. iii. 36) Numa's religious *fasti* were said to have been inscribed on oak until Ancus Marcius had them copied onto bronze pinakes.[1]

In any region of Greece where reasonably good stone was quarried, its great advantages as a medium could not be long overlooked. From early times certain standing stones had carried inscriptions; the classical Greek stele on which public documents were inscribed has a long history. Its prototype may be seen in the stone marker (σῆμα, ὅρος) of early times, a tall, roughly-hewn pointer erected to indicate a grave (as in the earliest examples at Thera) or to define a boundary. When an official inscription of any kind had to be set forth for attention, it was natural that the use of the standing stone should be extended to serve this purpose also. The earliest extant examples are stout four-sided pillars inscribed on all sides *boustrophedon*; cf. those found at Prinias in Crete (p. 313, **12**), at Kleonai (p. 148, **6**), and the so-called 'Forum Inscription' at Rome, whose shape no less than its alphabet is derived from a Greek original.[2] It may have been a mixture of convention (based on the original conception of these stones as primarily tall markers, carrying brief inscriptions only) and of technical convenience which caused the Greeks to maintain the somewhat narrow proportions of these pillars, which made it necessary for the tall archaic letters to be written in long lines vertically up and down, rather than in brief lines horizontally.

From this pillar the shape of the classical inscribed stele developed. The Greek instinct for visual effect which decreed that the tall pillar-bases for offerings, the sculptured grave-stelai, and the shafts of columns should all decrease slightly in their width upwards caused the inscribed stele also to retain its original taper; but the taper became less marked, the shape grew steadily flatter, the top was squared off (sometimes with the addition of a crowning member; cf. the Chian example **41**). The inscriptions were still cut on all four faces of the stone, and often still cut vertically on one of the wide faces[3] (as well as perforce on the narrow), although the practice of inscribing the wider faces horizontally was bound to become universal in the end.

---

[1] For the temporary wooden σανίδες used in Athens in the 5th c. and later, cf. Wilhelm, 229 ff.

[2] Sandys and Campbell, *Latin Epigraphy*[2] (1927), 37 ff.; Rehm, *Handb. d. Archäologie* (ed. Otto) i (1939), 209, n. 1.

[3] For examples of vertical cutting still practised in the late archaic period at Athens, cf. the Salamis decree, *IG* i². 1 (= Wade-Gery, *CQ* xl (1946), 101 ff.) and the first inscription on the stele from Marathon, *SEG* x. 2; cf. also the stele at Olympia carrying the text of the Peloponnesian dedication after their victory at Tanagra in 457 (pp. 129 f., Corinth **38**).

I have described the stele, sometimes called a 'kurbis', from Chios (41) (*c.* 575–550?) in some detail in Part III, pp. 336 ff.; it is an excellent example of the type which in development stands half-way between the archaic style of Crete 12 and the final stages exemplified in Miletos 39 (p. 335; *c.* 500–480?), which is a true classical stele in its proportions, but retains the early tradition by carrying the inscribed lines over every face, including the top.[1] The Chian stele is inscribed horizontally on one face, vertically on three. Other examples of the same period or later in the sixth century are the so-called 'Hymn to Athena' (p. 192, Lakonia 23), and the fragment from Tiryns (p. 149, 8).

In describing these early stelai or pillars I have refrained from using the Greek word κύρβις, because the real meaning of the term, and its application by the Greeks, have been disputed since the fourth century B.C.,[2] if not earlier; the problem has been fully set forth and discussed by Guarducci,[3] Oliver,[4] and Holland.[5] For Guarducci, the kurbeis were stone pillars, the Athenian examples carrying a part only of Solon's code (viz. that bearing on θυσίαι; the main code being, of course, contained on the famous wooden axones); for Oliver, the true meaning of the word kurbis is abstract, the 'Law of the land', and it was the later grammarians who, misled by the Athenian usage of the word (i.e., as though it meant a concrete object like the stelai), tried to reconstruct 'a kurbis' as though it were something material like an axon; while for Holland the kurbeis were triangular metal prisms, first produced by Peisistratos to codify religious laws introduced during his rule, and thence extended to embrace secular laws also.

There is no satisfactory etymology for the word κύρβις, although both ancient and modern scholars have sought hard to find one.[6] The most significant facts about it seem to be the following. Firstly, the Greeks themselves were not certain whether to treat the word as masculine or feminine; for example, it is feminine in Ar. *Av.* 1354, Lys. xxx. 20, and the manuscript of Plut. *Solon* 25 (citing Kratinos); masculine in Achaios of Eretria *ap.* Athen. 451d (F 19 N²), *Ath. Pol.* 7. 1, and Apoll. Rhod. iv. 280. Secondly, the only other words in Greek with the root κυρβ- are apparently foreign: κύρβη, an unknown silver object dedicated on Delos (*IG* ii². 161 and 199); κυρβασία, a tall hat, such as the tiara of the Persian king (Ar. *Av.* 487), or the hat worn by the Sakai of Scythia (Hdt. v. 49, vii. 64); Κυρβισσός, Κύρβασα, places in Caria; a Κύρβα in Rhodes, and also in Crete; and Κύρβαντες/Κορύβαντες, the name of priestly worshippers in an orgiastic cult attested in Crete, Phrygia, and Samothrace.[7] It may therefore be hazarded that κύρβις also is a non-Greek word, borrowed either from Anatolia or, perhaps even more likely, from the pre-Greek language of Crete; for Crete's well-established pre-eminence in the framing of

---

[1] The practice of using the narrow sides as well continued on occasion after the archaic period: e.g. on the Halikarnassian decree, p. 353, 42 (460–450); the stele from Lemnos (pp. 299 f., 59); *IG* i². 842.

[2] The first quoted explanation of the word appears to be that of Theophrastos (κύρβις < κορύβαντες); Photius, s.v. κύρβις 2.

[3] *Rend. Acc. Pont.* vii (1931), 101 ff.

[4] *Hesperia* iv (1935), 5 ff.

[5] *AJA* xlv (1941), 346 ff., with a convenient (though not always quite accurate) Appendix of ancient references; cf. also the bibliography by Kahrstedt, *Klio* xxxi (1938), 29 f., n. 2.

[6] κορυφή? (Apollodoros; see p. 54, n. 4, and LSJ s.v.); <κορύβαντες? (Theophrastos; see n. 2); <*κυπρις, copper? (Holland, op. cit. 358 f.); <*ku̯erb = to turn? (Boisacq, *Dict. Etym.*³ s.v. καρπός II); <√kurb found also in Anatolian place-names? (Fick, *Vorgriechische Ortsnamen*, 33, 126).

[7] Hesych, s.v. κύρβαντες; cf. Schwenn, *RE* xi, s.v. Korybanten, 1441.

laws during the archaic period may rest ultimately upon the great law-givers of the Minoan period (p. 310). In its original tongue the word may have meant either 'a law, command, instruction', or the object on which the law was written; and until we know the true meaning of the word, it is impossible to resolve the problem as to which meaning it had originally for the Greeks. All that we know at present is (*a*) that in some[1] of the examples of its use in ordinary or poetic speech (which are dated from the fifth century B.C. onwards) it appears to mean 'ancient laws', or perhaps rather 'ancient commandments, instructions'—which speaks neither for nor against an original material object as the meaning of the word; but in others[2] the meaning of a material object does seem to be implied; (*b*) that, at least from Theophrastos' time onwards, learned Greeks sought to explain what a 'kurbis' meant, and most of them had no hesitation in assuming as their basis that it was a concrete object. They sometimes confused their reconstruction by equating a 'kurbis' with other perfectly distinct and undoubtedly material objects—the wooden axones on which Solon wrote his laws, the whitewashed boards (σανίδες) used sometimes for special purposes, and the bronze pinakes or deltoi which were frequently used for the inscribing of legal texts from the sixth century onwards (pp. 55 f.).[3] When these alien elements have been removed, the statements of Apollodoros[4] remain, and fit what we know from the literary evidence and the surviving archaic inscriptions: πᾶσαν δημοσίαν γραφὴν καὶ νόμους κύρβιν καλεῖσθαι, ὅτι οἱ ἀρχαῖοι λίθους ἱστάντες τὸ δόξαν ἀνέγραφον, οὓς ἀπὸ μὲν τῆς στάσεως στήλας ἐκάλουν, κύρβεις δὲ ἀπὸ τῆς ἐς ὕψος ἀνατάσεως: the Greeks called public documents of all kinds κύρβεις, and in the early days they wrote them on upright tapering stones. It is only Apollodoros' presumed explanation of these facts (that κύρβις comes from the same root as κορυφή) which modern critics are uncertain of accepting. Thus we are brought back to our starting-point: that 'kurbis' could be and was used for any kind of law, commandment, or instruction; that the Greeks on occasion also used the word for the object on which it was written; and that we still do not know, any more than Apollodoros did, which was in fact the original meaning of the word. A possible clue to this meaning may be in the inference of some of the ancient writers[5] that in Athens the 'kurbeis' meant the sacred laws only, the axones the secular. This derives some support from the stock phrase θυσίαι ἐκ κύρβεων;[6] but it may be only an example of religious conservatism. Whereas new or different words

---

[1] Achaios of Eretria *ap.* Athen. 451d; Ar. *Av.* 1354; Kallimachos F 103 (Pfeiffer); Polemon *ap.* Athen. 234e–f; Ps.-Arist. *De Mundo* 400b; calendar of sacrifices of the *gens Salaminia* (Ferguson, *Hesperia* vii (1938), 5 (l. 87) and 67).

[2] Ar. *Nub.* 448; Kratinos *ap.* Plut. *Solon* 25; Lysias xxx. 17–18, 20; Plato, *Pol.* 298d; *Ath. Pol.* 7. 2–4; Didymos *ap.* Harpokration, s.v. ὁ κάτωθεν νόμος; Apoll. Rhod. iv. 280; and lastly the phrase 'ἐπικύρβια ἐνέχυρα' in the inscription from Amorgos *SIG*³ 1198, for which one possible translation is 'securities certified on kurbeis'.

[3] Eratosthenes (*Et. Mag.* s.v. κύρβεις; Schol. Apoll. Rhod. iv. 280–1); Aristophanes of Byzantion (*Et. Mag.* loc. cit.); Polemon (Harpokration, s.v. ἄξονι);

Zenobios iv. 77; Pollux viii. 128; Schol. Ar. *Nub.* 324.

[4] *FGH* ii, no. 244, F 107 (Harpokration and Photius, s.v. κύρβεις; Schol. Ar. *Nub.* 324; *BCH* i (1877), 150). I have not included the derivation by Phanias of Eresos and Asklepiades (*Et. Mag.* loc. cit.) from a mythical Kurbis, ὁ τὰς οὐσίας ὁρίσας. If the οὐσίας of the text is to be preferred to the variant θυσίας, there must be a reference here to some 'kurbis' concerning property (Holland, op. cit. 353, 360).

[5] Aristophanes of Byzantion (*Et. Mag.* loc. cit., reading θυσίας); Schol. Plato, *Pol.* 298d; 'some authors (ἔνιοι)' (Plutarch, *Solon* 25. 2); cf. Guarducci, op. cit.

[6] Lysias xxx. 17–18, 20; calendar of the *gens Salaminia* (see n. 1 above).

('axones' and the like) were applied to secular laws whenever occasion arose, the old word might stay unchanged in any reference to religious ordinances, merely by force of the conservative element which is instinctive in such details; as we, for example, retain the old noun in speaking of the Ten Commandments.

In addition to pillars and stelai, marble column-shafts or single drums were occasionally used for legal texts, the lines cut within the channels of the flutes. Several examples survive from the sixth and fifth centuries: a fragment from Paros (p. 294, **24**), a broken shaft from Naxos (pp. 292 f., **13**), another from Thera (p. 319, **14**) and part of a column-drum from Mantinea (p. 214, **28**). The island examples are all of the sixth or early fifth century and cut *boustrophedon*; the Arkadian belongs to the middle or third quarter of the fifth.

Lastly may be mentioned the old-established practice of inscribing legal texts upon the walls of buildings or freestanding walls (cf. Plato, *Laws* 859a). Most of the examples, including the earliest and finest, have been found in Crete (p. 310), at Dreros (**1**), Axos (**21–23**), Knossos (**13**), and above all at Gortyn (**2–5, 7–8**), their dates varying from the seventh to the fifth centuries. Others are known from the sixth century at Eretria (p. 84, **9**) and Miletos (pp. 334 f., **33**), from the fifth at Mantinea (**29**) and Athens.[1]

The bronze plaque (pinax or deltos) was widely used for the inscription of treaties and laws or, more rarely, of dedications, from the sixth century onwards. I do not know of any example as early as the seventh century, even of a dedication (such as Lakonia **19**, which may have been nailed up beside a trophy of arms, or Attica **21**, the dedicatory record by a body of treasurers of bronze objects dedicated on the Akropolis). The practice probably first gained popularity in some sanctuary such as Olympia, where the local stone was too coarse and shelly to make good stelai. The other advantages of bronze are obvious. A plaque occupies far less space than a stele, and the vast number of duplicate copies of treaties deposited at Olympia could hardly have been housed had they been on stone; moreover, when the text has finally become obsolete, bronze still possesses an intrinsic value as metal which makes it a source of profit to the temple officials. In addition to the large number of Elean and other plaques which have survived at Olympia, examples have been found in Athens, Megara, Ozolian Lokris, Arkadia, Achaia, Sikyon, Lakonia, Argos, Hermion, Mycenae, in Sicily near Leontinoi, and in the Achaian colonies round Kroton. The western Greeks apparently passed on the practice to the Latin and Etruscan peoples, for the Roman use of *aes tabulare* is well known (Pliny, *NH* xxxiv. 97). The most famous instance is that of the Twelve Tables, *c.* 450 (tabulae, δέλτοι), but earlier instances are recorded, beginning with Ancus Marcius.[2] Although no examples of the seventh century have yet been found, it may be noted that the Greeks themselves appear to have had a tradition that texts of really prehistoric antiquity were (or should be) inscribed on bronze. Thus Agesilaos of Sparta, on opening a tomb at Haliartos traditionally ascribed to Alkmene, found there, according to report, a small bronze bracelet, two clay amphorae, and a πίναξ χαλκοῦς covered with barbaric characters which resembled Egyptian (Plut. *De Gen. Soc.* 5). Akousilaos the Argive historian was said to have

---

[1] On the 'walls of stelai' erected in 410–404, see Oliver, op. cit. 5 ff.; Ruschenbusch, *Historia* v (1956), 123 ff.

[2] Dion. Hal. iii. 36 (cf. p. 52, n. 1). Other early examples are cited in Sandys and Campbell, *Latin Epigraphy*², 3 ff.

compiled his genealogies from δέλτοι χαλκαῖ which his father found while digging on his premises (*FGH* i, no. 2, T1). When Lucian's Alexandros went to Kalchedon to stage an elaborate piece of deception, he and his accomplices arranged to excavate δέλτοι χαλκαῖ of incredible age from the old temple of Apollo there, containing alleged statements by Asklepios and Apollo his father (*Pseudomantis* 217). If the first two examples were actually Mycenean inscribed tablets, as seems possible, one may suspect that the material was clay, turned to bronze in the crucible of the Greek imagination.

No gold plaques from the archaic period have survived in Greece, but a fifth-century inscription at Selinous (p. 271, **39**) appears to mention one vowed to the deities by whose aid the city won her victories. Lead was used in scroll form in the late Hittite Empire,[1] and this usage may possibly have spread to the Greeks, for Pausanias saw what he thought was a very old text of Hesiod inscribed on lead at Helikon (ix. 31. 4; cf. Pliny, *NH* xiii. 11. 21); but the earliest surviving examples are of curses (*defixiones*) of the fifth and fourth centuries B.C.[2] Silver is used for a plaque dedicated at Ephesos in the middle of the sixth century (p. 339, **53**), and a smaller one found at Poseidonia in Italy (p. 252, **4**).

The use of papyrus in Greece has sometimes been employed as an argument in discussions of the composition of the Homeric poems, on the grounds that they could not have been written down until this material was known to the Greeks[3] (a view which ignores the use of leather for this purpose; cf. pp. 57 f.). To those who maintained that the Greeks could not have known the papyrus roll until the time of Psammetichos I, or even until the formal cession of Naukratis to the Greeks,[4] it was pointed out in reply that the name for the papyrus roll in Greek was βύβλος, βυβλίον (βιβλίον), which shows clearly that their original source for it was not Egypt itself, but the Phoenician port of Gebal, which they called Byblos.[5] The date of the Greeks' first acquaintance with the Phoenician middlemen of Byblos may be a matter for dispute, but in any case knowledge of it would offer little help for the immediate question, for it gives only a *terminus post quem* for the introduction of the papyrus roll. The earliest reference in Greek literature to papyrus is the ὅπλον βύβλινον in *Od.* xxi. 390–1. When once the Greeks had learnt the word βύβλος for the papyrus plant, it was established in their language, and any secondary uses of the plant, wherever and at whatever date they encountered such uses, would still be described by the same word. Since the Phoenician scribes made use of the papyrus roll,[6] it may well be that the Greeks learnt this usage also when they first learnt the alphabet; but we cannot rule out the other possibility, that they did not become familiar with it until Greek merchants had gained a footing on the western side of the Nile delta in the last years of the seventh century, and there persisted until, about fifty years later, Greek interests in Egypt were officially recognized by Amasis' formal grant of Naukratis. We can be certain that thereafter the papyrus roll was a familiar article to the Greeks; but our only direct evidence as to their use of it is that it was the accepted form of writing-material in

---

[1] Bossert, *Altanatolien* (1942), 77, nos. 973–4, 983–90.

[2] For a list of 5th-c. *defixiones* see Jeffery, *BSA* l (1955), 72 ff.

[3] Birt, op. cit. 277; Bethe, *Forschungen u. Fortschritte* 1939, 103 f.; *Buch u. Bild* (1945), 11 f.

[4] Mazon, *Introduction à l'Iliade* (1942), 71.

[5] Dornseiff, *Hermes* lxxiv (1939), 209 f. Cf. also Lorimer, *Homer and the Monuments*, 527; Albright, *AJA* liv (1950), 165 f.

[6] Driver, 82 f.

Herodotos' day (Hdt. v. 58; Aesch. *Suppl.* 947), and that even in the late fifth century it was an expensive import, costing eight obols a χάρτη in Athens.[1]

Before papyrus became the accepted medium, the Ionic Greeks at least had been accustomed to employ leather for the same purpose. The chief evidence for this is the well-known passage in Herodotos (v. 58): καὶ τὰς βύβλους διφθέρας καλέουσι ἀπὸ τοῦ παλαιοῦ οἱ Ἴωνες, ὅτι κοτὲ ἐν σπάνι βύβλων ἐχρέωντο διφθέρῃσι αἰγέῃσί τε καὶ οἰέῃσι· ἔτι δὲ καὶ τὸ κατ' ἐμὲ πολλοὶ τῶν βαρβάρων ἐς τοιαύτας διφθέρας γράφουσι: in the old days, for lack of papyrus, the Ionians used to employ the skins of goats and sheep.[2] Herodotos does not suggest any upper limit in date for the prevalence of this practice; but there are two clues from other sources which seem to me to offer some evidence. The first lies in the character of eastern Ionic lettering as we see it in surviving inscriptions on stone from Samos, Miletos, and Chios about the second quarter of the sixth century. Compared with the contemporary lettering of mainland Greece it is small, hasty, and often untidy. We have only to compare (for example) Attica **18** with Samos **4** to see how marked the difference is. The Ionic approximates to a cursive script; and it may be inferred that this was not due to chance alone, but that in Ionia the practice of writing on διφθέραι had become sufficiently common for the contemporary cursive hand to influence the formal lettering of the masons. If the early inscriptions from Miletos and Chios are in fact to be dated in the first quarter of the sixth century or even earlier, as has been maintained,[3] this would extend the date for the influence of the cursive script on stone inscriptions back well into the seventh century; but there is, as far as I can see, no evidence for the higher dating of the inscriptions, and I do not think that in this instance we can say more than that the practice of writing on διφθέραι was well established by *c.* 575. The second clue, however, takes it back at least to the middle of the seventh century. We may recall the *skutale*, best known as the method of sending dispatches employed by the Spartans; it consisted of a staff or baton (σκυτάλη) round which was wound a roll of leather, which they used as a code simply by wrapping it in a particular way, writing the message across the result, and then sending the unwound strip to the receiver, who re-wound it on a similar staff to read it. We do not know how early the Spartans adopted this particular method of coding; σκυτάλη is used simply for a dispatch, without further details, by writers of the fifth and fourth centuries,[4] and the explanations of the stick and leather, and the coding system, all come from late writers.[5] It seems at least possible, or even likely, that in using these materials the conservative Spartans were merely re-taining a practice which had once been normal in Greece generally, of writing messages on leather rolls, because leather was then the normal writing-material, and winding them round a stick for transport.[6] When Pindar called the leader of his chorus σκυτάλα Μοισᾶν

---

[1] *IG* i². 374. ll. 279–81: χάρται ἐονέθεσαν δύο ἐς ἃ τὰ ἀντίγραφα ἐνεγράφσαμεν, ⊢⊢||||.

[2] The alternative rendering of ἐν σπάνι βύβλων, 'during a scarcity of papyrus', can hardly be right, even if it should be what Herodotos himself meant to say; a temporary inability to obtain a familiar article would not have driven its name from the Ionic dialect even after the article itself became available again. Cf.

Wendel, op. cit. 81 ff.; Lorimer, op. cit. 527.

[3] See pp. 333, 337, for a discussion of the dating of the early inscriptions of Miletos and Chios.

[4] Thuc. i. 131; Ar. *Lysist.* 991; Xen. *Hell.* iii. 3. 8.

[5] Plut. *Lysander* 19; Apoll. Rhod. *ap.* Athen. 451d; Schol. Pind. *Ol.* vi. 154; Hesych. s.v. σκυτάλη Λακωνική; Aul. Gell. xvii. 9.

[6] Cf. Hesych. loc. cit.

(*Ol.* vi. 154), the dispatch-staff of the Muses, he may not have had only the Spartan practice in mind; perhaps he was deliberately using a word with archaic associations to describe the Muses' message. For it will be recalled that Archilochos also used the word (F 81 Diehl):

Ἐρέω τιν' ὑμῖν αἶνον, ὦ Κηρυκίδη,
ἀχνυμένη σκυτάλη·
πίθηκος ᾖει θηρίων ἀποκριθείς (κτλ).

Here the 'gloomy message' is apparently pictured as itself addressing the recipient. Whether Archilochos actually sent the poem to his friend in the form of a σκυτάλη must be left to the imagination; the important point is that he was already familiar with the practice in about the middle of the seventh century, and it may be conjectured that at this time leather was the normal writing-material of the Greek scribe, used for messages as well as other writings. It will be recalled also that the oracles of Apollo at Delphi were at one time recorded on leather scrolls, according to Euripides (F 627 Nauck):[1]

Εἰσὶν γάρ, εἰσὶ διφθέραι μελαγγραφεῖς
πολλῶν γέμουσαι Λοξίου γηρυμάτων,

which again suggests a survival of an ancient practice, and indicates further that it was not confined to the Ionic Greeks. The word διφθέρα seems to have become synonymous with 'venerable records',[2] and finally lost its literal meaning, so that a later writer, Sokrates of Argos, could speak of διφθέραι χαλκαῖ (Plut. *QG* 25).

Wendel has suggested[3] that the Greeks derived the usage from the Phoenicians, and further that the widespread use of the leather scroll in Assyria and Persia also came from Phoenicia; and this seems very likely. It cannot have been a cheap product, for, though there was no need for Greece to import the material, the process of preparing it—the scraping, stretching, tanning, and then smoothing—was laborious, and the hides of sacrificed animals usually went to the temple officials, who were not likely to re-sell at a loss. When once a scroll was prepared, however, it could be used over and over again, like a wax tablet, for the ink could always be wiped off.

### III. *The Subjects of Early Greek Inscriptions*

I do not propose to do more here than touch upon some of the many subjects illustrated in the surviving inscriptions of the sixth century and earlier. A sketch of this kind cannot be free from distortion, because (even apart from the good or ill luck of excavations) the chances of survival vary greatly according to the material used; by this I do not mean only the truism that a poem on papyrus will perish faster than a decree on stone, but also that the same type of inscription will survive in one city but not in another. The questions and oracular replies at Delphi were apparently written on leather scrolls (below, n. 1), and therefore survive only in fragments in the literary tradition; those at the oracle in Dodona

---

[1] I see no reason for taking this description as poetic licence. We know that the questions and answers at Delphi must have been written on something perishable, for none has survived there, as they have, for example, at Dodona, where they were written on bronze and lead. Amandry suggests that they may have been written on wax tablets (*La Mantique apollinienne à Delphes* (1950), 149 ff.).

[2] Cf. Suidas, s.v. Ζεύς: ὁ Ζεὺς κατεῖδε χρόνιος εἰς τὰς διφθέρας: also the proverb, *ap.* Suid. s.v.: ἀρχαιότερα τῆς διφθέρας λέγεις.

[3] Op. cit. 81 ff.; cf. also Driver, 82 f.

were written on small bronze (later lead) plaques, and therefore some few at least have survived. The laws of Crete in the seventh and early sixth centuries survive because they were written on the walls of the temples; those of the same period at Athens were probably all, like Solon's, written on wood, for no traces have been found. Obviously, therefore, nobody would assume that a class of inscription did not exist in one state because, despite extensive excavation, it has not been found there. But the case is different when, despite the amount of excavation now achieved in Greece, a class of inscription still remains unrepresented in any area: namely, public chronicles of political events.[1] No archaic example, even of the briefest type, has yet been found in any state, on either stelai or walls, or on bronze plaques; yet it is hard to believe that, despite the variety of material used for public inscriptions, such chronicles were kept in every case on perishable substances only. Records of names are a different matter; there can be no doubt that certain lists of this kind, some of them used for purposes of dating, were written up in public at least as early as the sixth century. As is well known, the lists of Olympic victors, Spartan ephors, and Athenian and Parian archons are traced back in the literary sources to the eighth and the early seventh centuries; we must only be cautious of assuming that, because the names were known in a continuous list from 776 or 756 or 683, the first names were actually written up in those years. The memories of succeeding 'remembrancers' may have preserved them for generations before it was considered necessary to write them down in any form of list (pp. 20 f.). I give here the scattered evidence of the archaic inscriptions, as far as it is known to me, for such lists;[2] and I have included in it those inscriptions which record particular events (laws passed, temples repaired, gifts made) under the name of an eponymous official, conjecturing this to mean that, if the official's name was used in this way, a written list of these officials was being kept at the time. The total is meagre, but it may help to throw a little light on the kind of sources which were available for those historians of the late fifth century who first made use of such lists as a chronological basis for a narrative of historical events: Hellanikos of Lesbos, Hippias of Elis, Charon of Lampsakos.

There is nothing early from Olympia yet to suggest a prototype for Hippias' *Olympionikai*, but a fragmentary bronze plaque survives (*Ol.* v. 17) which from its lettering should belong to the end of the fifth or the early fourth century; it contains the beginning of a victors' list, with the names of the demiourgoi in office (all lost except for the ending of the principal demiourgos' name), and part of the number of the Olympiad:

Ενικασαν επι [τōν περι - - - ] -

-να δαμιοργοϋ[τōν - - -][3]

μēδεν ποτεχε[ν? - - - το - - - ] -

-κοστ(ο) Ολυμπια[σιν αγōνος?]

Λαμπυριōν : Αθ[αναιος?]

...ες : Α[- - -]

[- - -]

---

[1] Cf. Jacoby, *Atthis* (1949), 176 ff.

[2] I have not included the late epigraphic evidence for early lists of this kind, as those from Miletos (Rehm, *Milet* iii (1914), 230 ff.) and Halikarnassos (*SIG*³ 1020); cf. Jacoby, op. cit. 180 and n. 26.

[3] Cf. the formula on a somewhat later plaque from

Olympia, *Ö.Jh.* i (1898), 198 f.: [- - -] οσσα κα υ|σταριν γενωνται των περι Πυρρωνα δαμιοργων. The restoration of —μēδεν ποτεχε— is quite uncertain, though Roehl suggested that it might be part of some oath sworn (*IGA* 122 and add. p. 181; cf. *SGDI* 1170).

In Lakonia, two name-lists have been found at Sparta, and two more at Geronthrai (p. 195, **44–47**); they belong probably to the second half of the sixth century, and I surmise that they may be lists of victors rather than grave-monuments or lists of officials, for the Spartan examples were found in the precinct of Athena Chalkioikos, and the rare name Αϝαναξ occurs twice in six names on **46** (Geronthrai); if it is the same man, he is not very likely to have held office twice in rapid succession. If they are indeed athletic records, there may have been similar disjointed records of the victors at the Karneia, on which Hellanikos could draw for his *Karneonikai*. The only trace of any ephor-list seems to me to be in the dedicatory inscription of Damonon (**52**; *c*. 450–431?), in which towards the end the long list of victories suddenly begins to be reckoned by eponymous ephors (ὑπὸ δὲ ᾽Εχεμένη ἔφορον, κτλ), as though during his lifetime some publication (or republication) of an ephor-list had been reflected in the official victory-lists at the time. At Argos there are as yet no traces of the Priestesses of Hera; but an inscription (pp. 156 ff., **7**) dated *c*. 575–550, on a door-post (?) found on the acropolis, records nine names under the preamble: [τοιδεν?] εννͿεϝα δ]αμιοργοι εϝανασσαντο, which I suggest tentatively may be those of the boards of demiourgoi who (like the Athenian king-archon) in the fifth century were called βασιλεύς, and were eponymous (pp. 157 f.). Another (**8**) near it in date records that work was done in the precinct 'when [six names] were demiourgoi'. The names of two officials are mentioned, apparently as a date, in a fragmentary text at Phleious (p. 147, **1**). At Aigina *c*. 550–540 an inscription records that building was done in the precinct [επι Κλ?]εοιτα ιαρεος εοντος (pp. 110 f., **4**). In Athens, in addition to the now famous fragment of an archon-list found in the Agora (*SEG* x. 352), referring to the years 528/7–522/1 and itself dated *c*. 425–400, part of a sixth-century name-list written (in columns) on a poros stele has also been found (p. 74, **28**). It was found on or near the hill Sikelia, south of the city, and it may equally well be a grave-stele; but I include it tentatively here with the Agora fragment, conscious that, had the latter not chanced to include some well-known archons' names, we should probably have classed it also among the public grave-stelai. In Eretria a law was passed *c*. 550–525 επι Ͳολο αρχ[οντος] (p. 84, **9**). In Thebes a bronze phiale was dedicated by an official body of Thebans in the archonship of Phloax: Ͱιαρον Καρυκεϝιο· ΦλοϝαͿος απαρχοντος λεͿτοι{ς} ΘεͰαιοι{ς} ανεθεαν (p. 92, **7**); it may belong to the end of the seventh or first half of the sixth century. In the shrine of Ptoios at Akraiphia, also in Boiotia, a series of inscribed columns has been found which once carried tripods dedicated by the Akraiphian state; the earliest (**13**) may belong to the last years of the sixth century: Σιμονιδα αρχοντος τοι Ͱεροι τοι Πτοιοι Ακριφιες ανεθεαν. A similar public dedication, some years later in date, was made by the state of Halai in Opountian Lokris (p. 107, **11**): Θεαγενεος καριστομενεος και Φσανο αρχοντον Ͱαλεες ανεθεαν τἀθαναι· ΣͿοπα εστασε. In the Ionic cities no original lists of this period have come to light; but in Teos' colony Abdera the names of eponymous officials (priests of Apollo?) appear regularly on her coinage, which was first issued in the second half of the sixth century, possibly not long after the date of her foundation (p. 364, **28**). At Kyzikos, a Milesian colony, the last lines of an honorific decree of the late sixth century have been preserved on a broken stele, and a complete copy of the inscription made later on the same stone reveals that the decree was headed επι Μαιανδριο (p. 367, **51**).

These scattered traces are, I think, sufficient to indicate that the practice of inscribing in lists the names of those who held certain secular or religious offices, or who won the prize at the local festivals, was in force at least as early as the sixth century.

Other classes of public inscription have survived in clearer detail. The earliest legal texts appear to be those from the temple at Dreros in Crete (p. 311, **1**), which are of the seventh century, and deal with a variety of subjects, both sacred and secular. The relics of sixth-century codes from many other parts of Crete, notably Gortyn, amply confirm the early reputation of the Cretans as law-givers (pp. 310 ff.). The nearest secular rivals to these in age are the constitutional document from Chios (pp. 336 f., **41**), the fragment **9** (p. 158) from Argos, and the fragment bearing three laws from Eretria (pp. 84 f., **9**). Early sacral laws are more abundant: examples occur at Corinth (p. 128, **18**), Phleious, Kleonai, Tiryns (pp. 146 f., 148 f., **1, 6, 8**), Thessaly (p. 97, **1**). No very early treaties have been found as yet; the oldest are those found at Olympia, none of which is earlier than the last quarter of the sixth century; e.g. those between Elis and Heraia (p. 219, **6**), Megara Hyblaia and Selinous (p. 271, **36**), Zankle and an unknown state (p. 243, **5**); the agreements between Ozolian Lokrians at Naupaktos (?) and an ἐποικία of Opountian Lokrians (pp. 105 f., **2–3**) are probably of the late sixth and early fifth century.

Records of public work by a body of officials or an individual are attested at an early date. Mention has been made of the inscriptions which record the building done in the precinct of Aphaia at Aigina *c.* 550–540, and in the precinct of Athena at Argos some years earlier (p. 60). At about the same time the hieropoioi at Athens recorded on stelai the holding of the first and two later Great Panathenaia, and the establishment of the dromos (p. 72, **18**; *DAA* 326–8); and the archontes at Eleusis did likewise for Demeter and Kore (*IG* i². 817). A private benefactor, while holding the office of δικαστής, built or repaired a building in Thessaly during the sixth century (p. 97, **2**); an early telesterion at Eleusis (*IG* i². 805), a temple at Syracuse (p. 265, **3**), and the column of a temple at or near Sidene on the Propontis (p. 367, **50**) bear inscriptions by the men responsible for their making or repairing. Records by temple treasurers of valuables collected for the temple in about the middle of the sixth century have been found at Ephesos (p. 339, **53**) and Athens (p. 72, **21**), the latter in the form of a dedication.

The practice of marking monuments with the names of the dead probably goes back to a very early period. The primitive type of σῆμα, the rough stone marker or stele, is well illustrated in the necropolis at Thera (p. 317, **3–4**), whose earliest examples (bearing the name only) should not be later than the middle of the seventh century. Similar stelai, equally early in appearance and lettering, have been found in Aitolia (p. 225, **1**) and Achaia (p. 222, **1**). The magnificent series of Attic relief-stelai of the sixth century, which arose from these rough markers, bear their epitaphs at the top (**15**) or bottom of the shaft, or on the base (**32, 42**); but their predecessor in the seventh century, the stele of Keramo (**8**), carries the inscription in the field of the shaft, beside traces of a relief (?). The stele of Deinias at Corinth (*c.* 650?) may have had a painted figure on the shaft below the inscription (p. 127, **6**); but in those of her colony Korkyra the whole shaft is occupied with the epitaph (pp. 232 f., **8, 11**). The sculptured stelai of sixth-century Sparta were not inscribed, unless they belonged to a heröon (p. 193, **26, 29**). The Ionic stelai from Samos

(p. 329, **8–12**) and Prokonnesos (pp. 366 f., **43**) carry their inscriptions on the shaft, un-adorned save for a crowning member; but a stele from Kalchedon shows beneath the epitaph a clumsy relief apparently showing the scene of death, which is, as far as I know, unique at this date (*c.* 550–540?; p. 366, **41**).

Epitaphs form no small part of the total of early Greek inscriptions. The instinct for marking the grave of the dead in this way is strong. It is matched by the instinct, equally strong, for marking personal property, of men or of deities, a practice which is responsible for the largest part of this total. Some of the earliest-known inscriptions are owners' names scratched on pottery (pp. 347, 69, 238: Rhodes **1**, Attica **4**, Kyme **3**). Gifts to gods were marked sometimes with the same formula, τοῦ δεῖνά εἰμι, but more often with a dedication in verse; for, while the simple formula fulfilled the prime duty of guarding the object against theft,[1] the metrical dedication recorded the piety of the donor as well, and showed due honour to the god. Though the donor or the priest could incise an inscription on pottery, dedications on stone or metal objects had to be cut with the tools of the makers; it was therefore profitable to the early mason or bronze-worker to learn to write, and to pass on the knowledge to his son as part of the craft. Some may have been illiterates, who copied a draft made by the client; but the ingenious plotting often shown in fitting one or more hexameters into a limited and irregular space suggests that for the most part the craftsmen were themselves literate. A clear case can be made at least for the vase-painters in the first half of the seventh century, who sometimes added the names of the figures depicted (pp. 125, 110, 291: Corinth **4**, Aigina **2**, Naxos **1**), a practice naturally followed in the painting of clay plaques also, as well as in large-scale architectural painting and reliefs (pp. 71, 225 f., 101 f.: Attica **11**, Aitolia **2–3**, Phokis **8–9**). The practice of signing vases began very early (e.g. by Kallikleas, Ithake **2** (pp. 230 f.); Pyrrhos, Eretria **22** (pp. 83 f.); Aristonothos,[2] all of the seventh century); in these signatures the verb used is ποιεῖν, which suggests that these craftsmen both made and painted the pot; signatures which emphasize the pot-painter as a specialist (ὁ δεῖνα ἔγραψε) have not as yet been found before the early sixth century; e.g. Timonidas of Corinth (p. 126, **15**), Sophilos and Kleitias of Athens (**14, 16**). The earliest sculptors' signatures found as yet belong to the very end of the seventh century, or to the early sixth (except for a doubtful case, the Boiotian kore signed by —otos (p. 92, **4**), which may be *c.* 650–625). This is perhaps owing to the hazards of survival, but another possible reason may be suggested from a comparison with medieval sculpture. It was not until the close of the thirteenth century in England that the specialized craft of 'imager' became distinct among the skilled masons who carved both the blocks for the buildings and the sculpture which adorned them. It may be surmised that when the demand for stone temples and images began in Greece about the middle of the seventh century, replacing earlier works in wood and clay, the masons who made statues were not at first distinct from those who made build-ings. Daidalos himself, it will be recalled, was both builder and sculptor: ἀρχιτέκτων ἄριστος καὶ πρῶτος ἀγαλμάτων εὑρετής (Apollod. iii. 15. 9; cf. Diod. iv. 76). It may be,

---

[1] Cf. Lucian, *Hermotimus* 39, on the theft of an un-marked phiale from a temple.

[2] *MuZ* i. 110 f. It is not known where Aristonothos'

krater (found at Caere in a grave) was made; possibly he was a Greek colonist of Kyme; cf. Kirk, *BSA* xliv (1949), 121, n. 31 and below, p. 239, **24**.

therefore, that statues were not signed until the specialized craft of ἀγαλματοποιός was fully established. Apart from the above-mentioned Boiotian example, the earliest signatures are those of Euthykartides of Naxos *c.* 620–600 (p. 291, **3**),—medes of Argos *c.* 600 (pp. 154 f., **4**), Terpsikles of Miletos *c.* 600–575? (pp. 332 f., **23**). The earliest Attic signatures are those of the sculptor Phaidimos, of which two may belong to the decade *c.* 560–550 (**20, 23**) and one to *c.* 540 (**31**). The latter is cut by a different hand, indicating that Phaidimos either sold the work unsigned, for a local mason to add the client's inscription, or himself employed a lesser craftsman for lettering. It is clear from Attic inscriptions of the late sixth century that by this time some masons specialized in lettering, for the same hand can sometimes be detected alike in public inscriptions and in private dedications made by different sculptors.[1]

Writing was never regarded as an esoteric craft in early Greece. Ordinary people could and did learn to write, for many of the earliest inscriptions which we possess are casual graffiti. Kleisthenes' law of ostracism in 508/7 presupposes that the average person could write, but it is not known at what date reading and writing became a normal part of the education of children;[2] it can only be guessed that the trade of the γραμματιστής existed long before he joined the paidotribes and the kitharist as a regular instructor of the young.

## IV. *Letter-forms as Evidence for Dating Inscriptions*

In archaic Greek lettering no less than in other scripts there is a distinction between the formal and the informal or cursive style. It is not a conspicuous difference, like that between a formal inscription on stone from Pompeii and a contemporary graffito on one of the house-walls; and for that reason it is apt to be overlooked in modern commentaries on the chronological development of the Greek alphabet. But it is essential to remember that caution must be used when we compare the lettering of any inscription on stone or bronze with that of any painted inscription. The letter-forms used by the vase-painter will almost certainly be considerably more developed than those cut by a contemporary mason.[3] This is at once obvious if one compares, for example, the inscriptions painted on Attic black-figure vases during the years *c.* 570–550 by the painters Kleitias (**16**) or Nearchos (**24**) with the inscriptions cut on the Panathenaic dedicatory stelai of about the same period (*DAA* 326–8: **18**). The stelai show tailed *epsilon*, closed *heta*, crossed *theta*, small *omikron*; the vases, tailless *epsilon*, *heta* closed or open, dotted *theta*, normal *omikron*. The letters on stone or bronze are narrow in proportion to their height, those of the vases more squarely proportioned; that is to say, the painters are using forms which are not normal in formal inscriptions until the third quarter of the century, or even later.[4]

[1] *DAA*, 436 ff.

[2] Marrou, *Histoire de l'éducation dans l'antiquité*, 76 f.

[3] Cf. Peters, *Studien z. d. panathen. Preisamphoren* (1942), 17 f.

[4] The attempt of Loewy to lower the accepted date for the beginning of the RF style in pottery was based partly on this discrepancy, for he assumed that vase-inscriptions showing the same letter-forms as those of dated inscriptions on stone could not be earlier than the latter (*Sb. Ak. Wien* 216–17 (1936–7); *AE* 1937, 559 ff.; *Scritti . . . B. Nogara* (1937), 247 ff.; cf. Raubitschek, *AJA* xliii (1939), 710 ff.; Peters, loc. cit.).

It is a well-known fact that painting with a brush produces a faster and therefore more cursive script than any made by cutting; and, as painted letters are written faster, they tend to become smaller, so that simplification is sometimes necessary. For a vase-painter writing letters only 4 millimetres high it was difficult to paint such shapes as closed *heta*, crossed *theta* without blotting them; hence the first is simplified to H, and the second to dotted *theta*. In the same way tailed *epsilon* becomes tailless, because a wider space between the cross-bars lessens the chances of blotting, and tailed *upsilon* expands to V. It is possible, in short, that these changes in the Greek letters were first made by writers with brush or pen, and then adopted by the masons.

The only archaic painted texts which have survived are those on vases and clay or wooden plaques; but it is obvious that all those lost texts which were written in ink on leather or papyrus must have followed the same course, and to their scribes, even more than to the vase-painters, should be assigned, in all probability, the credit for evolving the simplified letter-forms, together with the credit for first breaking away from the *boustrophedon* system (pp. 48 f.). Traces of their influence are to be seen, I think, in early Ionic inscriptions. It is certain that lettering on stone in Ionia in the second quarter of the sixth century is distinctly smaller and more hasty than the contemporary script of the mainland. We may contrast the dedicatory inscription of Cheramyes of Samos to Hera (p. 328, 4) with that of the earliest base signed by the Attic sculptor Phaidimos (p. 72, **20**). The difference is striking; but Cheramyes' dedication may be compared with an Attic vase-inscription of the period without any such obvious discrepancy. As I have said above (p. 57), the Asiatic Greeks may have been pioneers in the use of leather and, later, papyrus as materials for writing among the Greeks; the example of their non-Greek neighbours in Asia Minor and Syria encouraged them in the use of both materials, which resulted in a style of writing formed by and for the brush or pen rather than the chisel.

A painted inscription, then, cannot be judged by the same standards as one cut by a mason, for whom each letter is a separate shape to be chiselled out in a series of strokes, not traced in a succession of rapid streaks with a brush. But even the painted inscriptions may vary in their degrees of informality. At first the names of the figures were held to be an important feature in the picture, and the writing was large and careful; as, for example, the names on the Protocorinthian pyxis Corinth 4, or the Attic plaque **11**. But as the labelling of figures became more customary and common, the lettering tended to become smaller and more hasty; the label was now taken for granted as an adjunct of the drawing. In Corinthian pottery we see the large, neat lettering on Early Corinthian vases (*c.* 625–600) give place to small, untidy script on Late Corinthian (*c.* 575–550). But a dedicatory inscription, which is *ipso facto* an important part of the whole, tends to preserve the formal characteristics of size and neatness; hence the lettering of painted dedications on Corinthian plaques of the late sixth century is often more archaic in appearance than that written on a vase a generation earlier (pp. 119 f.).

Graffiti also must be judged by special standards, for they are not the work of craftsmen, as are inscriptions on stone or bronze or vases; they may be the work of anybody, from an expert writer to one barely literate. In the development of letter-forms they stand mid-way between painted and chiselled inscriptions; for a scratched line cannot be done with the ease and speed of a painted one, although it is unlike the chiselled line in that it is done freehand. Hence graffiti sometimes retain the forms closed *heta*, crossed *theta* when a contemporary vase shows open *heta*, dotted *theta*; but the general proportions of the letters tend to resemble those of the painter rather than the mason. An interesting example may be seen on the François Vase, painted by Kleitias (Attica **16**). All the painted *thetas* but one are dotted; but when the word θακος is incised on the black paint of a seat in one of the pictures, crossed *theta* is used.

In trying to estimate the date of an inscription by its letter-forms, therefore, we have to remember these different streams of development, and in particular to use caution in comparing painted letters with the mason's script. In addition to the more obvious forms of development, as those of *heta* and *theta*, clues for a date or a provenance may be found in such details as the tilt of the cross-bar in *alpha*, or the length of the second stroke in *lambda*; but whereas such variations can be significant in the deliberate process of the mason, they may often mean nothing in the hasty strokes of the graffito or painted inscription.

Little remains to be said on the chronological development of the local alphabets in general, before their treatment in detail in Part III. The development has a double course; it is visible, firstly, in the changes within the actual letter-form (as those described above), which come from the Greek instincts for simplification and symmetry; secondly, in the gradual loss of obsolete letters (as *vau*, *qoppa*) or of local peculiarities (as Corinthian *beta* and *epsilon*, Argive *lambda*, Eretrian *mu*, Lakonian *sigma*, and many others) which disappear gradually in the fifth century beneath the spread of a standardized system, the Ionic script. Occasionally an old letter may be retained, but archaism of this kind is very rare. It occurs chiefly on coins, in cases where a brief legend has become part of the issuing city's badge, whereby the coin is recognizable to the rest of the Greek world: as *qoppa* for Corinth, *san* for Sikyon, Bυ (with local *beta*) for Byzantion.[1] But apart from these instances coin legends in general reflect the script in use at the time when the die was cut—the informal script, probably, rather than the monumental; for a die-cutter, like a vase-painter, might well prefer to use simple forms for his tiny letters.

[1] Cf. Rumpf, *Chalkidische Vasen*, 43; Payne, *NC*, 38 f., n. 5.

# PART III

# THE LOCAL SCRIPTS

## CENTRAL GREECE

### ATTICA

| α | β | γ | δ | ε | F | з | η | Ͱ | θ | ι | κ | λ | μ | ν | ξ | ο | π | M | φ | ρ | σ | τ | υ | φ | χ | ψ | ω | P | |
|---|---|---|---|---|---|---|---|---|---|---|---|---|---|---|---|---|---|---|---|---|---|---|---|---|---|---|---|---|---|
| 1 | ⋏ | B | Λ | Δ | Ɛ | Ϝ | I | - | 日 | ⊗ | ϟ | Ͱ | Γ | M | M | χϩ | ο | Γ | - | ϙ | P, | ϟ | T | Y | φ | X | φϩ | - | ⫶ | 1 |
| 2 | A | B, | Λ | Δ | Ɛ | Ϝ | | H | ⊕ | I | Ͱ | L | M | N | | | | | | P | ϟ | | Y | φ | + | | | ⫶ | 2 |
| 3 | A | B | | | Ɛ | | | | ⊙ | | Ͱ | L | M | N | | | | | | D | ϟ? | | Y | ⊕ | | | | ⫶ | 3 |
| 4 | Λ | | | | Ɛ | | | | | | | | | N | | | | | | R, | | Y | | | | | | ⫶ | 4 |
| 5 | Ͱ | | | | | | | | | | | | | | | | | | | R | | Y | | | | | | | 5 |
| 6 | Λ | | | | | | | | | | | | | | | | | | | | | V | | | | | | | 6 |
| 7 | A | | | | | | | | | | | | | | | | | | | | | | | | | | | | |

FIG. 26. Attica

*Notes on letter-forms*

αι is unique (**1**). The curved α2 appears on some of the earliest graffiti (**2–4**). α3 is the usual archaic form, developing sometimes to α4 by the mid-6th c. and commonly later. The exaggerated α5 occurs roughly *c.* 525–500 (**35**; *IG* i². 487). α6 occurs at all periods, but rarely. α7, the developed classical form, appears (like ε4) in a few inscriptions *c.* 520–500 (**36–39**; see p. 75).

In the earliest form β1 the loops do not join at the centre (**3c** and the Agora fragment cited on p. 69, n. 3, no. 81).

δ1 is abnormal, occurring in the very early graffiti **3a–b** (see also p. 24, and early Eretrian).

ε4, the developed classical type, occurs first in BF vase-inscriptions; e.g. in Exekias' work, p. 74; it appears also, with α7, in a few inscriptions *c.* 520–500 (see above).

Though it does not occur in the normal script of Attica, *vau* is written in the early abecedaria (p. 69), and twice in the diphthong αυ in metrical inscriptions (**7, 23**).

Ͱ1 is still used on BF vases *c.* 575–550 (**14, 16**), Ͱ2 *c.* 550 (**24**), but Ͱ1 still by the Amasis painter *c.* 550–525 (p. 74). The masons seem to have adopted Ͱ2 early in the period 550–525 (**30**; *IG* i². 971; D. M. Robinson, *Hesperia* xvii (1948), 142, pl. 35, 3).

θ1–2 is still used on BF vases, e.g. by Sophilos, *c.* 575–550 (**14**), θ3 by Kleitias (**16**) and Nearchos (**24**). The masons continued to use θ1–2 until the 5th c., but stray examples of θ3 occur already *c.* 550–525 (**30**; *IG* i². 989). See also *omikron*.

ι1 is unique (**1**).

κ1, the earliest form, has a long tail and short struts. The curved κ2 is perhaps one mason's habit rather than a normal form (**31, 32**).

λ2 is normal; λ1 occurs in **1** and very rarely later (*IG* i². 487). In the second and third quarters of the 6th c. it is often tilted (λ3), in both vase-painting and formal lettering (**14, 15, 22**).

μ1–2 is the normal archaic form to the end of the 6th c.; μ3 occurs also, but very rarely before the mid-6th c. (**15, 22, 32, 35, 37**).

The cutting-compass was in use for *omikron* and *theta* from the early 6th c. onwards (**13, 15, 17, 25, 30, 37**).

*Qoppa* is regular in Attic until about the mid-6th c.; e.g. it appears in **21**, but not in **22, 29**.

ρ1–2 is normal. ρ3, legless *rho*, occurs in the period *c.* 550–525 (**32**; *DAA* 63; *IG* i². 970, 972). ρ4–5 appears in the last years of the 6th c. and the early part of the 5th c. (**44**; Jeffery, *Hesperia* xvii (1948), 88 for other examples).

σ1 is normal, sometimes reversed (**21, 30**). σ2 occurs occasionally, especially in early painted inscriptions (**6**, Nessos amphora; **11**); σ3 appears once only, in the very early graffito on stone **2**, and may not in fact be a true letter (p. 69, n. 10).

υ1 is used until the second quarter of the 6th c., by both vase-painters and masons; a variant υ2 appears in **12**. The later form υ4–5 appears *c.* 560 on Sophilos' vases (**14**), the first Panathenaic stele (**18**), and Tettichos' gravestone **19**; **20** shows υ3, and **21** υ1. *C.* 550–500 υ6 is the form most commonly found, but υ3 is also used, particularly in carefully cut inscriptions (**36, 41**, *IG* i². 485).

χ1 is the form generally used until *c.* 550, χ2 *c.* 550–500; but exceptions to this order are fairly frequent. *Xi, psi,* and *omega* were not used in the Attic alphabet; for their first sporadic appearances in the 5th c., see *DAA*, 447 f.

*Punctuation* is common in Attic of the 6th c., 1 (three dots) being the most usual form. It appears first on the painted sherd **5c** (no. of dots uncertain). Though rarely necessary in the brief inscriptions on BF vases, it is used, for example, by Sophilos (**14a**). In formal inscriptions examples occur only from *c.* 600 onwards: on **12** (forms 1 and 2); **17** (2); **18, 21, 23, 25** (1); the rarer two-dot type 4 occurs on **31, 34**, and the Burgon amphora (p. 72). 3 occurs thrice in the 6th c. (*c.* 550–525?), on a BF fragment (GL 2134, pl. 94; incised), a poros dedication (*DAA* 2), and a funeral base (*IG* i². 984). Cf. *DAA*, 441 ff.

The script of Attica might be described as a cross between those of her two neighbours Aigina and Eretria. Whether this was in fact its parentage cannot be decided until more is known of the history of Athens in the eighth century; for, while the literary tradition suggests that she was then an agricultural state with few overseas interests, the warships painted on her Geometric pottery, and the wide distribution of this pottery, seem to reflect an interest in shipping no less strong than that of her two commercial neighbours. If the latter is a true picture, it is possible that the alphabet was brought to Athens by Attic venturers direct from some source in the south-eastern Aegean; otherwise, the people of Attica may well have become sufficiently familiar with the scripts of Aigina and Eretria to create a literate element in Athens before the end of the eighth century. Most of the letters of the Attic alphabet are common to both of the others; where the letters of Aigina and Eretria are not the same, Attic shows the Aiginetan *delta, mu, xi, chi,* but the Euboic *lambda* (except on **1**, discussed below).

Thanks to the generations of labour which have been spent in the excavation of the Akropolis, Agora, and Kerameikos at Athens, as well as in many scattered cemeteries and temples in the Attic demes, there is far more material available for the study of the early Attic alphabet than for that of any other state. The three most common types of early inscription—dedications, epitaphs, and graffiti or dipinti on pottery—are all well represented. The largest harvest comes from the pottery; it provides most of the earliest examples of Attic script until the late seventh century, when the first inscribed grave-stele

appears (**8**), the forerunner of a long series of Attic grave-monuments. The earliest inscription on stone (judged by its letter-forms) from the dedications on the Akropolis (**7**) must also belong to the seventh century; it too heralds a great series of similar inscriptions. There is also a large number of little inscribed bronzes from the Akropolis, but none of the published examples, as far as I am aware, is demonstrably earlier than the middle of the sixth century;[1] and so (since a full list of the archaic inscriptions of the seventh and sixth centuries together would require a separate book) the bronzes are here omitted, together with much else of the sixth-century material. Vase-inscriptions of the sixth century are not included, except for those few which can be considered as landmarks from the epigraphic point of view. Nor have I included the coinage,[2] whose brief legend ΑΘΕ with crossed or dotted *theta* gives little epigraphic help to establish the date of its beginning; all that can be said is that probably the lettering of the die-engravers should be classed in its development with that of the vase-painters rather than the stone-masons (p. 65). A few of the dedications are by public bodies (**18, 21, 27**), but no early legal texts, sacred or secular, have yet been discovered in Attica, on either stone or bronze; the earliest found as yet belong to the late sixth or the early fifth century (*IG* i².
1, 3–4, 5; *SEG* x. 2; Thompson, *Hesperia* xviii (1949), 223; **44**).

Every survey of early Attic inscriptions must start with the Dipylon oinochoe (**1**). It was found during illicit digging of tombs in or near the Kerameikos in 1871, and was offered to the Greek Archaeological Society with other material, after much had been already scattered; the rest of the grave-contents which accompanied this oinochoe, if there were any, are therefore unknown.[3] On its shoulder was incised (after firing) the retrograde hexameter: Ϝος νυν ορχ̄εστον παντον αταλοτατα παιζει, followed by an attempt at a second verse, which struggles up to stop near the handle. It reads ?τοτοδεκλμιν; possibly another, worse writer tried his hand here: τοῦ τόδε κ—, tailing off into the *stoichos* λ, μ, ν, with μ and ν each prefaced by a false start. This graffito differs from all later Attic lettering in its sidelong *alpha*, crooked *iota*, and *lambda* with its hook at the top; one may ask whether it is not Attic, but was inscribed, perhaps to show his prowess, by an outsider—possibly even from Posideion (?) itself, or one of the earliest Greek-writing colonies in those parts (p. 16). The date of this type of oinochoe should be somewhere in the second half of the eighth century,[4] and it still remains the only example of pottery found in Attica which is certainly Geometric and also carries an undoubted inscription. Another inscription on Geometric ware which may well be Attic was found in Aigina; J. Boardman, who found and published it, has pointed out that in fabric and style it is

---

[1] The earliest appear to be *IG* i². 433 (base of a statuette) and 436 (wool-carder's dedication); also the inscriptions *en pointillé* on bowls, Bather, *JHS* xiii (1892–3), pl. 6. 35 and 37.

[2] Seltman, *Athens: its History and Coinage* (1924), pls. 1 ff.; Jongkees, *Mnemosyne* xii (1945), 81 ff. See now Kraay, *Num. Chron.* 1956, 43 ff., pl. 13, who argues strongly that the date for the first Athenian 'owls' should be lowered to the last quarter of the 6th c.

[3] For references to the other material found during the digging and later published, cf. Koumanoudes, *Athenaion* ix (1880), add. to p. 50.

[4] A similar oinochoe (Athens, NM 152) was dated *c.* 800–750 by Kahane, *AJA* xliv (1940), 477, 482; Nottbohm suggests a date contemporary with the work of the painter of Athens 804 (*c.* 760–40), or slightly later (*JdI* lviii (1943), 19, n. 1). Dunbabin, to whom I owe the above references, adds: 'I think one can now say "second half of the eighth century". . . . The inscribed jug is stylistically rather later than Athens 152, and I think typical poor Late Geometric.'

indistinguishable from Attic, and that an Attic or Aiginetan traveller might have commissioned the object in Athens for dedication in Aigina; see p. 110, Aigina **1**. A sherd (Akrop. 309) carrying parts of three painted retrograde letters -ν τ ε- has been classed alternatively with Geometric and with early Protoattic (i.e. first quarter of the 7th c.).[1] An amphora from the Agora, certainly Geometric, carries an isolated sign not unlike a fifth-century *epsilon*.[2] Two small fragments, also from the Agora, with parts of undoubted graffiti retrograde (-ιβ- and -μ-) may be either Geometric or Subgeometric;[3] and lastly there is the very important series of graffiti from Hymettos (**3**), on small cups or bowls of a plain fabric and type, which is thought to have lasted from the Geometric period almost to the end of the seventh century.[4] The example here illustrated as **3a**, written retrograde round the cup, agrees well in the extreme archaism of its letters with other very early inscriptions such as Boiotia **1** (statuette dedicated by Mantiklos), Ithake **1** (oinochoe, Orientalizing); indeed, the Attic graffito apparently reads not unlike the Ithakesian dipinto: [. . .]εμ' α⟨ν?⟩δρο[ς μ]α[λισ]τα φιλει τε[- - -].[5] The correspondence with these scripts is confirmed by R. S. Young's date of the cup (by its shape) to the early seventh century; while the cup of **3b**, a vituperative graffito in lettering plainly later, was assigned (by its more developed profile) to the third quarter of the century.[6] **3c** shows a fragmentary abecedarium. Another shows the start of two, written perhaps by master and pupil; its curved, straggling letters recall the very early Euboic and Corinthian examples on an oinochoe from Kyme; see Corinth **2**, pp. 116 f. Parts of other abecedaria remain unpublished, but are reported to contain *vau*.[7] Most of these graffiti from Hymettos are not the formulae of dedications, but (when intelligible) consist of the simplest remarks common on such ware: 'I am X's', 'X wrote me', 'X gave me to Y', 'Drink this up', and attempts at the alphabet. The deity to whom they were dedicated is thought to be Zeus Ombrios,[8] but the circumstances of dedication remain obscure. A skyphos of the same ware found in the Agora, inscribed Θαριο ειμι ποτεριον (**4**), was dated by its shape in the middle of the seventh century,[9] and the script, again, appears to bear this out; the letters, though still tailed, are no longer tall and spidery like those of **3a**.

The lettering of **3a** may be compared with the graffito on a flat piece of slate-like stone from the Akropolis (**2**), bearing parts of two lines written *boustrophedon*, which, from the angle of their approach, suggest that only about ten letters may have been contained in the lost turn, or loop, of the lines. The scribe wrote retrograde well: [- - -]ενκεκαλ[υπται?], but forwards much more awkwardly: [- - -α]νϕτοεροισιν ε[- - -].[10] It is undoubtedly the

---

[1] It is set among the Geometric ware in GL i. 30, pl. 11; but Young (*Hesperia*, suppl. ii. 229) compares the decoration with that of Akrop. 345 (uninscribed), an amphora dated 'fairly late in Early Protoattic' by J. M. Cook, *BSA* xxxv (1934–5), 185.

[2] Young, op. cit. 181 f., 228, figs. 131, 144.

[3] Shear, *Hesperia* ii (1933), 563, nos. 81–82, fig. 23; cf. Young, op. cit. 226, n. 1.

[4] Young, op. cit. 227.

[5] Cf. also Beazley, *AJA* xxxi (1927), 352 f., and the 5th c. Attic example there cited, *IG* i². 924.

[6] Young, *AJA* xlvi (1942), 47.

[7] Report cited in *AJA* xlvi (1942), 124 f. I under-

stand that a second fragment has been found to join that showing the two abecedaria, for which see Young, *AJA* xliv (1940), 8, fig. 10. 9.

[8] Young, op. cit. 3.    [9] Young, *Hesp.* sp. ii. 124.

[10] The restorations are those of *IG* i². 484. From the photograph it will be seen that the signs taken for zigzag *sigma* and the last *iota* in line 2 are fainter than the other letters, which suggests that they may possibly be flourishes of the pen, so to speak, the word being ανϕοτεροιν. The hexameters (if such they are) find an echo in the Homeric *Hymn to Demeter*, ll. 42: κυάνεον δὲ κάλυμμα κατ' ἀμφοτέρων βάλετ' ὤμων, and 182: [ἡ δὲ] στεῖχε κατὰ κρῆθεν κεκαλυμμένη (κτλ).

earliest Greek inscription on stone which we possess, though 'inscription' is perhaps too formal a term for these scratched letters.

Painted inscriptions have been found on Protoattic pottery from the second quarter of the seventh century onwards until its development into the BF style late in the century (**5a–e**);[1] and two classes of graffiti on pottery may also be mentioned here, for the earliest examples should belong to the seventh century, and deserve to be better known than they are. The first (**10a–h**) is the series of personal names in the Attic alphabet scratched on the shoulders of big wine and oil amphorae of the kind called 'SOS' from their decorated neckbands. The fabric has been shown to be Attic, and they were exported all over the Mediterranean area in the late seventh and first half of the sixth centuries; the inscribed examples are: Ϙλōπετιōν⟨ο⟩ς from Gela (**10a**); -πετ- from Tell Defenneh (**10b**); Μυρμε̄ϙος from Caere (**10c**); Αριος Αριονος (BM, unpublished; **10d** and Addenda); Χαροπιο from the Kerameikos (unpublished; **10e**); all these should not be later than the seventh century by their lettering. One in later lettering may be of the sixth century: Περαδο ειμι from Caere (**10f**); another from Caere has an odd name, Λασαργαδο (**10g**), and the sherd of a third from Caere, inscribed Ϙοραϙος ειμ[ι], has recently come to light (**10h**). Were these the names of the exporting merchants, or of Attic travellers who took them abroad?

The other interesting class of graffito consists of names on sherds (sometimes cut into a rectangle or circle), which resemble the series of fifth-century political ostraka, but are palpably earlier than the fifth century (**9a–e**). In publishing a number of the latter found in the Agora, E. Vanderpool has added several of the earlier kind, rightly pointing out that on palaeographical grounds they can hardly be as late as the fifth century, several being found, moreover, in closed deposits of the sixth century.[2] Chief of these early graffiti is the well-known sherd inscribed retrograde with the name of Peisistratos (**9e**); I have no doubt that Vanderpool is right in divorcing it from any possible grandson of the tyrant, and ascribing it instead to the seventh or sixth century; indeed, if it is placed beside the early graffiti which we have been discussing, it falls into place among those of the first half of the seventh century, and, if it is to be connected with any known historical figure, may be ascribed to that Peisistratos who was archon in 669/8.[3] The exact significance of these graffiti is unknown; as Vanderpool says, they may be idle scribbles, or they may be survivals from some early method of voting of which we know nothing. One example (**9c**), reading *boustrophedon* Εγεστρατος | Ϝα⟨ι⟩σιμιōνι, was perhaps a label accompanying a gift; another (**9d**, Θρασυκλε̄ς) looks like early seventh-century work.

In Attic black-figure painting, which grew out of the old Protoattic style, the earliest script recognized as yet is that of the Nessos painter, *c.* 625–600. In the list of his identified works two bear painted inscriptions, the Nessos amphora and the Harpy krater (**6a–b**): part of the rim of another krater (?) (**6c**) has the remains of a dedication, scratched *boustrophedon*: [- - - γλα]υϙπōιδι (*sic*) ϙ[ορε̄ι]. It is interesting to compare this graffito with the painter's own script; we could hardly have a better illustration of the advanced appearance

---

[1] I have omitted from the Attic list of inscribed Protoattic ware the inscription Μενελας on a krater-stand from Aigina, which seems more likely to be in Aiginetan: cf. Aigina 2, p. 110.

[2] *Hesperia*, suppl. viii, 407.

[3] Paus. ii. 24. 7; cf. Cadoux, *JHS* lxviii (1948), 90.

of letters made by the painter's brush compared with those of a less-practised contemporary writer (cf. pp. 63 ff.).[1]

Apart from the small fragment **2** the earliest inscription on stone, judged from its appearance, is the fragmentary object of Naxian marble **7**, found among the Akropolis dedications, with parts of two lines written *boustrophedon* and a third at right angles. The surviving letters include *vau*: [- - -]ν αϝυτ̣[αρ? - - -] (cf. αϝυταρ in **23**), and it might be of any date from the middle of the seventh century onwards. The earliest grave-inscription is of the same century, perhaps towards the end (**8**). Plain stone stelai erected over graves have been found in the Kerameikos, and elsewhere in Greece, from the Geometric period onwards,[2] the most complete inscribed series being those from Thera. The stele of Keramo (**8**) is the earliest inscribed example from Attica, and is apparently the prototype of the fine series of Attic funeral reliefs of the sixth century. The inscription is cut on the field of a fragment of a stele of hard bluish stone, bearing faint traces of a raised surface identified tentatively as the remains of a relief. There was plenty of room to cut the hexameter in a single looping line, but it has been deliberately written in two separate retrograde lines, each starting (beside the relief?) with a name: Ενιαλο θυγατρ[ος Σπουδιδ]ọ | Κεραμος στελε̄: that is, the names were perhaps attached to two figures in profile, who may have been Keramo and her (already deceased?) father Enialos. The lettering, with its archaic long-tailed *upsilon* and small *omikron* may be compared with the graffito **3b**; even if we allow for the difference in medium, **8** can hardly be later than *c.* 625–600.

From the mass of sixth-century material it is impossible to do more than select those examples which seem to illustrate best the gradual development of Attic script within the somewhat arbitrary divisions of twenty-five-year periods. For the years *c.* 600 there is a clay plaque with a relief of Achilles and an Amazon Ainia (**11**); the lettering of this and of contemporary vases[3] is large in comparison with the small lettering of later generations of painters. The altar dedicated by Chairion on the Akropolis (**12**) should not be much later than 600; it may be compared with the Naxian dedication on Delos (Naxos **3**, p. 291), as showing the first Attic example of punctuation (1, 2) on stone. The remains of a well-cut dedication (**13**) on the abacus of an Ionic capital which bore a fragment of sculpture (seated animal?) made in one piece with it may be equally early—or indeed earlier, for the mason ruled all the lines of his letters carefully, which gives it a developed look that may be in fact delusive. Towards the end of this period there are the inscribed vases of the painter Sophilos (**14a–d**), in which the following points may be noted: *heta* is still closed, *qoppa* in use, *upsilon* is approaching its later, short-tailed form 4, and punctuation 1 is used. If Sophilos' inscriptions represent the painter's script of *c.* 575, the grave-inscription **15** should certainly not be earlier: [. .]λινο : μνε̄μα : ειμι. Yet the monument, a seated sphinx, is dated early in the first quarter of the century;[4] perhaps it remained in the sculptor's yard for some little time before it was bought and the inscription added.

The following period, *c.* 575–550, is represented in vase-painting by the painter

---

[1] Dunbabin drew my attention to an inscribed sherd of the same period and near in style to the Nessos painter, showing part of a centaur's name, Πετρ[αιος]: *CVA* Wien, 14, pl. 5, 2–3: Beazley, *AJA* xlv (1941), 596 and *JHS* lxix (1949), 122.

[2] Cf. *AAG*, 7 ff.; to the examples there cited may be added now the stele published in *Corinth* xv. 1 (1948), 8.

[3] e.g. the fragments GL i. 603–4 and the early BF dinos in *Hesperia* iv (1935), 430 ff.

[4] *AAG*, 16.

Kleitias, whose masterpiece the François vase (**16**) shows ⊢ı and ϙ still in use, and both θ2 (rarely; incised) and 3 (painted) (p. 65). θ3 is used also on the Burgon amphora, the earliest inscribed Panathenaic prize-amphora,[1] presumably *c.* 566 or not much later, and (with υ5) in the neat script of the painter Nearchos, about the middle of the sixth century (**24**); it may be noted that he wrote the two lines of his signature from left to right; the *boustrophedon* system is on the wane. A fine example of the formal script of *c.* 570–560 is the dedication on the base of the marble Calf-bearer from the Akropolis (**17**), by [Rh]onbos(?) the son of [P]alos(?).[2] A poros pillar from the Akropolis (**18**) has been ascribed to the same decade, for it commemorates the establishment of a δρόμος by a board of eight men whom Raubitschek has identified as the board of ἱεροποιοί who arranged the first Panathenaia in 566;[3] the inscription is written *boustrophedon* with punctuation ı, and shows on stone the later form of tailless υ6 which was already in use among the vase-painters. υ5 occurs on the funeral base of Tettichos (**19**), which perhaps held a stele,[4] and is, I think, the finest example of Attic *boustrophedon* lettering yet found. Had Nearchos been a sculptor, as well as potter and painter, he would have inscribed marble thus. The base of another funeral stele is of about the same date (**20**); it bears the earliest of the three surviving signatures of the Attic sculptor Phaidimos. Here also should belong our only surviving early Attic bronze plaque (**21**), which records the dedication to Athena of some bronzes (χαλκία) collected by a board of five, six, or eight treasurers. The bronze is broken on the right, and possibly half of it lost. It is perhaps the earliest example in Attic of an inscription written consistently from left to right, combining with this feature the archaic forms of ⊢ı, υı, and *qoppa*. The lettering is very like that of the Attic inscription on the stele erected in memory of Phanodikos of Prokonnesos at Sigeion (pp. 366 f.). This latter was cut *boustrophedon*, with long-tailed *upsilon* ı but open *heta* and no *qoppa*: *phi* also appears to be in the later form 3, whereas closed *heta*, *qoppa*, and tailed *phi* were still normal, even in the rapid painter's script, *c.* 575. I do not think therefore that the Attic inscription on this stele at Sigeion can be earlier than *c.* 575–550; and if this is so, it cannot be used to support the tradition of an Attic colony in Sigeion in the last years of the seventh century.[5] With **21** may also be compared the capital of a pillar(?) erected by Kylon in memory of his two children (**22**); it is written from left to right, but the last line (a half-line?) may have run from right to left, as there is a *vacat* below the left-hand part of the lowest surviving line, and traces of letters below the right-hand part.

The second signature of Phaidimos occurs in a funeral epigram (**23**) carved on the top stone of a stepped base from a tomb at Vourva. This base apparently bore a kore of the solid archaic Attic type best illustrated by the well-known statue now in Berlin.[6] Only the feet of Phaidimos' kore survive, side by side in thick-soled sandals, but (though the

---

[1] Peters, *Studien z. d. panathen. Preisamphoren* (1942), 14 f., n. 100; Beazley, *AJA* xlvii (1943), 441 and *DABF* 88 ff.

[2] Payne and Young, *Archaic Marble Sculpture from the Acropolis*², pl. 3 and, especially for the names, p. 67 (Beazley). Βόμβος (alt. Βόμβρος) and Ἴταλος, both attested in Boiotia (Pape-Benseler, s.vv., *IG* vii. 1119), may also be suggested; ıτ fits the space better than π.

[3] *DAA*, 352 f.

[4] The deep rectangular cutting on the top is modern.

[5] Cf. Strabo 599–600 and Leaf, *Strabo on the Troad*, 187 f.; Brouwers, *REG* xli (1928), 111 f.; Berve, *Miltiades* (1937), 30; *AAG*, 21 f. The alternative view which, based on Hdt. v. 95, would ascribe it to Peisistratos' tyranny in the third quarter of the 6th c., was advocated by Guarducci, *Ann.* iii–v (1941–3), 135 ff.

[6] Blümel, *Kat. Skulpt. Berlin* ii. 1, A1.

treatment of the details is more advanced) they correspond so closely in stance and general aspect with those of the Berlin kore that there is little doubt that the grave-statue was of this type.[1] It should be noted, therefore, that this disposes of the suggestion, advanced in *IG* i². 1012 to explain the use of *vau* in the epigram (αϝυταρ), that the sculptor Phaidimos came from Naxos; a kore made by a Naxian artist *c.* 550 would surely be connected not with the static, sandalled Berlin kore, but with Philippe, barefooted and just perceptibly advancing, made by Geneleos of Samos (Samos **6**, p. 329). Phaidimos made a typical Attic kore, and *vau* is attested in early Attic abecedaria and on the Akropolis fragment **7**; evidently, therefore, the letter could be used on occasion (at least in the diphthong αυ) in Attic poetry as well as in Naxian.

The mason who cut this epigram ended it *boustrophedon* in the last half-line, a practice occasionally used after *boustrophedon* proper had gone out of fashion. He was, I think, also the cutter of the earliest extant Attic *stoichedon* inscription, the epitaph of Phrasikleia (**29**), inscribed on a base which bears on its adjacent side the signature (in Attic script) of Aristion of Paros. The lettering of **23** and **29** is very similar, and in both the mason has been careful to end each line with a complete word—a practice which, though possible in **29**, could not long survive the introduction of *stoichedon*. If the Berlin kore belongs to the years *c.* 570, and Phaidimos' is *c.* 550, Phrasikleia's epitaph may fall within the years *c.* 540. A fragment which should be close to it in date is the dedication **26** from the Akropolis, which is inscribed (in the same delicate, fine lettering) *boustrophedon* and *stoichedon* and has a moulded frame round the inscribed face which recalls the incised frame round Phrasikleia's epitaph. Another inscription cut both *boustrophedon* and *stoichedon* is the dedication on the Akropolis by two Alkmeonidai, —ος and Alkmeonides, inscribed on a poros Doric capital which once bore a metal bowl (**25**).[2] Except for the circles (made by a cutting-compass) the lettering is ragged and untidy in comparison with that of **26** and **29**; it should not be much, if at all, later than 550. The other athletic dedication perhaps by the same Alkmeonides, inscribed on a Doric capital which once bore a statue of Apollo at the Ptoion in Boiotia (**30**), may have been erected when the Alkmeonidai went into exile after Peisistratos' return *c.* 546. We may guess that this Alkmeonides, son of Alkmeon, had won the chariot race at the Panathenaia in that year, and had to leave Attica before he could make his dedication on the Akropolis; the inscription shows dotted *theta*, but otherwise its appearance suggests a date round about 540. The script is Attic; cf. Attic *gamma*, and the open form of *heta*, which would be abnormal in a Boiotian inscription before the late archaic period. Two other fragmentary inscriptions which may also belong to the decade 550–540 deserve mention, since both are public documents and not well known. One is a dedication by the deme of Sounion ([Ͱοι Σ]ουνιες) inscribed on part of the thigh of a kouros (**27**), found with some similar fragments in the deposit by the temple of Athena at Sounion, not far from the area which produced the better-known Sounion kouroi.[3] This inscription, written from left to right in

---

[1] Eichler, *Ö.Jh.* xvi (1913), 86 ff.; Rhomaios, *AD* iv (1928–9), 25.

[2] The top of the capital shows a single round cutting, for the base of a bowl. Raubitschek notes that, since each dedicator won a prize, there should be two bowls; he therefore suggests that the offering is not an actual prize, but a gift made in commemoration. It is also possible that the capital held two bowls, stacked.

[3] Stais, *AE* 1917, 202 f.; Richter, *Kouroi*, 66 ff.

two lines, is the only Attic example, as far as I know (apart from an even smaller fragment from the same deposit), of an inscription cut on the marble statue itself, a practice common enough in other parts of Greece. The other inscription deserving of mention is on a poros fragment apparently from the top of a plain stele (**28**). It was found by the modern slaughter-houses near the hill Sikelia, on the south-west side of Athens; it bears the remains of two columns of names, separated by a vertical line. The lettering was apparently *stoichedon*, but the use of poros for a stele suggests that its date should not be long after the middle of the sixth century, at latest. It may be a list of officials (even of archons?), or of prize-winners at some recurrent festival, or, since it comes from an area where many graves have been found, of the dead on some public memorial; whatever its nature, it is of interest in being apparently the earliest example from Athens of a separate list of this kind as distinct from a series of names within the text of an inscription, like those in **18** and **21**.[1]

Although the tradition of tall, regular, long-tailed lettering lasted almost to the end of the sixth century, an alternative type was already growing up during the third quarter, which in its general effect is shorter and less regular; it is perhaps the work of inferior masons, and may for that reason reflect in some degree the ordinary, non-professional script of the time. As an example may be cited the inscription on the base of the funeral stele in New York depicting a boy and girl (**32**), which has been tentatively dated by its style *c.* 540. We may note the clumsy lettering, the circles made by punch-points joined together. A no less awkward script occurs on the marble stele bearing the third signature of Phaidimos (**31**), which one is tempted to attribute to some inferior mason employed in the sculptor's workshop. A casual graffito on a tile-sherd (**33**) from the filling of a well in the Agora, which also belongs to the years 550–525, may be cited here as an example of contemporary writing to set beside **31**; it reads Ͱερμειμαγαλμα, and may be an imperfect draft of an inscription for a sculptor who was making a Hermes statue for some client— not, presumably, a Herm proper, for that particular type was apparently introduced into sculpture in the time of Hipparchos son of Peisistratos.[2]

In so general a survey there is little to be said of the vase-painters' inscriptions during this period. The archaic closed *heta* and crossed *theta* are still used in inscriptions by the Amasis painter,[3] but the later types, with ε4, in the exquisite lettering of his contemporary Exekias.[4] The one existing joint signature of the potter and painter Sotes and Paideros (*c.* 550)[5] is written *boustrophedon*—a rarity in vase-inscriptions, although a name which was just too long for the available space might be turned back *boustrophedon* for the last few letters, like the end of a line in **23**.[6] On Little Master cups the lettering is used for decoration,[7] and a pleasant version of the *stoichedon* style appears in the signature of Thypheithides.[8]

[1] A list of names appears on one side of a poros stele of about the same period from near Anavysos in southern Attica, which bears an additional inscription on the narrow side; Jeffery, *BSA* xxxix (1938–9), 90 ff. It also comes from an area where many graves have been found.

[2] Lullies, *Typen der griechischen Hermen* (1931); Goldman, *AJA* xlvi (1942), 58 ff. The Agora sherd may read: Ͱερμει μ' αγαλμα . . . .

[3] Cf. *MuZ* iii, figs. 218–19; *DABF*, 57 ff.

[4] Technau, *Exekias* (1936), pls. 1, 2, 16, 20, 25; *DABF*, 63 ff.

[5] Roebuck, *Hesperia* ix (1940), 225 f., fig. 43.

[6] Cf. the name Κ̄εδαλῑο̄|νος, *boustrophedon* on a sherd of a Little Master cup, Roebuck, op. cit. 200 f.

[7] Austin, *Stoichedon Style*, 5; *DABF*, 53 ff.

[8] Beazley, *JHS* lii (1932), 193 f., fig. 17.

By the last quarter of the century the numbers of marble-sculptors and masons in Attica must have been considerable, judged by the output of sculpture in the round and reliefs during the period; and this fact may help to explain a certain variety in the inscriptions. Mostly the tall, tailed lettering persists; a good example is that on the base for a statue made by Antenor and dedicated by Nearchos, *IG* i². 485 = *DAA* 197. It is a problem whether this should be dated shortly before or after 525.[1] The fragment from the base of the offering made after the defeat of Chalkis and Boiotia in 506 (**43**) shows α3, ε3, ν1–2. The grave-stele of Lyseas, also dated from its style in the years *c.* 510–500, shows α3, ε1, ν1 in the epitaph (**41**). The stele of Aristion, assigned to the same period, shows *nu* both 1 and 3, with a marked difference in quality between the sculptor Aristokles' sloping signature on the stele and the fine vertical lettering of the mason who inscribed the base (**42**). In contrast with these inscriptions, the beautiful lettering on the altar dedicated by Peisistratos son of Hippias to commemorate his archonship (**37**) shows such developed types of *alpha* and *epsilon* (7, 4) that one authority has interpreted it as the work of an Ionic craftsman,[2] while others have sought for possible reasons to date it in the early fifth century.[3] Peisistratos dedicated it as a 'memorial of his office' (μνῆμα τόδε ἧς ἀρχῆς . . .), which does not necessarily mean an immediate memorial; but even so, it can hardly be later than 511/10, unless we are to believe that he returned and held office under the democracy, a view for which there is no ancient authority. The anomaly is further stressed by the contrast between the same[4] mason's lettering on the base of a dedication by Hipparchos at the Ptoion in Boiotia (**38**), and the untidy inscription **35** (with α5, ε2) on one of the Herms erected by Hipparchos in the country demes; both these inscriptions must be earlier than 514. A parallel example of ε4 in the sixth century has been pointed out in a signature of the painter Eumares (**36**);[5] and a similar α7 occurs on the base of a dedication at Delphi by the elder Alkibiades, contemporary of Kleisthenes (**39**); but the only other example of the sixth century which shows both α7 and ε4 is the inscription (which cannot be compared for technical excellence with those of the Peisistratid mason) on the base for a lost grave-stele made by Endoios (**40**). In conclusion, therefore, we can only infer that this Peisistratid mason modelled his lettering on the symmetrical script of the vase-painters; he must have been one of the best craftsmen of the time, if he worked for the Peisistratidai, and he may therefore have been technically in advance of other craftsmen.

Even in Athens the remains of the *boustrophedon* system persisted to the end of the archaic period. In the epitaph of Antigenes, assigned to the last quarter of the sixth century from the style of the relief, the last six letters return *boustrophedon* instead of starting a second line from left to right (**34**); the same practice is seen on the gravestone *IG* i². 990 of about the same period. Furthermore, the full *boustrophedon* system is found on two fragmentary blocks of marble (altars?) from the Eleusinion at Athens (**44**), which, judged by their lettering, should belong somewhere around the end of the sixth or the

---

[1] See further *DAA* 197: '*c.* 525–10'. The statue which may belong to the base was dated *c.* 530 by Payne (op. cit. 33).

[2] Welter, *AA* 1939, 34 ff.

[3] Meritt, *Hesperia* viii (1939), 62 ff.; Dinsmoor,

*Studies in the History of Culture* (1942), 195 ff.; Raubitschek, *DAA*, 449 f.

[4] The identity was pointed out by Raubitschek and Meritt, *Hesperia* viii (1939), 65, n. 1.

[5] *DAA* 108 and p. 499.

early fifth century. They appear to be amalgamated versions of earlier, briefer *leges sacrae* written *boustrophedon*, and imply that the *boustrophedon* system was retained in the copies through religious conservatism, as in English printing the Gothic type was still used for religious and legal works in the eighteenth century, long after its use had ceased in the normal way.[1]

The developed Attic script of the fifth century is not included in this survey. The public inscriptions raise historical problems outside the province of plain epigraphy, requiring a separate and more detailed study; and a large selection of the private inscriptions is discussed and illustrated in *DAA*.

## SELECT CATALOGUE

**1.** Graffito on a Late Geometric oinochoe from a grave in Athens; *c.* 725? Furtwaengler, *AM* vi (1881), 106 ff., pl. 3. *IG* i². 919. *SEG* iii. 51. R. S. Young, *Hesperia*, suppl. ii (1939), 228. *IIA²* 1, pl. 1. Friedlaender 53. Athens, NM 192. PL. 1

**2.** Graffito on a stone fragment from the Akropolis; 8th c.? *IG* i². 484. *DAA* 310. Peek, *AM* lxvii (1942), 37 f., pl. 1. Athens, EM 5365. PL. 1

**3a–c.** Graffiti on a series of small cups and bowls from a shrine on Hymettos; first quarter? to end of 7th c. Blegen, *AJA* xxxviii (1934), 10 ff., figs. 1–10, pls. 1–3; xliv (1940), 1 ff. Young, op. cit. 227. NM and Agora Mus. PL. 1

**4.** Graffito on a similar skyphos from the Agora; *c.* 650. Shear, *Hesperia* v (1936), 33, fig. 34; Young, op. cit., 124 ff., 226 f. Agora Mus. P 4663. PL. 1

**5a–e.** Painted inscriptions on Protoattic pottery from Athens; *c.* 675–625. (*a*) Amphora sherds, Akrop. Mus. 368*a*, *c*. GL i. 38, pl. 13. J. M. Cook, *BSA* xxxv (1934–5), 194, n. 8, pl. 54b (part only). (*b*) Similar fragment, Akrop. 380. GL i. 39, pl. 13. (*c*) Lip of a similar vase, Agora Mus. A–P 177. Pease, *Hesperia* iv (1935), 242, no. 38, fig. 14. (*d*) Skyphos, *c.* 675–650, Agora Mus. P 7014. Shear, *AJA* xl (1936), 194, fig. 10. Young, op. cit. 151 f., 226. (*e*) Fragment from a large vase, *c.* 650–625, NM 2226. Beazley, *AJA* xxxix (1935), 475. Cook, op. cit. 196, 205, pls. 54 f.

**6a–c.** Inscriptions, painted and incised, on early BF pottery by the Nessos Painter; *c.* 625–600. (*a*) Nessos amphora, NM 1002. *AD* i, pl. 57. (*b*) Harpy krater, Berlin F 1682. *CVA* Berlin i, pl. 47. (*c*) Rim with incised dedication, Akrop. Mus. 391. GL i. 41, no. 391*a–c*, pl. 14 (*a–c*). Beazley, *Hesperia* xiii (1944), 38 ff., nos. 1, 4, 9; *ABV*, 4 ff. PL. 1

**7.** Dedication on Naxian marble fragments, Akropolis; *c.* 625–600? *IG* i². 672. *DAA* 376. EM 6394. PL. 2

**8.** Stele of Keramo, from Athens; *c.* 625–600? Conze i. 21. Wilhelm, 1 ff. *IG* i². 997. EM. PL. 2

**9a–e.** Graffiti names on ostraka, 7th c.–early 6th c. (*a*) Akrop. Mus. N 48, 268. *IG* i². 913. (*b*) Akrop. Mus. 1316. GL ii. 3, 116, no. 1316, pl. 92. (*c–e*) Agora Mus. P 15.555: P 4661: P 3629. Vanderpool, *Hesperia*, suppl. viii, 394 ff., nos. 10, 17, pls. 58, 10a (*c*): 59, 17 (*d*): 60 (*e*). PL. 2

---

[1] The *boustrophedon* writing painted on a papyrus roll in a school scene on a RF sherd by Onesimos (*c.* 480; *ARV* 222, no. 55) was perhaps intended to show the antiquity of the roll.

**10a–h.** Graffiti names on SOS amphorae, late 7th c. to first half of 6th c. (*a*) Gela, Syracuse Mus. 21210. (*b*) Tell Defenneh, BM 48. 6–19. 9. (*c*) Caere, Louvre, Campana 2429. (*d*) BM, unpublished. (*e*) Kerameikos Mus., unpublished. (*f*) Caere, Louvre, Campana 2432. (*g*) Caere, Louvre, Campana 2449. (*h*) Caere, Villa Giulia. (*a–h*) Jeffery, *BSA* l (1955), 67 ff., fig. 1.    PL. 2

**11.** Clay plaque (Achilles and Amazon); *c.* 600. Richter, *Bull. Metr. Mus.* i (1942), 80 ff. *AGA*, 8, fig. 9. Von Bothmer, *Amazons in Greek Art* (1957), 3, pl. 1. 2. New York, MM 42.11.33.

**12.** Poros altar dedicated by Chairion, Akropolis; *c.* 600–575? *IG* i². 467. *IIA* 4, pl. 2. *DAA* 330. Akrop. Mus.

**13.** Dedication on a poros Ionic capital, Akropolis; *c.* 600–575? *IG* i². 466. *DAA* 1. Friedlaender 12a. EM 6216.    PL. 2

**14a–d.** Inscribed BF vases by Sophilos; *c.* 575–550. (*a*) Akrop. 587; GL i, pl. 26. (*b*) NM 15499; Karouzou, *AM* lii (1937), pl. 53. (*c*) NM 2035; Wolters, *JdI* xiii (1898), pl. 1. (*d*) NM 2035; *CVA* Athens i. 3, pl. 1. (*a–d*) Beazley, *Hesperia* xiii (1944), 50 f., *DABF*, 17 ff. *ABV*, 39 f., 42.    PL. 2

**15.** Grave-monument of -linos, Attica; *c.* 575? *AAG*, 14 ff., figs. 30–32. *SEG* x. 450. *MMNYC* 10. New York, MM 24.97.87.

**16.** François Vase, painted by Kleitias; *c.* 570. FR, pls. 1–3, 11–13. *DABF*, 26 ff. *ABV*, 76. Florence, Arch. Mus. 4209.

**17.** Dedication of [Rh?]onbos, Akropolis; *c.* 570–560. *IG* i². 469. *IIA* 5, pl. 12. *DAA* 59. Payne and Young, *Archaic Marble Sculpture from the Acropolis²*, 67, pl. 3. Akrop. Mus. 624.    PL. 2

**18.** Poros stele perhaps dedicated at the establishment of the Panathenaia in 566. *IG* i². 463+475. *DAA* 326. Friedlaender 12 f. EM 6212+6225.    PL. 3

**19.** Grave-monument of Tettichos, Attica; *c.* 560 ? *IG* i². 976. *SEG* x. 431. Friedlaender 135. Peek i. 1226. EM.    PL. 3

**20.** Grave-monument of Chairedemos, made by Phaidimos, Attica; *c.* 560–550. *SEG* iii. 55. *AAG*, 43 ff., fig. 65. Friedlaender 62. *MMNYC* 14. Peek i. 159. New York, MM 16.174.6.    PL. 3

**21.** Bronze plaque recording a dedication on the Akropolis by the Treasurers; *c.* 550? *IG* i². 393. Wilhelm, 23. Ferguson, *Treasurers of Athens* (1932), 6, n. 1; *IIA* 7, pl. 3. NM 6975.    PL. 3

**22.** Grave-monument of the children of Kylon, Attica; *c.* 550? *IG* i². 1016. *SEG* x. 454. Peek i. 147. Liopesi (H. Ioannes).

**23.** Grave-monument of a kore, made by Phaidimos, Attica; *c.* 550? Eichler, *Ö.Jh* xvi (1913), 86 ff., fig. 55. *IG* i². 1012. Pezopoulos, *AE* 1937 (ii), 539 f., fig. 2. Friedlaender 68. *SEG* x. 451. Peek i. 155. NM 81.

**24.** BF kantharos signed by Nearchos, Athens; *c.* 550. GL i. 71 f., no. 611, pl. 36. *DABF*, 40 f. *ABV*, 82. Akrop. 611. NM.    PL. 3

**25.** Poros capital with a dedication by two of the Alkmeonidai, Akropolis; *c.* 550? *IG* i². 472. *DAA* 317. *SEG* xiv. 13. EM 6222.    PL. 3

**26.** Fragment of a dedication from the Akropolis, inscribed *boustrophedon* and *stoichedon*; *c.* 550–540? *IG* i². 665. *DAA* 195. EM 6389+6454+6492.

**27.** Dedication on a fragmentary kouros by the deme of Sounion; *c.* 550? Stais, *AE* 1917, 202 f., fig. 14. *IG* i². 830. Picard, *RA* ii (1940), 28, n. 3. *SEG* xvi. 18. NM.

**28.** Fragment of a name-list from Athens; *c.* 550? Peek, *AM* lxvii (1942), 13, pl. 8. EM 420.          PL. 3

**29.** Grave-monument of Phrasikleia, Attica; *c.* 540. *IG* i². 1014. Raubitschek, *Bull. Bulgare* xii (1938), 148 f. Austin, *Stoichedon Style* (1938), 10 f. Friedlaender 80. Peek i. 68. Merenda (Panagia).          PL. 3

**30.** Marble capital with a dedication by an Alkmeonid at the Ptoion, Boiotia; *c.* 546–527. Bizard, *BCH* xliv (1920), 227 ff., figs. 1–3. *IG* i². 472. Friedlaender 167. Thebes Mus., 633+633a.

**31.** Grave-monument of Archias and sister, made by Phaidimos, Attica; *c.* 540. Pezopoulos, *AE* 1937 (ii), 538 ff., fig. 1. *SEG* x. 452a. Peek, op. cit. 85 ff., pl. 3; Friedlaender 169. Peek i. 74. Liopesi Mus.          PL. 4

**32.** Grave-monument of a boy and girl, Attica; *c.* 540. *IG* i². 981. *AAG* 64 ff., fig. 83. Friedlaender 61*b*; *MMNYC* 15. Peek i. 148. New York, MM 11. 185.          PL. 4

**33.** Graffito for the dedication of a Herm (?), from a well in the Agora; *c.* 550–525. Shear, *Hesperia* viii (1939), 258, no. 9, fig. 15. Agora Mus. P 12629.          PL. 4

**34.** Epitaph on the grave-stele of Antigenes, Attica; *c.* 510. *AAG*, 107 f., figs. 23, 104. *MMNYC* 20. New York, MM 15.167.          PL. 4

**35.** Herm inscribed with an epigram by Hipparchos, Attica; *c.* 520–514. *IG* i². 837 add. Peek, *AM* lxii (1937), 1 ff., pl. 1. *IIA* 11, pl. 5. *SEG* x. 345. Friedlaender 149. Koropi Mus.

**36.** Fragmentary signature (?) of Eumares, from the Akropolis, *c.* 525? Raubitschek, *Ö.Jh.* xxxi (1938), Beibl. 23. *DAA* 108. Akrop. Mus.          PL. 4

**37.** Altar dedicated in the Pythion at Athens by Peisistratos son of Hippias; *c.* 520–510? *IG* i². 761. *IIA* 11, pl. 5. Meritt, *Hesperia* viii (1939), 62 ff. *DAA*, 449 f. *SEG* x. 318. EM 6787.          PL. 4

**38.** Base for a tripod (?) dedicated at the Ptoion in Boiotia by Hipparchos; *c.* 520–514. Bizard, *BCH* xliv (1920), 237 ff., figs. 4–5. Meritt, op. cit. 64 f. Thebes Mus.

**39.** Base for a dedication by Alkibiades the elder at Delphi; *c.* 525–500? Daux, *BCH* xlvi (1922), 439 ff., figs. 1–5. *IG* i². 272. Delphi Mus. 2152.

**40.** Base for the grave-stele of Lampito, made by Endoios, Athens; *c.* 525–500. *IG* i². 978. *DAA* 494. Friedlaender 75. Peek i. 286. EM.          PL. 4

**41.** Epitaph on the grave-stele of Lyseas, Attica; *c.* 510. *IG* i². 1025. *SEG* iii. 61. Conze i. pl. 1. *AAG*, 103 ff. Peek i. 140. NM 30.

**42.** Epitaph on the grave-stele of Aristion, made by Aristokles, Attica; *c.* 510. *IG* i². 1024. Conze i. 2, pl. 2. *AAG*, 99 f. Friedlaender 164. NM 29.

**43.** Epigram on the base of a bronze four-horse chariot dedicated by Athens for a victory in 506 over Boiotia and Chalkis; Akropolis; *c.* 506. *IG* i². 394 II. *DAA* 168. Friedlaender 145. EM 6286.          PL. 4

**44.** *Leges sacrae* inscribed *boustrophedon* on two blocks (altars?) from the Eleusinion at Athens; *c.* 500–480. Jeffery, *Hesperia* xvii (1948), 86 ff., pls. 29–32. Agora Mus.          PL. 4

# EUBOIA

α β γ δ ε ϝ ζ η ʰ θ ι κ λ μ ν ξ ο π Μ ϙ ρ σ τ υ φ χ ψ ω Ρ

| | | | | | | | | | | | | | | | | | | | | | | | | | | | | | | | |
|---|---|---|---|---|---|---|---|---|---|---|---|---|---|---|---|---|---|---|---|---|---|---|---|---|---|---|---|---|---|---|---|---|

*Notes on letter-forms* (C = Euboic Colonies, Chalkidic (pp. 241 ff.); CE = ibid., Chalkidic–Eretrian (pp. 235 ff.).)

FIG. 27. Euboia and Colonies

The curved α3, normal in Boiotian, occurs rarely in Euboic (Eretria **9**). Inverted *alpha* appears once, probably in error (Eretria **22**).

γ1, the earliest version, is used in the abecedaria from Marsiliana d'Albegna (CE **18**) and Kyme (CE **2**), and in the Eretrian legal text **9**. It had evidently developed into γ2 or γ3 at Kyme before the end of the 7th c. (CE **19–21**), and in Chalkidic at least by the middle of the 6th (**7**). Only γ2 or 3 is attested in the Chalkidic colonies. By the 5th c. one may find in Euboia γ5 (the Attic type; Chalkis), or (Ionic) γ4 (Styra, **26**), as well as the normal γ2 or 3.

δ1 or 2 is the common form. It was used already in Kyme in the early 7th c. (CE **2**, CE **18**), and is invariable in the inscriptions of Chalkis and her colonies. Eretria, on the other hand, shows δ4 in the 6th c. (**10, 11, 24**), or a compromise, δ3 (**9**; cf. also Pithekoussai, CE **1**). This may be due to the influence of Attica or the islands. In the 5th c. δ4 occurs sometimes both at Chalkis and Eretria, doubtless by Attic influence; once possibly at Kyme (CE **14**).

At Kyme *epsilon* developed an exaggerated tilt forwards (ε3) in the 6th c. and early 5th (CE **4, 7, 8, 9, 11**).

The shape of *vau* follows that of *epsilon*: ϝ1 until the middle of the 6th c. or later (Eretria **9** and **22**), then ϝ2 (Leontinoi(?), *c.* 525: C **2**), finally ϝ3 (Rhegion *c.* 467, C **8**). ϝ3 appears in the second half of the 6th c. in the rapid script of vase-painters, e.g. on the 'Chalkidic' vases **7**.

ʰ2, the normal archaic form, is still in use in the second half of the 6th c. (Chalkis **7**; Leontinoi(?) C **2**). It is open probably by the turn of the 6th and 5th c. (Kyme, CE **7**; cf. also C **20**), but the unidentified inscription C **22**, which from its other letter-forms should not be earlier than the beginning of the 5th c., still shows closed *heta*. The form ʰ1 appears in the Marsiliana d'Albegna abecedarium (CE **18**), and also on an oinochoe from Eretria, here classed as Boiotian (p. 85). ʰ4 occurs once in the 5th c., in the script of Rhegion (C **8**).

An early example of θ3 appears in Eretrian in the third quarter of the 6th c. (**9**); it is used also on the unidentified text C **22**, in the early 5th c.; otherwise it appears to have replaced θ1, θ2 about the middle of the 5th c.; cf. Kyme (CE **12, 23**); Rhegion (C **14**). θ1 and 2 still appear in the text ascribed to Himera and dated *c.* 450 or shortly after, which is in the Ionic script (C **19**).

λ1 is the regular form: at Eretria (**9**), and especially at Zankle and Rhegion (C **5, 8, 11–13**), it may be tilted, λ2. The Ionic λ3 occurs at Styra *c.* 475? (**26**), replacing earlier λ1 (**25**).

μ1, developing to μ3 in the late archaic period, is regular in Eretria and Kyme until the start of the 5th c., when μ4 replaces it. μ1 is also doubtfully attested at Leontinoi (?) (C **2**). All other examples of Chalkis and her colonies show μ2 or μ4: see pp. 81 f.

The 'red' ξ2 or 3 is normal. χσ occurs in the 5th c. (Eretria **15, 16**) in two inscriptions which may be in Attic. ξ1, apparently an elaborated form of 三, appears in the place of *xi* in the early Etruscan abecedaria derived from Kyme; see pp. 32, 236. The proper form of Ionic *xi* 三 first appears in **21**, the gravestone of an Aiginetan in Eretria.

*San* is never used as a living form in Euboic inscriptions, but it continues to appear by convention in the abecedaria derived from Kymean (CE **18–23**) from the 7th to the 5th c.

*Qoppa* had disappeared by the time of the earliest Kymean coinage, in the early 5th c. (CE **10**); the coins seem to show the earliest examples of its omission, for it was still used on the 'Chalkidic' vases (**7**) in the second half of the 6th c., at Leontinoi (?) (C**2**) *c.* 525, and in C **22** in the early 5th c.

ρ1 or 2 is normal everywhere in the archaic period; the earliest examples of ρ3 are on some of the 'Chalkidic' vases (**7**). By the 5th c. ρ3 is normal, and examples of ρ1 or 2 in Euboia are probably due to Attic influence (**4, 5, 14, 16, 18, 20**).

σ1 is the more common form, but σ2 is used on rare occasions in the archaic period (e.g. on the 'Chalkidic' vases **7**, where it frequently sinks to an uncertain zigzag, and on certain of the abecedaria derived from Kyme, CE **19, 20**). σ2 appears in Eretria in the 5th c., perhaps from the islands (**18, 19**). At Rhegion (and Zankle) a rounded type σ3 is used in the first half of the 5th c. (C **7, 8–10, 11, 12–14**).

υ2 appears very early at Kyme in a graffito of the 7th c. (CE **3**).

*Phi* is normal except in Eretria **9**, where it is φ3.

The 'red' form of *chi* is used, developing from χ2 in the late archaic period to χ3; the last form is regular in the 5th c. (Kyme CE **9, 12**; Rhegion, C **8**), and occurs (rarely) in the rapid script of the 'Chalkidic' vases (**7**) in the second half of the 6th.

*Psi.* The Ionic ψ2 occurs on coins of Himera (C **17**), perhaps through external influence; see p. 246.

*Punctuation.* P1 is used in Eretria (**9, 20**; 6th and 5th c.) and Kyme (CE **13**; 5th c.); P2 in Pithekoussai (CE **1**; *c.* 700?), in Eretria (**9**; **15**, 5th c.) and Leontinoi (?) (C **2**; *c.* 525).

*Direction of script.* The very early graffito CE **1** is written in three lines consistently retrograde (pp. 45, 235 f.). It is to be noted further that, although only the two earliest abecedaria are retrograde (i.e. those from Marsiliana d'Albegna and Kyme, CE **18** and **2**, perhaps of the first quarter of the 7th c.), the convention of the retrograde start apparently remained strong in Euboic for some time; cf. **6, 22, 9, 10**; CE **2, 3**. The *boustrophedon* system in formal inscriptions seems to have lasted until the end of the 6th c. (cf. **2**, C **5**, CE **9**); the brief inscription on the impression from the scaraboid seal **24** is the first example of two lines running from left to right. The *stoichedon* style is used in CE **9**, and in the 5th c. inscriptions **5** and **15**, which may be in the Attic alphabet; also on the Eretrian base at Olympia (**19**), *c.* 480?, and possibly on the early 5th-c. gravestone from Styra (**25**). Among the leaden plaques from the latter place (**26**), four of the total number of names (over 400) are written retrograde, perhaps by left-handed writers (p. 47).

The island of Euboia is in effect a long slab of the eastern mainland, split off from it by wedges of sea driven in from the north-west and south-east. Her northern end reaches up to Thessaly, her southern ranges along the coast of Attica; in the centre, Euboian Chalkis faces directly on to Boiotian territory, with only the narrow channel of the Euripos between.

The early history of the island was centred mainly on the commercial enterprise and rivalry of her two chief states, Chalkis and Eretria. From their respective positions, the mainland interests of Chalkis lay naturally with Boiotia and Thessaly, while Eretria turned rather to her neighbours Attica, Oropos (where the dialect was similar to the

Eretrian, both places having the habit of rhotacism),[1] and the near islands of the central Aegean. Andros, Tenos, Keos, and others not named are said to have been at one time included in her thalassocracy (Strabo 448).

The dialect of Euboia was in the main Ionic, with a small admixture of elements from Attic and probably also from Boiotian.[2] Her archaic script is linked in a general way with that of her continental neighbours Attica, Boiotia, and Opountian Lokris, in their common form of *lambda*. But it is distinguished from that of Attica, in that it uses the 'red' forms of *xi* and *chi*, forms common also to Boiotian and Opountian Lokrian. Indeed, as far as Chalkis is concerned, her surviving inscriptions, with those of her Sicilian colonies, are remarkably like the Boiotian and Opountian Lokrian, except for the peculiar Boiotian 'crooked' *alpha*; all use the *vau* and tilted *delta* 1–3. But the surviving archaic inscriptions of Eretria differ (*a*) in using the rare five-stroked *mu*, and (*b*) in occasionally using a *delta* like the Attic, instead of the normal tilted form. The archaic inscriptions of Pithekoussai and of Kyme in Italy, which were joint foundations of Chalkis and Eretria, show the same form of *mu*, sometimes with *delta* 2–3. The existing inscriptions from Chalkis herself and her Sicilian colonies do not appear to be earlier than the last quarter of the sixth century; and in the fifth century Eretria also (under Attic influence?) and Kyme were using the normal *mu* 2, 4. It is therefore unsafe to conclude definitely that Chalkis' archaic alphabet did differ in this respect from the Eretrian, until we have more early material from Chalkis herself. Nevertheless, I think it possible that the five-stroked *mu* did not in fact achieve a place in the archaic script of Chalkis, for the following reasons. Firstly, the inscribed 'Chalkidic' vases (**7**), which are dated from *c.* 550 onwards through the second half of the sixth century (p. 83), are unanimous in showing the ordinary four-stroked *mu*. Their combination of Ionic dialect with a 'red' alphabet using *vau* and *lambda* 1–2 means that they must have been inscribed by Euboians, whether in Euboia or the West, and, since Eretria and Kyme certainly used the five-stroked *mu* at this time, a Chalkidic source seems to be the only obvious alternative. A graffito on a sixth-century vase from Olympia (**6**) shows the same alphabet, and the Ionic dialect; again, therefore, this inscription must be Euboic, but not from Eretria. Secondly, one might expect that the earliest surviving inscriptions of Chalkis' colonies in Sicily would show examples of the five-stroked *mu* if the mother-state used it. As it is, the only possible examples of five-stroked *mu* occur in the *boustrophedon* script on the plaques from Monte San Mauro (Chalkidic colonies **2**), that is, in copies drawn from badly damaged bronze fragments, which show, apparently indiscriminately, both five- and four-stroked *mu*; they are discussed below, p. 242. The only other *boustrophedon* fragment (Chalkidic colonies, **5**, p. 243; Zankle), which may be in the last years of the sixth century or *c.* 500, shows the four-stroked type.

In the following discussion, therefore, I have provisionally attributed the 'Chalkidic' vases to Chalkis,[3] and to Eretria such inscriptions from other provenances as appear in general to be Euboic, and in particular to show five-stroked *mu*.

[1] Buck, 57, 143.
[2] Buck, 143, 192. *Vau*, normal in Boiotia, was used also in Euboic, but was very rare in the Ionic of Athens and the Aegean islands, occurring only in verse (Attica 23; Naxos **10**).
[3] For recent studies which renew the claims of her colony Rhegion, see p. 244, n. 3.

When we come to consider the problem of the source whence Euboia first received the alphabet, the *lambda* and *mu* may provide a clue. Five-stroked *mu* occurs otherwise (as yet, at least) only in the southern islands—Crete, Melos, Sikinos; Euboic *lambda* is also attested at Dreros, Eltynia, Praisos, and Knossos in northern Crete (p. 308). Nothing else in Euboic is particularly like Cretan, but the 'red' letters *xi* and *chi* were used in Rhodes, Crete's Doric neighbour to the east (p. 346). 'A mixture of Rhodian and Cretan' would be an arbitrary way of describing Eretrian, but it would be a plausible one. Since the people of Chalkis and Eretria were active seafarers from an early period, and must have been as familiar as any with the trade-routes of the southern and south-eastern Aegean, some of them (Eretrians?) may well have brought an early version of the alphabet thence to Euboia at some time before the close of the eighth century. Chalkis may originally have used the same letter-forms as Eretria; or (as I should prefer to think) she may have done as Thera apparently did (p. 15) and received (whether from Eretria, or herself independently from the south-eastern Aegean) a *mu* which altered in the transmission from five to four strokes, and a variant *delta* 1–3. This hypothesis would have at least the merit of providing an explanation of the source of the Boiotian alphabet; for Boiotia was literate at a surprisingly early period (pp. 90 f.), and shows these forms from the beginning. The Boiotian script differs in several points from its neighbours in Attica, Phokis, and Thessaly; but, as was said above, it agrees well with Euboic in all things except the Eretrian five-stroked *mu*. On general grounds also, both geographical and historical, Chalkis seems a likely source to have introduced the alphabet to Boiotia; they were close neighbours, and allies against Athens in the sixth century.

The Eretrian version of the Euboic alphabet was already in use at Pithekoussai and Kyme, and among Kyme's non-Greek neighbours, in the first half of the seventh century, perhaps even before 700 (pp. 235 f.); but no surviving inscriptions from Euboia herself are as early. There are no epigraphic records from the protracted struggles of the Lelantine War; the only inscription which is certainly as early as the seventh century is that on a small aryballos attributed to Eretria (**22**). The literary tradition records, however, that in the precinct of Artemis at Amarynthos near Eretria there was a stele which preserved a military compact between Chalkis and Eretria during that war, of which an actual phrase is apparently quoted: μὴ χρῆσθαι τηλεβόλοις.[1] Another stele recorded the arrangements for the πομπή held at the festival of Artemis, which must have rivalled in its magnificence the Athenian Panathenaia: τρισχιλίοις μὲν ὁπλίταις, ἑξακοσίοις δ' ἱππεῦσιν, ἑξήκοντα δ' ἅρμασι ποιεῖν τὴν πομπήν.[2] The date of this stele is unknown except that it must surely be referred to Eretria's days of prosperity before the arrival of the Persian forces in 490.

## CHALKIS

The coins of Chalkis (**1**), which bear the legend Χαλ (occasionally from right to left; ΧΙ or 2) have been dated in the period *c.* 511–445.[3] One very rare issue, inscribed Χαλκ

---

[1] Strabo 448; cf. A. R. Burn, *JHS* xlix (1929), 33 and H. L. Lorimer, *BSA* xlii (1947), 114, 118.

[2] Strabo, loc. cit.; Lorimer, op. cit. 118.

[3] Regling *ap. IG* xii. 9, p. 172 II; cf. Rumpf, *Chalki-*

*dische Vasen* i (1927), 43. An earlier date was indicated by B ii. 1. 663 ff. (middle of the 6th c.), though left indeterminate by Head, *HN²*, 357 f.

and dated in the first half of the fifth century, has been assigned not to Euboic Chalkis but to the Chalkidike. The identification is of some importance, for, if the coin belonged to the Chalkidike, it would mean that the federation called οἱ Χαλκιδῆς already existed at this early period. The lettering is correct for Euboia; what scripts the colonists and local peoples of the Chalkidike used before the mid-fifth century is discussed below (pp. 363 f.). There is no good evidence as yet for the Euboic script in those parts, and it seems safer therefore to follow Gaebler in assigning this issue to Chalkis in Euboia.[1] The earliest of the few known inscriptions from Chalkis is a prism-shaped stele found near the river Arethousa, with a cutting for some lost object on top, and the dedication inscribed *boustrophedon*: Ευφēμος ανεθ[ε]∥κεν (**2**). The forms of *epsilon, nu, upsilon*, suggest the late archaic period, perhaps *c.* 500. Three others belong probably to the first half of the fifth century: a grave-stele inscribed Επικυδειδēς (**3**), a base bearing a metrical dedication, apparently from a precinct of Paieon (**4**), and a lost stele showing part of a list of names (**5**). It may be noted that **4** uses the Attic *gamma*, according to the copy, and **5** the Attic *delta* also. An Athenian settlement had been established in Chalkidic territory since the defeat of Chalkis and Boiotia in 506 (Hdt. v. 77), and probably this new element influenced the local script; Attic letters occur also in Eretrian inscriptions of the fifth century (p. 86).

As was said above (p. 81), the class of black-figure vases called 'Chalkidic' (**7**) is included here because, while their combination of Euboic letters (*delta, vau, lambda, xi, chi*) with the Ionic dialect (e.g. Αντιϵς, Οϝατιϵς, Αθēναιē) indicates that they must have been made either in Euboia or in one of her colonies, their script never shows the typical *mu* of sixth-century Eretrian;[2] and for the same reason the graffito Σēμονιδēς μ' ανεθēκεν on a vase (**6**) from Olympia (which from its description appears to be a Late Corinthian aryballos or alabastron, and which has been placed by Roehl among his Attic inscriptions) is here attributed to Chalkis; for the use of tilted δι shows that it should not be Attic. The western colonies of Chalkis—Rhegion, Zankle, Leontinoi, Katane, and Naxos—all appear to have used the same alphabet, though for Naxos the evidence is extremely slight (pp. 241, 247). For northern colonies in the Chalkidike it is equally tenuous; they have shown as yet no positive trace of any Euboic alphabet, nor (except for Skione) of any script other than the Ionic (presumably taken from one or other of the many Ionic colonies in the area? cf. further pp. 363 f.).

## ERETRIA

The earliest inscription which can be tentatively ascribed to Eretria is that painted on an aryballos of Early Protocorinthian style (provenance unknown) in Boston (**22**): Πυρος

[1] See Gaebler, *Zeitschrift für Numismatik* xxxv (1925), 193 ff.; D. M. Robinson, *Olynthus* ix. 292 ff.; Gomme, *Commentary on Thucydides* i. 203 ff. Bradeen (*AJP* lxxiii (1952), 363 f.) and Raymond (*Studies . . . D. M. Robinson*, ii (1953), 197 ff.) support the view that the coin was minted in the Chalkidike, as does Head, *HN*², 208.

[2] The script of the vases is ably discussed and the inscriptions reproduced by Rumpf, op. cit. 40 ff.; he does not discuss in particular the difference of the *mu*, but makes an excellent case on other grounds for ascribing the vases to Chalkis. He dates them in the period *c.* 550–510 (138 ff.). The alternative attribution of the vases to a group of potters of Chalkidic stock in Agylla (Caere) leaves the Chalkidic character of the inscriptions undisputed: H. R. W. Smith, *The Origin of Chalcidian Ware* (1932), 85 ff., esp. 124 f. See also p. 81, n. 3 above, and Addenda.

μ' ἐποίεσεν Ἀγασιλέϝο. It is generally agreed to be unlike true Corinthian in both clay and technique,[1] and the alphabet has been identified as Euboic.[2] The letter-forms may be compared with those of **9** below, particularly *gamma*, *vau*, and *mu*. The date is uncertain, for a copy need not of necessity fall within the same period as would the original (i.e. *c.* 700 or very little later); nor does the lettering suggest so early a date, even if full allowance is made for the skilled hand of the potter. It might have been executed as late as the second half of the seventh century, on the analogy of such Attic potters' inscriptions as Attica **5, 6**; but this would mean that the ovoid shape of aryballos persisted very late in Eretria. A painted vase-inscription which is certainly Eretrian is the brief θεα on an amphora from the necropolis, dated in the last quarter of the seventh century or possibly after 600 (**8**).

The most interesting inscriptions from Euboia are the three legal texts on two adjoining stone blocks (both broken in half) which, with a much smaller inscribed fragment, were rebuilt into a city gate in the later system of walls at Eretria (**9**).[3] The original structure was itself presumably a wall of some kind on which these and, doubtless, other like texts were cut. As far as can be judged none of these particular texts extended beyond the two blocks unless we conclude the opening of the first (A1) to be too abrupt, and infer that it continues from a lost block above. It deals with the payment of fines in 'approved moneys' (χρέματα δοκιμα),[4] a statement of particular interest in view of the early date of the inscription. *Epsilon* has only a very small tail, sometimes none at all, and the one *theta* is dotted; but apart from that it shows the archaic forms of tailed υι and χ1, and *phi* also (φ3) is in the early tailed form, though actually the vertical stroke has not been carried through the circle. The earliest inscribed coinage of Eretria, generally dated *c.* 511, bears her initial, with tailed ε3; but even so, the inscription **9** can hardly be as late as this, unless in all other details Eretrian masons were very much more conservative than their Attic counterparts; we may suggest a date *c.* 550–525, and the χρήματα referred to may then be the Attic, or whatever heraldically stamped coinage the Eretrians used before Eretria issued the series stamped with the city's initial.

The second text (A2), cut beneath A1 in smaller letters, begins with the name of the ἄρχων then in office: Επι Γολο αρχ[οντος---]. The letter-forms are similar except that the punctuation is 2, not 1 as in A1, and a cutting-compass is used. Part of the text is lost in the later recutting, but the end is clear: that, if the wrongdoer does not pay, the ἀρχοί are to inflict punishment according to the laws (ἀπὸ ῥητῶν), under penalty themselves of paying the same fine if they fail to do so.

The third text (B) was cut in more careless letters down the sides of the two

---

[1] Johansen, *Les Vases sicyoniens* (1923), 171. Boardman notes that Protocorinthian ware was much imitated at Eretria (*BSA* xlvii (1952), 12).

[2] Buck, 192. The inverted *alphas* are odd, and I can only suggest that the aryballos may have been upside down on the wheel when the potter painted in both the bands and the inscription, and so confused the execution of the letters.

[3] Cf. Papabasileiou, *AE* 1913, 210 ff. I have not included here the small fragment (*IG* xii. 9. 1275),

which is apparently of later date (first half of the 5th c. ?) and uncertain content.

[4] Volkmann points out (*Hermes* lxxiv (1939), 99 ff.) that this is the first attested usage of the word χρήματα as meaning 'money', and cites various passages to illustrate the use of δόκιμος = 'approved', of which the most famous is that in Ps.-Aristotle, *Oec.* ii. 2: Ἱππίας . . . τό τε νόμισμα τὸ ὂν Ἀθηναίοις ἀδόκιμον ἐποίησε (κτλ).

blocks when they were already in position one above the other; for the mason had to avoid two unsatisfactory places on the surface of the sides, and the continual 'inversion' of the letters suggests that he fell into difficulties in cutting his lines vertically downwards. The text apparently concerns payment in connexion with shipping and harbourage.

The remaining archaic inscriptions from Eretria are considerably shorter. The rim of a clay lebes (?) bearing a dedication to Herakles (incised before firing) was found in some filling within the temple of Apollo Daphnephoros (10). It reads from right to left: [- - -]δρος τōι ⱶερακλει ποιϝ[ēσας ανεθēκεν ?]. The connexion, if any, of a precinct of Herakles with Apollo's temple is uncertain; the temple was apparently begun c. 550.[1] The inscription may be of about this date, or even a little earlier, for *heta* is still the closed form; the cult of Herakles at Eretria is attested again in the first half of the fifth century (?)[2] by a bronze lebes, a prize from Herakles' games: Ερετριαθεν αθλον : παρ' ⱶερακλεος (16). A scaraboid chalcedony seal reading Χαρι|δēμο (24) shows the characteristics of Eretrian, not later than of the third quarter of the sixth century. A poros stele (11), found in a necropolis to the west of Eretria, and inscribed *boustrophedon* [- - -] τοδε : σēμα | τετυκται, is probably to be dated not earlier than the late archaic period, c. 525–500, by the more developed, tailless forms of μ3 and υ2.

Here should be mentioned an oinochoe in Bonn, which came from Eretria, and has been dated about the middle of the sixth century. If the inscription incised on the handle is indeed Eretrian, it shows that four-stroked *mu* could on occasion be used there also. Certain minor points incline me to think, however, that it may rather be Boiotian (see Boiotia 22); the unusual forms of *heta* and *pi* are found in Boiotian (though this may be only coincidence), and the inscription appears to read: ⱶēμιτριτον Π{o}τōιοδōρο: 'One-sixth of a *chous*: property of Ptoiodoros.' Πτωιόδωρος is well-attested for Boiotia, with its famous precinct of the Ptoian Apollo, but not for Euboia; and nothing else seems to make sense of the letters π.τ.ι.δ.ρ.[3]

I do not think that the inscriptions on a plain amphora (6th c.?) from Eretria are Eretrian either: Καλλιμ[.]ν⟨ι⟩ς καλα and κ[. . . .]ελεια κ[α]λα. The dialect is not Euboic Ionic, but could, like the script, be Boiotian or from Opountian Lokris. I have, therefore, assigned the writer tentatively to Boiotia (23), although the vase itself appears to be Eretrian in fabric.

In the first half of the fifth century a standardizing influence, which is probably that of the Attic alphabet, appears in Eretrian (as in Chalkidic), and the five-stroked *mu* disappears; cf. the gravestone of Menephron (13), which probably belongs to the first years

[1] Robertson[2], 325.

[2] Neugebauer (*RM* xxxviii–ix (1923–4), 405) places the lebes itself within his 'ripe archaic' period, but does not suggest an absolute date. I infer that the inscription is not earlier than the 5th c. from the open *heta* and upright *nu*.

[3] Rehm, describing this graffito (*CVA* Bonn i (1938), 47), thought that the two dots following π and τ were both casual, and left the translation after ⱶεμιτριτον undecided. I had read it as Ποτοιοδōρο, until Dr. Tod

suggested to me by letter that the name should be rather Πτωιόδωρος, possibly misspelt Π{o}τοιοδορος: 'The cult of the hero Πτῶιος, later fused with Apollo, was very popular in Boeotia and gave rise to a number of personal names in Πτωι—, but in Euboea (to judge by the Index of *IG* xii. 9) the sole example is Πτωίων, which occurs once.' See also Jacobsthal, *JHS* lix (1939), 151, where the jug is called Boiotian without comment, and Πτῳοδώρου is read.

of the century.[1] A small fragment (18), in neat lettering of about 500–475, shows the 'red' *chi* still; it is sad that so little survives, for it seems to have been part of a military epitaph in verse: [- - -]οισα[- - -|- - - -]ου εχει[- - -|- - - ? μαρ]ναμενο[- - -|- - - -]αισχρες ⱶει φ[- - -]. The following inscriptions are in lettering indistinguishable from Attic: **17** (grave-monument of Pleistias, who was born in Sparta, grew up in Athens, and died in Eretria; the first quarter of the fifth century?): **14** (gravestone of Philon, shipwrecked off the Euboic coast: *c.* 500–480?): **20** (from Aulon near Eretria: the top of an altar or table, dedicated by Chairigenes and his daughter Eudeine, probably near the middle of the fifth century). A proxeny-decree of the first quarter of the fifth century (**15**) might equally well be in Attic or Eretrian: the *xi* χσ suggests Attic, but the closed *heta* would be abnormal in Attic, perhaps slightly less so in Eretrian, at this date. The base for a bronze bull (**19**) dedicated by the Eretrians at Olympia (*c.* 480?) shows the Ionic *lambda* (λ3). The latter occurs on another inscription of about this period found at Eretria, the gravestone of Mnesitheos of Aigina (**21**), which also shows the Ionic form of *xi*; and Ionic *lambda* is used also in Styra at this time (**26**).

Eretria appears to have adopted the full Ionic alphabet by 446/5; for it is used in the Athenian copy of her treaty with Athens in that year,[2] and it was certainly not normal then in Athens. The Ionic alphabet also occurs on the gravestones *IG* xii. 9. 300, 465, *IG* xii, suppl., 579, 580, all apparently earlier than the fourth century; and it is used in two curses against a man named Daiton, scratched on kantharoi which were buried in a grave at Chalkis; the vases themselves are, as far as I know, unillustrated, and the graffiti might equally well be of the late fifth or the early fourth century.[3]

### SOUTHERN EUBOIA

A certain number of minor inscriptions have been found at various sites south-east of Eretria. At Styra a grave-stele was discovered of the solid, archaic type sometimes described as a 'cippus', inscribed in letters of the late archaic period Λυσικ|ρατεος (**25**). The Euboic *lambda* may be noted, for it is no longer used in the next series from Styra, the famous set of small leaden labels (**26**), each bearing a man's name scratched on it (sometimes above another half-obliterated name or on the reverse side of the label). They were apparently all found in a clay vase beside a square monument of some kind,[4] and their purpose is unknown. Though the lettering varies from one to another in its general appearance (presumably according to the handwriting of different individuals), they all show open *heta*, crossed *theta*, Ionic *lambda*, four-stroked *mu*, no *qoppa*, tailed *rho*, three-stroked *sigma*, and 'red' *xi* and *chi* (except for one 'blue' *chi*, *IG* xii. 9. 56, no. 96, Εχε-κρατēς). The change of *lambda* to the Ionic form has its parallel at Eretria in the first half of the fifth century (**19, 21**); the labels may be dated tentatively *c.* 475.

---

[1] The 6th-c. gravestone of the Athenian Chairion in Eretria (*IG* xii. 9. 296) is in Attic script: Χαιριōν | Αθē-ναιος | Ευπατριδōν | ενθαδε κει|τα(ι). Cf. Raubitschek, *Ö.Jh.* xxxi (1939), Beibl. 46.

[2] *IG* i². 17; cf. Schweigert, *Hesperia* vi (1937), 317 ff., no. 1.

[3] *IG* xii. 9. 1166–7.

[4] Cf. *IG* xii. 9. 56: 'prope monumentum quadratum [τετραγωνικόν τι μνημεῖον] (fortasse aram), ut recte Koerte interpretabatur, cum priores de sepulchro cogitaverint.'

Two fragmentary dedications have been found at Platanistos. One (**27**) is too battered to show anything except that it bore a two-line dedication ([- - -]μ' εστεσ[εν?- - -]) followed by a signature ([- - - εργα]σατο); the tailed *epsilon* was still in use, according to Lolling's copy, but not according to Ziebarth's, made for *IG* xii. 9. 42 (which gives three versions in all). If we accept Ziebarth's, the date may be anywhere in the first half of the fifth century. The second (**28**) is from a dedication to Aphrodite, and shows the Attic χσ for *xi*, with Euboic δ1 and tailed ρ3. **28** was, according to copies, inscribed *stoichedon*; the dedication of **27** may have been also *stoichedon*.

Karystos is represented by four small leaden strips bearing two names, [Α]ρισστομενες and Σοσικλες, which encircled a small stone column from a grave (**30**), and by the legend on her coinage (**29**), which began in the last years of the sixth century: Καρυστιο[ν], with ρ3, υ2. Lastly, from Zarax there is a rough stele (**31**), clumsily inscribed with a list of four names from right to left, probably of the last years of the sixth or the early fifth century.

## SELECT CATALOGUE

### CHALKIS

**1.** Series of coins inscribed Χαλ, dated from *c.* 511 onwards. B ii. 1. 670 ff., pl. 31. *HN*², 357 f. Gaebler, *Zeitschrift für Numismatik* xxxv (1925), 193 ff. Rumpf, *Chalkidische Vasen* i (1927), 41, 43.

**2.** Black stone stele, prism-shaped, found near the Arethousa, bearing a dedication by Euphemos; *c.* 500? *SGDI* 5262 (a). Roehl³, 77. 11. *IG* xii. 9. 922. Chalkis Mus.　　PL. 5

**3.** Grave-stele of Epikydeides; *c.* 500–450? *IG* xii, suppl. 656. Chalkis Mus.　　PL. 5

**4.** Base for a dedication to Paieon by Hagesippos; *c.* 500–450? *IG* xii, suppl. 675 and p. 218. Politika.

**5.** Part of a list of names (script possibly Attic?); *c.* 500–450. *IGA* 375. Roberts i. 172. Roehl³, 78. 3. *IG* xii. 9. 923. Chalkis Mus.

*Inscriptions attributed to Chalkis*

**6.** Dedication by Semonides inscribed on a small Corinthian alabastron found at Olympia; *c.* 550? *IGA* 1. *Ol.* iv. 201 and v. 262. Roehl³, 70. 5. Olympia Mus. 355.　　PL. 5

**7.** Names painted on 'Chalkidic' vases; *c.* 550–510. Roberts i. 188–94. *SGDI* 5293–5300. Kretschmer, *Griechische Vaseninschriften*, 63 ff. Rumpf, op. cit. 40 ff.　　PL. 5

### ERETRIA

**8.** Painted inscription on a grave-amphora from Eretria; *c.* 625 (or later). Boardman, *BSA* xlvii (1952), 21, 26 f., figs. 20, 21e, pl. 5. NM 12128.

**9.** Legal texts concerning (A) the payment of fines in money, (B) shipping, inscribed on two blocks of a wall in Eretria; *c.* 550–525? *IG* xii. 9. 1273–4. *DGE* 800. Ziebarth, *Beiträge z. Geschichte d. Seeraubs u. Seehandels* (1929), Anhang ii. Volkmann, *Hermes* lxxiv (1939), 99 ff. *IG* xii, suppl., p. 204. Eretria Mus.　　PL. 5

**10.** Fragment of a clay vase made and dedicated by —dros to Herakles, from filling-material in the temple of Apollo Daphnephoros at Eretria; *c.* 550? Kourouniotes, *AE* 1911, 34 f., fig. 25. *SGDI* iv. p. 851. *IG* xii. 9. 257. Eretria Mus.　　PL. 5

**11.** Part of a grave-stele from a necropolis west of Eretria; *c.* 525–500? Kourouniotes, op. cit. 37, fig. 31. *SGDI* iv. p. 852, n. 4. *IG* xii. 9. 288. Peek i. 60. Eretria Mus.              PL. 5

**12.** Two fragments of a skyphos from the temple of Apollo Daphnephoros at Eretria, with remains of a graffito; 6th c. Konstantinou, *PAE* 1952 (1955), 163, fig. 11. Eretria Mus.

**13.** Grave-stele of Menephron from Eretria; *c.* 500–480? Kourouniotes, op. cit. 37 f., fig. 32. *SGDI* iv. 852, n. 5. *IG* xii. 9. 297. Eretria Mus. 400.              PL. 6

**14.** Grave-stele of Philon, from Eretria (Attic alphabet); *c.* 500–480? *SGDI* 5302. Roehl³, 75. 1. *IG* xii. 9. 287. *DGE* 801. Friedlaender 79. Peek i. 320. Eretria Mus.

**15.** Part of a proxeny-decree from Eretria (Attic alphabet?); *c.* 500–475. Peek, *AM* lix (1934), 73 ff., Beil. v. 3–4. Wallace, *Hesperia* v (1936), 273 ff. *IG* xii, suppl. 549. Eretria Mus.

**16.** Bronze lebes, inscribed *en pointillé* on lip as a prize from Herakles' games at Eretria; *c.* 500–475? *IG.* xii. 9. 272. Neugebauer, *RM* xxxviii–ix (1923–4), 405. NM 1318.

**17.** Grave-pillar of Pleistias, from Eretria; *c.* 500–475? Roehl³, 75. 3. *IG* xii. 9. 286. Volkmann, *Klio* xxxi (1938), 244 f. *IG* xii, suppl., p. 186. Friedlaender 77. Peek i. 862. Eretria Mus.              PL. 6

**18.** Fragment of a military epitaph from Eretria; *c.* 500–480? Roehl³, 76. 8. *IG* xii. 9. 255. Eretria Mus. 299.

**19.** Base for a bronze bull, made by Philesios and dedicated by the Eretrians at Olympia; *c.* 480? *IGA* 373. Roberts i. 170. *Ol.* v. 248. *SGDI* 5305. Roehl³, 76. 7. *DGE* 802. Olympia Mus. 118.              PL. 6

**20.** Top of an altar(?) dedicated by Chairigenes and his daughter Eudeine, from Aulon near Eretria (Attic alphabet?); *c.* 450? *SGDI* 5303. Roehl³, 75. 4. *IG* xii. 9. 124. Friedlaender 20. Prinakion.

**21.** Gravestone of Mnesitheos, an Aiginetan, from Eretria; *c.* 450? *SGDI* 5304. Roehl³, 76. 6. *IG* xii. 9. 285. *IG* xii, suppl., p. 186. Friedlaender 140. Peek i. 1210. Eretria Mus.

*Inscriptions attributed to Eretria*

**22.** Imitation of a PC aryballos, by Pyrrhos son of Agasileos; *c.* 650? *SGDI* 5292. Johansen, *Les Vases sicyoniens*, 171. Hoppin, *Handbook of Greek BF Vases* (1924), 1. Buck, 192, no. 9. Lejeune, *REA* xlvii (1945), 103. Boston, MFA 98. 900.              PL. 6

**23.** Euboic name Demotheres on a bronze lebes from Thebes; see Boiotia 5, pp. 91 f.              PL. 7

**24.** Scaraboid chalcedony seal; *c.* 550–525? Wilhelm, 4. Richter, *MMNYC Engraved Gems* (1956), no. 32, pl. 5. New York, MM 42.11.14.              PL. 6

### SOUTHERN EUBOIA

**25.** Gravestone of Lysikrates, from Styra; *c.* 500? *SGDI* 5347. Roehl³, 76. 9. *IG* xii. 9. 67. Private coll.?

**26.** Collection of small leaden strips from Styra, bearing a personal name on one or both sides; *c.* 475? *IGA* 372. Roberts i. 169. *SGDI* 5345. Roehl³, 76 f. 8. *IG* xii. 9. 56. *DGE* 813. NM, Berlin Mus., Louvre, Basel Mus.              PL. 6

**27.** Part of a base from Platanistos, bearing a dedication and sculptor's signature; *c.* 500–450? *IGA* 371. Roberts i. 168. *IG* xii. 9. 42. Platanistos.

**28.** Part of a block from Platanistos, bearing the remains of a dedication to Aphrodite, and a sculptor's signature; *c.* 450? *IGA* 7. *IG* xii. 9. 43. Lost?

**29.** Coinage inscribed Καρυστιο[ν], from Karystos; late 6th c. onwards. *HN²*, 356. B ii. 1, 691 ff., pl. 32.

**30.** Small column found in a grave at Karystos, the top encircled with leaden strips, including the names [A]ristomenes and Sosikles; 5th c. *IGA* 6. *IG* xii. 9. 41. Lost?

**31.** Marble block from Zarax, bearing a list of names inscribed from right to left; late 6th–early 5th c. *IG* xii. 9. 75, pl. 1. Arvanitopoullos, *Epigraphike* i. 74, fig. 36. Chalkis Mus.

# BOIOTIA

| α | β | γ | δ | ε | ϝ | ζ | η | ᚺ | θ | ι | κ | λ | μ | ν | ξ | ο | π | M | ϙ | ρ | σ | τ | υ | φ | χ | ψ | ω | Ρ | |
|---|---|---|---|---|---|---|---|---|---|---|---|---|---|---|---|---|---|---|---|---|---|---|---|---|---|---|---|---|---|
| 1 | A | B, | Γ | D, | ᚱ | ᚨ | I | – | ⊟ | ⊗, | ι | Κ | ᒻ | ᛖ | Γ | Χᚄ | O | Ρ | – | φ | Ρ, | ᚄ | T | ᚤ | φ | Ψ | φᚄ | – | : | 1 |
| 2 | A | ᛒ | Γ | D | ᚱ | F | | ⊟ | ⊕ | | Κ | | ᛖ | ᚪ | Υᚄ | | Γ | | φ | Ρ | S | | V | ⊘ | Ψ | | ⚌ | 2 |
| 3 | A, | | | | ᛖ | Ϲ | | Η | ⊙ | | | | ᛖ | ᚪ | + | | Γ | | | Ρ, | | | Υ, | ᛦ | | | 3 |
| 4 | A | | | | Ε | | | | | | | | | | | | | | | Ρ | | | Υ | ᛦ | | | 4 |
| 5 | A | | | | ᚺ | | | | | | | | | | | | | | | | | | | Ψ | | | 5 |

FIG. 28. Boiotia

*Notes on letter-forms*

The curved or crooked α1–2 is characteristic of Boiotian at all periods.

The tailed ε2 still occurs in the first half of the 5th c. (**17**). A special letter ε5, apparently a hybrid form between E and I, is attested at Thespiai *c.* 424 (**19***a*) for the close sound (approaching ι) of ε before a vowel (Buck, 18 and 22).

For ζ (*ds, sd*) δ (medial δδ) was used in Boiotian; cf. **1** and **17**; Buck, 71. The normal ζ was in use by *c.* 424 (**19***a–b*).

ᚺ1 occurs only in **2** and **22** (the latter not certainly Boiotian). ᚺ2 was still in use late in the 6th c. (**13** and *IG* vii. 2455 = Neugebauer, *Kat. Bronz. Berlin* i (1931), no. 206, pl. 35). ᚺ3 was in use by *c.* 475–450 (**17**).

**1** shows unexpectedly the late type θ3; perhaps the cross was omitted in error. Otherwise θ1–2 is used as late as *c.* 470 (**16**), though θ3 is found already *c.* 500 (**15**). The form in **11** is clearly an error.

Isosceles μ2 is rare, but occurs on one of the early lebetes from the Athenian Acropolis (**3***b*), and in the inscription of Dermys and Kittylos from Tanagra (**8**).

ξ1 occurs only in **1**; otherwise ξ2 is normal. ξ3 is not common, but may be found sometimes (e.g. *IG* vii. 3435 = Roehl³, 83. 8, Ευξιθιο).

The curved or crooked forms π1–2 are normal in the 7th and 6th c.; thereafter π3 becomes regularly used.

The coins of Koroneia, if they are correctly dated, give a rough date for the disappearance of *qoppa*. It is used on the issues whose lower date is 480, but not on those which begin *c.* 456 (*HN²*, 345).

The tailed ρ3–4 is normal throughout the 5th c. and in the last quarter of the 6th (**12–15**). Earlier than *c.* 525 the common form is the tailless 1–2.

σ1 is normal in the early inscriptions; σ2, which occurs sporadically before *c.* 550 (**2**), appears to become the common type during the second half of the 6th c.

Boiotian *upsilon* nearly always has a tail of some kind; the late archaic type υ2, so common elsewhere, is not common in Boiotian inscriptions. The early form ʋɪ persists into the second quarter of the 5th c. (**17**); ʋ3–4 are used in the casualty-lists **19***a–b*, *c*. 424; ʋ2 is found occasionally, especially in graffiti (e.g. on a kantharos, Stavropoullos, *AE* 1896, 244, pl.).

*Psi* and *omega* occur in two abecedaria of the last quarter of the 5th c., in shapes only half-understood (**20**); but they were not used in ordinary inscriptions until the 4th c.

*Punctuation* is rare in Boiotian inscriptions. Pɪ occurs in **10** (*c*. 550–525?), P2 in **17** (*c*. 475–450?). The earliest example of *stoichedon* script seems to be **14** (*c*. 510–500).

At the narrowest point of the Euripos the distance is only 65 metres from Chalkis across to Boiotia. Even Hesiod, with his hatred of all seafaring, went to Chalkis to compete at the funeral games of Amphidamas (p. 91); and the trading connexion of Chalkis with Thebes was strong in the sixth century, at least until their joint defeat by Athens in 506.[1] But the greatest proof of intimacy lies in their scripts; for it is, I think, almost certain that Boiotia received her alphabet from Chalkis. The similarity between the two scripts is closer than that between Attic and Boiotian, in their mutual use of 'tilted' *delta* δɪ–2 (as against Attic Δ) and the 'red' *xi* and *chi*. It is true that Boiotian inscriptions show no sign of the five-stroked *mu* of Euboia, but this form has not yet been attested in early Chalkidic either, though it was certainly used in the script of Eretria and the joint Eretrian and Chalkidic colonies of Pithekoussai and Kyme (pp. 81 f.).

The extant epigraphic material from all the cities of Boiotia is overwhelming, and much of it is perforce omitted here. I have concentrated mainly on the inscriptions of the seventh and sixth centuries, confining my selection thereafter to a very few examples to indicate the general lines of development after the end of the sixth century. There is no essential difference, as far as I can see, between the scripts of the various cities, and therefore they are all discussed together here, such minor variations as may appear being shown in the notes on letter-forms above. Because of this necessary compression, the three largest sources of Boiotian inscriptions *c*. 510–400 are barely touched on here. These are (*a*) the innumerable grave-stelai, notably from Tanagra, bearing simply the name of the deceased; (*b*) the equally countless graffiti of owners' names and καλός-inscriptions on local pottery, chiefly black-glazed kantharoi; and (*c*) the vast store of graffiti dedications to the Kabiroi on minor objects from the Kabirion at Thebes.

The earliest datable inscription from Boiotia may belong to the first quarter of the seventh century; it is the dedication to Apollo by Mantiklos on a large bronze statuette of a belted warrior, who once wore a helmet and probably carried a spear and shield (**1**). It is said to have come from Thebes. If this is true, it may have been dedicated in the Ismenion, the most important sanctuary of Apollo in Thebes. The figure recalls the Orientalizing types of men on early Protoattic vases,[2] or on relief pithoi from Boiotia,[3] and a helmeted head of a statuette somewhat like this one has been found at Delphi.[4] In dating it *c*. 700–675,[5] we may compare the general aspect of the lettering—tall and

---

[1] Cf. P. N. Ure, *BSA* xiv (1907–8), 226 ff., esp. 236 f.

[2] Cf. J. M. Cook, *BSA* xxxv (1934–5), pls. 39, hydria (*c*. 700) and 53, jug (*c*. 650).

[3] Cf. Hampe, *Frühe griechische Sagenbilder in Boiotien*, 56 ff., no. R4, there dated *c*. 650–625.

[4] Lamb, *Gk. and Roman Bronzes*, pl. 15d; Hampe, *Die Antike* xv (1939), 22 ff., fig. 4.

[5] A date *c*. 700 was suggested as a possibility by Richter, *Kouroi*, 41, and Karo, *Greek Personality in*

spidery, with long tails and very small circles—with that of the earliest Attic inscriptions. In particular the use of the characteristic Boiotian 'crooked' αι may be noted. Though one might expect the inscription to begin from right to left at this early period, it starts from left to right—perhaps because a shield on the left arm would overshadow the left thigh, so that the bronze-worker began to cut the lettering on the right thigh instead (p. 47). He used a variety of chisels, and a small ring-punch for the circles.[1]

Perhaps the most interesting archaic inscriptions from Boiotia are those on the relics of bronze tripods or plain lebetes, the customary prizes offered at funeral games in early Greece. Fragments of nine such offerings have been found. Normally the bowl bore two inscriptions; the first (inscribed by the donor) commemorated the actual games: τῶν ἐπὶ τῷ δεῖνα ἄθλων εἰμί, or: ὁ δεῖνά μ' ἔδωκεν ἐπὶ τῷ δεῖνα ἄθλον: the second was dedicatory, added by the prize-winner when he duly offered his prize in some sanctuary. Hesiod, having won his tripod in the funeral games of Amphidamas at Chalkis, dedicated it in a sanctuary of the Muses (and Helikonios?) on Helikon,[2] where a fragment from the rim of an archaic bronze lebes has in fact been found, with part of the dedicatory inscription (6): [ͱιαρον ε]μι το Ελιϙōν[ιο - - -]; the lettering may be of the seventh century (cf. the archaic *qoppa* ϙι), but hardly as early in the century as that of **1** or of some of the other lebetes described below. Parts of five more Boiotian prize lebetes were found on the Athenian Akropolis, with traces of their commemorative inscriptions. The script is clearly Boiotian, and we may wonder to which city the Athenians went to compete. Only one appears to retain a fragment of the Athenian victor's dedication (**3b**): τōν επ[ι] Δ⟨α⟩ μ⟨α⟩σιδαι α̣[ιθλōν εμι] (= Boiotian), and below: [ὁ δεῖνα - - -] τ' εθ⟨ε̄⟩κεν (= Attic). A second lebes (**3c**) was used twice as a prize; the earlier inscription was written round the top just below the rim and, like **3b**, is perhaps of the late seventh century: τōν επι Γελαν-[ορι ? - - -]οπιδες || ειμι. Over this lettering a handle was nailed and a second text cut below, apparently some years later: [- - -]οιραχσιαδ[ας με εδōκε? ε]π' Ε̣υπε̣δοσθενιδαι. The third example is only a small fragment (**3d**): [ὁ δεῖνα ἐπὶ τῷ δεῖνα]α αιθλον με [εδōκε]; the fourth (**3a**), which from its spidery lettering appears to be the earliest, apparently bore the names of several dead, written in a spiral round the bowl: [Επι ?- - -]ε̣ [. . .]αιεͱυ [*c.* 4]εϝ[- - -]μοριōι και Χιχιδαι κα̣[ι- - -]. The latest (**3e**) is written *boustrophedon*, perhaps because the first line met the heavy handle or 'ear' of the tripod, nailed to the rim: [- - -]αδα[ς με ?] εδōκε επ[ι] | Δαμαλαι.

Two more fragments of similar prizes were found in Thebes. One (**2**) was offered at the funeral games of Ekpropos (επι Εκπροπōι, (*a*)) and dedicated to (Apollo) Pythios by a victor named Isodikos, (*b*); the lettering of the commemoration (*a*) looks no later than that of **1**, i.e. first quarter of the seventh century (?). The dedication (*b*) looks somewhat later in date, but Keramopoullos, who published the fragment, believed that (*a*) and (*b*) were by the same hand, and that only a second commemoration was by a different hand ((*c*), τōν επ- unfinished). The other fragment (**5**) has a dedication to Apollo Kerykeios

---

*Archaic Sculpture*, 70 f.; in the first quarter of the 7th c. by Jenkins, *Dedalica*, 62, Pfeiff, *Apollon*, 23 f., Grace, *Archaic Sculpture from Boeotia*, 49 f. and Homann-Wedeking, *Die Anfänge d. griech. Grossplastik*, 36 f.; in the first half of the same century by Lamb,

op. cit. 74, Casson, *AJA* xxxix (1935), 511 f.

[1] Casson, loc. cit.

[2] *OD* 654–9. Cf. *Certamen*, 210–4, and Paus. ix. 31. 3.

(end of the seventh century?) and bears also the name Δε̄μοθερε̄ς in larger letters, inscribed separately (Euboia **23**). This latter inscription is not Boiotian but Euboic (cf. five-stroked *mu* and the Ionic form of the name; the shape of *sigma* is uncertain throughout, according to Keramopoullos). We cannot tell whether this Euboian was the donor, the dead man or the dedicator; indeed it may not have been a funeral prize at all, though this seems likely in view of the other examples. The last example of such prizes (**9**) is that on a lebes found at Delphi, which bears a commemoration in Boiotian lettering and dialect: Λαϝοϙοϝος μ' επι παιδι εϝο̄ι αιθλα εδο̄κε Ευμ[ε]ι̣νο̄ι. Traces of a second inscription, presumably that of the man who won it and offered it at Delphi, are also reported.[1] The date should not be very early, perhaps *c.* 550.

The phiale mesomphalos **7**, which from its lettering should belong to the end of the seventh or the first part of the sixth century, is particularly interesting in that it is the earliest example of a public dedication by the officials of a Boiotian town (Thebes), which records further the name of the eponymous local magistrate, Phloax: ⊢ιαρον το Καρυκε̄ϝιο Φλοϝαϙος απαρχοντος λεϙτοι{ς} Θε̄βαιοι{ς} ανεθεαν.[2] It was apparently found at Tanagra, where there was a sanctuary of Hermes Kerykeios (Paus. ix. 20. 3). Later, the public dedications of tripods to the hero Ptoios at Akraiphia also testify to this practice (p. 93).

The fragmentary kore apparently of late 'Daedalic' type (**4**) from the Ptoion, the famous sanctuary of Apollo Ptoios which succeeded the local hero Ptoios' shrine, bears an inscription which may be rather earlier, perhaps *c.* 650–625: first the dedication, then the earliest signature of a Boiotian sculptor known as yet: [- - -]οτος εποιϝε̄σε. Indeed, if this headless kore is rightly dated, this is the earliest extant signature of any Greek sculptor (p. 62); but it may be a late Boiotian echo of a style already out of fashion elsewhere. Certainly later (i.e. *c.* 600–575?) is the well-known grave-inscription on a funeral monument from Tanagra (**8**): Αμφαλκε̄ς εστασ' επι Κιτυλο̄ι εδ' επι Δερμυι. The two sculptured kouroi, represented almost in the round against a stele, have their names added on the background of the stele, like those of figures in a painting; cf. the script on the stele of Keramo, Attica **8**. As for early Boiotian vase-inscriptions, little can be said of the signatures of the potters Gamedes, Pithiades, Mnesalkes, Menaides,[3] except that they suggest a general date somewhere about the middle of the sixth century, if we assume that here, as elsewhere, the potters wrote in a more cursive and developed script than that of formal inscriptions on stone. Mnesalkes should be the earliest, if we may judge by his use of σ1; the others use σ2 (p. 89). I should ascribe to about the third quarter of the century the dedication written vertically in false *boustrophedon* on a clay tile (?) from the Ptoion (**10**). It has been dated earlier, but three features seem to me to preclude a date before 550: the punctuation-sign 1 and the three-stroked σ2, which are normal features of the alphabet from the end of the archaic period onwards, here appear for the first time, and it is in false, not true *boustrophedon*.[4]

---

[1] Keramopoullos, *BCH* xxxii (1908), 447. He adds that the letters appear to be later in date than those of the commemoration.

[2] The use of a dative here is so hard to explain that I have bracketed the *sigma* in both cases as an error.

The λεϙτοί Θηβαῖοι may perhaps have been the βουλή.

[3] For discussion of these vases and their dates, cf. Hoppin, *BF Vases*, 17 ff.; Greifenhagen, *AA* 1936, 399 f.; P. N. Ure, *Hesperia* xv (1946), 46 ff.

[4] The offering, described as a καλὸν ἄγαλμα, was

The earliest federal coinage of the Boiotian cities has been assigned to the middle of the sixth century (*HN*², 343 ff.); the solitary letters on their reverses (αι, ε2, ⊦2, θ2, ϙ2, τ, φ2) can offer little help towards a more precise date. It has been further suggested[1] that the earliest of the inscribed columns found in the sanctuary of the hero Ptoios at Akraiphia (near the great Ptoion of Apollo) belongs to the same period, i.e. *c.* 550. These columns supported bronze tripods which were periodically dedicated to the hero by the people of Akraiphia, the name of the local archon being added to date the series; the earliest (**13**) may be cited to illustrate the formula: Σιμōνιδα αρχοντος τōι ⊦ερōι τōι Πτōιōι Ακριφιες ανεθεαν. This inscription cannot be as early as *c.* 550 (cf. the late archaic forms of ε2, ρ3, and χ3: see Euboia, p. 80); it should be set rather with the funeral stele of Agathon and Aristokrates from Thespiai, securely dated by its sculpture *c.* 510–500 (**14**), and with the beautiful kouros from the Ptoion dedicated by Pythias of Akraiphia and A(i)schrion (*c.* 500; **15**). The lettering on the kouros is unusually small, and the lines are set in decorative antithesis: two down the left thigh, retrograde, and two down the right, from left to right. At about the same time (judged by its lettering) a trophy of arms was offered by Tanagra at Olympia, after some defeat of an unknown foe; part of the shield survives, inscribed: Ταναγραιοι τōν [- - -] (**12**). An earlier Boiotian dedication of the same kind is that made by the Orchomenians after defeating Koroneia. It is inscribed on a helmet at Olympia (**11**), which may be as early as the third quarter of the sixth century; cf. ει, μι, νι, χι, ρ2: Ερχομενιοι ανεθειαν τōι Δι τὀλυ⟨ν⟩πιōι ϙορōνεια[θεν ?]—a campaign otherwise unrecorded, like the Tanagran.[2]

For the fifth century there is a mass of inscriptions which cannot be listed here. A few only may be mentioned to illustrate Boiotian script during that century. There is a bronze hydria dated *c.* 470 on stylistic grounds, a prize from the games at Thebes (**16**); *theta* is still crossed, θι. There is also a base at Delphi (**17**) which is signed by Hypato- doros and Aristogeiton, who also made a group of the Seven against Thebes at Delphi for the Argives in the second quarter of the fifth century (Argos **23**). The base at Delphi which bore their joint work was dedicated by Epizelos of Orchomenos, and is of about the same date as **16**, judged by its letters. The top is broken, but traces remain of a deep square cutting for a tenon, perhaps for the advanced left foot of a bronze statue. The tailed *epsilon* and *upsilon* give a look of archaism to the inscription, which is belied by the late forms of *heta* (⊦3) and *theta* (θ3). The graffito of Mogeas to Eucharis on a kantharos from Thespiai (**18**) is dated by the type of kantharos *c.* 450 or a little later.[3] A polyandrion found at Thespiai has been ascribed, from the heavy casualties, to the battle of Delion in 424. Above the dead stood a stone lion and eight marble stelai bearing ninety-four names —the flower of Thespiai, as Thucydides called them (iv. 133). The shallow lettering

---

sent by at least three donors. It can hardly have been merely the tile or plaque itself; was this to be inserted in some larger object (as a base or column), or can it be perhaps the draft of an inscription, sent with the ἄγαλμα for a local mason at the Ptoion to copy on the base?

[1] Guillon, *Les Trépieds du Ptoion* ii (1943), 67. The other examples, ibid., belong apparently to the first half of the 5th c.

[2] A Corinthian helmet now in Berlin is described by Kukahn (*Der griechische Helm* (1939), no. 33) as bear- ing the inscription: -λυνπιανμ-. It shows Boiotian λι and πι, and suggests a Boiotian dedication similar to **11**: [- - - Ζευ Ο]λυνπι' αγα[λμα ?].

[3] Mrs. A. D. Ure has kindly informed me of this date.

(**19***a*) is a good example of the fine, sophisticated work that could be produced for a public monument by a mason with an individual style; we may note the sweeping curves in *lambda*, *nu* (rarely), *sigma*, *upsilon*. A special letter ε5 is used to represent a short vowel-sound midway between ε and ι (p. 89). The casualty list on a large, dark stone block from Tanagra (**19***b*) is usually identified as those from Tanagra who fell at Delion: sixty-three, including two Eretrians. This lettering is less distinctive. It retains three-stroked *sigma*, and lacks the elaborate tailed *phi* of **19***a*. Clearly the local script was still normal *c.* 424. It is used also for the name ῾Ρύνχων on a painted funeral stele (**21**), which from its style cannot be earlier than the last quarter of the fifth century, and may be no earlier than *c.* 400. The graffiti dedications on local pottery from the precinct of the Kabiroi at Thebes also provide evidence that as late as the end of the century the local alphabet was still in use.[1] But the Boiotians were aware by this time that additional letters existed; for an attempt at the Ionic forms Ψ and Ω appears at the end of the *stoichos* in the lower of two abecedaria painted on a Boiotian cup of unknown provenance (**20**). A. Ure sets the *floruit* of this type of cup *c.* 420.[2]

## SELECT CATALOGUE

**1.** Bronze statuette of a warrior, dedicated to Apollo by Mantiklos, probably from Thebes; *c.* 700–675? Froehner, *Mon. Piot* ii (1895), 137 ff., pl. 15. Friedlaender 35. For other authorities, see pp. 90 f., n. 5. Boston, MFA 03.997.                                            PL. 7

**2.** Rim of a lebes (funeral prize) from Thebes; *c.* 700–675? Kourouniotes, *AE* 1900, 109 f. Roehl[3], 83. 16 (part only). *IG* i[2]. 402, n. *DGE* 440. 12. Buck 38. 2. Athens, private coll.          PL. 7

**3***a–e*. Fragments of five similar lebetes from the Athenian Akropolis; *c.* 700–600? Bather, *JHS* xiii (1892–3), 128 f., nos. 58–59, 62–64, pl. 7. *IG* i[2]. 401 (*a*), 406 (*b*), 402–3 (*c*), 404 (*d*), 405 (*e*). Raubitschek, *Hesperia* viii (1939), 155, n. 1. NM.                            PL. 7

**4.** Kore dedicated at the Ptoion; *c.* 650–625? Holleaux, *BCH* x (1886), 77 ff., pl. 7 and xii (1888), 398, n. 8. *IG* vii. 2729. *DGE* 539. 1. Picard, *Manuel* i. 231 f., fig. 72. Grace, *Archaic Sculpture from Boiotia* (1939), 53. *AGA*, 23, fig. 40. NM 2.                             PL. 7

**5.** Fragment of a lebes from Thebes, *c.* 625–600? Kourouniotes, op. cit. 107 ff. *DGE* 440. 10. Buck 38. 1. Athens, private coll.                             PL. 7

**6.** Similar fragment from Helikon; *c.* 625–600? Plassart, *BCH* l (1926), 385 f., fig. 1. NM 10.850.
                                                                          PL. 8

**7.** Phiale dedicated to Apollo Kerykeios by the Thebans, from Tanagra; *c.* 610–550? Stavropoullos, *AE* 1896, 243. Roehl[3], 84. 17. *DGE* 440. 1. NM.                             PL. 8

**8.** Funeral stele of Dermys and Kittylos from Tanagra; *c.* 600–575? *SGDI* 857. *IG* vii. 579. Collignon, *Les Statues funéraires* (1911), 60 f. *DGE* 455. Picard, *Manuel* i. 508 f. Lullies, *JdI* li (1936), 150. Grace, op. cit. 53 f., fig. 69. *Kouroi*, 23, 50, 77 f., figs. 57–58. Friedlaender 4. Peek i. 137. NM 56.

**9.** Fragment of a funeral lebes, from Delphi; *c.* 550? *FD* v. 70, figs. 228, 228*a*. Keramopoullos, *BCH* xxxii (1908), 445 ff. and (1909), 440 f. Buck, *Festschrift für Wackernagel* (= *Antidoron*, 1924), 133, n. 1. Friedlaender 156. Delphi Mus.

---

[1] Wolters and Bruns, *Das Kabirenheiligtum bei Theben* i (1940), 43 ff., pls. 5, 10; cf. further Kirchhoff[4], 143; Larfeld[3], 264; Fraser and Rönne, *Boeotian and West Greek Tombstones* (1957), 369.

[2] *JHS* xlvi (1926), 57.

**10.** Clay tile (?) bearing a dedication, from the Ptoion; *c.* 550–525? Buck, *CP* iv (1909), 76 ff. *DGE* 538. Friedlaender 37. Buck 37. NM.

**11.** Helmet dedicated by the Orchomenians at Olympia; *c.* 550–525? Oikonomos, *AE* 1925–6, 87 ff., figs. 1–2. Robert, *Coll. Froehner* i. 35. *SEG* xi. 1208. NM. 15155. (See Addenda.) PL. 8

**12.** Shield dedicated by the Tanagrans at Olympia; *c.* 525–500? Kunze and Schleif, *JdI* liii (1938), *Olympiabericht* ii. 69, 72, fig. 42 and pl. 21. *SEG* xi. 1202. Olympia Mus. PL. 8

**13.** Earliest of the tripod-dedications made by the Akraiphians in the sanctuary of Ptoios; *c.* 525–500? Guillon, *Les Trépieds du Ptoion* i (1943), 49 f. and Appendix ii. 54, pl. 15, 1; ii (1943), 67 f. Thebes Mus. PL. 8

**14.** Grave-stele of Agathon and Aristokrates from Thespiai; *c.* 510–500. *IG* vii. 1890. *DGE* 479. i. Oikonomos, *AE* 1920, 56 f. *AAG*, 102 f. Peek i. 59. NM 32. PL. 8

**15.** Dedication on a kouros at the Ptoion by Pythias and A(i)schrion; *c.* 500. Holleaux, *BCH* x (1886), 269 ff. and xi (1887), 275 ff., 287. *Kouroi*, 213 f., 225 f., figs. 363–7. *AGA*, 153. NM 20. PL. 9

**16.** Prize hydria from the games at Thebes; *c.* 470. Jacobsthal, *Diskoi* (1933), 21 f., figs. 10–11. D. M. Robinson, *AJA* xlvi (1942), 180 ff., figs. 12–13. Providence, Rhode Is. School of Design. PL. 9

**17.** Base for a dedication at Delphi by Epizelos, made by Hypatodoros and Aristogeiton; *c.* 475–450? Roberts i. 204. *SGDI* 1130. Roehl[3], 86. 24. *SIG*[3] 60. *DGE* 443. *FD* iii. 1. 388 f., pl. 12. Marcadé i. 8, pl. 4. 1. Delphi Mus. 852. PL. 9

**18.** Graffito by Mogea(s) on a Boiotian kantharos for Eucharis, from Thespiai; *c.* 450–430. *SGDI* 1133. *IG* vii. 3467. Roehl[3], 84. 22. *DGE* 441. *Louvre, Encycl. photographique de l'art* ii (1936), 277. Friedlaender 177*h*. Buck 38. 5. Paris, Louvre. PL. 9

**19*a–b*.** (*a*) Grave-stelai from the polyandrion of the Thespians who fell at Delion, 424. Stamatakes, *PAE* 1882, 71 f., pl. A. *IG* vii. 1888*a–i*. Keramopoullos, *AE* 1920, 18 ff. Roehl[3], 85. 26. *DGE* 478. Thebes Mus. 2016–23. PL. 10

(*b*) Gravestone from the polyandrion of the Tanagrans who fell at Delion. *IG* vii. 585. *IGA* 157. Keramopoullos, op. cit. 19 ff. *DGE* 451. Skimatari Mus. 271. PL. 10

**20.** Two abecedaria on a Boiotian cup, provenance unknown; *c.* 420. Kalinka, *AM* xvii (1892), 101 ff., pl. 6. Roehl[3], 86. 30. A. Ure, *JHS* xlvi (1926), 57, fig. 4. NM CC 1116. PL. 10

**21.** Grave-stele of Rhynchon, *c.* 425–400. Vollgraff, *BCH* xxvi (1902), 554 ff., pl. 8. Keramopoullos, op. cit. 1 ff. *MuZ*. i. 665, fig. 633. *DGE* 468. 16b. *SEG* ii. 187. NM. PL. 10

*Inscriptions attributed to Boiotia*

**22.** Graffito on handle of an oinochoe from Eretria; mid-6th c.? *CVA* Bonn i, 47, pl. 40. 1, 3: Boardman, *BSA* xlvii (1952), 44. Bonn Mus. 1092. See p. 85. PL. 10

**23.** Painted inscriptions on an amphora from Eretria; mid-6th c.? Boardman, op. cit. 43 f., fig. 25. Eretria Mus. See p. 85.

## THESSALY

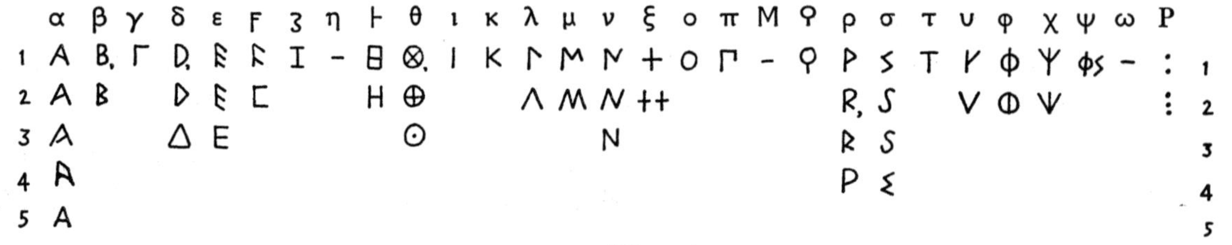

FIG. 29. Thessaly

*Notes on letter-forms*

α3 occurs in **7** and in a 5th-c. inscription from Phalanna, *IG* ix. 2. 1236. α4, the Boiotian *alpha*, is used occasionally in **6**, also of the 5th c.

Like the Boiotian, the Thessalian local script used *delta* to express the ʒ sound; cf. **10**, εξξανακαδ(δ)εν (ἐξαναγκάʒειν).

Ͱ1 is still used in **4**, which may belong to the early 5th c.; there is as yet no example of its occurrence later in the century.

λ2 is already in use in **4**, though isolated examples of λ1 still occur later (**12**).

The doubled form ξ2 occurs in the 5th c. (**6, 10**).

σ2 occurs in the 6th-c. inscription **2**, and the developed type σ3, though not common, appears occasionally in the 5th c. (**4, 8**). σ4, rare before *c.* 450 (**6**), is common thereafter (**10–14**).

*Punctuation* is rare: 1 is used rarely in the 5th c. (**8**, *IG* ix. 2. 975, 1203, 1240), 2 appears on the stele **14**. The *boustrophedon* style probably lasted until late in the 6th c. (**3**), though archaic inscriptions are too few as yet for a precise date to be possible. The *stoichedon* style is not attested before the 5th c.; the first complete example is **6** (*c.* 475?), in which the horizontal and vertical lines of the chequer are still visible.

The Thessalian alphabet is obviously derived from those of the states which lay south of Thessaly herself and her dependencies. It corresponds with the Chalkidic–Boiotian type, using *gamma* 1 (as in Boiotian and early Euboic) and *sigma* 1 (as in Euboic, in contrast with early Boiotian); but for *lambda* it shows not the Euboic–Attic but the more common forms 1–2, which may be directly due to Thessaly's southern neighbour Phokis; or it might be merely an error in transmission from a Boiotian or Euboic source.[1] Like all the states of central Greece except Attica, Thessaly also used the 'red' forms of *xi* and *chi*. No local variants are visible in the inscriptions of her four tetrarchies or among her perioikic territories of Perrhaibia, Magnesia, and Achaia Phthiotis, and therefore I have treated them all together here. No early inscriptions have yet been found in the southern dependencies Malis, Doris, and Ainis.

Very few inscriptions have been found which are earlier than the fifth century, as against a large number extant from that century. From this it might be inferred that conservative Thessaly was late in learning the alphabet from her neighbours, though it

[1] The Chalkidic *lambda* apparently occurs in an inscription from Thessalian Eretria (Achaia Phthiotis), *IG* ix. 2. 199: Μεθιστας Πιθουνειος Απλουνι. But this is known only from a 19th-c. copy, and so cannot be checked. It is the only example. This type of *lambda* is not said to be Thessalian by either Kirchhoff or Larfeld, as is stated by Lejeune, *REA* xlvii (1945), 99 f. Cf. further Corinth, p. 125, n. 3.

should be remembered that Pausanias saw at Delphi (x. 16. 8) a statue dedicated by Echekratidas of Larisa (presumably one of the Aleuadai), which the Delphians held to be the earliest dedication made there. The few extant inscriptions are all from the Magnesian peninsula or the coast of Achaia Phthiotis to the south—that is, broadly speaking, from the district round the Gulf of Pagasai. Of these the first inscription (**1**) is written *boustrophedon* on the lower part of a wide, rough stone stele found in the precinct of Apollo at Korope in Magnesia; it was obviously intended to be read vertically, for the tops of the letters continually oppose each other within the same line (see pp. 49 f.), and there is a vacant space left at the surviving narrow end, for insertion in the ground. The extant parts of the text have been interpreted as concerning the provision of food for some ritual meal, but they suggest to me rather a law against stealing or misusing the temple utensils for sacrifice. The abrupt opening without preamble: αι κε αφελετοι, 'if anyone causes to be removed . . .' is to be noted as characteristic of archaic laws; we many compare, for example, the Ozolian Lokrian: τον ξενον με Ϝαγεν (Lokris **4***a*). The fine of 'fifty ——' mentioned in the last line, whatever the units were, cannot refer to any local Thessalian coinage, for there is no evidence of its existence before the first decade of the fifth century, when the Aleuadai of Larisa medized and struck a coinage on the Persian standard.[1] From the look of the letters, the temple-inscription may belong somewhere in the middle of the sixth century, or even *c*. 550–525, if the Thessalians were conservative in all things. We may note the archaic tailed forms of *upsilon* and *chi*. The same approximate date may be ascribed to a roughly shaped stele (**2**) found at Orminion (?), which apparently records the generosity of a citizen who during his tenure of the office of judge (δικαστώρ) provided the roof for a public building (or possibly the whole building): ΑνδροϘυδες εϘρουσε· | Ϙολουρος δικαστορευϘον | ετευξε ο Παισιαδας (genitive?) το τεγος.[2] The first clause, whose meaning is uncertain, is separated from that following by the start of a fresh line for the latter; for other examples of this system for paragraphs, cf. pp. 44, 50.

A third inscription from the southern end of Magnesia, also *boustrophedon*, is a fragment of a narrow stele, broken above and below (**3**). It is clearly later than **1** and **2**, but may still be earlier than the fifth century. Interpretation of the brief remains is risky; but possibly the central letters are part of a Thessalian patronymic adjective, and the inscription was a funeral epigram: [- - -? θ]ανατōι, Να|υκιδαι|ōνιε, σταλα. Of a fourth inscription, from Thebai in Achaia Phthiotis, so little is legible that nothing can be made of it save the bare fact that the lettering seems to be archaic.[3]

There is a considerable amount of fifth-century material, but very little to suggest any precise dates. One at least may be clarified, the base for a funeral column from Demetrias (**8**), bearing a fragmentary epitaph. This was identified by Peek[4] as a metrical address to

---

[1] Hermann, *Zeit. f. Num.* xxxv (1924), 1 ff.; cf. Westlake, *JHS* lvi (1936), 12 ff.

[2] For examples of the genitive -ας from a nominative masculine ending -α in Boiotian and north-western Greek, cf. Buck, 87. This rendering seems to me preferable to that of the editor (Arvanitopoullos, *Polemon* i (1929), 216 ff.): Α. εϘρουσε· Ϙ. δικαστορευϘον· ετευξε ο Π. το τεγος: 'A.? built (this); K. was dikastes (= epony-

mous official for the year); P. made the roof.' The interpretation of the verb ἔκρουσε is uncertain. If it is from κρούειν, the meaning might be that of κολάπτειν, i.e. 'cut (this record)'. If it is a misspelling of ἐκύρωσε, it would mean 'ratified (this)'. Neither is satisfactory.

[3] *IG* ix. 2. 140. The traces of letters are much less certain than the facsimile in *IG* suggests.

[4] *Gnomon* xiv (1938), 472 ff.

a sphinx which originally crowned the column, and her reply. It cannot be much, if at all, earlier than the middle of the fifth century. The letters are neat and squared, with open *heta* and dotted *theta*, and the lines are partly *stoichedon*. It is certainly not earlier than the brief inscription Πολυξεναια εμμι on the funeral stele of Polyxena (**7**); this latter bears a relief of rustic quality showing a young girl, which Johansen describes as 'probably some-what older than the middle of the fifth century'.[1] The lettering suggests a date *c.* 475–450, probably near the lower date. The unusual α3 occurs elsewhere (p. 96). A second figured stele, also from Larisa, shows a youth in three-quarter profile, with the title Ϝεκεδαμος (**9**); this can hardly be earlier than the middle of the fifth century, and may well be some decades later.[2] These two stelai show that, at Larisa at least, the local *delta*, *vau*, *xi*, and *sigma* were still in use about the middle of the fifth century. An inscription clearly older than any of these is the epitaph of the soldier Pyrrhiadas from Kierion (**4**), cut on two sides of the base for a stele (?). Here the *boustrophedon* system is no longer used, but *epsilon* is still tailed, *heta* closed, *theta* crossed. If it is set in the first years of the fifth century that should not be far wrong, though the campaign must remain unknown. The part of a law from Atrax or Argoura, inscribed *stoichedon* (**6**), may lie between this in-scription and the stele of Polyxena. In the bronze plaque from Thetonion (**10**) which records honours paid to a Corinthian benefactor named Sotairos, the younger forms δ3, θ3, σ4 have replaced the older; but *vau* and the 'red' *xi* and *chi* are still in use. At some time after 450, but before the 'red' *chi* had gone, the Ionic form of *xi* came in. It is used in the artist's signature (Προνος εργαξατο) on a stele dedicated near Larisa (**11**) and on the grave-stele of a man named Gastron from Pelion (**12**); the latter has also the later forms δ3 and σ4, but *theta* is still crossed. Ionic *eta* appears, sometimes confused with *epsilon*, in an epitaph from Chyretiai (**13**), which also shows *vau* and crossed *theta*, to-gether with δ3, σ4, and a letter □ possibly intended for *omega*; *xi* and *chi* are not repre-sented. (See also Addenda.)

The general conclusion therefore is that the local script lasted until well after the middle of the fifth century; but more precise dates cannot be given. The coins offer little help. On those of Larisa the older ρ2–3 and σ1 are said to change to the ρ4 and σ4 '*c.* 450';[3] but is this conclusion itself based only on epigraphic arguments? Ionic *xi*, as we have seen, appears before Ionic *chi*, *psi*, *omega*. *Eta* also is used comparatively early; for it occurs in **13** and on the grave-stele of Kineas and Phrasimede from Pherai (**14**). This stele bears a relief which is dated by Johansen to the start of the Parthenon period, i.e. *c.* 440–430;[4] it is not the work of a provincial mason, but of a well-trained sculptor, and the lettering matches it; δ4 and σ4 are used as well as *eta*, and only in the *nu* and *phi* does it lag behind the best script of any other Greek state of the time.

### SELECT CATALOGUE

**1.** Stele with the text of a sacral law, from the Apollonion at Magnesia; *c.* 550? *IG* ix. 2. 1202. Roehl[3], 94. 1. *DGE* 603. Lejeune, *REA* xlvii (1945), 100 f. Volos Mus.     PL. 11

---

[1] *The Attic Grave-reliefs* (1951), 134 f.
[2] Cf. Brommer, *AM* lxv (1940), 115.
[3] *BMC Coins*, Thessaly, p. xxiii.
[4] Op. cit. 144.

**2.** Stele bearing the record of a roof (or building?) provided by Kolouros as judge, from Orminion (?), Magnesia; *c.* 550? Arvanitopoullos, *Polemon* i (1929), 216 ff., figs. 71–72. Volos Mus. 782.    PL. 11

**3.** Fragment of a grave-stele (?) from the district of Spalauthra and Olizon, Magnesia; *c.* 525–500? *IG* ix. 2. 1209. Roehl³, 94. 2. Volos Mus.    PL. 11

**4.** Epitaph for Pyrrhiadas on a base, Kierion; *c.* 500–480? Roberts i. 237. *IG* ix. 2. 270. Roehl³, 94. 4. Friedlaender 160. Peek i. 69. Destroyed.    PL. 11

**5.** Earliest inscribed coinage of Larisa; *c.* 492. *HN*², 297 ff. Hermann, *Zeit. f. Num.* xxxv (1924), 1 ff.

**6.** Stele with part of a sacral law, Atrax (?); *c.* 475? Giannopoullos, *AE* 1934–5, 140 ff., fig. 1. Larisa Mus. 588.

**7.** Funeral stele of Polyxena, Larisa; *c.* 460–450? Brunn, *AM* viii (1883), 81 ff., pl. 2. *IG* ix. 2. 663. Roehl³, 95. 13. *DGE* 584. 1. Brommer, *AM* lxv (1940), 111 f., pl. 76. 1. Johansen, *The Attic Grave-reliefs* (1951), 134 f., fig. 67. Buck 29a. NM 733.    PL. 11

**8.** Base for a funeral column with sphinx, Demetrias; *c.* 450? Arvanitopoullos, *Polemon* ii (1934–8), 47 ff., figs. 14–15. Peek, *Gnomon* xiv (1938), 476. Brommer, op. cit. 108, n. 1. Friedlaender 139A. Peek i. 1831. Volos Mus. 650.    PL. 11

**9.** Funeral stele of Echedemos, Larisa; *c.* 450–425? Brunn, op. cit. 81 ff., pl. 3. *IG* ix. 2. 662. Roehl³, 95. 10. *DGE* 584. 2. Brommer, op. cit. 111, 115, pl. 77. 1. Buck 29b. NM 733.

**10.** Bronze plaque granting honours to Sotairos of Corinth, from near Kierion; *c.* 450–425? *IG* ix. 2. 257 and add. Roehl³, 96. 11. Kern, pl. 10. *SIG*³ 55. *DGE* 557. Buck 35. NM 11716.    PL. 11

**11.** Stele dedicated by Aristion and the συνδαυχναφόροι, Larisa; *c.* 450–425? *IG* ix. 2. 1027. Roehl³, 97. 18. Buck 30. Village of Salsilar?

**12.** Grave-stele of Gastron, from Pelion; *c.* 450–425? Arvanitopoullos, *Polemon* i (1929), 37 f., fig. 11. Peek i. 77. Volos Mus.

**13.** Base of a funeral monument for Euethides, from Chyretiai; *c.* 450–425? Arvanitopoullos, *AE* 1917, 135. Karousos, *Epitumbion Tsounta* (1941), 5, 576. Volos Mus.

**14.** Grave-stele bearing a relief inscribed with the names of Kineas and Phrasimede; *c.* 440–430. *IG* ix. 2. 426. *DGE* 575. Brommer, op. cit. 112, pls. 79–80. Johansen, op. cit. 144, fig. 75. Halmyros Mus.    PL. 11

# PHOKIS

FIG. 30. Phokis

*Notes on letter-forms*

α1 is most frequent, α2 not uncommon. Crooked α3 occurs in **2, 3,** and **11.**

Ͱ2 is already in use *c.* 475–450 (**17**), but Ͱı is re-introduced in an inscription *c.* 400 (**20**) to serve as the aspirate when 2 is used for Ionic *eta*.

θı–2 is still used in **17**, but has been replaced by 3 in **18** (*c.* 430?).

λ2 is in use in the first quarter of the 5th c. (**15**).

The use of *san* in Phokian is doubtful; see below.

*Qoppa* is attested as yet only in inscriptions which also contain *san* (see below).

*Punctuation* is not often used. It is attested in one inscription apparently of the 6th c., known only by copy (*IG* ix. 1. 186); in the 5th c. it appears in the dedication of the 'Tyrrhanoi', *c.* 475–450 (Flacelière, *FD* iii. 4. 199 f., no. 124, fig. 2 and pl. 22. 1), and *c.* 430 (?) in **18**. *Boustrophedon* is attested as yet only in **1** and *IG* ix. 1. 186, a scarcity probably due only to the rarity of 6th-c. texts of any length. *Stoichedon* is used partially in **15** (*c.* 479); a well-cut example is **17**.

Since the oracle of Apollo at Delphi was the most famous and one of the oldest in mainland Greece, attracting inquirers not merely from all the other Greek states, but even from the wealthy rulers of Phrygia and Lydia, it is possible that the alphabet was introduced into this part at least of Phokis at a very early period, though there is little direct evidence for this. The custom of recording the answers of the oracle on leather may have begun before the middle of the seventh century, since the use of διφθέραι can be traced back so far at least (pp. 57 f.); but our knowledge of any other early records at Delphi is very scanty. The names of the local archons for 590/89 and 582/1 (Gylidas and Diodoros) are known,[1] which may mean that a consecutive archon-list was already kept at this time; but a late inscription seems to indicate that the full list of the Pythionikai was not composed until the second half of the fourth century.[2]

The early inscriptions at Delphi have not yet all been published, but a comprehensive work on the archaic Delphic script has been projected,[3] and therefore it is treated here merely in brief and general terms. I have made selections only from the great number of fifth-century dedications (often mere fragments) by various states which were inscribed in the local script of Delphi.

At present no inscriptions can be certainly ascribed to an earlier period than the sixth century, and they present an unresolved problem on the use of *san* in Phokis. With three exceptions the alphabet used in Phokian inscriptions of the sixth and fifth centuries is clearly of the same family as Boiotian and Thessalian, showing *lambda* as in Thessalian, 'red' *xi* and *chi*, and four-stroked *sigma* as in early Boiotian; it differs only in the use of lunate *gamma*, and in the lack of *qoppa* (cf. Lakonian). Since Boiotia certainly learnt the alphabet very early—probably from her commercial neighbours in Euboia—it is possible that Phokis acquired her script from Boiotia (*gamma* and *lambda* being altered in transmission) and passed it on to her western neighbour Ozolian Lokris (p. 105) and (in part at least) to Thessaly (p. 96)—possibly even to Lakonia (p. 185). But this must remain pure hypothesis until more early inscriptions are found, and it can then be decided

---

[1] Daux, *Chronologie delphique* (1943), 9 (= *FD* iii, suppl.). There may also have been some archaic document which recorded the oracle and instructions of the Pythia for the First Sacred War (Aischines, *In Ctes.* 107 ff.; see Parke, *JHS* lxxvii, pt. 2 (1957), 276).

[2] *SIG*³ 275. Cf. pp. 59 f.

[3] Lerat, *RA* 1944, 5, n. 2.

whether the *san* was regularly used in early Phokian, as is generally assumed,[1] or whether the three examples known are not in the local Phokian, but from other *san*-using scripts (see p. 223 for a fourth example, sometimes ascribed to Phokis). The first—the inscriptions on the plinths of the Argive statues of Kleobis and Biton at Delphi—is undoubtedly Argive (p. 155). The second is the series of names cut by different hands on tufa blocks of an archaic building (once ascribed to the Thebans) between the Theban and Athenian Treasuries at Delphi (5). They did not show when the blocks were in position, and may be the names either of donors of small sums for the erection of the building, or of masons.[2] All show the 'red' *xi* and *chi*, and most show *san* 1 or 2 ,with *qoppa*; but some show normal Phokian *sigma* and lack of *qoppa*, and appear to be no later in date than the others;[3] they all appear to belong to the second half of the sixth century, the earliest in the third quarter, the latest in the fourth. Are these the names of Phokian and non-Phokian masons, imported to erect this building? Or are they alien donors and Phokian masons? Or are they all Phokians—i.e. was *san* used in some parts of Phokis, and not in others? I hesitate to accept the last hypothesis, if the appearance of *san* in Phokis should prove in fact to be confined to Delphi, where examples of non-Phokian scripts naturally abound. The third example of *san* does little to determine the question. This is on the lost base for a dedication to Athena and Hera (1),[4] which from the use of ρι and χι must be certainly earlier than the late archaic period, possibly earlier than *c.* 550. The inscription is known from nineteenth-century copies only. Its original provenance is unknown, for it was found on the site at Hagios Georgios (once identified as classical Krisa), which Jannoray has shown to have been unoccupied between the Mycenean and Byzantine periods;[5] it may therefore have been brought to that site in modern times for building-material, and may well have been originally dedicated in the precinct of Athena Pronaia at Delphi. If this is the case, there is, again, the possibility that the original dedicator was not a Phokian. A script showing *san* might be attributed to parts of Aitolia, whose alphabet shows strong Achaian influence (p. 225); but further speculation is idle.

The archaic examples of what may perhaps be termed the standard Phokian script—i.e. without *san* or *qoppa*—can be only briefly mentioned here. The dedication by the sons of Charopinos the Parian on the base of a (lost) kouros (4) may be dated *c.* 550–540 from the shape of the plinth and traces of the feet which survive;[6] we may note also the use of the early ρι. This inscription is certainly Delphic, not Parian; but I hesitate to include also here the dedication of one Thaumis on the lip of a bronze lebes found at Delphi, which has been described as Delphic; for it shows the Doric dialectal form Ἀπέλλων, and I suspect that it may rather be Lakonian (p. 190, n. 5). The gravestones of Charimedes and Chion (2–3), known only from copies, would appear to be not later in date than 4. The names painted beside the figures in the reliefs of the metopes from the Treasury of

---

[1] Roberts i. 233; cf. *SIG*³ 5; *GHI*² 3; Lejeune, *REA* xlvii (1945), 114.

[2] Bourguet inclined to the view that they were donors rather than masons (*FD* iii. 1. 220 f.).

[3] Early examples showing *sigma* are *FD*, nos. 374 (pl. 9. 18); 381 (pl. 9. 6); 385 (pl. 9. 3): *BCH* lxii (1938), 347, fig. 8.

[4] The most recent interpretation is that the base held a dedication of spits (δραχμαί) and perhaps other temple utensils, as cauldrons: Raubitschek, *Yale Studies* xi (1950), 295 f., with a résumé of earlier theories.

[5] *BCH* lxi (1937), 40, n. 1.

[6] *Kouroi*, 172 f.

Sikyon (*c.* 575–560? **8**) and of the frieze from the Treasury of Siphnos[1] (*c.* 530; **9**) appear to be in Phokian of the late archaic period, for they show ρ3 and Ͱ2; it is thought that the reliefs must have been repainted more than once.[2] The inscription Κοριν[- - -] from the Treasury of the Corinthians has been classed as Corinthian of the archaic period; this is impossible, for Corinthian would show *qoppa* and crooked *iota*. If it is of the archaic period, it must be in the local Delphic script (**21**). A marble votive capital with a few letters of its dedication surviving on the abacus must certainly belong to the sixth century; it appears to read: [- - -] Αλκιμαχ[- - -] (**6**). Another fragment yields the attractive restoration [- - - ανεθε̄]κε Ροδ[ο̄πις] (**7**). It was cut on the bottom step of a base with some lost crowning member above, on which perhaps were laid the spits which Rhodopis sent to Delphi as a tithe from her earnings (Hdt. ii. 134). The script is Phokian (cf. δ1), and should belong to the second half of the sixth century, for *rho* is in the late archaic, tailed form ρ2; it is evidently later than **4** (*c.* 550–540). This does not contradict what we know of Rhodopis' life from other sources:[3] that she flourished in the reign of Amasis (569–529), and—presumably after her retirement—left an outstanding offering to Delphi as a memorial of her prosperous career as a courtesan. This may have been as much as forty to fifty years after Sappho's brother Charaxos had established her independently at Naukratis by paying off her first owner; which would permit a date *c.* 530 or even a little later for the inscription. Sappho called her Doricha, but Rhodopis was evidently the name by which she chose to be remembered at Delphi, and which is given by Herodotos, who must have seen the inscription.

The earliest inscribed specimens of the federal coinage of Phokis (**10**) are dated tentatively *c.* 520 (Φο̄κι); the separate coinage of Delphi (**14**) apparently began *c.* 480 (Δαλφικον).

The bronze Snake Column now in Istanbul once upheld a golden tripod, offered by the Greeks after Plataia (**15**; its uninscribed base survives at Delphi). It must be dated *c.* 479 or not long after, and script and dialect are Phokian rather than Lakonian;[4] cf. non-Lakonian *gamma*, *sigma*, and the non-Lakonian forms [ε]πολεμ[ε]ον, Φλειασιοι (for normal Lakonian επολεμιον, ΦλειαͰιοι). It shows tailless ε3, λ2, υ3; according to this, the dedication of 'pelanos' by the Pierians (?)[5] should be some years earlier (*c.* 500?) and the gravestone of the doctor Charon from Teithronion about the same (**11**). The well-known statement of accounts by the Labyad phratry (**13**) should then come in date between these and the Snake Column. The fragmentary prohibition which mentions a penalty of one obol for selling ἱερεῖα in a forbidden area (**16**) may be roughly contemporary with the Snake Column (i.e. *c.* 480–470?); the text concerning the unlawful removal of sacrificial wine (**17**) may perhaps be a little later (*c.* 470–450?).[6] The dedication of the Metapontines, sons of Phayllos (**23**), may be 450 (cf. p. 256, where it is suggested that the lettering is Phokian). Another dedication at Delphi by Achaian colonists—the Krotoniates—may be slightly earlier; it too is here taken to be in Phokian script (**22**; cf. p. 258).

---

[1] I have omitted the disguised signature (?) cut on the shield of one of the figures (Wilhelm, 137), since the letters have been worked over too elaborately to show any local characteristics.

[2] *FD* iv. 1. 26; iv. 2. 94, 109; La Coste-Messelière *BCH* lxviii–ix (1944–5), 10 f.

[3] See Page, *Sappho and Alcaeus* (1955), 49, and (below) Corinth, p. 124.

[4] Carpenter, *AJA* xlix (1945), 456.

[5] The ethnic was thus restored by Guarducci, *Riv. Fil.* xxv (1947), 244 f. If this is correct, the script might equally well be Thessalian.    [6] See Addenda.

18, a list of theorodokoi resident in Arkadia, Achaia, and Boiotia, indicates that the local script was still used *c.* 430; for it gives a series of names in Phokian (δ2, ξ1, χ3), but after the last entry Πασιχος κα[ι] | οι παιδες a postscript has been added giving two names which are assumed to be those of the sons; this would presumably be done about a generation later, and the script of the addition is the standard Ionic, of about the end of the century. υ2, the developed form, in the main inscription is hardly likely before *c.* 430. The stele bearing the laws of the Labyad phratry (20) also shows the standard Ionic (*c.* 400?); the decree concerning the 'pelanos' offered by the Phaselites (19), which has Ionic *delta* and *chi*, but not *eta* or *omega*, should then be some years earlier, in the last quarter of the fifth century.

## SELECT CATALOGUE

1. Dedication to Athena and Hera, found on the site of Mycenean (not classical) Krisa; possibly not Phokian; *c.* 600–550? *IGA* 314. Roberts i. 228. *SGDI* 1537. Roehl³, 87–89. 1. *DGE* 316. Friedlaender 44. Raubitschek, *Yale Studies* xi (1950), 295 f. Lost.                                            PL. 12

2. Gravestone of Charimedes, at Stiris; *c.* 550–540? *IG* ix. 1. 49. Roehl³, 91. 10. Once at Hosios Loukas; lost?                                                                                                        PL. 12

3. Gravestone of Chion, at Abai; *c.* 550–540? *IG* ix. 1. 81. Roehl³, 91. 11. *DGE* 348. Abai?    PL. 12

4. Dedication of the sons of Charopinos the Parian, at Delphi; *c.* 550–540. Roberts i. 230 *bis*. *SIG*³ 16. *FD* iv. 1. 54 ff., no. 23, fig. 24. Roehl³, 90. 7. *DGE* 318. *Kouroi*, 172 f., fig. 282. Marcadé i. 21, pl. 5. 4. Delphi Mus. 2278.                                                                                         PL. 12

5. Names inscribed on blocks of the so-called 'Theban' building at Delphi; *c.* 550–500? (some possibly not in Phokian script?). *FD* iii. 1. 219 ff., nos. 369–90, pl. 9. Bousquet, *BCH* lxii (1938), 347 f., figs. 8–9. Delphi.                                                                                              PL. 12

6. Fragmentary votive capital with dedication, Delphi; *c.* 550? La Coste-Messelière, *BCH* lxvi–lxvii (1942–3), 38 ff., fig. 7. Delphi Mus. 4741.

7. Fragment of the base for Rhodopis' offering at Delphi; *c.* 530? Mastrokostas, Ἑταιρεία Μακεδονικῶν σπουδῶν ix (1953), 635 ff., pl. 31. *SEG* xiii. 364. Delphi Mus. 7512.                                       PL. 12

8. Names repainted on the Sikyonian metopes at Delphi; *c.* 525–500? *FD* iv. 1. 26. La Coste-Messelière, *Au Musée de Delphes* (1936), 195 ff.

9. Names repainted on the Siphnian frieze at Delphi; *c.* 525–500? *FD* iv. 2. 94, 109. La Coste-Messelière, op. cit. 342, n. 5, 357 and *BCH* lxviii–lxix (1944–5), 5 ff., figs. 1–3. Mastrokostas, Νεὸν Ἀθηναῖον i (1955), 100 ff. and *AM* lxxi (1956), 74 ff., figs. 1–3.

10. Inscribed federal coinage of Phokis; *c.* 520(?) onwards. B ii. 1. 977 ff., pl. 42. *HN*², 338.

11. Grave-inscription of Charon from Teithronion; *c.* 500? Klaffenbach, *Sb. Ak. Berlin* 1935, 702. Friedlaender 86. Chaironea Mus.                                                                             PL. 13

12. Base for a statue dedicated as 'pelanos' by the Pierians(?) at Delphi; *c.* 500? Amandry, *BCH* lxiii (1939), 216 ff., figs. 2–4. Guarducci, *Riv. Fil.* xxv (1947), 244 ff. Delphi Mus. 4673+6325.

**13.** Statement of accounts by the Labyad phratry at Delphi; *c.* 500–480? Roberts i. 229. *SGDI* 1683. Roehl³, 90. 8. *DGE* 320. Guarducci, *L'Istituzione della fratria* ii (1938), 109 ff. Buck 49. Lost.

**14.** Inscribed coinage of Delphi; *c.* 480 onwards. B ii. 1. 993 ff., pl. 42. *HN²*, 340.

**15.** Snake Column dedicated by the Greeks at Delphi after the battle of Plataia; *c.* 479. Roberts i. 259. *SGDI* 4406. *SIG³* 31. Roehl³, 101. 16. *DGE* 11. *GHI²* 19 and p. 259. *ATL* iii. 59 ff. Istanbul. (Base: Bourguet, *Les Ruines de Delphes* (1914), 160 ff., figs. 49–50; *RE* suppl. iv, 1406 ff.)     PL. 13

**16.** Stele bearing remains of a prohibition, from Delphi; *c.* 480–470? Daux, *BCH* lxxiii (1949), 255 f., pl. 6. Jeffery, *BSA* l (1955), 77 f. Delphi Mus. 3873.

**17.** Sacred law inscribed on the wall of the stadion at Delphi; *c.* 470–450? Roehl³, 90. 9. Fournier, *REA* xxiv (1922), 1 ff., pl. 1. *DGE* 321. Buck 50. Delphi, stadion.     PL. 13

**18.** List of theorodokoi, Delphi; *c.* 430? *SIG³* 90. Daux, *REG* lxii (1949), 4 ff., pl. 1. Delphi Mus. 3134.

**19.** Decree concerning the 'pelanos' of the Phaselites at Delphi; *c.* 425–400? Pomtow, *Ph. W.* 1909, 252. *DGE* 322. Daux, *Hesperia* xviii (1949), 64, pl. 1. Buck 51. Delphi Mus. 3970.

**20.** Laws of the Labyad phratry at Delphi; *c.* 400. Homolle, *BCH* xix (1895), 5 ff., pls. 21–4. *SGDI* 2561. Roehl³, 91. 14. *DGE* 323. Guarducci, op. cit. 105 ff. Buck 52. Delphi Mus. 31.

*Inscriptions attributed to Delphic masons* (see also Addenda)

**21.** Fragmentary dedication on a block from the Corinthian treasury at Delphi; 6th c.? *FD* iii. 3. 128, no. 153, fig. 16. *NC* 160, n. 2. Jeffery, *BSA* xliii (1948), 205. Delphi Mus. 4073 (4686).     PL. 13

**22.** Base for a dedication at Delphi by the Krotoniates; *c.* 475? *SIG³* 30. *FD* iii. 1. 1, fig. 1. Delphi Mus. 974+2373+3158+3252.

**23.** Base for a dedication by the sons of Phayllos from Metapontion at Delphi; *c.* 450? Pomtow, op. cit. 251. *SIG³* 25. Delphi Mus.     PL. 13

## LOKRIS, OZOLIAN AND OPOUNTIAN

+=Ozolian X=Opountian

FIG. 31. The Lokrides and Lokroi Epizephyrioi

*Notes on letter-forms* (E = Epizephyrian Lokrian, pp. 284 ff.)

αι is the common form; 3 occurs rarely (**1, 17**).

Ͱ2 is used already in Ozolian **2**, i.e. *c.* 525–500 (?); but the closed form 1 is still used in Opountian **11** (early 5th c.?).

Both crossed and dotted θ are used in **4a–b**; (*b*), the later text (*c.* 450?), uses 3 exclusively, (*a*) (*c.* 475–450?) uses both 1–2 and 3.

The early form λ1 is still used in **4a**, the later λ2 in **4b**. Opountian Lokris uses λ3, like her neighbour Boiotia.

*Qoppa* is not used in Ozolian **2**, which might suggest that Ozolian, like Phokian, had no use for it; but it does occur in Ozolian **3**. It appears to be regular in Opountian (**11**), and is used also in the colonial inscription E**2**.

Like Boiotian, Opountian shows σ1 in the earliest inscriptions (**7–8**), σ2 thereafter (**10, 13–16**); **11** reverts to 1. Ozolian appears to have used only 1.

ψ1, Ozolian *psi* (**2, 3, 4a**), occurs also in Arkadian (p. 207).

*Punctuation.* 1 occurs in both mainland areas (**3, 4a, 8**); 2 once, on the *verso* of **2**; 3 in E**3. 2, 7** and E**1** are the only examples of *boustrophedon*, **7** being 'false' (pp. 49 f.). There are as yet no examples of proper *stoichedon*, though E**3** shows it in part.


## OZOLIAN LOKRIS

The scripts of the two Lokrides betray their origins fairly clearly. That of Ozolian Lokris corresponds in general with Phokian, except in two points: (*a*) that *qoppa* was sometimes (not always) used (cf. **2** and **3**), and (*b*) that a rare form of *psi*, ψ1, was also in use. This has not yet been attested anywhere else in central Greece, but is found in Arkadian (pp. 213 ff., where it is suggested that the form may possibly have come from one of the towns of Achaia, which lay between Lokris and Arkadia). The earliest inscription is perhaps the gravestone of Charilaos found at Tritea (**1**); and we may note that *rho* is in the late archaic tailed form 3, which suggests that it should not be earlier than *c.* 525. Then follows a series of three bronze plaques all bearing legal texts. The first (**2**) should be earlier than the fifth century, for it is written *boustrophedon*; there is no *qoppa*, *heta* is 2, *chi* both 1 and 2, *upsilon* 2; the main text (A) may belong to the last quarter of the sixth century, the addition (B) on the back being perhaps some few years later than the first.[1] The plaque was said by one informant to have come from the area of Naupaktos; by another, from Psoriani in Aitolia, over the border. Thus both reports agree that it came from the western end of Ozolian Lokris, though some scholars have suggested that it deals with a settlement at the place called Polis, which they would set near the Phokian border, east of Amphissa.[2] The script is Lokrian, not Aitolian; so, if the report about Psoriani should be right, the settlers will have been Lokrians who spread over the Aitolian border. The law defines the inheritance of pasturage-rights for the families settled in an area which has already[3] been divided up into ἀπότομα and δημόσια, called 'the plain of Ὑλία and Λισκαρία'. They have already a temple to Apollo, Leto, and Artemis, and a council of elders and a citizen assembly, which suggests that these are not new settlers from another

---

[1] I have followed here the view of the first editor, Pappadakes, that the phrase κομιзοιεν–χρειзοι was omitted from the main text A at the point where A reads OIION partly erased, and had to be added on the back of the plaque. OIION looks like careless dittography, and the erasure looks deliberate. For different views and interpretations, see Wilamowitz, *Sb. Ak. Berlin* (1927), 13 ff.; Buck 59; Georgacas, *CP* 1956, 249 ff.

[2] Chatzes, *AE* 1927–8, 181 ff.; Buck 59. In his comprehensive study of Ozolian Lokris (*Les Locriens de l'ouest* i–ii (1952), Lerat argues (ii. 9 f.) that one should accept the report about Psoriani and regard this text as Aitolian, since at three points the dialectal forms differ from those of the other Lokrian plaques. The script, however, is Lokrian—unless one sees a single, stray *san* in l. 5, rather than (as I should suspect) a *mu* cut in error.

[3] As Wilamowitz observed (op. cit. 9 f.), the text gives no details about the division and distribution.

area, but members of an existing settlement who are assimilating some adjoining newly acquired stretch of agricultural land. The usual curses are called down in the law on anyone who in future demands a redistribution (δαιθμός) of this land; but it is also said that, under the dire necessity of war, if 'the Hundred and One chosen ἀριστίνδην' so vote, a maximum of 200 new settlers of military age (ἀξιόμαχοι) may be invited to settle there: half the land to go then to the new settlers. The law B, written in a different hand on the back of the plaque, defines the punishment for a demiourgos who makes unlawful profits from his office.[1] It is tempting to accept the report that this text came from the district of Naupaktos, for then it can be linked with the similar bronze plaque (3) which was found many years ago on the eastern side of Lokris, at Galaxidi, a place formerly believed to be the ancient Oianthea, but now more plausibly identified with Chaleion.[2] This plaque 3 carries the laws defining the political relationship between an ἐποικία sent to Naupaktos and the two places which sent out the ἔποικοι, Opountian Lokris and Chaleion. Judged by their letters, the two plaques should not be far apart in date. 3 is not *boustrophedon*, but shows *qoppa* still; it might belong to the first quarter of the fifth century. Though we happen to have the copy made for Chaleion, the body of its text concerns simply the new Naupaktians from Opountian Lokris and their mother-state; only at the end is a clause added to say that 'all the above applies also to the Chaleian settlers who came out with Antiphates'. But the script is not Opountian Lokrian, and so the three copies needed may have been made by a bronze-worker among the Lokrians already living in Naupaktos. Was this fresh influx to Naupaktos the 'additional settlers up to 200', foreshadowed in the law on plaque 2 for the unidentified settlement? At all events, the new Naupaktians will not have long enjoyed their change, since presumably they were evicted *c.* 460 by the Athenians, and their site occupied by others no less ἀξιόμαχοι, the exiled rebels of Messenia (Thuc. i. 103). A third plaque (4), also from Galaxidi, bears the text (A) of a συμβολή between Oianthea and Chaleion, establishing the rights of the Chaleian or Oianthean ξένος against seizure in the other city.[3] Though some editors have dated it in the second half of the fifth century, it should from its lettering be only a little later than 3; cf. its γ3 (abnormal in Lokrian), ε2–3, θ2–3, λ1–2, ν1, χ3. The following text (B), in a different hand, shows throughout ε3, θ3, λ2, ν3, and may well belong to the third quarter of the century; it is clearly an addendum, legislating against unjust proxenoi, for alien plaintiffs in legal cases, and for citizens involved in δίκαι ἀπὸ συμβολῶν.

After these legal texts, the only remaining inscriptions from Ozolian Lokris are the dedication of the demiourgos Euphemos and his colleagues on a bronze vase-handle from Galaxidi, probably about the middle of the fifth century (5), and the gravestone of Nikarchos of Amphissa, probably also of the fifth century, judged by the type copy (6). A miniature bronze wheel now in Boston (17), bearing a dedication by one Phalas to Apollo, was said to have been found at Galaxidi; but the script is not that of Ozolian Lokris. It

---

[1] This sentence was held by Wilamowitz to be the tail end of another law cut on a separate plaque; op. cit. 11.    [2] Lerat, op. cit. i. 198 ff.
[3] I follow here the interpretation tentatively given by Tod, *GHI²* 34, taking τον Οιανθεα in apposition to τον ξενον: 'No one shall carry off the Oeanthian stranger from the territory of Chaleum nor the Chalean from that of Oeanthea. . . .'

shows λ3 and σ2, and, with its crooked *alpha*, should belong to either Boiotia or Opountian Lokris. If the provenance is correct, it may be a dedication made by an Opountian in the other Lokris. The lettering suggests a date in the third quarter of the sixth century; *rho* is still 1, but *sigma* is already the three-stroked type 2. (See Addenda.)

No Attic or Messenian inscriptions have yet been found on the site of Naupaktos; see further pp. 204 f.

OPOUNTIAN LOKRIS

The script of Opountian Lokris is the same as those of its neighbours Boiotia and (as far as it is known) Chalkis. The two earliest examples are dedications from the akropolis at Halai. The first (7) is inscribed in false *boustrophedon* on three of the vertical faces of a block which has a narrow rectangular cutting for a tenon on one horizontal face. If this face is taken as the top of a base (as the editor does),[1] the first line of the inscription is upside down; so the block is perhaps more likely to be the crowning member of a pillar, with a mortise on its underside whereby it was set upon a lost shaft as thick as itself, on which possibly a flat figure (of a kore?) was carved in relief or incised, like the lower halves of such figures later found on this site.[2] The dedication shows σ1, as in the earliest Boiotian, and the second line has to be read upside down, like that on the grave-stele of Deinias from Corinth (Corinth **6**, p. 127): Ευϝανδρος μ' ανεθēκε [τυπ ?]ον Ͳερι[κ]αλεα Ͳο[ιϝ|ō]ν χερσι φιλαισιν, εδō[κε τ' Αθα]γαιαι [Ͳ]ολιοχ[ōι].[3] The lettering suggests a date not later than the first half of the sixth century. It is considerably earlier than that of **8**, a Doric capital which was once the top of a pedestal-base: Ϝασιōν μ' ανεθēκε : Διακριος μ' εͲοιϝēσα (*sic*). This may perhaps be dated *c.* 540; the flat archaic bulge of the echinus suggests an earlier date, but I do not think that the inscription could be earlier than the middle of the sixth century. I can only suggest that perhaps a provincial sculptor of Halai did not keep pace with the development of the true architectural capital (cf. pp. 159, 233). The gravestone of Minades (**9**) may be earlier than the end of the sixth century as far as can be judged from the copy. The other extant inscriptions from this area all appear to belong to the first quarter of the fifth century. Of five brief grave-inscriptions (**12–16**) the first (**12**) is on a relief stele whose style resembles that made in Boiotia by the sculptor Alxenor of Naxos *c.* 490 (p. 292, Naxos **12**); the rest are on plain stelai. The graffito of Panteles on a skyphos should be of about the same date (**10**). Lastly, a base for a marble statue dedicated by the people of Halai on their akropolis (**11**), dated by the names of three archons (cf. the similar public dedications from Akraiphia in Boiotia, p. 93), may belong to the first years of the fifth century; it shows ⊢1 and *qoppa*, but ε3 and θ3.

The script of Lokroi Epizephyrioi, the Lokrian colony in Italy, is the same as that of

---

[1] Goldman, *AJA* xix (1915), 439 f.
[2] Goldman, *Hesperia* ix (1940), 413 ff., figs. 57–58, 242. Two other stelai, that of Dermys and Kitylos from Tanagra (p. 92, Boiotia **8**) and of a 'Daedalic' head from Malessina on the Lokrian–Boiotian border (Jenkins, *Dedalica*, 71), are advanced examples of the same technique, the first being almost in the round.

[3] I suggest this restoration in preference to that of Friedlaender 45: Ευϝανδρος μ' ανεθēκε· [καμ]ōν Ͳερι[κ] αλεα κο[ρο]ν | χερσι φιλαισιν εδō[κεν Αθα]γαιαι Ͳ[ο]λιοχ[ōι]. One would expect Ϙο[ρο]ν, but the first letter cannot be *qoppa*; a kouros is not a normal dedication to Athena (unless Euandros was an athlete as well as a sculptor); and the asyndeton before καμών seems a little harsh.

Ozolian Lokris (pp. 284 ff.). This is significant, for it is not clear from the ancient authorities which of the mainland Lokrides sent out the settlement.

## SELECT CATALOGUE

### OZOLIAN LOKRIS

**1.** Gravestone of Charilaos from Tritea; *c.* 525? Lerat and Chamoux, *BCH* lxxi–ii (1947–8), 78 f. Lerat, *Les Locriens de l'ouest* (1952) i. 168. Kolopetinitza.　　　　PL. 14

**2.** Bronze plaque from near Naupaktos (?), bearing a law concerning inheritance of pasture-rights for settlers; *c.* 525–500? Pappadakes, *AE* 1924, 119 ff., pl. 3. Wilamowitz, *Sb. Ak. Berlin* 1927, 7 ff. Chatzes, *AE* 1927–8, 181 ff. Meillet, *Rev. Phil.* 1928, 185 ff. Nilsson, *Historia* iii (1954), 270 ff. Georgacas, *CP* 1956, 249 ff. NM.　　　　PL. 14

**3.** Bronze plaque from Galaxidi (Chaleion), concerning an additional colony sent to Naupaktos; *c.* 500–475? *IG* ix. 1. 334. *BMC Bronzes* 262. *SGDI* 1478. Roberts i. 231. *SIG*³ 47. Roehl³, 92. 1. *BMI* 954. *DGE* 362. *GHI*² 24 and p. 259. Lerat, op. cit. ii. 29 ff. Buck 57. BM.

**4a–b.** Bronze plaque from Galaxidi (Chaleion), concerning an agreement with Oianthea; *c.* 475–450? *IG* ix. 1. 333. *BMC Bronzes* 263. *SGDI* 1479. Roberts i. 232. Roehl³, 93. 2. *BMI* 953. *DGE* 363. *GHI*² 34 and p. 261. Lerat, op. cit. ii. 31 ff. Buck 58. BM.　　　　PL. 15

**5.** Dedication by Euphemos and colleagues, from Galaxidi; *c.* 450? *IG* ix. 1. 335. *SGDI* 1480. Roberts i. 233. Roehl³, 93. 3. *DGE* 364. NM.　　　　PL. 14

**6.** Gravestone of Nikarchos, *c.* 450? *IG* ix. 1. 326. Roehl³, 93. 4. Amphissa, church of Hagia Trias.

### OPOUNTIAN LOKRIS

**7.** Dedication of Euandros at Halai; *c.* 600–550? Goldman, *AJA* xix (1915), 438 ff., figs. 1–4. Friedlaender 45. Thebes Mus.

**8.** Dedication of Asion at Halai; *c.* 550–540? Goldman, *Hesperia* ix (1940), 428 ff., fig. 80. Thebes Mus.　　　　PL. 14

**9.** Gravestone of Minades from near Zeli; *c.* 525–500? *IG* ix. 1. 307. Roehl³, 87. 2. Peek i. 153. Lost?

**10.** Graffito of Panteles on a skyphos from a grave near Livanatas; *c.* 500–475? *IGA* 307. *IG* ix. 1. 303. *SGDI* 1493. Roberts i. 236. Roehl³, 87. 1. *DGE* 361. Friedlaender 177a. Private coll.　　　　PL. 15

**11.** Dedication by the people of Halai; *c.* 500–475? Goldman, *AJA* xix (1915), 442 ff., figs. 5–6. *DGE* 359. Thebes Mus.

**12–16.** Gravestones of Againetos, Nausiteles, Exainetos, Polydamas, Agasinos; *c.* 500–475? *IGA* 309–13. *IG* ix. 1. 291–5. *SGDI* 1491–2, 1495–7. Roehl³, 87. 4–8. *DGE* 360. **12**, a fragmentary relief stele, is illustrated (drawing only) in *AM* iv (1879), pl. 14. Once at, or near, Livanatas, Kyparission, Atalanti, Korseia.

*Inscription attributed to Opountian Lokris*

**17.** Bronze votive wheel dedicated by Phalas to Apollo; said to have come from Galaxidi (Chaleion); *c.* 550–525? Caskey, *AJA* xl (1936), 310 f., fig. 5. Wade-Gery in *Greek Poetry and Life* (1936), 64, n. 3. Lerat, op. cit., p. xi. *SEG* xvi. 336. Boston, MFA 35.61.　　　　PL. 15

## AIGINA

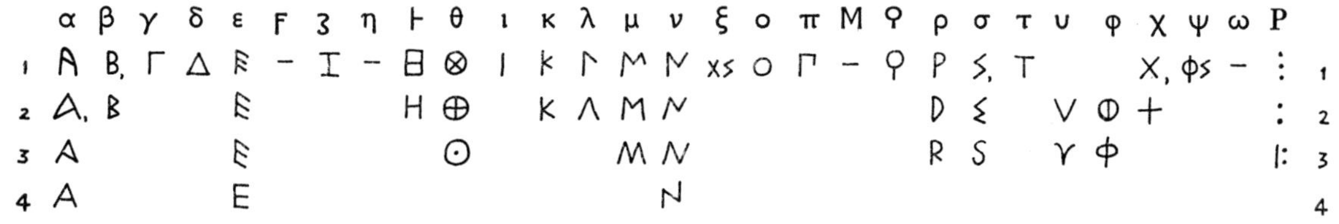

| α | β | γ | δ | ε | ϝ | ʒ | η | ├ | θ | ι | κ | λ | μ | ν | ξ | ο | π | M | ϙ | ρ | σ | τ | υ | φ | χ | ψ | ω | P | |
|---|---|---|---|---|---|---|---|---|---|---|---|---|---|---|---|---|---|---|---|---|---|---|---|---|---|---|---|---|---|
| 1 | Α | Β, Γ | Δ | ⯂ | F | - | I | - | ├ | ⊗ | I | Κ | Γ | Μ | Μ | xs | Ο | Γ | - | ϙ | Ρ | Ƨ, Τ | | | Χ, φs | - | | : | 1 |
| 2 | Δ, β | | | ⯂ | | | | | Η | ⊕ | | Κ | Λ | Μ | Ν | | | | | | Ρ | Ƨ | | V | Φ | + | | : | 2 |
| 3 | Α | | | ⯂ | | | | | | ⊙ | | | | Μ | Ν | | | | | | Ρ | S | | Υ | Φ | | | Ⱶ: | 3 |
| 4 | Α | | | Ε | | | | | | | | | | | Ν | | | | | | | | | | | | | | 4 |

FIG. 32. Aigina

*Notes on letter-forms*

α2 is characteristic. The archaic curved α1 occurs in **3** (7th c.?).

├2 is in use in graffiti *c.* 510 (**9**).

θ3 is in use before the end of the 6th c. (**6, 7**).

λ1 has developed to λ2 by the first quarter of the 5th c. (**12, 13**).

μ2 occurs in the building record of the mid 6th c.? (**4**), but μ1 in the dedication **5**; more early examples are needed before we can say which was the normal archaic form.

The Attic *xi* was used. This is attested in two of the graffiti on sherds from the precinct of Aphaia: [- - -] ευχσα[μενος ? - - -] and Αρχσινα[- - -]θε ται [Αφαιαι ?], which from their lettering may belong to the late 6th c. (*Aegina* i. 466, nos. 371, 392, pl. 121. 65–66).

*Qoppa* is used in **4** (mid-6th c.?). There are no further examples in the existing inscriptions; it may have disappeared, as in Attic, before the end of the century.

ρ1 is the early form. From the late archaic period onwards, ρ2 is very common; ρ3 occurs rarely (**12, 13**).

The normal form of *sigma* appears to have been σ1, as in Attic; but σ2 also occurs (**10**; *IG* iv. 71, 177). The curved σ3 is used in **4**.

*Punctuation.* 1 is used in **4** (mid-6th c.?), and continues in use throughout the period (**11, 12, 16**). 2 is also found in the 5th c. (**13, 15**), and 3 once, *c.* 470–50? (**18**). The *boustrophedon* system appears to have gone out of normal use about the middle of the 6th c., as in Attic, for it is no longer used in **4**; but the present material is too scanty to provide any details of its decline. One of the best examples ever produced of the erratic setting of letters in a vertical inscription is the grave-stele of Hermaios, **18** (cf. p. 50).

The alphabet of Aigina is kin to that of several neighbouring scripts, but identical with none; so that it cannot be said definitely whether she received it from one of the mainland states which shut her into the Saronic Gulf on all sides save one, or from that one open side which led out of the gulf to the Cyclades and the trade-route to the East. The closest resemblance is to Attic, from which Aiginetan differs chiefly in its forms of *gamma* and *lambda*; the next closest seems to be to Cycladic, from which it differs in its *beta* and also in having no signs for the long vowels *eta* and *omega*. The script of Epidauros, the traditional mother-city of Aigina (Hdt. viii. 46; Paus. ii. 29. 5), is not yet fully attested (pp. 179 ff.); but Epidauros certainly used a different *delta* (p. 180), and possibly *san* also, neither of which is Aiginetan. Troizen, Methana, and Hermion used the 'red' *chi*, and the scripts of Corinth and Megara belong to a wholly different group. The present evidence therefore gives some slight grounds for the conjecture that both the Aiginetan and the

Attic script are derived from the same source, namely, the route through the Cyclades from the eastern Aegean. Priority cannot be established for either; Attic may have been taken from Aiginetan, with an added element of Euboic; or possibly Aiginetan from Attic, with an added element of Cycladic; or each may have been acquired independently. But at least we can infer that both states were among the earliest on the western side of the Aegean to receive the new art of writing. Athens' proof is shown directly in her inscribed pottery, Aigina's indirectly in her early history (and perhaps directly in the plaque **1**). Doric and independent, made expert in seafaring by their geographical position, the Aiginetans carried the produce of other states to every quarter of the Greek world, shaking off their filial bonds with Epidauros (Hdt. v. 83), and apparently thriving in an atmosphere of perpetual hostility alike from Athens near at hand, and from their more distant rival Samos (Hdt. iii. 59; v. 83).

The earliest inscription which can be assigned to Aigina is a painted fragment on a sherd from a clay votive plaque, dated by the style of the warriors' heads on it to the years shortly before 700 (**1**). The style is indistinguishable from Attic, and there is nothing definitely unAttic in the few surviving letters, but I have listed it here because it was found beside the temple of Apollo on Aigina, and the letters agree with Aiginetan script (see pp. 68 f.). The next earliest inscription that can be attributed to Aigina is the name Μενελας painted on a Protoattic krater-stand of the mid-seventh century (**2**), found with other early Attic pottery on Aigina. I have observed elsewhere[1] that the provenance, the Doric form of the name, and the non-Attic *lambda* all combine to suggest that the painter was Aiginetan. That an Aiginetan should have been employed on Attic pottery in the midst of the ἔχθρη παλαιή is not impossible, for the unbroken series of Attic ware from the eighth century onwards found at various sites on the island shows that, whatever were their feelings of hostility towards each other, Aigina did not cease to have commercial intercourse of some kind with Athens.[2] A boundary stone inscribed Ϝἕρακλεος (**3**) from a precinct of Herakles somewhere in the south-eastern part of the island may also be ascribed tentatively to the seventh century; we may note the archaic appearance of the *alpha* with curved leg, and the disproportionately small *omikron*.

Several sherds of Chian ('Naukratite') chalices were found in the temple of Aphaia at Aigina.[3] The fragmentary painted dedications show in two cases the Ionic *eta* of Chios; none of the inscriptions is certainly Aiginetan. Perhaps they were inscribed by the makers for Aiginetan purchasers to dedicate in their own temple on their safe return (p. 338). In this precinct of Aphaia was also found the earliest public record of any kind from Aigina, the stone which commemorates the building and other work done in the precinct during the priesthood of a man named (Kl?)eoitas (**4**). A similar record has been found in the temple of Athena at Argos (p. 158, Argos **8**). The Aiginetan inscription was cut on a single long thin slab of soft limestone, fragments of which were later built into the foundations of the eastern terrace wall.[4]

---

[1] *JHS* lxix (1949), 26.

[2] Dunbabin, *BSA* xxxvii (1936–7), 83 ff., esp. 84.

[3] *Aegina* i (text), 478 ff., pl. 129; Price, *JHS* xliv (1924), 202 f.; Cook and Woodhead, *BSA* xlvii (1952), 159 ff. Boardman, *BSA* li (1956), 59.

[4] *Aegina* i. 367 f. The meaning is uncertain at several points: 'When [Kl?]eoitas was priest, the temple to Aphaia was [built], and the altar, and the ivory was added (= the altar was adorned with ivory plaques?), [and the treasure?] was laid up.' I suggest the last, the

The date of this inscription, if it may be compared with Attic texts, should lie in the middle of the sixth century, perhaps some few years later than 550. It cannot be as early as the seventh century, as Furtwaengler maintained.[1] Though he did not suggest a date, Thiersch, in his careful analysis,[2] observed all the features which indicate its comparative lateness: the fact that it is not *boustrophedon*, the scrupulous avoidance of divided words at the ends of lines, the competent cutting of the letters, with small-tailed ε2 and symmetrical μ2. Its best parallels in Attic are the bronze plaque of the Treasurers (p. 72, Attica **21**), the epitaph bearing the second signature of the sculptor Phaidimos (Attica **23**), and the epitaph of Phrasikleia (Attica **29**). But its provenance presents a difficulty; for the lower part (into which it was found rebuilt) of the eastern terrace wall has been dated in the third quarter of the sixth century.[3] This would mean that its original life was remarkably short. On the other hand, the upper part of this wall belongs certainly to the period *c*. 500–480[4] (shortly after the existing temple was built), and the inscription was found on the inner face of the wall, where the construction, according to the excavators, was very unequal;[5] it is possible, therefore, that the stone, though apparently belonging to the original lower part, was actually built in during the erection of the upper part. The existing temple's predecessor is held by Welter to have been built *c*. 550,[6] and probably it is this predecessor which is the οἶκος which the inscription commemorates, not (as is usually held) the little building which in its turn preceded this predecessor.[7]

The remaining inscriptions of Aigina may be briefly summarized. A rough poros pillar bears a retrograde dedication by Thales to a deity or hero whose epithet is θεβασσιμαχος[8] (**5**); the lettering indicates a date near that of **4**, perhaps early in the third quarter of the sixth century. Two stone omphaloi **8**, inscribed φρα and Προσσαριδōν, are apparently to be connected with the cults of the local phratries;[9] they may also be of the second half of the sixth century, but the lettering is inconclusive. A series of funeral inscriptions (name, or name with patronymic, rarely with εἰμί) on the walls or cover-slabs of underground chamber tombs (**10**) should belong mainly to the first half of the fifth century, though some may be slightly earlier (e.g. according to the copies, *IG* iv. 55–57, 63). The masons' graffiti on the foundation blocks of the existing temple of Aphaia (*c*. 510–500?) show ⊦2 already in use, with ε 2 and 3 (**9**). The famous school of Aiginetan bronze-sculptors which flourished in the late sixth and first half of the fifth century has left few surviving signatures; one of the few, a base signed by Glaukias at Olympia (**12**), may be

normal meaning of περιποιεῖν, as a possible alternative to the interpretation of previous editors: '[and the ?coping, precinct, etc.] was made round (it).'

[1] *Aegina* i. 480 ff.    [2] Op. cit. 367 f.
[3] Op. cit. 483; Welter, *AA* 1938, 6: '*c*. 540.'
[4] *Aegina* i. 86.    [5] Op. cit. 86.
[6] *AA* 1938, 6.
[7] Orlandini also suggests that the inscription refers to the 6th-c. temple (*Arch. Class.* ii (1950), 57 f.). I cannot be convinced by Furtwaengler's argument (*Aegina* i. 480 ff.) that the soft limestone ('Mergelkalkstein') was only used in the buildings of the 'first period' (i.e. the little building and the earliest altar), and therefore the inscription must belong to this building, which he dated

in the seventh century. Even if the use of the limestone is thus confined, a suitable block of the first building or the old altar might have been re-used for the inscription in the second.

[8] The epithet is not otherwise attested. Perhaps the Aiakidai might claim it, having been sent once to Thebes to lend divine aid to the Thebans against the Athenians in 506 (Hdt. v. 81); but their aid proved disastrous, and in any case the inscription should be earlier than this. Inscriptions from Aigina which appear to be in Boiotian script are those stamped, with devices, on three tiles published by Welter (*AA* 1938, 485 ff., nos. 5, 7, 8). They are archaic, but the meaning is uncertain.    [9] Welter, op. cit. 494.

assumed to illustrate good Aiginetan script of the period *c.* 485, for the dedication was by Gelon for a victory in 488, while he was still ruler of Gela (p. 266). In **12** the dedication is in a different script (presumably Geloan or Syracusan), but on the base of another lost work by an Aiginetan sculptor both dedication and signature are in the sculptor's script, for both show the typical α2. This is the base for a bronze bull, made by Theopropos and dedicated at Delphi by the Korkyreans (**13**): it may be slightly later than **12**. A third signature, also at Delphi, is only partly preserved (**11**): [- - -ε]ποιε ⠅ Αιγιναι; the lettering is slightly earlier again than that of **12** (cf. ε2); the name of Onatas may be suggested.[1] A bronze hydria (**16**) dedicated to Zeus Hellenios, found in a well in his precinct on the Oros, is dated by its shape *c.* 470;[2] and to this period *c.* 475–450 may belong also the altar dedicated to the Koliadai (**17**), the gravestones of the Athenian Antistates (**19**) and the Aiginetan Hermaios (**18**),[3] and the stone anchor inscribed: Μē κινε τοδε (**20**); but precise dating is impossible. We have a sure *terminus ante quem* in the year 431, when the island was occupied by an Athenian settlement, and **19** and **20** may equally well be dated 450–431. The bronze plaque (**21**) from a dedication made by Pherias, winner of the boys' wrestling at Olympia in 464, should, from its lettering, be later than that date. With ν4 and φ2, it suggests rather a time in the 440's; perhaps Pherias was already adult when he made his commemorative offering (cf. Addenda, and pp. 167, 246).

　　The script of Aigina was used by Kydonia in Crete, the city occupied by Aiginetans *c.* 519 (Hdt. iii. 59). Tombstones of the early fifth century found on the site show the typical Aiginetan script, sharply distinct from the contemporary Cretan (p. 314).

## SELECT CATALOGUE

**1.** Painted dedication on a sherd from the Apollo temple at Aigina; *c.* 710–700? Boardman, *BSA* xlix (1954), 183 ff., pl. 16, 1. Athens, BSA Coll.　　　　　　　　　　　　　　　　　　PL. 16

**2.** Name 'Menelas' painted on a Protoattic krater-stand; *c.* 650. Karo, *26 Hallische Winckelmanns-Programm* (1928), 10 ff. J. M. Cook, *BSA* xxxv (1934–5), 189 ff., 205, 208. *CVA* Berlin i. 24 f., pls. 31–33. Jeffery, *JHS* lxix (1949), 26. Berlin, Antiquarium.　　　　　　　　　　PL. 16

**3.** Boundary stone from a precinct of Herakles on Aigina; 7th c.? Keramopoullos, *AE* 1932, Ἀρχ. χρον., 6; Welter, *Aigina* (1938), 122; Jeffery, op. cit. 25 f., fig. 2. *SEG* xi. 3. Welter, *Polemon* iv (1949), 145 ff., fig. 3. Aigina Mus.　　　　　　　　　　　　　　　　　　PL. 16

**4.** Record of building on a stone from the precinct of Aphaia; *c.* 550? *IG* iv. 1580. Furtwaengler and Thiersch, *Aegina* i (text), 367 f., fig. 292, pl. 25. Roehl[3], 66. 3. *DGE* 111. Welter, *Aigina* (1938), 69 f. and *Polemon* iv (1949), 151 f., fig. 2. Orlandini, *Arch. Class.* ii (1950), 50 ff. Aigina Mus.　　　PL. 16

**5.** Poros pillar bearing a dedication by Thales, Aigina; *c.* 550–525? Peek, *AM* lix (1934), 42 f. *SEG* xi. 1. Aigina Mus.　　　　　　　　　　　　　　　　　　　　　　PL. 16

---

[1] The only extant signature of Onatas is at Athens, in Attic script (*IG* i². 503 = *DAA* 236). For part of a later copy of another, cf. Fraenkel, *Inschriften von Pergamon* i, no. 48.　　　[2] Welter, op. cit. 8 ff.

[3] In the Transliteration of Plates I assume that the wide face bearing the dead man's name begins the inscription. Previous editors read: Σαμα τοδε | ⊢ερμαιο | το Κυδōνικο το Αγριτα.

**6.** Limestone basin, dedicated to Aphaia; *c.* 550–500? *Aegina* i. 368, no. 7, pl. 25, 4. *IG* iv. 1582. Aigina Mus.

**7.** Signet ring of Thersis; *c.* 550–500? *IG* iv. 179. Furtwaengler, *Antike Gemmen* ii. 36, pl. 7, 66. *DGE* 118. Seltman, *Greek Coins*, 27. Breslau Mus.

**8.** Stone omphaloi used in the cults of local phratries; *c.* 550–500? *IG* iv. 61. Welter, *AA* 1938, 494, 2–3, figs. 21–23. *SEG* xi. 5–6. (*a*) Aigina Mus. (*b*) Lost.

**9.** Masons' graffiti on the foundations of the temple of Aphaia; *c.* 510–500? *Aegina* i. 23, 369, figs. 9, 295.

**10.** Names of the dead on walls or slabs of chamber-tombs, Aigina; *c.* 500–450? *IGA* 351, 353, 357–8, 363–6. *IG* iv. 55–58, 62–65, 70, 73, 1590. Roehl[3], 67. 9. Welter *AA* 1932, 162 f.; 1938, 497 ff.; *Aigina* (1938), 58, fig. 49.

**11.** Signature of unknown sculptor on a base at Delphi; *c.* 500–480? *FD* iii. 1. 324 f., figs. 43–44. Marcadé i. 120, pl. 23. 1. Delphi Mus. 1809.                                                         PL. 16

**12.** Signature of Glaukias on a base for a dedication by Gelon at Olympia; *c.* 485? *IGA* 359*b–c.* *Ol.* v. 143. Roberts i. 126. *SGDI* 3410. *SIG*[3] 33. Roehl[3], 68. 6. *DGE* 115. 2. See also Doric colonies 5, p. 266. Olympia Mus. 382*a–b.*                                                         PL. 16

**13.** Signature of the Theopropos on base for a bronze bull dedicated by the Korkyreans at Delphi, *c.* 480. *SIG*[3] 18. *DGE* 115. 1. *FD* iii. 1. 3 f., no. 2, pl. 1. Marcadé i. 106, pl. 20, 3. Delphi Mus. 1198.                                                         PL. 16

**14.** Stone anchor of a ship, perhaps named after Aphrodite Epilimenia, from Aigina; *c.* 475? Welter, *AA* 1938, 489 f., fig. 11. *SEG* xi. 18. Aigina Mus.

**15.** Dedication of Philostratos, Aigina; *c.* 480–470? *IGA* 354. Roberts i. 122. *IG* iv. 7. *SGDI* 3409. Roehl[3], 67. 7. *DGE* 113. Aigina Mus.

**16.** Bronze hydria dedicated to Zeus Hellenios on Aigina; *c.* 470. Harland, *AJA* xxix (1925), 76 ff., figs. 1–2. Welter, op. cit. 8 ff., figs. 3–4. D. M. Robinson, *AJA* xlvi (1942), 180. *SEG* xi. 7. Aigina Mus.                                                         PL. 17

**17.** Altar dedicated to the Koliadai on Aigina; *c.* 475–450? *IGA* 352. Roberts i. 120. *IG* iv. 6. *SGDI* 3408. Roehl[3], 67. 4. *DGE* 112. Aigina Mus.

**18.** Gravestone of Hermaios, Aigina; *c.* 475–450? *IG* iv. 47. Roehl[3], 67. 5. *DGE* 114. 1. Friedlaender 9*a.* Peek i. 56. Aigina Mus.                                                         PL. 17

**19.** Gravestone of the Athenian Antistates from Aigina; *c.* 450? *IGA* 368. *IG* iv. 50. Roehl[3], 69. 14. Friedlaender 76. Peek i. 1209. Athens, EM 10626.                                                         PL. 17

**20.** Stone anchor of a ship from Aigina; *c.* 450–431? *IG* iv. 176. Roehl[3], 69. 12. Hereiotes, *AE* 1914, 92 ff. *DGE* 117. Welter, op. cit. 489, figs. 14–15. Aigina Mus.

**21.** Bronze plaque from the base for a dedication at Olympia by Pherias of Aigina; *c.* 450? Kunze and Schleif, *JdI* liii (1938), *Olympiabericht* ii. 129 f., fig. 80. *SEG* xi. 1231. Olympia Mus.                                                         PL. 17

*Inscription attributed to Aigina*

**22.** Signature of maker, Απολλας εποιε, incised on an iron (*sic*) mirror once in the Muret collection; *c.* 500–475? *AZ* July 1862, 302 f., pl. 166. 2. I know this only from the publication, but its α2 suggests Aigina, and the other letters are all Aiginetan also.

## CORINTH

| α | β | γ | δ | ε | ϝ | ζ | η | ⊢ | θ | ι | κ | λ | μ | ν | ξ | ο | π | M | φ | ρ | σ | τ | υ | φ | χ | ψ | ω | P | |
|---|---|---|---|---|---|---|---|---|---|---|---|---|---|---|---|---|---|---|---|---|---|---|---|---|---|---|---|---|---|
| 1 | A | ⅃ˀ | Γ | Δ | B | ᚱ | I | – | ⊟ | ⊗ | ξ | K | ᒋ | M | Ͷ | ‡ | O | Γ | M | φ | P | – | T | Υ | φ | X | Ψ | – | ⋮ |
| 2 | A | Ш | C | | B | F | ⊐ | | H | ⊕ | �ϟ | K | Λ | M | ᐽ | ⊞ | | | | | R | | | Υ | ⊕ | + | Ψ | | : |
| 3 | A | ᒃ | < | | ᚱ | | | | | ⊙ | I | | Λ | | N | | | | | | ◌ | | | V | | | | | |
| 4 | | | | | E | | | | | | | | | | | | | | | | P | | | | | | | | |

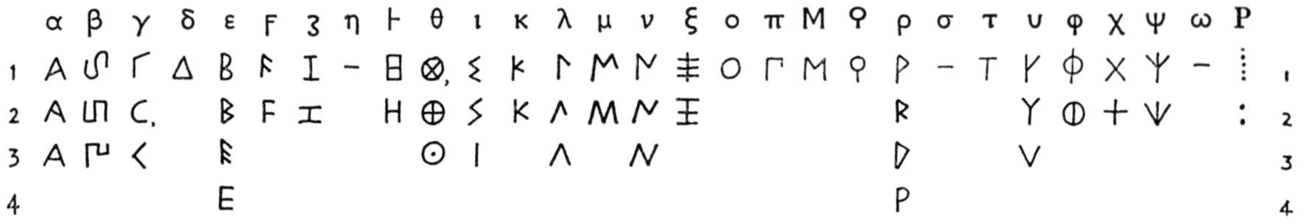

FIG. 33. Corinth and Korkyra

*Notes on letter-forms*

αι is normal in the earliest examples, but not invariable; on some of the 7th-c. vase-labels and graffiti α2 is used. In the 6th and early 5th c. α2 is the normal form. α3 is in use before the middle of the 5th c. (**37**).

The Corinthian *beta* has been called an artificial derivation from *pi*, to avoid confusion with the *epsilon*.[1] I incline to think rather that it arose from an incorrect rendering of the primitive *beta*-type in which the 'hooks' are not closed (as in Thera, Naxos–Paros, Argos, Gortyn in Crete), the lower hook of the Corinthian *beta* being twisted in the reverse direction.[2] This may have been done deliberately, because of the *epsilon*; but in Melos, where the *epsilon* is normal, the twisted *beta* is also used, and so it is perhaps more likely that it was an original error, and that the curious Corinthian *epsilon*, which I assume to be a doublet from closed *heta*, slipped into its form the more readily because there was no cause for confusion with *beta*. The proper direction should then be given by the top hook, but the distinction is not always observed (cf. the painter Timonidas, **15**). By the early 5th c. its ambiguous appearance had been solved by the extension of one vertical (β3), after the pattern of the *pi*.[3]

γ2–3 is normal; γ1 appears on **5** (*c.* 675?) and **17** (*c.* 600–550?). On the vase-label by Chares (**19**: *NC*, no. 1296) the Achaian *gamma* is used; see Fig. 42, γ1.

ε3–4 is used for the false diphthong ει; here Corinthian does not differ from other early Greek alphabets. It also used a single letter to express both the long and the short *e*-vowels, and was thus apparently at one with the majority of other Greek alphabets in making no difference in spelling between these two vowels; but the letter which it used for them was the freak form ε1–2, which some scholars have held to be a deliberate misuse of the unemployed *beta*-form, others a development from the normal *epsilon* produced by the cursive strokes of a pen or brush,[4] and others, again, a variation of the closed *heta*. I think that this last is the most likely solution: that Corinth accepted from the south Aegean alphabet

[1] Kirchhoff[4], 102; Roberts i. 134; Carpenter (*AJA* 1933, 20) holds that the *beta* was derived from the *pi*, and also suggests that this alteration was made because the Semitic form of *bêt* too closely resembled the Greek *rho*.

[2] This abnormal form occurs also in the Semitic alphabet. In the inscriptions of Shafatba'al and Abdo from Byblos the lower curve of *bêt* is turned back in the same way (Dunand, *Byblia Grammata*, 146, 152 ff.; Driver, 104, 106).

[3] I have not considered here the doubtful *betas* on two inscriptions published among the Corinthian in

*IG* iv. 354, a gold leaf seen near Corinth and hastily copied, and 357, a bronze frog said to be from the Peloponnese. 354 was read as φ[ο]ιβοι (why not φ[α]ινοι?); 357 was attributed to Corinth because the false diphthong was written in full and because of a theory that the frog was sacred to Apollo at Corinth. Αμον Σονοου Βοασονι is an unconvincing reading for 357; I take it to be a jargon inscription (not necessarily Corinthian), like the Ἐφέσια γράμματα; see *BSA* l (1955), 76.

[4] Kretschmer, *Die griechischen Vaseninschriften*, 34.

the closed *heta* which represented both aspirate and vowel, and formed from it a doublet, which was used to express the vowel, both short ε and long η. Since the difference in sound between all these vowels and diphthongs can never have been very great, it is not surprising that the Corinthians should originally have made the error of assigning to ει the E and to ε and η the B, nor that they occasionally confused the letter-forms (writing the false diphthong in full, ε+ι, and using E for the true diphthong) —nor that in Phleious, Kleonai, and Tiryns the values were shuffled, producing B = η but not ε (p. 144, Fig. 36). From the late 7th c. onwards inscriptions on vases and plaques show the shape as sharply angled (ε2) and this is also the form on nearly all the archaic stone inscriptions (perhaps because it was easier to cut); but on vases of the first half of the 7th c. it is more rounded (ε1); I have therefore used this as a factor in dating the two stone inscriptions which show this rounded form (**6, 7**), but with some reserve, since the rounded form is still found occasionally in vase-labels and graffiti of the 6th c. (cf. *AD* i, pl. 8. 15). The letter appears to have gone out of use in Corinthian during the second quarter of the 5th c. (pp. 129 f.).

*Vau* was apparently still in use at Corinth in the last years of the 5th or even the start of the 4th c. (**39**).

32 is 5th c. (**37**); there are as yet no examples to show us more precisely when this flattened type came in.

ͱ1 is usually small in proportion to the other letters (see also *theta, omikron,* and *chi*). In graffiti the change to ͱ2 (and normal size) apparently took place late in the 6th or early in the 5th c., which should give a *terminus post quem* for the appearance of ͱ2 in stone inscriptions.

θ1 is still used in formal inscriptions *c.* 480 (**29**). It is usually smaller than the other letters, particularly at the end of the 6th and beginning of the 5th c. (cf. also Argive examples).

The four-stroked ιι is regular; the type used in the south Aegean islands was always the three-stroked 2, a form which occurs in Corinthian only on vases of the LC period (575–550), and even then rarely, and on three stone inscriptions whose dates are not certain (**12, 17, 18**). But since Achaia and Korkyra, whose alphabets are presumably derived from the Corinthian, also use the three-stroked type, it is possible that (as happened elsewhere with *sigma*) the earliest Corinthian version of *iota* was simply a zigzag line which chanced to be transmitted to Korkyra and Achaia in one form, while the other happened to become the convention in Corinth itself, and persisted through the 6th c., although the LC vase-painters occasionally used the more cursive ι2, and one particular painter of round aryballoi habitually made the letter with five strokes (*NC*, 164, nos. 23–26). I have sought to show elsewhere[1] that the straight ι3 was not used in normal Corinthian during the 6th c. (as is sometimes asserted), but appears to have superseded the crooked type *c.* 500 B.C.

λ1 is still used in formal inscriptions of the first part of the 5th c. (**30, 37**), but λ2 is found in the unofficial cursive of graffiti by the end of the 6th c. (**28**).

The Corinthians, like the Ionians, used the single letter *xi* (ξ) to express guttural+sibilant. The south Aegean alphabet expressed this sound simply by *kappa+san*, but the letter-form Ξ was known in the south Aegean and used in Thera for the initial letter of the name Zeus (p. 317), in Crete for an Eteocretan sound whose exact value is not known (p. 309); perhaps the *xi* may have come to Corinth in the abecedarium, bearing a value which to the Corinthian ear seemed nearer to the guttural+sibilant than to anything else.[2] The earliest type 1 is tailed (**4**), the later tailless.

---

[1] *BSA* xliii (1948), 201 ff.

[2] The suggestion of Drerup (*Musée Belge* v (1901), 142 ff.) that the Corinthians originally used the 'red' forms X = ξ and Ψ = χ until Periander's connexions with Ionia caused them to adopt the 'blue' forms is unacceptable now, because the increased numbers of early inscriptions from Thera and Corinth clearly show that the use of Ψ for ξ in Thera (one of the chief links in his argument) begins much later than that of Ψ for ψ in Corinth; and now that Corinthian vases have been comprehensively studied we know that the 'blue' X = χ was in use long before the reign of Periander. Cf. Payne,

O was used, as elsewhere, to express both long and short vowel; but the false diphthong ου, which other Greek states normally spelt as the monosyllabic O, was spelt out in full at Corinth like the true diphthong, which suggests that in the early days of writing at Corinth perhaps the false diphthong was in fact pronounced as a dissyllable.[1] At the end of the 6th c. and later, here as elsewhere in the Peloponnese (e.g. Argos), the letter may be disproportionately small (**35**).

*San* was apparently supplanted by *sigma* some time in the first half of the 5th c. (**37–38**), but, as with the other original *san*-users, the name 'san' continued to be used for the new sign; cf. p. 33.

*Qoppa* apparently disappeared from general usage in the first half of the 5th c. (**38**), but was retained as part of the city badge on the coinage until the 3rd c. (*HN*², 403, 417); cf. *beta* on the coinage of Byzantium and *san* on the Sikyonian.

ρ2 appears in the late archaic period, and also ρ3 (**29**), which is like the type regular in Megarian. By the mid-5th c. ρ4 is apparently common, as elsewhere.

υ1 is the normal archaic type in formal inscriptions. On vases and graffiti υ2 is found as early as the 7th c. (**1, 9**), evolving in the 6th c. to the more cursive υ3 (already present in embryo on **9**), which was finally adopted in formal inscriptions also by the beginning of the 5th c. (**29**).

I have suggested (pp. 35 f.) the hypothesis that the letters Φ, Χ, Ψ may have existed in the earliest Cretan abecedaria of the 8th c., though we should then have to postulate that they had been dropped even from the abecedaria by the time that the alphabet reached Thera and Melos. It must be stressed again that this is pure conjecture; but it would provide an explanation of the appearance of these letters in the Corinthian alphabet. Neither Thera nor Melos could be compared with Corinth as flourishing centres of trade in the 8th c., and may therefore have been later in receiving the alphabet; but if the full formal alphabet arrived very early in Corinth from Crete, the Corinthians might have got φ, χ, ψ thus, and their dialect would find a practical use for all the aspirated forms. The simpler alternative is to infer that the Corinthian alphabet received these forms from a different source—one of the alphabets of the eastern Aegean, that of Samos perhaps—and grafted them on to her own abecedarium. Like *heta*, *theta*, and *omikron*, archaic *chi* is often smaller than the other letters (**9, 18**).

*Punctuation* is very rare in Corinthian inscriptions. The only instances known to me are the multiple dots (1) between the names on the early sherds from the Potters' Quarter (**1**), and a double-dot (2) on one plaque from Penteskouphia, which is not yet adequately illustrated (*IG* iv. 249) and, from the lettering, might be late 6th or early 5th c. The surviving inscriptions are admittedly either brief or incomplete; but even so, had punctuation been used at Corinth with anything like the frequency of the examples at Argos or Kleonai or Tiryns, it would certainly be seen in many of the surviving dedications on the Penteskouphia plaques.

*The order of the letters in the Corinthian abecedarium.* Two incomplete examples of the Corinthian abecedarium survive. The earliest (**2**) is a graffito on a conical oinochoe of PC style, which was found in a grave at Kyme, and has been dated in the first half of the 7th c. On the base of this vase is scratched an inscription which appears to be a later addition in Etruscan, and beneath it are the beginnings of two abecedaria, one written below the other, with a horizontal line drawn to separate them. The lower (which is the better written) is probably Kymean, i.e. Euboic (see p. 237). The upper must be Corinthian, from the unmistakable *beta*; but it is plainly by a bad scholar. Although the *stoichos* runs from left to right, like that immediately below it, the letters themselves face from right to left; there are

---

*NC*, 159. Drerup's further suggestion that ⊞ was originally a form of double sibilant *ss* (shown in the spelling ⊞ευς for Zeus in three plaques) and only received the value ξ in Periander's day was likewise disproved by Payne (ibid.), who observed that the plaques in question were later than vase-inscriptions which showed the normal ⊞ = ξ.

[1] The alternative, more intricate explanation is that the false diphthong was always pronounced as a monophthong, and that in Corinth the true diphthong very early became a monophthong also, and extended its own spelling to the false diphthong: cf. Buck, 30 ff.

omissions, and some letters are so badly shaped that their value is not clear. It begins with *beta*; then follows what is apparently meant for *gamma*, but rather resembles *lambda*, as though the writer had confused both letters. Then follow a wavering trapezoidal shape, *vau*, and another trapezoid; they may be meant for *delta*, *vau*, *heta* (central cross-bar omitted), and if so, *ei* E has been omitted, like *alpha*. The local *epsilon* may have ranked among the supplementary letters after *tau*. After *zeta* both abecedaria fail; in the last three letters they are very alike, as though one was a direct copy of the other; but which was written first is uncertain, as the oinochoe appears, from its description, to have been made in Kyme, either by an immigrant Corinthian or by a local potter copying an imported type.[1]

The second Corinthian abecedarium (**16**) is that on a plaque from Penteskouphia, which may be of the early 6th c.[2] It is complete from *ei* (E) to *tau*. The letter E occupies its normal place before *vau* in the *stoichos*, which suggests that the local ε may have been added on with the other non-Phoenician letters at the end. The other feature of interest is the treatment of the sibilants. The (unused) *sigma* is missing, *san* has been moved into *sigma*'s place, and *xi* into *san*'s. The merits of this arrangement are obvious; *sigma* was not only unused, but identical in appearance with *iota*, and would be a cause of confusion to learners; while the assonance of *mu, nu, ou, pei, xei* makes an easier mnemonic than *mu, nu, xei, ou, pei*. To shift *san* into *sigma*'s place instead of merely leaving the *stoichos* to continue *xei, san, qoppa, rho, tau* might seem unnecessary, but a parallel case of this kind of *horror vacui* appears in the early Roman alphabet, where the doublet G, instead of either following C or being added at the end of the abecedarium, was put in the place of the disused *zeta*.[3] Whether this rearrangement was made when the alphabet was first established in Corinth, or whether it was the work of some later γραμματιστής, it is impossible to tell.

*Direction of the script.* The practice of starting the *stoichos* from left to right appears in some of the earliest of the inscribed sherds (**1, 2, 3**); in fact, they outweigh the number which begin from right to left, but this may well be accidental. It may be noted, however, that where the beginnings of the early inscriptions on stone are preserved, they start from right to left without exception (**6, 7, 12, 17, 18**). It is possible that the formal art of the mason here preserved the original tradition (that an inscription should *start* always from right to left) for a considerable time after the less conventional writers had ceased to be bound by it (cf. pp. 47 f.). Three of the early inscriptions—the name-list on the skyphos-fragment from the Potters' Quarter (**1**), the pyxis-fragment from Syracuse (**3**), and the latest kerbstone from Perachora (**17**)—appear to be written in lines running consistently from left to right (**1, 3**) and right to left (**17**); but the first two are probably single lines which spiral round the body of the vase,[4] and the third I believe to be an example of 'false' *boustrophedon*, in which the letters of the succeeding lines are rolled over so as to continue in the same direction as the first line (pp. 49 f.). The system of 'false' *boustrophedon* appears also on the stele of Deinias (**6**), and is much practised in the brief two-line inscriptions on the Penteskouphia plaques and on vases (*AD* i, pl. 7. 1; ii, pls. 24. 21; 30. 10; **9**, owner's inscription on Aineta's aryballos; **19**, signature of painter Chares on pyxis). Very rarely, a name written ἑλιγμῷ on a vase may be in true *boustrophedon* (**10**, *NC* 482), but the first satisfactory

---

[1] Gàbrici, *MA* xxii (1913), 230 ff., fig. in text: 'ventre di lekythos a base conica e lungo collo (mancante) di argilla rossastra con ingubbiatura color crema.' The description of the clay and slip suggests that it was a local copy of a PC original. The longest inscription reads: ⲏιγαμενετιννυνα (retrograde), and the attempts of various scholars to make it read as Greek are unacceptable; cf. Lejeune, *REA* xlvii (1945), 102 and n. 1. I take it to be Etruscan, and to give the name of the vase's owner. For other Etruscan remains at Kyme, see Carpenter, *AJA* xlix (1945), 456.

[2] The general appearance suggests the early 6th c., but it might be anywhere in the first half of that century (I owe this information to T. J. Dunbabin).

[3] Cf. Schmidt, *RE*, s.v. Alphabet, 1623; Sandys and Campbell, *Latin Epigraphy*[2] (1927), 35.

[4] As on the aryballos of Tataie from Kyme (p. 238; **3**) and the conical oinochoe from Ithake (p. 230; **1**). The name-lists on the skyphos and Aineta's aryballos obey the convention that all name-lists should run from left to right (p. 50).

example of this system is the sacral fragment from the temple of Apollo (18), which may be dated somewhere in the second quarter of the 6th c. The only other examples of which I know are the fragment of a plaque, *IG* iv. 215, whose date cannot be assessed more accurately than as late 7th or first half of the 6th c., and the second abecedarium 16, which may also be in the first half of the 6th c.

The earliest example of consistent left-to-right is the signature of the painter Timonidas on a MC plaque (*c.* 600–575; 15); here, as elsewhere, the vase-painters (and writers on papyrus?) were probably the pioneers who popularized the left-to-right style (p. 48). The earliest stone inscription which shows it is the enigmatic fragment 27, which appears to be late in the 6th c. By the first quarter of the 5th c. the *boustrophedon* system had certainly disappeared, as the Salamis gravestone shows (29). But until more inscriptions are forthcoming, the date of its disappearance cannot be stated more accurately than 'middle or second half of the 6th c.'.

The alphabets employed throughout the north and north-east Peloponnese (excepting only the coastal cities of the eastern Argolid) are all variations on a common theme which may have been derived ultimately from the Doric islands of the south Aegean (pp. 42, 310). These Peloponnesian variations differ somewhat in detail, both from each other and from their common source; but the mutual resemblances (abnormal *beta* forms, crooked *iota*, use of *san*, and the *epsilon–eta* complication: see *Notes* above) suggest that the south Aegean script was introduced into one or two of the Peloponnesian cities, and radiated thence, with divers alterations, over the whole collection of states in this part of the peninsula, which had had close dealings with each other, whether friendly or hostile, from early times.

Within this area, as the text-figs. 33–37, 42 show, there are no two local alphabets which can be called identical, except perhaps those attested for Tiryns and Kleonai. They are here separated into three groups by the following criteria:

The Corinth group (= Corinth, Sikyon, Megara, Phleious, Kleonai, Tiryns) all show a particular connexion with each other in the use of an odd vowel-letter for *epsilon/eta*; 'twisted' *beta* (p. 114) is also confined to certain of its members. The Argos group (Argos, Mycenae) use a different form of *beta*, 'curved' *delta*, and a peculiar *lambda*. Achaia, while using the crooked *iota* and the *san*, differs from both the other groups in using the 'red' forms for *xi* and *chi*.

One reason for the individual differences is, I think, geographical. Nearly all these states have land frontiers which at some point touch those of another state using a quite different alphabet. Megara touched Attica and Boiotia; Sikyon bordered (narrowly, it is true) on Arkadia, and was also open to influences across the gulf; Achaia bordered on Arkadia and Elis; Phleious on Arkadia; Argos on Arkadia and the eastern coastal cities. Corinth alone was unaffected, surrounded by Sikyon, Phleious, Kleonai, and Megara; and Corinth's is the script which has, in sum, the greatest number of likenesses to that of the south Aegean 'Primitives': *beta, delta, iota, san*, and perhaps also the use of *heta* for both vowel and aspirate (see pp. 114 f.). This may mean that the south Aegean alphabet came first into Corinth and spread thence to the other members of the north and north-eastern Peloponnese; and that, in proportion as these latter had contact with other local alphabets, so the type which took root in each shows certain variations from the Corinthian;

thus Argos uses the *delta* and *iota* of Arkadia and the eastern Argolid, Achaia the *xi* and *chi* of Arkadia and Elis, Megara the *iota* and *sigma* of Attica or Boiotia or even Aigina, and so on. On the other hand, we must note that an alphabet very close to the Argive occurs on pottery, apparently of some East Greek fabric, found in the Dodekanese at Rhodes and Kalymna (pp. 153 f.). Argos may then have got her script independently of Corinth, both being varieties of the same south Aegean script.

It is possible that Corinth was the first receiver of the alphabet in these parts. The policy of commercial expansion pursued by the Bacchiad prytaneis in the late eighth and early seventh centuries sent the Corinthians eastwards on trading expeditions as well as westwards to colonize. The shape and decoration of Protocorinthian pottery show that her trade connexion with Crete existed in the second half of the eighth century, and grew closer in the first half of the seventh.[1] At the end of the eighth century her shipbuilder Ameinokles was making ships for Samos (Thuc. i. 13), and Protocorinthian ware has been found there and in every main port of the south-eastern Aegean.[2]

Whether this (south Aegean) Corinthian–Argive version was the first alphabet to arrive in the Peloponnese, anticipating the other types used in Lakonia, Elis, Arkadia, and the east Argolid, there is as yet no way of telling. From Corinth's pre-eminence in extra-Peloponnesian affairs at this early period, it seems very possible. However that may be, the hypothesis of contamination suggested above (p. 118) makes it necessary to infer that, by the time the alphabet had spread from the commercial states to the outer fringe, the other type of alphabet existed in the adjoining states (Arkadia, Elis). The source whence Corinth herself derived her 'blue' supplementary letters *phi*, *chi*, *psi* is discussed above (pp. 35 f., 116).

Inscriptions on pottery and clay plaques, both painted and incised, provide by far the largest body of evidence for the chronological development of the early Corinthian alphabet. There are also a small number of grave-inscriptions and dedications on stone and metal, among which are two commemorating events of public importance, the Kypselid phiale dedicated at Olympia (**13**) and the epitaph of the Corinthians who fell at Salamis (**29**); whether the dedications of spits at Perachora also reflect a historic event is discussed below (pp. 122 ff.). There is also a small fragment of a sacral list of offerings (**18**). None of the stone and metal objects on which these are written shows any features distinctive enough to help in their dating. The Salamis gravestone offers a definite terminus from which to work backwards, and the Kypselid phiale gives a date within very wide limits; but apart from these two any general chronological survey must depend chiefly on the copious evidence of Corinthian pottery as dated by the accepted authorities Johansen and Payne,[3] and of the long series of clay plaques from Penteskouphia, for which (in the absence as yet of any definitive publication) Payne's work provides the latest chronological discussion (*NC*, ch. viii). See also Addenda.

From the detailed comparison of the pottery and plaques (see below, pp. 126 f.) an interesting fact emerges: that, whereas in the pottery of the Late Corinthian period (*c.* 575–550) the lettering had become noticeably smaller and more cursive, of little importance

[1] *NC*, 53, 67; Carpenter, *AJA*, xlii (1938), 69.
[2] Cf. *VS*, 88 and index, 190 f.
[3] K. F. Johansen, *Les Vases sicyoniens* (1923); H. G. G. Payne, *NC* (1931).

now in the design, on many of the plaques even to the end of the sixth century the lettering continued in the archaic tradition of tall, careful script; one has only to compare the plaque **8**, dated before 625 (*NC*, 97), with **25**, which is late sixth century (*NC*, 112, n. 4)[1] to see how little the style of the letters has altered in a hundred years. In other words, the vase-labels here, as elsewhere, show the informal script of every day, whereas for the plaques, with their dedicatory inscriptions, the formal style was evidently considered more suitable by some painters (p. 64). The reason for this is obvious: they reflect in miniature the great tradition of free painting at Corinth (*NC*, 93), for which the use of formal lettering would be natural. In any attempt to date other inscriptions, therefore, the series of dated plaques gives precise evidence for the contemporary formal script; but since this evidence shows that no marked changes in the letter-forms occur until the start of the fifth century, we are not much better off in our search for criteria; the difference between a short stone inscription of the seventh century and one of the late sixth can be seen only in such details as the *ductus* of the lines (the earlier being straggling and uneven), or small differences within the same letter-form. The discovery of more material to swell the present number of inscriptions on stone, whose meagreness does scant justice to the size and importance of ancient Corinth, will obviously lessen the difficulty. Meanwhile it must be remembered that the plaques are not the only datable evidence for the conservative tendency of the Corinthian script; the archaic lettering of the Salamis gravestone **29**, whose date is happily beyond question, offers final and convincing proof.

According to the present dating of Corinthian ware, the Oriental influence first appears in the second half of the eighth century;[2] whether it came by Crete or by another intermediary, it reflects that contact with the trade-routes of the south and east Aegean which must have brought the art of writing to Corinth. A date in the eighth century has been suggested for two sets of inscriptions, with which we may therefore begin our survey.[3] The first is the set of three sherds (A–C) found in the Potters' Quarter at Corinth in 1930 (**1**), which are still the subject of controversy. All are from plain glazed cups; C has four letters from a graffito, almost certainly the owner's name (e.g. [Προκ]λεος [ειμι ?]). A and B, both from the same cup, bear part of a list of names incised within zones round the body. A and C were found in a bedding of broken pottery laid for a drain, B elsewhere on the site; the excavator claims[4] that they belong to the second half of the eighth century on the grounds (1) that the sherds are of typical Corinthian Late Geometric fabric, and the rest of the bedding consisted entirely of such Late Geometric ware, among which were

---

[1] Even better examples for the second half of the 6th c. are the wooden plaques from near Sikyon, not yet published; cf. Jeffery, *BSA* xliii (1948), 207, n. 3; *AGA*, 85.

[2] The absolute chronology proposed by Payne and Johansen has since been criticized on the grounds that it is too high to fit the chronology now being evolved for the early pottery of south Italy and Sicily, on the one hand (A. Åkerström, *Der geometrische Stil in Italien* (1943), 32 ff.), and that of Cyprus, on the other (E. Gjerstad, *Swedish Expedition to Cyprus* iv. 2. 208, n. 1, 425). I am not qualified to judge if these doubts

are justified, and therefore follow the Johansen–Payne chronology throughout, only noting the occasional vases whose inscriptions do not appear to fit that chronology. Cf. further the discussion by Dunbabin, *The Western Greeks*, 435 ff.

[3] Single signs appear on the bases of two conical oinochoai and the inside of a cup from a Geometric stratum at Perachora (*Perachora* i. 66, pl. 123. 9–11). They are presumably potters' or owners' marks, but not necessarily letters.

[4] A. N. Stillwell, *AJA* xxxvii (1933), 605 ff.; *Corinth* xv. 1 (1948), 12.

uninscribed fragments of similar skyphoi; (2) that the drain which sealed the deposit was from its position earlier, perhaps much earlier, than the fifth-century house beneath whose floor it chanced to lie. The late-sixth-century date which was proposed as an alternative[1] rested on the arguments (1) that, until the drain can be proved to be eighth century, the sherd-bedding cannot be regarded as a closed deposit; whenever it was laid, the numerous disused dumps in the Potters' Quarter could easily provide a homogeneous bedding of eighth-century fragments into which a few later strays filtered during the laying-down; (2) that two of the names listed, Amyntas and Angarios, could not be earlier than the sixth century; and (3) that the letter-forms themselves were characteristic of the late sixth century.

Neither the bedding-sherds nor the inscribed set have yet been fully published, but a significant observation has already been made concerning their style:[2] that traces of a triple band of added colour on C may suggest a date well down towards the middle of the seventh century, and that the expert use of incision on AB (stressed by the excavator also) is hardly to be expected of a potter before that century.[3] There can be no doubt that the potter himself wrote the list, even if the cup was not re-fired afterwards; it was set upside down on the wheel, the zones were incised as it revolved slowly, and the names were then added while the vase was still upside down, the lowest zone at the rim being probably filled first, and so upwards to the *vacat* at the top; the whole was done with a fine-pointed instrument so expertly handled that the glaze has been scarcely chipped, and the writing must have formed an effective decoration. Perhaps it was a way of listing the members of some club (cf. that at Sikyon, **8**); or perhaps the cup was (part of?) a present given to somebody by a collection of people.

Since the drain may have been laid at any time before the fifth century, and the names give little help historically,[4] the date can only be decided by the fabric and style of the sherds, and the lettering. The final verdict on the fabric—Geometric or Subgeometric?— must be left to the experts. If it is demonstrably of the eighth century, then the graffiti should be also. If it extends into the seventh century, then the graffiti have good parallels in the inscribed cups from Hymettos and the Athenian Agora, whose single-line inscriptions also run sometimes from left to right (Attica **4**, **5**d). As for the lettering of AB, its α and ε have some likeness to those of the very early seventh-century fragment from Syracuse (**3**), its υ to that in the name-list on Aineta's aryballos, *c.* 625 (**9**); it is less like the vase-labels and graffiti of the sixth century. I therefore list these fragments under the date '*c.* 700', a fence from which the epigraphist may ultimately climb down on one side or the other.

---

[1] R. Carpenter, *AJA* xlii (1938), 58 ff.

[2] R. S. Young, *Hesperia*, suppl. ii (1939), 227, n. 2.

[3] Practised incision (as against the very rare examples of its usage on early Orientalizing ware) comes in with the early BF style at the start of the 7th c.; Payne, *Protokorinthische Vasenmalerei* (1928), 12 f. and *NC*, 7.

[4] The arguments used by R. Carpenter (n. 1) are that *Amyntas*, the title given to the Macedonian 'protector' of the Chalkidic peninsula, would come into Corinthian circles only after the foundation of Poteidaia, and *Angarios*, which resembles the Median Aggares from a conjectured Aramaic form *\*aggara*, only after the Greeks had come into contact with the Persians. But Amyntas, 'protector', may be a personal name quite independent of any connexion with an official title (cf. Archon), like any of the other names formed from the root αμυν- (Fick-Bechtel, 56 and Pape-Benseler, s.v. Ἀμύντας): while Angarios might conceivably be from a non-Greek language other than Median; what of the Ancus, Ancharius, &c., of the natives of Italy?

The three spit-dedications I–III from Perachora (**7, 12, 17**) have also been cited as possibly eighth century;[1] this is an inference drawn from the original publication, in which a *terminus ante quem* of *c.* 650 was proposed from the archaeological evidence, and a closer date in the beginning of the seventh century was suggested on historical grounds, with the possibility (stressed as uncertain) that II, the most archaic in looks, might be still earlier.[2] Since these dedications are, by their nature, involved in the vexed question of the date of Pheidon of Argos, they are here discussed more fully than would be justified were it simply a question of arguing whether the eighth-century date can be correct. It will be recalled that they are parts of three limestone dedicatory stelai which were later reshaped and used as kerbstones (κρατευταί) round an ashpit altar in the floor of the temple of Hera Limenia, where they were found *in situ*, the altar still full of fine ash; the fourth kerb (of hard schist, which possibly replaced a worn limestone predecessor) had beneath it two fragments of a Middle or Late Protocorinthian kotyle (*c.* 675–640?), and traces of ash round it; whereas the floor under and round the limestone kerbs was bare; the ash in the altar contained 'two or three sherds; these appeared to be either Protocorinthian or archaic Corinthian, but were not distinctive or exactly datable'.[3] It was concluded, therefore, that the existing ash in the pit accumulated after the limestone kerbs had been laid down, but before the schist block was laid; which, from the sherds beneath the schist and in the ash, would give a *terminus ante quem* of *c.* 640 for the re-use of the limestone stelai; and a further reason for dating this re-use about the middle of the seventh century was the conclusion that, since the earliest existing roof-tiles were dated *c.* 650, and the temple itself was demonstrably earlier, a tiled roof had at this time replaced a previous thatch, perhaps destroyed by fire, and that in this time of restoration the pit was cleared and the kerbs laid down. Thus the date of the original dedications would be earlier than the mid-seventh century; perhaps many years earlier, since there was no reason to suppose that the stelai were cut down for re-use shortly after their erection.

This argument must rest on the assumption that, when once the last kerb (the schist block) had been laid, none of them was moved thereafter, nor was the pit cleaned out again; which seems to me impossible. The temple was in use until the fourth century at least,[4] and, since no other altar was found and there was still ash in the pit at the end, it is to be concluded that it continued in use throughout the period.[5] No pit would hold the amount of ash produced in the passage of over 250 years; furthermore, the slope of the site from east to west meant that the temple precinct was subject to floods in rainy seasons, so that the temple-dumps were washed away and scattered,[6] which must have meant that the whole temple floor had sometimes to be cleaned up for that cause alone. The only practical way to clean out the pit would be to roll back one or more of the kerbs each time. Hence it seems to me to be impossible to regard the sherds in the ash as evidence for dating, and most unlikely that the schist block was never moved throughout the period. When we recall the scattered state of the temple-dumps, with their mass of early pottery, it is not surprising that the sherd or two which strayed under the block on the last occasion

---

[1] Friedlaender 10; *SEG* xi. 223; *AGA*, 17.
[2] *Perachora* i. 257, 262 f.      [3] Op. cit. 112.
[4] From the dates of some of the dedicatory graffiti; cf. *Perachora* ii. 393 ff.

[5] Examples of post-archaic ashpit altars occur at Kos (cf. *Perachora* i. 111 f.) and at Samothrace (*Hesperia* xix (1950), 5 f.).
[6] *Perachora* i. 116 f., 119.

when it was moved happened to be of early date. In my opinion, the only practical clue of this kind which we have is that enough time elapsed between the first laying-down of the kerbs and the final disuse of the altar (after the fourth century) for the limestone edges to become very worn from the friction of the iron spits on which the roasting victims were turned.

The nature of the original dedications was proved in a detailed analysis by the first editor, which showed them to be vertical stelai, each with an unworked butt-end for insertion into a socket or the ground, and one (**17**) bearing traces of the cutting for a clamp which had held a bundle of spits vertically against the stele. **12** may preserve the full length, but **17** and **7** were shortened for their re-use; all were apparently sliced in half longitudinally. This explains, I think, the position of the last three letters [- - -]λαι of **17** (Pl. 20). The dedication began from right to left at the right lower edge, ran up to the top (where the tops of the spits may have projected above the stone), down the opposite edge, and finally overlapped on to the front edge again. It is most unlikely that, had the dedication finished, but for three letters, in a single line at the lost right upper edge, the mason would have gone right to the bottom again for the tail-end; he would have cramped them in somewhere near the end of the main line.[1]

The opening words of **17**, Δραχμα εγō Ⱶερα λευϞ[ōλενε - - -], identified the offering as a drachma, i.e. a set of six spits,[2] and, taken in conjunction with the early seventh-century dating, this suggested that these offerings were dedications made in the Heraion at Perachora at the same time as the similar offerings of Pheidon in the Heraion of Argos, when iron spits ceased to have the value of currency. But it has now been shown by W. L. Brown that the traditional attribution of the first Greek (Aiginetan) coinage to Pheidon was almost certainly the invention of Ephoros in the fourth century, not an historical fact; Aiginetan coinage did not begin before the end of the seventh century; so that, if Pheidon in the first half of that century (on the orthodox dating) dedicated some spits in the Argive Heraion, he was offering either the currency of the time, or spits for use.[3] On the epigraphical side I would strongly support this view, having long felt that Pheidon's famous dedication has exercised undue influence over the interpretation of all other examples of spit-dedications. That every temple included 'drachmai' of spits among its cooking utensils needs no stressing,[4] and presumably they were the gifts of individuals no less than were the other ἱερὰ χρήματα—valuable gifts, moreover, from the amount of iron in them. The fourth-century temple inventory of ἱερὰ χρήματα of a Heraion found at Chorsiai in Boiotia,[5] which includes sets of spits and cauldrons among the other utensils, still uses the

---

[1] Cf. p. 75, Attica **34**.

[2] Dr. J. G. Milne suggested (*CR* lviii (1944), 18 f.) that the dedication may have been one of the new 'drachma' coins introduced by Pheidon. I cannot believe that a stele of this size held one small coin.

[3] *Num. Chron.* 1950, 177 ff.; cf. R. M. Cook, *Historia* vii (1958), 257 ff.

[4] Cf. the examples cited in *Perachora* i. 259–61; also *IG* ii². 1425B, 404, 407. Herodotos has an interesting note on the μάχαιρα, ὀβελοί, and λέβης used in the Greek temple (ii. 41).

[5] M. Feyel and N. Platon, *BCH* lxii (1938), 149 ff. One cauldron and one bundle (δαρχμά) of spits evidently formed a set: ll. 4–7, λέβετες τριάκον|τα πέντε, ἐχῖνος, ὀβελίσσκω|ν δαρχμαὶ τριάκοντα πέν|τε: ll. 25–26, λέβετες| τρίς, ὀβελίσκων δαρχμαὶ τρίς: ll. 26–27, λέβετε (*sic*) δύο, ὀβελίσκω|ν δαρχμαὼ δύο. I can see no reason for taking these as the relics of early currency-dedications (as the editors, op. cit. 162 f., and M. Guarducci, *Riv. Fil.* xxii–iii (1944–5), 177). The number of spits is high, but so is that of other items (ll. 22 f.: κλιντῆρες πεντήκοντα, l. 24: τρεπέδδαι τριάκοντα) in the lists of ordinary utensils

term δαρχμαὶ ὀβελίσκων for the bundles of spits, so that it might have been used on the Corinthian stelai without any monetary significance. Nor do I see why (as is generally inferred) the dedication of Rhodopis-Doricha at Delphi had necessarily a similar significance (p. 102).[1] She wished to make a memorable gift; may it not have been the size and quantity which made it so?

It seems therefore quite likely that the dedications to Hera Limenia were actual temple furniture; after the racks in which they were offered had proclaimed the donors' piety for a suitable time they were re-used as κρατευταί, and thereafter saw long service until the temple and altar were disused. If this is so, there is, again, nothing to date them closely within the archaic period except their letter-forms. It was observed by the editor that **7** has particular features which suggest that it is the earliest: the *ductus* is straggling, *upsilon* has a curve, *delta* is uncertain, *epsilon* has not yet the sharp angles of the later examples; it should, on these grounds, be earlier than the formal writing on the earliest plaque (**8**; 640–625?), but there is no earlier formal writing with which to compare it except perhaps that of the Aigina pyxis in the second quarter of the century (**4**), and that of the Deinias stele (**6**), in both of which the *epsilon* has still the rounded form (p. 115 above). The dedication may have read something like the following:

[–◡◡– παιδες με ανεθεν· τυ δε ποτνια Ϝερα]
[ε]υμενεοι|σα Ϝυποδ[εξαι ◡– τοδε αμενφες αγαλμα].

**12**, the next oldest, may be some decades later—that is, *c.* 625 if we set **7** very tentatively *c.* 650. The lettering of **12**, badly damaged though it is, has some general resemblance to the tall, regular script of the Early Corinthian vases and the plaques from Early Corinthian onwards. It has also the particular feature of the three-stroked *iota*, a simplified form which in the dated sequence of the vases first appears in the Late Corinthian period (*c.* 575–550) on a few examples.[2] It does not appear on any of the plaques throughout the archaic period, but in stone inscriptions it occurs on the Perachora dedications **17** and **12**, and on the list of offerings from the temple at Corinth (**18**), the letter being reversed in all three instances. Until more archaic material is available, it is hardly justifiable to pin any faith to the three-stroked *iota* as a criterion of date; it was the regular form in Korkyra, and, for all we know to the contrary, these particular inscriptions might have been cut by masons from that region, or the dedications at least made by Korkyreans, from whose copies the Corinthian masons worked. That it does not occur on vases before the Late Corinthian period may prove to be significant; but one would hesitate on those grounds alone to bring all three inscriptions down to *c.* 575–550. I do not think that we can go farther than to say that **12** might equally well be late in the seventh century or anywhere in the first third of the sixth; and that **17**, whose finer limestone, better condition, and smaller lettering, all point to a date after **12**,[3] might be anywhere from *c.* 600 to the mid-sixth century.

and furniture in which they occur. This view is suggested independently by Brown, op. cit. 191, n. 62.

[1] Hdt. ii. 135: Athen. 596: Plutarch, *De Pyth. Or.* 14. Cf. Karo, *J. Int. Arch. Num.* x (1907), 289 f.;

Pomtow, *RE*, suppl. v. 74 ff., no. 128; *Perachora* i. 259 f.

[2] Cf. Jeffery, *BSA* xliii (1948), 203, n. 2.

[3] *Perachora* i. 257.

The reading of **12**, in its battered state, is uncertain; it may perhaps have originally carried two lines, as has been suggested of **17** (p. 123).[1]

There are also two graffiti in Corinthian script from the West, dated *c.* 700–675 by the style of the pottery on which they are written. One is the fragmentary Corinthian alphabet **2**, incised above its equivalent (in Euboic script) on the base of a conical oinochoe from a grave at Kyme (Kyme **1**; see pp. 116 f.). The other graffito is that on a pyxis fragment from the Athenaion at Syracuse (**3**). I think that this inscription is undoubtedly in the Corinthian alphabet; it was probably incised in a single spiral round the body of the pyxis from left to right, and appears to read: [- - -]παρε̣ [- - -]ανκλασε̣[- - -]. It is possible that this fragment should be classed among the Syracusan inscriptions; if so, it is the only piece of evidence yet to suggest that the Syracusans ever used the Corinthian alphabet, and as evidence it loses a little value by being written on an object itself from Corinth. It is true that virtually all our other examples of Syracusan script are dated only from the late sixth century onwards (pp. 264 f.), but in view of the fact that the other western colonies which used their mother-alphabets continued to use them well into the fifth century, it is hard to believe that the Syracusans once had the Corinthian but forsook it; and I have concluded therefore that this pyxis was already inscribed before it left Corinth.

With the Protocorinthian pyxis found in Aigina (**4**) we reach somewhat firmer ground. The style of its drawing is dated provisionally in the second quarter of the seventh century; the fragmentary labels are painted in large, careful letters occupying the available field-space to the full.[2] The circular base was evidently quartered like a wheel, and between the four spokes more letters were inscribed—perhaps the names of four people, though only δεια and ξε remain. ει should be noticed, and also the archaic ξι; by *c.* 625 *xi* has lost its tail in painted inscriptions, according to the names on Aineta's aryballos (**9**).

In speaking of inscriptions earlier than *c.* 650, mention should be made of one of the list of inscribed Protocorinthian vases given in *NC*, 38,[3] the ovoid aryballos from Megara

---

[1] If this is so, tentative restorations on the following lines may be made:

**12**: [Δραχμαι ταιδε - - - - - - - - - - ματρος ?]

Ορσιας ποταγοντο θεαι λευϙολενōι [Ⱶ]ε̣ρα̣[ι].

The disappearance of all the other halves could be accounted for by the following hypothesis: **12**, split longitudinally, was used for the two long sides of the altar; a suitable length was cut off **7**, halved, and used for the short sides, the remaining stump being thrown out or re-used elsewhere. After many years one-half of **7** broke up and was replaced by a section of **17**, the rest of which was re-used or thrown out; and later again, one-half of **12** broke up and was replaced by the schist block, there being now no more archaic disused stelai to serve the purpose.

[2] The only names restored so far are those of the horses Θοας and Δ[ιας], and the man preceding them Τ̣ε̣λ̣ε̣[σ]τ̣ροφο̣ς. The names of the riders in the chariot (Amphiaraos and Eriphyla?), were probably written in the field by the heads of the figures, and the letters running into the wheel will then be the name of a figure following the chariot, [- - -]μαιναϙ[ο - - -].

[3] Of the other inscriptions mentioned in this list, that from the Argive Heraion is discussed on p. 139 (Sikyon). The inscriptions on the Chigi vase are not in the Corinthian alphabet (p. 264). The pointed aryballos inscribed on the handle απλουν may be compared with the two examples illustrated *NC*, fig. 8, A and B, pp. 22 ff., which are described there as a late continuation of the PC style found in association with Corinthian at Selinous and elsewhere. The date may then be round about the third quarter of the 7th c. Though the equation Απλουν = Απολλον suggests the Thessalian dialect (cf. Pottier, *Vas. Ant. Louvre* ii. 469; Lejeune, *REA* xlvii (1945), 97 ff.), an inscription painted on a vase of Corinthian fabric and showing no non-Corinthian letters is more likely to be Corinthian than Thessalian; probably a syncopated version of the owner's name, Απλουν[ιος ?], as Lejeune suggests.

Hyblaia bearing on its rim a painted nonsense-inscription which includes a Corinthian *beta*. It was found with Corinthian pottery, and Johansen suggests that it is a late example of its type (which, by his dating, came to an end *c.* 650; *VS*, 172, 185); the letters look so small and squared when compared with the letter-height of the other early inscriptions mentioned above, that it would be a relief to epigraphists if this particular aryballos could be brought down below the middle of the seventh century.[1] We should recall, however, the surprisingly neat lettering on the very early cup from Pithekoussai (pp. 235 f.).

The aryballos of Aineta (**9**), dated as Early Corinthian (625–600) by Payne with the proviso that it could be rather earlier,[2] is our next landmark. The painter began with large letters for the first name, but had to cramp the rest to fit into the small space available. We may note ϟ2,[3] the small *chi*, ∪2, ε2, and compare the general appearance with the plaque **8**, which Payne dated before 625. ε2 evidently remained fashionable throughout the sixth century.

Payne's catalogue of vase-inscriptions in ch. xi of *Necrocorinthia* provides a clear picture of the development of the vase-painter's script from the last quarter of the seventh to the middle of the sixth century.[4] The painted names on Early Corinthian, Payne, op. cit. (his nos. 366, 480–2, 499–500, 780), show a large, careful script, as on Early Corinthian plaques (**10** and **11**). In the following period, 600–575, the inscriptions on Middle Corinthian vases show the genesis of a more cursive style. Most of them still have the large, careful lettering; cf. Payne, op. cit., 807, 861, 996, 958 (not 998, as on his p. 163), 1196 and **14a**; but here and there the lettering, though carefully executed, is becoming proportionately smaller (cf. Payne's 1179 and the Louvre kotyle showing komasts, **14b**); in one case— 996—definitely more hurried and cursive. It is not, I think, merely the difference between good letterers and bad; the painter of 1196 was a bad letterer, but wrote his names as large as possible; whereas for the man who painted Nebris and Glyke (996) it was evidently no longer the convention to spend much care on the inscription. There can be no distinct chronological line drawn at the point of change; the change was 'in the air'. The plaques show the same variation; contrast the formal lettering of *AD* i, pl. 7. 21 and pl. 8. 25–26 with that of pl. 7. 1, 6, 17, or with the untidy writing of the painter Timonidas and the graffito dedication on his plaque (**15**).

A survey of the Late Corinthian vases (Payne, cat. inscr. nos. 21–75) shows that the monumental style of lettering has now been abandoned by the vase-painters; the labels are noticeably smaller, more rapidly written, and often untidy; the name is important now for identification only, not as a formal part of the decoration.[5] But on the plaques the

---

[1] A similar nonsense-inscription is painted round the shoulder of an unpublished globular aryballos in Paros Museum, and here again the letter-forms look much later than the early date established for this type of vase (before *c.* 700): Payne, *Protokorinthische Vasenmalerei*, 20; Dunbabin, 460, 466. 'The vase may be Cycladic, not Corinthian' (Dunbabin, by letter).

[2] *NC*, 162, 287.

[3] In *NC*, 162, n. 1, the initial *xi* of Ξευϝōν is read wrongly as the 'red' form X.

[4] The conclusions are based on the available illus-

trations of each vase as cited by Payne in his vase catalogue, *NC*, 269 ff. For some of the vases no good reproduction is available, but I think that the illustrations as a whole justify the conclusions drawn here.

[5] The lettering of the pyxis by Chares (**19**) is a notable exception; large and sprawling, it resembles EC. The painting is described as Subgeometric in style, with little or no incision (*NC*, 322). If Payne's date for the pyxis is right, the lettering must be an archaism like the rest.

formal tradition frequently persists; compare *AD* i, pl. 7. 25; ii, pls. 24. 9: 29. 22: 30. 12: 39. 12—all late in the sixth century—with the more cursive *AD* ii, pl. 29. 4, 23, and finally with the graffito of Anthesilas at about the end of the sixth century, **28**.

I have already spoken of the conservatism of the Corinthian formal script (pp. 119 f.), noting that this tendency is shown at its best on the Salamis gravestone **29**, in which the general scheme of the letters is still very archaic, although by this time the crooked *iota* had been changed to the straight, ʋɪ had become ʋ3 (a change long anticipated by the vase-painters), and the *boustrophedon* style of writing had been abandoned, as one might expect for the early fifth century. As evidence for the latter period, it is invaluable; but for the dating of the other fragments on stone and metal which must be earlier than *c.* 480 there is little to help us.

Of these, the two earliest should be the kerbstone **7** from Perachora (p. 124) and the grave-stele of Deinias (**6**), a limestone slab with a horizontal overhang at the top,[1] and the epigram cut below this. It probably carried a picture below, painted and perhaps faintly incised as well, like the seventh-century limestone stelai from Prinias in Crete;[2] for over 60 cm. of its shaft were broken off by the peasant who found it because it bore no ostensible design. The inversion of the second line is interesting; it suggests that the mason was given a copy to follow which was written in a single line from right to left, and, feeling unequal to reversing the letters of the second line unaided, he surmounted the difficulty awkwardly by cutting it in this way, in 'false *boustrophedon*', which would have been perfectly normal had the inscription read vertically. I put the date of this as about the same date as the Perachora kerbstone **7**. The kerbstones **12** and **17**, as we have seen (p. 124), cannot be closely dated, but might even come down into the sixth century.

No less difficulty besets the dating of the gold phiale from Olympia (**13**), the sole survivor of the many costly dedications made there and at Delphi by the family of Kypselos.[3] The Kypselidai who defeated Herakleia and dedicated the phiale to Zeus may either have been those sons of Kypselos who were sent out to colonize the route to the west, or the next generation, contemporaries of Psammetichos Kypselos at Corinth; the latter's downfall came early, but his cousins in the west may have remained in power for some time afterwards. I have listed the phiale here rather than in the north-western colonies

---

[1] Earlier publications describe the overhang as triangular, but on inspection of the stone it seemed to me that the right-hand slope was due only to a break, weathered smooth. A horizontal projection of the same kind occurs on archaic relief-stelai from Boiotia and Lokris; it obviously served as a frame or protection for the sculpture or other decoration on the shaft below, and matched a similar projection at the base (cf. the sculptured stelai illustrated by R. J. H. Jenkins, *Dedalica*, 71; H. W. Goldman, *Hesperia* ix (1940), 414, fig. 57, and above, p. 107, n. 2).

[2] Pernier, *Mem. Ist. Lombardo* xxii (1910–13), 59 ff., pls. 4–5; cf. Johansen, *The Attic Grave-Reliefs* (1951), 80 ff.

[3] At Olympia: (1) a gold statue bearing an epigrammatic statement similar to that of the Naxians' colossal statue at Delos (p. 292):

εἰ μὴ ἐγὼν ὦναξ παγχρύσεός εἰμι κολοσσός,

ἐξώλης εἴη Κυψελιδῶν γενεά

(Overbeck, *Die antiken Schriftquellen* (1868), 295–301); (2) a chest inlaid with ivory, Paus. v. 17. 5. At Delphi: (1) a bronze palm-tree with frogs and snakes at the root (Plut. *De Pyth. Or.* 12 and *Sept. Sap.* 21). No satisfactory interpretation of the meaning of this dedication has yet been offered; can it perhaps have reference to the hill Phoinikaion and Athena Phoinike at Corinth? (p. 128, n. 5); (2) a treasury, which originally bore the name of Kypselos himself as dedicator; but after the fall of the Kypselid dynasty the name was altered to that of the Corinthian people. A block attributed to this treasury survives, inscribed Κορɪν— apparently by a Delphic mason; see p. 102, **21**. See also Addenda.

(p. 228), because surely this superb offering was made and lettered by an expert goldsmith in the metropolis; but admittedly the point is debatable. Historically then the extreme limits for the date would be the last quarter of the seventh century, and the third quarter of the sixth.[1] Nor can the phiale itself be dated even within a half-century.[2] As for the inscription itself, as formal lettering it compares equally well with the plaque **8** (third quarter of the seventh century?), and with the late-sixth-century plaque **25**; nor, as far as I know, can it be dated by the instruments employed.[3]

We may include in this discouraging review nos. **21, 22,** and **23,** none of which seems to me more closely datable than 'sixth century'. **23,** the grave-trapeza of Patrokles, shows only that at this time Krommyon belonged to Corinth (Strabo 380). The brief fragments **21** and **22** cannot even be dated by the fine stucco which covered them, for this stucco seems to have been used over a long period.[4] A more interesting fragment is the corner of a poros block inscribed on both faces, found near the temple of Apollo (**18**); it bears part of a list of sacrifices to be offered, listed either under the months, or under the deities concerned,[5] and is the work of a mason who bevelled the edges of his stone, ruled guide-lines, and made his circles with a cutting-compass. The three-stroked *iota*, though it is the regular form in Achaia and Korkyra, is not common in Corinth. As was said above (p. 124), it is not used on any of the plaques, and on vases appears first in the Late Corinthian period (*c.* 575–550), where it occurs, together with the four-stroked type, on 17 of the 39 examples in which *iotas* are used.[6] On stone it is used here and on kerbstones **12** and **17** from Perachora. If the early date first suggested for the kerbstones is right, then the vases certainly cannot provide a *terminus post quem* for the use of the three-stroked *iota* at Corinth; even if the kerbstones are later, the evidence of the vases remains doubtful (p. 124). In the case of the sacral list, the use of fine limestone and the technical skill employed may indicate that it is later than the seventh century. If it is placed in the first half of the sixth, it cannot have belonged to the existing temple but must be assigned to its predecessor.[7]

In the battered fragment **27**[8] the *san* is still used, together with the four-stroked *iota*

---

[1] According to whether we accept the traditional chronology of the Kypselids at Corinth, 657–584 (see *CAH* iii. 764 f.), or that of Beloch followed by Lenschau (*Philologus* xci (1936–7), 278 ff.), which would give 614–541, or that of Smith (*The Hearst Hydria* (1944), 254 ff.), who suggests 622–549.

[2] Cf. *NC*, 211 f.; Smith, op. cit. 258. Luschey, *Die Phiale* (1939), 136 f., puts it late in the 7th c., but appears to derive this mainly from the 7th-c. date given to the Kypselidai; he notes that examples of this type are found as late as the 5th c.

[3] The letters were punched into the gold with a chisel, used vertically, and a ring-punch (Casson, *AJA* xxxix (1935), 513).

[4] **21,** the right-hand corner of a block, may perhaps have been from a grave-cover, the inscription running round three sides and ending something like: [ματρος εφεμ]οσυναις: for the wording, cf. *SEG* x. 440. **22,** on the shaft of a small Doric column, may have been either

dedicatory or funeral. The use of local limestone and fine stucco instead of imported marble lasted on for some time after the archaic period; cf. the series of stuccoed stelai published in *Corinth* xv. i. 63 ff.

[5] Two interpretations are possible for the first line φοινικ—; either the month Φοινικαῖος (Meritt, *Corinth* viii. i. 2), or else Athena Phoinike—or whatever deity was concerned with the hill Phoinikaion at Corinth (Dow, *AJA* xlvi (1942), 69 ff.; Will, *Korinthiaka* (1955), 143 f.).

[6] *NC* 160; cf. Jeffery, *BSA* xliii (1948), 205.

[7] The existing building is now held to date from the middle or third quarter of the 6th c.; Weinberg, *Hesperia* viii (1939), 191 ff. Traces of an earlier building have been reported (*JHS* lxxv (1955), suppl. 6).

[8] The lines apparently read: [Λα?]στρατο το Μανδ| [---]ππος α . . vετοι[---]. In the first publication (Smith, *AJA* xxiii (1919), 359 ff.) it was tentatively interpreted as the base for a grave-statue, though this means

and characteristic *epsilon*; but the *boustrophedon* system is no longer in use, and the general proportions of the letters are more uniform than any of those hitherto discussed. The date may be set very tentatively at the end of the sixth century, the *terminus ante quem* being the Salamis stone. For this period, some further clues are furnished by the vase-graffiti. In addition to that of Anthesilas already mentioned (**28**), a sherd from Perachora,[1] dated to the end of the sixth or the early fifth century, has still the local *beta*, *epsilon*, and *iota*. At about this time also the open *heta* supplanted the closed form, at least in the informal script of the graffiti; for another graffito from Perachora with a *terminus post quem* in the third quarter of the sixth century shows the closed form, whereas one from the early fifth century shows the open.[2] The closed form may well have lasted longer on formal inscriptions on stone, but none of the extant examples happens to show the *heta*. Closed *heta* occurs, however, on a bronze mirror-handle (**34**), which has also the later forms ι3 and ∪3, as on the Salamis stone; cf. *BSA* xliii (1948), 207, n. 9.

On the Salamis gravestone (**29**) the advances in lettering are ι3 and ∪3; the formally inscribed plaques of the late sixth century still have the earlier ∪ι, so that the change to the more cursive form—already well established in the vase-labels and graffiti—evidently took place in the formal script somewhere about the turn of the century. The local *epsilon*, crossed *theta*, *qoppa*, and *san* are still in use. The gravestone of Xenyllos (**30**) is of the same period, perhaps by the same hand. Other inscriptions which may be placed in the first quarter of the fifth century are those on the fragment of a bronze bowl from the Potters' Quarter at Corinth (**35**),[3] the ten-stater weight found in Attica (**36**), and the graffiti on a pyxis, a plate, and a late black-figure lekythos (**31–33**).

After the *iota*, the next local letter to disappear was the *san*. On the horos from the temple area at Corinth (**37**) the *beta* and *epsilon* remain, but the *sigma* is now in use; it should therefore be later than *c.* 480; perhaps early in the second quarter of the fifth century. Other points to be noticed are the flat 32 (there are as yet no other fifth-century examples for comparison), and the long-tailed β3; the latter form occurs also on the first sherd from Perachora mentioned above, and is apparently characteristic of the first half of the fifth century.

The inscription on the dedication which the Peloponnesian League made at Olympia after defeating the Athenians and their allies at Tanagra *c.* 458 (**38**) is generally held to be in the Corinthian script, from the use of 'blue' *chi*, the ∪ diphthong, δι and γ3, none of which are Lakonian forms.[4] If it is indeed Corinthian, the *epsilon* has now become the

---

regarding the *omikron* as standing for ∪; which would be unusual, but paralleled by the αστ∪ Ϙορινθο on the Salamis gravestone. I have taken the last six letters of l. 1 to be part of the patronymic rather than το ϙαμ[α] (ed., ibid.), because the letters read there as *san* and *mu* (?) are *mu* and *nu* (verified on the stone).

[1] *Perachora* ii. 398, no. 109.

[2] Idid., nos. 102, 111.

[3] In *Corinth* xv. i, it is observed that the bulk of the deposit in which the bowl was found appears to be datable in the second half of the 6th and the early 5th c.

(p. 115), and noted further that the vases and figurines are mostly of the first quarter of the 5th c. (p. 23). Cf. further Jeffery, op. cit. 208, n. 2.

[4] The surviving fragment is from a contemporary stone stele bearing a copy of the dedication, which was on a golden shield (Paus. v. 10. 4). The nature of the offering perhaps explains why the Corinthian script was used instead of Lakonian or Elean; the shield may have been made and inscribed by a Corinthian, since Corinth was pre-eminent in metalwork.

usual type ε4, and *qoppa* has gone—although on the coinage it survived as an integral part of the city's badge until the third century (*HN²*, 403, 417).

When *epsilon* became normal, *beta* might follow suit. The old form may, however, have lasted beyond the middle of the fifth century, for it occurs on a bronze statuette of Poly-kleitan type found at Bologna, which has been attributed both to Taras and to Selinous (**40**). The script cannot be Tarantine, and the Selinountine *beta* is different (p. 262). It seems simplest to regard the bronze as a dedication by a Corinthian at one of the Pelo-ponnesian sanctuaries, which was taken to Bologna in the post-classical period.[1] As a *terminus ante quem* we may note that a kotyle fragment from the Asklepieion at Corinth, assigned to the late fifth century, shows [Αισ]χλαβι[ōι] with normal *beta*.[2]

The *vau* evidently lasted as late in Corinth as it did elsewhere in the Peloponnese. One of the seats in the Greek theatre (re-used during the Roman period) was inscribed κορϝαν (**39**). The theatre was built, according to the archaeological evidence, in the last quarter of the fifth century, or at latest in the early years of the fourth.

The course of the Corinthian alphabet among the Corinthian colonies can be pursued, though the details are still very scanty. It is attested directly at Korkyra, at Leukas, and at Potidaia; though no demonstrably Corinthian inscriptions have yet been found at Am-brakia, Anaktorion, or Sollion (pp. 227 f.), we see in the script of Dodona the influence of Corinthian letters which must have come from Ambrakia; and a lost fifth-century inscription in Corinthian letters copied in northern Akarnania (p. 228, **8**) must have come from either Anaktorion or Sollion. It has often been remarked that the script used at Syracuse, the oldest Corinthian colony after Korkyra, is not Corinthian; and it has been further argued that Korkyra may not have received the alphabet until the time of Peri-ander, and that the alphabet at Syracuse is not Corinthian simply because *c.* 734 the Greek alphabet did not yet exist, and so the Syracusans took their script later from a neighbouring colony; and the same practice is claimed for practically all colonies founded before the end of the eighth century. I shall discuss this argument in more detail elsewhere (pp. 250 f., 263 f.), and therefore merely note here that it is not necessarily valid; Kyme, Taras, the first Achaian colonies, all traditionally founded before 700, all use their mother-alphabets, and so some other reason must be found to explain why Syracuse did not.

## SELECT CATALOGUE

**1.** Graffiti on three sherds (A–C) from Potters' Quarter, Corinth; *c.* 700? A. Stillwell, *AJA* xxxvii (1933), 605 ff., fig. 1. Carpenter, *AJA* xlii (1938), 58 ff. R. S. Young, *Hesperia*, suppl. ii (1939), 227. Rehm, *Handbuch d. Archäologie* i (1939), 196. Lejeune, *REA* xlvii (1945), 106 ff. *Corinth* xv. i (1948), 12. *SEG* xi. 191–3. Corinth Mus.                                                                                            PL. 18

**2.** Graffito on conical oinochoe of PC style from Kyme, Italy; *c.* 700–675? Gàbrici, *MA* xxii (1913), 230 ff. Ribezzo, *RIGI* iii (1920), 241 ff. *VS*, 171. Blakeway, *JRS* xxv (1935), 138 ff. Lejeune, op. cit. 102. Buchner and Russo, *Rend. Linc.* 1955, 221 f., n. 4. Naples Mus.                                    PL. 18

---

[1] If the statue is meant to show Asklepios himself, it might be possible to locate the sanctuary, since cults of the youthful Asklepios were not common. Pausanias mentions one at Phleious (ii. 13. 5), one at Sikyon (ii.

10. 3), and one at Gortys in Arkadia (viii. 28. 1). See also Furtwaengler, *Samml. Somzée*, 55 f.

[2] *Corinth* xiv (1951), 135, no. 68, pl. 51. The statuette might be from this sanctuary.

**3.** Graffito on PC pyxis from Syracuse; *c.* 700–675? Orsi, *MA* xxv (1918), 608 f. Syracuse Mus. PL. 18

**4.** Painted names on PC pyxis from Aigina; *c.* 675–650. Studniczka, *AM* xxiv (1899), 361 ff. *NC*, 98 and 161. Lejeune, op. cit. 102. Kraiker, *Aigina* (1951), 50, pl. 19. Aigina Mus.   PL. 18

**5.** Graffito on sherd from Perachora; *c.* 675? *Perachora* i (1940), 98, pl. 131, 7. *SEG* xi. 229. NM.   PL. 18

**6.** Grave-stele of Deinias, from Bartata, south of Acrocorinth; *c.* 650? Lolling, *AM* i (1876), 40 ff. *IGA* 15. *IG* iv. 358. *SGDI* 3114. Roberts i. 85. Roehl³, 41. 1. *DGE* 24. Friedlaender 2. Buck 91. Peek i. 53. Athens, EM.   PL. 18

**7.** Spit dedication on kerbstone from Perachora; *c.* 650? *Perachora* i, 256 ff., pls. 36, 132. *SEG* xi. 223–5. NM.   PL. 18

**8.** Plaque from Penteskouphia; *c.* 650–625. *AD* ii, pl. 24. 21. *NC*, 97. Friedlaender 11. Buck 92a. Berlin Mus.   PL. 19

**9.** Aryballos of Aineta from Corinthia; *c.* 625. *IG* iv. 348. *SGDI* 3121. *NC*, cat. vases 480. BM 65.12.13.1.   PL. 19

**10.** EC vases, *c.* 625–600. *NC*, cat. vases 366, 481, 482, 499, 500, 780.   PL. 19

**11.** EC plaques from Penteskouphia; *c.* 625–600. *AD* ii, pl. 24. 10; pl. 39. 1a. *NC*, 101. Berlin Mus.   PL. 19

**12.** Spit dedication on kerbstone from Perachora; *c.* 625–575? (see **7** above). NM.   PL. 19

**13.** Gold phiale dedicated by Kypselidai, from Olympia; *c.* 625–550? Caskey, *Bull. MFA Boston* xx (1922), 65 ff., figs. in text. *NC*, 161, 211 f. Casson, *AJA* xxxix (1935), 513. H. Luschey, *Die Phiale* (1939), 87, 102, 133 ff. *Perachora* i (1940), 151, 10. H. R. W. Smith, *The Hearst Hydria* (1944), 258. *AGA*, fig. 18. *SEG* xi. 1201. Boston, MFA 21.1843.   PL. 19

**14a–c.** MC vases; *c.* 600–575. (*a*) *NC*, cat. vases 791, 807, 861, 958, 995, 996, 1072, 1178–9, 1187, 1196. Hopper, *BSA* xliv (1949), 162 ff. (*b*) Komast Kotyle. Amandry, *Mon. Piot* xl (1944), 23 ff., pls. 3–4. Louvre. (*c*) Aryballos of Pyrrhias. Roebuck, *Hesperia* xxiv (1955), 158 ff., pls. 63–64. *SEG* xiv. 303. Corinth Mus.

   PL. 19

**15.** MC plaques from Penteskouphia; *c.* 600–575. *AD* i, pl. 7. 1, 6, 17, 21: pl. 8. 15 (Timonidas), 25, 26; ii, pl. 29. 2. *NC* 104. Berlin Mus.   PL. 19

**16.** Plaque with alphabet from Penteskouphia; *c.* 600–550. *AD* ii, pl. 24. 23. Berlin Mus.   PL. 20

**17.** Drachma-dedication on kerbstone from Perachora; *c.* 600–550? (see **7** above). NM.   PL. 20

**18.** List of sacral offerings from temenos of temple of Apollo, Corinth; *c.* 575–550? *Corinth* viii. 1. 1. Roehl³, 41. 3. Dow, *AJA* xlvi (1942), 69 ff. *SEG* xi. 53. Corinth Mus.   PL. 20

**19.** LC vases; *c.* 575–550. *NC*, cat. vases 1263, 1296 (pyxis by Chares), 1340, 1340a, 1359, 1373–4, 1389–90, 1396, 1399, 1408, 1410, 1412, 1419, 1422, 1431, 1436, 1439, 1443, 1446, 1447–51, 1453, 1456, 1459, 1461–2, 1464, 1467, 1471–2, 1474–5, 1477–8, 1481, 1483. *AGA*, 81, fig. 137.   PL. 20

**20.** LC plaques from Penteskouphia; *c.* 575–550. *AD* i, pl. 7. 11, 13; ii, pl. 29. 13: pl. 30. 9. Hoppin, *Handbook of Gk. BF vases* (1924), 10 f. *NC*, 108, 160 ff. Berlin Mus. and Louvre.   PL. 20

**21.** Fragment of slab (grave-cover?) from Corinth; 6th c. Meritt, *Corinth* viii. 1. 26. Corinth Mus.

**22.** Shaft of Doric column from Corinth; 6th c. Meritt, op. cit. 27. Corinth Mus.

**23.** Grave-trapeza from Krommyon; 6th c. Peek, *AM* lix (1934), 44 f. Lejeune, op. cit. 110. Hagioi Theodoroi, school-house.   PL. 20

**24.** Plaques from Penteskouphia; *c.* 550–525. *AD* i, pl. 7. 28; ii, pl. 24. 9: pl. 29. 10, 22: pl. 30. 12: pl. 39. 12. *NC* 112, 160. Berlin Mus.                              PL. 20

**25.** Plaque from Penteskouphia; *c.* 525? *AD* i, pl. 7. 25. *NC* 112, 160. Berlin Mus.              PL. 20

**26.** Plaque from Penteskouphia; *c.* 510–500. *AD* ii, pl. 29. 23. *NC* 113. Friedlaender 36*a*. Berlin Mus.
                                                                                PL. 20

**27.** Fragmentary block from Corinth; *c.* 550–500? Meritt, op. cit. 61. Corinth Mus.

**28.** Graffito of Anthesilas on black-glazed oinochoe; *c.* 510–500. Campbell, *Hesperia* vii (1938), 584, no. 63, fig. 11. Corinth Mus. 949.                                      PL. 20

**29.** Gravestone of Corinthians at Salamis, *c.* 480. Roehl³, 44. 8. *IG* i². 927. *DGE* 126. *GHI*² 16 and p. 259. *SEG* x. 404a. Peek i. 7. EM 22.                              PL. 21

**30.** Gravestone of Xenyllos; *c.* 480? *Corinth* viii. 1. 28. Corinth Mus.

**31.** Graffito of Xenokles on late BF lekythos; *c.* 500–475? *IG* iv. 353. *IGA* 23. *SGDI* 3155. *NC*, 160. NM.

**32.** Graffito of Xeniadas on black-glazed pyxis from Corinth; *c.* 500–475? *IG* iv. 352. *NC*, 160. Now lost?

**33.** Graffito of Timeas on black-glazed plate from Corinth; *c.* 500–475? *IG* iv. 351. NM 2492.

**34.** Bronze mirror-handle from Perachora; *c.* 500–475? *Perachora* i (1940), 180. Jeffery, *BSA* xliii (1948), 207, n. 9. *SEG* xi. 228. Perachora ii. 401, no. 167. NM.

**35.** Fragment of a bronze bowl, Corinth; *c.* 500–475? Newhall, *AJA* xxxv (1931), 1 f., fig. 1. Jeffery, op. cit. 208, n. 2. *Corinth* xv. 1 (1948), 115, no. 1. *SEG* xi. 200. Corinth Mus.        PL. 21

**36.** Bronze ten-stater weight from Attica; *c.* 500–475? Hultsch, *J. Int. Arch. Num.* 1905, 5 f. *NC*, 160. Jeffery, op. cit. 205 f. NM.

**37.** Horos of a temenos, Corinth; *c.* 475–450? Meritt, op. cit. 22. *DGE* 126a. *SEG* xi. 65. Corinth Mus.                                                                      PL. 21

**38.** Stone copy of a dedicatory inscription commemorating the battle of Tanagra, Olympia; *c.* 458. *Ol.* v. 253. Roehl³, 44. 11. *NC*, 160. *GHI*² 27 and p. 259. Olympia Mus. 1067+40+830.      PL. 21

**39.** Theatre-seat, Corinth; *c.* 400? T. L. Shear, *AJA* xxxiii (1929), 521 f. *SEG* xi. 145. *Corinth* ii (1952), 27, 56, 110, figs. 49b, 86. Corinth.                          PL. 21

*Inscription attributed to Corinth*

**40.** Bronze statuette dedicated to Asklepios, from Bologna; *c.* 450–425? *IG* iv. 356; xiv. 2282. Furt-waengler, *Samml. Somzée* (1897), 55 f. *DGE* 127. Jantzen, *Bronzewerkstätten in Grossgriech. u. Sizilien* (1937), 64, no. 9, pl. 17, 67–68. P. W. Lehmann, *Statues on Coins* (1946), 21. Paris, Bib. Nat. 98. PL. 21

## MEGARA

FIG. 34. Megara

*Notes on letter-forms*

α1 occurs in a graffito *c.* 550–540 (1): but by the end of the 6th c. and during the 5th c. α2 is normal

(**2, 3, 4, 5, 6, 7?, 11**); the same 'reversed' *alpha* appears in the inscriptions of Aigina, at about the same date (p. 109). α3 occurs once, on a bronze plaque, *c.* 446? (**8**), perhaps for technical reasons.

There is no example of *beta* as yet attested at Megara, but it is to be expected that, as the 'freak' *epsilon* is plainly derived from Corinth, so the *beta* would be of Corinthian type also. This is confirmed by the appearance on Byzantine coins of the late 5th c. of β1, which is apparently a 5th-c. version of the old 'twisted' *beta*, stylized to resemble something like an offshoot of *pi*, as happened to Corinthian *beta* also in the 5th c. The Selinountine form (p. 262) may also be derived from the Megarian, but if (as is possible) the same form was used in Syracuse (pp. 269 f.), then perhaps Megara Hyblaia and Selinous originally took their script from Syracuse, not from their mother-city; for there is no trace of any other distinctive Megarian letters at Selinous.

ε1–2 is used for both ε and η, undoubtedly taken from the Corinthian. It continued in use after the middle of the 5th c., but probably was given up during the third quarter (**11**). ε3, here as at Corinth, represents the improper diphthong ει.

Ⱶ1 is still in use shortly after the middle of the 6th c. (**1**); but texts of the early 5th c. show the open form already in use (**2, 4, 6**).

θ1 seems to have continued throughout the 6th c., θ2 replacing it in the early 5th (**4**).

The earliest Megarian example of *lambda* does not antedate the late 6th c. (**3**); it is the later, isosceles type by that time.

ρ1–2 is normal, though ρ3 occurs in **2** (*c.* 500). It is met occasionally elsewhere *c.* 500–480 (Corinth **29**; Sikyon **8, 14**) but nowhere else consistently as at Megara, sometimes in the exaggerated form ρ2 (**4**). It had evidently gone out of fashion by the end of the 5th c. (**14, 15**).

σ1 is used, except on the statuette **6**, which shows σ2. Although the latter is the normal form in Attic, later Boiotian, and Aiginetan (from one of which places, it is suggested, Megara derived her use of *sigma* instead of *san*), there are occasional examples of four-stroked *sigma* in Attica and Aigina; in Boiotia it is regular in the earliest inscriptions.

ʋ2 is already in use in the graffito **1** (*c.* 550–540?), and continues throughout the 6th and 5th c.

Both false and true ει-diphthongs are written E in **3**, where the spelling is uncertain more than once (p. 136, n. 1). In **7** the true diphthong is written in full ει, and in **11** EI is written in full for the diphthong produced by broadening an original ῑ (MⱵιλο–>MⱵειλο–: *SGDI* iv. 3. 337). The false diphthong ου is always written O, as in Attica and elsewhere.

*Punctuation.* ː is quite frequent in Megarian (**1, 2, 3, 5, 13**). It is likely that this practice was borrowed from Attica, as punctuation is extremely rare in any Corinthian inscriptions.

*Direction of the script.* There is little to be said of this, since all the examples begin comparatively late. All are written from left to right except the name on the statuette **6**, which is from right to left; this might be for symmetry, as it is possible that it formed part of a little bronze group which contained other figures also labelled with their names. The *boustrophedon* style had evidently lost favour by the end of the 6th c. (**3**), and the *stoichedon* style was already known (**3**; cf. also **4** and **8**).

It was recorded in the Atthis that a famous horos had once stood at the Isthmus of Corinth, bearing on its west side the verse: τάδ' ἐστὶ Πελοπόννησος, οὐκ Ἰωνία, and on its east: τάδ' οὐχὶ Πελοπόννησος, ἀλλ' Ἰωνία. According to the version in Strabo, it was erected as a limit by both parties when the Dorian invaders drove the Ionians from the rest of the Peloponnese, leaving Megaris still an Ionic territory; according to Plutarch, Theseus set it up after annexing Megaris to Attica. Later, the tradition continued, when Kodros reigned, the Peloponnesians attacked Attica and wrested Megaris from her; it was thenceforward a Dorian state, and they made away with the horos (ἠφάνισαν τὴν στήλην).[1]

What gave rise to this tale of an opisthographic stele marking Megara as Attic property, which had already disappeared many hundreds of years before the time of the Atthidographers, can only be guessed;[2] but the general circumstances described may be correct, that the original Ionic inhabitants of Megara were expelled or swamped by a further expansion of the Dorians who had already spread from the Argolid and settled Corinthia.[3]

The Megarian alphabet has the general character of the Corinthian group in the use of the 'blue' forms of *xi, chi, psi,* and also the peculiarly Corinthian letters for *beta* and *epsilon*. But it differs in other details from the Corinthian; its use of the straight *iota*, of *sigma* instead of *san*, and O (not ου) for the false diphthong suggests that—as might be expected of a corridor-state wedged between Corinth, Boiotia, and Attica—the Megarian alphabet is a mixture, taken from her neighbours, the influence of Corinth predominating. It must be stressed that no Megarian inscription has yet been published which is earlier than *c.* 550–540; but as the Corinthian alphabet at that time still retained the crooked *iota* and *san*, it seems likely that from the beginning the Megarians used the *iota* and *sigma* of their neighbours in Boiotia and Attica.

The present harvest of early Megarian inscriptions is very meagre. Our loss is the more tantalizing in that the equally fragmentary record of her early history shows her as no less energetic in her colonial expansion than were the other Doric dwellers round the Saronic Gulf. During the eighth century, despite her struggles with Bacchiad Corinth,[4] she gained a footing in Sicily with her colony Megara Hyblaia; but the earliest inscription found so far on the latter site shows that the colony used an alphabet which is certainly not Megarian, and could perhaps be Syracusan (pp. 269 f.). Only in Megara Hyblaia's colony Selinous may a possible trace of the Megarian alphabet be preserved in the *beta* (pp. 262, 269). Blocked by Corinth from further colonizing in the west, Megara turned north and laid her chain of daughter-cities and their daughters in the Propontis—Astakos, Kalchedon, Byzantion, Selymbria. Here again the epigraphic evidence is of the slightest. A single sixth-century inscription from Kalchedon shows not the Megarian but the Ionic script (p. 366); while of Byzantion's early alphabet we know nothing except that her

[1] Androtion, *FGH* iii, no. 324, F 61; Strabo 171 and 392–3; Plutarch, *Theseus* 25.

[2] Was the tradition wholly fanciful, or was there in fact some Mycenean monument here, which later Greeks professed to interpret as a horos, and which disappeared early enough for the Atthidographers to retain only the tradition of a vanished stele, putting its loss also in the heroic age and embroidering the recollection with a suitable couplet? At all events, the Emperor Hadrian was evidently inspired by the 'interpretation' when he erected his arch which led out of old Athens into his new suburb, and inscribed it:

Αἵδ' εἰσ' Ἀθῆναι, Θήσεως ἡ πρὶν πόλις.
Αἵδ' εἰσ' Ἀδριανοῦ καὶ οὐχὶ Θήσεως πόλις.

cf. Frazer, *Pausanias* ii. 188 and Judeich, *Topographie v. Athen*², 123.

[3] Cf. Dunbabin, *JHS* lxviii (1948), 62 ff.; Hammond, *BSA* xlix (1954), 93 ff.

[4] The only epigraphic link in the tradition of her early feud with Corinth is the copy, made probably in the Hadrianic period or shortly after (*IG* vii. 52), of an epitaph commemorating Orsippos of Megara, who commanded the Megarians in war against an unnamed, encroaching foe, which could hardly be other than Corinth. The date of Orsippos' victory at Olympia in the stadion is given variously as *Ol.* 15 (= 720; Euseb. *Chron.* i. 195 (Schoene); Dion. Hal. *AH* vii. 72. 3) or *Ol.* 32 (= 652; *Et. Mag.*, s.v. Γυμνάσια). Pausanias also records the inscription (i. 44. 1). The epitaph was set up in obedience to a command from the Delphic Oracle and cannot from its diction be much, if at all, earlier than the 5th c.; Boeckh thought that it might be by Simonides (*CIG* 1050).

silver coinage of the late fifth century, bearing the legend Βυ, shows that here certainly a form of *beta* survived which can only be derived from the Megarian (p. 366).

In Megara itself there are as yet no inscriptions surviving from the late seventh century, the probable date of Theagenes' tyranny, and nothing from the first part of the sixth, when she contested with Athens for Salamis and lost it finally on arbitration—a contest of which one alleged relic at least was still extant in Pausanias' day, the bronze akroterion of an Athenian ship, dedicated by the Megarians in their temple of Zeus Olympios (Paus. i. 40. 5). The earliest inscription is a graffito (**1**), which, according to the context in which it was found, may perhaps be dated shortly after the middle of the sixth century. It was scratched on the base of a skyphos found in the rubbish dump of a house under the later Agora at Athens. It was apparently sent as a message to somebody: [. . . .]: καθες: ⱶυπο τōι ⱶοδōι: τας θυρ[ας τ]ας το καπο: πριον[. .], and its special interest lies in the hint which it gives of intercourse between Athenians and Megarians at this time.

Towards the end of the sixth century the Megarians built a Treasury at Olympia of which only a number of damaged blocks now survive, one bearing the late inscription ΜΕΓΑΡΕΩΝ,[1] and others the remains of a Gigantomachy in the pediment, as described by Pausanias (vi. 19. 12–15). The Treasury is at present dated *c.* 510 B.C.,[2] and I mention it here because of the inscribed shield, now lost, which was set as akroterion above the pediment. According to Pausanias the inscription recorded that the Megarians dedicated the Treasury from the spoils of a war against Corinth. Pausanias wished to identify this war with the very early strife between the two places, though he admitted that the building itself was many years later in date.[3] But a Treasury finished in the last decade of the sixth century, with a dedicatory inscription stating that it was offered from the spoils of Corinth, should mean rather that at some time in the late sixth century Megara and Corinth fought an engagement not otherwise recorded, from which the Megarians won considerable spoils. In view of this it would be interesting to know if the Argives were allies of Megara at the time, for Pausanias says that 'they were said to have helped the Megarians in the deed'; but it is not clear whether he is here making a reference of his own to the eighth-century war to which he sought to refer the dedication, or whether he is actually citing further from the inscription on the shield. The surviving parts of the panoplies which Argos dedicated at Olympia 'from the spoils of Corinth' at once come to the mind, but they appear to be some years later in date (p. 162).

One of the best Megarian inscriptions extant is that on a silver phiale mesomphalos found in a grave near Kozani (Beroia) in Macedonia—evidently part of some spoil taken from Megara at a later date (**2**). The excavators suggest a date in the last years of the sixth or the early years of the fifth century, a period indicated alike by the style of the phiale itself and by the lettering (cf. open *heta*, as on the statuette **6**). The earliest inscription yet found in the Megarid itself is the grave-stele of ?Lakles (or Eukleitos?), son of Prokles (**3**), which was found in the necropolis which bordered the road to Corinth

---

[1] *Ol.* ii. 50 ff.       [2] Robertson², 326.

[3] Loc. cit.: ταύτην Μεγαρεῦσιν ἡγοῦμαι τὴν νίκην Ἀθήνησιν ἄρχοντος γενέσθαι Φόρβαντος . . . λέγονται δὲ καὶ Ἀργεῖοι μετασχεῖν πρὸς τοὺς Κορινθίους Μεγαρεῦσι τοῦ ἔργου. τὸν δὲ ἐν Ὀλυμπίᾳ θησαυρὸν ἔτεσιν ὕστερον τῆς μάχης ἐποίησαν οἱ Μεγαρεῖς. He may have inferred his early date for the war partly from the offerings inside the Treasury, which were the work of Dontas, an artist one generation later than Dipoinos and Skyllis, who were traditionally pupils of the half-legendary Daidalos.

(Paus. i. 44. 6). It may be dated *c.* 500 B.C.—hardly much later, if its tailed *epsilon* may be compared with that on the bronze statuette **6**; nor earlier, for the lettering is *stoichedon* throughout, a practice which even in Attica is found only occasionally before the last decade of the sixth century.[1] Two inscriptions published by Peek may be rather later in date, but one at least is almost certainly by the same cutter (**4**): it differs only in using the dotted instead of the crossed *theta*, and is probably to be dated within the first quarter of the fifth century. As Peek observed, the six marine-sounding names which it records may be those either of some lost sailors, or of some local heroes whose precinct it once marked. The other (**5**) is a grave-stele to Athenades son of Theonikos, with punctuation 1 (as on **2**, **3**), and *phi* cut in error for *theta*.

As I have said elsewhere,[2] the inscription on the bronze statuette of Herakles in the Benaki Museum (**6**) appears to be Megarian from the letter-forms *alpha*, *epsilon*, *rho*, and *sigma*, and the unusual genitive form of the name (Buck, 87); if this is correct, the date of the statuette (*c.* 490–480), offering a control for that of the inscription, confirms that by the early fifth century Megara had adopted Ⱶ2 (cf. **2**, **4** above).

Unlike the gravestone of the Corinthians, the epigram commemorating the Megarians who fell in the Persian war survives only in a late copy.[3] The inscription on a rough un-worked horos from a shrine of Apollo Lykeios (**7**) is not closely datable, but may belong to the second quarter of the fifth century; cf. ν2. The only surviving inscription from a military dedication of any kind is a single hexameter on a small bronze plaque (**8**) which perhaps once served as a label nailed beside some spoils consecrated in one of the three sanctuaries of Athena in Megara (Paus. i. 42. 4): [τ]οιδε απο λα[ι]|στἁν δεκατα[ν] | ανεθἑκαν Αθαναι. This inscription has been dated variously in the sixth or fifth centuries.[4] That it is not earlier than the second half of the fifth is indicated by the form ν3, which appears in Attica after the middle of the fifth century (p. 325). α3 was used occasionally by fifth-century vase-painters for technical reasons; its use on stone or bronze is very rare (cf. Achaia **8**; Arkadia **37**).

It does not seem likely that Megara would retain her 'freak' *epsilon* for long after the middle of the fifth century, when Corinth had apparently already discarded it (pp. 129 f.). It occurs still in three inscriptions which are published only in majuscule type, and can therefore only be given the widest date in the fifth century: the marble plaque found in Megara (**9**) inscribed ευφρονες, with a later inscription Ρινωνος added below;[5] two

---

[1] Austin, *Stoichedon Style* (1938), 6 ff. The first part of the inscription is lost, and the reading of what remains is still uncertain; the chief difficulty is that the cutter has made certain errors: E corrected to the local form in l. 5, and *nu* for *lambda* in εντπιδες, l. 3, following the *nu* in the line above (ἐντπίδες as a dialectal form is unattested elsewhere; Buck, 65). It is therefore possible that there is some dittography in ll. 4–5, καααλει: καικαλει. To read [Ευ]κλειτον Προκλεος rather than the generally accepted [Λα]κλη τον Προκλεος would rescue the cutter from the suspicion of writing E for the local form once again.

[2] *JHS* lxix (1949), 31 f.     [3] *GHI*² 20 and p. 259.

[4] It was read as απο λα[ια]ς ταν δεκαταν and attributed

to the wars of the 6th c. by Ernst Meyer, *RE*, s.v. Megara, 187; to the 5th c. by Highbarger, *A History of Ancient Megara* (1927), 45 f.: to the middle of the 5th c. by the first editor Korolkow, *AM* viii (1883), 182. The reading ἀπὸ λα[ι]|στᾶν was made by Peek (**8**, bibliography).

[5] As was implied by Earle (*CR* v (1891), 344), the plaque was apparently re-used in the 4th c. as the grave-stone of Rhinon, though it must have made a very small one, from the measurements (0·14 m. × 0·07 m.). Its original use is not clear to me. The Ionic feminine Εὐφρόνη is not likely for Megara (as suggested ibid.); it might be from the shrine of some deities like the Eumenides, though I can find no other example of the epithet εὐφρονες so used.

fragments of a stele (**10**), inscribed Ⱶερο—, found in a shrine identified tentatively as that of Zeus Aphesios;[1] and the signature of an artist named Myron (**13**):Μυρōν : επ[οιε]. The famous Myron of Eleutherai would not himself sign a work in the Megarian script, but this could be associated with him, if we assume that the base was made by a local mason. From the shrine of Zeus came also the lip of a plate (**11**), which shows, together with αι, the non-Megarian *epsilon* in the diphthong of ΜϜειλο - - -.

Two final examples should be included among the pre-Ionic inscriptions of Megara. One is the gravestone known only from a copy by Lenormant, from an unidentified church between Megara and Eleusis (**14**): Σαμα τοδε Ὑψικλεος· Μεγαρες τονδ' ε[νθαδ' εθα-ψαν]. Its authenticity has been doubted,[2] but, as far as the letters go, they agree perfectly well with those of **15** below, showing the last stages of the local alphabet, in which normal *epsilon* is used, with γι, υ2, and the 'blue' *psi* of the Corinth group.

The last inscription is that on a marble grave-stele found in the Peiraieus: Απολλοδ|ōρος Διο|κλεδα |Μεγαρευς (**15**). γι is used, and Ionic *omega* is not yet known. If the suggestion is right which identifies the dead man as the Megarian Apollodoros who killed Phrynichos and was rewarded with a grant of land which he sold again in 404 (Lysias vii. 4), then the inscription can hardly be earlier than *c*. 400, and the adoption of the Ionic script at Megara will not have taken place until the fourth century.

## CATALOGUE

**1.** Graffito on the base of a skyphos from the Agora at Athens; *c*. 550–540? H. Thompson, *Hesperia* xvii (1948), 160, pl. 41, 2. Agora Mus. P 17824. PL. 22

**2.** Silver phiale dedicated to the Megarian Athena, from Kozani near Beroia; *c*. 500? Kallipolites and Feytmans, *AE* 1948–9, 92 ff., figs. 8–9. *SEG* xiii. 306. Kozani Mus.? PL. 22

**3.** Grave-stele of [Eu?]kleitos son of Prokles, from Megara; *c*. 500? Wilhelm and Solmsen, *AM* xxxi (1906), 89 ff., 342 ff., pl. 13. Kern, pl. 9. Roehl[3], 52. 1. *DGE* 148. Highbarger, *History of Ancient Megara* (1927), 23 f., n. 75. *SEG* xiii. 311. Peek i. 2068. Eleusis Mus. PL. 22

**4.** Stele bearing a list of six names, Megara; *c*. 500–475? Peek, *AM* lix (1934), 52 ff., no. 10, Beil. iv. 3. *SEG* xiii. 300. Dunst, *Archiv Papyr.* xvi (1958), 169, n. 2. Eleusis Mus. PL. 22

**5.** Gravestone of Athenades, Megara; *c*. 500–475? Peek, op. cit. 54, no. 11. *SEG* xiii. 314. Megara Mus. PL. 22

**6.** Bronze statuette of Herakles, *c*. 490–480. Payne, *JHS* liv (1934), 163 ff., pl. 7. Lejeune, *REA* xlvii (1945), 105, n. 5. Jeffery, *JHS* lxix (1949), 31 f. *SEG* xiii. 305. Athens, Benaki Mus. PL. 22

**7.** Rough horos from the temenos of Apollo Lykeios, Megara; *c*. 475–450? *IG* vii. 35. Roberts i. 113. *IGA* 11. Roehl[3], 52, 2. *DGE* 149 (1). PL. 22

**8.** Bronze plaque for a dedication of spoils, Megara; *c*. 450–440? *IG* vii. 37. *SGDI* 3001. Roberts i. 113a. Roehl[3], 53. 3. *DGE* 149 (2). Highbarger, op. cit. 45 f. Friedlaender 23. Peek, *Studies . . . D. M. Robinson* ii (1953), 325 f. *SEG* xiii. 307. NM. PL. 22

---

[1] Paus. i. 44. 9. The identification was confirmed by the discovery of a sherd inscribed —φεσ— (*AE* 1890, 46 and pl. vi. 7; *IG* vii. 3494, there shown inverted), which from the lettering appears to be 4th c.

[2] It is classed among the 'inscriptiones dubiae vel spuriae' in *IG* vii, on the grounds that Lenormant's copies, like those of Fourmont, were not always above suspicion.

**9.** Marble tablet inscribed ευφρονες, Megara; 5th c. Earle, *CR* v (1891), 344. Roehl³, 53. 6. Lost?

**10.** Fragment of stone stele from the shrine of Zeus Aphesios, near Megara; 5th c. Philios, *AE* 1890, 45 f., n. 2. *IG* vii. 3492. Roehl³, 54. 5. Megara Mus.?

**11.** Graffito dedication on the lip of a plate, from the above shrine; 5th c. Philios, op. cit. 45 f., pl. 6, 6. *IG* vii. 3493. Roehl³, 54. 4. *DGE* 151. *SEG* xiii. 301. Megara Mus.?

**12.** Horos stone from Megara, inscribed Διος Μιλιχιο Πανφυλο: 5th c. Richards, *JHS* xviii (1898), 332. Lost?

**13.** Artist's signature, seen near Megara; 5th c. Preuner, *AM* xlix (1924), 121. *SEG* xiii. 325. Lost?

**14.** Gravestone of Hypsikles, near Megara; late 5th c. *IG* vii. 3478. *IGA* 14. Roberts i. 115. Friedlaender 3*b*. Peek i. 61. Lost?

**15.** Gravestone of Apollodoros, son of Diokleides; *c.* 400? *IGA* 13. Roberts i. 114. *SGDI* 3002. Conze 1491. *DGE* 150. EM.

# SIKYON

FIG. 35. Sikyon

*Notes on letter-forms*

The freak ει, peculiar to Sikyon, is used for both ε and η. It was perhaps a deliberate alteration of the Corinthian *epsilon*, to avoid confusion with *beta*. It appears to have been still used in the second quarter of the 5th c. (**16**), but to have disappeared by about 450 or soon after, according to the evidence of the coins.

Medial *vau* seems to have disappeared during the first years of the 5th c. (**12**), but initial *vau* still occurs in the masons' marks on the Treasury at Olympia **15***b* (second quarter of 5th c.?).

ⱶ2 is already in use in the earliest example, *c.* 500? (**7**).

θ3 was already appearing *c.* 500? (**7**). In the 5th c. an angled form θ2 came into fashion, probably because it was easier to cut in stone or bronze. Sporadic examples of this practice appear in other places, but only in Sikyonian could it be called consistent; cf. *omikron*.

λ2 is still in use, as in Corinthian, about the middle of the 5th c. (**16**).

ο2 is used in all the 5th-c. examples (polygonal in **12**); cf. *theta*.

*San* seems to have been replaced by *sigma* in the first years of the fifth century (**13**).

*Qoppa* has already disappeared *c.* 500? (**8**).

Towards the end of the archaic period ρ2 appears twice (**8**, **14**); cf. this type in Megarian and Corinthian (pp. 116, 133).

*Diphthongs* ει, ου. The true ει is spelt out in full, the false, as in Corinthian, is denoted by ε2; both true and false ου are spelt in full, as in Corinthian.

*Punctuation* is rare, as at Corinth. In a late archaic inscription (**7**) a short stroke (1) is used; this is, so far, the only example of punctuation in Sikyonian.

*Direction of the script.* The early graffito from Delphi (**2**) is written from right to left; the other early inscriptions **1** and **3** are incomplete, and their direction uncertain, **3** being probably a single line from a longer text written *boustrophedon*. Though the prescript of **8** (*c.* 500?) is written consistently from left to right, the *boustrophedon* system occurs still in a dedication (**7**) which should be of about the same date, which suggests that the practice was dying out in Sikyon in the last years of the 6th c. The *stoichedon* style was in use in the second quarter of the 5th c. (**16**), but not yet properly established at the start of the century (**13**). Guide-lines were sometimes used (**3, 13**), as in Corinthian.

Sikyon, situated in the fertile area adjoining the western boundary of Corinth, lived at peace with her powerful neighbour; her antagonism was directed rather against the cities of Achaia on her western frontier,[1] and the dependencies of Argos to the south.[2] Although she herself was theoretically dependent on Argos, as part of the heritage of Temenos (and it has been inferred that this subserviency was actually enforced during the rule of Pheidon of Argos),[3] her anti-Argive feelings culminated in open hostility under the direction of the tyrant Kleisthenes early in the sixth century (Hdt. v. 67).

The alphabet of Sikyon is like that of Corinth, except in three details. It used the straight *iota*, as did its southern neighbour Kleonai. Its *beta* was not the 'twisted' but the normal form; it is true that this letter has not yet been attested earlier than *c.* 500 (**8**), but at that date Corinth was still using the 'twisted' form. The Achaian *beta* was also normal, and Sikyon may have got hers thence; but whencesoever it came, it clearly had some influence on the *epsilon*. The unique Sikyonian ει can hardly have arisen from anything but the 'freak' Corinthian type, deliberately altered to avoid confusion with Sikyonian *beta*.

The earliest datable Sikyonian inscription is the fragment —φε— (or —εϙ—?) painted on an aryballos from the Argive Heraion of the Late Protocorinthian period, *c.* 650–640 (**1**); it was presumably a name either of a figure in the drawing or of the vase's owner, and its chief interest lies in showing that in the seventh century there were Sikyonians among the potters who worked in the prolific factories of Corinthian ware, as there were also in the sixth century (cf. **4**, pp. 140 f.).

Pausanias records (vi. 19. 1–4) a lost Sikyonian inscription of the seventh century, which he read on the smaller of the two bronze θάλαμοι which the tyrant Myron, son of Orthagoras, dedicated at Olympia after winning the chariot race in Ol. 33 (648); he paraphrases the epigram: ἐπιγράμματα . . . ἐστί . . . ἐς μὲν τοῦ χαλκοῦ τὸν σταθμόν, ὅτι πεντήκοντα εἴη τάλαντα, ἐς δὲ τοὺς ἀναθέντας Μύρωνα εἶναι καὶ τὸν Σικυωνίων δῆμον. If his paraphrase is close, it shows that a tyrant in the seventh century used the same stock formula as did the tyrants of the fifth century; the name is given without title, as of a private citizen joining with the other citizens in the offering. The Treasury itself in which these 'thalamoi' were housed is not earlier than the fifth century (**15**), although Pausanias believed it to have been dedicated by Myron also; but another Sikyonian fragment was tentatively connected by Purgold[4] with Myron's dedicatory inscription for the 'thalamoi': a narrow strip cut in later times from a bronze inscribed plaque without regard

---

[1] e.g. Pellene (*Ox. Pap.* x. 1241 and xi. 1365: Aelian, *VH* vi. 1) and Aigeira (Paus. vii. 26. 2, where the campaign is dated before the Dorian Invasion).

[2] At Delphi Pausanias saw a bronze group representing a procession and sacrifice dedicated by the people of Orneai after defeating the Sikyonians at an unknown date (x. 18. 5); Plutarch preserves the text of the dedication: Ὀρνεᾶται ἀπὸ Σικυωνίων (*De Pyth. Or.* 15).

[3] Strabo 358; cf. Skalet, *Ancient Sikyon* (1928), 48 ff.; Andrewes, *The Greek Tyrants* (1956), 40 f.

[4] *AZ* xxxix (1881), 179.

for the inscription written on the plaque, and pierced by four nails for its re-use (**3**). The original text was probably inscribed *boustrophedon* between guide-lines, and the strip was cut along the lines. Nothing of its subject can be made out from the surviving letters.[1] On general grounds it might be dated in the first half of the sixth century by comparison with Corinthian and Argive inscriptions of that period. Guide-lines do not occur in seventh-century inscriptions on stone or bronze, as far as I know.

The graffito ΣεϞυϝōνιιος on a poros block at Delphi (**2**) may well be earlier than either of the two inscriptions just discussed (**1** and **3**); it is extremely archaic in appearance (cf. Ϟι, υι), though awkward writing may be partly responsible for this.[2] The building from which it came has not been identified,[3] so that we do not know if this was scratched by some Sikyonian visitor, or by a mason working on a building for the Sikyonian state. The earliest recorded Sikyonian activity at Delphi is that of Kleisthenes, who aided the Amphiktionic League in the First Sacred War by blockading Krisa (Paus. ii. 9. 6; x. 37. 6; Schol. Pind. *Nem.* ix, preface). If it is also true that he helped to reorganize the Pythian Games in 586, as well as winning the chariot race in Pyth. 2 (Paus. x. 7. 6; 582 B.C.), he may well have erected a building or buildings there. In the foundations of the fifth-century Treasury of Sikyon lay older blocks and metopes which have been assigned to an early sixth-century monopteral building and a tholos, and assumed to be the works of Kleisthenes.[4] The inscribed block does not belong to either of these, but it should be remembered that their attribution to Sikyon, though eminently reasonable, is not absolutely certain, and there remains the remote possibility that they may belong to another Treasury, and the inscribed block to some erection by Kleisthenes.

In the late seventh and early sixth centuries Corinth with her colonies was opening up the semi-barbaric areas of Aitolia and Akarnania, and evidence of Corinthian intercourse is plain in the temples at Thermon and Kalydon (pp. 225 f.). Though there is no record of any Sikyonian colony, it seems likely that Sikyonians accompanied the Corinthians to these parts, for Pliny records (*NH* xxxvi. 4) the tradition that the Cretan sculptors Dipoinos and Skyllis settled in Sikyon, but, having quarrelled with the Sikyonians over the contracts for some temple images, left Sikyon and settled for a time in Aitolia; and, as though in confirmation of what might otherwise have been disputed as one of Pliny's many confusions of places, two inscriptions have in fact been found near Thermon which show a form of letter resembling the Sikyonian *epsilon* (**19**, **20**).[5]

Mention has already been made (p. 139) of the Late Corinthian krater in Berlin (**4**)

---

[1] It was formerly read as [- - - σ]ταθος ταριστερον πυρ-ροι, το [δε δεξιον - - -] referring to some rules for sacrifice; but the *tau* is uncertain, and the hyperdorism σταθος for στῆθος very dubious; cf. Lejeune, *REA* xlv (1943), 184, n. 1, and 191 f.

[2] This is so far the only example in Sikyonian of the 'on-glide' ι between *iota* and the following vowel frequently attested at Argos in the early period; cf. p. 152.

[3] Daux (following Courby) suggests as a possibility the earlier temple of Apollo, which was burnt down in 548; *BCH* lxi (1937), 58, n. 3, and 60, n. 1.

[4] La Coste-Messelière, *Au Musée de Delphes* (1936),

19 ff., esp. 77 ff.; Dinsmoor (*BCH* xxxvi (1912), 443 ff.) and Pomtow (*RE*, suppl. iv. 1248 ff.) both sought to assign the early remains to a Syracusan Treasury.

[5] The little clay table (?) **19** was found at Baltsa, north-east of Thermon, where there was a small shrine, apparently to a female deity, for the bulk of the dedications comprised terracotta 'korai' statuettes (none earlier than the 6th c.). The inscription incised on the table was read by the excavator Δορὸ Ϙυλία ἀρὰν ἄξε, with Sikyonian *epsilon*, but 'red' *xi*. All suggested readings are dubious, but the final ει is clear. The graffito on a pithos found at Thermon (**20**) has only been illustrated in majuscule type, but with ει twice.

which shows the duel of Achilles and Memnon, with their names in the Sikyonian script; and for the third quarter of the sixth century there is the incised inscription Επαινετος μ' εδōκεν Χαροπōι on an Attic black-figure dinos (**5**), which bears the signature of Exekias. The Attic potter who sold it to his Sikyonian client may have incised the inscription himself from the client's copy, for it is in a neat professional hand like that of the signature. There are also a number of Sikyonian dedications among the Corinthian in the temple of Hera Limenia at Perachora. Some are on fragments of sixth-century kotylai, too small to be more closely dated (**6**). The most important is on a bronze bull-calf (**7**), which itself may be by a Sikyonian craftsman, for Payne noted that the style differed in some points from the Corinthian.[1] He suggested a date in the last quarter of the sixth century, and this is borne out by the lettering of the inscription, in which the two lines, though not continuous, are *boustrophedon* in their direction, and *san* is still used; while, on the other hand, the open *heta*, dotted *theta*, and *v*2 suggest the end of the archaic period (*c.* 500 B.C.?). There appears to be an attempt at punctuation by a short chisel-stroke after the *san* of Ναυμαχος, and again after the last *epsilon* of ανεθēκε.

To the period *c.* 500 belongs also, I think, the most important Sikyonian inscription yet found, the large bronze plaque which lists in five columns the seventy-three members of an association which had a common ἑστιατόριον (**8**). The prescript is written consistently from left to right, and the open *heta* is used, but the forms of *mu*, *nu*, and diphthong ε2 are archaic still, and it has crossed *theta*. *Vau* (both initial and medial) is still used spasmodically, but *qoppa* has disappeared.[2]

The *san* occurs on three other inscriptions: a stone base for a stele bearing two or more names, [Εχ?]ετιμος and Θελξαγορας (**9**), a marble slab with the letters -πισθυι- (**11**), and a bronze spear-butt found at Olympia inscribed Σεκυōνι[οι] (**12**), which from its *v*2 looks later than the earliest of the inscriptions showing *sigma* (**13** below). Medial *vau* is not used, nor *qoppa*. If it is about the turn of the sixth and fifth centuries, it might possibly be attributed to the campaign of Sepeia (494?), since we are told by Herodotos (vi. 92) that Sikyonians not only provided ships for the Spartans, but also joined in the landing. **9** and **10** may also be from the start of the fifth century; but this is very uncertain.

The earliest example of *sigma* appears to be on the corner-fragment from a base or a stele inscribed on at least two faces, which recorded the many victories of a contestant, Agatha[rchos]?,[3] at Delphi, the Isthmos, Nemea, Sikyon, Athens, and elsewhere (**13**), anticipating the feats of his later compatriot Sostratos in 355 B.C. (Paus. vi. 4. 1). The fragment is not in full *stoichedon* order, but ll. 1–2 and 5–7 apparently fall into the order. The μι and νι are still archaic, and θ2 is used, the angled form which was easier to cut than the circular, and to which the Sikyonian workmen seem to have been especially addicted (**15, 16, 21**(?)). The surviving adjacent face was ruled, like the front, with guidelines, ready for more victories to be recorded; but only one survives, [- - -]οις in l. 4. On top are the remains of a square cutting for the tenon of a bronze statue. I do not think it can be later than the first quarter of the fifth century.

---

[1] *Perachora* i. 136.
[2] For full details of this inscription cf. the excellent commentary by Lejeune, *REA* 1943, 185 ff.

[3] The alternative αγαθα [τυχα] is suggested in *SEG* xi. 257, but rightly rejected in Moretti 12.

The date when *sigma* replaced *san* should give a *terminus ante quem* for the earliest coins of Sikyon, for there is no doubt that the letter which appears in the incuse on the reverse is *san*;[1] this indicates that at the time when the type was first chosen (obverse a dove, reverse M for Sikyon) this was the normal sign for the sibilant—though obviously it continued in use for many years after *san* had been dropped from the normal alphabet, like Corinthian *qoppa* and Byzantine *beta*, because it formed part of the badge whereby outsiders recognized the place of origin of the currency.[2] A sherd from Perachora which belongs to the first half of the fifth century (**14**) shows, with *sigma*, the triangular *rho* which, apart from its constant use at Megara (p. 133), occurs on two Corinthian inscriptions of the early fifth century (Corinth **29** and **34**), and occasionally on the bronze plaque **8**. In view of this, and of the lettering of the victory-list **13**, I should hazard the guess that the loss of *san* took place here rather earlier than at Corinth, *c.* 500–480. *Sigma* was certainly in use when the Sikyonian Treasury at Olympia was built and the inscription was cut on the western anta (**15***a*). The date for this building may be about the second quarter of the fifth century; we may note the ν2 and ο2 of the dedication, and the initial *vau* still used in the masons' marks (**13***b*). This was the Treasury which Pausanias saw, in which were housed the bronze θάλαμοι of Myron; it may perhaps have been built from the spoils of the Persian War.[3] The date of the later Treasury at Delphi is disputed as between the beginning and the end of the fifth century,[4] and the masons' marks are not sufficiently characteristic to incline the balance in either direction.

Lastly, there is the list of names (now lost) found at Moulki near Sikyon (**16**), which is cut *stoichedon*, and has α2 and ν2. It may be slightly later than the Treasury at Olympia, that is, somewhere late in the second quarter of the century. I hesitate to put it lower than 450, from comparison with the Corinthian script, which has apparently lost its 'freak' *epsilon* by 458 or shortly after (pp. 129 f.); but such an argument may well prove invalid. The only other clue comes from those coins which show on the obverse a dove and the letters ΣΕ for Σεκυών, on the reverse the old *san* ornamented with a palmette, and which are dated by Babelon in the middle of the fifth century (**17**).

---

[1] It is described as *sigma* by Babelon (ii. 1. 815 ff.), and Head (*HN*², 409), who attribute the first issues tentatively to *c.* 480 (Babelon) or rather earlier (Head): but Payne rightly pointed out that the long parallel legs of the sign are those of typical *san* (*NC*, 38, n. 5).

[2] The sign on the shields of the Sikyonian army, which Xenophon calls *sigma*, may have been in reality the *san* (*Hell*. iv. 4. 10); and it is an attractive suggestion that the breed of horse called the σαμφόρας may have come from the horse-breeding plains of Sikyon, as perhaps the κοππατίας did from Corinth (Böttiger, *Kleine Schriften* ii. 162; Daremberg-Saglio ii. 800; above, p. 33, n. 1).

[3] It was ascribed to the first half of the 5th c. by Purgold, on epigraphical grounds (*Ol.* v. 649); Dörpfeld, while observing that in general its architectural features agreed with those of the temple of Zeus at Olympia (*c.* 465?), inclined to a date in the second half of the century, because of a detail ('kleiner Rundstab') on the metopes and triglyphs, which he believed to have been first used on the Parthenon (*Ol.* iv. 43). Dyer disputed this in favour of an earlier date, between 480 and 450 (*JHS* xxv (1905), 309, and 1906, 80 f.).

[4] *c.* 500, after the fall of the last tyrant of Sikyon? (La Coste-Messelière, *Au Musée*, 60 ff., 78); or at the end of the 5th c. after the Athenian disaster in Sicily (Pomtow, *RE*, suppl. iv, s.v. Delphi, 1248 ff., '*c.* 412'; Robertson², 328, '*c.* 405').

## CATALOGUE[1]

**1.** Painted inscription on late PC aryballos from the Argive Heraion; *c.* 650–640? Waldstein, *AH* ii. 185, fig. 101. *VS*, 103, fig. 55. *NC*, 38. Lejeune, *REA* xlvii (1945), 102, n. 3. Nauplia Mus.

**2.** Graffito on poros block at Delphi; 7th c.? *FD* ii. 191, fig. 146 and pl. ii, e. Daux, *BCH* lxi (1937), 57 ff., fig. in text. Lejeune, *REA* xlv (1943), 183, 191. Delphi.          PL. 23

**3.** Strip cut from a bronze plaque at Olympia; *c.* 600–550? *Ol.* v. 714. *IGA* 21. *SGDI* 3163. Roberts i. 94. Roehl[3], 49. 1. *DGE* 130. Lejeune, op. cit. 184, 191. *SEG* xi. 1216. Olympia Mus. 611a–b.  PL. 23

**4.** LC krater; *c.* 575–550. *SGDI* 3165. Furtwaengler, *Katalog*, 1147. *NC*, cat. vases 1170. Rodenwaldt, *Korkyra* ii (1941), fig. 106 and p. 119. Lejeune, op. cit. 184, 191. Berlin Mus.          PL. 23

**5.** Incised inscription on Attic BF dinos from Caere; *c.* 550–525. Roberts i. 95. *SGDI* 3164. *IG* iv. 424. Roehl[3], 49. 2. Mingazzini, *Vasi Coll. Castellani* (1930), no. 446. Technau, *Exekias*, 15. Lejeune, op. cit. 184, 191. *ABV*, 146, no. 20. Rome, Villa Giulia Mus.

**6.** Four sherds from the temple of Hera Limenia, Perachora; 6th c. *Perachora* ii. 398, nos. 99–101, 103. NM.

**7.** Bronze statuette of bull-calf from the same temple of Hera Limenia; *c.* 525–500. Payne, *JHS* li (1931), 194. Lejeune, op. cit., 183. *Perachora* i. 136, pl. 43. 5–7. *SEG* xi. 226. NM.

**8.** Bronze plaque listing members of an association; *c.* 500? Orlandos, Ἑλληνικά x (1937–8), 5 ff., fig. 1. Peek, *AM* lxvi (1941), 200 ff. Lejeune, op. cit. 185 ff. *SEG* xi. 244. Buck 96. NM.          PL. 23

**9.** Bluish stone base with cutting on top for a stele, bearing two names in two lines, Sikyon; *c.* 500–480? Orlandos, *PAE* 1951, 189 f., fig. 4. *SEG* xiv. 309. Sikyon Mus.

**10.** Base of a late BF lekythos from a grave (?), Sikyon, with graffito Ϝερōος: *c.* 500–475? Orlandos, op. cit. 191, n. 2. *SEG* xiv. 313. Sikyon Mus.

**11.** Marble slab; *c.* 500–475? Orlandos, Ἑλληνικά x (1937–8), 12 ff. Lejeune, op. cit. 189, 191. *SEG* xi. 259. Sikyon Mus.          PL. 23

**12.** Bronze spear-butt from Olympia; *c.* 500–475? *Ol.* v. 245. Roberts i. 126. *SGDI* 3126. *IGA* 27a. Roehl[3], 49. 3. Lejeune, op. cit. 184, 191. Olympia Mus. 331.          PL. 23

**13a–b.** Part of an opisthographic stele listing victories at the Games; *c.* 500–475? Orlandos, *PAE* 1932, 70, fig. 8. Lejeune, op. cit. 183, 191. *SEG* xi. 257, xiv. 310. Moretti 12. Sikyon Mus.          PL. 23

**14.** Graffito on a sherd from the temple of Hera Limenia; *c.* 500–475? *Perachora* ii. 398, no. 113.

**15.** (*a*) Inscription on anta and (*b*) masons' marks on blocks from the Sikyonian Treasury at Olympia; *c.* 475–450? *Ol.* ii. 43 and v. 668. *IGA* 27b–c. *SGDI* 3166–7. Frazer, *Pausanias* iv. 57 f. Roehl[3], 50. 4. Lejeune, op. cit. 184.

**16.** Stele bearing list of names found near Sikyon (Moulki); *c.* 460–450? Earle, *Papers American Sch. Athens* v (1890), 39. *IG* iv. 425. Roehl[3], 50. 6. Lejeune, op. cit. 183, 191. Lost?          PL. 23

**17.** Coins of Sikyon with *san* on reverse; *c.* 450 onwards? B ii. 3. 515 ff., pl. 219.

**18.** Masons' marks on the later Treasury of Sikyon at Delphi; late 5th c.? Pomtow, *Zeitschrift f. Gesch. d. Architektur* iii (1910), 129 f., fig. 26. La Coste-Messelière, *Au Musée de Delphes* (1936), 19 ff. Lejeune, op. cit. 184.

---

[1] I have omitted from this list the very fragmentary inscription on an anta-block from the Sikyonian treasury at Olympia, *Ol.* v. 650 (= *SEG* xi. 1218). The interpretation is uncertain, and the lettering unlike that of **15a**.

*Inscriptions attributed to Sikyon*

**19.** Inscription on a clay object (trapeza?) found near Thermon, Aitolia; 6th c.? Rhomaios, *A. Delt.* vi (1920–1), 65 ff., fig. 2. *SEG* iii. 438. *IG* ix². 1. 93. Vollgraff, *BCH* lviii (1934), 145. Lejeune, op. cit. 184 f., n. 4 and 1945, 111.

**20.** Graffito on the lip of a pithos from Thermon, 6th c.? Soteriades, *AE* 1903, 94. *IG* ix². 1. 84. Lejeune, op. cit. 184 and 1945, 111 f. Thermon Mus.

**21.** Inscription [Διο]ς Ολυμπιου on a bronze spear-butt from Olympia; *c.* 500–475? *Ol.* v. 699. *IGA* 24. Roehl³, 44. 10. It is generally ascribed to Corinth, because of the use of *san* and ου for the false diphthong; but these are equally valid for Sikyonian, and the angled *omikron* seems especially characteristic of 5th-c. Sikyon; cf. **12, 13, 15, 16** above. Olympia Mus. 552.                     PL. 23

# PHLEIOUS, KLEONAI (WITH NEMEA), TIRYNS

FIG. 36. Phleious, Kleonai and Nemea, Tiryns

*Notes on letter-forms*

β1 (Kleonai) is similar to the Corinthian, with one stroke less in the upper 'twist' and one more in the lower. There are no examples yet from the other places, but it is probable that they used either a like form, or the Argive type.

Tiryns shows γ1, as in the alphabets of the eastern Argolid, Lakonia, and (modified) Argos; it is not yet known whether the other places also used this form, or the lunate type of the Corinthian.

All these places were familiar with both the freak *epsilon-eta* and the normal form, but turned them to different uses from the Corinthian, employing the normal letter for ε and the freak for η. It is impossible to say whether this is a confusion of the Corinthian usage, made by the first receiver and so transmitted to the rest, or whether it reflects directly a form of script received without the agency of Corinth (E = ε, and Ɇ (>B?) = η), which would imply that the alphabet of this part of the Peloponnese came by another entry, independently of Corinth. The latter hypothesis has the attraction of simplicity, but is quite unprovable. There is good evidence that the alphabet arrived in Corinth very early; the most likely place of entry for the other version would be Nauplia (spreading thence past Tiryns upwards), and nothing at all is known of the Nauplian alphabet.

ι1 is used at Phleious, probably under the influence of Achaian and Corinthian; but at Kleonai and Tiryns the straight form 2 is always used.

The characteristic μ1 has both vertical strokes parallel (**5, 6**).

The Phleiasian text **1** shows still the archaic ξ1, the others ξ2.

In the stone inscriptions of the first half of the 6th c. a cutting-compass is used, forming an *omikron* with central dot (used also for *theta, qoppa*). The circle may be disproportionately small (cf. **6, 7, 8, 11**).

The date of *san*'s disuse is not yet evident, but presumably it was replaced by *sigma* about the end of the 6th or the early 5th c., as elsewhere in this part of the Peloponnese.

At Phleious the archaic ϙ1 is used, the circle being made with a cutting-compass; the Kleonaian ϙ2 shows the central dot from the compass left still visible.

φɪ (made with the cutting-compass) is used in the first half of the 6th c. In the second half of the century the coins of Phleious show the later form φ2.

χɪ is current at Phleious and Kleonai, χ2 at Tiryns.

There are two possible instances of ωɪ; see Phleious **1** and p. 147, n. 1.

*Diphthongs.* The true diphthong εɪ is only attested once (Kleonai **5**), spelt in the normal way EI; it was presumably the same in the other places. At Kleonai the false diphthong was also spelt EI (**6**), but at Phleious E (as Corinthian; Phleious **1***b*); there is no example yet from Tiryns. The true diphthong ου is, again, not yet attested, but was presumably spelt in full; the false is attested at Kleonai (**5**), and probably also in **11**, spelt with *omikron* only, as in Argive.

*Punctuation* does not occur in the examples from Phleious, but Kleonai and Tiryns both show ɪ, as at Mycenae and Argos. Guide-lines are used in Kleonai **6**.

*Direction of the script.* Most of the examples fall within the first half or middle of the 6th c., when the *boustrophedon* system was at its height. The very early graffito **11** is retrograde; so is Phleious **3**, which cannot be closely dated.

The alphabets of the smaller places which lay between Corinth and Argos are as yet known only in part. Archaic inscriptions have been found at Phleious, Kleonai (with Nemea), Mycenae, and Tiryns, though none of the scripts is yet fully attested, the nearest to complete being those of Kleonai and Mycenae. No archaic inscriptions have yet been found at Tenea, Orneai, Midea, or Oinoe; or south of Argos at Lerna, Hysiai, and Nauplia. As the companion of letters shows, the scripts of Phleious, Kleonai, and Tiryns seem to have been derived principally from the Corinthian; but the Mycenean differs in several letters, which set it apart from this group as a whole, though geographically it lies right in the centre. It is remarkable that at Tiryns the alphabet was not taken direct from that of her close neighbour Argos, but is in all respects like that of Kleonai. It looks as though a form of the Corinthian alphabet, developing as it went variations in the *iota* and *epsilon-eta*, spread southwards towards the Argolic Gulf, but in Argos some other influence prevailed, and the Argive type extended (for political reasons, perhaps) to Mycenae. Such an explanation is very lame, but with the present gaps in our knowledge it is hard to find one which will fit all the facts; if future excavations reveal the scripts of such places as Tenea and Orneai, on the one hand, and, on the other, Oinoe and Nauplia before the latter fell into Argive hands, the problem of this curious distribution of scripts should at last be solved.

### PHLEIOUS

Of the history of Phleious before the fifth century it is known that, according to tradition, in the second half of the seventh century a body of emigrants under Hippasos went thence to Samos (Paus. ii. 13. 1–2): that in the second half of the sixth century there was a tyrant Leon established in Phleious, whose name is preserved only because he allegedly conversed with the philosopher Pythagoras, great-grandson of Hippasos (D. L. *Prooimion* 12 and viii. 1. 1, 8; Cicero, *Tusc. Disp.* v. 3. 8–9): and that at some time in the sixth century, possibly during her tyranny, Phleious began to coin silver on the Aiginetan standard, marked with a *phi* of late archaic type (**4**). Of her early political relations with Corinth and Argos we know nothing directly, but her fifth-century history shows that (unlike Kleonai, her closest neighbour) she was essentially pro-Corinthian and anti-Argive. Like Mycenae and Tiryns she sent her quota of troops to Thermopylai, the Isthmos and Plataia, defying the neutrality of Argos and pro-Argive Kleonai; and she took the side of Corinth and Sparta before and during the Peloponnesian War.[1]

The Phleiasian script is known to us from several inscribed blocks which, though now scattered about the site or re-used in modern buildings, all belonged originally to some large structure, of which a good many uninscribed blocks also remain. Two (possibly three) of the inscribed blocks are known only from Fourmont's sketches (**1e–f**); another, built into a church, was published by Ross and others in the nineteenth century (**1g**); the remaining four were found by the American excavators of the site in 1923 (**1a–d**). Though too little now remains for any certain restoration of the monument or the inscription, a few points may be noted. Firstly, no block contains more than a single line of writing, except in one of Fourmont's copies (**1e**); and, as his original was built into a church wall and he copied the second line as being inverted, it is possible that there were two blocks one above the other, both inscribed along their lower edges, and the second built in upside down (cf. Fraenkel, *IG* iv. 439: *IGA* 28). Secondly, the letters of **1a**, which reads from left to right, are slightly larger than those whose measurements are known, which read from right to left.[2] Thirdly, all whose measurements are known are of considerable width;[3] and lastly, the late inscription which survives in part on one of the blocks (**1c**) refers to sacrifices to Apollo, and the things 'which they used to offer in former times'.[4]

It is therefore possible that the structure was a large altar made of stone slabs, like the small one illustrated on the François vase (FR, pls. 1–2);[5] and the archaic inscriptions might be (*a*) a dedication written from left to right in large letters, e.g. [Ηιππōνα]ξ και Ηιπποκρατ[ε̄]ς εθ[εταν - - -] (**1a, d**), and (*b*) instructions concerning the oaths sworn over the victims, written from right to left in a long single line round the sides of the altar, perhaps starting on the opposite side from the dedication: [- - -Η]ορϘος ενδετō· αι λο̣ι τον το[- - -]αι τ' ΗορϘον οτια οφελ[- - -] δεχεται τον ΗορϘον [- - -]τọ τọις ΗορϘιọ[ις- - -]

---

[1] Hdt. vii. 202; viii. 72; Thuc. i. 27. 2; iv. 70. 1; v. 57 ff.; Diod. xi. 32. 1; Plut., *De Mal. Her.* 42. A relic of a defeat of Phleious by an unknown adversary is the *paragnathis* from Olympia (Robert, *Coll. Froehner* i (1936), 35, no. 30, pl. 32 = *SEG* xi. 1212): [ΔιϜ]ος ολυ[υπ]ιου ΦλειϜονταθεν. The letters (cut with a chisel and circular punch whereby the circular letters are occasionally set out of alinement) suggest a date about the second quarter of the 5th c. They have no marked characteristics except that *lambda*'s hook is slightly lowered from the top, as in the Argivo-Mycenean type. A battle between Phleious and Mycenae or Argos sounds plausible; but it is risky to build a battle on a possible slip of the chisel.

[2] **1a**, letter-height 0·04–0·07 m.; **1b–c**, 0·03–0·05 m.; **1d**, 0·03–0·05 m. (incomplete); **1g** is given as 0·05–0·07 m. by Roehl, *IGA* 28c, but Scranton, who re-

measured them in 1936, states that 'the measurements agree perfectly with those discussed above' (i.e. **1b–c**).

[3] **1a–c** measure respectively: length 0·81 × width 0·67 m., length 0·77 × width 0·77 m., length 0·74 × width 0·77 m.

[4] *Hesperia* v (1936), 241: [- - -αρ]χοντος ωστε θυειν τωι Απολλ[ωνι - - -|- - -] εν τε τοις προτεροις χρονοις εδιδο-[σαν - - -|- - -] τωι θεωι των κρατιστευοντων βοα[- - -], κτλ: cf. *SEG* xi. 276.

[5] Whether the curious system of channels and grooves cut on some of the blocks (described in detail, op. cit. 235) is to be connected with the ritual arrangements of such an altar is dubious (cf. Jeffery, *Hesperia* xvii (1948), 92, n. 23, and 91 f. for other instances of inscribed altars). They seem to be too elaborate merely for haulage, but they may be only from some later re-use of the stones.

δεκατας αι τε κ[- - -]: and recording at the end two officials, priestly or secular, during whose office it was done: [- - -]ς και Λαστρατος αρχε[ταν?] (**1** *b, c, e–g*).

The alphabet shows crooked II, facing always to the right; the rest is also like the Corinthian in all respects except that *epsilon*, as well as the false diphthong, is represented by the normal E; what Phleious used for *eta* is still uncertain, but it may have been the freak Corinthian form, as at Kleonai and Tiryns. The archaic forms of ?ι and ξι may be noted (in contrast with the cutting, which is sharp and competent, with a cutting-compass used for the circles); also the curious double circle on one of the blocks, perhaps to express ω.[1] Punctuation is not used. The date may be somewhere in the first half of the sixth century.

The only other archaic inscriptions from Phleious are the lost fragment **2**, which differed in measurements, trimming, and letter-height from the other blocks, and was judged by the excavators not to belong to the same structure,[2] and a fragmentary block found at Hagios Georgios reading Αρταμ[ιτι?], which cannot be closely dated from the illustrations, but is inscribed from right to left (**3**). Pausanias mentions a dedication by Phleious at Delphi, of Zeus carrying off the nymph Aigina, and a larger composition at Olympia of Zeus, Aigina, and her family; but dates and artists are unknown.[3] By the last part of the fifth century the coinage shows that the local alphabet had been abandoned; ΦΛΕΙΑΣΙΟΝ is the legend on the series dated in *HN*², 408, as '430–322'.

## KLEONAI, NEMEA

Phleious did not lie on any major traffic route, except that from Sikyon to Arkadia by way of Alea and Mantinea. But Kleonai lay close to the main road from Corinth to Argos. The resemblance between the Kleonaian and Corinthian alphabets can be seen in the

---

[1] A similar duplication of *omikron* to express ω was published by Ross from a gravestone at Corinthian Asprokampo: Δρωπιδου τοδε σαμα (cf. Jeffery, *JHS* lix (1939), 139). The Phleiasian letter has been explained as a mistake corrected by the mason (Scranton, *Hesperia* x (1941), 371). While welcoming the note, ibid., which (by establishing as modern the stone published as ancient in *Corinth* viii. i. 267) corrects my own reference in *JHS*, l.c., I must nevertheless join issue, on behalf of Ross, with the further statement (op. cit. 372): 'Other copies of the Asprokampo inscription quoted by Miss Jeffery, however, show only a single circle or rectangular mark for the letter in question, and Ross's copy may for any of various reasons be unreliable.' Ross's reading 8 was reproduced by Roehl (*IGA* 18), Fraenkel (*IG* iv. 414), and Kirchhoff (*Geschichte*³, 88). Forchhammer copied the letter as ◇ (*Halcyonia* (1857), 14) and to Roehl (loc. cit.) this reading seemed to make better sense. Le Bas, from whom came Rangabé's copy, only saw the stone after the first five letters, including the debatable one, had been lost (Le Bas, *RA* i. 174 and *Voy. Arch.* ii. 77, pl. iv. 6; Rangabé, *Ant. Hell.* no. 319); a stone, possibly the

same, was seen, reading only -ΟΔΒΜ-, by Payne (*Perachora* i. 7 and *SEG* xi. 243). There are thus only two originals to consider, those of Ross and of Forchhammer, who was not an epigraphist; and I am not prepared to reject Ross's as unreliable without further reasons; he commented in his text on the oddness of the letter, and his accuracy over other inscriptions is well attested. For the same reason I believe that his drawing of the 5th and 6th letters in the name is accurate, but that the letters are to be read as υλ (so Roehl, after Forchhammer) to give Δρωπυλου ([Μαν]-δροπυλου, Roehl; but cf. Δρωπυλίων). This avoids the non-Doric genitive Δρωπιδου, against which Roehl rightly protested.

[2] *Hesperia* v (1936), 244 f. The second line appears to read, from right to left, [- - -]ν προ τας [- - -]: the direction of the first may be the same, but is not certain, and nothing can be made of the reading.

[3] v. 22. 6 (Olympia) and x. 13. 6 (Delphi). Pomtow suggested that they were offered after the battle with Argos in 416 (Thuc. v. 115. 1; cf. *RE*, suppl. iv. 1402 f., no. 5); but this is quite uncertain.

types of *beta* and *delta*, and the use of the freak vowel; the differences lie in the *iota* and in the fact that at Kleonai the freak letter was used to denote *eta* (as at Corinth), but not *epsilon*, for which the normal E was used, as at Phleious. Kleonai also denoted the false diphthong ει by EI, and the false ου by O. As far as the extant evidence goes, the only differences between the scripts of Kleonai and Phleious lie in the *iota* and the false ει.

The early history of Kleonai is less obscure than that of Phleious. Politically she sided with Argos as a loyal member of the traditional Argive hegemony, which involved her in hostilities possibly with Sikyon,[1] certainly with Corinth[2] and Mycenae. Her antagonism with the latter was either begun or strengthened by disputes over the control of the Games at Nemea, which belonged by tradition to Kleonai.[3] One of the earliest inscriptions found at Nemea[4] is the dedication of the Kleonaian Aristis son of Pheidon (**5**), four times victor in the pankration there, which gives a *terminus post quem* of 567 B.C. for the inscription, since the Games were trieteric.[5] Of about the same date, i.e. the middle of the sixth century or rather earlier, is the lower part of a poros stele (**6**) which was found in the modern village of Hagios Basilios, south of Kleonai, inscribed in vertical *boustrophedon* on three sides (the fourth side being now broken or worn away). It came from some precinct, for its text concerns the ritual of purification. The wide face A, which has a modern socket for a door-post, and was evidently used as a threshold, is badly worn, but may have lost only one line (the topmost, adjoining the lost side D). The reading appears to be continuous from A on to the adjoining narrow face B, and thence on to C; so that the text probably started in the lost top line(s) of A, and ended on the last lines of C or on the lost D. The letter-forms resemble those of the altar (?) at Phleious (**1**), and the *lex sacra* from the temple of Apollo at Corinth p. 128, **18**), though the turn of the lines on the latter is more primitive than in the example from Kleonai. Guide-lines and a cutting-compass have been used; the circular letters are small in proportion to the rest, the legs of *mu* are parallel (as also in contemporary inscriptions from Argos; contrast the more splayed form used at Athens and elsewhere). The triple-dot punctuation is used throughout, as at Mycenae and Argos.

[1] This has been deduced from the passage in Plutarch, *De Ser. Num. Vind.* 7, which refers to a boy victor of Kleonai whose citizenship was disputed by the Sikyonians, who tore him to pieces during the struggle. For this wantonness, Zeus chastened Sikyon with the bitter but powerful medicine (φάρμακον) of the Orthagorid dynasty; whereas Kleonai, which never experienced such a draught, for the same reason never reached any greatness. It is never suggested that Kleonai was in any way subject to Sikyon.

[2] Ion, *ap.* Plutarch, *Cimon* 17; the date of the aggression is not there given, but it was coupled with a similar attack on Megara, and is therefore inferred to be during the years shortly before *c.* 460 when Megara allied herself to Athens. The statement that Corinth (as well as Kleonai and Argos) once held the Nemean Games is made by the Schol. Pind. *Nem.* Hypothesis, c and d; cf. Hanell, *RE*, s.v. Nemea, 2324.

[3] Mycenae, before her downfall in the 5th c.,

asserted a counter-claim to control the Games (Diod. xi. 65). Kleonai thereafter helped Argos in her destruction (Strabo 377).

[4] The inscription *SEG* xi. 291 should from its alphabet belong to Olympia, rather than to Nemea as has been suggested by Meritt (*AJP* lix (1938), 500). A fragment of the temple accounts found at Nemea (Blegen, *Art and Archaeology* xxii (1926), 130, 132 = *SEG* xi. 294) is dated 's. Vᵃ' in *SEG*; I have seen the stone, and from the look of the letters (e.g. *sigma* and *upsilon*) and the use of *eta* and *omega* would date it rather in the early 4th c.

[5] I saw the stele in 1953, and add the following detail: on top, two rectangular cuttings (0·08 m. × 0·11 m., depth 0·005 m.), set wide apart, midway between front and back, and very near the two side faces. They appear to be for the tenons of a crowning member, perhaps a flat capital on which Aristis' dedication, whatever it was, was set.

These two inscriptions establish the type of script used at Kleonai; and in view of these I should ascribe tentatively to a Kleonaian hand the very early graffito χος ηεμι (*sic*) incised on a two-handled cup of Subgeometric type (**11**), dated in the first years of the seventh century, which was found in a small early shrine excavated in the area of the great Argive Heraion. It might also be Tirynthian; but it cannot be Argive, because of the freak *epsilon* used.[1] Some explanation is also required for the inscription *IG* iv. 484 (**7**). This stone, found built into a ruined chapel south of Nemea, is inscribed [- - -]ι εφοδιαι, with ει, 12; and the freak letter for *epsilon* is not normal for Kleonai. Judged by the epithet it probably came from some shrine of Hekate or Persephone or Artemis in the neighbourhood of the sanctuary of Nemean Zeus, and from the illustration there is nothing to show if it is sixth-century or early fifth. It might be assigned to the period of Corinthian control, *c.* 470–460?, when Corinth 'broke into Kleonai without knocking', and held the Nemean Games for a time (see p. 148, n. 2); or it may be simply a mis-spelling for E by a Kleonaian mason.

### TIRYNS

The archaic fragment found at Tiryns (**8**) comes from a stele of the same kind as the *lex sacra* from Kleonai, and may have been erected in the temple of Hera, the chief sanctuary at Tiryns. It was inscribed on at least two adjoining faces; the other two faces, and the top and bottom, are broken away. The surviving edge is bevelled (like those of the *lex sacra* from Corinth (Corinth **18**)), and a single line in smaller letters was cut on the bevel; it is not clear if this was intended, or if there was not enough room left on the last face for the last line, so that the mason resorted to this device; it may even be a later addition of something omitted when the text was cut. The instructions have to do with a religious body, for the official called the ἐπιθέτας is mentioned, but nothing further has been made out of the fragmentary text.[2] The letters are very neatly cut, resembling those of the Kleonaian *lex sacra*, except that the Tirynthian differs in the form of *chi* (χ2), and has no guidelines. They cannot be far apart in date, and mark the high standard of technical ability maintained by the masons of the Peloponnese at this time.

We know that in the first half of the fifth century, about a generation after the battle of Sepeia (494?) and probably after 468, the Tirynthians were defeated in an attack, and their city occupied, by the slaves of Argos, who held it at first under Argive control, and later, after an unsuccessful revolt, yielded it to the Argives.[3] Any inscription found there in the Argive alphabet would help to narrow down the dates of these events; but so far

[1] The meaning is not clear. χος {η}εμί gives the best sense, but the measure of a χοῦς (12 kotylai) was far larger than this small cup, at least in Attica. Dunbabin, however, pointed out to me that some local Peloponnesian measure current in these parts might have been smaller than the Attic; and that anyway the word need not refer to a measure, but might merely describe the cup.

[2] I saw the stone in 1953, and add the following minor points to the previous publications: (1) Peek thought that a small piece of the original back remained; I think not. (2) Measurements: max. height 0·32 m.; width 0·365 m.; thickness 0·17 m. (3) There may not be a vacat above l. 1; the surface is too battered to show. (4) L. 3, Peek: —καν ፡ μη—, J.: —καν ፡ νη—. L. 5, Peek —καθ—, J.: —ν καθ—.

[3] Hdt. vi. 83; cf. Seymour, *JHS* xlii (1922), 24 ff.

only two graffiti on sherds have been found at Tiryns, one still unillustrated (**9**), and the other, described as 'probably fifth-century', reading only —φροφ— (**10**).

## CATALOGUE

### PHLEIOUS

**1.** *a–g*. Seven inscribed blocks from an archaic structure (altar?); *c.* 600–550? (*a–d*) Scranton, *Hesperia* v (1936), 235 ff., nos. 1–3, 7, figs. 2–6, 9a. Jeffery, *JHS* lix (1939), 139. Scranton, *Hesperia* x (1941), 371 f. *SEG* xi. 275–6. (*e–f*) (known only from Fourmont's drawings): *IG* iv. 439a–b. *IGA* 28a–b. Roehl³, 51. 1a–b. Scranton, *Hesperia* v (1936), 239 f., fig. 7. (*g*) *IG* iv. 439c. *IGA* 28c. Roehl³, 51. 1c. Scranton, loc. cit., Heraklion (Nemea) Mus.                                    PL. 24

**2.** Fragment, now lost, from the excavations at Phleious; *c.* 600–550? Scranton, op. cit. 244 f., no. 8, fig. 9. *SEG* xi. 284.

**3.** Block from a statue-base (?) found at Hagios Georgios; *c.* 550? Bilco, *BCH* vi (1882), 444. *IG* iv. 440. *SGDI* 3171. Lost?

**4.** Coinage of Phleious with letter φ; second half of 6th c.? B ii. 1. 813 f., pl. 33. 12. *HN*², 408 f.

### KLEONAI (with NEMEA)

**5.** Dedication of Aristis son of Pheidon, from Nemea; *c.* 560? Blegen, *AJA* xxxi (1927), 432 f., fig. 10. Peek, *AE* 1931, 103 f. Macgregor, *TAPA* lxxii (1941), 275. *SEG* xi. 290 and xiv. 314. Friedlaender 103. Buck 97. Moretti 3. Heraklion (Nemea) Mus.                                    PL. 24

**6.** *Lex sacra* on a poros stele from Hagios Basilios; *c.* 575–550? Dickerman, *AJA* vii (1903), 147 ff., figs. 1–3. *IG* iv. 1607. Roehl³, 45. 12. *DGE* 129. Peek, *AM* lxvi (1941), 200, pl. 71. *SEG* xi. 296. EM 585.                                    PL. 25

**7.** Stele bearing a dedication [- - -]ι εφοδιαι: 6th–5th c.? Roehl³, *AM* i (1876), 229. *IGA* 26. *IG* iv. 484. *SGDI* 3161. Roehl³, 45, 13. Lost?                                    PL. 25

### TIRYNS

**8.** Fragment of stele bearing a *lex sacra* from Tiryns; *c.* 600–550? Peek, *AM* lxvi (1941), 198 ff., no. 5, pl. 70. *SEG* xi. 369. Nauplia Mus. 2463.                                    PL. 25

**9.** Dedication to Athena, Αθαναιας εμι on the rim of a glazed vase from Tiryns; 6th c.? K. Müller, *AM* xxxviii (1913), 90 f. Karo, *RE* s.v. Tiryns, 1466.

**10.** Graffito on the rim of a large glazed Attic (?) plate; 5th c.? Frickenhaus, *Tiryns* i (1912), 105, no. 226, fig. 43.

*Inscription attributed to Kleonai or Tiryns*

**11.** Graffito on a Subgeometric cup from an early shrine in the precinct of the Argive Heraion; *c.* 700–675? Blegen, *AJA* xliii (1939), 425 f., fig. 13. *SEG* xi. 306. Nauplia Mus.?                                    PL. 25

## ARGOS

| α | β | γ | δ | ε | ϝ | ζ | η | ⱶ | θ | ι | κ | λ | μ | ν | ξ | ο | π | Ϻ | ϙ | ρ | σ | τ | υ | φ | χ | ψ | ω | P | |
|---|---|---|---|---|---|---|---|---|---|---|---|---|---|---|---|---|---|---|---|---|---|---|---|---|---|---|---|---|---|
| 1 | A | Γ | D | ⱶ | F | I | | ⱶ | B | ⊗ | I | K | ⋏ | M | ⋎ | ⵣ | O | Γ | M | ϙ | P | — | T | Y | Φ | X | | — | ⋮ | 1 |
| 2 | A | Γ | ⋀ | D | F | | | | ⊞ | ⊕ | | K | ⱶ | M | ⋏ | ⧻ | ⊙ | Π | | ϙ | R | ξ | | Y | Ⴔ | + | Ψ | | ⋮ | 2 |
| 3 | A | | ⋀ | | E | | | | H | ⊙ | | | | M | ⋏ | ⧻ | ◇ | | | | R | | | V | Φ | | Ψ | | ⋮ | 3 |
| 4 | | | Γ | | | | | | | | | | | | N | | | | | | R | | | Y | | | | | ⁝ | 4 |
| 5 | | | | | | | | | | | | | | | N | | | | | | | | | | Y | | | | ≡ | 5 |
| 6 | | | | | | | | | | | | | | | | | | | | | | | | | | | | | ) | 6 |

FIG. 37. Argos and Mycenae

*Notes on letter-forms, including those of Mycenae*

α1 is the normal archaic form, α2 rare. α3 becomes the standard form in the second quarter of the 5th c., though examples of it occur already in the 6th c., e.g. Mycenae **1**. The Argive coinage, which began comparatively late, shows both α2 and α3 on its reverse in different examples of the early issues; whether the coinage began in the first years of the 5th c. (cf. B ii. 2. 825 ff.) or during the Argive expansion *c.* 468 (*HN²*, 437 f.), in either case it falls within the years when the archaic and late forms were used side by side.

Argos and Mycenae used a form of *beta* with its 'hooks' left open (β1), as in Corinthian, Melian, and, an extreme example, the lunate type used by the Naxian group (p. 289). The earliest example of the Argive *beta* so far attested appears to belong to the last quarter of the 6th c. (**15**); β2 was still in use in the third quarter of the 5th c. (**46**). Both forms occur in texts of about the middle of the 5th c. (**30, 39a–b**), so that it cannot be said with certainty that β1 is always the more archaic.

During the second quarter of the 5th c. γ1 developed to γ2 (**26**). The evidence for its further changes in the second half of the century comes firstly from the inscription *en pointillé* on the prize dinos for the Games of Hera Argeia (**43**), probably belonging to the third quarter of the century, where the *gamma* appears still to be 2; secondly, from the coins. A type which was first struck in 421 to mark the alliance of Argos and Elis, bearing the head of Polykleitos' new cult-statue of Hera Argeia, shows on one of its earliest issues the legend Αργειον with γ2 (B ii. 3. 458 and pl. 215, 11); later issues, from the end of the 5th or the beginning of the 4th c., show the Ionic form 4, with *omega*. This is also the form on the public dedication **48**, which may be from the end of the 5th or the beginning of the 4th c. We may note here also the forms 1 and 4 on the decree **39b**, whose lettering is a mixture of archaic and later forms.

Medial *vau* still occurs spasmodically *c.* 460 and later (cf. αεθλον in **17**, αϝεθλον in **26**, αϝρετευε in **40**). Initial *vau* was certainly still in use *c.* 457 (**30**), probably still in the third quarter of the century; cf. Vollgraff, *BCH* xxviii (1904), 429, no. 11, where *vau* is used apparently with the later forms θ3, φ3.

ⱶ1 was still used in the third quarter of the 5th c. (**46**); the earliest example of ⱶ3 used for the aspirate appears to be the inscription on the rim of a bronze phiale from the Heraion (*AH* ii. 284 and 337 f., no. 1994, pl. cxvi = *SEG* xi. 308), dated in the 6th c. If the open *heta* is correct in the drawing (there is, unfortunately, no adequate photograph), the use of the late form is remarkable. The one example of Ionic *eta*, from the last years of the century (**49**), shows the open form. It may be assumed that in Argos, as elsewhere in the Peloponnese, the letter was used with both values for some time before the aspirate was finally abandoned.

In the second quarter of the 5th c. the older θ1–2 and newer θ3 were in use together (cf. **26, 28, 30, 34, 39a**); 3 was normal in the second half, except for the 2 of **39b**, which, as noted above, contains several other early forms.

*Iota* was also used during the 6th c. and presumably earlier to express the 'on-glide', ͺ used between *iota* and a following vowel (θίͺοιν, Σικελίͺας, ἅλιͺος), but by the last years of the century this practice seems to have been given up (cf. **17**, Θιοπος and Buck, 52).

The peculiar λ (shared by Mycenae) was probably evolved from the normal type, to distinguish it from Argive *gamma*. The direction of the cross-bar follows those of *alpha, epsilon, vau*; that is to say, it slopes (λı) until the second quarter of the 5th c., but has become horizontal (λ2) *c.* 460–450.

In μı the last bar may sometimes depart slightly from the vertical, but never very much. At the end of the 6th c. it was losing its rigidity and spreading out (cf. the various forms in **15, 16, 17**); by *c.* 460 it had become μ3.

νı lasted into the 5th c., though *c.* 500–480 the later ν2 may appear in the same inscription (**17**); *c.* 460 the form still varies between 1, 2, 3; by the third quarter it has become the later type 4–5, with both its side-strokes vertical.

Five inscriptions to be dated between 475 and 450 show a sidelong ξ2, which may be attributed to a fashion of the time perhaps set by a single mason (**22, 30, 31, 32, 39a**); 3, a variation of this type, appears on a tripod-base from the Heraion (**33**). Chance has preserved one early example of Argive ξ1 (**9**, εξπριͺασθαι); so possibly this sidelong type may be a standard form of the 5th c.

In the early inscriptions *omikron* is sometimes small in proportion to the other letters (**1, 4**), or varies in size (**7**); but in most of the inscriptions throughout the 6th c. it is normal. At the end of the century it sometimes reverts to the very small type, a tendency which becomes stronger in the first half of the 5th c. (**19, 20, 21, 26, 28, 29, 30**; Mycenae **3, 5, 6**). The use of the cutting-compass, producing an *omikron* with central dot, is sporadic during the 5th c. (**7, 30, 39a, 42**); I do not know of any Argive example certainly earlier than **17**, but it may have been used during the 6th c. also, as elsewhere in the Argolid; cf. Mycenae **1, 7**.

In the decade *c.* 470–460 π2 appears on a bronze hydria (**26**), and again on the stele **32**, and sporadically with π1 on the Tanagra stele (**30**), which is probably by the same mason.

As far as can be judged, *san* was displaced at Argos by *sigma* during the last years of the 6th c. (**15, 16**); it is not as yet attested at Mycenae, but this may well be due only to the lack of early material (pp. 171 f.).

*Qoppa* is still used in the proper names on the Tanagra stele **30**, but not in the treaty **39a**, which must be very close in date.

ρ1 is normal in the earliest inscriptions. ρ2 first appears sporadically, on dedications from the Heraion (**11, 12, 14**). By the beginning of the 6th c. ρ1 was still sometimes used (**17, 18, 20**), but the tailed form was rapidly displacing it (**19, 21, 23, 24**), first as 2, and later, during the second quarter of the century, as 3–4. 3 or 4 remained the normal type until the end of the 5th c. (**48, 49**); the series of Argive didrachms which began in 421 (see *gamma*) show in two examples, which might be from the late 5th or the early 4th c., the tailed *rho* still used with Ionic *gamma* and *omega* (B ii. 3. 458 f., pl. 215. 13–14).

*Sigma*, used at Argos instead of *san* from the end of the 6th c. onwards, is regularly σ2. Roberts (i. 117) speaks tentatively of a three-stroked example in one of Fourmont's copies, and a single example is cited in *AH* i. 197, no. 1, but in view of its total absence in any of the adequately illustrated inscriptions of Argos, I should venture to doubt both these copies. Mycenean *sigma* also is σ2.

The early types of υ in Argos (as in Corinth) are 1 (**4, 8**) and 2 (**2, 5, 9**). The earliest example of υ3 appears to be on a bronze antyx (?) (**13**). Thereafter υ3 seems to have been the normal form in Argive until about the middle of the 5th c., except for the finely cut stele **17**, where υ2 is still used. About the middle of the century, or just after, the tailed form was again adopted (**4**), and thence continued, very occasionally in the form 5 (cf. **39b** and *AH* i. 205, no. 6), until the end of the period.

φɪ occurs still in the last quarter of the 6th c. (**15**). The next examples of the letter, from the first quarter of the 5th c., show 2 (**20, 21**). About the middle of the century (as with *upsilon*) the tailed form reappears (3), and continues in use to the end of the period.

χɪ and 2 are both used in the first half of the 6th c. The next examples occur in the first half of the 5th c., when the type used is 2 (**17, 20, 30, 36**); ɪ reappears in **39a–b**, and presumably becomes the regular type for the rest of the 5th c., as elsewhere.

ψ2 is used in the last quarter of the 6th c. (**15**), and in the treaty **39a**, shortly before the middle of the 5th c. In **39b** ψ3 is used; no other examples occur, but we may conclude that *psi*, following in general the same development as *upsilon*, remained in this form thereafter. It is not yet attested in Mycenean inscriptions.

*Punctuation* by multiple dots is very characteristic of Argive inscriptions. ɪ occurs already on a 7th c. sherd from the Heraion (**1**), and 2–3 in other inscriptions frequently throughout the 6th and 5th c., both Argive and Mycenean; 4 is rarer (**8, 9**, both in the first half of the 6th c.). 5 occurs once in the 5th c., on the bronze hydria **26**. 6 is used in a Mycenean graffito of the 5th c. (Mycenae **6**).

*Guide-lines* were not used in the long inscriptions (**7, 9**); but they occur in the last quarter of the 6th c. on the capital **15**, faintly and apparently not meant to be seen. Deeply cut lines, evidently meant to show, were used on Mycenae **7** (*c.* 525?), and in the Argive dedication **17**, in the first years of the 5th c.

*Direction of script.* Apart from the bases of Kleobis and Biton (**4**), where the direction of the lines is ordered by the need for symmetrical effect, the earliest Argive inscriptions, whether single-line or *boustrophedon*, begin from left to right (**1, 2, 5, 7, 8**) more often than right to left (**3, 6**, and probably **9**, though the latter text may be a continuation from another bronze plaque). The *boustrophedon* system is still in force after the middle of the 6th c. (**11**), but by the last quarter it appears to have gone out of fashion in monumental stone-cutting (**15, 16, 17**). The *stoichedon* system first appears on stone inscriptions in the first quarter of the 5th c. (**17, 19**), and by *c.* 460–450 has become customary in good work (**30, 39a–b**).

The kinship between the alphabets of Argos and Corinth is apparent in their common use of the *san* and the 'blue' forms for *xi*, *chi*, and *psi*. The Argive differs from the Corinthian in its *beta*, *gamma*, *delta*, *epsilon*, *iota*, *lambda*, and false diphthong ου; and it differs again from the Tirynthian group (Fig. 36) in its *gamma*, *delta*, lack of the freak *eta*, and *lambda*. It remains possible that both the Argive alphabet and that of the Tirynthian group may have been taken ultimately from the Corinthian, acquiring their different details as they spread farther from the original source. Thus the Argive rounded *delta* may have come from Arkadian or Lakonian; straight *iota* from the same source, or from that of the Tirynthian group; *gamma* from any of her neighbours (Lakonia, Tiryns, the eastern Argolid) which used a like form. The Argive *gamma* being identical with the normal *lambda* as used elsewhere, the peculiar Argive *lambda* is probably the result of a deliberate alteration made to avoid confusion, by lowering the top stroke of the *lambda* to half-mast. This form is used also in Mycenean, which is plainly an offshoot from Argive (p. 171); and it is further attested on pottery from the Dodecanese, a fact which may be of importance for the origin of the Argive script. For a long time there was only one example. The Euphorbos plate, as is well known, was found in Kamiros and belongs by style to a fabric attributed tentatively to Rhodes herself, certainly to a manufacturing centre in the eastern Aegean area. The date of the plate is somewhere in the second half of the seventh century, possibly at the end.[1] Hektor and Menelaos are depicted, fighting over the body of Euphorbos. It is the only example as yet of this ware which shows heroic figures as decoration, and when one looks at the design it is plain that all the elaborate filling-motives characteristic of the style were painted in, and the picture finished, before the inscriptions were inserted; for they are squeezed in just as the motives leave room for them. They are in a Doric dialect (Μενελας), but the alphabet is certainly not Rhodian; all the letters correspond with those of the Argive alphabet as we know it, except for the normal, un-Argive *beta* of Ευφορβος. It is true that, by chance, the first example of *beta* in Argos itself is late sixth century (**15**); but that a normal *beta* should change during the sixth century into the abnormal Argive type is a development for which there seems no reason; and, as the plate itself has been held to be the work of somebody who followed the conventional designs of these plates, but for the main picture copied some imported design like those on the Argive bronze relief strips (pp. 158 f.), so one might suggest that the script also is hybrid, such as might be written by Argive workmen settled in Rhodes, or wherever in that area the plates were made. We now have more examples of east Greek pottery inscribed in the same alphabet. On Kalymna in a rich dump of early sherds and terra-cottas beneath the temple of Apollo Pythios were found two sherds from the same vase, which appear to be in the style called 'Rhodian geometric' of the early seventh century.[2] Each sherd has preserved part of the same name, painted under the figure of a bull: Αλκιδαμ[ος?], r. to l. The Argive *lambda* is unmistakable. Another sherd, described as 'geometric in type', shows a fragmentary graffito including the letter *san*. Does the Argive script then come from one of these Doric islands of the Dodecanese? The curious Argive open *beta* has its closest likeness in the open *beta* of the Cycladic islands Paros and Naxos (p. 289); yet the *beta* on the Euphorbos plate is not the Argive type. It is useless to speculate until we know more of the island scripts (see further pp. 353 f.).

The archaic Argive inscriptions cover a fairly wide field. It is true that as yet no Argive pottery has yielded painted inscriptions comparable with those of Corinth, but there is a far richer diversity of material, and some of it on objects which can themselves provide a control for the epigraphical dating: as statuary (**4, 5**), bronze relief strips (**10**), a Doric capital (**15**), a base signed by the son of a known sculptor (**19**), a bronze hydria (**26**), a public war-memorial (**30**). The use of the local alphabet extends to the last years of the fifth century, and so far there is nothing from Argos which is certainly datable before the second half of the seventh.

We may begin with the famous statues of Kleobis and Biton dedicated by the Argives at Delphi (**4**), which are generally assigned to the turn of the seventh and sixth centuries.[3] Over their partly obliterated inscriptions disputes have risen which develop fresh aspects —epigraphical, philological, historical—with every archaeologist who studies them. I re-state the problem here not because I can pretend to offer any new contribution of

[1] *MuZ* i. 139; Buschor, *Griech. Vasen*, 51 ff.
[2] The style was identified for me by Dunbabin.
[3] *Kouroi*, 23, 51 ff., 78 ff.: 'c. 615–590, perhaps to-

wards the end of the period'; Jenkins, *Dedalica*, 74 f.: *c.* 600.

importance, but because there are certain basic facts about the inscription which are apt to be lost in the increasing literature.

The statues were made in island marble, and one, B, is signed by an Argive sculptor (Poly?)medes. Their foot-plinths are carved as small rectangular bases, which was apparently the normal Doric technique at this time; we may recall the similar support on which the rather earlier 'Auxerre kore' stands,[1] and those of the two small bronzes **5** and **6**, though the former has been assigned by some scholars to an east Greek school (p. 156, n. 5). The anathyrosis on the bottom of plinth A (ascribed to the statue of Biton) shows that they were set on a larger base, presumably of local Delphian stone. Whether they were placed side by side on the same base, or facing each other on each side of a path or entry (as suggested in *SIG*³ 5), is not certain; but if there is indeed any continuity between the surviving lines on plinths A and B (which seems to me unlikely), they must have been set side by side as close as possible, so that the reader could track the inscription from one to the other. The sculptor signed his name in the Argive script along the right-hand (outer?) edge of B, from right to left, matching the corresponding line along the left-hand (outer?) edge of A; and I may say at once here that I hold that all the writing on these plinths is contemporary and in Argive, not that (as has been suggested) all but the sculptor's signature is in Phokian dialect and script, added by the Delphians to explain the dedication to the visitor. The use of the triple-dot punctuation is typical of archaic Argive, but not of Phokian; the *gamma* in B is Argive, not the lunate Phokian type; as for the alleged Phokian dialect, careful studies of the inscriptions[2] reveal plainly how tenuous is the interpretation of everything but the sculptor's signature. It is evident that on A the letters are quite uncertain after [- - -]τον ⫶ τọ[- - -]; the ταν ματαρα read by von Premerstein is entirely conjectural, and the very existence of a second line on A (unhesitatingly interpreted by a former editor) is doubtful; while on B the line between Kleobis' feet appears to begin (r. to l.) with the *epsilon* and to end with τοιδυιοι, i.e., to be a short independent line—not the continuation of one which (as was once thought) extended to the back of the plinth, and so might be the continuation of something on plinth A. We do not know how much explanatory matter was written on the lost lower base or bases of these plinths; but if we cast away the preconceived notion that there must have been a long inscription on the plinths, from which the vivid details of the story could be taken, and then judge these inscriptions by the general standards of the period, they suggest something as follows. The line along the outer edge of A might be a brief description: [Κλεοβις και Βι]τον ⫶ το [patronymic?]; or it might even be the signature of another sculptor from the same workshop (for we are not bound to conclude that (Poly?)-medes made both statues, but only that they were deliberately made to look alike, except in one or two details): [- - -]τον ⫶ τọ[δε εποιϝε]. The line between the feet on B and (if it exists) any similar line on A might then be short 'labels' placed beside the figures as the names issue from the figures on vases; as the names of Dermys and Kittylos are placed beside their statues on the grave-monument from Tanagra (Boiotia **8**). What such 'labels'

---

[1] Collignon, *Mon. Piot* xx (1913), 5 ff. The sculptors of Attica and Ionia preferred to cut a small flat plinth, sometimes following the lines of the feet, which was then let into the base proper; cf. *Kouroi*, 22 ff.

[2] G. Daux, *BCH* lxi (1937), 61 ff.; La Coste-Messelière, *BCH* lxxvii (1953), 177 f.

might say, I cannot pretend to decipher; the worn remains on B appear to give ε αγαγον-τοιδυιοι, whence can be extracted at the end τοιδ' υιοι or τοι δυ' ιοι. It is likely that some part of the dramatic story recorded by Herodotos (i. 31) after seeing the statues at Delphi was indicated on the base proper, and perhaps elaborated in detail by his guide.

The punctuation by multiple dots, which is a feature of archaic Argive, occurs again on a small fragment of a dinos from the Heraion (1). It bears a painted dedicatory inscription which with its tall, straggling letters should not be later than the seventh century: [- - -]νδρος ⁚ με αν[εθεκε]. Another brief inscription which probably belongs to the seventh century is incised on a label-shaped plaque of bronze (2), which was apparently cut from a larger bronze strip and inscribed τὸνυϝαλιο ιαρα (sc. σκῦλα, or a similar neuter plural?). It was plainly meant to adorn some offering of war-spoil to Enyalios, whose sanctuary in Argos is attested by ancient authority.¹ The style of the horse and rider engraved on the original strip suggests the second half of the seventh century,² and the dedication itself may well be before the end of the century; it can hardly be later than the early sixth. A small bronze aryballos (3), allegedly found in Sparta but with an inscription clearly Argive, should by its shape be also of the late seventh century;³ it was offered by one Chalkodamas (perhaps the bronze-worker who made it) to the Twin Gods (θιιοιν), that is, probably to Kastor and Polydeukes.⁴ The bronze kouros statuette⁵ dedicated by Poly-krates (5) has been dated c. 590–570, i.e. a generation later than the two statues at Delphi; the inscription is clearly later in date than 2. The rectangular plinth of a similar statuette, of which only the feet survive (wearing ἐνδρομίδες, like those worn by Kleobis and Biton), may be of about the same date; it was dedicated by the sons of Nirachas to the ϝανακε (perhaps, again, the Dioskouroi), and the triple-dot punctuation is used (6).

Within the first half of the sixth century should probably be placed the three longest and most important archaic Argive inscriptions yet found. The first (7) is the stele or (probably) door-post from the acropolis on the Larisa (Paus. ii. 24. 3), a stone block which was rebuilt into the Venetian citadel there, copied by Fourmont and several later travellers in the eighteenth and nineteenth centuries, and finally re-discovered by Voll-graff in 1928. The first two lines, which run *boustrophedon*, beginning from left to right, were read by him: ενν[εϝα δ]αμιοργοι εϝ|ανασσαντο,⁶ and then followed the list of nine names: Ποταμος | και Σθενελας Ϝοχιδαμιδα | και Ιπομεδον | και Χαρον Ϝο Αρχεσιλα | και Αδραστος | και Ϝορθαγορας | και Κτετος Ϝο Μιντονος | και Αριστομαχος | και Ιχονιδας. Since many of the names have a flavour of Argive epic (as Sthenelas, Adrastos, Aristo-machos), and Potamos is not usual, Vollgraff suggested that it might be a list set up by Pheidon of Argos of the past rulers of the state in heroic times, Potamos being Inachos,

¹ Plutarch, *De Mul. Virt.* 245c–f. According to this tradition the sanctuary was not founded until the defeat of Kleomenes of Sparta by the Argive women under Telesilla; but the mixture of fact and legend in the story leaves the true origin of the sanctuary uncertain.

² Cf. *NC*, 71 ff. and cat. vases 496, fig. 18b.

³ This aryballos is mentioned briefly by Payne, *NC*, 211, but without reference to its date. I am indebted to Dunbabin for the date suggested here.

⁴ A sanctuary of the Dioskouroi lay between Argos and Lerna (Paus. ii. 22. 5 and 36. 6). The miniature wheel dedicated in the 5th c. τοι⟨ν⟩ ϝαναϙοι⟨ν⟩ (28) may have come from the same sanctuary, where it would be an appropriate offering to Kastor the horse-tamer.

⁵ Dunbabin pointed out that the style of the statuette itself is east Greek—another small link between Argos and the E. Aegean.

⁶ There is room for a few letters in the break before ενν[εϝα]: e.g. [τοιδ]⟨εν⟩ ενν[εϝα], or [τοιδ'] ενν[εϝα].

who was traditionally the first king and gave his name to the river (Paus. ii. 15. 4). But it is, I think, impossible to regard this lettering as belonging to the first half of the seventh century—or even to the later part of that century, if Pheidon's date should be finally brought down so far. Nor is there necessarily any significance in the heroic echoes called up by certain of the names; a fifth-century dedicator at the Heraion is called after Belos, father of Danaos (**25**). The meaning of the inscription lies rather in the phrasing of the prescript, for one must decide whether the combination of the words δαμιοργός and ϝανάσσομαι is merely a loose, poetic form of speech, as Vollgraff suggested, or has a precise technical meaning, as I should prefer to believe. The demiourgoi were a body of high officials in the archaic Argive constitution, although it is not known what were their numbers, nor what their precise duties. If it is a list of the nine who chanced to be in office at the time when a particular event took place, one might expect the past imperfect tense: τοίδεν ἐννέϝα ἐδαμιόργεον, or δαμιοργοὶ ἦσαν, or at least ἐϝανάσσοντο. But the verb here is the aorist ἐϝανάσσαντο, which in official language should mean 'held the position of anax', i.e. 'prince' or 'ruler'. The dynasty of the Temenid kings of Argos ended, according to Pausanias (ii. 19. 2), with Meltas, son of Lakedas (Leokedes), and a Leokedes, son of Pheidon, wooed Agariste of Sikyon in the first third of the sixth century, according to Herodotos (vi. 127).[1] Nevertheless, in the first quarter of the fifth century the Argives still had a figure whom they called their king, who led them in war (Hdt. vii. 149), and whose name was used to date decrees (e.g. **39a**, where he is called βασιλεύς), which suggests that he was annually elected. Was he perhaps chosen from the demiourgoi, and, if so, can this be a list of those who held the office of 'king' in the nine years which followed the deposition of Meltas? I suggest this with reserve, for it is not certain that Meltas' father Leokedes was that Leokedes who wooed Agariste, and pure hypothesis that, if so, Meltas himself was

---

[1] Mention may be made here of the theory advanced by Vollgraff, *Le Décret d'Argos relatif à un pacte entre Knossos et Tylissos* (1948), 85 f. Observing that there is a flagrant discrepancy between (*a*) Pausanias' remark that the Argives deposed from kingship Meltas, son of Lakedas, tenth descendant of Medon (i.e. at some time in the first half of the 6th c.), and (*b*) Herodotos' that the Argives were led in war by their king at the time of the Persian invasion (vii. 149), Vollgraff seeks to correct this by removing Μήδωνος from Pausanias' text, and taking 'Meltas' to be a scribe's error for the βασιλεύς Melantas mentioned in the mid-5th c. text **39a**, concluding that what Pausanias meant was: Μέλανταν δὲ τὸν Λακήδου δέκατον ἀπόγονον τὸ παράπαν ἔπαυσεν ἀρχῆς καταγνοὺς ὁ δῆμος. This would mean that the last Argive king was ejected between *c.* 450 and 431; Vollgraff argues that the kingship must have gone before the latter year, for Thucydides does not use a king's name to date the start of the Peloponnesian War (ii. 2). But a tenth descendant of that Leokedes who sought the hand of Agariste in the first third of the 6th c. would live in the 4th or even the early 3rd c., not in the middle of the 5th. The reconciliation between Pausanias' and Herodotos' statements is better met by the hypothesis that with Meltas ended the autocratic (perhaps also the hereditary?) aspect of kingship, but, as at Athens and elsewhere, the title of king was retained for the annual holder of certain traditional royal offices, military and religious.

Professor Andrewes suggests that Pausanias' 'Meltas son of Lakedas' was the grandson of the great Pheidon, and was exiled and fled to Tegea in the late 7th c. during the second Messenian war (*CQ* xliii (1949), 76 f. and 1951, 44). Herodotos' 'Leokedes son of Pheidon', wooer of Agariste, will then have been a Leokedes III, son of a Pheidon II who will have been a brother of Meltas. Where then are we to fit Demokratides, who was king of Argos during the second Messenian War (Paus. ii. 24 and 35)? I would suggest rather the following tree: Pheidon I (fl. *c.* 670); Demokratides (fl. *c.* 640); Pheidon II (fl. *c.* 610); Leokedes (fl. *c.* 580); Meltas (reigned very briefly, deposed *c.* 560?). We know nothing about Leokedes' age when he wooed Agariste; he may have been a widower with a near-adult son. Nor, necessarily, need he have been an exile from Argos to think of wooing a Sikyonian princess; he may have been hoping for a reconciliation of Argos and Sikyon, and been disappointed in this by a still-hostile Kleisthenes. See Addenda.

deposed at least ten years before the middle of the sixth century (see the tree suggested on p. 157, n. 1; the lettering of the inscription can hardly be later than *c.* 550); nor, if the 'anakes' were eponymous, is there any obvious reason why the Argives should have recorded the first nine names together at the end of the ninth year, and then left the rest of the stele blank. On the other hand, if the verb is here colourless and means only that 'these nine demiourgoi held office', does it refer to those who held it in a single year, the total number of the officials being nine (like that of the archons at Athens), and if so, why was there a different number, six, in office not very many years later (in **8**)?

A few technical points may be noted: the archaic looped turn of the lines in the prescript (the line-ending in the two following inscriptions may be contrasted), the doubled consonants in ϵϝϝϵϝα and ϵϝαναϭϭαντο (as in the περικαλλϵϛ of **3** above), though not in Ιπο-μϵδον, and the writing of the name-list consistently from left to right in contrast with the *boustrophedon* prescript. Lastly, we may note the varying size of the *omikron*, also an archaic feature.

The next inscription, from Athena's temple on the Larisa, is of similar appearance and measurements (**8**). It may well be by the same mason at a later stage of development, perhaps about the middle of the century. The text is cut in a smoothed panel, which was perhaps meant to give the effect of a plaque nailed to the stone. The *boustrophedon* leaves no loop in turning, and the *omikron* is of a standard size; punctuation 3 and 4 are used, as 4 is also in the next inscription (**9**). The text falls into two parts: a statement that during the office of six demiourgoi, whose names are appended in a list, certain improvements were made in the sanctuary, and a sacral law that no private person (ϝΗϵδιϵϭταϛ) should use the temple utensils outside the temenos (though public officials might do so);[1] the demiourgoi were to be responsible for inflicting the penalty, and the temple-servant (αμφιπολοϛ) was to 'have the care of these things'—that is, presumably, to look after the property and bring accusation against offenders.

The third inscription is on a bronze plaque from the Argive Heraion (**9**); only the middle piece survives, with the hole for a central nail between the letters of ταδϵν in l. 1. The bronze-worker uses the same tall, careful lettering as did the mason of **8**, and the two inscriptions must be close in date. The double punctuation 4 is used frequently between phrases. The text refers first to the penalties for defacement, and then follows the main law, which appears to be a list of those major crimes against the state which were punishable by cursing and death or exile, like the famous Teian Curses (p. 340, **62**).[2]

The next series for discussion are the inscribed bronze relief strips of the style conventionally called 'Argivo-Corinthian' (**10**), which have been the subject of a detailed and illuminating study by Kunze.[3] The designs on the strips show sometimes an obvious connexion with the figure-styles of archaic Corinth, but the names of the figures are always written in Argive, and it seems probable that the original workshops were in Argos.

---

[1] I follow the reading of Schwyzer for ll. 9–10, taking δαμοϭιον as a collective singular used as the subject of the plural χρονϭθο (*Rh. Mus.* lxxix (1930), 321 ff.; cf. *SEG* xi. 314).

[2] In *IG* iv. 506 the reading is restored as if very little were gone from the right-hand edge; but the view of the editor in *AH* ii (no. 1826) seems preferable, that there is a considerable amount missing from both sides. In default of a complete text, some suggestions towards restoration are made in the Transliteration of Plates.

[3] *Olympische Forschungen* ii (1950).

By far the greater number of the examples come from the arm-bands of shields dedicated at Olympia, and the inscribed reliefs have been listed and dated by Kunze.[1] Of all the mythical subjects treated on the extant strips, only the following pictures bore inscriptions: (1) Boxing-match of Mhopsos (*sic*) and Admetos, *c.* 600–575 (?); (2) Man seizing woman (inscription illegible), *c.* 600–575?; (3) Death of Ajax, attended by an otherwise unknown hero Aristodemos, *c.* 575–550?; (4) Adrastos stopping the fight between Amphiaraos and Tydeus (same date); (5) Herakles meeting Theseus and Peirithoos in the underworld (same date); (6) Duel of Achilles and Penthesila (*sic*), from three different matrices (*c.* 575–550), one showing dotted *theta* 3, and one showing crossed *theta* 2; (7) Contest of Herakles and the Old Man of the Sea (Ͱαλιμος γερōν), *c.* 555–540; (8) Herakles bringing the boar to Eurystheus (illegible, *c.* 550–525). Kunze notes that this comparative dearth of inscriptions is very unlike the habits of Corinthian artists, and suggests that the Argive matrix-makers only added the names when the subject might otherwise be ambiguous: the practice reached its height *c.* 575–550, and thereafter went out of fashion.[2] As far as the brief material offers any points for comparison, the lettering of the names agrees with that of other inscriptions of the same date; cf. in particular υ2, here and in **2**, **5**, and **9**. θ3 in (6) is perhaps due to the technical difficulty of producing a crossed *theta* on a sheet of bronze hammered into a matrix.

Argive inscriptions of the second half of the sixth century present fresh complications. As a start, we may take the small Doric capital found south-west of the Heraion, which formed a grave-monument like that of Xenares at Korkyra (p. 233, Ionian islands **13**), commemorating Hyssematas, killed in war (**15**). It was cut by an awkward writer who could not centre his letters (cf. *alpha* and *upsilon*), but there are several points in the script which show that it should be distinctly later than the middle of the century. It is not written *boustrophedon*; it has υ3, ψ2; *epsilon* varies between 1 and 2, and *rho* has a tail (3); on the other hand, there is no gemination of consonants (Ͱυσεματαν, Ͱιποδρομοιο). The capital itself appears to rank with those which a recent study sets in the last quarter of the century.[3] Any attempt to date it closely must be regarded with reserve, since these votive model capitals may have developed more slowly than the architectural ones which they follow (pp. 107, 233). Its discoverer compared it with those of the Athenian Treasury at Delphi; he also noted its resemblance in size and proportions to another small capital, votive or commemorative, from the Heraion (**16**). On the abacus of this latter capital is a mutilated inscription listing the places where the athlete concerned had won his victories, and the lettering is not unlike that of the monument of Hyssematas; but in the donor's inscription cut across the flutes of the shaft of **16** (Τιμοκλēς μ' εθēκε) *sigma*, not *san*, is used. Both may belong then to the last quarter of the sixth century, but **15** near the beginning and **16** near the end.

The tailed *rho*, normal in the fifth century, also occurs before the fifth century on a silver pin (**14**), on a bronze mirror-handle (**11**) inscribed *boustrophedon* Αριστεια εκε .|. . οι ανεθēκε, and once (with ρι) on a small bronze votive plate (**12**), all from the Argive

[1] Op. cit. 212 ff.; dates given 242 f.
[2] Op. cit. 213 f.
[3] La Coste-Messelière, *BCH* lxvi–lxvii (1942–3),

22 ff. Cf. the profile of **15** with that of the Alkmeonid temple at Delphi (*c.* 510), op. cit. 56, fig. 12.

Heraion. The pin is of a type which is dated anywhere between *c.* 650 and 575 (see **14**, bibliography, s.v. Jacobsthal); the mirror-handle should, from its design, be somewhere about the middle of the sixth century; the plate, undecorated, is hardly datable. Elsewhere in the Peloponnese the tailed *rho* does not appear before the last third of the sixth century (Corinth, Lakonia, Arkadia), and I have therefore classed it as a mark of the late archaic period, like tailless *upsilon* and *psi*. I should place these three inscriptions tentatively in the years between *c.* 550 and 525, the plate possibly the earliest; whence one would have to conclude that the mirror was dedicated in its owner's old age, and that the pin perhaps belonged to the wardrobe of Hera's statue, and was marked by the temple officials against theft after it had been in use for some time.

There follows a series of inscriptions which, because of the use of *sigma*, should be later than those discussed above, but which from the rest of their lettering are clearly earlier than the chief landmark among Argive inscriptions of the fifth century, the grave-stele of the Argives who fell at Tanagra *c.* 458 (**30**). We may begin with two whose dating is slightly helped by factors other than epigraphical. The first is the base at Olympia signed by the Argive sculptors Atotos and Argeiades son of Ageladas (**19**). The monument consists of five blocks of marble, which were laid in line on five larger blocks of stuccoed tufa, to form a stepped base; both these rested, again, on a lower foundation of tufa which, from its rough appearance, was evidently not meant to be seen. The dedication was made by an Arkadian, Praxiteles, who had emigrated to Sicily (p. 211, Arkadia **20**). The actual offering was apparently a set of bronze statues in a row, probably a group like some of those described by Pausanias in his visit to the sanctuary—the Homeric gods and heroes, Zeus and the daughters of Asopos, a chorus of boys, and so on (Paus. v. 22. 2; 22. 6; 25. 4–5; 25. 8; vi. 12. 1, &c.). This set stood on rectangular mounts only slightly smaller than the marble blocks, for the shallow cuttings made to receive such mounts are still visible on the top of the marble blocks. The dedication has a definite *terminus ante quem* established for it, because the building-rubbish from the temple of Zeus (begun *c.* 465) lay over the stuccoed tufa blocks, which were still *in situ*; the first erection must therefore have been before the temple was built, even if we suppose that the group was removed only a short while after its erection, when it was found to interfere with the planning of the temple, and set up again elsewhere farther from the building. The work was signed by four sculptors in all, who worked in two pairs. We cannot tell how many figures each produced. The end block on the (spectator's) left is signed by the sculptors Athenodoros 'an Achaian', and Asopodoros of Argos. This inscription is generally described as Argive, because it is not in Achaian, nor in the 'red' alphabet of the dedicator (see below and pp. 211, 267); but it should not rank as true Argive, because it uses the non-Argive lunate *gamma*. In fact, it corresponds with what we know of the alphabets of Syracuse and Kamarina (p. 267). An illustration is given on Pl. 28, [**19**].

The next two blocks (described further on p. 211) bear the dedicatory inscription of the donor, Praxiteles son of Krinis, who describes himself as being of Syracuse and Kamarina, having migrated to Sicily from Mantinea. The city of Kamarina was destroyed by Gelon of Syracuse in 484 (Hdt. vii. 156), and her citizens were settled in Syracuse to increase that city's population, until Kamarina was rebuilt *c.* 461, after the fall of the

Deinomenids (Diod. xi. 76. 5). Since the dedication was set up before *c.* 465, Praxiteles was evidently not a citizen of the later Kamarina, and the editors of *Olympia* maintained a date before 484 for the base, on the grounds that between 484 and 461 anyone transplanted from Kamarina into Syracuse would describe himself as Syracusan only, whereas before 484 he might quite possibly have held the citizenship of both places. The opposite hypothesis seems, however, to be the simpler and more obvious; that he called himself 'of Syracuse and Kamarina' precisely because he *was* one of those transplanted: in his time he had lived in Mantinea, Kamarina, and finally Syracuse. If this is so, it sets the limits of the base between 484 and 461, which seems a reasonable period for it on other counts; for it is hard to consider the developed lettering of the dedicatory inscription as earlier than 484 (see p. 211), and the fresh state of the tufa foundation suggests that it had not been erected for very many years before its burial under the building-rubbish.[1] The second pair of sculptors, whose joint signature covers the last two blocks, were the Argives Atotos and Argeiades son of Agelads, and this inscription is undoubtedly in Argive characters (**19**). Agelads' life-time is not certainly known, but his commissions seem to have extended from *c.* 520 to *c.* 460.[2] Nothing except this base is known of his son's work, but if he were born *c.* 500, he could have been executing commissions by 475.

On these counts, therefore, a date *c.* 480–475 would be suitable for the base. The script is plainly considered earlier than that of **30** (*c.* 458/7), for it shows αι, γι, ε2–3, λι, ρ2. The use of *vau*, closed *heta*, and small *omikron* persisted throughout the first half of the fifth century, and so cannot help to date it closely; on the other hand, it is not likely to be much earlier than 480, for the first part of it is cut *stoichedon*, and the other two contemporary inscriptions on the base are both *stoichedon* throughout.

The bronze plaque inscribed in Argive characters (**20**), which was said on doubtful authority to have been found at Hermion, appears to be of about the same date as the signature of Atotos and Argeiades. It shows the same regard for the ending of lines with complete words, and the current convention of writing a small *omikron* has been freely exploited here by the bronzeworker, who saved himself much trouble by simply making all these letters with the pointed head of his punch. The text apparently refers to an occasion when a president of the Argive Boule named Ariston and his fellow councillors were empowered to use the treasures of Athena to meet some emergency, and were protected by this law from any subsequent impeachment on the grounds of illegal procedure. Another inscription which, from the similarity of its lettering, may also be ascribed to the first quarter of the fifth century is the base for a lost bronze statuette from the Heraion (**21**), dedicated by four ἱαρομνάμονες, presumably one from each of the four tribes. The inscription reads: τοι ιαρομναμονες τōν [εκ] το Ηιππο|δρομο ανεθεν: Κριθυλο[ς: Α]ϝακτο[ς: |

---

[1] This was observed by Furtwaengler, *AZ* xxxvii (1879), 45.

[2] His earliest recorded work is the statue of Anochos of Taras, whose victories were won in Ol. 65 (522; Paus. vi. 14. 11); the latest, the Zeus Ithomates made for the Messenians who were settled in Naupaktos *c.* 461/0 (Paus. iv. 33. 2). His Herakles Alexikakos in Attica was made (according to the scholiast on Ar. *Ran.* 504) for the great plague in 430; but as this one late date conflicts with everything else recorded about him, it is probable that the statue commemorated some earlier visitation. Nothing else is known of the other two sculptors, Athenodoros from an Achaian state and Asopodoros of Argos: the sculptors with these names mentioned by Pliny (*NH* xxxiv. 50) in a list of Polykleitos' disciples should, if he is right, be of the end of the fifth century; cf. Paus. x. 9. 8. See further V. Poulsen, *Der strenge Stil* (1937), 115.

Φιλεας ⋮ Γναθις ⋮ 'The hieromnemones dedicated (this) from the proceeds of the hippo-drome.'[1] It must refer to the games celebrated in honour of Hera at the Heraion, though what the 'proceeds' were is uncertain. There are two other fifth-century dedications by four hieromnemones in the Heraion, **32** and **36**. Another inscription which I should ascribe tentatively to the years *c.* 475 is the proxeny-decree on a bronze plaque found in the Agora at Argos (**22**): αλιαιαι ⋮ εδοξξε ⋮ προ|[ξε]νον ⋮ εμεν ⋮ Γνοσστ|αν ⋮ τον Ϝοινοντιον | τοις Αργειοις ⋮ αϝρε̄|τευε ⋮ Επικρατε̄ς ⋮ Π|ανφυλος ⋮ Ρινο̄νος ⋮ | Ϝυιος. The lettering is very like that of **20**, with *gamma, vau, epsilon, lambda, nu* all of types 1–2. It shows also a side-long ξ2, such as occurs also in Argive stone inscriptions of about the second quarter of the fifth century (**30, 32, 39***a*); this may have been a fashion set by one mason (p. 152 above).

It will have been noted that the general appearance of the above group of inscriptions is not impressive, either in the plotting or in the execution of the letters. But some Argive masons of this period could do good work, as is evident from the stele **17**, which was erected by the athlete Aischyllos son of Theops (Thiops in the Argive dialect) to record his seven victories at the public games (the Heraia). This inscription is written almost completely *stoichedon*, without regard for the ending of the line with a complete word, as shown on the base **19**; the latter method being, in any case, hardly practicable on a narrow stele. In certain letters this inscription is more archaic than the early fifth-century series discussed above (e.g. ν1, ρ1, ε2); in others (α3, υ4) it is more advanced. A date *c.* 500–480 would probably not be far wrong. With this style of script may be compared the dedications on surviving parts of the trophies of arms sent by the Argives to Olympia to commemorate a defeat of the Corinthians (**18**). The inscribed pieces consist of two helmets and parts of at least six shields, the latter found during the German excavations on the site. All bear, whole or in part, the same verse for the dedication: τἀργειοι ανεθεν το̄ι Διϝι τον Ϙορινθοθεν. The pieces of armour were dated *c.* 500—possibly a little earlier or later—by Kunze and Schleif in their study of the bronze weapons found at Olympia;[2] and, with allowance for the difference in the tools used, the lettering is very similar to that of **17**; it may be noted that the ring-punch used by the bronze-worker for all semicircles as well as for circles has resulted in a rather odd *rho* on the helmet in the British Museum (Pl. 27).

For the following period, *c.* 475–450, a considerable group of inscriptions may be formed round the two securely dated examples, a bronze hydria in New York (**26**) and the grave-stele for the battle of Tanagra (**30**). There is, however, one inscription which, from its lettering, should come somewhere between these two groups in date. This is the dedication Αργειοι ανεθεν τἀπολλο̄νι inscribed on three blocks from a base of local stone at Delphi (**23**). It will be noted that the letters are distinctly more archaic than those of what may be called the Tanagra group; we may contrast the types of *gamma, epsilon, lambda, nu, rho*. The base has been tentatively ascribed by Bourguet (after Pausanias) to the battle of Oinoe, for the following reasons. Somewhere near the dedications of the

---

[1] The reading given by Walter, *Ö.Jh.* xiv (1911), Beibl. 141 f. is: τοι ιαρομναμονες τον[δε] το Ϝ[ιπ]ο|δρομο, κτλ; but the sense of τόνδε τοῦ ἱπποδρόμου is dubious.

[2] *JDI* lvi (1941), *Olympiabericht* iii, 76 ff.; or perhaps *c.* 500–475 (Kunze, *Bericht* v (1956), 36).

Athenians after Marathon (lost in the past) and the Wooden Horse dedicated by the Argives in 414 after Thyrea (**47** below) Pausanias saw and described (x. 10. 3–5) three Argive dedications: (1) a group of the Seven against Thebes, by the Theban sculptors Hypatodoros and Aristogeiton, 'which were made, as the Argives themselves declare, from the spoils of victory which the Argives and their Athenian allies won over the Lakedaimonians at Oinoe in Argolis': (2) a group of the Epigonoi, 'from the spoils of the same battle, as I believe' (from which it may be concluded that the inscription did not mention the place of the defeat nor the names of the defeated, so that Pausanias was forced to guess them, unfortunately without recording his reasons for his conclusion); (3) a group of the Kings of Argos, erected *c.* 369 B.C., which he says was opposite the group of the Epigonoi. The semicircular substructure of (3) has been identified,[1] and opposite it across the Sacred Way is a substructure similarly shaped, which can hardly be other than that of (2). The three inscribed blocks in question (**23**), which were not found *in situ* but rebuilt into the Sacred Way farther on, have been assigned by the excavators to this substructure (2) accordingly, on the grounds of general probability; they do not look out of place upon it, but, as Bourguet is careful to point out, the attribution cannot be regarded as certain. If the archaeologists are right in assigning these inscribed blocks to the semicircular foundation, which from its position must belong to the monument of the Epigonoi, then the campaign which this group commemorated should not, according to the letter-forms of the inscription, be as late as *c.* 460, the earliest likely date for the battle of Oinoe. The precise year of this battle is unknown; it was fought against the Lakedaimonians by the Argives and Athenians in alliance, and commemorated by the Athenians in a painting in the Stoa Poikile at Athens (Paus. i. 15. 1).[2] It is believed to have been fought between 461 and 451, when Athens and Argos were in alliance against the Lakedaimonians;[3] if this date for the battle is right, then this dedication at Delphi should have nothing to do with the battle of Oinoe, in spite of Pausanias' suggestion. From its letters it should belong to a campaign during the years *c.* 480–465, or a year or two later at most; but, since the precise chronology of Peloponnesian affairs during this period is still disputed, little more can be said. Two victorious campaigns of the Argives during the decade 470–460 are possibilities: the final defeat of the 'slaves' who had been settled in Tiryns, and the destruction of Mycenae.[4] Diodoros records that the Argives dedicated a tithe of their Mycenean captives to 'the god', that is, to Apollo at Delphi;[5] they may well have set up a permanent memorial of their victory there as well. The first set of statues, the Seven against Thebes described by Pausanias as certainly

---

[1] *FD* iii. 1, no. 90.

[2] The Stoa Poikile was built perhaps *c.* 460 (cf. I. T. Hill, *The Ancient City of Athens* (1953), 68 f.), and on its completion (or possibly some years later) was adorned with paintings by Polygnotos, Mikon, and perhaps Panainos, all of whom flourished in the 2nd or 3rd quarters of the 5th c. It is nowhere recorded who painted the scene at Oinoe, and some authorities have suggested that the campaign and painting should belong to the Corinthian War of 394; cf. Hobein, *RE* iva, s.v. stoa, 17.

[3] Cf. Gomme, *Commentary on Thucydides* i (1945),

370, n. 1.

[4] Diodoros' date for the destruction of Mycenae (xi. 65: 468/7) has not yet been proved wrong, though the general unreliability of his chronological system lays it open to suspicions; cf. Gomme, op. cit. 408 f. The Argive seizure of Tiryns from their slaves is generally set a few years before 470 (Seymour, *JHS* xlii (1922), 28 ff.).

[5] Diod. xi. 65. For a full discussion of the custom of dedicating tithes of captives at Delphi, cf. Parke and Wormell, *The Delphic Oracle* i (1956), 49 ff.

commemorating Oinoe, has not survived; but the base of a private dedication made for a Boiotian by the same sculptors Hypatodoros and Aristogeiton was found also at Delphi, and is to be dated in the second quarter of the fifth century (p. 93, Boiotia **17**; see also p. 167, n. 2).

**25**, whose lettering (as far as can be judged by the publications) resembles that of the bronze hydria **26**, is a dedication on a pillar-base by one Βᾶλος ᾿Αργεῖος to (Hera), child of Kronos; it was found not far from the Heraion and is probably a stray from the precinct. This citizen Belos, bearing a name renowned in Argive saga, reminds us of Sthenelas, Hippomedon, and Adrastos on the stele of the demiourgoi **7** (p. 156). Mitsos has pointed out[1] that an Argive is most likely to have added his ethnic to an offering in the Heraion in the years between 494 and 468, when Argos was in eclipse after Sepeia and Mycenae claimed rights in the administration of the Heraion before her own destruction (see p. 171).

The bronze hydria **26**, offered as a prize at the games of Hera, is dated *c.* 470–460 by Dr. Richter on the triple basis of the shape of the vase, the style of the small protome of a kore set between rim and handle, and the comparison of its lettering with that of the Tanagra stele **30**. Here the *gamma* is spreading out from the archaic 1 to the later 2; the bars of ε and λ are now horizontal, *nu* is ν2, and an exaggeratedly small circle is used for both *theta* and *omikron*. The *nu* of the hydria is earlier in shape than those on the Tanagra stele. In a grave at Sinope on the Black Sea a hydria of the same pattern was found, with a like inscription, probably by the same hand: παρ Ϝέρας Αργειας εμι τōν Ϝαϝεθλōν (cf. also **43**); a further, damaged inscription, also in Argive, is reported below the first.[2] Little needs now to be said about the Tanagra stele **30**, since its detailed and convincing reconstruction by Meritt (see **30**, bibliography). The date should fall very soon after 458/7, though naturally we do not know how long it took to assemble the full list of the dead under their four tribes and to choose the epigram (for which, as Meritt points out, the mason left a space at the top which proved to be too small). The letter-forms vary slightly in the excellence of their cutting (contrast, for example, *Kerameikos* iii, pl. 10, 4 with pl. 11, 2), but not enough to suggest that it was the work of more than one mason. *Xi* is sidelong (2) as on the bronze plaque **22** (p. 162).

The characteristic style of this mason, whom for convenience we may call the Tanagra mason, is reflected in several other inscriptions which must be of about the same period. A stele from the Heraion looks like a poorer example of his work (**32**). It bears in its centre a cutting for a bronze plaque, now lost, and on the stone above the plaque a state-ment that both the bronze (Ϝα σταλα) and the stone frame (Ϝο τελαμō⟨ν⟩) were the pro-perty of Hera Argeia, followed by the names of the four hieromnemones then in office, who presumably made the offering. In this inscription the fourth and sixth lines have been carried on down the right-hand edge of the stone in the same way as the lines of the epigram on the Tanagra stele, apparently in an attempt to give a full line to each name, one under the other, as was normal for a list of names. Here the letter-forms are all similar to those of the Tanagra stele (in particular π2; see p. 152), except for the Ϝ2 on

---

the Tanagra stone, which was evidently an error or correction, for elsewhere in the inscription the normal form ⊦ɪ is used.

Another inscription which looks like the same man's work, with the same *xi*, is the fragmentary list of names **31**, part of a public inscription found on the Larisa, perhaps a casualty-list. One name, Derketos, recurs twice on the Tanagra stele; can **31** be part of the local Argive copy, or was this a common name? The sidelong *xi* also occurs on the two parts of a stele found by Vollgraff rebuilt into a later structure in the Agora of Argos (**39a**), which bears the details of an agreement between the two adjacent Cretan cities Knossos and Tylisos, which was drawn up by Argive arbitrators to settle a series of disputed points—the establishment of their common boundary, the division of spoils after allied operations, mutual conditions for import and export, allocation of the duties and perquisites in certain sacrifices, and so on. Vollgraff rightly noted that, where the lettering differs in detail from that of the Tanagra stele, it suggests a slightly later date (as β2, θ3, loss of *qoppa*). In the last six lines (which record that the stele was set up when Melantas was βασιλεύς and Lykotadas of the tribe Hylleis president, and then add a rider to the main decree) the more developed forms υ4 and φ3 are used;[1] which may mean either that it was an addition made by a different mason at a later date, or—since the sidelong *xi* is retained—that the same mason added it later, having meanwhile adopted some newer styles. In a masterly survey which should become the definitive edition for both texts Vollgraff[2] has put forward the attractive hypothesis that the fragments **39b** are in fact a part of the same decree. These fragments were found at Tylisos and bear part of a similar text concerning an alliance between Knossos and Tylisos, drawn up in the Argive dialect and script, and mentioning Argive participation at certain points in the alliance. In Vollgraff's reconstruction of the decree the main Tylisian fragment and a small 'floater' come from the first part of the text, the Argive fragment from the latter part. If they are really part of the same decree, the two copies were cut by different masons: **39b** shows a curious mixture of earlier and later forms: β1, γ1 or 4, θ1, υ4–5, υ3, φ3, ψ3. ν5 is not normal even in Attic before the third quarter of the fifth century. This would not quite suit Vollgraff's thesis, which seeks to date the decree to the end of the decade of the Argivo-Athenian Alliance, but before the Argivo-Spartan Thirty Years' Peace was signed in 451. It is perhaps easier to imagine Argos active in Crete during her alliance with Athens than after her peace with Sparta; but in that case the Argive mason who cut the copy for Tylisos was in the forefront of fashion with his ν5.

Three sculptors' signatures may be mentioned here, which all appear to fall within the

[1] It is generally said by the editors of **39a** that a change of letter-forms from Θ, V, Φ to O, Y, Φ begins at αλιαια εδοξε, the start of the rider proper; but actually, though the *omikron* is still Θ, the *upsilon* V has already changed to Y in the two lines above, containing the end of the main decree (⊦α σταλα εσστα, κτλ), and, as there chances to be no example of *phi* in this sentence, for all we know the *phi* might have changed then also.

[2] *Le Décret d'Argos relatif à un pacte entre Knossos et Tylissos* (1948). Vollgraff believes that the small fragment *IC* Tylisus ɪγ (= Vollgraff 3) repeats a piece of the Argive text, ll. 33–34. But there is a *nu* in the first line of the Tylisian fragment, which will not suit the Argive text. If one re-alines the Argive text to fit the Tylisian fragment, it reads:

εμ<u>α</u>τα⊦οπαισυνγνοιεν⊦οιΚ
νο⊦ιοικαιτοιΑργειοι⊦ουτ
οε<u>μεν</u>τοιΑρεικαιταφφροδιτ
αι(κτλ).

But the Tylisian fragment reads:

. ν . . . . .
ο⊦ιοι..
. . . ν τ οι

second quarter of the fifth century. The earliest (**24**) is on the fragment of a base found at Olympia, showing the latter halves of a sculptor's signature [- - - ε]ποϝεϝε ⋮ Αργειος and of a dedication in Ionic lettering: [- - -] ανεθηκαν. αι, ε2, and γι indicate that it is some years earlier than the Tanagra group, perhaps *c*. 475; the artist may have been any one of the several Argive bronze-workers then flourishing. The second signature is that of Dorotheos of Argos on the base of a bronze horse dedicated to Demeter Chthonia in Hermion (**34**). The dedicatory inscription by a Hermionian is described below, pp. 178 f.; the signature itself has all the marks of the years *c*. 460–450 which we have been discussing —α3, γ2, ε3, θ3. The third signature is on the fragment of a base at Delphi (**35**): Δο̣[- - -] | Αργ[ειος]. It has been restored tentatively as the dedication of an unknown Argive; Pomtow first suggested that it was another signature by Dorotheos, combining it with a Rhegine dedication (Chalkidic colonies **15**, p. 245). Although his combination was wrong,[1] the attribution of this fragment to Dorotheos may well be right; the few remaining letters resemble those of the other signature in their development (α3, γ2). The dedication was probably a group in some dramatic pose, for there remains the cutting for the right foot of a bronze statue very near the upper edge of the base, too near for the foot of a single statue centred on a single block, as in a normal athletic dedication.

Several other minor inscriptions should belong to the same decade, including two from Argive dedications at the sanctuary of Asklepios at Epidauros (**37, 38**); further reference may be made only to one (**36**), a pillar[2] which once bore a statuette dedicated in the Argive Heraion by four men whom one may conjecture to have been the hieromnemones of the four tribes (cf. nos. **21, 32**). The dedication may be restored as: [τ]ας ϝερας ε[μι ϝια]|ρον εκ το ϝιπι[ϟο], *or* ϝιπι[ο?]· | Αρχεκρατες ⋮ Σμο[θος?] | [Α]ρεφιōν ⋮ Συλιχ[ος]—that is, a dedication by the officials from the proceeds which accrued to them from some part of the Games, either the men's footrace called the ἵππιος δρόμος or the horse-racing, like that made 'from the hippodrome' in **21** above.[3]

There is a considerable number of fragmentary public inscriptions of the fifth century— decrees, name-lists, records of sales—some of which are known only from rough copies made by Fourmont in the eighteenth century, and others in preliminary publications without satisfactory illustrations; and little therefore can be said of them here. A record of sale dated by Vollgraff in the second half of the century (**40**) may be compared with Fourmont's sketch *IG* iv. 553, which, with its φ3, should be later than the Tanagra stele. A tantalizing fragment of a decree rebuilt into a building in the Agora at Argos mentions the Epidaurians (**41**). A small fragment (**42**) from a large stele, fully published by Voll- graff, might be contemporary with **39**. A single contemporary signature survives of the great Argive sculptor Polykleitos, on the base of an athlete's statue dedicated at Olympia by the pentathlete Pythokles of Elis, whose victory was won in 452 (**45**). Polykleitos' period of activity apparently extended over the greater part of the second half of the fifth century; writers in the next generation called him a contemporary of Pheidias, and Pliny's estimation of his *floruit* as *c*. 420 is generally accepted, since his great work, the

---

[1] Cf. the refutation by Bourguet, *FD* iii. 1. 327, no. 502.

[2] It appears to be of the kind described as Type B (i.e., with cavetto capital) by Raubitschek, *DAA*,

[3] The reading of the first publication gives for line 2: εκ το ϝιδ̣ι[ο] and for the names [Α]ρχεκρατες ⋮ Σμο[ιος ⋮ Β- *or* Ε]ρεφιον ⋮ Συλιχ[ος]. See now *SEG* xvi. 244.

Hera for the Argive Heraion, was presumably commissioned to replace the cult-statue destroyed in the burning of the Heraion in 423. Both dedication and signature of Pythokles' offering were re-cut at a later period, when (as the double set of cuttings on top of the base show) another statue was erected, perhaps a copy of the original. A fraction of Pythokles' original dedicatory inscription survives on the front of the base, and on top along the edge Polykleitos' name, in neat Argive letters, the *omikron* in the rhomboid form 3, a device not usual in Argive. In the absence of the rest of the inscription it is difficult to judge whether this signature belongs to the third or the fourth quarter of the century. The third is perhaps more likely, though athletic dedications were not always erected shortly after the victory; sometimes it might only be possible late in the athlete's life. (It is tempting but unsound to conjecture that a statue of an otherwise unknown Elean victor may savour more of Polykleitos' early days than of the years after 425, when he was given such contracts as the cult-statue of Hera Argeia *c.* 423, and that of Zeus Meilichios in Argos (Paus. ii. 20. 2).) To the third quarter of the century should also belong the base of an offering at the Heraion by two Argives, Hybrilas and one whose name has perished (**46**); it can hardly be earlier, with the upright ν4.

In the fourth quarter of the fifth century the local forms of the letters were apparently still in use; the *lambda* at least certainly, as may be seen from the base of the Wooden Horse dedicated at Delphi by the Argives after the fighting at Thyrea in 414 (**47**),[1] which shows δ2 for the normal form, possibly the idiosyncracy of one mason.

Another block from a base at Delphi, reading only Αργειοι (**48**), is from a dedication not yet certainly identified, but which appears to have been renewed at some time after the fifth century, for the cuttings for the iron clamps have been altered from the earlier form ꓶ to the later ꓮ.[2] The lettering shows γ4 and *alpha* with a very high cross-bar, which is not normal in fifth-century work; but none the less it might still be of the fifth century, for the Ionic *gamma* was used in the decree **39b** above.

While the local letter-forms were still in use, the Ionic *eta* was introduced. Its first appearance as yet is on the stele bearing a relief of Artemis with torch, bow, and quiver, dedicated by Polystrate (**49**): Πολυστρατα ανεθηκε, the *eta* being in the open form. The relief was dated after 403 by Kirchhoff[3] because of the use of the Ionic letter, a date repudiated by others in favour of one not later than 430, on the grounds that the general pose resembles that of Artemis on vases of the mid-fifth century, the eye, moreover, being drawn as frontal in the archaic manner.[4] It seems, however, that second-rate Argive art of the late fifth century was, like Lakonian, very backward, for the frontal eye appears on another Argive relief in the same clumsy style, which from its general appearance can hardly antedate the end of the fifth century, and shows *omega* in the battered inscription above it.[5] On general grounds, therefore, Polystrate's relief might be dated in the last

[1] Thuc. vi. 95. It was wrongly supposed by Pausanias to refer to the 6th-c. battle at Thyrea (x. 9. 12).

[2] It is suggested by Bourguet that it might be from the group of the Seven against Thebes (described by Pausanias x. 10. 4; cf. pp. 162 ff. above), erected after Oinoe, but renewed (the base at least) after Thyrea (*FD* iii. 1. 386 f.).  [3] Kirchhoff[4], 100.

[4] Furtwaengler, *Meisterwerke*, 415; Bluemel, *Kat. Skulpt. Berlin* iii. 56.

[5] The relief is published by Vollgraff, *Argos et Sicyone* (1947), 7 ff., pl. 1. It is there described as a funeral stele of the 4th or 3rd c., bearing a humble copy of a 5th-c. group (perhaps by Ageladas) of Herakles and Hebe, part of the dead person's name being

years of the century, without necessarily accepting Kirchhoff's precise limit 'after 403'.

## SELECT CATALOGUE

**1.** Fragment of a dinos from the Heraion, with painted inscription; 7th c. Heermance, *AH* ii. 185, no. 2, fig. 102. NM.

**2.** Bronze plaque from the Larisa at Argos, re-used as a label for a dedication; 7th c.? Vollgraff, *BCH* lviii (1934), 138 ff., fig. 1. *SEG* xi. 327. NM.　　　　　　　　　　　　PL. 26

**3.** Bronze aryballos dedicated by Chalkodamas; late 7th c.? *IG* v. 1. 231, pl. 1. *DGE* 77. De Ridder, *Bronzes ant. du Louvre* ii. 127, pl. 102. Karouzos, *Epitymb. Tsounta* (1941), 540, 571. Bloesch, *Agalma* (1943), 23. Friedlaender 16. *SEG* xi. 678. Paris, Louvre MNC 614.　　　　　　PL. 26

**4.** Statues of Kleobis and Biton at Delphi; c. 610–580. *FD* iv. 5 ff., figs. 4–9, pls. 1–2. Von Premerstein, *Ö.Jh.* xiii (1910), 41 ff. *DGE* 317. *GHI*[2] 3 and p. 257. Daux, *BCH* lxi (1937), 61 ff. *Kouroi*, 78 ff., pls. 18–19, 23. Van Groningen, *Mnemosyne* lxvii (1945), 34 ff. Buschor, *Frühgriech. Jünglinge* (1950), 35 ff. Marcadé i. 115, pl. 24, 1–3. Delphi Mus. 4672, 980.　　　　　　　　PL. 26

**5.** Bronze statuette dedicated by Polykrates; c. 590–570. *IG* iv. 565. *IGA* 31. Roehl[3], 37. 4. *Kouroi*, 100 and 117 f., pl. 41. *SEG* xi. 335. Leningrad, Hermitage.　　　　　　　　PL. 26

**6.** Part of a bronze statuette dedicated by the sons of Nirachas; c. 590–570? Roberts i. 72. *IG* iv. 564. *SGDI* 3262. Roehl[3], 36. 1. Neugebauer, *Kat. Bronz. Berlin* i (1931), 78 f., pl. 28, 179. *DGE* 79. Berlin Mus. 7837.　　　　　　　　　　　　　　　　　　　　　　　　PL. 26

**7.** Stone bearing a list of nine demiourgoi, on the Larisa at Argos; c. 575–550? *IG* iv. 614. *IGA* 30. *SGDI* 3260. Roehl[3], 37. 3. Vollgraff, *Mnemosyne* lvi (1928), 321 ff. and lix. 369 ff. *SEG* xi. 336.　　PL. 26

**8.** Stone bearing a sacral law from the temple of Athena Polias on the Larisa; c. 575–550? Vollgraff, *Mnemosyne* lvii (1929), 206 ff. Boissevain, *Mnemosyne* lviii (1930), 13 ff. Schwyzer, *Rh. Mus.* lxxix (1930), 321 ff. *SEG* xi. 314. Buck 83. Argos (Larisa).

**9.** Bronze plaque from the Heraion, bearing part of a law; c. 575–550? Rogers, *AJA* v (1901), 159 ff. DeCou, *AH* ii. 273 f., 333 f., no. 1826, pls. 106–7. *IG* iv. 506. *SEG* xi. 302. NM.　　　　PL. 27

**10.** Fragments of inscribed bronze relief strips from the armbands of shields, found at Olympia, Delphi and Orchomenos; c. 600–525. Kunze, *Olympische Forschungen* ii (1950), *passim*, esp. 212 ff., pls. 14, 43, 54; Beil. 7, 12, 13.

**11.** Mirror-handle from the Heraion; c. 550–525? DeCou, *AH* ii. 265 and 332, no. 1581, pl. 96. NM.

**12.** Miniature bronze plate from the Heraion; c. 550–525? DeCou, op. cit., 277, 366 f., no. 1877. NM.

**13.** Bronze antyx (?) from the Heraion; c. 550–525? DeCou, op. cit. 298, 338, no. 2252. NM.

**14.** Inscription cut later (?) on a silver pin of the 7th or early 6th c. from the Heraion; c. 550–525? DeCou, op. cit. 339. *IG* iv. 508. *BMC Jewellery*, 1250, pl. 14. Jacobsthal, *Greek Pins* (1956), 31, fig. 84. BM.　　　　　　　　　　　　　　　　　　　　　　　　　　　　　　　　PL. 27

**15.** Capital from the tomb of Hyssematas, near the Heraion; c. 525–500? Daly, *Hesperia* viii (1939), 165 ff., figs. 1–4. Friedlaender 136. *SEG* xi. 305. Peek i. 305. Argos Mus.

preserved above, Θεωρ [- - -]. In the photograph there appears to be a *vacat* after the fourth letter, and it is hard to see why a group of Herakles and Hebe should be reproduced on a grave-stele. Should it not rather be a dedication, offered to an unnamed minor deity (θεωι) shown receiving a suppliant, the line at his neck being not the paws of a lion-skin, but merely a clumsy rendering of the clavicle?

**16.** Capital erected by Timokles, from the area of the Heraion; *c.* 525–500? Richardson and Wheeler, *AH* i. 202, no. 3. *IG* iv. 510. Daly, op. cit. 165, n. 2. Moretti 7. *SEG* xiv. 315. EM?  PL. 27

**17.** Stele dedicated by Aischyllos, from Argos; *c.* 500–480? *IG* iv. 561. *IGA* 37. *SGDI* 3267. Roehl³, 38. 48. *DGE* 82. Vollgraff, *Mnemosyne* lviii (1930), 30 ff. Friedlaender 51. *SEG* xi. 328. Moretti 10. *SEG* xiv. 317. EM.  PL. 27

**18.** Helmets and shields from a trophy dedicated at Olympia; *c.* 500–480? *Ol.* v. 250. *SGDI* 3263–4. *BMC Bronzes*, 251. Roehl³, 36. 5. *DGE* 80. Vollgraff, *Mnemosyne* lix (1931), 22 f. Kukahn, *Der griech. Helm* (1939), 47. Kunze and Schleif, *JdI* liii (1938), *Olympiabericht* ii. 68, 73, pl. 20; *JdI* lvi (1941), *Olympiaber.* iii. 76 ff., 81 ff., pls. 20–23; *Olympiabericht* v (1956), 35 ff. *SEG* xi. 1203. Brommer, *Ant. Kleinkunst im Schloss Fasanerie* (Adolphseck, 1955), 5 f., fig. 7. Friedlaender 174. BM, Olympia Mus., and Schloss Fasanerie.  PL. 27

**19.** Base for a dedication at Olympia by Praxiteles son of Krinis, signed by the Argive sculptors Asopodoros, Atotos, and Argeiades; *c.* 480–475? *Ol.* v. 630–1. *SGDI* 3720–1. Roberts i. 80–81. *DGE* 80, 3. Vollgraff, *Argos et Sicyone* (1947), 4 f. Friedlaender 153. *SEG* xi. 1250. Olympia Mus. 23, 28; 30, 12.  PL. 28

**20.** Bronze plaque bearing a law concerning the treasures of Athena, said to have been found at Hermion; *c.* 480? Froehner, *RA* 1891 ii, 51 ff., pl. 19. *IG* iv. 554. Roehl³, 39. 12. *DGE* 78. Vollgraff, *Mnemosyne* lviii (1930), 26 ff. *SEG* xi. 315. Buck 84. NM.

**21.** Base for a bronze statuette dedicated by the four hieromnemones at the Heraion; *c.* 480–475? Walter, *Ö.Jh.* xiv (1911), Beibl. 141 f., fig. 72. *DGE* 96(3). EM?  PL. 28

**22.** Bronze plaque bearing a proxeny decree for Gnostas of Oinous, from the Argive Agora; *c.* 475? Charneux, *BCH* lxxvii (1953), 395 ff., fig. 3. *SEG* xiii. 239. Argos Mus.

**23.** Dedication on a base at Delphi, perhaps for a bronze group of the Epigonoi; *c.* 480–460? Homolle, *BCH* xxi (1897), 401. Karo, *BCH* xxxiv (1910), 196 ff. Pomtow, *Klio* viii (1908), 199 ff. *SIG*³ 28. *DGE* 81. *FD* iii. 1. 54 ff., no. 90, pl. 3, 1 and fig. 23. Delphi Mus. 3962–3+2720.  PL. 28

**24.** Unknown Argive sculptor's signature at Olympia; *c.* 475? *Ol.* v. 632. *SGDI* 3273. *IGA* 44a. Roehl³, 27. 32. Olympia Mus. 946.

**25.** Pillar-base for a dedication by Belos, from the Argive Heraion; *c.* 494–468? Koumanoudes and Oikonomides, *Polemon* v (1952–3), 67 ff., fig. 1. Mitsos, Ἐπετηρὶς τῆς Ἐταιρείας Βυζαντινῶν Σπουδῶν 1953, 150 f. *SEG* xiii. 246. Chonika, outside church of Hagioi Anargyrioi.

**26.** Bronze prize hydria from the games of Hera Argeia; *c.* 470–460. Richter, *Antike Plastik (Festschr. Amelung*, 1928), 183 ff., fig. 8. *NC*, 219 ff. V. Poulsen, *Der strenge Stil*, 15 ff. D. M. Robinson, *AJA* xlvi (1942), 178 ff. *SEG* xi. 355. New York, MM. 26.50.  PL. 29

**27.** Bronze cup from the Larisa; *c.* 475–450? Vollgraff, *Mnemosyne* lx (1932–3), 231 ff., pl. 1. *SEG* xi. 329. NM?

**28.** Bronze wheel from a sanctuary of the Dioskouroi(?); *c.* 475–450? *IG* iv. 566. *SGDI* 3274. Roehl³, 40. 17. *BMC Bronzes*, 253. Vollgraff, *Mnemosyne* lviii (1930), 29. BM.

**29.** Fragment of a bowl bearing a graffito from the Heraion; *c.* 475–450? Heermance, *AH* ii. 186 f., no. 13, pl. 69. NM?

**30.** Gravestone from the Athenian Kerameikos for the Argive allies who fell at Tanagra; *c.* 458–457. *IGA* 36. Roehl³, 37. 7. *IG* i². 931–2. *GHI*² 28 and pp. 259 f. Peek, *Kerameikos* iii. 34 ff., pls. 10–11. Meritt, *Hesperia* xiv (1945), 134 ff. and xxi (1952), 351 ff., fig. 2, pl. 89. *SEG* x. 407. EM 10274–6. BM. Agora Mus. I 2006*a–c*, 551*a–b*, 39, 4893, 3285. Kerameikos Mus.  PL. 29

**31.** Part of a stele bearing a list of names from the Larisa; *c.* 460–450? Vollgraff, *Mnemosyne* xlvii (1919), 161 f., no. 6. Argos Mus. 274.　　　　　　　　　　　　　　　　　　　　PL. 30

**32.** Stele erected by the four hieromnemones in the Heraion; *c.* 460–450? *IG* iv. 517. Richardson and Wheeler, *AH* i. 197 ff., no. 2. Roehl³, 39. 14. *DGE* 96 (1). Vollgraff, *Mnemosyne* lviii (1930), 28 ff. *SEG* xi. 303. Buck 82. EM.

**33.** Base for a tripod, inscribed Δεξξιλος, from the Heraion; *c.* 460–450? Richardson and Wheeler, op. cit. 205, no. 6. *IG* iv. 515. Roehl³, 40. 18. EM.

**34.** Signature of the sculptor Dorotheos of Argos on the base of a dedication at Hermion; *c.* 460–450? *IG* iv. 684. *IGB* 51. Philadelpheus, *PAE* 1909, 174. Peek, *AM* lix (1934), 45 ff., no. 8*b*. Marcadé i. 31, pl. 7, 1. (See also p. 178, E. Argolid 9.) Hermion.　　　　　　　　　　　　PL. 33

**35.** Signature of Dorotheos of Argos on the base of a dedication at Delphi; *c.* 460–450? Pomtow, *Klio* ix (1909), 170. *FD* iii. 1. 326 ff., no. 502, fig. 46. Peek, op. cit. 47. Marcadé i. 30, fig. 34. Delphi Mus. 3840.

**36.** Base for a dedication at the Heraion, perhaps by the four hieromnemones; *c.* 460–450? Walter, *Ö. Jh.* xiv (1911), Beibl. 139 ff., fig. 71. *DGE* 96 (2). Mastrokostas, *Neon Athenaion* ii. 24. *SEG* xvi. 244.

**37–38.** Graffito and inscription from the Asklepieion at Epidauros; *c.* 460–450? *IG* iv². 1. 137, 139.

**39a–b.** Argive (*a*) and Tylisian (*b*) copies of an agreement between Knossos and Tylisos, drawn up by Argos; *c.* 460–450? Vollgraff, *BCH* xxxiv (1910), 331 ff. and xxxvii. 279 ff., pl. 4. *SIG*³ 56. *DGE* 83. *GHI*² 33 and p. 261. *IC* i, Cnosus, 56 ff., no. 4, and Tylisus, 307 f., no. 1. Kahrstedt, *Klio* xxxiv (1942), 72 ff. Vollgraff, *Le Décret d'Argos relatif à un pacte entre Knossos et Tylisos* (1948), 1 ff. *SEG* xi. 316. Buck 85. Argos Mus., Heraklion Mus.

**40.** Part of a stele bearing a record of sale, from the Larisa; *c.* 450? Vollgraff, *Mnemosyne* lvii (1929), 245 f., no. 29. *SEG* xi. 339. Argos Mus.

**41.** Fragment of a stele bearing a decree referring to the Epidaurians; *c.* 450–425? Vollgraff, *Mnemosyne* xlvii (1919), 160 f., no. 5. Argos Mus.?

**42.** Fragment of a stele bearing a decree from Argos; *c.* 450–425? *IG* iv. 555. *IGA* 38. *SGDI* 3272. Roehl³, 38. 9. Vollgraff, *BCH* lxviii–lxix (1944–5), 392 ff., fig. 1. *SEG* xi. 317. Private coll.?　　PL. 30

**43.** Bronze prize dinos from the games of Hera Argeia, from a grave in Attica; *c.* 450–425? A. H. Smith, *JHS* xlvi (1926), 256 f., fig. 3 and pl. 14. Vollgraff, *Mnemosyne* lviii (1930), 33 f. *SEG* xi. 330. BM.

**44.** Base bearing a dedication by Telestas at Nemea; *c.* 450–425? *IG* iv. 486. *SEG* xi. 295. Lost?

**45.** Base of the dedication of Pythokles at Olympia, signed by Polykleitos; *c.* 450–425? *Ol.* v. 162–3. *IGB* 91. *SGDI* 3275. Richter³, 246 f. Olympia Mus. 675.　　　　　　　　　　PL. 30

**46.** Base for a dedication by Hybrilas and another, at the Heraion; *c.* 450–425? *IG* iv. 514. Richardson and Wheeler, *AH* i. 203, no. 4. Roehl³, 39. 13. EM.　　　　　　　　　　　　PL. 30

**47.** Base for the Wooden Horse dedicated by Argos at Delphi after the battle of Thyrea; *c.* 414. *FD* iii. 1. 56 and 384 ff., no. 573, fig. 62, pl. 12, 3. Delphi 4897*a–c*.　　　　　　　PL. 30

**48.** Block from a dedication of the Argives at Delphi; *c.* 415–400? *FD* iii. 1. 56 f. and 386 ff., no. 91, fig. 24, pl. 4, 1. Bourguet, *REG* xxxii (1919), 50 ff. Delphi Mus. 733.　　　　　PL. 30

**49.** Sculptured stele dedicated to Artemis by Polystrate; *c.* 415–400? *IGA* 45. *IG* iv. 567. *SGDI* 3276. Roehl³, 40. 19. *DGE* 87. Furtwaengler, *Meisterwerke*, 415. Bluemel, *Kat. Skulpt. Berlin* iii (1928), 55 f., pl. 67. Berlin Mus. 682.　　　　　　　　　　　　　　　　PL. 30

**50.** Prohibition on a stele, 5th c. Rhomaios, *PAE* 1950, 237.

*Inscription attributed to Argos*

**51.** Bronze fragments, Tegea museum (*IG* v. 2. 560. Honorific decree? cf. [ευ]ϝεργεταν). Only a few letters are legible, but they resemble Argive of the second quarter of the 5th c. (cf. especially *gamma*).

## MYCENAE

*Letter-forms*; see Argos, pp. 151 ff. and Fig. 37.

Little is known of the history of Mycenae between the destruction of her Homeric citadel towards the end of the twelfth century, and the time of the Persian invasion, when she sent a troop of eighty men to Thermopylai and (jointly with Tiryns) 400 to Plataia (Hdt. vii. 202; ix. 28; Paus. ii. 16. 5). Strabo says (372, 377) that she was under the control of Argos from the Return of the Herakleidai onwards; and this is generally held to be true in principle, though in practice the waxing and waning of Argive power between the eighth and fifth centuries must have caused the degree of control to vary greatly. In 480, at least, Mycenae and Tiryns acted as though they were wholly independent of Argos, and it is inferred that they had broken loose from all ties with her after the defeat of the Argive army by the Spartans at Sepeia *c.* 494.

The destruction of Mycenae followed not long afterwards. Pausanias attributed it simply to the jealousy of the Argives over her part in the Persian War (ii. 16. 5; cf. Strabo 377); but according to Diodoros (xi. 65) the Myceneans had shown further their defiance of any Argive authority by claiming the right to administer the Games at Nemea (which were under the control of Argos' satellite Kleonai), and actually disputing over the ritual of the Argive Heraion. Mycenae was besieged by the Argives and their allies, the troops of Tegea and Kleonai, and finally taken in 468 according to Diodoros; a date which may be correct, though Diodoros' system of chronology is not reliable.[1] The city was plundered and razed, the population evicted or enslaved, and from the captives a tithe was sent to Apollo at Delphi.[2] The base of an Argive dedication there of about this date may possibly have some connexion with these events (p. 163). The Argives resettled the area later, for a community existed there in Hellenistic times, as building and inscriptions show;[3] but Mycenae proper had ceased to exist, and Pausanias (ii. 16. 5–7) and Strabo (372) speak of the site as desolate.

Three inscriptions on stone, one on bronze, and two brief graffiti on sherds have been recovered in and round Mycenae. They show that the local alphabet was identical with that of Argos after the adoption of *sigma* by the Argives, an event which has been attributed tentatively to the last years of the sixth century (pp. 159 f.). Five of these inscriptions are of the fifth century; but one (**1**) may be early in the last quarter of the sixth, which

---

[1] An alternative date suggested by modern authorities is 460; cf. Kolbe, *Hermes* 1937, 254 ff.; Gomme, *Commentary on Thucydides* i. 408 f.

[2] Diodoros, loc. cit. He says only that the people were enslaved; but Pausanias has a more interesting version (vii. 25. 6), that some fled to Kleonai, others to Keryneia in Achaia, and others to the protection of Alexandros I of Macedon.

[3] Wace, *Mycenae* (1949), 24.

would mean either that Mycenae for some reason gave up the use of *san* before either Argos or Corinth, or that the local Mycenean script differed from the Argive in this one particular, and used the *sigma* from the beginning. If this is so—and it seems to be supported by a sixth-century inscription from Nemea, here attributed to Mycenae (p. 173)— she may have taken the use of *sigma* from one of the states of the eastern Argolid, since her other neighbours, Kleonai and Phleious, used the *san*. Here once more, as elsewhere, we must wait for archaic material from other cities of Argolis and Corinthia before we can see how far, in fact, the use of *san* extended.

The best-known of the Mycenean inscriptions is the bronze plaque found on the north-west side of the citadel near the summit, and presumably belonging to the archaic temple (**2**). It is usually termed 'sixth-century',[1] but according to the standards of the Argive inscriptions it should rather be dated in the early years of the fifth (cf. γ2, ε2, ν2); the nearest parallel in Argive would be the stele dedicated by Aischyllos (**17**) and the signature of the sculptors Atotos and Argeiades (**19**). The text concerns a suppliant named Phrasiarides, but no satisfactory translation has yet been proposed.[2]

If this plaque is to be dated in the early years of the fifth century, it is clear that the other inscription from the Mycenean citadel (**1**) must belong to the sixth, for its letter forms are demonstrably earlier, as, for example, γι, μι, νι, υι. The exact nature of the monument on which it is inscribed remains unexplained: it is a circular crowning member for some structure, with a wavy moulding running round it and two sets of holes on top, each set joined by horizontal channels cut below the surface. Another channel leads from the top to an outlet on the vertical face, and was thought by the excavator to be meant to ease its haulage.[3] The bottom of the stone is smoothed, for setting on another stone below, and the main inscription was written either on this stone or on another lost one above, for the surviving line: αι με δαμιοργια ειε τος ιαρομναμονας τος ες Περσε το⟨ι⟩σι γονευσι κριτερας εμεν κατ⟨τ⟩α ϝεϝρεμενα is plainly a last clause, added here because there was no room for it elsewhere. The stone must have come originally from the fountain-house which was cleared by Wace, and identified by him as the Περσεία κρήνη, the spring of Perseus, described by Pausanias (ii. 16. 6).[4]

---

[1] e.g. by Fraenkel, *IG* iv. 492; Kern, p. viii; Buck 80; Wace, op. cit. 86.

[2] The usual interpretation is that it is the reply of an oracle in a temple of Athena, delivered to one Phrasiarides: 'Phrahiaridas a Mycenis ex arce a Minerva supplex missus est' (Fraenkel); 'Phrahiaridas Mycenaeus a Minerva ex arce supplex (= a Minerva, arcis Argis praeside, ad quam supplex, ut oraculum peteret, missus est) iam Mycenas rediit' (Vollgraff and Buck). The sense of the next part is generally agreed upon: '—in the magistracy [or priesthood?] of Antias and Pyrrhias. (The reply was) "Let Antias and Kithios and Aischron be (the judges, or whatever the question had asked)".' Apart from the ambiguity of the first sentence, a further difficulty is that (as Levi has rightly pointed out, *AJA* xlix (1945), 301 f.) there is no evidence that any shrine of Athena either at Mycenae or Argos was ever oracular; and the wording of the text is unlike that of any other written oracular response so far known, in that, in spite of the other detail given, it does not quote the question asked. A possible way out of the difficulty would be to read ειεν as an error for Ͱιεν, from ἵημι, taking this as the shorter -ν ending of the third plural (secondary) used in many dialects, Argive among the rest (as ἀνέθεν for ἀνέθεσαν, cf. Buck, 112 and Thumb-Kieckers, *Handbuch*², 122). The text might then be translated: 'Phrasiarides from Mycenae at the instance of Athena became a suppliant (sent away) from his city, during the (priestly?) office of Antias and Pyrrhias; and Antias and Kithios and Aischron sent him (let him go?)'—and thereafter recorded their action on a plaque placed in Athena's temple.

[3] Tsountas, *AE* 1892, 67. Wace suggests (*BSA* xlviii (1953), 19 ff.) that the holes and channels had to do w th the installation of water.  [4] Loc. cit.

A fragment of a sixth-century dedication found near Nemea should perhaps also be assigned to a Mycenean hand (7), for it shows the characteristic letter-forms, i.e. Argive *lambda* with *sigma*. It was said to come from Tourkovrysi, about an hour's walk southeast of Hagios Georgios. The tall, careful script suggests a date about the same as that of 1, perhaps *c.* 525. Guide-lines and a cutting-compass are used, and the text begins with a sculptor's signature, [.ᶜ·⁴·]ιαδε̄ς με εποιϝε̄σε, written from left to right and occupying the first line, followed by a vertical stroke for punctuation, and *vacat*.

The text then begins again, from left to right, with the dedication, which is inscribed in false *boustrophedon*, so that the lines continue from left to right throughout:[1] [Κ]λεανδρος δε ανεθε̄κε και ℎι[δρυε?- - - | - - -κ]αλον αγαλμα · εμι δε το [ᶜ·³·|ᶜ·³·]εια καλονι ℎειδομ[- - -].

The remaining four inscriptions appear somewhat later in date than the bronze plaque of Phrasiarides, and may be only a few years earlier than the destruction of the city, if that event took place in 468. The first (3), found at Asprochoma near Mycenae, is the right-hand part of a small limestone tablet; it may have been meant to imitate a bronze plaque, for it is only 2 centimetres thick, and the *omikron* has been made by a small drilled hole, like those of the Argive bronze plaque 20. The inscription, which is carelessly cut, records that a body of hieromnemones (at least five offerings survive or may be restored) dedicated—in an unknown temple—a series of sets of armour (ασπιδα, ϙυνιαν, αϙοντιον). The letters are typical of the period round about 475: ε3, ν2–3, ρ2, while *qoppa* and the late archaic form υ2 are still present. The odd appearance of the *beta* in the name Βυτιος (l. 3) may be partly due to the carelessness of the writing. The first *alpha* in ιαρομναμονας has been omitted, and then added. The inscription ορος ℎεραιας on a boundary-stone (4) found built into the Hellenistic fountain-house Perseia may be of about the same date.

The last two inscriptions are graffiti on two sherds of black-glazed pottery, one found below the citadel, the other on it. The former (5) reads: πενπυλος,[2] probably a name scratched on the already-broken sherd rather than one written when the vase was still entire. The latter (6) is part of a dedication: το ℎεροος] εμ[ι]. The hero might be either Perseus or Agamemnon, if the sherd has strayed.[3] We may note the 'bracket' type of punctuation here, which resembles the Lakonian (p. 184).

---

[1] Some minor observations on the first publication may be noted: (1) the script cannot be Corinthian, as the editor suggests; it has none of the characteristics. (2) Since the false *boustrophedon* leaves every alternate line inverted, and the inscription is otherwise expertly cut, is it possible that it read vertically, and that the one preserved face (bearing a cutting, and therefore taken by the editor for the top) is actually the side, with a later mark of re-use? (3) I hesitate to follow him in the suggested restoration [Μικκ]ιαδες for the sculptor's name, since there is as yet no satisfactory evidence that the Mikkiades whom Pliny mentions as the father of Archermos was in fact his father, and not simply the dedicator in the epigram from which Pliny appears to have derived his names (see further, pp. 294 f.). If there was indeed a sculptor Mikkiades of Chios, one might expect him to sign himself ὁ Χῖος, as Archermos did.

It would, of course, be a local Mycenean mason who actually cut this signature, and one would have to assume that he altered an original signature: Μικκιαδης εποιησεν ὁ Χιος (on the statue?) to Μικκιαδες εποιϝεσε, or else that the work had no signature anywhere, and the local man added one. (4) The monument should be dedicatory, not funerary, from the use of the dedicatory verb ἀνέθηκε: for epitaphs the verb used is normally ἐπιτιθέναι or κατατιθέναι.

[2] I follow the reading of Tsountas, *AE* 1887, 155, as against Περιπυλος in *IG* iv. 494, for the reason (admittedly not conclusive) that in the latter case one would have expected the tailed form of the *rho* at this date.

[3] The shrine of Agamemnon lay about 1 km. south-south-west of the acropolis of Mycenae; see J. M. Cook, *BSA* xlviii (1953), 30 ff.

## CATALOGUE

**1.** Final clause of a law added on the crowning stone of a structure from the fountain-house Perseia; *c.* 525? Tsountas, *AE* 1892, 67. *IG* iv. 493. Roehl³, 52. 2. *DGE* 98. *SEG* xi. 300. Wace, *Mycenae*, 41 and *BSA* xlviii (1953), 19, pl. 14b. Buck 81. Athens, EM 218.        PL. 31

**2.** Bronze plaque concerning the suppliant Phrasiarides, from the citadel; *c.* 500–480? *IG* iv. 492. Roehl³, 51. 1. Kern, pl. 8. *DGE* 97. Vollgraff, *Mnemosyne* lvii (1929), 221 f. Levi, *AJA* xlix (1945), 301 f. *SEG* xi. 299. Wace, *Mycenae* (1949), 86. Buck 80. NM.        PL. 31

**3.** Part of a limestone plaque with a list of armour dedicated, from Asprochoma near Mycenae; *c.* 475? Mitsos, *Hesperia* xv (1946), 115 ff., fig. 1. *SEG* xi. 298. Nauplia Mus. 2907.        PL. 31

**4.** Boundary stone from a precinct of Hera, now built into the Hellenistic fountain-house Perseia; *c.* 475? Woodhead, *BSA* xlviii (1953), 27 ff., fig. 5. Nauplia Mus.

**5.** Graffito on a black-glazed sherd found below the citadel; *c.* 475? Tsountas, *AE* 1887, 155. *IG* iv. 494. *SGDI* 3314. Roehl³, 52. 3. NM.        PL. 31

**6.** Dedication incised on part of a black-glazed saucer from the shrine of 'the Hero'. *c.* 475? *IGA* 29. *IG* iv. 495. *SGDI* 3313. Roehl³, 52. 4. Kern, pl. 8. NM.        PL. 31

*Inscription attributed to Mycenae*

**7.** Fragment of a plaque (? or base or stele?) said to come from Tourkovrysi near Hagios Georgios (Nemea), in private possession; *c.* 525? Androutsopoulos, *Polemon* iv (1949), 73 ff., fig. 1.

## THE EASTERN ARGOLID

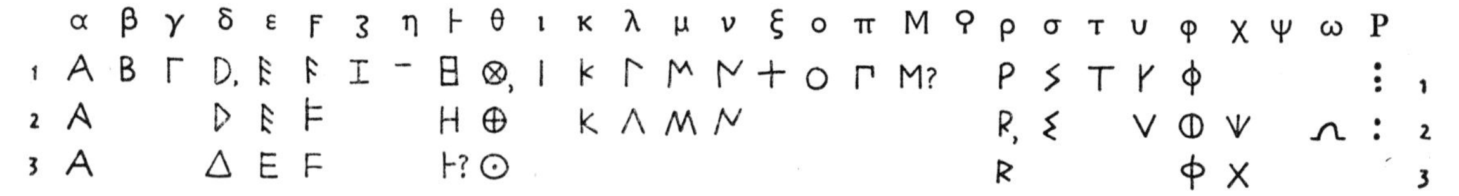

FIG. 38. The Eastern Argolid

(Since there is still uncertainty over many points, discussion of the letter-forms is kept to the text and notes, to avoid repetition. For some general conclusions, see pp. 176 ff.).

In studying the inscriptions of this area, we have to start from the obvious historical fact that, though the inhabitants spoke the Doric dialect, and the peninsula itself was called Argolic, none the less their natural interests lay seawards, towards the Saronic Gulf or the opposite coast of eastern Lakonia, rather than inland over the hilly centre of the peninsula back to the Argive plain. Epidauros, Methana, Troizen, and Hermion were all settlements made on or very near the coast, and, although their Doric-speaking population must have arrived there in some early eastward expansion of Dorians from the Argive plain soon after the Dorian Invasion, these places persistently retained their tradition of non-Doric connexions. From the time of Theseus onwards Troizen had had links with Attica, which caused her to give shelter to the non-combatants of Athens when the Persian invasion threatened Attic territory.[1] Epidauros at an early date had expanded

[1] Cf. Paus. ii. 30. 9 and 31. 7; Hdt. viii. 41; Welter, *Troizen u. Kalaureia*, 53.

eastwards and colonized the island of Aigina, and earlier still, by her own accounts, had participated in the eastward migrations which colonized the Doric Hexapolis and Samos (Hdt. i. 146; vii. 99; viii. 46; Paus. vii. 4. 2). The people of Hermion on the southern coast were said to be originally Dryopes from central or northern Greece; Asine, the other state called Dryopian, was overwhelmed by Argos at the close of the Geometric period, and did not revive until Hellenistic times;[1] and the Hermionians lived secluded from history, making their living chiefly by their purple-fishing, and practising a curious chthonic cult of Demeter and Persephone, which was evidently a relic of their Dryopian origins (Hdt. viii. 43. 73; Strabo 374). The early ties of all these places with the opposite mainlands of Lakonia and Attica are further confirmed by the existence of the Kalaureian Amphiktiony, a group holding a common cult of Poseidon on the island of Kalaureia off Troizen. The cult can be traced back to the Late Geometric period from the finds on the site of the temple, and the original members were Epidauros, Aigina, Hermion, Prasiai (replaced during the seventh century by Sparta), Nauplia (replaced in the same way by Argos), Athens, and Boiotian Orchomenos.[2]

It is not surprising, therefore, that the inscriptions found on the Argolic peninsula do not show the Argive alphabet. We might expect rather to find the same alphabet as that used on Aigina, or even a version of the Attic; but from the inscriptions themselves epigraphists have concluded that the influence came from the other side of the peninsula and that Epidauros, Troizen, Methana, and Hermion all used the same form of alphabet as did Lakonia.[3] This is certainly true of Troizen and Methana in the sixth century, and probably of Hermion too, but for Epidauros the case is not clear. It is therefore best to consider the evidence separately.

## METHANA AND TROIZEN

The earliest inscription found as yet in the eastern Argolid is the gravestone of Androkles, son of Eumares, which was discovered on the peninsula of Methana (1). It is inscribed *boustrophedon* on a rough block of trachyte, starting from left to right and turning with a loop at the end of the lines. At the first turn the mason continued in false *boustrophedon*, but righted himself half-way along, and thereafter proceeded in the usual way. Von Premerstein suggested[4] that originally the stone stood vertically as a stele; but, as there

[1] Cf. Paus. ii. 36. 4–6 and iv. 34. 9–12; Strabo 373. Asine helped Sparta under King Nikandros to ravage the Argolid, and in reprisal later the Argive king Eratos sacked the city; the surviving inhabitants were ultimately given sanctuary by Sparta in Messenia, in a new Asine. The Swedish excavations on the original site confirmed this (Froedin and Persson, *Asine* (1938), *passim*); there was continuous habitation there until the end of the Late Geometric period (*c.* 700?), and thereafter nothing until Hellenistic times. But in a small sanctuary on Mount Barbouna a preliminary excavation revealed some 7th-c. material, and this has been identified with the shrine of Apollo Pythaios, which Pausanias says expressly was spared by the

Argives (ii. 36. 5). The site has not yet been further excavated; but presumably any inscriptions found there are likely to be Argive.

[2] Ephoros *ap*. Strabo 374. Troizen herself is not mentioned in the list (because she administered the cult?). The inclusion of Boiotian Orchomenos has suggested to some scholars that the Amphiktiony must go back to Mycenean times; but, though Mycenean relics have been found in the graves on Kalaureia, there has been nothing earlier than Geometric, and that very scanty, from the site of the temple itself (cf. Welter, op. cit. 45).

[3] Kirchhoff[4], 160; Roberts i. 285.

[4] *AM* xxxiv (1909), 358 f.

is no extension at either end for bedding it in the ground, it is more likely that it lay flat above the grave like the archaic Theran gravestone of Rhexanor and others (pp. 317 f., Thera **5**);[1] and, as a stone lying flat might be read by the spectator with equal ease, or difficulty, whether inscribed up and down like a pillar, or horizontally like a base, the mason was at first in two minds as to how it should be treated, finally deciding, as we have seen, to inscribe it like a base. The archaic looping of the *boustrophedon* and the early forms ɑɪ, ɛɪ, ʋɪ, ϕɪ suggest a seventh-century date; ϝ2 may be a trick of the mason's own, as it does not recur elsewhere. Even if we assume some backwardness in the technique of Methanian stone-masons, the inscription can hardly be later than the second quarter of the sixth century.

The same letter-forms appear on the earliest inscription from Troizen (**2**), a state whose political activity in the archaic period is slightly better known than that of Methana, though only in three brief notices: she claimed the foundation of Halikarnassos in the Doric Hexapolis (Hdt. vii. 99; Paus. ii. 30. 9 and 32. 6); at the end of the eighth century she joined with the Achaians of Helike to found the western colony Sybaris, whence the Troizenian element was later expelled (Arist., *Pol.* 1303a; Ps.-Skymn. 340), without leaving any trace of its existence in the alphabet of Sybaris (cf. p. 251); and *c.* 525 she acquired the island Thyrea (Hydra), previously the property of Hermion, from that band of freebooting Samian exiles who later went on to found a short-lived colony at Kydonia in Crete (Hdt. iii. 59). The inscription is on an octagonal pillar 3·5 m. high, which, with two others, was found re-used in a Hellenistic cistern. The pillar bears a mortise on top for the tenon of a lost capital, which carried a tripod won, according to the epigram, by 'Damotimos the son of Amphidama' in a race at the Games in Thebes. These were perhaps the games held in honour of Apollo Ismenios, or one of those funeral games in which, as we have seen, Athenians also competed and won tripods (pp. 91 f.). Is it mere chance, or does it reflect the general outlook of Troizen and her neighbours, that this one recorded prize should have come not from any of the numerous athletic contests of the Peloponnesian sanctuaries, but from across the Saronic Gulf?

The inscription is written vertically up and down two faces of the pillar in false *boustrophedon*, which curves round decoratively at the top; it does not rise very far above eye-level, and must have required some careful plotting. Octagonal supports are rare among archaic monuments; a few only occur among the dedications on the Athenian Akropolis, all dated in the last decades of the sixth century.[2] The best-preserved example there is much more developed in detail than the Troizenian pillar, but it does suggest, I think, that the type itself is not particularly early. Though *upsilon* and *phi* of **2** are still in the archaic form ɪ, the lettering as a whole has nothing of the true archaic unevenness, and, taking this in conjunction with the use of the false *boustrophedon*, I should prefer to give this monument a wide date within the third quarter of the sixth century, rather than *c.* 550, as is usually suggested.

A second inscribed grave-monument was found at Troizen, beside the road from Galata to Damala (**3**): a round, unfluted column 2·15 m. in height, bearing on its top

---

[1] If this is so, the remains of four letters observed on the back of the stone in 1921 would be from some later time (as their shape, indeed, suggests); cf. *SEG* xi. 391.
[2] *DAA* 181, 183.

an oblong cutting for the plinth of a marble statue[1] with a commemorative epigram to the dead man, Praxiteles, inscribed in two complete lines running vertically down from left to right, the second turning over at the bottom in a brief spilling on to a third line in false *boustrophedon*. The first line being written below the second, it is clear that the monument stood originally on the left side of the path whereby the spectator came up to it, so that the nearer (i.e. lower) line would naturally be read first. The letter-forms show ξ1 and χ2, both in the 'red' forms; this is the chief difference between this local alphabet and those of Aigina or of the Argive-Corinthian group, and links it closely with Lakonia and the rest of the Peloponnese. The date may be *c.* 500. It is plainly later than **2** from the forms of the letters, particularly μ2 and ν2; *chi* also is in the late archaic form 2, though *upsilon* is still 1 and *epsilon* has a small tail (2); *alpha* is also 2.

At about this time or slightly later, that is to say in the first quarter of the fifth century, may be placed the inscription on a spear-butt found at Olympia, which records an otherwise unknown defeat of the Lakedaimonians by the people of Methana (**4**): Μεθανιοι απο Λακεδαιμονιōν. It has been connected with the dedication of another butt, also by the Methanians (Μεθαν[ιοι]), which was found in the precinct of Apollo Korythos at Korone in Messenia; but I have suggested elsewhere (see p. 204, n. 1) that this latter should be connected with the perioikic town known to late writers as Methone or Mothone, since it is hard to see how a public dedication by Argolic Methana could have arrived at a local shrine in the heart of Messenia. The inscription **4** is carelessly incised, but *epsilon* is still 2, and *mu* and *nu* vary between 1 and 2, as in other inscriptions of the period *c.* 500–475 or a few years later.

The only other inscription from Methana which may be held to antedate the arrival of the Ionic alphabet is the gravestone *IG* iv. 859, which, according to the copy (in majuscule type only), shows *alpha* with sloping bar, and tailed *rho*, as elsewhere in the Peloponnese in the fifth century. Troizen provides two more examples of pre-Ionic script. One is the legend TRO on her earliest coins (**5**), which are struck on the Attic standard and bear a curious frontal head of Athena, which can hardly be later than the middle of the fifth century, even if it is archaizing in the sense that it is a deliberate copy of an archaic cult-statue.[2] The other inscription is the stele dedicated by Euthymides (**6**), which records the question and answer given at an oracular shrine which is assumed to be that of Asklepios at Troizen. It shows Ͱ2 in l. 3, but Ͱι (for η) in l. 6, and Ͱι (= Ͱ) in l. 8, while *omega* is used for both long and short *o*, except once in l. 4, θεōν. The inscription thus has a distorted resemblance to the vowel system used in the islands Paros, Thasos, Siphnos (Ω = o, O = ω, H = η and occasionally ε), but otherwise the letters are Troizenian (cf. δ1, χ2), and the best explanation seems to be that the mason was trying to use the new letters, without understanding fully the rules for their use. The date is

---

[1] Welter (op. cit. 40) describes the column wrongly as eight-sided, with a round hole on the top for a capital, which suggests a confusion with the pillar of Demotimos. In 1954 I found the top of the column, now broken across, protruding slightly out of the earth of an olive-yard in the spot described by Welter, loc. cit. I could only probe down about 25 cm., and do not know if it is broken off, or buried whole. The measurements are: diam. 1·08 m.; cutting, width 0·26 m., length 0·38 m. (originally 0·47), depth 0·055 m. (see Pl. 32).

[2] *HN*², 443: '*c.* 430–400 or earlier'; B ii. 3. 495 ff., pl. 217: '*c.* 460–400'. E. S. G. Robinson tells me that in his opinion they belong to the first quarter of the 5th c.

usually disputed as between the early or the late fifth century. For the latter date many of the letter-forms, judged by normal standards, would be too archaic; but the wavering *ductus* of the lines suggests the work of an inferior craftsman, and it is clear that the *omega* which he was taught was not the early fifth-century type with curled struts (pp. 37 f., Fig. 24), but that used in the Ionic alphabet of the middle and second half of the century (Fig. 38, ω2). Without going to the lower extreme, therefore, we may suggest that the inscription should be set somewhere in the third quarter of the century. We may note also σ2 and δ3, which are different forms from those of the archaic period (see below).

### HERMION

The earliest inscriptions at Hermion may belong to the decade 460–450; they show δ3, σ2, and, with one exception, the 'red' *xi* and *chi*. Probably, then, she should be classed with Troizen and Methana as one whose early script changed in some details in the fifth century through outside influence, δ3 being normal in the islands, and σ2 also, as well as elsewhere in the Peloponnese. The script is known from three statue-bases, all bearing offerings typical of the chthonic cult which was the chief religion of Hermion, and all to be dated approximately between the years 480 and 450. The first is a block of local stone at Delphi (**7**), with cuttings on the top for a lost bronze statue of Persephone, mounted by two bronze tenons under each foot in the style characteristic of the first part of the fifth century (cf., for example, the dedication by Kallias on the Athenian Akropolis, *DAA* 111). The block, which has a smoothed frame round the inscribed face (as occurs also on the base from the Akropolis) is similar in measurements to other Delphic bases of the second quarter of the century—those of the charioteer (p. 206, **9**), the Korkyrean dedication (p. 233, **15**), and the signature of Sotades of Thespiai (the latter block has been assigned to the dedication of Hermion; cf. *FD* iii. 4. 221 f.); evidently the local mason or masons who supplied the mounts for the bronzes which were erected in the sanctuary at about this time produced a standard size to crown the parapet of the Ischegaion.[1] Another block once joined it to the right, as the clamp-cuttings show, and doubtless held a companion statue of Demeter, completing symmetrically the *stoichedon* dedicatory inscription. The occasion for the offering is unknown, but it might well have been erected *c.* 475 or a few years earlier, as a thank-offering for the Persian Wars, to which Hermion had contributed three ships and 300 hoplites (Hdt. viii. 43; ix. 28).

The other two bases **8** and **9**, found at Hermion itself, have been discussed in detail by other authors, and it is enough here to recall that they are single blocks, each bearing cuttings at the top for a bronze cow and dedicated to Demeter Chthonia by Alexias son of Lyon and Aristomenes son of Alexias. The first bears the signature of Kresilas of Kydonia, the second of Dorotheos of Argos (see pp. 165 f.). Peek pointed out[2] that the lettering of the two dedications differs in some details each from the other, that of Aristomenes showing the more archaic forms; and suggested that they might be *c.* 20 years

---

[1] Hampe's attempt to assign the Charioteer to Sotades, which rested partly on the similarity between the two blocks, was refuted by La Coste-Messelière (*RA* 1941 ii, 150 f., quoting *FD* ii. 1. 142 ff. and 235 f.). Cf. further pp. 266 f. (Syracuse) and Chamoux, *FD* iv. 5. 34 ff.

[2] *AM* lix (1934), 45 ff.

apart in date, the offerings of different generations in the same family. They suggest to me rather the work of two masons in the same workshop, one perhaps being younger than the other, and using a more developed form of *nu* (2), the 'blue' χ3, and punctuation; the unusual curved *heta*, which occurs on both, is hardly likely to have been copied by the second mason if he cut his base twenty years after the first. In this case the dedicators might have been first cousins, sons of two brothers Lyon and Alexias. Dorotheos' signature is in Argive letters of the period *c.* 460–450 (p. 166), which should therefore give the date for both offerings. Kresilas' is not in the Aiginetan of Kydonia (p. 314), but in the same lettering as the dedications. It will be recalled that Kresilas' other signatures vary according to the alphabets of the places where his works were dedicated,[1] which suggests that he sent no signature with his bronzes from his foundry, or that the local masons did not always copy an artist's signature exactly from the draft. Dorotheos', on the other hand, was reproduced accurately; but he may have come over from Argos to see his work erected, and signed the base himself.

There are no further inscriptions from Hermion, though we may hope that some day will be found the local copy of the treaty between her and Athens in the middle of the fifth century, of which a fragment of the Athenian version has been discovered (*SEG* x. 15). Meanwhile the bases show that by *c.* 460–450 *heta* had become open and *theta* dotted; and that, though the alphabet normally used the 'red' form of *xi*, the 'blue' use of X for *chi* was not unknown.

### EPIDAUROS

Nearly all the existing evidence for the alphabet of Epidauros comes from her famous precinct of Asklepios, which lay some distance west of the town, with the small precinct of Apollo Maleatas adjoining it on Mount Kynortion. The cult of Asklepios was not introduced here from Thessaly until the second half of the sixth century, whereas that of Apollo Maleatas goes back at least to the seventh.[2] The only inscriptions as yet from the older shrine are a graffito on a black-glazed sherd, not yet fully published,[3] and the ill-written inscription which must be classed as a graffito on the bronze stepped base of a lost statuette (**12**), which was bought in Ligurio, and resembles the small bronzes found in Apollo's precinct rather than anything from the Asklepieion;[4] the bad spelling makes its translation uncertain (p. 180), and the open *heta* suggests a date not earlier than the second quarter of the fifth century.

None of the inscriptions from the Asklepieion itself looks demonstrably earlier than

[1] Cf. *DAA* 512 and Marcadé i. 62 ff. M. Jameson suggests (**8**, bibliography) that Kresilas drafted both dedication and signature in the Aiginetan script of Kydonia; the 'blue' *chi* would then be correct, and the 'red' *xi* the local mason's error. Attractive though this theory is, I find it hard to square with Kresilas' other signatures. Nor do I find the view of Orlandini easy to accept (**8**, bibliography), that this work should be dated a little after 430.

[2] Papademetriou, *BCH* lxxiii (1949), 361 ff., especially 380 f.; cf. *IG* iv². 1, p. xiii.

[3] Papademetriou, op. cit. 377; the graffito is given as λαδες, with *lambda* as in Attic, and sibilant *san*. If this is right, it would, on the one hand, bear out the suggestion on p. 180 that the early alphabet of Epidauros used the *san*; on the other hand, the *lambda* would be wrong for Epidauros, and the name should be in the non-Attic form Ladas.

[4] This suggestion, first made by Furtwaengler (*50 Winckelmannsprogramm* (1890), 126), was supported by Papademetriou, op. cit. 370 f., from the similarity of the small bronzes found in his excavation.

the fifth century. The earliest is, in my opinion, the bronze phiale (?) **10**: τõι Αισκλαπιõι ανεθēκε Μικυλος. It is included among the Argive dedications at the sanctuary in *IG* iv². 1. 136, presumably because the letter *s* is expressed by the *san*; but it has not the *qoppa*, which one would expect in an Argive inscription which showed also tailed *epsilon* and *san*, and the *lambda* is not the Argive form. It thus presents an alphabet not at present exactly identical with that of any state in this area, and, in default of more evidence, it may be tentatively assumed that this dedication is local, and that the early script of Epidauros, unlike that of the other states in the eastern Argolid, was sufficiently influenced by that of the Argivo-Corinthian group to use the *san*, at least until the early fifth century, for this inscription can hardly be earlier than *c*. 500. It is not yet evident that any other Epidaurian letters differed thus sharply from those of the Methana-Troizen group, but it should be remembered that there is still no proof that Epidaurian used the 'red' forms of *xi* and *chi*; for the only examples are the + on the base **12**, whose value is uncertain, and X = χ on the base **13**, which, in the absence of other typical letters, might be either Epidaurian or Argive (below).

The remaining inscriptions of Epidauros range through the fifth century, and little can be said of individual specimens. The dedication το Απολλōνος εμι το Πυθιο (**11**) on the lip of a bronze lebes from the building E, believed by Kavvadias to be the oldest in the precinct, is called 'sixth-century' in *IG* iv². 1. 142, but the shapes of the letters ε3 and λ2 suggest rather the early fifth. The graffito on the base **12**, if it comes from the shrine of Apollo, should be dedicated to that deity or possibly to Asklepios, or both; but not to Athena, as is required if we accept the dubious reading ανφοξυν (= ὀξυδέρκη?) as an epithet of Athena. The dedicatory verb in the plural (ανεθēκαν) is clear, but the subject, plainly mis-spelt in some way, has been rendered variously as Ϝοι φροροι, or επιπρροροι, or εμφροροι, or as the citizens of an otherwise unknown place in the Argolid.[1] In such a confusion there is no reason why it should be assumed that the + must be the 'red' *xi*. The block inscribed Μαχαονος (**13**), judged by its ν2 and α2, should be earlier than the middle of the fifth century. It might be Argive, but, whereas the other Argive inscriptions in the sanctuary are private dedications, this stone, which must be either a small altar or a horos marking the precinct assigned to Machaon, offers by its nature a prima facie case for being local. If so, this would put it beyond a doubt that the Epidaurian alphabet, unlike that of Troizen and Methana, followed the Argivo-Corinthian group in using the 'blue' *xi* and *chi*.

The hollow bronze handle found in or near Epidauros (**14**) and the dedications **17** and **18** from the Asklepieion show the local forms of *gamma* and *delta*; the dotted *theta* was already in use by the third quarter of the century (**17**), but in formal inscriptions at least the closed *heta* persisted until late in the fifth century (cf. **18**; **19**, a fragment known

---

[1] For detailed discussions of the suggested readings cf. Neugebauer, *Kat. Bronz. Berlin* i. 180 and *IG* iv². 1. 141. Ϝοι φροροι = 'custodes fani' is the most commonly accepted. Another possibility (see the Transliteration of Plates) is to read Ϝεπρορος as Ϝιροποιοι mis-spelt, and ανφοξυν as ανφοιυν (= ἀμφοῖν), the form of the dative dual which is attested for Arkadia (Buck, 89); the dual deities would then be the Dios-kouroi, who had a place in the precinct; cf. *IG* iv². 1. 129 (l. 6), 510, 511. There is no evidence that this dialectal form was used in Epidauros; but as far as the actual reading is concerned, *iota* is possible as well as *xi*; Neugebauer's pl. 28 shows that the crossbar, barely crossing the vertical, may possibly have been an inadvertent stroke made by the unskilful wielder of the incising tool, like the inadvertent prolonging of the *phi*.

only from a sketch in Kavvadias's notebook, is probably of about the same date, i.e. last quarter of the fifth century). ρ2–3 was apparently in use in graffiti of the early fifth century (**12**), and in formal inscriptions by about the middle (**16**). *Sigma* in the fifth century, here as in the other cities of the Argolid, was the four-stroked type. It appears from the name Μικυλος (**10**) that the Epidaurian alphabet did not use the *qoppa*, or, if it did, it lost the use of the letter much earlier than did the Argivo-Corinthian group; we may compare the similar lack of *qoppa* in Lakonian and Phokian (pp. 100, 183). By chance, the extant early inscriptions from Troizen and Methana show no occasion for its use; but, as they resemble the Lakonian and Phokian strongly in other respects, it may be conjectured that they also had no use for it.

Here should be mentioned the bronze fragment *IG* iv². 1. 151 from the Asklepieion, which reads (right to left): Ϝαισκλαπιει μ—, with Ϝ3, as in the later Greek script of S. Italy. Neither this nor the form Αἰσκλαπιεύς occurs elsewhere in Epidaurian inscriptions, so the dedication may be by somebody from another state. The date should not be much later, if at all, than *c*. 500. If the shape is not an error, it is by far the earliest attested instance of this letter (p. 29).[1]

It is uncertain when the use of *boustrophedon* died out. The grave-pillar **3** shows that *c*. 500 the practice of writing consistently from left to right was in use at least for vertical inscriptions. The curious spacing of the graffito on the base from Ligurio (**12**) might suggest that in the early fifth century the *boustrophedon* system was still practised; but, as there was enough space on either the upper or the lower step for the dedication, once started, to be ended in the same line, it is evident that the writer wanted to separate the word ανφοξυν and attach it, so to speak, to the lost offering, like the label in a vase-painting; hence, probably, the retrograde direction of the word. The dedication proper was then written in the usual way, beginning at the front of the base. The *stoichedon* system occurs on the base dedicated by the Hermionians at Delphi *c*. 480–475?, though not on the slightly later bases found at Hermion; also on the bronze plaque dedicated by the μάγειρος Kallistratos at the Asklepieion about the middle of the century (**16**), and (to some extent) on the stele granting ἀσυλία to the daughter of Kalliphanes (**17**), which can, from its φ3, be dated securely after the middle of the century. Punctuation, when it is used at all, is of the common dotted types: 1 in the sixth century (**2**), and 2 in the fifth (**8**).

## CATALOGUE

### METHANA AND TROIZEN

**1.** Gravestone of Androkles from Methana; *c*. 600? Premerstein, *AM* xxxiv (1909), 356 ff. *DGE* 105. Friedlaender 27. *SEG* xi. 391. Peek i. 158. EM?                                    PL. 32

**2.** Grave-pillar of Demotimos, Troizen; *c*. 550–525? Legrand, *BCH* xvii (1893), 84 ff., 627 (van Herwerden). *IG* iv. 801. Roehl³, 110. 6. Arvanitopoullos, *Epigraphike* i. 88. *DGE* 102. Welter, *Troizen u. Kalaureia* (1941), 39 ff. and 54, pl. 22d. Friedlaender 30. *SEG* xi. 388. Peek i. 216. Troizen.    PL. 32

[1] Hiller suggests that it should be read also on    this might equally well be M̄, or even the drachma-
Sikyonian coins of the 5th c., Ϝ Σ (*IG* iv². 1. 151); but    sign Ϝ.

**3.** Grave-pillar of Praxiteles, Troizen; *c.* 500? Legrand, *BCH* xxiv (1900), 179 ff. *IG* iv. 800. Roehl³, 110. 7. *DGE* 101. Welter, op. cit. 40. 54. Friedlaender 29. *SEG* xi. 387. Peek i. 165. Troizen.   PL. 32

**4.** Bronze spear-butt dedicated at Olympia by the Methanians; *c.* 500–475? *IGA* 146. *Ol.* v. 247. Roberts i. 286. *SGDI* 3369. Roehl³, 110. 5. *DGE* 106. Kunze and Schleif, *Olymp. Forschungen* i, pl. 63a. Olympia Mus. 10.   PL. 33

**5.** Coinage of Troizen, with legend Τρο—; *c.* 500–475? B ii. 3. 495 ff., Pl. 217. *HN*², 443.

**6.** Stele bearing the response of an oracle, dedicated by Euthymides at Troizen; *c.* 450–425? Legrand, *BCH* xvii (1893), 86 ff. *IG* iv. 760. Roehl³, 110. 8. *SIG*³ 1159. *DGE* 103. EM?   PL. 33

### HERMION

**7.** Dedication by the Hermionians to Apollo at Delphi, perhaps made by Sotadas of Thespiai; *c.* 480–475? *FD* ii. 1. 234 f., fig. 186; iii. 4. 221 f., no. 147, pl. 25. 3 and 26. 1. Delphi Mus. 2501.   PL. 33

**8.** Dedication to Demeter Chthonia at Hermion by Alexias; *c.* 460–450? *IGB* 45. *IG* iv. 683. Peek, *AM* lix (1934), 45 ff. Orlandini, *Mem. Acc. Linc.* (1952), 273 ff. Jameson, *Hesperia* xxii (1953), 149 ff., pl. 50. Marcadé i. 63. *SEG* xi. 378.   PL. 33

**9.** Similar dedication by Aristomenes. *IGB* 51. *IG* iv. 684. Peek, loc. cit. Orlandini, loc. cit. Jameson, loc. cit. Marcadé i. 31. *SEG* xi. 379. See Argos **34**.   PL. 33

### EPIDAUROS

**10.** Phiale (?) dedicated by Mikylos in the Asklepieion; *c.* 500–475? Kavvadias, *Fouilles d'Épidaure* i. 8. *IG* iv. 1202; iv². 1. 136. NM 10870.   PL. 34

**11.** Fragment of a bronze lebes dedicated to Apollo Pythios, from the Asklepieion; *c.* 500–475? Kavvadias, op. cit. 9. *IG* iv. 1169; iv². 1. 142 and p. xiv. Lost?

**12.** Stepped base of a lost bronze statuette, from Ligurio (?); *c.* 500–475? *IG* iv. 1611 (= vii. 4249); iv². 1. 141. Roehl³, 109. 1. *DGE* 110. *SIG*³ 998, adn. Neugebauer, *Kat. Bronz. Berlin* i (1931), 180, pl. 28. Papademetriou, *BCH* lxxiii (1949), 370 f. Berlin Mus. 8096.   PL. 34

**13.** Altar (?) of Machaon, from the Asklepieion; *c.* 475–450? *IG* iv². 1. 152. *In situ*?

**14.** Bronze handle (?) found in or near Epidauros; *c.* 475–450? *IG* iv. 1342. Wilhelm, 10. *IG* iv². 1. 146. Louvre.   PL. 34

**15.** Pedestal-base for a statue dedicated by the sons of Philomelos, from the Asklepieion; *c.* 475–450? Kavvadias, op. cit. 249. *IG* iv. 1205; iv². 1. 143.

**16.** Dedication on a bronze plaque by Kallistratos, from the Asklepieion; *c.* 450? Kavvadias, op. cit. 12. *SGDI* 3324. *IG* iv. 1204. Roehl³, 109. 3. *DGE* 107. *IG* iv². 1. 144. NM 8166.   PL. 34

**17.** Stele granting asylum to the daughter of Kalliphanes, from the Asklepieion; *c.* 440–425? *IG* iv. 913. Wilhelm, 7. Roehl³, 109. 2. *IG* iv². 1. 46. EM?   PL. 34

**18.** List of offerings to be made to the deities in the precinct, from the Asklepieion; *c.* 425–400? *IG* iv. 914. Roehl³, 109. 4. *SIG*³ 998. *DGE* 108. *IG* iv². 1. 40–41. Buck 89. EM?

**19.** Fragment of a stele from the Asklepieion, known only from a copy in Kavvadias's notebook; *c.* 415–400? *IG* iv². 1. 145.

## LAKONIA

| α | β | γ | δ | ε | ϝ | з | η | ⱶ | θ | ι | κ | λ | μ | ν | ξ | ο | π | Ϻ | ϙ | ρ | σ | τ | υ | φ | χ | ψ | ω | Ρ | |
|---|---|---|---|---|---|---|---|---|---|---|---|---|---|---|---|---|---|---|---|---|---|---|---|---|---|---|---|---|---|
| 1 | A | B | Γ | D | Ɛ | Ϝ | I | – | Ⱶ | ⊗ | I | K | Λ | M | Ͷ | X | ο | Γ | M? | ϙ? | Ρ | ϟ | T | Ѵ | Φ | Ψ | Φϟ | – | ) | 1 |
| 2 | Ꝑ | | Γ | Ⅾ | ⅀ | Ϝ | | | H | ⊕ | | K | Λ | M | Ν | + | | Γ | | | Ρ | ϟ | | Ѵ | ⊙ | Ѵ | | | I | 2 |
| 3 | | | Δ | Ꝑ | Λ | | | | Ⱶ | ⊙ | | | | | Ν | Xϟ | | | | | | ϟ | | Υ | | Ψ | | | • | 3 |
| 4 | | | | Ɛ | | | | | | | | | | | Ν | | | | | | | | | | | | | | | 4 |
| 5 | | | | E | | | | | | | | | | | Ν | | | | | | | | | | | | | | | 5 |

FIG. 39. Lakonia and Taras: Messenia

*Notes on letter-forms, including those of Messenia and Taras*

α1 is normal. α2 appears in several inscriptions all apparently of the same period; *c.* 600–550 (p. 190).

δ3 occurs in **54** (before 431 ?), but is not normal before the 4th c.

ε2 appears in some 6th-c. inscriptions (pp. 189 f.), and the 'archaistic' ε3 in the late 6th and early 5th c. The standard form ε5 comes in gradually in the second quarter of the 5th c.; but **62**, a public document of the years 403–399, reverts to the earlier type 3. At Taras, ε1 or 3 is still in use *c.* 443–433 (Taras **10**).

ϝ2 is in use by the end of the 6th c. (**28**). By the third quarter of the 5th, the letter apparently survives only in archaic words, e.g. the epithet of Poseidon γαιάϝοχος in **52**, where the letter is tilted (ϝ3).

ⱶ1 is still used towards the end of the 5th c., when the Ionic value η of the letter was already known (**57**). ⱶ3, the S. Italian form probably from the Tarantine, is not yet attested before *c.* 400 (p. 29).

θ1–2 is still in use at the end of the century (**61**), though rare examples of θ3 are found very occasionally in informal inscriptions (e.g. on a vase-fragment, *BSA* xxx (1928–30), 241 f., fig. 1. 19; a stone ἁλτήρ, p. 191). Square or rhomboid shapes will be found sometimes on bronze inscriptions (e.g. **11**, **14**), obviously because the angled shapes were simpler to cut. At Taras, θ1 is still used *c.* 443–433 (**10**), but θ3 on coins *c.* 450–430, and on a fibula **12**, which may be of the mid-5th c.

Unlike most other scripts of the mainland, Lakonian shows, from the earliest examples onwards, a *mu* whose four strokes are approximately equal in length (μ1).

ν 1, 2, and 3 are used erratically throughout archaic Lakonian, the last in some of the earliest inscriptions (**5, 9, 10**), the former two even in the 5th c. (**48**). The form sometimes varies in the same inscription (e.g. **23, 30, 48, 50**).

ξ3 occurs once, in a graffito on the throne of Apollo at Amyklai (**32**); possibly the workman who wrote it was not Lakonian.

A very small circle is used for *omikron* in the early inscriptions **5** and **9**. On bronzes, for technical reasons, angled forms may occur, as in other places (cf. *theta*).

π2 occurs occasionally, with α2 and ε2 (p. 190).

*San*, though not used in any of these scripts, kept its place apparently in the abecedarium of Taras (**15**, p. 283).

*Qoppa* has not been attested so far in Lakonian, Tarantine, or Messenian except in the abecedarium used on the Vix krater **66**, and the Messapic (Tarantine) abecedarium of Vaste (Taras **15**).

ρ1 is normal (but cf. p. 188, n. 1), ρ2 appears occasionally in the 5th c. (*IG* v. 1. 700, 1107a, 1120, 1135).

There is no constant version of *sigma* in Lakonian (see pp. 186 f.). The characteristic type is long σ2, usually of five strokes, but on occasion even of eight (**10**). The earliest datable examples occur in the first half of the 6th c. (**6, 7, 8**); it apparently reached its zenith of fashion in the late 6th and early 5th c. σ1 also is found continually from the earliest inscriptions onwards, and occasionally σ3 (**23**). σ3 seems to have replaced 1 somewhere about the middle of the 5th c. (cf. **51, 52**). The long *sigma* has been attested in archaic Messapic script, though not yet in Tarantine; p. 279, n. 4. The coin-legends of Taras suggest that the change there from σι to σ3 occurred during the period *c.* 475–450 (p. 280). No example of long *sigma* has yet been found in Messenian, where the normal form seems to have been σι.

υι is common until at least the beginning of the 5th c. (**50**), although υ2 occurs in some informal inscriptions from about the middle of the 6th c. onwards (e.g. **16, 17, 35–36**). υ3 occurs occasionally in the late archaic period (**32, 64,** *IG* v. 1. 824) and in an inscription which is probably of the early 5th c. (**49**). From about the middle of the 5th c. onwards it becomes common, though 2 is still used in an epitaph *c.* 418 (**60**).

A stray *omega* occurs in an inscription dated in the third quarter of the 5th c. (**54**); but it does not appear regularly until after the period here discussed. It appears at Taras also on coins in the third quarter of the 5th c. (p. 282).

A letter-form like Sikyonian *epsilon* appears in *IG* v. 1. 828, an inscription cut *boustrophedon* between guide-lines in lettering which otherwise resembles Lakonian of the second half of the 6th c. The inscription itself appears meaningless in Greek; but if it is a modern forgery, it is a good one as far as the actual lettering goes.

*Punctuation.* The typical Lakonian form is 1, which seems to be a local development. The earliest examples known as yet may belong to the third quarter of the 6th c. (**19, 20**), and it is fairly frequent thereafter. 2 is used in one example (**43**); 3 is Tarantine (p. 279). Messenia shows one doubtful case of 1 (**2**). Guide-lines are often found in Lakonian inscriptions of the second half of the 6th and the early 5th c. (e.g. **12, 22, 23, 31, 43, 45**).

*Direction of the script.* Apart from those examples whose direction is governed by motives of symmetry, the earliest surviving inscriptions seem to begin indifferently from right to left or left to right. The *boustrophedon* system, both true and false, lasts through the 6th c.; indeed, the latest example apparently belongs to the first quarter of the 5th (**50**); but the method of consistent left-to-right was established well before this date. Its earliest usage is in the end of the 7th or the early 6th c., in a painted inscription on a plate (**2***a*); and at about the same time a dedication on a bronze handle is written vertically in two lines retrograde (**5**). The earliest formal stone inscription written consistently from left to right (vertically) is **24**, in the last quarter of the 6th c.; and (apart from **61**, where the retrograde direction is probably followed for reasons of symmetry) the latest inscriptions written consistently from right to left seem to be **45**, *c.* 500?, and *IG* v. 1. 700, which I take to be not earlier than the 5th c. from the use of ε5.

The scripts of the Argivo-Corinthian group may be traced with reasonable conviction to sources in the southern or south-eastern Aegean, for here the epigraphist is aided by certain distinctive letter-forms; but the source or sources whence came the 'red' script of the rest of the Peloponnese presents a harder problem. The alphabets of Lakonia, Messenia, Arkadia, Elis, and the cities of the eastern Argolid are sufficiently close to each other to suggest that one of them received it from the outside and passed it on to the rest; but the immediate source is not obvious. Similar 'red' scripts were used in Rhodes, in Phokis, Lokris (Ozolian), Thessaly, and in the western colonies settled by Rhodes and Lokris. Was there sufficiently close connexion between Doric Rhodes and Sparta in the Orientalizing period for the alphabet to have come by this route? There are some differences in detail (i.e. in *delta*, *heta*, *qoppa*); and, though the sixth-century pottery of Lakonia was exported in moderate quantity to Rhodes,[1] the evidence is still too scanty to bear much

---

[1] Lane, *BSA* xxxiv (1933–4), 179 f.

weight. Another possible candidate is Delphi.[1] The strips of hide, or whatever material bore the oracles which were preserved at Sparta from generation to generation by the four Pythioi, have all perished; but it may well have been during their recurrent visits to Delphi that these representatives from Sparta learnt the script of Phokis, and so Lakonia became literate. The resemblance between Phokian and Lakonian is certainly very close, only *gamma* and *sigma* differing. When once the alphabet had entered Lakonia, it would not be long before it had been passed thence to Olympia. I think that, on the present evidence, this is a more likely process than the reverse; for although the Olympic Games were apparently already attracting athletes from beyond the Peloponnese in the early seventh century, if we view Olympia as the pioneer of literacy, we fall into worse difficulties. Olympia's 'red' script does not come from Achaia, her nearest and most obvious source; nor had she any especial connexion with Delphi, apart from the help traditionally given by the Pythia to the 're-founding' of the Games in the eighth century. Hence it is not easy to see whence she could have received it, if not from Lakonia.

A large number of archaic inscriptions has been found throughout Lakonia, and all show the same alphabet, whether they have come from the near or far side of Parnon, from the parts bordering on Argos and Arkadia, or from parts as far south as Tainaron and the island of Kythera. As there seem to be no visible local differences, they are all discussed together here. Most of the material consists of dedications, especially from the two great Spartan sanctuaries of Artemis Orthia by the Eurotas and Athena Chalkioikos on the citadel, and from the heröon of Menelaos on the south side of the town. In addition there are inscribed offerings from the precincts of Apollo at Amyklai, Thornax, Tyros, Hyperteleaton, Prasiai, Gythion, and Geronthrai; of Artemis at Limnai, and Pleai near Gythion; of the Dioskouroi at Sellasia, Athena at Geronthrai, Poseidon at Tainaron and near Amyklai. There are also several Spartan dedications at Olympia, two at Delphi, and one (unpublished) from the Heraion in Samos.[2] These offerings consist mostly of bronze statuettes and implements, and various small objects; but one particular type of dedication, which occurs in the late sixth and the fifth centuries, is especially characteristic of Lakonia, reflecting vividly her pride in the prowess of her athletes. This is the stone stele dedicated by a victor, bearing a detailed list of all the contests which he won in Lakonia and elsewhere. Similar recitations occur occasionally at Argos (pp. 159, 162), but they pale beside such records as that of the anonymous runner who at the Hekatombaia (at Geronthrai?) won the *stadion*, the *diaulos*, the *dolichos*, the *pente dolichoi*, and the hoplite-race (*IG* v. 1. 1120): or that of the victories won by the stables of Damonon, and by Damonon himself and his son (**52**). There are also fragmentary lists of names, which I have conjectured may be those of local victors (p. 195). Further, there are plain stelai or roughly-worked stones, some bearing only a personal name (as *IG* v. 1. 699, 926; *AE* 1911, 193 f., fig. 1), some with the patronymic or the title ἱαρός added (as *IG*. v. 1. 1337, 1338, 1590); these may be gravestones. If Plutarch's tradition is right (*Lycurgus* 27), even this simple form of commemoration was only allowed to serving soldiers, and to priestesses (and priests?) who died in office. The latest example of this is the polyandrion of the Spartan soldiers buried in the Kerameikos at Athens in 403 (**61**). There is also the

---

[1] Carpenter, *AJA* xlix (1945), 455.

[2] Lane, op. cit. 179.

famous series of Lakonian relief-stelai, which began in the sixth century and lasted into the Hellenistic period. Several of the sixth-century examples bear inscriptions (**24, 25, 26, 29**). In a careful analysis of these stelai, Andronikos has argued[1] that they do not represent dead persons heroized, as the common interpretation holds, but show those chthonic powers who sometimes actually had precincts in or beside the cemeteries, and who must be propitiated by offerings from the families of the deceased. There is no doubt that these stelai were erected for the cult of chthonic powers, whether deities (as Kore (Persephone), **25**) or heroes (as the Dioskouroi, **24**). In the series which shows an enthroned pair receiving offerings, the chthonic aspect is shown above all by the snake which accompanies them (as in **26**); also, the odd shape of the stelai is worth comment. The masons of the time could make normally-shaped stelai when they wished (cf. **22, 23, 30, 31**); but for these it was evidently the custom that they should have irregular edges following roughly the outline of the scene depicted, and should all taper downwards—in fact, should retain as far as possible the look of a primitive stone marker. Andronikos denies that any of the figures represent dead men heroized; but there is no doubt that the Spartans sometimes followed this practice, for Pausanias noted sanctuaries to the ephor Chilon (iii. 16. 4), and to soldiers who fell in campaigns abroad (ibid. and iii. 12. 9; see p. 193); and I find it hard to accept the figure labelled [Χ]ιλōν (**26**), or the young spearman (**29**), as other than heroized men.

Only two Spartan pot-painters as yet have proved their literacy by vase-labels, the Arkesilas painter and the Hunt painter (pp. 189 f.); but others of them must have been literate to some extent, because nearly all the dedications on pottery are painted, not graffiti. The only certain examples of public notices of any kind so far (if we except the possible victor-lists, and the polyandrion in the Athenian Kerameikos) are the list of donations for the Peloponnesian war (**55**), the guarantee of asylia for Delos (**62**), and a prohibition against quarrying sacred rock (*IG* v. 1. 1155). No laws, sacred[2] or secular, have yet been found, although it may be inferred that some at least were written up in the early period, as, for example, the famous prose fragment, archaic both in dialect and expression, which was attributed to Lykourgos' constitution by Aristotle (Plutarch, *Lycurgus* 6), and which is perhaps a genuine fragment of ancient legislation, though disguised as a prose oracle.[3]

Although it might appear at first sight that the Lakonian alphabet is hardly distinguishable from the rest of the large and widely-scattered family of 'red' scripts, it has in fact certain peculiarities which, when present, make a Lakonian inscription both easy to identify and difficult to date. The best-known is the Lakonian *sigma*, a long zigzag whose strokes vary between five and eight. Its appearance is not confined to any one place in Lakonia, though most of the examples come from Sparta; and, though it seems to have been fashionable during most of the sixth century and well into the fifth, its use was never universal; in the archaic period, the three-stroked *sigma* was often employed (as in the other alphabets of this group), and occasionally the four-stroked, until the latter became

---

[1] *Peloponnesiaka* i (1956), 253 ff.

[2] Except for the brief notice incised on a rock, *IG* v. 1. 1316, in lettering of about the middle or third quarter of the 5th c. Cf. also Beattie, *CQ* 1951, 46 ff., for a reconstruction of the lost stone *IG* v. 1. 722 as an archaic sacred law.

[3] Cf. Wade-Gery, *CQ* 1943, 62 ff.; 1944, 1 ff. and 117 ff. I cannot agree with the 9th-c. date for this law suggested by Hammond, *JHS* lxx (1950), 64.

the normal form after the middle of the fifth century. It looks as if to the earliest Lakonian writers *sigma* was not a fixed letter-form, but merely a zigzag of three or more strokes, which could be extended as the writer chose—just as, in Ithake, the Achaian crooked *iota* was elongated to six strokes (p. 230). Lakonian is also distinctive in its *alpha*, whose cross-bar is always horizontal, and in its *mu*, whose outer strokes are equal, unlike the archaic form normally used elsewhere. *Gamma* is the Ionic type, in contrast with that of other 'red' alphabets (cf. also those of the eastern Argolid and the places round the Gulf of Nauplia). *Qoppa* has not yet appeared in any Lakonian inscription, though it is attested for Arkadia and Elis in the sixth century. The only other notable Lakonian characteristic is a punctuation mark like a bracket, ), often used in conjunction with guide-lines, of which the Lakonian writers made considerable use (**12, 22, 23, 29, 31, 41, 42, 43, 45**). Lastly, attention may be drawn to the neatness and competence shown in many inscriptions of the late sixth and early fifth centuries. Perhaps they are indeed closely related, for the trade of stone-mason and letterer may have been confined to one particular family as an hereditary profession, as Herodotos observed was the custom with certain trades in Sparta (vi. 60).

Lakonian inscriptions are thus particularly difficult to date by their letter-forms alone, presenting as they do a deceptive mixture of forms normally considered as advanced (as the *alpha* and *mu*) with others which, normally hall-marks of the archaic period (as long-tailed *epsilon* and *upsilon*, or closed *heta*), are still in use in the fifth century for formal inscriptions. The development of Lakonian pottery has now been established on a firm basis,[1] which gives valuable evidence for the informal style of script about the middle of the sixth century; but the chronology of the relief-stelai is still insecure, except for one fragment, securely dated in the last decade of the sixth century from its obvious kinship to Attic work of the Leagros period (**29**). Had we among the surviving Spartan dedications any which could be connected with the campaigns of Thyrea *c*. 546 or of Plataia in 479 (for the Snake Column at Delphi is in Phokian script), the whole series of Lakonian inscriptions would then fall into place. As it is, we begin with the dedications from the sanctuary of Orthia, for they include what is probably the earliest surviving Lakonian inscription (**1**).

At some time during the archaic period, presumably after the Eurotas had risen unusually high and swamped the low-lying precinct of Orthia, a layer of river-sand was laid down over the remains of the early sanctuary, and a new temple was built above it. The date of the layer was established by the stylistic development visible between the pottery which lay below it (Lakonian I and II) and that which lay above (Lakonian III and later). The start of Lakonian III was brought down by Lane from that first proposed (*c*. 600) to 'well into the Middle Corinthian period', i.e. *c*. 590–585,[2] on the evidence afforded by tomb-groups elsewhere, and by Payne's revised dating for Corinthian ware. Since, as Lane further pointed out, several lakainai of early Lakonian III style had in fact been found *under* the sand-layer, this gave the latter a *terminus post quem* of *c*. 585, or even some five years later.[3]

---

[1] Lane, op. cit. 99 ff.; Shefton, *BSA* xlix (1954), 306 ff.

[2] Op. cit. 135.

[3] Cf. further Searls and Dinsmoor, *AJA* xlix (1945), 72.

The inscribed material found under the layer consisted, first, of the well-known ivory plaque showing the departure of a ship and her crew (**1**), with the name Ϝορθαια scratched retrograde on the ship's bow. The style of the clumsily carved picture seems to belong to the late seventh century, a date with which the straggling height of the letters agrees well.[1] In addition to this, two plates (**2a–b**), some fragments of bone flutes (**3**), and some carved limestone plaques (**6**), all inscribed, were found in two deposits immediately below the sand at a point north-east of the later temple, close to two blocks which apparently formed part of another building, at a higher level than that of the early temple and its altar. The excavators noted that the material from these deposits, though presumably earlier than that found above the sand, was, from its appearance, later in date than the rest of that found below.[2] The date for the plates ranges from Lakonian I to III.[3] The dedications, inscribed in white paint before the firing and so, presumably, the work of the pot-painter, are so developed in appearance that Kolbe hesitated to class them in the sixth century at all;[4] and, even if allowance is made for the characteristics of Lakonian lettering, and for the skilled brush of the painter, a *terminus ante quem* of 580 may well seem startling to epigraphists, especially if the script is compared with that of the Arkesilas painter (**8**; *c.* 570–560). Nevertheless, unless we are prepared to disregard the excavators' clear statement that these deposits were sealed by the sand-layer,[5] these inscriptions must be accepted as belonging at latest to the early years of the sixth century. They show us that at this date Lakonian informal lettering could be small and squarely proportioned, with ε4 and ν3 (**2a**); and that, though doubtless the *boustrophedon* system was universal on monumental stone inscriptions at this time, the left-to-right style was already practised, at least on occasion, by less formal writers. Two other inscriptions give additional support to this picture. One is a fragmentary dedication painted on a sherd from the neck of an oinochoe, from the precinct of Athena Chalkioikos on the Akropolis of Sparta (**4**); its style has been classed by the excavators as intermediate between Lakonian II and III, in the earliest years of the sixth century. The other is a dedication to Apollo by one Dorkonida(s) or Dorkoilida(s), incised on a hollow bronze handle, found in an unstratified layer of ash in the Amyklaion (**5**). The handle ends in a lion's head of archaic type, described as seventh-century by the excavators.[6] This is the earliest inscription which gives an occasion for the use of *qoppa*, a letter of which, as was said above, there is as yet no trace in Lakonian. *Omikron* is very small, and *epsilon* has a short tail, as in **2b**; otherwise, the general appearance of these inscriptions, especially the tailless *nu*, accords

[1] On the faults in the lettering, cf. *AO*, 370: *phi* for *theta* (as on the Aristonothos krater, p. 239), *omikron* incomplete, scratches over *iota* and *rho*; for even in Lakonian of the 5th c. tailed *rho* is so uncommon, that I assume it to be a casual scratch here. Perhaps the writer meant to show that the ship itself was called Orthia as well; cf. 'Ορθεία, a ship of the Athenian fleet in the 4th c. (*IG* ii². 1623. 76).     [2] *BSA* xiv. 22 ff.

[3] They are plain, with a ribbed edge, which in the case of **2b** is painted white. Droop classed them as Lak. II, though noting that the paint resembles that of a lakaina now assigned to early Lak. III (*AO*, 76: cf. also

p. 187, nn. 1–2). Lane described **2a** in his Lak. I series (op. cit. 117), but admitted that the style might continue into the Lak. III period.

[4] *IG* v. 1. 1587: 'VI saec. tribuebat editor, quem sequi dubito.'

[5] It has also to be inferred that the layer as a whole was laid down at the same time; but this, as far as I know, has never been disputed.

[6] An earlier version of this type appears on the handle of an oinochoe from Perachora, dated tentatively between *c.* 650 and 550, 'perhaps seventh century': *Perachora* i. 140 and pl. 144. 10.

with those on the plates. The brief graffiti on the bone flute or flutes from the same deposit (**3**) are more carelessly written;[1] we may note, however, the tilted *epsilon*, which occurs also on both the plates, **2a–b**, in the fragment **4** and on some of the formal inscriptions which have early features (**11, 15**). In Ionia (p. 325) and at Kyme in Italy (p. 238) the tilted *epsilon* is a distinct feature of the early alphabet, and it may be true of Lakonia also; but here examples are fewer.

It is recorded that this deposit also contained some of the many little carved limestone plaques and figures which were apparently a cheap and popular form of dedication here for a considerable time. Unfortunately, it is nowhere evident in the publication of the site which of the inscribed plaques (which are all described together) were those belonging to this particular deposit. Most of the plaques were found scattered through the sand-layer, or above it, or rebuilt into the Roman theatre at the point where its foundations disturbed the sand-layer. The general conclusions stated in *AO* 187 ff. are that they are all close in date, perhaps made from chips of the stone brought to build the later temple (which, if so, would mean that those found under the sand-layer are out of place); and, as far as can be judged from their clumsy style, any date in the first half of the sixth century is possible. In their lettering, we may note the absence of *qoppa*: σι–3: υι–2: and *nu ephelkustikon*, of which an earlier example occurred on the oinochoe-fragment **4**.

Human figures very rarely make an appearance on Lakonian vases before the period of Lakonian III; then, with the increasing popularity of this motif, appears also the practice of labelling the figures—an idea perhaps copied, like the notion of figure-drawing, from contemporary Corinthian art.[2] Two literate painters have been so far identified. The earlier produced the famous kylix whose tondo shows King Arkesilas of Kyrene watching the weighing and storing of silphion (**8**). If this is Arkesilas II (died in 568?), the vase may be dated *c.* 570–560; the date and the names and speeches of the figures have been fully discussed by Lane and others,[3] and it need only be noted here that this is the first example of the long Lakonian *sigma* which can be closely dated. Its use on two of the limestone plaques dedicated to Orthia offered no closer date than the first half of the century. Apart from this its earliest appearance seems to be in the name Τελεσστας, cut carefully round the rim of a fragmentary bronze hydria (**7**), now in Mainz. The vertical handle rises from the head of a kore in high relief, dated by its style in the early years of the sixth century. The fragments were said to come from Lebadea in Boiotia, but hydriai of this particular type have been found on many different Greek sites, and the expert view holds that they were manufactured in Lakonia. The latest publication of this vase seeks to establish that the name is not the possessor's, but is the maker's signature, the maker being that Lakonian bronze-sculptor Telestas who, with his brother Ariston, made a bronze Zeus eighteen feet high for the people of Kleitor in Arkadia to dedicate to Zeus at Olympia (Paus. v. 23. 7; see further p. 210).[4] But it may be doubted if that Telestas

---

[1] The name, read usually as Αχραδατος (*BSA* xxiv. 115; *AO*, 370) with an unexpected 'blue' *chi*, should, I suspect, be rather Αυταρετος; the nearest parallel would be Ἀμφάρετος.          [2] Cf. Lane, op. cit. 129 f.

[3] Cf. Lane, op. cit. 162; Beazley, *Hesperia* xii (1943), 88; Mazzarino, *Fra Oriente e Occidente* (1947), 150 ff.,

315 ff.; Chamoux, *Cyrène* (1953), 258 ff.; Shefton, op. cit. 309, n. 9.

[4] Hafner, *Charites* (1957), 119 ff. Neugebauer (*AA* 1938, 330 ff.) also thought that it might be the maker's name. Richter (*AJA* xliii (1939), 200 f.) suggested a date *c.* 500 B.C. for Ariston and Telestas.

would sign a single small bronze hydria,[1] or, if he did, would omit the significant verb. It is safer to infer only that this is the owner's name, cut by the bronze-worker either to safeguard his property, or because he was going to dedicate it; for another possible example of a dedicator's name without ἀνέθηκε, see **27**, the stele of Anaxibios (p. 193).

The Arkesilas painter (**8**) also used the long-tailed υι and χι, whereas his pupil the Hunt painter employed the later υ2 and χ2 on his hydria from Ialysos (**16a**).[2] The hydria has been dated *c.* 560, though the work of the Hunt painter extended well into the second half of the century.

Before proceeding from the neat script of the Hunt painter to the fine work of Lakonian stone-cutters in the second half of the sixth century, we may consider a group of inscriptions which are all on objects not in themselves datable, and which appear to have a certain similarity in the treatment of some of the letter-forms, which inclines me to date them fairly close together, and to set the group, as a whole, somewhere *c.* 575–550, not because I can offer any convincing resemblances to the minor inscriptions which we have so far considered, but because they have even less in common with such inscriptions as are held on reasonably likely grounds to be later than the middle of the century. The common features are a large, sprawling script and, in particular, a marked tilt in the formation of certain letters (α2, ε2, π2). The first example is on a piece of bronze from the ash-deposit in the Amyklaion, interpreted as part of a helmet (**9**): [(ὁ δεῖνα) ανεθεκε τōι Α]μυκλαιō[ι].[3] *Omikron* is very small, as on **5** from the same sanctuary, and the tilt of *alpha* is marked.

Both α2 and π2 occur on the lip of a bronze lebes dedicated by the Spartans at Olympia (**10**), and on a similar fragment (**11**) bearing a dedication by —das son of Dexippos at Delphi—perhaps one of the Pythioi? This latter also shows the tilted *epsilon* once.[4] The others are tiny fragments from a bronze plaque inscribed *boustrophedon* between guide-lines at Olympia (**12**), with α2, π1: a block from a dedication to Artemis(?) found near the Menelaion (**13**), with α2: a small bronze disk (**14**) from Hagios Elias, which is probably the site of the sanctuary of Apollo Pythaios (or Pythaieus) at Thornax,[5] with π2: and lastly, the marble seat found at Olympia (**15**), inscribed in the Lakonian alphabet: Γοργος Λακεδαιμονιος προξενος Fαλειōν, where the tilt in the *alpha* is slight, in the *epsilon* more noticeable. In all these inscriptions *sigma* varies between 1 and 2, and *nu* is never the same twice—even in the same inscription; which is a further disconcerting feature for those seeking to date the early Lakonian alphabet.

[1] Hafner (op. cit. 125 f.) cites for comparison the tripods made by the famous sculptor Gitiadas (Paus. iii. 18. 7; iv. 14. 2); but these were large works, with sculptured supporters.

[2] The painter has incised the rider's name Συνις upon his horse's black back, among the painted labels; in the same way, the word θακος is incised on a black seat on the François vase. In spite of the arguments in *Clara Rhodos* (**16**, bibliography), for reading Σινυς, I have no doubt that Συνις is correct, since names on vases normally read outwards away from the figures.

[3] It is not mentioned by Kukahn, *Der griech. Helm* (1939). A smaller, shapeless fragment has [- - - Αμυκ]λαιōι

and a third (not illustrated, but apparently later) [---τōι Α]μυκλαιōι ανεθεκε: *AM* lii (1927), 64.

[4] Lerat, publishing this fragment, was uncertain whether to class it as Lakonian or Delphic: but there can be no doubt that it is Lakonian. Closed *heta* is written with four horizontal bars; Lerat cites for analogy that of the Marsiliana alphabet (p. 237, Kyme **18**), and it occurs also on a lebes from Thebes (Boiotia **2**) and a small jug from Euboia (Boiotia **22**). It is not attested again in Lakonian, and may be an error here.

[5] Another lebes at Delphi (**65**) shows apparently Lakonian script of this type (from Aigaiai in Lakonia?): Αιγ[α]ιευς Θαυμις ανεθεκε Fεκαβολōι Απελōνι.

To the third quarter of the sixth century should belong the bronze statuette dedicated by Chimarides to Artemis Daidale (**67**), which, though found at Mazi in northern Triphylia, has been identified as Lakonian on grounds of style;[1] a conclusion confirmed by the neat lettering, which has all the characteristics of Lakonian rather than Elean or Arkadian. To the same period I should assign tentatively the phiale **18**, and a strip of bronze of unknown provenance (possibly Olympia), which evidently formed a label nailed up beside a trophy of arms (**19**): [Δι Κρονιδαι ανεθε̄]κε ) Ευρυστρατιδας ) ταδε τα ⊦οπλα ) τ[ο Λα|κεδ]αιμονιο ) τυ δε τō‌ι χαριν αιες ⊦[υπαρχοις]. For the first time we see the typical Lakonian punctuation-sign ı and may notice further ε3 with exaggerated tail which, though used in the early period (**7**), seems to become particularly fashionable in the late archaic period—again, in defiance of the normal rules of development elsewhere. If the saying of King Kleomenes related in Plutarch is true (*Apophth. Lac.* 18), that the Spartans did not follow the general custom of dedicating the armour of their beaten enemies, we should have to conclude that these ὅπλα belonged to Eurystratides himself, and are not necessarily to be connected with an actual battle, since he may have dedicated them for a variety of reasons—e.g. on ceasing to be of military age, or even (if the bronze can be dated after 520 and assigned to Olympia) on winning the hoplite-race. Another military offering to Olympian Zeus is **64**, a fragmentary helmet; the inscription Διος Ολυνπιο has the look of typical Lakonian, with zigzag *sigma*, and I have no hesitation in assigning a Lakonian origin to this dedication.

The punctuation ı occurs again on a ἁλτήρ from Olympia (**20**), dedicated by one Akmatides for a victory in the pentathlon.[2] Three other Spartan halteres may be mentioned here for the sake of completeness: a fragment of one in white marble from the precinct of Chalkioikos at Sparta (**21**), bearing the owner's name Kleocha(res) in letters of about this date, and hitherto described as 'a ram's horn'; another fragment of greenish stone from Olympia (**63**), again with the owner's name Κοιρις;[3] and one from the precinct of Chalkioikos (possibly of the early fifth century, for it shows the dotted *theta*), dedicated to Athena by Paitiades (*BSA* xxvii (1925–6), 251 ff.).

The great Greek bronze krater found in 1953 at Vix in France (**66**) gives valuable evidence for the dating of Lakonian script. The krater itself is dated on its style somewhere in the late years of the period 550–525, and Rumpf has argued persuasively, on his analysis of the features of the vase as well as its lettering, that in the volute-krater, of

[1] Ernst Meyer suggests, however, that she may be a local dedication from the predecessor of the 4th c. temple at Mazi (*Neue peloponnesische Wanderungen*, 46). She is dated *c.* 540–510 by Lamb, *G. and R. Bronzes*, 90, n. 5: 'not earlier than the middle of the sixth century' by Neugebauer, *Ant. Bronz.* 44. Her appearance suggests a Lakonian contemporary of the Peplos Kore (no. 679) from the Athenian Akropolis (Payne and Young, *Archaic Marble Sculpture*, pls. 29–33; *c.* 540–530). Her way of wearing the peplos, with the fullness of the skirt all brought round to the back in pleats, seems to have been fashionable in the Peloponnese at about this time, for it is found on various small bronzes both earlier and later in style:

cf. *BSA* xxviii (1926–7), 100, pls. 11–12 and 101, pl. 12; *BCH* xlv (1921), pl. 13 (Tegea): part of a cult statue of Artemis from Lousoi (*Ö.Jh.* iv (1901), 35, fig. 23); a small bronze from Lousoi (ibid., figs. 20–22); and the kore who forms the knob on the strainer of the Vix krater, **66**.

[2] The curious form ἀσσκονικτεί (for the usual ἀκονιτεί) may be an error of metathesis for ἀκονιστεί; the latter is not attested, but the stem κονισ- as well as κονι- is used in kindred words: cf. LSJ, s.v. κόνισμα *or* κόνιμα = a wrestling-arena.

[3] The fragment is read as Κϙδιας or Κοιριας in *Ol.* v. 720, and not recognized there as Lakonian: but the six-stroked *sigma* and lack of *qoppa* make the attribution certain.

which Vix has now produced so superb an example, we should recognize the κρατὴρ Λακωνικός mentioned by ancient writers.[1] The frieze of chariots and hoplites which runs round the neck of the vase was cast separately, and letters of the alphabet were cut on the backs of the figures and in the corresponding places on the neck, to help the assembler to set each figure in its proper place. The letters used are: αβγδεϝϝ3ϝθικ—ϙοτξ ('red') χ ('red'). They are undoubtedly Lakonian; for example, one *sigma* is four-stroked, the other five-stroked; *alpha, gamma, delta* are good Lakonian. The presence of *qoppa* in an abecedarium is to be expected, though no Lakonian inscription shows it actually in use; for abecedaria habitually preserved 'fossilized' forms (pp. 25, 236).

To the late third or early fourth quarter of the sixth century may be ascribed the first of the extant series of stelai recording victories at games—all of them good works by skilled masons, reflecting equally the merits of Sparta's athletes and stone-workers during the late archaic and early classical periods. The earliest appears to be the stele found near the temple of Apollo Karneios, bearing the dedication of Aigletes, who won the *makros dolichos* five times, the *dolichos* thrice, and probably other races as well (**22**).[2] The disposition of the lines here is typical of Lakonian; they do not continue to the edge of the stone, but the tops of the guide-lines join in a curve, forming a continuous belt along which the letters run (cf. **31**). Here, because the inscription is to be read horizontally, the true *boustrophedon* is used; had it been cut vertically it would probably have been in the false. A cutting-compass was used for the circles, leaving a central dot; *sigma* is 1 or 3; and the slope of *nu* alters perpetually. The same mason may have cut the so-called 'Hymn to Athena' found on the Akropolis, presumably from the sanctuary of Athena Chalkioikos (**23**). Here the three extant sides of the stele are all inscribed, the wider horizontally, the narrower vertically, all *boustrophedon*; and here again is the cutting-compass, the variant *sigma* and *nu*, the guide-lines (not continuous). The narrow side bears part of an apostrophe to Athena; the wider sides have so far defied restoration, for not one complete word seems to have survived; but from the fragments I should hazard the guess that it is not a hymn, but another victor's dedication, in which the actual dedicatory couplet is written on the narrow side, while the wider sides bear the details of his successes. To the same date (early in the last quarter of the sixth century?), may be ascribed two of the relief-stelai discussed above, pp. 185 f.: that dedicated by Pleistiades to the Dioskouroi, found near Sellasia (**24**), inscribed from left to right vertically,[3] and that in Brussels (**25**), which shows three korai, wearing the peplos pleated behind in the same style as **67**, the bronze Artemis Daidale, and with their hair curiously dressed.[4] The inscription κορας σōτιας is usually translated as the dedication of one Sotias to the 'korai',

---

[1] *Charites* (1957), 127 ff. See Addenda.

[2] The last letter in l. 6 seems to give a better reading if taken as ϝ instead of ϝ (as in *IG* v. 1. 222). The top of the stele is said to have two shallow holes, presumably to support the ἄγαλμα (*BSA* xv. 81). It might also have had some crowning member, like that of the stele **30**, the whole monument then being the ἄγαλμα.

[3] Langlotz dated this stele *c.* 560, citing the figures on the François Vase: *FGB*, 86, 91; Wace has pointed out that this date is too early (*AE* 1937, 219). If a

comparison with vases is needed, we may cite the long-legged flute-player on a kylix of Lak. IV style (*c.* 525?), Lane, op. cit., pl. 46a.

[4] i.e. combed to the top of the head and tied there, falling thence in a horse's tail behind (a fashion still adopted in modern days, particularly in hot weather). A somewhat similar, though more elaborate, effect is seen in a relief from the parapet of the archaic temple at Ephesos (late 6th c.): *BMC Sculpt.* i, B 215.

meaning Eumenides or else nymphs; but, if σωτία can be regarded as a Lakonian hypo-coristic form for the normal σώτειρα, it should perhaps be taken rather as being in the genitive, which would enable us to assign the stele to the precinct of Kore Soteira, seen by Pausanias near the Spartan agora (iii. 13. 2). The three figures would then be dedicators, holding offerings. To this group of stelai should belong also the fragmentary relief from the heröon of the ephor Chilon (26), which has been assigned on historical and stylistic grounds to *c.* 525;[1] and for the last decade of the century we have another relief, almost certainly from a heröon, which is one of the very few Lakonian inscriptions that can be securely dated from external evidence. This is the famous relief from Magoula, now in Berlin (29), which bears the upper part of a young man in the style of the Leagros period (*c.* 510–500). The large snake depicted opposite him indicates that this is some heroized person; the inscription might be restored: Κορōι Θιοκλενα μ' [ανεθēκε]. We may compare the heröon made for some part of the contingent who went in Dorieus' ill-fated expedition to Sicily, and the precinct of the brothers Maron and Alpheios, who won ἀριστεῖα at Thermopylai (Paus. iii. 12. 9 and 16. 4).[2]

A stele found in the temenos of Athena Chalkioikos (27), bearing the name Ϝαναξιβιος and a relief of a kore holding a lotus-flower, is also to be dated in the last quarter of the century, perhaps as late as the Magoula relief 29; though little can be seen of the detail, the profile of the left leg, as though the skirt were pulled taut, shows a marked advance in style on the relief 25, 27, being found in a precinct of Athena and depicting a kore, can hardly be other than a dedication, in spite of the absence of the verb. I should also set in the last years of the sixth century the stele dedicated to Athena Chalkioikos which bears a lotus-bud in relief on its capital; the inscription reads *stoichedon* (30): Ετεοι[τας] | ανεθε[κε τ']|Αθανα[ιαι]. The significant letter here is ε3, with its long tail but strictly horizontal bars, which may perhaps be interpreted as the last phase of the archaic *epsilon*, the 'tidying-up', as it were, before the tail was finally abandoned. It occurs again on what is evidently the shaft of a similar stele (28), with a cutting on top for the dowel of a separate capital, now lost.[3] Here the inscription runs vertically between guide-lines in a mixture of true and false *boustrophedon*: [- - - νι]κασας ) τ[α] | πεντε [- - - | - - - δ]υō ) τον | δολιχ[ον - - -]: ε3 is even more exaggerated here, and *nu* is 1 throughout, whereas it varies on 30 between 1 and 2. 28 may therefore be rather earlier than 30. A third stele of like proportions (31), but with no cutting for a capital, is inscribed in false *boustrophedon* along a continuous belt of guide-lines, as in 22 above. It has one archaic letter, ϝ1; the one visible *nu* is 3, but what a second would have been like is quite conjectural. Its exact provenance is not recorded, but I do not think that it can be a grave-epigram, as is usually held, for that would be inconsistent with the other evidence for Lakonian memorials, which (apart from sculptured reliefs for the heroized dead) bear only the dead man's name (see p. 185 above). It is more likely to be yet another victory-inscription,[4]

---

[1] Wace, op. cit. 217 ff.

[2] The text of iii. 16. 4 is corrupt: Ἀθηναίων ρω. Wade-Gery has suggested Ἀθηναίων ρ, i.e. 100 Athenians; see Dunbabin, 352.

[3] The editors in *BSA* xxvii. 249 wrongly restore the stone as a horizontal base with a hole in the left side.

[4] For completeness' sake I add here a fragment from another victory inscription, probably a stele, which was found in the Amyklaion (von Massow, *AM* lii (1927), 61, fig. in text; *SEG* xi. 693). Very little is left, but we can restore (between guide-lines) [---]τον τρις τα [πεντε ? --- ϝ]αμα Αθα[ναιοις ---]) ταν [ϝοπλιταν ? ---].

dedicated perhaps to Athena Chalkioikos; the following conjectural restoration would occupy a length of shaft about equivalent to the extant piece: Γλαυκατ[ιας νι|κας το] μναμα | καλας α[νεθēκ|ε Πραξ]οιδα Ϝυι|υς ) παι[δι Διος μ|εγαλο] *vacat*.

As evidence for cursive writing (graffiti) in the last years of the sixth century, there are several masons' names incised on architectural fragments from the Throne of Apollo at Amyklai, which was made by the craftsman Bathykles and is now dated to the end of the century (32).[1] There are also great numbers of brief inscriptions incised on small bronzes (mostly animals) from the many sanctuaries of Lakonia, which I am unable to date more closely than 'second half of the sixth century': as examples may be cited a bull and a fish from a Poseideion somewhere near Amyklai (33–34), a goat from the Apollonion at Hyperteleaton (35), a bronze handle from a precinct of Apollo Pythaieus, probably that at Thornax (36),[2] a warrior and a ram from that of Apollo Maleatas at Prasiai (37–38), several small phialai[3] to Artemis Limnatis, found near Mistra (39), and various minor bronzes from the Apollonion at Tyros (40).[4] The late archaic υ2, which was already used by the Hunt painter (p. 190), occurs on several of these graffiti dedications, of which one at least can hardly be later than the third quarter of the century (17). Its first appearances on stone are in the fragments 41 and 42, both of which I should not put earlier than the last quarter of the century.[5] About the turn of the century—perhaps in the first years of the fifth—may be placed a fragment from the round pedestal of a perirrhanterion, or perhaps the pedestal-base for a statue, from Hyperteleaton (43). It has been restored as a dedication by the wife of Arkesilas IV of Kyrene: [Αρκεσιλα μ' αν]εθēκε | δαμαρ [βασι-λισσα] Κυρανας [Απολλōνι Ϝανακτι]· Κυραναιος | δε μ' επο[ιει]. The order of the words in the first line is uncertain, cut as they are in a circle and partly mutilated. I should suggest instead: Δαμαρ[ετος, or the like, με αν]εθēκε |, the punctuation | separating the start from the finish; κυρανας should, I believe, be removed altogether from the text, for Hondius's drawing and comment suggest that it is in fact modern, scratched in above the κυραναιος of l. 3. He wrote: 'the letters are so faintly cut that the lines hardly show. The fine cutting contrasts oddly with the bold strokes of line 1. The line has apparently only one word, κυρανας. The stone is undamaged, and therefore various undecipherable lines which appear on the squeeze are probably not letters'.[6] He saw the stone in the yard of a private house in Phoinike, 'in imminent danger of destruction'; as far as I know, it has

---

[1] Lane, op. cit. 157.

[2] The inscription on this handle was ascribed to the 5th c. by Kolbe, *IG* v. 1. 928; Neugebauer, apparently accepting this, called the ornament on the handle an example of the provincial retention of more archaic forms (*RM* xxxviii–ix (1923–4), 369); but the carelessly-cut inscription might well be dated at the end of the 6th c.

[3] These small bronze objects are usually termed 'cymbals' in the epigraphical publications, but phialai of one type or another are a favourite dedication to goddesses.

[4] I would set *c.* 510–500 the graffito on a small mug from Kythera (*IG* v. 1. 945). 'In Attica this shape (VIII A) lasts from c. 510–c. 450' (J. D. Beazley).

[5] Both have ε3 (cf. p. 193), guide-lines, and punctuation. The texts of both are very fragmentary; 41, inscribed from left to right, consists chiefly of numbers: (a) [---] Ϝιαρα Ϝεξ [---]ν τοι[---], (b) [---] δυο [---Ϝε]π-τ[α? ---]. 42 has even less to identify it: [---]μεσο αι[---]ν τον) δαμ[οσια?---]ον τουτο γ[---|---] προ-τερον[---]. They might be more victory-dedications, but this is far from certain.

Roberts (i. 262) and Walters (*Hist. Anc. Pottery* i. 135) call it 5th c. Cf. Young, *Hesperia* viii (1939), 280, n. 38.

[6] *BSA* xxiv (1919–21), 137. Chamoux (*Cyrène*, 201) doubts the attribution to a queen of Kyrene, the text being so mutilated: 'on attendrait d'ailleurs dans une dédicace de ce genre le nom de la reine à côté de son titre.'

not been seen since. After the dedication, Κυραναιος δε μ' επο[ιϝε] follows as part of the sculptor's signature ending a hexameter.

We may note also here two lists of names from Geronthrai, one faintly cut (**45**), the other much more clearly (**46**). The second list is particularly interesting, for the unusual name Αϝαναξ occurs twice, with three other names between. If this is the same man, the list will hardly be either a funeral inscription or a list of any officials, since it was not customary in Greek states to hold office twice, at least within a short period. We may therefore suggest that this and perhaps **45** also are lists of victors at the local games, and, in this connexion, note also a fragment of a similar but earlier list, found on the Akropolis at Sparta (**44**); here the names are listed in pairs,[1] and the last pair are clearly written by a different hand from the rest. There is also one other very small fragment of a list in the Museum at Sparta (**47**), containing only the endings of three names: -ευς | -οφας | -σ[ος]. If they are indeed victors' lists—which is, I think, at least as likely an identification as any other, especially in view of the elaborately recorded victors' dedications described above—it may perhaps have been from such stelai as these that Hellanikos (or his informants) drew part at least of the data for his *Karneonikai* (pp. 59 f.).

The first datable inscription to show the later ε5 appears to be a fragment of a sculptured stele from Amyklai (**51**), bearing a frontal relief of a discus thrower in action. Von Massow dated it *c.* 475 by the style, and suggested that this is the stele bearing a likeness of Ainetos, a pentathlete who died while being crowned at Olympia, which Pausanias saw (iii. 18. 7) in the Amyklaion.[2] The very fragmentary inscription suggests a typical victory-list: [- - - νικαϝ]ας δεκα ) κα⟨ι⟩ ϝενατον | [- - -]. Although *epsilon* is clearly 5 in the photograph, *nu* is still 1 and *sigma*, from its traces, 2. The inscription which seems to me to be the link between this stele and the preceding group (which showed the 'archaistic' ε3) is **48**, part of a long inscription on a block of white marble from Magoula, which reads like a verse-dedication to Athena by yet another athlete: [- - -χαι?]ροσα ορεν δ' [- - - | - - -]τ' αυτος νικασ[ας - - - | - - - τα]χυτατος εδ[ραμε? - - - | - - -]ε χαριζομεν[ος - - - | - - -] ενθαδε παις π[ρατος? - - - | - - - τ]οι και {ε}ευφρον[εοσα? - - - | - - - παι Δ]ιος αιγιοχο. It shows ε5 once, ε3 otherwise, the later υ3, and νι–2; according to the present hypothesis, we may (provisionally) set it early in the first quarter of the fifth century.

The offering of the Lakedaimonians to Zeus at Olympia (**49**) and the fragment **50** have both been assigned to the decade *c.* 460–450, the first as a dedication made during the great Helot Revolt, the second as the memorial of a man of Crete,[3] killed in the battle of Tanagra. Although the latter inscription shows the developed ε5 throughout, the use of *boustrophedon* after 458–457, even in conservative Sparta, seems a little dubious. In fact,

---

[1] The alternative interpretation is that each pair consists of name and patronymic (cf. *BSA* xxvii. 253 f.); but then in the last pair (Δαμοξενιδα[- - -] | Αλκιπος) we should have to conclude that the patronymic was put first, which is not usual in such lists. Although the untidy writing makes dating uncertain, the early forms of *epsilon, phi, upsilon* suggest that it may be as early as the third quarter of the 6th c.

[2] v. Massow, *AM* li (1926), 42. *Ox. Pap.* 222 gives other names for the winners of the pentathlon at Olympia for the years 476, 472, and 468, so that, if this stele does represent Ainetos, he must have won his victory in 480 or earlier.

[3] Guarducci has shown that the adjective Ἐρταῖος which occurs in two epigrams from Crete (Knossos and Gortyn, second to first century B.C.) has no reference to an actual place, but is a poetical term for 'Cretan' (*Historia* vi (1932), 593 ff.).

the only reason for dating **50** after 458–457 lies in the reading [Ταν]αγραι for the last line, which other scholars read as —αιραι; nor is there any valid reason for bringing in a Cretan, since the lines in question, instead of [- - -]ρθαι· | Ερται[ος] would surely be as easily read: [- - -]ọθ' αι[π]|ερ ται[- - -]. The inscription may then be no later than the first quarter of the fifth century.[1]

As for the offering at Olympia (**49**), Pausanias described it (v. 24. 3) as a 12-foot-high bronze Zeus made at the time of the second Messenian revolt, i.e. *c.* 464–460. But the sloping ε4 and tailed υ1 seem rather archaic types for this date (the other letters give no help). Moreover, the base itself is a hollow cylinder, as though made for some tall cylindrical core to be thrust down it, and this suggests a bronze pillar-statue of the archaic style favoured by the Spartans, like the Apollo at Amyklai, the Apollo Karneios, and the Athena Chalkioikos. But such a primitive work *c.* 464–460 seems rather unlikely, even for the conservative Spartans. Yet the lettering cannot belong to the time of the seventh-century revolt; the period *c.* 500–490 may therefore be suggested, when other evidence indicates that the Spartans had trouble with their subjects.[2]

The famous stele of Damonon (**52**) is usually dated in the third quarter of the fifth century, partly by the style of the battered relief at the top. This is the crowning example of the type of victory-list of which we have already reviewed so many incomplete examples. Beneath a relief showing a four-horse chariot racing, Damonon records firstly a total of thirty-five racing victories won over an unknown period of years at the Games in seven local sanctuaries: secondly, the victories of his son when a boy at the *stadion* and *diaulos* in three local Games: thirdly, his own similar victories as a boy in six such Games. Then, having given no indication of date in these accounts, other than παῖς ἰών or πρᾶτος παίδων, he abruptly starts a new arrangement, giving the names of three (or four?) ephors—Echemenes, Euippos, Aristeus, Echemenes—during whose years of office he won various horse races, and his son (no longer described as παῖς) various foot races. Since we know from the *Hellenika* of Xenophon the names of the eponymous ephors from 431 to 403, these men, who do not figure in that list, must have held office before 431. The writing has the same general appearance throughout; that is to say, it does not suggest that the final part, using the ephors' names, was added at some later date. Why then did Damonon suddenly begin to cite them for these victories, though he had not done so for the previous ones?[3] I hazard the suggestion that in the earlier period, during his own and his son's youth, the official method of recording the victories did not yet extend beyond the simple record of the victors' names in lists; but that during Damonon's later life, and some time before 431, it became the official practice of the recorders to cite the ephor's name at the head of the annual list of victors, and Damonon not unnaturally described his victories as they were recorded in the official lists (p. 60). The ephors'

[1] The provenance is not recorded. Were it from a precinct, it might be yet another victory-dedication from scattered words here and there: [---]τε δα[μοσια? --- ενικασεν?]ανδρα[ς] | ⊢ελον[- - -αλλ]ọθ'? ⊢αι[π] | ερ ταị [- - -]αịραι.

[2] For a more detailed discussion of this trouble, see Jeffery, *JHS* lxix (1949), 26 ff. and Wallace, *JHS* lxxiv (1954), 32 ff.

[3] It has been suggested (*BSA* xiii. 179 ff.) that the victories given under the ephors' names are the same as the preceding victories, in a new arrangement; but Kolbe has pointed out (*IG* v. 1. 213, p. 74) that in l. 72, under the ephor Echemenes, a victory is mentioned at a festival which does not occur among those previously named.

names, none of which occurs in the series incorporated in Xenophon's *Hellenika* ii. 3. 9–10, make it certain that all the victories were won before the start of the Peloponnesian War; and, though naturally we cannot overlook the possibility that Damonon made his offering many years after his last victory, it is natural to infer that the stele also was erected before 431. The relief is too damaged to offer any closer dating. We may note the letter *nu*, still varying somewhat: *sigma*, already settled in the standard form ϵ: *upsilon* ϒ, as current elsewhere by the second half of the century: and the curious tilted Ϝϵ, which occurs only in Poseidon's epithet γαιαϝοχος.

Two of the stelai from Tainaron recording the manumission of slaves have also been referred to the years before 431; the first (**53**) is slightly more archaic in its lettering than Damonon's stele (cf. *upsilon* and *chi*), and was erected in the ephorate of Daiochos, of whom nothing is known; the second (**54**) was erected in the ephorate of Aristeus, who may well be the official also mentioned by Damonon. The lettering of **54** is rather more advanced than that of Damonon's stele, particularly in its use of δϵ and *omega*; but the latter, set out of alinement as though by an unpractised hand, has the curved hooks of earlier types, not the wide horizontal bars of the late fifth century (cf. pp. 37 f.).

The stele of manumission *IG* v. 1. 1231 has been dated in the year 427/6 because the name Hegesistratos, recorded in Xenophon, *Hell.* ii. 3. 10, as that of the ephor in that year, is also the name of the ephor on the stele; but from its lettering the stele cannot be earlier than the fourth century, in spite of the absence of *omega*. The *epsilon* with short central bar, the open *eta*, the curved lines of many of the letters, the small loop of *rho* and *omikron*, would be advanced even for the end of the fifth century (cf. the Ionic lettering on the Delian stele, **62** below); they are utterly alien from anything as early as *c.* 427/6, not merely in Lakonia, but anywhere else. It is sufficient to compare the lettering on the fragmentary stele recording contributions in money and kind to the Lakedaimonians in the Peloponnesian War (**55**), which has been dated by Adcock with great probability to the year 427/6.[1] Fourmont's copy of part of this stele, made when the stone was in better condition than it is now, is naturally unreliable in detail—*delta*, for example, is given as ϵ throughout—but the extant fragment is enough to show that the letters are similar in general to those of Damonon's stele. Although the stone itself was found rebuilt into a church some distance south of modern Sparta, it may be suggested that it was originally erected in the precinct of Athena on the Akropolis; for a small fragment of marble, found in the precinct in 1907 (**56**), which has hitherto passed in obscurity as the remains of some dedication in verse, bears in its extant letters so striking a resemblance to the text of the list of gifts that I think there can be little doubt that it is part of the same monument.[2]

Several typical grave-inscriptions may be attributed with confidence to the Peloponnesian War: the memorials of Ainetos (**57**), of Telephanes (**58**), of Hairesippos (**59**), where for the first time *heta* is used for η as well as Ͱ; that of Eualkes (**60**), who fell at Mantinea, is somewhat archaic in its *nu* and *upsilon*, but presumably belongs none the

---

[1] *Mélanges Glotz* i. 2 ff.

[2] It appears to read: [---τ]οι Απελλ[--- | ---εδον τοις Λακεδ]αιμονιο[ις ---]καλλοσι[ --- ὁ δεῖνα] εδōκε [ποτ τον πολεμον ?--- | ---εδ]ον ποτ [τον πολεμον ---]εν ερ[---] θαι αρ[γυριο ? ---].

less to the battle of 418. The gravestone of the Spartan force under the polemarchs Thibrakos and Chairon, which suffered disaster near the Peiraieus in 403, and was given honourable burial by the Athenians in the Kerameikos, shows that in formal inscriptions of this date crossed *theta* and 'red' *chi* were still used (**61**); the retrograde direction of the letters, which under normal circumstances was not used at this time in Lakonia any more than elsewhere, is here undoubtedly due to the position of the long slab on the right side of the path for one walking through the outer Kerameikos towards the Dipylon, the entrance to the city (p. 44).

Among the many doubtful points which beset the chronology of Lakonian inscriptions, the last and perhaps the most curious is that of the stele erected on Delos between the years 403 and 399, whereby the Lakedaimonian authorities guaranteed ἀσυλία to the island (**62**). There is, as we have seen, sufficient evidence that ε3 and σ2 were no longer in use in the second half of the fifth century; but they reappear in the decree on this stele, which is cut *stoichedon*. The fine, careful lettering and the use of crossed *theta* and 'red' *chi* cause no surprise, for the former is typical of many Lakonian masons, and the latter is still in use on the Kerameikos gravestone also. The only other significant letter is the *nu*, which is the type 5 generally in use elsewhere on the mainland (though not in other Lakonian examples) in the latter part of the fifth century. The lists which follow the text of the treaty, giving the names of those in office at Sparta and Delos (the latter names lost) are in the complete Ionic script, and presumably cut by a Delian. It is possible that a Delian mason cut the whole stele, closely following a Lakonian original for the text of the treaty, in which, for some reason, the old letter-forms were used. The Spartans may have retained them for public documents by convention, although one wonders then why they did not employ them for the public gravestone **61** also; or perhaps they used them at Delos to symbolize the new Spartan hegemony.

## SELECT CATALOGUE

**1.** Ivory plaque of a ship, from the site of Artemis Orthia; late 7th c. Droop, *BSA* xiii (1906–7), 100 ff., pl. 4. *AO*, 370, 169.25, pls. 109–10. *IG* v. 1. 252b. Kirk, *BSA* xliv (1949), 121 f. NM.　　PL. 35

**2a–b.** (*a*) Plate dedicated by Ϝριθιοα, from the same site. (*b*) Plate with fragmentary dedication, from the same site; late 7th–early 6th c. Dawkins, *BSA* xvi (1909–10), 28. *AO*, 73 f., 169, and 371. *SEG* ii. 84, 86. *IG* v. 1. 1587–8. Sparta Mus.　　PL. 35

**3.** Fragments of bone flutes, from the same site; late 7th–early 6th c. Woodward, *BSA* xxiv. 115. *AO*, 370, 169. 26–27, pl. 161. 2 and 4. *SEG* ii. 82–83. Sparta Mus.　　PL. 35

**4.** Neck of an oinochoe with remains of a dedication, from the precinct of Athena Chalkioikos; early 6th c. Droop, *BSA* xxviii (1926–7), 70, fig. 13. Lane, *BSA* xxxiv (1933–4), 174. *SEG* xi. 666. Sparta Mus.

**5.** Bronze handle of a dedication by Dorkonidas(?), from the Amyklaion; late 7th–early 6th c.? Von Massow, *AM* lii (1927), 34 f., 63, Beil. viii. 15. *SEG* xi. 689. Sparta Mus.　　PL. 35

**6.** Inscribed limestone plaques from the site of Orthia; *c.* 600–550; *AO*, 15, 367 ff. *SEG* ii. 64–80. Sparta Mus.　　PL. 35

7. Bronze hydria with name Telestas; *c.* 600–575? Neugebauer, *AA* 1938, 330 ff., figs. 1–2. D. M. Robinson, *AJA* xlvi (1942), 173, 188. Hafner, *Charites* (1957), 119 ff., figs. 1–2. Mainz University, Archaeological Institute.                                                                     PL. 35

8. Lak. III kylix painted by the Arkesilas painter, from Vulci; *c.* 570–560. Lane, op. cit. 140, 161 f. Buschor, *Griech. Vasen* (1940), 75, fig. 84. *CVA* Paris, Bib. Nat. i, pls. 20–22. FR iii, pl. 151. H. R. W. Smith, *The Hearst Hydria*, 251 f. Beazley, *Hesperia* xii (1943), 88. Mazzarino, *Fra Oriente e Occidente* (1947), 313 ff. Chamoux, *Cyrène* (1953), 258 ff. Shefton, *BSA* xlix (1954), 301, 309, n. 9. Paris, Cab. Méd.                                                                                               PL. 35

9. Fragment of bronze from a helmet, dedicated at the Amyklaion; *c.* 600–550? Von Massow, op. cit. 37, 64, Beil. vii. 8. *SEG* xi. 690. Sparta Mus.                                                  PL. 35

10. Rim of a lebes dedicated by the Spartans at Olympia; *c.* 600–550? *Ol.* v. 244. Roehl³, 99. 12. *IG* v. 1. 1563. *SEG* xi. 1204a. Olympia Mus. 718+849.

11. Rim of a lebes dedicated by —das son of Dexippos at Delphi; *c.* 600–550? Lerat, *RA* 1944, 5 ff., figs. 1–2. *FD* v. 70, figs. 228a–b. Delphi Mus. 6036.                                          PL. 35

12. Fragment of a bronze plaque dedicated at Olympia; *c.* 600–550? *Ol.* v. 263. *IG* v. 1. 1561. Olympia Mus. 625.

13. Block inscribed Αρταμ from near the Menelaion; *c.* 600–550? Woodward, *BSA* xv (1908–9), 87, 91. *IG* v. 1. 224. Sparta Mus.

14. Bronze disk dedicated by Melas from Kosmas (Thornax?); *c.* 600–550? Th. Arvanitopoullou, *Polemon* iii (1948), 152 ff., fig. 1. *SEG* xi. 890. Private coll.

15. Marble seat belonging to the Lakonian Gorgos, proxenos of Elis, at Olympia; *c.* 600–550? Kunze and Schleif, *Olympiabericht* iv (1944), 164 ff., pl. 67. *SEG* xi. 1180a. Olympia Mus.          PL. 36

16. Lak. III hydria (*a*) and three sherds (*b–d*) inscribed by the Hunt Painter; *c.* 560–550. (*a*) Laurenzi, *Clara Rhodos* viii. 85 ff., figs. 71–80, pl. 4. Rhodes Mus. (*b*) Beazley, *AJA* liv (1950), 313, fig. 2. Cyrene Mus. (*c*) Technau, *AM* liv (1929), Beil. xvi. 1. Samos, Tigani Mus. (*d*) J. M. Woodward, *JHS* lii (1932), 26, fig. 2. Leipzig Mus. Cf. Lane, *BSA* xxxiv (1933–4), 143, 163, 166; Shefton, *BSA* xlix (1954), 306 ff.                                                                                            PL. 35

17. Bronze handle of a mirror (?), dedicated to Apollo Hyperteleatas; *c.* 550? *IG* v. 1. 989. *SEG* xi. 908. NM?

18. Bronze phiale dedicated to Artemis Limnatis, presumably from Limnai; *c.* 550–525? *IG* v. 1. 1497. Roehl³, 98. 8. Berlin Mus.

19. Strip of bronze from a trophy of arms dedicated by Eurystratides, probably from Olympia; *c.* 550–525? Peek, *Philologus* xciv (1941), 330 ff., fig. 1. Friedlaender 36a. *SEG* xi. 1214. Olympia Mus.                                                                                                               PL. 36

20. Haltēr dedicated by Akmatides at Olympia; *c.* 550–525? Hampe and Jantzen, *JdI* lii, *Olympiabericht* i (1937), 82 ff., pl. 25. Moretti 8. *SEG* xiv. 355. Olympia Mus.

21. Haltēr belonging to Kleocha(res), from the precinct of Athena Chalkioikos, Sparta; *c.* 550–525? Woodward, *BSA* xiv (1907), 137. *IG* v. 1. 216, pl. 1. Sparta Mus.

22. Stele dedicated by Aigletes to Apollo, from Sparta; *c.* 530–500? Woodward, *BSA* xv (1908–9), 81 ff. *IG* v. 1. 222. *DGE* 9. Friedlaender 50. Moretti 9. *SEG* xiv. 329. Sparta Mus.          PL. 36

23. Stele bearing the 'hymn to Athena' (athletic dedication?) from the precinct of Athena Chalkioikos; *c.* 530–500? Woodward, *BSA* xxix (1927–8), 45 ff. *SEG* xi. 652. Sparta Mus.

**24.** Relief dedicated to the Tyndaridai by Pleistiadas, from Sellasia; *c.* 525? Tod and Wace, *Cat. Sparta Mus.* 447. Furtwaengler, *AM* viii (1883), 371 ff., pl. 18. 2. Roehl³, 99. 11. *IG* v. 1. 919. *DGE* 38. *FGB*, 86, 91. Wace, *AE* 1937, 219. Bloesch, *Agalma* (1943), 21. Friedlaender 95. Sparta Mus. 575.
PL. 36

**25.** Relief dedicated to Kore Soteira (?); *c.* 525? Froehner, *Coll. Tyszkiewicz* (1892), pl. 16. *FGB*, 86, 91, pl. 44d. Cumont, *Cat. Mus. Cinquantenaire* (1913), 50. Brussels, Mus. Cinquantenaire A 1150.
PL. 36

**26.** Relief inscribed (Χ)ιλōν, from near Sparta; *c.* 525? Woodward, *BSA* xv (1908–9), 80 f. *IG* v. 1. 244. Wace, op. cit. 217 ff., fig. 1. Bock, *Ö.Jh.* xxxv (1943), Beibl. 5 ff. *SEG* xi. 698. Andronikos, *Peloponnesiaka* i (1956), 264 ff.

**27.** Relief dedicated by Anaxibios, from the precinct of Athena Chalkioikos; *c.* 525–500? Woodward, *BSA* xiv. 136 f., 144, fig. 1. *IG* v. 1. 215. *FGB*, 86, 94. *SEG* xi. 651. Sparta Mus.                        PL. 36

**28.** Stele bearing part of an athletic dedication from the theatre area, Sparta; *c.* 510–500? Woodward, *BSA* xxvii (1925–6), 249 f. Sparta Mus.

**29.** Relief of a youth, found at Magoula; *c.* 510–500. Dressel and Milchhoefer, *AM* ii (1887), 314 f., pl. 25, 2. *IG* v. 1. 457. Tod and Wace, op. cit. 104, fig. 4. Roehl³, 98. 3. *DGE* 2. *FGB*, 91. Blümel, *Kat. Skulpt. Berlin* ii. 1 (1940), A 13, pl. 25. Johansen, *The Attic Grave Reliefs* (1951), 86, fig. 39. *SEG* xi. 772a. Andronikos, op. cit., 274 ff., fig. 7. Berlin Mus. A 13 (752).                        PL. 37

**30.** Stele dedicated by Eteoi(tas) to Athena Chalkioikos; *c.* 510–500? Woodward, op. cit., 250 f. *SEG* xi. 653. Sparta Mus.                        PL. 37

**31.** Stele dedicated by Glaukatias (?), recording an athletic victory (?), from Sparta; *c.* 510–500? *IG* v. 1. 720. *IGB* 22. Roehl³, 98. 5. *DGE* 6. Friedlaender 7. Peek i. 143. *SEG* xi. 863. EM.                        PL. 37

**32.** Graffiti (masons' names) on architectural blocks from the throne of Apollo at Amyklai; *c.* 510–500. Fiechter, *JdI* xxxiii (1918), 221 f., figs. 74, 76–87. Skias, *AE* 1919, 33. 4. *SEG* i. 84. *IG* v. 1. 823, 832. Von Massow, op. cit. 62. Hagia Kyriaki (Amyklai).                        PL. 37

**33.** Bronze statuette of a bull, dedicated by Amphimenides to Poseidon, from Amyklai (?); late 6th c.? Robert, *Coll. Froehner* i. 26 f., pl. 9. *SEG* xi. 955. Paris, Cab. Méd.

**34.** Bronze fish dedicated to Poseidon, found near the Amyklaion; 6th c. Von Massow, op. cit. 37, 63, pl. 1. *SEG* xi. 692. Sparta Mus.?

**35.** Bronze statuette of a goat dedicated to Apollo Hyperteleatas; 6th c. Robert, op. cit. 26, pl. 9. *SEG* xi. 905. Paris, Cab. Méd.

**36.** Bronze handle from a dedication by Menoitios to Apollo Pythaieus, at Tyros; 6th c. *IGA* 59. *IG* v. 1. 928. Rhomaios, *PAE* 1911, 254 f. Neugebauer, *RM* xxxviii–ix (1923–4), 369. Berlin Mus. 7268.

**37.** Bronze statuette of a soldier, dedicated by Charillos to Apollo Maleatas; *c.* 525? *IG* v. 1. 927. Lamb, *G. and R. Bronzes*, 91, pl. 28a. *FGB*, 89, pl. 49d. Karo, *Greek Personality in archaic Sculpture*, 154, 313, n. 99. NM 7598.

**38.** Bronze statuette of a ram dedicated to Apollo Maleatas; 6th c. *IGA* 89. Roberts i. 289. *SGDI* 4536. *IG* v. i. 929. NM 7666.

**39.** Bronze phialai dedicated to Artemis Limnatis; 6th c. *IG* v. 1. 226, 225. Robert, op. cit. 27, pl. 14. Berlin Mus. and Paris, Cab. Méd.

**40.** Minor bronzes from the Apollonion at Tyros; 6th c. Rhomaios, *PAE* 1911, 263 ff. *IG* v. 1. 1517 ff. *SEG.* xi. 893. NM?

**41.** Three fragments from a victory-dedication(?) at Sparta; 6th c., second half? *AO*, 354, no. 139a–c. Sparta Mus.

**42.** Fragment from a victory-dedication(?) from Mistra; 6th c., second half? Tod and Wace, op. cit. 72. *IG* v. 1. 2, pl. 1. Sparta Mus. 599.

**43.** Fragment from the pedestal of a perirrhanterion(?) dedicated by Demar(etos) at Hyperteleaton; *c.* 500–480? Hondius, *BSA* xxiv (1919–21), 137 f. *SEG* ii. 170. Chamoux, *Cyrène*, 201. Lost?     PL. 37

**44.** List of names in pairs(?) from the Akropolis at Sparta; *c.* 500? Woodward, *BSA* xxvii. 253. *SEG* xi. 638. Sparta Mus.                                                          PL. 37

**45.** Stele bearing a list of names, faintly incised, from Geronthrai; *c.* 500? *IG* v. 1. 1134. Roehl³, 99. 13. *SEG* xi. 919. Church of H. Ioannes Chrysostomos.

**46.** Stele bearing a list of names from Geronthrai; *c.* 500? *IG* v. 1. 1133. Roehl³, 97. 1. Hiller von Gaertringen, *Glotta* xxv (1936), 116 f. *SEG* xi. 918. Lost?                            PL. 37

**47.** Small fragment of a list of names from Sparta; *c.* 500? Tod and Wace, op. cit. 527. *IG* v. 1. 357. Sparta Mus. 527.

**48.** Block inscribed with a victory-dedication(?) from Magoula; *c.* 500–475. Tod and Wace, op. cit. 73. Roehl³, 99. 10. *IG* v. 1. 238, pl. 2. Sparta Mus. 611.

**49.** Base of an offering dedicated by the Lakedaimonians to Zeus at Olympia; *c.* 490? *Ol.* v. 252. *IG* v. 1. 1562. *SGDI* 4405. Roberts i. 261. Roehl³, 102. 20. *DGE* 7. Hiller, *Hist. griech. Epigramme*, 13. Arvanitopoullos, *Epigraphike* ii. 231 f. Friedlaender 113. Jeffery, *JHS* lxix (1949), 26 ff. Buck 68. *SEG* xi. 1203a. Olympia Mus. 43+510.                                                   PL. 37

**50.** Part of a stele bearing an inscription, possibly a victory-list; *c.* 500–475? Tod and Wace, op. cit. 75. *IG* v. 1. 721, pl. 2. Kirsten, *Das Insel Kreta* (1936), 12 f. Sparta Mus. 625.

**51.** Relief stele bearing part of a list of victories(?) from the Amyklaion, probably that commemorating the victor Ainetos; *c.* 475. Versakes, *AE* 1912, 188, fig. 16. Fiechter, *JdI* xxxiii (1918), 220, 222 f., figs. 74, 84. Von Massow, *AM* li (1926), 41 ff., fig. 1. *SEG* xi. 696. Sparta Mus.

**52.** Stele dedicated by Damonon in the precinct of Athena Chalkioikos; *c.* 450–431? Tod and Wace, op. cit. 64 and 176. *IG* v. 1. 213, pl. 2. Roehl³, 100. 17. Tillyard, *BSA* xiii. 174 ff. Moretti 16. *SEG* xiv. 330. Sparta Mus. 440.                                                          PL. 38

**53.** Manumission stele from Tainaron; *c.* 450–430? *IG* v. 1. 1228. Roehl³, 101. 19. *BMI* 139. *DGE* 52 (1). *SEG* xi. 939. BM.                                                            PL. 38

**54.** Manumission stele from Tainaron; *c.* 440–430? *IG* v. 1. 1230. Tillyard, op. cit. 182. Roehl³, 103. 27. *DGE* 52 (2). *SEG* xi. 941. EM 11526.                                           PL. 38

**55.** Stele recording contributions towards the Peloponnesian War; *c.* 427/6? *IG* v. 1. 1. Tod, *GHI²* 62 and p. 263. Adcock, *Mél. Glotz* i. 2 ff. *SEG* xi. 456. Church of H. Basilios.

**56.** Fragment of marble (part of **55**?), from the precinct of Athena Chalkioikos. Woodward, *BSA* xiv. 135 f. *IG* v. 1. 219. Sparta Mus.

**57.** Gravestone of Ainetos, from Magoula; *c.* 431–403. *SGDI* 4420. Roehl³, 102. 22. Tod and Wace, op. cit. 386. *IG* v. 1. 701. *DGE* 17. *SEG* xi. 862. Sparta Mus. 386.

**58.** Gravestone of Telephanes, Geronthrai; *c.* 431–403. Roehl³, 102. 23. *IG* v. 1. 1125. *DGE* 47 (2). *SEG* xi. 916. Private Coll.?

**59.** Gravestone of Hairesippos from Sparta(?); *c.* 431–403. Tod and Wace, op. cit. 387. *SGDI* 4421. *IGA* 85. *IG* v. 1. 702. Roehl³, 103. 28. *SEG* xi. 862. Sparta Mus. 387.

**60.** Gravestone of Eualkes, Geronthrai; *c.* 418. Roehl³, 104. 31. *IG* v. 1. 1124. *DGE* 47 (1). *SEG* xi. 915. Church of Koimesis Theotokou.                                                                                                PL. 38

**61.** Gravestone of the Spartans who were buried in the Kerameikos in 403. Karo, *AA* 1930, 90 ff. and 101 f., fig. 5. Van Hook, *AJA* xxxvi (1932), 290 ff. Kerameikos.

**62.** Stele bearing a decree of protection granted to Delos by the Spartans; *c.* 403–399. Homolle, *BCH* iii (1879), 12 ff. *SGDI* 4415. Roehl³, 103. 26. Kern, pl. 16. *IG* v. 1. 1564 and p. vii. *DGE* 15. *GHI* ii. 99. Amandry, *BCH* lxxi–lxxii (1947–8), 415, fig. 30. *ID* i (1950), 87. *SEG* xi. 963. Delos Mus. 506+597.
PL. 38

*Inscriptions attributed to Lakonia*

**63.** Haltēr belonging to Koiris, Olympia; 6th c. *Ol.* v. 720. Olympia Mus. 679.                        PL. 39

**64.** Part of a Corinthian helmet, 6th c. *Ol.* iv. 168. Kukahn, *Der griech. Helm* (1939), 34a, p. 66. Chase, *Bull. Boston MFA* xlviii (1950), 80 ff., fig. 5.                                                                            PL. 39

**65.** Lip of a bronze lebes at Delphi, dedicated by Thaumis; 6th c. *FD* v. 70, figs. 228b, 228 bis. Keramopoullos, *BCH* xxxiii (1909), 441 f. Friedlaender 14*a*. See p. 190, n. 5.

**66.** Letters incised on reliefs and neck of a bronze krater from Vix, France; *c.* 530–520? Joffroy, *Rev. Phil.* xxvii (1953), 1 ff. and *Mon. Piot* xlviii (1954), 1 ff. Amandry, *RA* xliii (1954), 125 ff. Rumpf, *Bulletin van de Vereeniging tot Bevordering der Kennis van de antieke Beschaving* xxix (1954), 8 ff., and *Charites* (1957), 127 ff. *SEG* xii. 483. Woodhead, *CR* 1955, 225. Chatillon Mus.                  PL. 39

**67.** Bronze statuette dedicated to Artemis Daidale by Chimarides, found near Olympia; *c.* 550–525? Lamb, *Gk. and Rom. Bronzes*, 90, pl. 35d. *FGB*, 87, 92, pls. 44e, 47a. Chase, *Guide Class. Coll. Boston*, 29, fig. 33. Meyer, *Neue peloponnesische Wanderungen* (1957), 46. Boston MFA 98. 658.   PL. 39


# MESSENIA

*Letter-forms*; see Lakonia, pp. 183 f. and Fig. 39.

Very few archaic inscriptions have been found as yet in Messenia, and of these not all are adequately illustrated. Among them they do not muster examples of more than two-thirds of the letters of the alphabet; but there is enough to indicate (as might be expected) that, just as the Messenians spoke a Doric dialect like that of the Lakonians (Thuc. iv. 3; Paus. iv. 27. 11), so they used a similar alphabet. Moreover, there was no neighbouring script with dissimilar characters to cause any contamination, for both Arkadian and Elean were basically the same as Lakonian. *Gamma*, their principal point of difference, is among the letters not yet attested in Messenian, and so we cannot tell if the lunate type of Arkadia and Elis was used, or that of Lakonia; *sigma* varied between three- and four-stroked, with no trace as yet of the exaggerated form frequently used in Lakonian.

The earliest datable inscription is probably the dedication to the river Pamisos, τōι Παμισōι Πυθοδōρος, on a little bronze warrior now in a private collection (**1**), which has been dated from its style 'around the middle of the sixth century';[1] but the inscription has not yet been published. A second inscription, which was found on a stone on the island of Prote, is plainly archaic, but so battered that it is barely half-legible (**2**). The first line runs from right to left, the direction of the second is uncertain; and little can be said of

[1] *AGA*, 90.

the letter-forms as given in the copy, since owing to the state of the stone it is plainly impossible to tell which are complete, and whether the curved lines are parts of letters, or (as the editor suspected) punctuation marks. The only other possible case of punctuation in Messenian occurs on the gravestone of two men whose title ἰαρός shows that they were officials of the Mysteries.[1] This inscription (**6**) is known only from a copy by Fourmont, and it is quite possible that the short strokes between the words were inserted by Fourmont himself to show that each word actually occupied a separate line. As often happens in his copies, the letters show discrepancies (ͱ1–2, ρ1–2, δ3); so that the date of this inscription is no more certain than that of **2**, though we may hazard that **2**, with its tailed *epsilon* and retrograde line, belongs to the sixth century, whereas **6** may belong to the first half of the fifth.

Three sites in Messenia have yielded a small series of inscriptions, if such a title can be given to the short graffiti of which they consist. In the bed of the river Nedon, in the district of Pherai, several names have been cut on a smoothed surface of rock (**5**); though not all legible, they appear to be dated about the end of the sixth or the early fifth century, showing ε 1 or 4, ρ1, χ1, and the lack of *qoppa* (in Κορφιατα, Κροφιατα), which is characteristic of Lakonian also (p. 183). Among the ruins of a small building north-east of Ithome near the modern village Vasiliko were found fragments of bronze and undecorated sherds, some of which bore graffiti, apparently the owners' names (**4**). If Valmin is right in suggesting that at some time the Arkadian frontier ran here, and that the building is an Arkadian fort, these graffiti should be listed among the Arkadian inscriptions; but the epigraphical arguments on which he partly bases his claim are not valid.[2] The dates, again, seem to extend from the end of the sixth into the fifth century.

Lastly, the temple of Apollo Korythos between Korone and Kolonides, described by Pausanias as one of the principal sanctuaries of Messenia (iv. 34. 7), yielded among its rich store of minor objects two inscribed spear-butts (**3, 10**), three fragments of pottery inscribed with their owners' names (**7**), and a small stone pillar-base (**11**). The first spear-butt **3** presents an historical problem. It is a plain, archaic type which cannot be dated precisely, bearing a dedication inscribed from right to left on its four faces: Μεθαν[- - -] | ανεθε[ν- - -] | Αθαναι[- - -] | λαιδο[ς - - -]. The obvious parallel, as the excavator pointed out,[3] is the butt from Olympia inscribed Μεθανιοι απο Λακεδαιμονιōν (p. 177, east Argolid **4**), which has been universally attributed to Argolic Methana, on the occasion of some otherwise unrecorded clash with Sparta (see p. 177). The butt from Messenia has therefore been ascribed to the same dedicators, and restored: Μεθαν[ιοι] | ανεθε[ν] | Αθαναι [εκ] | λαιδο[ς]. This interpretation, however, involves two difficulties: firstly, why should the Methanians of the eastern Argolid dedicate a spear in a local sanctuary of Messenia, and secondly, why should they make a dedication to Athena in a sanctuary of

---

[1] For a full commentary on this use of ἰαρός, cf. *SGDI* 4668.

[2] *Op. Arch.* ii (1941), 69 ff. He argues that Ευτρεσιο can only refer to a man from Eutresis in Arkadia, which may well be so; but I do not think that additional support can be found, as he suggests, in the graffiti -χαον and -χιλοι. For the first: 'blue' *chi* does not occur, as far as I know, in Arkadian in the 5th c., as he claims—nor,

indeed, in Messenian; the vase (black-glazed) might be Attic, or from the Argivo-Corinthian area, or (as he himself notes, p. 70, n. 1) may be later than the 5th c. For the second: the 'Attic' *lambda* is not (as he says) found in Arkadian; possibly the sherd should be read the other way up (right to left).

[3] Versakes, *A. Delt.* ii (1916), 115.

Apollo? The surviving letter-forms might belong equally to the eastern Argolid or to Messenia. They suggest a date not later than the first quarter of the fifth century. Judged on the standards of the Lakonian inscriptions, the spear-butt might be of about the same period as the relief from Magoula (p. 193, Lakonia **29**), i.e. *c.* 510–500; but the form of *nu* (inverted twice) on the butt is somewhat later in appearance than that on the relief, and the provincial craftsman's work might well be a generation later than that of the Lakonian sculptor. But if the spear was not dedicated by Argolic Methana to Athena, how is it to be restored? Given that it was found in a local temple of Apollo, the normal formula to be expected in such a dedication would be (*a*) the name of some local dedicators, from Korone or Kolonides, or at all events from somewhere in Messenia, (*b*) the verb, (*c*) perhaps the name of Apollo, (*d*) perhaps the name of the vanquished, (*e*) a description of the offering (tithe, part of spoils, &c.); e.g. Μεθαν[αιοι] | ανεθε[ν απ'] | Αθαναι[ōν τας] | λαιδο[ς]. But to restore the awkward lines 1 and 3 on this basis would produce equally great historical difficulties.[1] The dedication on the second butt fortunately contains none of these difficulties: Απελλōνος Ηιαρον (wrongly given as Ἀπ Η λλōνος in *DGE* 68a). It is certainly later than **3**, perhaps about the middle of the fifth century. The three graffiti on the rims of three vases (**7**) may be dated from the beginning to the middle of the same century (if not later), that of Hairantios being the earliest. Of the pillar-base **11**, inadequately described and photographed, it can only be said that the combination of dotted *theta* and tailed *rho*, but 'red' *xi* still, suggests a date late in the fifth century.[2]

We have even less evidence for their script from those Messenians who lived outside the Peloponnese—those who, after their vain attempts at revolt against the Lakedaimonians, found shelter overseas. The exiles who were invited by Anaxilas of Rhegion to seize Zankle in the early fifth century, though they caused Zankle's name ultimately to be changed to Messana, appear to have left no traces of their existence in the local alphabet, which remained the same as that of Rhegion (pp. 243 ff.). The exiles of the next generation, who were settled by the Athenians in Naupaktos after the great Helot Revolt (*c.* 464–460?),

---

[1] The nearest equivalent to the name Μεθαν[- - -] in this locality is that of the town called Mothone by late writers, on the west coast of the same peninsula. It was traditionally granted by the Lakonians to the people of Nauplia after their expulsion by the Argives at about the time of the Second Messenian War (Paus. iv. 24. 4). There is no direct evidence that this town was called Methana in Doric. But the evidence for the form Μοθώνη is all late: Hellenistic coins (*HN*[2], 433), an inscription of the third century A.D. from Argos (*IG* iv. 619), and the writers Pausanias, Plutarch, pseudo-Skylax, Ptolemaios, Porphyrios, Suidas s.v. (Meyer, *RE*, s.v. Methone, 1382). In Thuc. ii. 25. 1, our only 5th-c. authority, the form is Μεθώνη in all manuscripts (as it is also in the late writers Diodoros, Strabo, Cassius Dio, Eustathios, Steph. Byz. s.v., Suidas s.v.; cf. Meyer, loc. cit., and Frazer, *Pausanias* iii. 452 s.v.). It will be recalled that Thucydides also uses the Ionic form Μεθώνη for the Argolic town (iv. 45. 2; v. 18. 7), although its Doric name was undoubtedly Μεθάνα

(Meyer, loc. cit.). To postulate, then, a Messenian form Μεθάνα is reasonable; but why should the name have been changed later to Μοθώνη? In Pausanias' day the citizens derived it from 'Mothone, daughter of Oineus' (iv. 35. 1), or (his own view) from a rock called Μόθων which flanked the harbour. Here we can only walk among the pitfalls of conjecture, which grow even deeper in the second problem—the restoration of l. 3, Αθαναι[- - -]. Can the Athenians be brought into this context? In the First Peloponnesian War they suffered a reverse at Messenian Methone in 456–455 under the leadership of Tolmides (Diod. xi. 84). The Spartans might perhaps allow the people of Methone to put their name on an offering made in their own local sanctuary; but it is questionable whether the inscription can be brought down as low as this in date.

[2] These forms seem reasonably certain, from the photograph and the editor's commentary. According to his transcript l. 3 reads [αν]εθέκε, but l. 1 [Απ]ολλων[ι]; the photograph suggests O rather than Ω.

may or may not have retained their local script in the new surroundings. Since the Lokrian alphabet is of the same type, we should have difficulty in deciding this, even if we had examples (pp. 105 f.). As it is, no help can be gained from the dedication on the famous Victory at Olympia (12), offered by 'the Messenians and Naupaktians' after the defeat of the Spartans in the campaign of Pylos and Sphakteria in 425, for it is in the complete Ionic alphabet, like the sculptor's signature, and may have been drafted with the signature by the sculptor, Paionios of Mende (p. 365). The fragments of its counterpart restored at Delphi (13) are also in Ionic. A further trace of Messenian activity at Delphi has been restored by Daux[1] from several blocks with clamp-cuttings of unusual form, which once formed the base of a large dedication in the late archaic or early classical period, by donors who can hardly be other than the Messenians: [Απελλōνι] Πυ[θιōι] ανεθεν [Μεσ]σανιοι (8). The letter-forms of this inscription are archaic, but, as Daux points out, the technique employed shows that it is a late copy of an earlier inscription. Above it runs a version in larger letters dated in the first half of the second century B.C., and it is assumed that, after some prosperous undertaking at this time, the Messenians renewed an earlier offering, piously copying their original dedication, and adding their contemporary version: [Μεσσαν]ιο[ι Απο]λλω[νι Πυ]θιωι. The lettering of the first version, with ει, ϝι, υι, suggests, as Daux observes, a date not later than the middle of the fifth century, and possibly some years earlier;[2] and the occasion of its dedication remains one of the many riddles of Messenian history. Even if we accept the hypothesis that the Messenians were in revolt in the years after 500,[3] an offering of this size at Delphi at that time seems hardly credible. Yet the lettering does not suggest an original offering by the Messenians of Zankle, for the evidence of the coinage there indicates that the Doric form Μεσσάνα did not replace the Ionic (Chalkidic) Μεσσήνη until after the downfall of the tyranny at Rhegion c. 461,[4] a date at which *epsilon*, *nu*, and tailed *upsilon* would be very unlikely in the Chalkidic alphabet of the colony. If the offering was made by the Messenians of Naupaktos, the *terminus post quem* must be near the middle of the fifth century; the occasion could have been either their new settlement, or some local campaign like that against Oiniadai (which began, at least, with a victory for the Messenians), described by Pausanias (iv. 25. 1; v. 26. 1). Pausanias does not date this affair; but he suggests that it happened soon after the occupation of Naupaktos, and it is perhaps to be connected with the abortive attack on Oiniadai by the Athenians in 455/4, during the First Peloponnesian War (Thuc. i. 111. 3).

A final instance of Messenian activity abroad is 14, the gravestone of Σκο[τ?]εας Μεσ-⟨σ⟩ανιος found in one of the cemeteries of Athens. The dialect is Doric, and the combination of both four- and three-stroked *sigma* with tailed *epsilon* and *nu* suggests the script of Messenia rather than Athens. If that is correct, the date may be anywhere down to the mid-fifth century.

---

[1] *BCH* lxi (1937), 67 ff.

[2] The squared forms of *theta* and *omikron*, being easier to cut (or scratch) than circles, were occasionally used by archaic writers (especially on bronze), as we have had previous occasion to note. The slanting *iota* of the later copyist is remarkable; it occurs also in the graffito ⊢αιραντιος on a sherd from the temple of Apollo Korythos (7), though this may be only by coincidence.

[3] Cf. Jeffery, *JHS* lxix (1949), 26 ff. and Wallace, *JHS* lxxiv (1954), 32 ff.; above, p. 196.

[4] E. S. G. Robinson, *JHS* lxvi (1946), 18.

## SELECT CATALOGUE

**1.** Bronze statuette of a youth, dedicated by Pythodoros to the river Pamisos; *c.* 550? *AGA*, 89 f., fig. 154. Private coll.

**2.** Inscription from the island of Prote; 6th c.? Valmin, *Bull. Soc. Lund* (1928–9), 46 f., no. 29, fig. 13. *SEG* xi. 1005.

**3.** Dedication on a spear-butt from the precinct of Apollo Korythos, near Kolonides; *c.* 500–475? Versakes, *A. Delt.* ii (1916), 88 f., 114 f., fig. 24. NM?                    PL. 39

**4.** Graffiti on sherds from a building near the Arkadian border; *c.* 500–475? Valmin, *Op. Arch.* ii (1941), 66 ff., figs. 7–10.

**5.** Names incised on rock in the Nedon valley, *c.* 500–475? Skias, *AE* 1911, 112 f. *IG* v. 1. 1362a–g. *SGDI* iv, p. 756. *DGE* 67. *SEG* xi. 969.

**6.** Gravestone of Charop(i)nos and Aristodemos; *c.* 500–475? *IG.* v. 1. 1356. *SGDI* 4668. *DGE* 66. Lost.                    PL. 39

**7.** Graffiti on three sherds from the precinct of Apollo Korythos; *c.* 500–450? Versakes, op. cit. 114, fig. 62. NM?

**8.** Later copy of a 5th-c. dedication by 'the (Mes)sanioi' to Apollo at Delphi; (*c.* 500–450?). Daux, *BCH* lxi (1937), 67 ff. fig. 1. Delphi Mus.                    PL. 39

**9.** Gravestone of Chnoadas; *c.* 450? *IG* v. 1. 1357. *SGDI* 4669. Lost?

**10.** Dedication on a second spear-butt from the precinct of Apollo Korythos; *c.* 450? Versakes, op. cit. 90, 114, fig. 28. *DGE* 68a. *SEG* xi. 993.                    PL. 39

**11.** Stone pillar-base bearing a dedication to Apollo Korythos; *c.* 425? Versakes, op. cit. 115 ff., fig. 63.

**12–13.** Dedications (in the Ionic script) by the Messenians of Naupaktos at Olympia and Delphi; *c.* 424. Roehl³, 30. 45. *SIG*³ 80–81. *Ol.* v. 259. *IG* v. 1. 1568. *GHI*² 65 and p. 263. *SEG* xi. 1210. Olympia Mus. 5. See also N. Colonial area **33** (Mende).                    PL. 71

*Inscription attributed to Messenia*

**14.** Grave-stele of Sko(t?)eas of Messene from an Athenian cemetery; *c.* 500–450? *IG* i². 1030. EM.

# ARKADIA

FIG. 40. Arkadia, Elis

*Notes on letter-forms* (E = Elis)

α4 is used only in an informal script on clay counters (**37**).

ε5, a shorthand form, occurs on counters (**37**), and on two inscriptions from Lousoi (**35–36**), all of the 5th c.

Ϝ2 appears with ι2 in **38**, an inscription showing Achaian influence. *Vau* was still in use in the early 4th c. (*IG* v. 2. 3).

ʒ is used in Arkadia to express the sibilant σ in the plaques **2** and **27** (see p. 213). In Elean it expresses the initial letter of Ζεύς in the dative τōι Ζι (E **2**, E **3**); cf. also ʒεκα for δεκα, E **10**.

In formal inscriptions ⊢ι persisted, even into the 4th c. (*IG* v. 2. 3). The open ⊢3 occurs on the dedication **25** at Delphi. In less formally inscribed dedications on bronzes, ⊢2 appears spasmodically throughout the 5th c.; cf. **35, 36**, and the bronze by Hybristas, **39**. The aspirate was not used in the Elean dialect.

θ3 is established in cursive writing by the late 5th c. (**37**). It also occurs on the legal text **29** from Mantinea (middle of the 5th c.?), and on two inscriptions of the first half, which are not certainly Arkadian: the dedication of Tellon at Olympia (**22**), and the coin bearing a legend θαλι, doubtfully ascribed to the insignificant little state Thaliadai (cf. *HN*², 456).

The crooked ι2 appears only on three inscriptions, two (**2, 3**) certainly from Arkadia and one (**38**) found at Olympia; all probably come from a state very near the Achaian border (Pheneos?).

The doubled ξ3 occurs in 5th-c. Arkadian (**24**).

ϙ is normal in the 6th c. (**1**, E **1**). The plaque **2** in the late years of the 6th c. does not use it (δεκο Ϝετεα), nor the phiale **12** in the early 5th, nor the base **20**; but it had not completely disappeared by the 5th c., for it recurs at least once in the legend Αρκαδιϙον on the federal coinage **10**.

ρ2 becomes the normal type at the beginning of the 5th c. (cf. **11** and following).

σ2 is not common (**7, 12, 22**); for ʒ see pp. 212 f. σ2 is the normal type at Elis.

υι is used in the earliest inscription (**1**); thereafter, υ2.

φι is used in **2**, which is dated late in the 6th c.; thereafter, in the 5th c., φ2 is regular, being still used on the coins of Pheneos, which begin in the last quarter of the 5th c. (*HN*², 452).

χ3, the form found elsewhere (e.g. Euboia and colonies) in the 5th c., is attested in Arkadia and Elis from the second quarter of the 5th c. onwards: Arkadia **27**, Elis **10, 15**.

ψι is attested for Mantinea in the late 5th c. on two of the counters (**37**), and in Psophis on her coins, which begin at some time in the 5th c. It may well have been used elsewhere in Arkadia, not only in these two widely separated communities; but as occasion for its use is rare, there are as yet no examples. The type is attested also at Ozolian Lokris; cf. further pp. 213 f.

*Punctuation* is rare in both Arkadian and Elean. It appears in three Arkadian inscriptions of the 5th c.: the plaque from Olympia **38**, which has P2; the bronze key from Lousoi (**23**), which has Pι; and the legal text **28** from Mantinea, which varies between ι and 2. Pι occurs in E **17**, and P2 in E **6, 8, 9**.

The *direction of the script* varies; in **1, 6, 15, 18, 23**, retrograde, in **2–5** from left to right. The plaque **2** shows that already by the late 6th c. long inscriptions were being written consistently from left to right; cf. also E **4–6**. There is, in fact, as yet only one example of *boustrophedon* script from Elis (**2**), and one from Arkadia (excluding the false *boustrophedon* of **5**). This is the brief dedication Χαριλαος | Αχελōιōι on a little bronze bull bought in Tripolis; the style of the bull is described as '*c*. 400', and the 'blue' *chi* is used (*IG* v. 2. 284). By the end of the 5th c., then, an Arkadian could still write *boustrophedon* if it suited the demands of the surface on which he was writing, just as in the first half of the century inscriptions were still written retrograde, on occasion; cf. **15, 18, 23**, and pp. 47 f. The *stoichedon* style is not yet attested for Elis; it is used occasionally in Arkadian, e.g. on the well-cut dedications at Olympia and Delphi, **20** and **25**, *c*. 480–450, and on the legal text **29**—though not on **28**, which is equally well cut. On the whole, the general standard of Arkadian writing is not so high that the lack of interest in this technique should surprise us; but there are so few examples of Arkadian masons' work on stone, as compared with the number of brief dedications on bronze (often cut hastily on awkward spaces), that to generalize about their standards may well be premature. Elean lettering also, on the bronze plaques found at Olympia, sometimes looks untidy and scamped; but we should remember that the bronzeworker must often have had the monotonous task of making three copies, one for each contracting party, and one to be deposited at Olympia.

Confined within the mountainous centre of the Peloponnese, Arkadia can hardly have taken a leading part in the introduction of the alphabet. The type found in general use throughout the area is basically the 'red', which presumably came first to those Arkadian states which lay on the route from Lakonia to Olympia, and thence penetrated gradually throughout all Arkadia. Of these two sources, it is closest to the Elean, in its lunate *gamma* and the use of *qoppa*, which has not yet been found in Lakonian except in an abecedarium (p. 192); indeed, it is impossible to decide whether the script on the two bases dedicated by Arkadians at Olympia is in fact Arkadian or Elean (**22, 30**). There are occasional variations between the script of one Arkadian community and another, which seem to be the result of contamination from the script of one of the states which encircled Arkadia. For instance, the crooked *iota* occurs in three archaic inscriptions which I have attributed on this ground to some place on the borders of Achaia (Pheneos?) (**2, 3, 38**); and in Tegea there is an athletic dedication which, if not actually Lakonian, shows that the Tegeate masons must on occasion have copied closely the work of their Lakonian neighbours (**5**). In general, Arkadian inscriptions are not marked by any notable characteristics in their letter-forms or technique, except for an interesting attempt attested at Lousoi, Psophis, and Mantinea during the fifth century to introduce new symbols for *epsilon*, *mu*, *psi*, and a new sibilant-letter σ3 (pp. 212 ff.). Most of the inscriptions from Arkadia are short dedications. Many of them are on small bronzes—rustic figures of herdsmen (**7–8**), an apple (**1**), a herald's staff (**16**), a key (**23**); there are also a spear-butt offered from spoils (**11**), the bases of three dedications at Olympia (**10, 22, 30**), two from Delphi (**17, 25**), and others at Mantinea and Tegea, a single stone statue, headless, from Asea (**6**), a sacral law from an unknown state (Pheneos?) (**2**), and two fragments of legal texts from Mantinea (**28, 29**). The latter serve to remind us of the reputation enjoyed by the Mantineans as arbitrators among other states, both in and beyond the Peloponnese; cf. Hdt. iv. 161 and *Ol.* v. 16 (Elis **17**).

The earliest Arkadian inscription, according to its letter-forms, should be the bronze apple (**1**) inscribed from right to left: Ϙōμαδας υνεθēκε, with the Arkadian form ὑν- for ἀν- which betrays its origin, though the exact provenance is unknown;[1] ει, νι, υι recall Lakonian inscriptions of the sixth century, and the apple might be dated at any time from the middle of the century to the fourth quarter. This is, so far, the only Arkadian inscription which shows υι. If indeed it was acquired in Elis (n. 1), it may have come from an Arkadian town by the border, such as Heraia. The next in date should be the bronze plaque, said to have come from Kalavryta, which bears a sacral law concerning the behaviour of women in some precinct of Demeter Thesmophoros (**2**). It is cut between

[1] The dealers through whose hands it passed mentioned both Elis and Sparta as the original provenance. Robert (*Inscr. Froehner* i. 33) suggests southern Arkadia, in the region of Megalopolis. The fifth letter is surely *delta*, not *rho*, as previously read.

guide-lines, and the archaic character of the letters is self-evident; but it runs from left to right throughout, each line ending with a complete word, and has ʋ2, χ2, all of which points bear out Professor Robinson's date for it late in the sixth century.[1] I have sought to show elsewhere[2] that the remarkable use of the crooked *iota*, normal in Corinth and Achaia, probably means that it came from somewhere on the Achaian border. Kleitor, tentatively suggested by Professor Robinson, is unlikely if Miss Richter's attribution of **11** to that state is correct, for **11**, not many years later than **2**, has the normal *iota*. Pheneos may therefore be suggested as the provenance, for the following reasons: (1) Pausanias says of Kleitor only that it had a precinct of Demeter (viii. 21. 3), whereas of Pheneos he says specifically that it had an archaic sanctuary of Demeter Thesmia, some fifteen stades outside the town, under Kyllene (viii. 15. 4); a casual find in this neighbourhood might well be brought to Kalavryta; (2) the territory of Pheneos marched with that of Achaia (Paus. viii. 15. 8); (3) it is true that later Pheneate inscriptions show the normal *iota*, but none of these antedates the middle of the fifth century (**33, 34**). If this is accepted, we may assign to archaic Pheneos also the lip of a bronze lebes bought in Kalavryta (**3**), inscribed [ι]ερα τ⟨α⟩ι Αρταμ⟨ι⟩τι. This has been attributed to Achaia by some, by others to Lousoi, where there was an old and famous sanctuary of Artemis Himera; but this last hypothesis is not confirmed by the only archaic fragment certainly of the sixth century which we have as yet from the site of Lousoi (**4**)—a few letters *en pointillé* on a thin strip of bronze from the bouleuterion; the reading appears to be: [- - -]δει ιαρος [- - -]; tailed *epsilon* and straight *iota* are certain. In Pheneate territory, on the way northwards to the Achaian states Aigeira and Pellene, there was a sanctuary of Apollo Pythios and Artemis, and a place called τὸ ἐπ' Ἄρτεμιν marked the boundary between Pheneos and Aigeira (Paus. viii. 15. 5–8); moreover, the form ἱερά is Arkadian rather than Achaian (ἰαρά). The date may be about the same as that of the plaque **2**. The crooked *iota* occurs also on a fragmentary bronze plaque from Olympia (**38**), probably belonging to the first quarter of the fifth century; the dialect apparently contains forms both Arkadian ([γ]ενεσται for [γ]ενεσθαι) and non-Arkadian (αἰ for εἰ), which would suit an origin on the border such as Pheneos.

Another inscription which should also belong to the late sixth century is the narrow stele(?) from Tegea which bears part of a victor's dedication to Athena Alea (**5**). The technique strongly resembles that of contemporary Lakonian inscriptions, the neat lettering being written along a curious double-looped guide-line, recalling such inscriptions as Lakonia **22, 28, 31**. One cannot help suspecting that it is in fact a Lakonian offering; but the decisive letters *gamma* and *qoppa* are absent, the literary dialect of the verse prevents any positive evidence against Arkadian,[3] and the stone is described as Mainalian. It is therefore included here among the inscriptions of Arkadia, with the qualification that it undoubtedly shows a strong Lakonian influence. The seated, headless statue found near Asea (**6**), inscribed Αγεμο on the front of the footstool, can hardly be later than the sixth century, but should, I think, be placed towards the end of the century,

---

[1] *CP* xxxviii (1943), 191.

[2] *JHS* lxix (1949), 30 f.

[3] Had it been prose, we should have expected not ἀνέθηκε but ὑνέθηκε or ὑνέθυσε in an Arkadian dedica-tion. It may be noted that in the inscription *IG* v. 2. 101, on a fragment of a marble basin(?) also from Tegea, the reading should be [---υνε]θυσε τα[ι---], not [---]θυσει ι[---] as there given.

as a clumsy provincial work, rather than at the beginning, as its xoanon-like simplicity might at first suggest.[1] It has been disputed whether it is a cult-statue of Artemis Hegemo or a grave-statue; the true answer may lie halfway between: that it is the memorial of a heroized dead person, like certain of the stelai of Lakonia.[2]

The spear-butt dedicated to the Tyndaridai as part of the spoils from a victory over Heraia (**11**) shows υ2, υι or 3, and ρ3; tailed *rho* is henceforth the regular type in Arkadian. In dating the butt tentatively *c.* 500 or slightly later, Miss Richter has pointed out that there was a sanctuary of the Dioskouroi at Kleitor (Paus. viii. 21. 4): that the Kleitorians made a dedication for a victory to Zeus at Olympia in the archaic period (Paus. v. 23. 7), and, according to the numismatic evidence, the flourishing coinage of Heraia ceased *c.* 500, and only revived in the last quarter of the century, the Heraian mint perhaps producing in the interval the common coinage marked Ἀρκαδικόν, and small change for local use. On general epigraphical grounds the date for the butt may well be correct; but another dedicator—Mantinea—is also possible. Wallace has suggested[3] that Heraia's coinage ceased *c.* 500–490 simply because all the chief Arkadian cities but one formed an anti-Spartan federation then and replaced their local coins by the Ἀρκαδικόν series (possibly minted at Heraia), which lasts until the late fifth century. The one exception was Mantinea, whose coinage continues through the century. Mantinea refused to join the rest against Sparta at Dipaia (Hdt. ix. 35. 2); and she also had a precinct of the Dioskouroi (Paus. viii. 9. 2).

The early coinage of Heraia (**9**) shows ε both 2 and 3, and ρ2 and 3; the legend reads now right to left, now left to right (E, Eρ, Eρα, Eραι); the type of Despoina's head also varies between an archaic and a later version. The common coinage (**10**) shows both Ϙ and κ, ρ3, and δι–3.

Two other inscriptions are similar in character to that on the spear-butt, and so may also be dated in the first years of the fifth century. One is on a bronze phiale dedicated by Kamo, perhaps from Melpea: Καμō υνεθυσε ται κορϝαι (**12**); the other is on a stone stele from Tegea (**13**), with a peaked top, which is inscribed Διος Στορπαο, and was perhaps erected originally in some spot where lightning had struck, so that the place was thereafter fenced off as sacred to Zeus. Both these inscriptions show a disproportionately small *omikron*, like that on the butt. On the phiale the three-stroked *sigma* is employed, which is not usual in Arkadian. It is used also in the badly written dedication by Phauleas to Pan on a little bronze herdsman, which is thought to have been found in the sanctuary of Pan at Melpea in south-western Arkadia (**7**). The bronze is dated on grounds of style to the late archaic period, at the end of the sixth century; we may note ε2 and υ2. The other similar bronze, dedicated by Aineias (**8**), may be a decade or so later, according to what is visible of the badly worn inscription. The dedication on a bronze statuette of

---

[1] It is set early in the 6th c. by Homann-Wedeking, 122; cf. Matz, *Gesch. d. gr. Kunst* i (1949), 199.

[2] There was a widespread cult of semi-mythical, heroic founders of states throughout Arkadia; cf. Immerwahr, *Die Kulte u. Mythen Arkadiens* i (1891), 257 ff. An instance of the heroizing of ordinary mortals after death is the cult of the soldiers from Oresthasia, who were killed in battle helping Tegea in her early wars with Sparta (Paus. viii. 41. 1).

[3] *JHS* lxxiv (1954), 32 ff. Whether the Heraian coins do in fact cease at the start of the 5th c. is a point which a new study of the types might clarify. The coin shown in B i, pl. 38, 3, might from its lettering be no earlier than *c.* 475.

Apollo (**14**), which is almost certainly from the precinct of Artemis at Lousoi, should belong also to the early fifth century (*c.* 480?) from the style of the statuette.[1] The same date, or a few years later, should hold too for the bronze statuette of a youth, inscribed on the base with the maker's name: Ϝυβρισστας | εποιἐσε (**39**). It was allegedly found near Epidauros. Scholars have suggested both Lakonia and Arkadia as its place of origin; the type, with short, straight hair and clumsily moulded features, is common in Arkadian statuettes of the late sixth and early fifth century, and also in some of the statuettes found on Lakonian sites. If Hybristas was Arkadian (as one hopes, reluctant to assign so bad a work to the skilled bronze-workers of Lakonia), then perhaps he was a Tegeate, for the neat, splayed *alpha* of the inscription recalls the near-Lakonian of **5**.

Several other brief inscriptions from Arkadia may be dated very tentatively in the first quarter of the fifth century: the stele cut like a triglyph from near Kleitor, dedicated by Arminidas (**15**): the herald's staff of Thelpousa, found at Olympia, inscribed: καρυξ δαμοσιος Θελφοισιος (**16**): the dedication of a bronze statue, δεκαταν πολεμιὄν, by the people of Gortys (Kortys) at Delphi (**17**): the stele from Tegea which records the honour of προϜεδρα at the games to the Pasitimidai (**18**). This last inscription is repeated on each side of the stone, once horizontally from left to right, and once vertically and retrograde. The latter reads from the under line—presumably nearest to the spectator—to the upper, and the lettering on both sides looks close in date; perhaps the damage to the horizontal inscription occurred soon after the erection of the stele, and for that reason it was reinscribed.

The long base for a bronze group dedicated at Olympia (**20**) by Praxiteles 'of Syracuse and Kamarina, born in Mantinea' has been described in detail above, pp. 160 f. Though generally taken to be in the script of Arkadia, it has also been claimed for Syracuse.[2] It is certainly a debatable point, but I see no reason to deny an Arkadian origin. The alphabet conforms with the Mantinean script (for exceptions to the peculiar Mantinean *nu*, see p. 213), whereas I am not certain that enough is known of early Syracusan to be equally definite (pp. 263 ff.). What strikes the eye when looking at the whole base is that, though the inscription has a *terminus ante quem c.* 465, because the builders' waste from the temple of Zeus was laid over the foundation-blocks of the base, the lettering of the dedication appears noticeably more advanced than that of the sculptors' signatures which flank it on either side (pp. 106 f.). The latter can hardly be later than the first quarter of the fifth century (*c.* 480–475?); the *stoichedon* dedication suggests the following decade, *c.* 475–465. Was the script of Arkadia (or even of Syracuse) really so far in advance of its neighbours? Or was the dedication finally inscribed, and the monument erected, only just before the building of the temple began?[3]

---

[1] The dedication was read by Furtwaengler as τας Αρταμιτος αποβὄ|μιον τας Ϝἐμερας. Hiller (*IG* v. 2. 403) noted the odd shape of the letter which had been taken as *beta* (it resembles rather *lambda* with a nick across the vertical), and suspected that the inscription might be a forgery. Can it be απο Λο⟨υ⟩σιὄν? (For this form of the ethnic, see Steph. Byz., s.v. Λουσοί.) The letter read as *mu* might be *sigma*, for the line turns in 'false' *boustrophedon* at this point. But ἀπό should mean 'from the spoils of'; hardly likely in a precinct at Lousoi itself!

[2] Rhys Carpenter, *AJA* xlix (1945), 453; Guarducci, *Ann.* xxvii–ix (1949–51), 104 f.

[3] It is possible that the group, being a large one for which four sculptors were commissioned, took a long time to make, and that for some reason the sculptors' signatures were drafted onto their blocks of the base at an early stage of the work. The last line of the dedication could be interpreted to mean that Praxiteles himself was dead when it was composed, which would suggest that it was inscribed after the sculptors' work was finished.

The battered inscription on the base of a lost bronze statue (artist unknown; cf. Paus. vi. 10. 9), which was dedicated at Olympia by Tellon of Oresthasia (**22**), may be dated in the second quarter of the century; it combines ε3 (once only) and σ2 with a dotted *theta*, which one would not normally expect in any formal inscription from the Peloponnese before the middle of the century. The other offering by an Arkadian athlete at Olympia, the base of the statue of Kyniskos of Mantinea by Polykleitos (**30**), can hardly be much earlier than *c.* 450, in view of Polykleitos' activity during the last quarter of the fifth century. Both these bases, as was remarked above (p. 208) may equally well be Elean works.

Other inscriptions which may be placed conjecturally in the second quarter of the century are the bronze key, headed like a snake, dedicated in the Artemision at Lousoi (**23**), the base of an offering by Polyxena at Tegea (**24**), the dedication of the people of Kaphyia at Delphi for a victory (**25**), which shows the unusual Ͱ3, and the base at Tegea for two statues of Athena Astyochos (= Polias) and Herakles (**26**). The only inscription of any length is the bronze plaque which belonged originally to the precinct of Athena Alea at Tegea, and which contains two contracts (one cancelled by deliberate erasure) concerning deposits of money made there by Xouthias son of Philachaios (**27**). As the dialect of the text is not the true Arkadian, it is generally concluded that Xouthias was one of those Spartans who evaded the currency regulations of his state by depositing a sum outside Lakonia. In this event, he must have drawn up the terms of contract himself; but the plaque was inscribed in Tegea, for the alphabet is plainly Arkadian (cf. in particular lunate *gamma* and tailed *rho*); from their appearance, the second contract was made not long after the first. The crossed *theta* is still used, but *epsilon* has settled into the type with horizontal bars (4), and *nu* varies between sloping (3) and upright (4). In both an asymmetrical *upsilon* is used, which may be a particular trick of the cutter. It cannot be dated closely, but the occasional use of ν4 may be an indication that it should not be regarded as earlier than the middle of the century.

One of the most interesting problems in Arkadian is that of the new symbols which appear during the fifth century, at Lousoi and Psophis in the north, and Mantinea in the south. They are four in all: ε5, μ3, ψ1, and σ3. All are attested at Mantinea, at Lousoi the *epsilon* only (p. 213), at Psophis the *psi*. Since both the examples from Lousoi occur on dedications in the sanctuary of Artemis, it is conceivable that both were the work of outsiders, e.g. from Mantinea, and that we should exclude Lousoi from the category. The *psi* of Psophis is certain, for it is used on her coinage. The sibilant σ3 has been found so far only on a single stone block bearing two columns from an inscription which was originally cut in a series of columns on the wall of a building in the precinct of Athena Alea at Mantinea (**29**), in the same manner as the famous Gortyn Code. Its use for the dentals τ in τις and οτεδι, ειτε and the first *delta* of απυδεδομιν[ος] makes it clear that the Arkadian pronunciation of these dentals[1] was sufficiently different from the plain unvoiced τ and voiced δ for some innovator in Mantinea (if not elsewhere) to evolve a

---

[1] The unvoiced dental τ affected thus in Arkadian is that which denotes the original labio-velar *qu̯+front vowel (*qu̯is > τις > ϲις). The sibilant sound given to the voiced dental δ in απυϡεϡομιν[ος] may be dissimilation; cf. Buck, 62 f.

separate symbol to express it. The Arkadian sound was evidently a kind of palatal sibilant, such as is attested for the kindred dialect of Cyprus by the Hesychian gloss: σί · τί Κύπριοι: for the dental τ in τις, οτις, and τε is expressed by *zeta* in the archaic plaque **2** (as are also the dentals of δέ, δίκαια, Δί, and ϝειδός in early Elean; p. 207), and that of τετρακατιαι by *tau*+*zeta* on the plaque from Tegea (**27**). The letter-form has been interpreted, from its appearance and value, as a form of the *ṣāḏê*,[1] presumably handed on automatically in its place in the abecedarium. The theory is attractive, but why then should it not have been used instead of *zeta* in the other Arkadian inscriptions? Taking into consideration the symbols for *epsilon* and *mu*, which have very much the appearance of innovations, we may hazard the guess that all are the work of some innovator during the course of the fifth century, which did not survive the introduction of the Ionic alphabet in the early fourth. The case of the *mu* seems to be a clear one. Its appearance is confined as yet to Mantinea, where it is found in the legal texts **28** and **29**, and on one of the earliest of a large series of small clay counters inscribed with personal names (**37**). Fougères saw in it a descendant of the old Phoenician curving *mem*;[2] but there is no doubt that the Mantineans knew the normal *mu* also, for the latter is used always in the legend Μα on their coinage, which apparently begins in the early fifth century (**19**). The bases **20** and **30** also show μ2, but neither can be certainly termed Mantinean; a third base (**32**), however, which was found in Mantinea and has been ascribed to the campaign against Tegea and her allies in 422 (Thuc. iv. 134; cf. *IG* v. 2. 282), uses the normal μ2, and so does one of the earliest of the counters **37**. This suggests that the form was invented as a shorthand form of *mu* (like the straight line for *mu* which occurs at Axos in Crete, p. 309), but never succeeded in ousting the accepted form. The single stroke for *epsilon* is plainly a form of shorthand; it occurs in Lousoi on a bronze rim and an amphora-handle (**35, 36**), both inscribed with the usual formula ιερα Αρτεμι⟨τι⟩, and in Mantinea on (*a*) a stone stele or base (now lost) inscribed Αχελοιο from a precinct of the god of the Arkadian river Acheloos (*IG* v. 2. 285) and (*b*) all those counters which antedate the introduction of the Ionic script. The Lousoi examples of this *epsilon*, which both show also open *heta*, might be dated at any time between the early and the late fifth century; the counters are generally dated in the last quarter. Neither of the legal texts from Mantinea uses this letter, and it is possible that it was only invented after they were written. The *psi*, again, looks like a deliberate invention, presumably by someone who, himself using 'red' *chi* Ψ, had seen the use of Ψ for *psi* in the alphabet of the Argivo-Corinthian group, and evolved this simple variation. It is found in the legend Ψō on the coins of Psophis, which appear to start at some time in the first half of the fifth century (**21**), and twice on the counters at Mantinea. But it occurs also outside Arkadia; it is attested in inscriptions of the period *c.* 525–450 from Ozolian Lokris across the Corinthian Gulf (pp. 105 ff., **2–4**), and, although so simple a form might have been evolved from the Ψ (*psi*) independently in Lokris and Arkadia, it is tempting to conjecture that there is a connexion, and that the link may be through Achaia, lying between, whose script is a mixture of various elements—the crooked *iota*

---

[1] Larfeld[3], 220 ff. Apart from its use in 5th-c. Mantinean, the occurrence of this letter as a sibilant is doubtful: in Messapic (= Tarantine) on the kerykeion Taras **13** (where it might be an error for 3-stroke *sigma*), and in late Pamphylian with an uncertain value; cf. Neppi Modona, *RIGI* xi–xii (1927–8), 58 ff., and above, p. 40.

[2] *BCH* xvi (1892), 571.

and *san* of the Argivo-Corinthian group, with the 'red' forms of *xi* and *chi*. But as yet none of the inscriptions from Achaia or her colonies has given occasion for the use of the rare letter, except for one doubtful example (p. 259).

The law from the precinct of Athena Alea (**29**) was dated *c.* 480–460 by Vollgraff, on the evidence of the letter-forms.[1] All the circular letters are made with a cutting-compass, leaving a central dot, so that the dotted *theta* is indistinguishable from *omikron*. Its general appearance may be compared with two Argive texts (p. 165, Argos **39***a–b*), and, to be consistent with my dating of those, I should set this Arkadian text, with its dotted *theta*, a little later than 460. The content of the law has been already fully discussed by many scholars. It does not form part of a code, but records a particular verdict given over an involved case of homicide within the sacred precinct. The other legal fragment (**28**), found rebuilt into the later Bouleuterion at Mantinea, is cut on the shaft or drum of a Doric column, broken at one end and sliced across the diameter, so that we have only a mutilated fragment of the text left; it is defined in *IG* v. 2. 26 as a *lex sacra*, but even this rests only on the uncertain readings [χρε]σμο in l. 1 and χρε[σμοι] in l. 5. The crossed *theta* is still used, but otherwise it looks no earlier than **29**, and the two are probably fairly close in time to each other. Other examples of legal texts on column-shafts are found in the Aegean islands of Paros, Naxos, and Thera (p. 55).

The list of proxenoi from Lousoi (**31**), in which the *nu* sometimes approaches the upright form 4, should perhaps be dated on that account in or after the middle of the fifth century. The dedication to Apollo at Mantinea (**32**) has, as we have seen, been assigned to the last third of the fifth century, during the Archidamian War. The only other Arkadian inscriptions in the local alphabet which should be mentioned are on clay tesserae or counters found partly in the theatre, partly in the stoa at Mantinea, in lettering which ranges from the second half of the fifth to the third century (**37**). They have been associated with some constitutional procedure, possibly with the constitution drawn up by Nikodoros of Mantinea, the friend of the atheist Diagoras of Melos.[2] The dotted *theta* is used throughout, also α4 (cf. p. 136, Megara **8**), and once δ3.

SELECT CATALOGUE[3]

**1.** Bronze apple dedicated by Komadas; *c.* 550–525? *IGA* 556. L. Robert, *Collection Froehner* i (1936), no. 29, pl. 13. *SEG* xi. 1044. Paris, Cab. Méd.    PL. 40

**2.** Bronze plaque inscribed with a law concerning the ritual of Demeter Thesmophoros; *c.* 525? D. M. Robinson, *CP* xxxviii (1943), 191 ff., pl. 1. Beattie, *CQ* xli (1947), 66 ff. Jeffery, *JHS* lxix (1949), 30 f. Buck 16. *SEG* xii. 1112. D. M. Robinson Coll.    PL. 40

**3.** Lip of a bronze lebes dedicated to Artemis, bought in Kalavryta; *c.* 525? Purgold, *AZ* 1882, 393 f. *SGDI* 1600. *IG* v. 2. 401. Roehl[3], 118. 1. *SEG* xi. 1118. Private coll.    PL. 40

**4.** Fragment of a bronze strip from Lousoi; *c.* 525? Wilhelm, *Ö.Jh.* iv (1901), 77 f., no. 9, fig. 153. *IG* v. 2. 400. Lost?

---

[1] *Mél. Boisacq* ii. 338.

[2] Cf. Hiller, *IG* v. 2, pp. 47 and 65, *ad* n. 323.

[3] I have omitted in particular the following inscriptions, known to me only from the preliminary reports: bronze double-axe from Pallantion (Arvanitopoullos, *Epigraphike* ii (1939), 255); statue-base from Glanitsa (Lemerle, *BCH* lxii (1938), 460); and *IG* v. 2. 95 and 425, both known only from poor sketches.

**5.** Stele dedicated to Athena Alea by an athlete, Tegea; *c.* 525–500? Rhomaios, *BCH* xxxvi (1912), 353 ff. *IG* v. 2. 75. *DGE* 650. Friedlaender 155. *SEG* xi. 1065. Tegea Mus. 1310.                    PL. 40

**6.** Seated stone statue inscribed Αγεμο̄, from Asea, *c.* 525? Curtius, *AZ* xxxi (1874), 110. Koumanoudes, *AE* 1874, 480 ff. and pl. 71. *IGA* 92. *SGDI* 1185. Roberts, i. 274. Stais, *Cat. Nat. Mus. Athens*, 6. *IG* v. 2. 559. *DGE* 677. *SEG* xi. 1163. NM 6.                    PL. 40

**7.** Bronze statuette of a herdsman dedicated to Pan by Phauleas, from Melpea; *c.* 510–500? Studniczka, *AM* xxx (1905), 65 ff., Beil. and pl. 4. *IG* v. 2. 555. *DGE* 676. Lamb, *Gk. and Rom. Bronzes*, 93. Richter, *MMNYC Bronzes*, 93 and *AGA*, fig. 240. *SEG* xi. 1162. New York, MM 08.258.7.

**8.** Similar dedication by Aineas; *c.* 500? Richter, *AJA* xlviii (1944), 5, figs. 11–13 and *AGA*, fig. 241. *SEG* xi. 1043. New York, MM 43.11.3.

**9.** Coinage of Heraia; *c.* 525–500? B ii. 1. 835 ff., pl. 38. *HN²*, 447 f. Cahn, *Monnaies grecques archaïques* (1947), 15, 29, fig. 20.

**10.** Federal coinage inscribed Αρκαδικον; *c.* 500–417? B ii. 1. 843 ff., pl. 38. *HN²*, 448. Wallace, *JHS* lxxiv (1954), 32 ff.

**11.** Bronze spear-butt dedicated to the Tyndaridai from a victory over Heraia; *c.* 500–480? Richter, *AJA* xliii (1939), 194 ff., figs. 4–6. *SEG* xi. 1045. New York, MM 38.11.7.                    PL. 40

**12.** Bronze phiale dedicated to Kore by Kamo; *c.* 500–480? *IG* v. 2. 554. *SGDI* 373. Roehl³, 100. 14. *DGE* 676. Buck 15. *SEG* xi. 1161. NM 7959.                    PL. 41

**13.** Stone stele marking a precinct of Zeus the Thunderer; *c.* 500–480? Arvanitopoullos, *AE* 1906, 63 ff. Rhomaios, *AE* 1911, 150. 1. Kern, pl. 11. *IG* v. 2. 64. *DGE* 652. *SEG* xi. 1067. Tegea Mus. 217.

**14.** Bronze statuette of a youth, perhaps from the precinct of Artemis at Lousoi; *c.* 480. Froehner, *Coll. Béarn* i (1905), 21 ff., pl. 5. Furtwaengler, *Kleine Schriften* ii. 458 ff., figs. 2–3. *IG* v. 2. 403. Private coll.

**15.** Stele inscribed with the name Arminidas, from near Kleitor; *c.* 500–475? Meyer, *Pelop. Wanderungen* (1939), 88 ff., no. 1, pl. 27a. *SEG* xi. 1123. Olympia Mus.

**16.** Herald's staff from Thelpousa, found at Olympia; *c.* 500–475? Weber, *Ol. Forschungen* i (1944), 158 f., pl. 67a. *SEG* xiii. 270. Olympia Mus.

**17.** Dedication for a victory by Gortys, from Delphi; *c.* 500–475? *SIG³* 49. *FD* ii. 1. 247 f., fig. 194. *DGE* 671. *SEG* xi. 1168. Delphi Mus. 1657.

**18.** Stele giving the right of 'prohedra' to the Pasitimidai, from Tegea; *c.* 500–475? Mendel, *BCH* xxv (1901), 267 f. Wilhelm, 8 ff. *IG* v. 2. 113. Roehl³, 105. 1. *DGE* 651. *SEG* xi. 1074. Tegea Mus.

**19.** Coinage of Mantinea, *c.* 500 onwards (Mα, Mαv). B ii. 1. 861 ff., pl. 38. *HN²*, 449.

**20.** Dedication by Praxiteles of Mantinea, Syracuse, and Kamarina, at Olympia; *c.* 480–475? *Ol.* v. 266 and 630–1. Roberts i. 277. *SGDI* 1200. *IGA* 95. *IG* v. 2. 47. Friedlaender 142. Kunze, *Olympiabericht* v (1956), 152, fig. 60. *SEG* xi. 1222. Olympia Mus. 23+28.                    PL. 41

**21.** Coinage of Psophis (Ψ, Ψο̄, Ψο̄φι); *c.* 475 onwards? B ii. 1. 873 ff., pl. 38. *HN²*, 453.

**22.** Dedication of the victor Tellon of Oresthasia at Olympia; *c.* 475–450. *Ol.* v. 147. Olympia Mus. 254.

**23.** Bronze key, property of Artemis at Lousoi; *c.* 475–450? *IG* v. 2. 399. *DGE* 670. Boston, MFA.

**24.** Dedication by Polyxena at Tegea; *c.* 475–450? *IG* v. 2. 108. Roehl³, 106. 11. Tegea Mus.

**25.** Dedication for a victory by the people of Kaphyia, at Delphi; *c.* 475–450? *SIG*³ 48. *IG* v. 2, p. 73. *FD* iii. 4. 258, no. 191, pl. 29. 1. Delphi Mus. 1562.

**26.** Base for statues of Athena Astyochos and Herakles, at Tegea; *c.* 475–450? *SGDI* 1218. Roberts i. 278. *IG* v. 2. 77. Roehl³, 106. 6–7. *SEG* xi. 1066. Tegea Mus.

**27.** Bronze plaque recording sums of money deposited by Xouthias son of Philachaios with Athena Alea at Tegea; *c.* 450? *IG* v. 2. 159. Comparetti, *Ann.* ii (1916), 246 ff. Roehl³, 121 f., 1. Buck, *CP* xx (1925), 133 f. *SIG*³ 1213. *DGE* 57. *SEG* xi. 1083. NM.      PL. 41

**28.** Part of a legal text inscribed on the drum or shaft of a Doric column at Mantinea; *c.* 460–450? Fougères, *BCH* xvi (1892), 576 ff. *IG* v. 2. 261, pl. 2. Roehl³, 106. 8. Kern, pl. 11. *DGE* 661 (g). *SEG* xi. 1086. Tegea Mus.

**29.** Part of a legal text inscribed on a wall in the precinct of Athena Alea at Mantinea. Fougères, op. cit. 569 ff. and *Mantinée* (1898), 523 ff. Hiller, *Arkadische Forschungen* (1911), 15 ff. *IG* v. 2. 262. Comparetti, *Ann.* i (1914), 1 ff., pls. 1–3. Roehl³, 107. 9. Kern, pl. 11. *DGE* 661. Buck, op. cit. 136 ff. Vollgraff, *Mélanges Boisacq* ii. 335 ff. Buck 17. *SEG* xi. 1087. Tegea Mus.

**30.** Dedication by the victor Kyniskos of Mantinea at Olympia; *c.* 450? *Ol.* v. 149. Roehl³, 106. 10. Richter³, 247. Moretti 14. *SEG* xiv. 356. Olympia Mus. 165.

**31.** Bronze disk inscribed with a list of proxenoi, from Lousoi; *c.* 450–430? Wilhelm, *Ö.Jh.* iv (1901), 78 f., fig. 156. Pernice, *AA* 1904, 32. 47. *IG* v. 2. 387. Kern, pl. 21. *DGE* 669. Jacobsthal, *Diskoi* (1933), 29. *SEG* xi. 1114. Berlin Mus. 8721.

**32.** Base for a dedication to Apollo by Mantinea for a victory over Tegea (?) and allies at Mantinea; *c.* 422? Roberts i. 281. *SGDI* 1198. Roehl³, 106. 12. *IG* v. 2. 282. Lost?      PL. 41

**33.** Coinage of Pheneos (Φε, Φενικον); 5th *c.* B ii. 3. 598 ff., pl. 224. *HN*², 452.

**34.** Terra-cotta head of a boar, dedicated to Hermes at Pheneos; 5th c.? (possibly 4th). *IGA*, adn. 60. Farnell, *Cults* v. 80. *IG* v. 2. 360. Winterthur Mus.

**35.** Lip of a bronze vase, property of Artemis, said to be from Lousoi; 5th c. Robert, *Coll. Froehner* i (1938), 27, pl. 11. *SEG* xi. 1115. Paris, Cab. Méd.

**36.** Handle of a bronze amphora, property of Artemis, from Lousoi; 5th c. Perdrizet, *REA* i (1899), 281. *IG* v. 2. 402. *DGE* 670. Robert, op. cit. 26. Lost.

**37.** Series of clay counters inscribed with proper names, from Mantinea; *c.* 450–400. *IG* v. 2. 323. Tegea Mus.      PL. 41

*Inscriptions attributed to Arkadia*

**38.** Fragment of a bronze plaque from Olympia; early 5th c.? *Ol.* v. 27. Jeffery, *JHS* lxix (1949), 31, fig. 7. *SEG* xi. 1168a. Olympia Mus. 750.      PL. 40

**39.** Bronze statuette of a youth, made by Hybristas, said to have been found near Epidauros; *c.* 480–470? *IG* iv. 1476. Lamb, op. cit. 95, pl. 32a. Neugebauer, op. cit. 48 f., 129, pl. 27; *AA* 1938, 336 f., and 1942, 486. Elderkin, *AJA* xliv (1940), 232 and fig. 11. Paris, Dutuit Coll., Petit Palais.      PL. 41

## ELIS

*Letter-forms*; see Arkadia, pp. 206 f. and Fig. 40.

The archaic alphabet of Elis, known to us mostly from the many rhetrai on bronze plaques found at Olympia, resembles those of Lakonia and Arkadia, especially the latter; for it differs from Arkadian only in the use of three-stroked *sigma* (Arkadian normally using the four-stroked), and from Lakonian in the use of lunate *gamma* and *qoppa*. It has little in common with Achaian, and (as was said above, pp. 184 f.), if it is assumed that these three scripts are derived one from the other, it is perhaps more likely that Lakonia was the pioneer than Elis; for Lakonia had possible sources in Rhodes or Delphi, whereas there is no obvious external source for Elis.

In fact there is no reason for believing that the alphabet arrived very early in Elis, except for the literary tradition that the Olympic victor list began in 776, and for the undoubted existence among the treasures at Olympia of an archaic bronze disk, inscribed with the terms of the Olympic Truce, and bearing the names of Lykourgos, Iphitos, and Kleosthenes (see below). I have already referred to the problem of the old victor list (pp. 59 ff.). Even if the traditional date for the first Olympiad is proved to be roughly correct, as seems very possible,[1] and even if the traditional list of victors' names does go back to that date, we still have no evidence that the names were recorded in writing from the beginning; they may have been handed down in the memories of successive hieromnemones. When Hippias of Elis produced a list of Olympic victors as a chronological framework for his History, perhaps he had some written lists from the site on which to base it; but perhaps he had no more than a collection of bronze plaques like *Ol.* v. 17 (p. 59), one having been dedicated by the Hellenodikai after each Olympiad. Pausanias tells us that Paraballon, an Elean victor in the *diaulos*, caused the names of the victors to be inscribed in the gymnasium at Olympia; and Pausanias' wording hints that the inscription recorded that Paraballon was the first to do this, and left it as an incentive for the future (vi. 6. 3): ὑπελίπετο δὲ καὶ ἐς τοὺς ἔπειτα φιλοτιμίαν, τῶν νικησάντων Ὀλυμπίασι τὰ ὀνόματα ἀναγράψας ἐν τῷ γυμνασίῳ τῷ ἐν Ὀλυμπίᾳ. Euenorides of Elis, on becoming a Hellenodikes, also had the names of the victors publicly inscribed (Paus. vi. 8. 1). The dates of these two are unknown, and disputed.[2] The most important list (the victors in the stadion) must surely have been inscribed in public *c.* 400, or whenever Hippias produced it; these other people, if they lived later, may have compiled lists of *all* the victors at each Olympiad. But so far no inscribed blocks or plaques, early or late, bearing simply lists have been found.

There can be no doubt that the so-called Disk of Iphitos bore an archaic inscription. From the descriptions of Aristotle, Phlegon of Tralles, and Pausanias,[3] it was a bronze disk of unknown size—not necessarily an athletic disk, cf. Arkadia **31**—bearing an inscription written ἑλιγμῷ (spirally) which said that 'the terms of the Olympic Truce and Festival were thus and thus, drawn up by (or in the time of? ὑπό or ἐπί?) so-and-so'. The disk certainly bore the name of Lykourgos (Aristotle), and probably those of Iphitos and Kleosthenes of Pisa also (Pausanias, Phlegon). Was this a genuine document of *c.* 776? It is perhaps more likely that in the archaic period each of the spondophoroi, when they went forth to proclaim the coming Truce through the states of Greece, carried

[1] Cf. Hampe, *Die Antike* xiv (1938), 245.

[2] Förster, *Die Sieger in d. olympischen Spielen* ii. 7. 24, sets Euenorides doubtfully in the 3rd c. B.C. and leaves Paraballon undated. The Hellenistic period is suggested by Körte, *Hermes* 1904, 236 f. Jacoby believes that both may belong to the first half of the 5th c., or Paraballon even to the 6th; *FGH* iii, Elis u. Olympia: Einleitung, 225 f. and T1–2.

[3] Aristotle, F 146 Rose; Phlegon, *FGH* ii. 257, F 1; Paus. v. 20. 1.

such a disk as a badge of his identity, and read the text of the Truce from it; in Aristotle's day there was only one of these venerable disks preserved in the sanctuary, and it passed for the original document drawn up by the three whose names were mentioned on it.

I have omitted from the following discussion a number of little statuettes or utensils from Olympia bearing very brief inscriptions of the sixth or fifth century. The best evidence for the script at present comes from the series of bronze plaques which have survived, on which the Eleans wrote their 'rhetrai'—treaties of alliance (**6, 12**) and decrees approved by their ruling body (**4, 5, 10, 15**). Judged by the general standards of development attributed to the other Peloponnesian scripts, none of the Elean plaques should be earlier than the last quarter of the sixth century. The early history of Elis, Pisa, and Triphylia is little known, and that little subject to dispute. The plaques, far from solving any of the problems, have been themselves the cause of some of the uncertainty. Some authorities[1] have claimed that a plaque referring to a single Hellenodikes (**15**) should be assigned to the years before 580, because in that year, according to Pausanias and perhaps others,[2] the establishment of two Hellenodikai was decreed; and that a plaque referring to the people of Triphylian Skillous (**17**) must be earlier than 572, when Skillous was sacked by the Eleans.[3] In the other extreme, it has been maintained that the two Hellenodikai were not created until after 471/470 (the year when Elis was synoecized: Diod. xi. 54. 1), and that **17** should not be dated before 371/370.[4] As our concern is with the alphabet, we shall first seek only to suggest dates for the lettering of the plaques without reference to their possible historical connexions, and then see whether these dates are obviously incompatible with the content of the texts—though here there is admittedly a wide margin for error.

The rhetra **15** should, by appearance, be dated fairly early in the fifth century; the lettering may be compared, for general similarity, with that of the Arkadian dedication of Praxiteles at Olympia c. 480–465 (p. 211, Arkadia **20**), and with the epitaph of the Argives who fell at Tanagra c. 458/457 (p. 164, Argos **30**); we may note in **15** ε2 or 4, θ2, λ1–2, v3, ρ3, χ3; on the whole, it appears to resemble the Arkadian more closely than the Argive. As for the content, the mention of one Hellenodikes does not necessarily deny the existence of two, and ten mnai sounds an incredibly heavy fine for the early sixth century.[5]

The plaque **17** (referring to Skillous) shows θ2 and 3, v4, and punctuation 1; *rho* is tailless. It should not be earlier than c. 450. Elis apparently had trouble with Pisa and

[1] Kirchhoff[4], 162 f.; Busolt, *Griech. Staatsk.*[3] i. 148.

[2] Paus. v. 9. 4; Hellanikos and Aristodemos (two or twelve, β or ιβ? see *FGH* i. 4, F 113).

[3] Blass, *SGDI* 1151; Geyer, *RE*, s.v. Skillous, 526.

[4] Kahrstedt, *Gött. Gel. Nach.* 1927, 157 ff.

[5] The meaning of this rhetra is still disputed. The Transliteration of Plates gives the version which seems to me the better: that Patrias is the public secretary of the governing body of Elis, responsible for drafting this and all other rhetrai. Because he has been wrongly accused of abusing his office in some way, this rhetra is passed (*a*) to give him (with his family and property) immunity against any such irresponsible charges in future; (*b*) to define the procedure of punishment to be followed if anyone does so charge him, and if the judges do not enforce the penalty; (*c*) to punish any who maltreat a man on trial; and (*d*) to include Patrias himself in such punishments, if he does in fact abuse his office. In the alternative view (see, for example, Buck 61) πατριά = the gens (of an accused man), which, with his family, is now no longer to be bound by the primitive law which attached liability equally to the kin of the accused. But it is hard to believe that this primitive law had survived into the 5th c. at Elis; and who is the official called the 'scribe of the gens' (πατριᾶς ὁ γροφεύς), thus introduced in the final clause?

parts of Triphylia between the Persian and Peloponnesian Wars,[1] and it is conceivable that Skillous, which was certainly inhabited in 398 (Xen. *Hell.* vi. 5. 2), may have been repopulated already in the fifth century, and had some connexion with this struggle against Elis. At all events, I cannot think that the plaque should be dated as late as 371/370, for we have no particular grounds for assuming that the Elean script was especially backward, and in the fragment *Ol.* v. 36, which is securely dated in 364,[2] the full Ionic script is used. The fragmentary text **17** suggests that Elis is establishing two men as καταστάται to regulate the affairs of the Skillountines after some emergency. It is possible that the fragment **18** may also belong to the same period of strife; it records sums of money borrowed κα(τ) τον π[ολεμον?] from one Zeuxias, and has been referred tentatively to the Peloponnesian War.[3]

A single broken plaque is inscribed *boustrophedon* (**2**). This fact by itself does not preclude its being placed as late as *c.* 525, and a date in the late archaic period is suggested by the letter forms ε3, υ2, as against the earlier εɪ used in **4** and **5**, which are both inscribed from left to right. **5**, which concerns temple regulations and their alteration, refers to a Boule of 500, and Kahrstedt would therefore date it later than 470;[4] I can only say that if this is correct, then the date of the treaty between Elis and Heraia (**6**) ought also to be brought down below 470, for its lettering is, if anything, later than that of **5** (εɪ still, but υ2, χ2). In the above inscriptions **4–6**, *lambda* and *rho* are still in the early form ɪ; the later form 2 is attested, as we have seen, in **15**; between these may be placed the treaty between the Anaitoi and Metapioi (**12**; λɪ, ρ2) and the manumission list **13** (υɪ–2, ρ2). In the second half of the century the signature of the sculptor Kalon (**19**), whose *floruit* may have been in the third quarter of the fifth century (p. 245), shows *gamma* Γ, ρ3, and σ2; we may note the same letters (and δ3) in **20**, an agreement concerning the renting of land, which has been assigned to the last quarter of the century, or the early years of the fourth (cf. *DGE* 419).

Apart from the plaques there is little early Elean material. The retrograde signature Ϙοιος μ᾽ αποϝσεν (**1**) on a bronze aryballos in the shape of a helmeted head, which was bought in Pyrgos, may well be Elean, for the spelling α for ε suggests the Elean dialect more than any other.[5] The type of helmet is dated in the second half of the sixth century; if the attribution is correct, it shows that *qoppa* was once used in Elean, as in Arkadian, although it had apparently gone out of use before the date of the first surviving plaques. A public dedication by Elis on the rim of a bronze lebes (**3**) probably belongs to the sixth century (cf. υɪ): τōι Ζι Ολυνπιōι τοι Ϝαλειοι, and ιαρα Διος added later by another hand. A similar rim, inscribed [- - - ανε]θ̄κε : Δι Κρονιōνι Ϝανακτι, may be of the early fifth century (**11**). A special series of coins, bearing a Zeus of early fifth-century type, has the legend Ολυνπικον retrograde (**7b**); the normal coinage bears a winged Nike of late archaic type, with the legend Ϝα retrograde (**7a**). The fragmentary bronze strip recording a dedication by an athlete Kordaphos of Lepreon (**14**) should belong, as Kunze suggests, to the period 500–450; we may note the *stoichedon* lettering, and Һɪ still in use.

---

[1] Hdt. iv. 148; Paus. v. 4. 7; 10. 2; Strabo 355. Cf. *Ol.* v. 42 ff.; Philippson, *RE*, s.v. Elis, 2393 f.

[2] *Ol.* v, p. 73.

[3] Meister, *Die griech. Dialekte* ii. 27; *Ol.* v. 40.

[4] Op. cit. 164 ff.

[5] Buck, 23 f. I am indebted to Dunbabin for dating the helmet.

## SELECT CATALOGUE

**1.** Signature of Koios on a bronze aryballos bought in Pyrgos; *c.* 550–525. Greenwell, *JHS* ii (1881), 69 ff. *IGA* 557. Roberts i. 254, n. 1. *Ol.* v. 629. *SGDI* 1176. Maximova, *Les Vases plastiques* (1927), 155 f., pl. 37. Cambridge, Fitzwilliam Mus. GR. 15. 1864.                PL. 42

**2.** *Boustrophedon* fragment of a law on a bronze plaque; *c.* 525? *Ol.* v. i. *IGA* 109. Roberts i. 290. *SGDI* 1147. Roehl³, 111. 1. Olympia Mus. 554.                PL. 42

**3.** Dedication of Eleans on a bronze lebes-rim; 6th c. Kunze and Schleif, *JdI* liii, *Olympiabericht* ii (1938), 104 f., figs. 65–66. Olympia Mus.

**4.** Bronze plaque bearing part of a law on aliens and the Olympic ritual; *c.* 500? *Ol.* v. 5 (+6?). *IGA* 115. *SGDI* 1158. Roehl³, 113. 12. Olympia Mus. 130 (+565?)                PL. 42

**5.** Bronze plaque bearing part of a law mentioning procedure for alteration of the law by a Boule of 500; *c.* 500? *Ol.* v. 7. *IGA* 113c, add. Roberts i. 296. *SGDI* 1156. Roehl³, 113. 8. *DGE* 412. *SEG* xi. 1181. Buck 64. Olympia Mus. 1014.                PL. 42

**6.** Treaty between Elis and Heraia; *c.* 500? *Ol.* v. 9 and pp. 795 f. Roberts i. 291. *BMC Bronzes*, 264. *SGDI* 1149. Roehl³, 111. 2. *SIG*³ 9. *DGE* 413. *GHI*² 5. *SEG* xi. 1182. Buck 62. BM.                PL. 42

**7a–b.** (*a*) earliest inscribed coinage of Elis; *c.* 500 onwards? (*b*) series inscribed Ολυνπικον; first half of 5th c.? B ii. 1. 887 ff., pl. 39. *HN*², 419 ff.

**8.** Bronze plaque with a decree concerning one Deukalion; *c.* 500–475? *Ol.* v. 11. *IGA* 113. Roberts i. 294. *SGDI* 1153. Roehl³, 112. 6. *DGE* 415. *SEG* xi. 1186. Buck 63. Olympia Mus. 261.                PL. 42

**9.** Fragment of bronze plaque with a law referring to 'the ancient writ' (το γραφος τἀρχαιον); *c.* 475? *Ol.* v. 3. *IGA* 111. *SGDI* 1157. Roehl³, 112. 3. *DGE* 410. *SEG* xi. 1177. Olympia Mus. 442+715.

**10.** Bronze plaque bearing a law concerning the tenure of sacred lands by the theokolos; *c.* 475? *Ol.* v. 4. *IGA* 113b, add. Roberts i. 295. *SGDI* 1154. Roehl³, 114. 9. *DGE* 411. *SEG* xi. 1178. Olympia Mus. 1015.

**11.** Fragmentary dedication on a lebes-rim; *c.* 475? Robert, *Coll. Froehner* i. 38, no. 34, pl. 32. Meritt, *AJP* lix (1938), 500. Paris, Cab. Méd.

**12.** Bronze plaque with the terms of an alliance between the Anaitoi and Metapioi; *c.* 475–450? *Ol.* v. 10. *IGA* 118. Roberts i. 297. *SGDI* 1150. Roehl³, 116. 14. *DGE* 414. *SEG* xi. 1183. Olympia Mus. 703.

**13.** Bronze plaque with part of a manumission list; *c.* 475–450? *Ol.* v. 12. *IGA* 552. *SGDI* 1161. *DGE* 416. *SEG* xi. 1253. Olympia Mus. 445.

**14.** Dedicatory inscription of Kordaphos of Lepreon; *c.* 475–450? Kunze, *Olympiabericht* v (1956), 156 f., fig. 63. Olympia Mus. B 1290.

**15.** Bronze plaque bearing a decree concerning one Patrias (?); *c.* 475–450? *Ol.* v. 2. *IGA* 112 and add. Roberts i. 292. *SGDI* 1152. Roehl³, 112. 4. *DGE* 409. Kahrstedt, *Gött. Gel. Nach.* 1927, 159 f. *SEG* xi. 1176. Buck 61. Olympia Mus. 771.                PL. 43

**16.** Gravestone of Rhipis (?), from Koskina near Olympia; *c.* 475–450? *Ol.* v. 718. *IGA* 112a and add. *SGDI* 1165. Roehl³, 111. 5. *DGE* 421. Olympia Mus.                PL. 43

**17.** Fragmentary bronze plaque bearing part of a decree concerning Skillous; *c.* 450–425? *Ol.* v. 16. *IGA* 119 and add. Roberts i. 298. *SGDI* 1151. Roehl³, 116. 6. *DGE* 418. Kahrstedt, op. cit. 164 f. *SEG* xi. 1184. Olympia Mus. 434+1075+602.

**18.** Fragmentary bronze plaque bearing a text concerning a war-loan; *c.* 450–425? *Ol.* v. 15. *IGA* 114
and add. *SGDI* 1162. Roehl³, 114. 11. Olympia Mus. 569.                                    PL. 43

**19.** Signature of the sculptor Kalon of Elis on a base at Olympia; *c.* 450–425? *Ol.* v. 271. *IGA* 536.
*IGB* 33. *SGDI* 1169. Olympia Mus. 401+1055.                                               PL. 43

**20.** Bronze plaque bearing a private agreement concerning the renting of land; *c.* 425? *Ol.* v. 18.
*IGA* 121 and add. Roberts i. 300. *SGDI* 1168. Roehl³, 117. 19. *DGE* 419. *SEG* xi. 1185. Olympia
Mus. 564.

*Inscription attributed to Elis*

**21.** Fragment of a dedication by the Apolloniates of Epeiros at Olympia; *c.* 475–450? Kunze, *Olympiabericht* v (1956), 149 ff., pl. 80. Olympia Mus. (see p. 229).                              PL. 43


# ACHAIA

*Letter-forms*; see Achaian Colonies, pp. 248 f. and Fig. 42.

Although the Achaian alphabet has left its mark not only in the Achaian colonies of
Magna Graecia, but also along the trade-route which led thither through the Ionian
Islands, through lack of excavation very few archaic inscriptions have yet been found in
Achaia itself. From the twelve states mentioned by the ancient authorities[1]—Dyme,
Olenos, Pharai, Tritaia, Patrai, Rhypes, Aigion, Helike, Bura, Aigai, Aigeira, and Pellene
—the total material, as far as I am aware, is a grave-stele (**1**), a boundary-stone (**3**),
a single series of inscribed coins (**2**), and a bronze oinochoe whose inscription may be
in the Ionic, not the local alphabet (**4**). There are also the following possible attributions:
a very fragmentary bronze plaque said to have been found in northern Arkadia (**8**), two
helmets from Olympia (**6–7**), which might equally well be dedications from the Achaian
colonies in Magna Graecia, and a clay bobbin from Delphi (**5**). The fifth-century statue-
base at Olympia signed jointly by Athenodoros 'of Achaia' and Asopodoros of Argos is
not in the Achaian, or the Argive, script; see further pp. 160, 267.

   The known facts of Achaia's early history are as scanty as her inscriptions.[2] Apart from
the foundation of the western colonies, we know only that the Achaian states early formed
some kind of federation, of which Helike may have been the leading member; that they
were ruled by kings until the reign of one named Ogyges, after whom the constitution
became 'democratic'; that they took no part in the Persian War; and that at some time in
the first half of the fifth century the federation made a joint dedication at Olympia of a
bronze group representing the Achaian chiefs casting their lots for the duel with Hector.
Pausanias has preserved the dedicatory epigram (v. 25. 10):

Τῷ Διὶ τἀχαιοὶ τἀγάλματα ταῦτ' ἀνέθηκαν
ἔγγονοι ἀντιθέου Τανταλίδα Πέλοπος,

---

[1] Hdt. i. 145; Strabo 385–6; Polyb. ii. 41; Paus. vii.
6. 1.

[2] Cf. Strabo 384; Polyb. ii. 41. 5; Paus. vii. 6. 3;
and Larsen, *Studies . . . D. M. Robinson* ii. 797 ff.

and also that of the sculptor Onatas, which forms the only evidence for the date of the offering:

Πολλὰ μὲν ἄλλα σοφοῦ ποιήματα καὶ τόδ' Ὀνάτα
Αἰγινήτεω, τὸν γείνατο παῖδα Μίκων.

The earliest inscription is the gravestone of Demokedes (**1**), which was found by Wilhelm in western Achaia, in a village not very far from Kato Achaia, having evidently come from a group of ancient graves nearby.[1] Kato Achaia has been identified by some scholars with Dyme, and by others with Olenos.[2] It reads from right to left: Δαμοκαδεος τ[οδε σαμα], inscribed vertically on a rough stele 1·22 m. high, and from the wavering, archaic height of the letters I think that it is almost certainly to be dated in the seventh century. The coinage bearing the protome of a goat and inscribed (retrograde) Αιγ, with lunate *gamma* and three-stroked crooked *iota* (**2**), which was attributed to Aigai by Babelon and Head, but to Aigion by Imhoof-Blumer,[3] seems most likely to be from the latter place; the goat might well be used by either as a canting badge, but it is only at Aigion that we hear of a famous goat, the one which suckled the baby Zeus (Strabo 387); moreover, Dionysos, whose head appears on the reverse of the later series, had a precinct at Aigion (Paus. vii. 23. 9), and his head appears again much later on a series which belongs unquestionably to Aigion, dated after 146 B.C. (*HN*², 413). The first series, belonging to the late archaic period, shows *iota* and *gamma* as described above; lunate *gamma* is the type used by Achaia's neighbours Sikyon, Arkadia and Elis, but the western Achaian colonies use the straight form | (p. 248). The second series, which, from the style of Dionysos' head, appears to be not later than the first half of the fifth century, shows that by this time *iota* had become straight; whereas in the colonies the old crooked form seems to have persisted at least until the middle of the century (p. 249).

A small bronze oinochoe (**4**), found in a grave at Aigion, was inscribed on the body ιερ[ο]ν, and round its trefoil lip Αιγεος. The *nu* still slopes slightly, but *gamma* is in the Ionic form, and, unless there are very strong grounds for dating the type of vase to the period *c.* 450–440,[4] I should prefer to set this inscription some decades later, when the use of the Ionic alphabet was spreading over the Peloponnese.

The plaque **8** is generally set among the inscriptions of Arkadia. It was seen and copied in Kalavryta, with the report that it had been found at Lousoi;[5] its fragmentary state allowed only a partial reading: [- - - δα]ρχμας εϟοτον οϟλεν ℎιερας το Ε[- - -] (first line), and then follow two faint lines inscribed the other way up, perhaps an addendum like that inscribed in the same way on a plaque from Ozolian Lokris (pp. 105 f., **2**): [- - -] ϝικατι ται πολι ταλαντον [- - -]. Lousoi lay near the Achaian border, and an inscription has been found in that area which, while undoubtedly Arkadian, shows the Achaian crooked *iota*

---

[1] Wilhelm, 121 f.

[2] The alternative views are discussed by Bölte (*RE*, s.v. Olenos, 2436), who, while inclining to Dyme, leaves the question open.

[3] B ii. 1. 823 ff.; *HN*², 412; Imhoof-Blumer, *Monnaies grecques*, 157.

[4] This is the date suggested by D. M. Robinson, *AJA* xlvi (1942), 194.

[5] Cf. *IG* v. 2. 410. It was later bought by Vollgraff, and published as new in *Mnemosyne* xlvii (1919), 66 ff., with a less acceptable restoration; not knowing its provenance, he ascribed it tentatively to one of the Chalkidic colonies of Sicily; and hence arose the erroneous statement that the *san* was used in certain Sicilian alphabets (Pareti, *La Tomba Regolini-Galassi* (1947), 491, n. 30).

instead of the straight type normal in Arkadian (p. 209, Arkadia **2**); but as yet no Arkadian inscription has been found which shows the *san* as well, and so I am inclined to think that this plaque **8**, if indeed it came from Lousoi, was an agreement which concerned one of the nearby Achaian states (Aigai or Helike?), of a kind like that between Elis and Heraia for example (Elis **6**), which specified the fines to be paid for an infringement of the terms; it might then properly be termed Achaian, though the copy found happens to be the one which was deposited in the sanctuary at Lousoi. The alphabet shows, according to the copies, tailless *epsilon*, open *heta*, crooked *iota*, *san*, and *qoppa*; the circles of *qoppa* and *phi* have become angular, as being easier to cut, and *omikron* is merely a small dot, as on the plaque from Hermion ascribed to Argos (p. 161, **20**), and the stone plaque from Mycenae (p. 173, **3**), both of which have been dated in the first half of the fifth century. The Lousoi plaque probably belongs to the same period, perhaps the first quarter of the century.

The bronze helmet **6**, found at Olympia during the last century, which bears the inscription Ζὲνος Ολυντιο, should be dated somewhere in the last quarter of the sixth century, from the forms of its ε2, υ1. As was said above (p. 221), there is nothing to show whether it is from an Achaian state in the Peloponnese, or one of the western Achaian colonies. The same is true of the magnificent helmet found in the renewed excavations of Olympia shortly before the last war (**7**). The excavators describe the inscription το Διος εμι as Corinthian, but the rounded *delta* stamps it as Achaian. They further observe that the helmet itself is not the normal Corinthian type, but a mixture of the Corinthian and Chalkidic of a style which is worn by warriors on Attic vases of the Leagros period, *c*. 510–500. The neat *epsilon* of the inscription might suggest a rather later date, perhaps in the first quarter of the fifth century; the helmet may well have seen some years' service before it was dedicated.

A clay bobbin (**5**), scratched with sketches of a man and a scorpion, and with the name Μιριϙυθος (from right to left), was found at Delphi in strata which included material of both the seventh and sixth centuries. It is dated tentatively in the sixth century,[1] but the straggling height of its letters, especially ϙ1, υ1, suggests rather the seventh. It is further proposed that both bobbin and inscription may be Phokian, on the grounds that *san* occurs in early Aitolian and Phokian inscriptions, and it might well be that in these regions the crooked *iota* also was originally used. There is, in my view, no definite evidence for the existence of *san* in early Phokian (pp. 100 f.); and it is stated that the clay of the bobbin is distinctly finer than that of the innumerable similar examples from Delphi which are held to be local, though this might be due merely to chance. The alphabet corresponds with that of Achaia, or the earliest Aitolian (which, from the scanty examples, appears to be in some areas the same as the Achaian; cf. pp. 225 f.), or even Korkyrean; and, in view of the difference in the clay, I should ascribe it to a visitor from one of these places. The remarkable name (unattested elsewhere) might be a feminine Μιριϙυθώ in the genitive.

A limestone pillar found in Patras bears the end of an inscription [- - -]θεος (**3**). *Theta* is crossed still, but *epsilon* is tailless, and *sigma* appears for *san*. It should not be earlier than the middle of the fifth century.

[1] Lejeune, *REA* xlix (1947), 36 f.

The detailed commentary on Achaian letter-forms is reserved for the inscriptions of the colonies, pp. 248 f. As for the genesis of this alphabet, it seems likely that it was a mixture resulting from the fusion of the scripts of Sikyon and Corinth on the eastern border with those of Elis to the west and Phokis across the Gulf. Some of the Achaian states may have been late in receiving it; but one at least—perhaps at the eastern end of the chain?—must have been literate early, for the Achaian version of the alphabet had already reached Ithake in the early Orientalizing period (p. 230). Its influence is also visible in the scattered inscriptions which have been found in Aitolia, Achaia's northern neighbour on the opposite shore of the Gulf of Corinth.

## CATALOGUE

**1.** Gravestone of Demokedes, from Olenos or Dyme; 7th c.? Wilhelm, 121 f., fig. 69. Lost?

**2.** Coinage of Αιγ- (= Αἴγιον?); *c.* 500 onwards? B ii. 1. 823 ff., pl. 37. *HN²*, 412.

**3.** Limestone pillar from Patras; *c.* 450? Bingen, *BCH* lxxviii (1954), 400, no. 17, fig. 4. *SEG* xiv. 374. Patras Mus.                                                                                              PL. 44

**4.** Bronze oinochoe inscribed ιερ[ο]ν Αιγεος, from Aigion; *c.* 425? D. M. Robinson, *AJA* xlvi (1942), 194 ff., figs. 27–30. *SEG* xi. 1266. D. M. Robinson Coll.

*Inscriptions attributed to Achaia*

**5.** Clay bobbin inscribed Μιριϙυθος from Delphi; 7th c.? Lejeune, *REA* xlix (1947), 36 f. *SEG* xiii. 229. Kretschmer, *Glotta* 1954–5, 9 ff. Delphi Mus.                                                                    PL. 44

**6.** Helmet from Olympia; *c.* 525–500. Roberts i. 301a. *SGDI* 1599. *Ol.* v. 694. Roehl³, 120. 15. Bodkin, *Report of the Barber Institute of Fine Arts, Univ. of Birmingham* (1950), 12. Barber Inst.        PL. 44

**7.** Helmet from Olympia; *c.* 510–475? Kunze and Schleif, *JdI* lvi (1941), *Olympiabericht* iii. 79 and 112 f., pl. 45. *SEG* xi. 1233. Olympia Mus.                                                                            PL. 44

**8.** Fragment of a bronze plaque said to be from Lousoi; *c.* 500–475? *IG* v. 2. 410. Vollgraff, *Mnemosyne* xlvii (1919), 66 ff. and *Mélanges Boisacq* ii (1938), 339. *SEG* xi. 1121. Private coll.?

# NORTH-WESTERN GREECE

## AITOLIA

According to Strabo (450), Aitolia was divided geographically into two parts: ἡ ἀρχαία, the fertile area along the Gulf of Corinth, and ἡ ἐπίκτητος, the rugged inland country. It was presumably the latter area which gave her the reputation of a land of half-savages, who ate raw flesh and spoke an unintelligible dialect (cf. Eur. *Phoen.* 138; Thuc. iii. 94); for her coastal settlements were open to the civilizing influence of all the Greeks who from the eighth century onwards sailed along the shores of Lokris, Aitolia, Akarnania, in constant communication with their colonies in Italy and Sicily.

Among these pioneers Corinth was pre-eminent. The little ports of Molykreion, Makynia, and Chalkis were Corinthian settlements;[1] and excavations in the precincts of Artemis Laphria at Kalydon and Apollo at Thermon have revealed how strong was the influence of Corinthian painting and plastic art in these parts. There is no doubt that much of Aitolia's civilization came ultimately from Corinth; but it is important to remember also her close contact with Achaia, especially at the narrows between Rhion and Antirrhion, where traditionally the Herakleidai crossed from Aitolia to the Peloponnese (Paus. v. 3, 5–6), and Achaian Patrai later maintained close links with the Aitolians (Paus. iv. 31. 7; vii. 18. 6 and 20. 6). Lastly, in addition to Corinthian and Achaian, there are traces of Sikyonian interests also; the Sikyonian sculptors Dipoinos and Skyllis settled there (Pliny, *NH* xxxvi. 4), and one of the suitors of Agariste of Sikyon was Males of Aitolia (Hdt. vi. 127).

It is not surprising therefore that the few archaic inscriptions found in Aitolia show between them Achaian, Corinthian, and Sikyonian forms. There seems nothing to show that her eastern neighbour Ozolian Lokris contributed anything. The inscriptions showing Sikyonian letters may be the work of immigrant craftsmen, and so they are not included here (p. 140); but the rest, from the areas round Kalydon and Thermon farther inland, suggest what we might expect, namely, that some Aitolians learnt literacy from Achaian neighbours, and others from the Corinthian or Corinthian-influenced settlements of Akarnania and Epeiros. I have not therefore attempted to draw up a table of Aitolian letter-forms, but have merely noted the script of each inscription. The earliest found so far is the grave-stele of Promethos (**1**): Προμαθο τοδε σαμα φιλοξενο ανδρος. It was found near Vlachomandra, about two hours north of Molykreion; and it is in the Achaian alphabet, with the usual characteristics of extreme archaism, i.e. tall, straggling, long-tailed letters, with a very small *omikron*. Even if we allow for Aitolian backwardness, it should not be later than the seventh century. It was probably through such men as the hospitable Promethos that Aitolia was kept in touch with the passing traders of the outside world.

The painted names on the terra-cotta metopes of the seventh century from the temple

---

[1] Thuc. i. 108; iii. 102 (Molykreion and Chalkis); for Makynia, cf. Oldfather, *RE*, s.v., 817.

of Apollo at Thermon (**2**) show a mixture of letters, Achaian predominant. Although the style of painting has been established as Corinthian (*c.* 640–620), the metopes are in local clay;[1] the names of Chelidon, Iris, and the Charites appear to be in Achaian script (cf. the normal *epsilon*), that of Eileithyia in Corinthian.[2] The earliest inscriptions from the temple of Artemis Laphria at Kalydon also show variations. The painted names on the metopes (**3**) are unfortunately too fragmentary to establish anything, except for a fragment of Troilos' name in a picture of the famous ambush by Achilles; but on the underside of the sima (also of local clay)[3] instructions were incised, numbering the sections according to their positions to the east or west (**4**): μια επι ϝικατι πο εσπερας, and so on. These revetments have been dated in the first quarter of the sixth century;[4] all show Corinthian *epsilon* and *san*, one shows Corinthian four-stroked *iota*, and all the rest show a straight *iota*, which is not normal either at Corinth or in her north-western colonies Korkyra and Leukas, at so early a date. But the freak *epsilon* combined with straight *iota* is typical of the archaic script of Dodona, at least in the late sixth century (p. 228). The local script of Kalydon was evidently influenced by Corinthian; but the precise details of its origin must remain uncertain, until more archaic material becomes available from the sites of Aitolia, Akarnania, and Epeiros.

The two inscriptions from near Thermon showing Sikyonian *epsilon* have been discussed on p. 140 (Sikyon **19**, **20**), and are therefore omitted here. The later inscriptions from Thermon and Kalydon illustrate the gradual loss of the local forms. A bronze phiale from Kalydon shows *san* still, but *epsilon* E and the later, tailed *rho* (**8**);[5] the general appearance suggests a date *c.* 500–475. The rim of a krater (**9**) inscribed [Αρτε]μιδος Ϝιαρος shows open *heta* and four-stroked *sigma*; the latter occurs also on part of a gravestone from Ophioneis, north-east of Thermon (**10**), and both are presumably later therefore than **8**; but more than that can hardly be said. To enlarge further upon the letter-forms of Aitolia is useless until we have more material from the area; it may only be repeated that the chief sources of Aitolian script seem to be Achaian and Corinthian.[6]

## CATALOGUE

**1.** Grave-stele of Promethos, found north of Molykreion; 7th c.? Rhomaios, *A. Delt.* ii (1916), *par.*, 46, fig. 1. Klaffenbach, *Sb. Ak. Berlin* 1935, 714, and n. 2. Lerat, *Les Locriens de l'Ouest* (1952), i, p. xi and ii. 27. Peek i. 55. Lost?     PL. 44

**2.** Inscriptions on the metopes from the temple of Apollo at Thermon; *c.* 625? Soteriades, *EA* 1903, 71 ff. *AD* ii, pls. 50. 1 and 52*a*. 2–3. Koch, *AM* xxxix (1914), 237 ff. and *RM* xxx (1915), 111 ff. Payne, *BSA* xxvii (1925–6), 124 ff. and *NC*, 96, n. 3, and 160 f. *IG* ix². 1. 86. Lejeune, *REA* xlvii (1945), 111 ff. NM.     PL. 44

---

[1] Koch, *AM* xxxix (1914), 238, 248. For the date, cf. *NC*, 96, n. 3.

[2] Cf. Jeffery, *BSA* xliii (1948), 204, n. 3.

[3] Dyggve, *Das Laphrion* (1948), 163 f., 201 f.

[4] Op. cit. 223 ff.; cf. *NC*, 235.

[5] The reading of the dedication is disputed. I think it possible that the last seven letters of the dedication

have overlapped the first seven; and restore: [. . . . . . .] υστρετος ανεθεκε ται Αρταμι[τι τα]ι Λαφριια (*sic*).

[6] A careful study of the early Aitolian alphabet was made by Lejeune, *REA* xlvii (1945), 110 ff., but without knowledge of **1**; he makes no mention of a connexion with Achaian.

**3.** Inscriptions on the metopes from the temple of Artemis Laphria at Kalydon; *c.* 600–575? *IG* ix². 1. 153. Lejeune, op. cit. 109, n. 11. Dyggve, *Das Laphrion* (1948), 156 f., pls. 18, 20 α–β, 21. NM.

**4.** Inscriptions on the sima from the same temple; *c.* 600–575? Poulsen–Rhomaios, *Erster Bericht . . . Kalydon* (1927), 22 ff., pls. 25–29. Dyggve, Poulsen, and Rhomaios, *Das Heroon v. Kalydon* (1934), 292. *NC*, 235 ff. *IG* ix². 1. 152. Rhomaios, *Korkyra* i (1940), 123. Jeffery, *BSA* xliii (1948), 203 f. Dyggve, *Das Laphrion* (1948), 172 ff. NM.     PL. 44

**5.** Boundary-stone from the precinct of Apollo Laphrios, Kalydon; *c.* 550–500? Rhomaios, *A. Delt.* x (1926), *par.*, 39, fig. 14. *IG* ix². 1. 149. Lejeune, op. cit. 112. Dyggve, op. cit. 295 f., 340. Kalydon.

**6.** Fragment from the rim of a marble basin from Kalydon; *c.* 550–500? Dyggve, op. cit. 134, fig. 152*b*. NM.

**7.** Fragmentary bronze plaque from the temple of Apollo at Thermon; *c.* 500? *IG* ix². 1. 91. Lejeune, op. cit. 112. Thermon Mus.

**8.** Bronze phiale from Kalydon; *c.* 500–475? Dyggve, Poulsen, and Rhomaios, op. cit., 293, 296, fig. 3. Klaffenbach, op. cit. 708. Dyggve, op. cit. 340, fig. 307. NM.

**9.** Rim of a krater from Kalydon; *c.* 450? *IG* ix². 1. 150. Dyggve, op. cit. 339, fig. 308. NM.   PL. 44

**10.** Gravestone from Ophioneis; 5th c. Pappadakes, *A. Delt.* vi (1920–1), *par.*, 153, fig. 6. *IG* ix². 1. 197. *SEG* iii. 434. Lejeune, op. cit. 112. Peek i. 1414. Lidoriki school.

# AKARNANIA AND EPEIROS

## AKARNANIA

The culture of Akarnania, such as it was, must have come principally from the Corinthian colonies settled in those parts by the Kypselid dynasty: as Leukas, Anaktorion, Herakleia, Sollion.[1] Little excavation has yet been done on the sites, and only brief comments can be made on the few early inscriptions found. As far as the evidence goes, it indicates that the colonies used the script of Corinth; but at Stratos, the chief settlement of the Akarnanians, an archaic inscription has been found which, enigmatic though it is in all other respects, shows the script not of Corinth, but of Achaia (below, **2**). Probably in Akarnania, as in her flanking neighbours Aitolia and the Ionian Islands, the colonizing states of Achaia left a good many marks on their way to the west, though whether their script got to Akarnania directly or via her neighbours must remain an open question.

Of the Corinthian colonies, Leukas was traditionally settled during the reign of Kypselos, in the second half of the seventh century (*FGH* ii, no. 90, F 57; Strabo 451); here have been found a miniature bronze helmet-crest from a dedication to Athena, in Corinthian script which might be of any date in the sixth century (**1**): three gravestones inscribed Μικυθας, [· · · · ·]νεος and Βουλιαδα (**5–7**), which show Corinthian *beta*, *epsilon*, and *san*, with straight *iota*, and should probably therefore belong to the first half of the fifth century: and one of rather later date, showing *sigma* combined with Corinthian *epsilon*: [Ξ]ενοκρατες (**9**). Her coinage, which is not earlier than *c.* 500, shows only *lambda*

---

[1] Cf. Kirsten, *Neue Jahrbücher* 1940, 298 ff. and Klaffenbach, *IG* ix. 1². 2, Fasti Acarnanici.

during its early period, following the pattern set by the Corinthian series with its *qoppa*; cf. B ii. 1. 918 f.; ii. 4. 51 f., pls. 40, 273.

From Anaktorion, founded at about the same time as Leukas (*FGH* ii, no. 90, F 57), there is a broken gravestone probably of the fifth century, known only by copy: [- - -]ολλυο σαμα (**10**). Her coinage, also starting in the fifth century, kept its solitary *vau*, as Corinth kept her *qoppa*, long after the letter had passed from normal usage (B ii. 1. 914 ff.; ii. 4. 81 ff., pl. 277; *HN*², 329). A longer inscription, seen somewhere in northern Akarnania and known only from a single copy, apparently showed Corinthian *epsilon*, closed *heta*, straight *iota* and *sigma*, and may (judged on Corinthian standards) have been of the period *c.* 475–450 (**8**). Nothing else of significance has been found in the Corinthian colonies,[1] though it is probable that the Kypselidai who offered a golden bowl at Olympia from the spoils of Herakleia came from these parts (p. 127, **13**). At Palairos two small fragments of archaic grave-stelai were found (**3**), reading: (*a*): -μ' εμ- and (*b*): -ς σαμ- in Corinthian or Achaian; at Echinos (?: modern Paliambelo) is another fragment of a grave-stele, reading ανδρο-, with Achaian rounded *delta* and the late archaic tailed *rho* (**4**). At Stratos, the chief town of Akarnania, was found a broken slab containing about ten lines written in false *boustrophedon*, left to right (**2**). As false *boustrophedon* is most easily read if the lines run vertically up and down, it is likely that the stone was originally a stele. The letters show Achaian forms: rounded *delta*, normal *epsilon*, three-stroked *iota*, *san*, and a triple-dot punctuation; but the surface of the surviving fragments of the slab is so damaged that no proper sense can be made of the text, either as a decree (Kirsten) or as a verse epitaph (Klaffenbach).[2] Another inscription from Stratos has been dated tentatively in the last years of the fifth century (**11**). This is a proxeny-decree on a bronze plaque, which grants προξενία, προνομία, προπραξία, and ἀτέλεια to a Megarian, Lysias son of Kallias, and to his two sons and their descendants. The writer used 'blue' *xi* and *chi*, and *omega* but not *eta* (H serving still as aspirate). The letter-forms themselves all suggest the middle of the fifth century, or not long after. But the preamble εδοξε ται πολι των Στρατιων has an Attic flavour, and one would not expect Attic and Ionic influences to penetrate this area until the Peloponnesian War.

## EPEIROS

A solitary gravestone has been found at Ambrakia, the Corinthian colony founded in the late seventh century (Strabo 325, 452); it reads Αρμονοα, and looks fifth-century (**12**). At Dodona, where was the famous oracle of Zeus, a series of leaden plaques or strips was found, which bore the questions put to the oracle, and, occasionally, its answer. The nearest source for the script of Dodona was presumably Ambrakia; but all that can certainly be said as yet from these brief inscriptions is that a variant of the Corinthian script was used, showing the freak Corinthian ε/η and *san*, but straight *iota* (cf. Aitolia, p. 226). The archaic script (with *san*) is attested on a late archaic bronze statuette found in the precinct, inscribed: τōι Δι Ετυμο|κλεδας ἀνεθēκε (**14**), a plaque inscribed *boustrophedon*

---

[1] I have omitted the fragment *IG* ix 1². 2. 215 (two letters,—δα; from Anaktorion).

*IG* ix. 1². 2. 399, a gravestone (?) with the dubious reading κορδιρας apparently in archaic lettering.

[2] Another inscription from Stratos, omitted here:

(13), and another very fragmentary plaque (15). The later examples, i.e. those showing *sigma* and normal *epsilon* (17), are probably not earlier than the late fifth century, and those showing *sigma* but 'freak' *epsilon* lie between (16); cf. the inscriptions of Corinth, in which the local *epsilon* outlasted the *san*.

Part of a dedication by the colony Apollonia farther up the Illyrian coast has been found at Olympia. The complete verses are recorded by Pausanias (v. 22. 3), who also describes the offering, a great bronze set of gods and heroes of the Trojan War, the work of Lykios son of Myron. The *floruit* of Lykios is set tentatively *c.* 450, overlapping that of his father. The victory celebrated was over Thronion, a settlement of Lokrians some-where on the Illyrian coast; but its date is unknown. The lettering of the surviving fragment from the marble base suggests a date *c.* 475–450. It is not the script of either Corinth or Korkyra, the joint founders of Apollonia under the rule of the Kypselidai (Plut., *De Ser. Num. Vind.* 7; Ps.-Skymnos, 429 f.), nor the hybrid script of Dodona, nor the Attic such as Lykios should have used, nor the Ionic which he might have used, as Attic writers occasionally did at this time. The *vau* and other letters would fit the script of a local mason at Olympia, and so I have tentatively set this inscription among those attributed to Elis (Elis **21**).

## SELECT CATALOGUE

### AKARNANIA

**1.** Dedication of Euphaios from Leukas; 6th c. Preuner, *AM* xxvii (1902), 363 ff. Roehl³, 45. 16. *DGE* 141. NM 12345. PL. **44**

**2.** Stone slab with fragments of a decree or an epitaph from Stratos; 6th c. Kirsten, *Neue Jahrb.* 1940, 304, pl. 12. *IG* ix. 1². 2. 398. Agrinion, schoolhouse. PL. **44**

**3a–b.** Fragments of two gravestones from Palairos; 6th c.? Preuner, op. cit. 333. 3–4. Roehl³, 56. 1–2. *IG* ix. 1². 2. 459, 458. *a* EM 203. *b* lost.

**4.** Fragment of a gravestone from Paliambelo (Echinos?); *c.* 500? *IG* ix. 1². 2. 367. House of B. Yeses.

**5.** Gravestone of Mikythe, Leukas; *c.* 500–450? *IGA* 338. *IG* ix. 1. 544. Roberts i. 104. *SGDI* 3178. *DGE* 142. Leukas.

**6.** Gravestone of -neos, Leukas; *c.* 500–450? Kolbe, *AM* xxvii (1902), 369. 32. Roehl³, 45. 17. Leukas.

**7.** Gravestone of Bouliades, Leukas; *c.* 500–450? Kolbe, loc. cit. 33. Roehl³, 46. 20. Leukas.

**8.** Gravestone of Prokleides from N. Akarnania (Anaktorion?); *c.* 475–450? *IGA* 329. *IG* ix. 1. 521. Roberts i. 106. *SGDI* 3175. Roehl³, 45. 14. *DGE* 140. Friedlaender 64. Buck 95. Peek i. 70. *IG* ix. 1². 2. 214. Lost. PL. **44**

**9.** Gravestone of Xenokrates, Leukas; *c.* 450–425? Kolbe, op. cit. 368. 31. Roehl³, 46. 19. Leukas.

**10.** Gravestone of -ollyos, Anaktorion; 5th c.? *IGA* 330. *SGDI* 3176. *IG* ix. 1². 2. 216. Lost.

**11.** Bronze plaque with a proxeny-decree, Stratos: *c.* 425–400? Joubin, *BCH* xvii (1893), 445 ff. *IG* ix. 1. 442 and p. 211. *SIG*³ 121. Roehl³, 56. 3. *DGE* 394. *IG* ix. 1². 2. 390. NM 10760.

### EPEIROS

**12.** Gravestone of Harmonoe from Ambrakia; 5th c.? *IGA* 331. *SGDI* 3177 (there given wrongly as Ἀρμονία). EM.

**13.** Leaden plaque bearing an inquiry by Hermon from the oracular precinct at Dodona; *c.* 525–500?
Euangelides, *PAE* 1931, 89 f., fig. 7. Ioannina Mus.                                              PL. 44

**14.** Bronze statuette dedicated by Etymokleides from Dodona; *c.* 500? De Ridder, *Cat. Bronz. Louvre*
i. 22, no. 108, pl. 12. Lamb, *Gk. and Roman Bronzes*, 88, pl. 34. Langlotz, *FGB*, 82, pl. 42. *NC*, 238,
n. 5, 245. Jeffery, *BSA* xliii (1948), 206. Paris, Louvre.

**15.** Leaden plaque from Dodona; *c.* 500–450? Euangelides, ʼΗπειρωτικὰ Χρονικά (1935), 245 ff.,
no. 22. Ioannina Mus.

**16.** Leaden plaques from Dodona; *c.* 450–425? Euangelides, loc. cit., nos. 12, 35, 38, 40; *PAE* 1952,
299 ff., nos. 7 (2), 10 (3), 20 (5), fig. 29. Roehl³, 45. 15. Ibid.

**17.** Leaden plaques from Dodona; *c.* 425–400? Euangelides, loc. cit., nos. 10, 19, 16, 17. Ibid.

## THE IONIAN ISLANDS

FIG. 41. Ithake, Kephallenia

### ITHAKE

Ithake was well placed to be a port of call from early times for any ships which
emerged from the Gulf of Corinth to strike across the Ionian sea to Italy. The early
users of this route were Chalkis and Eretria, Corinth, and Achaia. The pottery found
at Aetos in central Ithake shows Corinthian imports and Corinthian influence on the
local ware from the Geometric period onwards, and it has been suggested by Professor
M. Robertson that the island may have been actually settled from Corinth, at some time
during the early days of exploration in the west before the foundation of the Italian and
Sicilian colonies.[1] Further excavation may decide this point; but meanwhile it should be
remembered that another influence is visible as well as Corinthian, for the alphabet used
in Ithake is very similar to the Achaian. There is as yet no other indication that the
Achaians frequented these waters before the foundation of their colonies in southern
Italy at the end of the eighth century; but the hall-mark of their script is plain in the few
early inscriptions of Ithake: the combination of the normal *epsilon* with the crooked *iota*
and *san*. The earliest inscription (**1**) is a fragmentary poem in hexameters painted in a
spiral from left to right round the body of an oinochoe which has been dated 'not much,
if at all, later than 700 B.C.'.[2] The letters show the long tails and small *omikron* of extreme
archaism, and two features deserve special comment: the use of Euboic *lambda* 1 and the
exaggerated *iota* 1, which stands to the normal three-stroked Achaian type as Lakonian
*sigma* does to the normal Greek letter. Neither letter recurs in later Ithakesian (which
corresponds exactly with Achaian), and Robertson has suggested the possibility of Chalkidic influence. A 'candlestick', also of local make, is dated not later than the second

[1] *BSA* xliii (1948), 122 f.                                    [2] Op. cit. 82.

quarter of the seventh century (**2**); it is inscribed round the neck: Καλικλεας ποιασε (*sic*), an interesting sidelight on the Ithakesian dialect. A fragmentary inscription on an oinochoe is too blurred to be either legible or datable.[1] No other early inscription has been discovered at Aetos, but at Polis in the north of Ithake a stone stele was found which bears an inscription cut, or rather scratched, *boustrophedon* within a smoothed surface enclosed by a rougher frame (**3**). It appears to record a dedication by some officials jointly to Athena Polias and Hera Teleia; the last word of line 1 was for some reason only drafted by the mason, and then cut as the first word of line 2: [- - - τας Α]θανας {τας} | τας Πολ[ιαδ|ος] κα[ι τ]ας Ⱶερ|ας τας Τελ[ει|ας] τοι [·]ερι̣πολ|[ο]ι με ε[πο]ι̣εσ[αν ·· | - - -]π̣ι[- - -].[2] The careless lettering makes it extremely difficult to suggest a precise date; it may be earlier than 550, but it equally well may be later, *c.* 550–525. The dedication may be compared with Phokis **1**, also a joint offering to Athena and Hera. The last archaic example, the word Ⱶιαρος on a fragment of a flute (**4**), shows the open form of *heta*, and therefore should not be earlier than the end of the sixth century.

## KEPHALLENIA

There is as yet only scanty evidence for the script of Kephallenia. It might be inferred that, as a close neighbour of Ithake, she would share the same alphabet; but this is not confirmed by an archaic inscription said to have been found in Kephallenia, the bronze disk dedicated by Exoides (**5**): Εχσοιδα μ' ανεθεκε Διƒος Ϙοροιν μεγαλοιο χαλκεον Ⱶοι νικασε Κεφαλανας μεγαθυμος.[3] It is not certain from this Homeric ending whether Exoides was himself a Kephallenian, or came from some neighbouring place to a festival on the island, and defeated the local entrants. On the whole, the first interpretation seems more likely, for in the second event one would expect Exoides to mention his own native town; but it should be remembered that the provenance of the disk is stressed as uncertain.[4] The same lettering occurs on a tombstone found in an archaic cemetery in Athens, which is written *stoichedon*, and therefore probably little if at all earlier than the fifth century (**6**): Δαμαινετο | το Παλεος; this may well be the Kephallenian town Pale. On the evidence of these inscriptions, the Kephallenian alphabet resembles Achaian (= Ithakesian) in using lunate *gamma*, rounded *delta*, normal *epsilon*, *san*, and 'red' *chi*; but it differs sharply in using straight *iota*. The unusual *vau* of **5** may also be noted. The only other evidence[5]

---

[1] Op. cit. 87 f., pl. 32.

[2] In 1949 I examined the stone in Polis Museum, and made the following notes on the lettering, from which the restoration given here is made: traces of the mason's first draft under ας of [Α]θανας in l. 1; πολ in l. 2 and τελ in l. 4 make the epithets πολιάς and τελεία reasonably secure; in l. 5 the final letter is λ or ρ, not crooked *iota*, and this disposes of the restoration [ι]ερο-[π]οι[ο]ι, which would, in any case, be inconsistent with the W. Greek dialect (cf. ιαρός, **4**): perhaps [π]ερι̣πολ[ο]ι? I find that Vollgraff (*BCH* xxix (1905), 165 f.) had already restored τελεια; he also suggests tentatively τοι [π]ερι Ⱶοιλεε· · (?) in l. 5, rejecting the editors' με ε[πο]εσ[αν] of l. 6.

[3] The letter preceding ανεθεκε is clearly *mu*, not *san*;

for the nominative singular masculine in -α, gen. -ας, in north-west Greek, see *DGE ad* 143, 430, and Buck, 87.

[4] Cf. *BMI* iv. 952; *BMC Bronzes* 3207; and especially *IG* ix. 1. 647. Cf. also, however, Kirchhoff[4], 167. He saw the disk briefly during its early career on the market, and had no doubt that, from what was told him, it came from Kephallenia.

[5] I omit here the inscription of three lines said to have been found at Kranion (*IG* ix. 1. 610 = *SEG* xiv. 471), for it is impossible to tell from the existing illustrations whether it is a modern forgery, or merely a very bad copy; the fragment *IG* ix. 1. 611 was specifically stated to be a forgery (Froehner, *RA* 1891, 47, n. 3).

comes from the coins struck by Kranion and Pale during the fifth century, with the legends Κρα, Κρανι, and Γ (**7**); *rho* is in the later, tailed form.

### KORKYRA

Korkyra was settled *c.* 734 by a band of emigrants from Corinthia, led by Chersikrates, an offshoot from the main body of settlers who, led by Archias, were making for Sicily to colonize Syracuse (Strabo 269–70; Plutarch, *QG* 11). An Eretrian settlement which had been made previously on the island was dispossessed, and Korkyra became Doric. Because of her strategic position, whence, if she chose, she could block the way for Corinthian shipping trading with the West, it was almost inevitable that hostility should develop between mother-city and colony. In 664 Korkyra defeated Corinth in the first recorded sea-fight (Thuc. i. 13), only to fall into the power of the Corinthian tyrant Periander two generations later.[1] The alphabet of Korkyra is the Corinthian, not that of Syracuse. It has been suggested that Korkyra's alphabet is Corinthian 'because she was retaken and administered by Corinth after a revolt in the seventh century',[2] i.e. that she did not become literate until the time of Periander; but even on the hypothesis that her first colonists brought no script with them, it is not necessary to descend to so low a date to find Corinthian influence in Korkyra. It is true that as yet very little Protocorinthian material has been found on the island, but this may be only because the earliest necropolis has not yet been located,[3] and modern excavation in Korkyra has been concentrated mainly on the great temple of Artemis at Garitsa, which was built in the early sixth century; already in the generation before Periander those Bacchiads who opposed the accession of his father Kypselos had emigrated to Korkyra (Nic. Damasc., *FGH* ii, no. 90, F 57), and it has even been suggested that the rhapsode Eumelos may have been there.[4]

The four metrical epitaphs found in Korkyra are longer and finer specimens of archaic Corinthian lettering on stone than anything yet found in Corinth herself; but they are peculiarly hard to date, because they have no accompanying material from the graves to provide a basis for comparison, and (as has been said already, p. 120) the individual Corinthian letter-forms show very little change from the early seventh to the late sixth century. The circular tomb of Menekrates (**9**), proxenos for Korkyra at Oianthea in Ozolian Lokris (p. 285), is believed to have contained (among other objects now lost) two olpai of Corinthian Transitional style (*c.* 640–625), now in the British Museum.[5] This, if correct, would provide a *terminus post quem* for the tomb and its inscription, but not a precise date, for the vases are thought to be of local make, and might therefore be as much as a generation later than their counterparts in Corinth. An unusual feature in the inscription is the triple-dot punctuation, for punctuation is almost unknown in Corinthian, and does not occur again in Korkyrean. The start of the long retrograde line is marked by a sign ◇, which was perhaps painted in a different colour from the letters, to attract the reader's eye.

The lost stele of Polynoe (**8**) should be earlier than **9**, if the copy is accurate, for it

[1] Hdt. iii. 52; cf. Rodenwaldt, *Korkyra* ii (1939), 170.

[2] R. Carpenter, *AJA* xxxvii (1933), 27.

[3] Rodenwaldt, loc. cit.

[4] Wilamowitz, *Hellenistiche Dichtung* ii. 240 f.; cf. Rodenwaldt, loc. cit.

[5] Rodenwaldt, op. cit. 171 f., n. 1.

shows one rounded 'freak' *epsilon* (the rest being angled), which in Corinthian seems to be earlier than the angled type (p. 115); and the very tall, careful letters cover the available surface with very little interlinear space, a kind of *horror vacui* which, again, is characteristic of early vase-inscriptions (e.g. Corinth **4**). The epitaph of Arniadas (**11**), on the other hand, has lettering very like that of **9**, though without punctuation; it has faint guide-lines. The battle by the river Arachthos, mentioned in the verse, may perhaps have been with the Kypselid colony Ambrakia which lay at its mouth: an event which might equally well have happened either before Periander's seizure of Korkyra, or after his death.

The last and hardest problem is the epitaph of Xenares, inscribed retrograde on a Doric capital which served as a grave-monument (**13**). It does not spread all over the abacus, as one would expect of a seventh-century inscription, but is cut in neat letters as small in proportion to the field as is the lettering of Late Corinthian vases (p. 126); and to this period, *c.* 575–550, I should assign the inscription. But the type of capital, with a painted leaf-and-point moulding at the base of the echinus, is generally agreed to be very early, and Schleif holds **13** to be stylistically the earliest of eight such capitals from Korkyra, among which are two rebuilt into the supporting north wall of the precinct of Artemis at Garitsa.[1] If these belonged to the temple itself, they would be securely dated *c.* 600–585; but if they were from votive, not architectural, columns, they would be later. In support of the date suggested above for the inscription, therefore, I can only suggest that votive capitals lagged behind architectural in their development (pp. 107, 159).

The Korkyrean dedication at Delphi (**15**) was inscribed on a wall dated by the excavators in the beginning of the fifth century;[2] it shows the local letter-forms *epsilon*, *iota*, *qoppa* still in use, although *upsilon* is now in its late archaic tailless form (cf. Corinth **29**); a graffito Ϙυνισϙ⟨ο⟩ς from Korkyra on the foot of a vase may be of the same date or slightly earlier (**14**). The funeral column[3] inscribed retrograde Λεξειατας (**16**) shows the 'freak' *epsilon* still, but straight *iota* and *sigma*; judged on Corinthian standards, it might be *c.* 475–450. The two boundary-stones inscribed ορϝος Πυθαιος (**17**) and ορϝος Ϝιαρος | τας Ακριας (**18**) may, from the developed, tailless form of *vau*, belong to the second half of the century.

## CATALOGUE

### ITHAKE

**1.** Fragmentary hexameters painted on a long-necked oinochoe at Aetos; *c.* 700? M. Robertson, *BSA* xliii (1948), 80 ff., pl. 34. Vathy Mus. PL. 45

---

[1] Schleif, *Korkyra* i. 76 ff. He gives a list of 20 archaic capitals from Korkyra, of which 1 (= **13**), 2–5, and 8–9 (the latter rebuilt in a wall of the precinct of Artemis) have similar moulding, while 7, one of the capitals from the temple of Artemis itself, has a leaf-pattern. 2–5 were also rebuilt into a late archaic wall (at Monrepos; op. cit. 75, 79). He would assign **13** to the 7th c.; cf. Puchstein, *Das ionische Capitell* (1887),

47 ff.; Rodenwaldt, *Altdorische Bildwerke in Korfu* (1938), 10 f.   [2] Courby, *FD* ii. 1. 228 ff., 246 f.
[3] This column, found near the grave of Menekrates, has a late inscription added: Διοσκουρων, and has therefore been described as a boundary-stone, Λεξειατας (ορϝος?); but the simpler explanation seems to be that it was originally a gravestone, re-used as a boundary-stone many years later.

**2.** Signature of Kallikleas on a clay 'candlestick' at Aetos; *c.* 675–650? Payne, *JHS* liii (1933), 283. Kretschmer, *Glotta* xxiv (1936), 63. Lejeune, *REA* xlvii (1945), 103 ff. M. Robertson, op. cit. 88 f., pls. 38–39. Vathy Mus.      PL. 45

**3.** Dedication to Athena and Hera on a stele at Polis; *c.* 550? *IGA* 336. Roberts i. 310. *IG* ix. 1. 653. *SGDI* 1669. Vollgraff, *BCH* xxix (1905), 165 f. Roehl³, 118. 4. Lejeune, op. cit. 104, n. 3. Polis Mus.      PL. 45

**4.** Fragment of a flute; *c.* 500? *IGA* 337. Roberts i. 311. *IG* ix. 1. 655. *SGDI* 1670. Roehl³, 119. 5. Schliemann Coll.?      PL. 45

### KEPHALLENIA

**5.** Bronze disk dedicated to the Dioskouroi by Exoides, probably from Kephallenia; *c.* 550–525? Froehner, *RA* xviii, 1 (1891), 45 ff., pl. 18. *IG* ix. 1. 649. *BMC Bronzes* 3207. Roehl³, 118. 2. *DGE* 430. Jacobsthal, *Diskoi* (1933), 22. Webster, *CQ* xxxiii (1939), 178. Friedlaender 43. Moretti 6. *SEG* xiv. 470. BM.      PL. 45

**6.** Gravestone of Demainetos of Pale, from Athens; *c.* 500–475? *IGA* 334. Roberts i. 308. Roehl³, 118. 3. *DGE* 431. *IG* i². 1070. 1. EM.

**7.** Inscribed coins of Kranion and Pale, 5th c. *HN*², 427. B ii. 1. 907 ff., pl. 39; ii. 3. 791 ff., pl. 237.

### KORKYRA

**8.** Epitaph on the grave-stele of Polynoe, Korkyra; *c.* 650–600? *IGA* 340. Roberts i. 96. *IG* ix. 1. 870. *SGDI* 3186. Roehl³, 46. 21. *DGE* 134. Friedlaender, 24. Peek i. 67. Lost.      PL. 46

**9.** Epitaph on the tomb of Menekrates, Korkyra; *c.* 625–600? *IGA* 342. Roberts i. 98. *IG* ix. 1. 867. *SGDI* 3188. Roehl³, 47. 26. *DGE* 133 (1). Friedlaender 26. Buck 93. Peek i. 42. Korkyra.

**10.** Dedication by Lophios on a bronze label; early 6th c.? *IGA* 341. Roberts i. 97. *IG* ix. 1. 705. *SGDI* 3187. *BMC Bronzes* 261. Roehl³, 46. 22. BM.      PL. 46

**11.** Epitaph on the grave-stele of Arniadas; late 7th or early 6th c. *IGA* 343. Roberts i. 99. *IG* ix. 1. 868. *SGDI* 3189. Roehl³, 46. 25. *DGE* 133 (2). *GHI*² 2 and p. 257. Friedlaender 25. Buck 94. Peek i. 73. Korkyra Mus.      PL. 46

**12.** Dedication of Mys; 7th–6th c. Six, *AM* xix (1894), 340 ff. *IG* ix. 1. 704. Roehl³, 46. 23. *DGE* 132. Korkyra Mus.

**13.** Epitaph of Xenares on a Doric capital; *c.* 575–550? *IGA* 344. Roberts i. 100. *IG* ix. 1. 869. *SGDI* 3190. Collignon, *Les Statues funéraires* (1911), 38. Roehl³, 47. 27. *DGE* 133 (3). Rodenwaldt and Schleif, *Korkyra* i (1940), 76 ff., pl. 19a; ii (1939), 195. Friedlaender 1. Peek i. 52. Korkyra Mus.      PL. 46

**14.** Graffito Ϙυνιοϙ⟨ο⟩ς on a sherd; *c.* 525–500? *Korkyra* i. 171, no. 8, fig. Korkyra Mus.      PL. 46

**15.** Korkyrean dedication at Delphi; *c.* 500–475? *FD* ii. 1. 228 ff., fig. 183.      PL. 46

**16.** Grave-column (?) of Lexeiatas; *c.* 475? *IGA* 345. Roberts i. 101. *IG* ix. 1. 696. Roehl³, 48. 28. *DGE* 135. Korkyra Mus.      PL. 46

**17.** Boundary-stone of a precinct of Apollo; *c.* 450–400? *IGA* 347. Roberts i. 103. *IG* ix. 1. 699. *SGDI* 3193. Roehl³, 48. 30. *DGE* 135 (3). Rhomaios, *BCH* xlix (1925), 211 ff., fig. 5. *Korkyra* i. 165 f., no. 5. Korkyra Mus.

**18.** Boundary-stone of (Hera) Akria; late 5th c.? *IGA* 346. Roberts i. 102. *IG* ix. 1. 698. *SGDI* 3192. Roehl³, 48. 29. *DGE* 135 (2). Korkyra Mus.

# THE WESTERN COLONIES

## THE EUBOIC COLONIES, ITALY (CHALKIDIC–ERETRIAN)

*Letter-forms*: see Euboia, pp. 79 f. and Fig. 27.

### PITHEKOUSSAI, KYME, NEAPOLIS

Kyme, the famous Greek outpost in Campania, stood apart from the later Euboic colonies in more ways than one. She was founded from Pithekoussai about the middle of the eighth century (i.e. some twenty years before Naxos, the earliest of the others), and the motives for her foundation appear to have been more ambitious than those of the rest. The steady flow of the Euboic and Achaian emigrants into Sicily and southern Italy from *c.* 734 onwards was directed principally towards good land on which to settle and raise crops, whereas Kyme's isolated position north of all the rest reveals what was probably the main motive of the pioneers who founded her—trade with the wealthy interior. Moreover Pithekoussai and Kyme were the only Euboic colonies in the west in which both Eretrians and Chalkidians took part. The tradition is somewhat confused, and the part played by Chalkis is heavily stressed, so that late writers spoke of Kyme often as a Chalkidic colony, but it seems certain that Eretrians and Chalkidians settled together originally on the island of Pithekoussai (Strabo 247; now Ischia), and that some of them moved thence to the mainland and founded a colony at Kyme, probably with some fresh settlers from the two mother-cities in Euboia (Livy viii. 22; Dion. Hal. vii. 3). Then the rivalry of the mother-cities developed into the long Lelantine War, and the Eretrian element dropped out of the story.[1]

On Pithekoussai the excavations of Dr. Buchner have shown that the Euboic settlement here continued for a long time after Kyme had been founded. In the necropolis in the Valle di San Montano a skyphos (1) was found of the Aegean 'bird-bowl' type known well from the abundant examples on Delos and other of the islands; three fragments also are noted from Eretria.[2] The skyphos, found with some aryballoi of Protocorinthian globular style, is of Late Geometric type, though whether it belongs to the Geometric period proper or verges on the Subgeometric must be left to expert decision. At least it may well belong to the last quarter of the eighth century, and can scarcely be later than *c.* 700. On its body is an amiable verse graffito, scratched in three lines retrograde. This is the only certain example of a really early inscription written thus in the Phoenician retrograde style (pp. 43 ff. above). It is unique in another respect: the inscription consists of a statement: Νεστορος: ε[ιμ?]ι[3] ευποτ[ον]: ποτεριο[ν], followed by two hexameters: Ϝος δ' α⟨ν⟩ τοδε π[ιε]σι: ποτερι[ο]: αυτικα κενον | Ϝιμερ[ος: Ϝαιρ]εσει: καλλιστε[φα]ν̣ο: Αφροδιτε̄ς. The statement and the two hexameters each occupy a separate line. I know

[1] Dunbabin, 6 f.; cf. Berard[2], 37 ff.
[2] Boardman, *BSA* xlvii (1952), 12.
[3] Other restorations (e.g. ἔρροι) have been made here and εἰμί rejected, because the standard Euboic spelling should be εμι, and the space requires 4–5 letters. I do not regard this as a serious difficulty: the standard Attic was also εμι, but cf. Attica **4, 10***h* (ειμι).

no other example of an archaic poem in which the lines are thus separately written. Punctuation is : , as in examples from Eretria (p. 84, **9**) and Leontinoi (p. 242, **2**); *lambda* is geminated; the lettering is not tall and spidery like that of other very early inscriptions, but small and neat, very like that on Tataie's aryballos from Kyme (**3**). It is even partly *stoichedon*, but that is probably due to the unusual arrangement of the separate lines. Some way beyond the end of the second line is a retrograde graffito νε̣ι or νϝ. Perhaps the writer began Νεστορος here with *nu*, started in error the aspirate *heta* after it, realized his mistake before finishing the letter, and tried to turn it into an *epsilon*, and then gave it up and started the line afresh farther back.[1]

According to this inscription the alphabet of Pithekoussai was, as we should expect, identical with that of Kyme. A Geometric krater with five painted letters is also reported by Buchner from the same necropolis.[2]

Apart from her share in the settlement at Zankle (p. 243) there are no recorded dates in Kyme's early history until the last quarter of the sixth century, when, under Aristodemos, she twice defeated the Etruscans in their attempt to dominate Campania (Dion. Hal. vii. 3–4); but the contents of her archaic tombs show that she flourished both commercially and artistically from the time of her foundation onwards. As is well known, the most valuable evidence for her early alphabet is that of the series of abecedaria found at various sites in Etruria, which range in date from the early seventh to the fifth century. In spite of the various dissentient views that have frequently been raised, there is very little doubt that Kirchhoff was right in maintaining that this alphabet is Euboic in origin, and must therefore have come from Kyme.[3] Every letter-form in the row has its parallel in the archaic inscriptions of either Kyme or Eretria, except the unique *xi* and the *san*. These are not found in actual use in any Euboic inscription, although the Etruscans found a use for *san*; but their significant positions in the places of *xi* and *san* (which occupied the place of Phoenician *ṣāḏē*; cf. p. 33) show clearly that this was how the Etruscans received the abecedarium from their original teachers, and therefore how the Kymeans themselves still learnt it. The two letters for which the Euboic peoples had no practical use were still repeated in the recitation and written in the row; and thus the Etruscans, at least, continued to write them in their abecedarium until the beginning of the fifth century, although by this time not only *san* had ceased to be used in any Etruscan inscriptions, but other letters also, such as *beta*, *delta*, *kappa*, and *qoppa*.[4] Whether it was the Etruscans, or the Kymeans, or even the people of Chalkis and Eretria, who were responsible for the 'closing' of the letter *xi* in a square, it is impossible to decide; the type is as yet unknown elsewhere, but it occurs persistently in the Etruscan abecedaria.

The oldest of these abecedaria is that on an ivory writing-tablet found in a grave rich in other ivories in an archaic necropolis at Marsiliana d'Albegna in northern Etruria; it

---

[1] The suggestion of Russo (*Rend. Linc.* 1955, 228) is that Ν is for the omitted *nu* of ϝος δ' α⟨ν⟩, which is added here, with the alphabetic numeral sign Ε for '5', to show that after the fifth letter *nu* must be added. This is hard to accept, for normally archaic Greek writers were quite happy to insert an omitted letter at the point of omission or above it.

[2] Buchner, *Rend. Linc.* 1955, 220 ff.

[3] Kirchhoff⁴, 127 ff.; cf. Rehm, *Handbuch d. Archäologie* (ed. Otto, 1939), 206 ff. For a careful discussion of the views both for and against, cf. Buonamici, *Epigrafia Etrusca* (1932), 133 ff., and Pallottino, *The Etruscans* (1955), 257 f.

[4] Cf. Buonamici, op. cit. 115 ff., 166.

should belong to the first half of the seventh century (18).[1] This is the only example of the series which is written from right to left and shows *gamma* in the early form γ1; with this agrees the fragmentary abecedarium incised on a conical oinochoe of Protocorinthian type, which was found in a grave at Kyme (2) and bears the first letters of a Corinthian abecedarium above it (see pp. 116 f., 125. A third inscription, scratched retrograde, on the oinochoe, Ϝιγαμενετιννυνα, is in Kymean (or Etruscan) script; as the text is clearly not Greek, I have omitted it from the catalogue.). *Heta* 1 (four cross-bars instead of three) likewise does not recur; other isolated examples are known, in Boiotian (Boiotia **2, 22**, pp. 85, 89), and Lakonian (p. 190, Lakonia **11**). In no script has it been found more than once (unless Boiotia **22** is certainly Boiotian; p. 85), and it therefore seems possible that it was an error of writing in each case. The remaining abecedaria are all written from left to right, and show a lunate γ2–3. The bucchero bottle from the Regolini–Galassi tomb (**19**) may be dated tentatively in the second half of the seventh century.[2] Here, as a further aid to the learner, a syllabary was inscribed spirally round the bottle (γι, γα, γυ, &c.); *mu* and *nu* have elaborated forms, with an extra stroke at the end; *qoppa* is omitted in the abecedarium, but perhaps in error, for it appears in the syllabary, used indiscriminately with the vowels (Ϙι, Ϙα, Ϙυ, Ϙε) in defiance of the Greek practice; *san* is damaged, and has been read as either M or Ϻ;[3] *sigma* is four-stroked, both here and in the two abecedaria (of teacher and pupil?) on a bucchero amphora from Formello near Veii, which appears to be of about the same date (**20**); and here probably belongs also the incomplete version (*alpha* to *kappa*) inscribed upside down on a little bucchero goblet from Narce (**21**), which was found in a tomb with Protocorinthian pottery,[4] and which shows the 'fossil' closed *xi* transposed to the place of closed *heta*. In all these examples the letters have retained the tall, straggling appearance of Greek script of the seventh century, with tailed forms of *epsilon* and *upsilon*; but in the example on a little bird-shaped bottle from Viterbo (**22**) the letters are shorter and neater, with the late archaic tailless forms of *epsilon* and *upsilon*. In this abecedarium *sigma* is repeated in the place of *chi* X (after *upsilon*), and *chi* Ψ, set at the end, is in the late archaic tailless form, tilted, like *upsilon*, slightly to the right.[5] Lastly, there is the alphabet which was painted with a syllabary on the wall of a tomb in Siena; it is known to us only from an incomplete copy made in 1698 (**23**). It can hardly be dated earlier than the first half of the fifth century, for *vau* (transposed with the lunate *gamma*) has the developed form Ϝ3, and *theta* is dotted. The odd *zeta* may be the copyist's error, as the *nu* certainly is.[6]

Kyme's alphabet had taken root and grown well in this barbaric soil. The Marsiliana abecedarium obviously provides a *terminus ante quem* for the arrival of the alphabet in

---

[1] I conclude this from Neppi Modona's description of the ivories as belonging 'al periodo più rigoglioso d'influsso orientalizzante' (*Rend. Linc.* 1926, 494 ff.; cf. Buonamici, op. cit. 128, n. 6) and Huls, *Ivoires d'Étrurie* (1957), 43 f.

[2] Pareti is of opinion that it came from the left-hand niche in the tomb, where there was material somewhat later in date than the rest: *La Tomba Regolini-Galassi*, nos. 321–73.

[3] Cf. Neppi Modona, *RIGI* 1927–8, 58 ff.

[4] Buonamici, op. cit. 112.

[5] E. Fiesel observed (*AJP* lvii (1936), 264 f.) that, as the Etruscan letter X appears to stand for a sibilant (ś) in certain early inscriptions, it is easy to write another sibilant in its place, in error.

[6] I have not included here the Capena abecedarium, the last of the archaic series (Buonamici, op. cit. 112 ff., pl. 5), which seems to be the work of a barely literate writer, and so offers no proper grounds for comparison.

Pithekoussai and Kyme; but we cannot tell whether the first settlers actually brought it with them about the middle of the eighth century, or whether it arrived at any time during the next half-century, brought by Euboic traders or additional emigrants. The earliest inscription after the graffito **1** and the Kymean abecedarium **2** is that incised on the Protocorinthian aryballos of Tataie (**3**), a vase which has been dated in the first quarter of the seventh century.[1] The letter-forms are not unlike those of the graffito **1**, but later in certain details: cf. the tailless *epsilon* and *upsilon*. A small bronze disk of unknown provenance, now in Naples, is generally agreed to be almost certainly from Kyme (**5**). The incised inscription reads in a spiral retrograde round the edge, and has been convincingly interpreted by Guarducci as a *sors* from the oracular precinct, written in the Ionic dialect of Kyme: Ͱε̄ρε̄ ουκ εαι{ι} επιμαντευεσθαι: 'Hera does not allow further prophecy.'[2] For Hera at Kyme Guarducci cites the inscription τε̄ς Ͱε̄ρε̄- (retrograde, but with open *heta* and tailed *rho*) on a sherd now lost, found at Kyme and published in 1860 (**6**). The inscription on **5** shows closed *heta*, and Guarducci would date it about the middle of the seventh century by comparison with the script of the Marsiliana abecedarium **18** and Tataie's aryballos **3**. This may well be right, though I would hesitate to compare closely an inscription cut on bronze with a well-written graffito on a miniature pot; one would expect the latter to be ahead of the formal lettering of its time, so that the disk might in fact be appreciably later.

Several of the archaic inscriptions of Kyme come from the large chamber-tombs in which the Kymeans buried their dead in the sixth and fifth centuries. The funerary inscription was cut along one or more of the wall-blocks inside the tomb, above the place where the remains were laid. The earliest (**4**) reads only Κριτοβ|ολε̄ς inscribed *boustrophedon*; the *epsilon* is tilted forward, a local characteristic which occurs again in four later inscriptions (**7, 8, 9, 11**), as well as independently elsewhere in Greece (Lakonia, p. 189; Ionia, p. 325). The next is inscribed along two wall-blocks of a large chamber-tomb (**7**); Ͱυπυ τε̄ι κλινε̄ι τουτε̄ι Λενος Ͱυπυ. It probably belongs to the last quarter of the sixth century, or even the first years of the fifth; *heta* is now ꓕ, and the script as a whole is similar to that on a bronze lebes from Kyme in the British Museum (**8**), which was given as a prize at the funeral games of Onomastos son of Pheidileos: επι τοις Ονομαστο το Φειδιλεο αθλοις εθεθε̄ν: here *mu*, *nu*, and *phi* are no longer in their tailed archaic forms. The lebes is plain, and therefore hard to date precisely; but a lebes-lid from the same grave, belonging perhaps to another vase—it does not fit this one well—shows runners of late archaic style, *c.* 500. The third grave-inscription (**9**) probably belongs also to the last years of the sixth century or the very beginning of the fifth. It is inscribed *boustrophedon*, but also *stoichedon*; *mu* (counting as two letter-spaces in the line) is now four-stroked (μ4), *rho* is in the tailed form ρ3, and *chi* has the tall vertical stroke (χ3) which is characteristic of the late archaic and early classical period in the scripts of Euboia and the western colonies (p. 80). The second block on which the inscription continued is lost; we have only: Δε̄μοχ|αριδος | εμι το | [- - -].

The coinage of Kyme (**10**), which started in the early years of the fifth century with the

---

[1] *VS* 16, n. 1, 75, 171, 188: Blakeway, *JRS* xxv (1935), 138: 'it is therefore probable that the incised    inscription which it bears is not later than *c.* 650 B.C.'

[2] *Bull. Comm. Arch. di Roma* lxxii (1946–8), 129 ff.

legends Κυμε̄, Κυμαιον, is of service in confirming that by this time the normal *mu* had ousted the older five-stroked type, and also that *qoppa* was no longer in use. To the first half of the fifth century perhaps belongs the graffito Ξενοφαντο εμι (**11**) on a black-glazed Attic kylix (the vase itself is not illustrated, as far as I know) from one of the tombs; the drooping *epsilon* is still in use. This feature has disappeared, however, by about the middle of the century or slightly earlier, the date to which we may assign **12**, the last and best-known of the grave-inscriptions, which was cut on a block from a large chamber-tomb, whose use was evidently restricted to initiates of Dionysos: ου θεμις εν|τουθα κεισθ|αι ι με̄ τον βε|βαχχευμε|νον. We may note θ3 and χ3; ι for ει, sometimes explained as crasis of ει with the preceding -αι, is surely a Euboic dialectal variant comparable with ἰάν for ἐάν at Eretria (Euboia **9**) and Leontinoi (**2**).

The three owners' inscriptions **13, 14, 15** —χαιριο ⁚ εμι on an amphora (**13**), Δε̄μο̄νος on a small bronze bowl (**14**), and Βιοτο on another plate (**15**)—have been illustrated in majuscule type only, and may belong somewhere in the middle years of the century; and this, or not long after, should be the approximate date of the leaden plaque containing a curse against Oporis and As(t)ron (**16**).[1]

I have assigned tentatively to a Kymean source the retrograde inscription Αριστονοθος εποι⟨ε̄⟩σεν on a Greek krater found at Caere, which is usually dated somewhere in the second quarter of the seventh century (**24**). Unfortunately the text contains no characteristic letter to identify its source. It could be colonial Euboic; the use of the Ionic *nu ephelkustikon* would support that, and four-stroked *sigma*, though not normal in Kymean, does occur in two of the abecedaria, **19** and **20**. Against the old theory that the vase is Argive both Ducati and Cultrera had long ago contended that it might well be Euboic or Kymean, a view recently reinforced by Kirk (see **24**, bibliography).

The general characteristics of the script of Kyme are discussed with those of Euboia and the other Euboic colonies, pp. 79 ff. Her colony Parthenope, refounded about the first quarter of the fifth century under the name Neapolis,[2] may have used the same script; the bare evidence comes from the Neapolitan coin-legends, which begin *c.* 450: Νεπολιτες, Νεοπολιτες, &c. (**17**), showing the Euboic *lambda*.

### CATALOGUE

#### PITHEKOUSSAI

**1.** Graffiti verses on a skyphos of Geometric type from a grave; *c.* 700? Buchner and Russo, *Rend. Linc.* 1955, 215 ff., pls. 1–4. Page, *CR* 1956, 95 ff. *SEG* xiv. 604. Ischia Mus.                    PL. 47

#### KYME

**2.** Fragmentary abecedarium on a conical oinochoe from a grave; *c.* 700–675? Gàbrici, *MA* xxii (1913), 230 ff. Ribezzo, *RIGI* iii (1920), 241 f. *VS*, 171. Blakeway, *JRS* xxv (1935), 138 ff. Lejeune, *REA* xlvii (1945), 102. Buchner and Russo, op. cit. 221 f., n. 4. Naples Mus.                    PL. 18

---

[1] It is ascribed to the 4th c. in *DGE* 792a; for other views, cf. Arangio-Ruiz, 22.          [2] Bérard², 57 ff.

**3.** Graffito on a PC aryballos belonging to Tataie, from Kyme; *c.* 675–650? *IGA* 524. *IG* xiv. 865. Roberts i. 173. *SGDI* 5267. Roehl³, 79. 23. Gàbrici, op. cit. 307. Ribezzo, op. cit. 243 ff. *DGE* 786. *VS* 16, n. 1, 75, 171. Blakeway, op. cit. 138. Lejeune, op. cit. 101. Friedlaender 177*c.* Buck 10. BM A1054.                                                                                                             PL. 47

**4.** Tomb-inscription of Kritoboule, from Kyme; early 6th c.? *IGA* 527. *IG* xiv. 869. Roberts i. 176. Gàbrici, op. cit. 571, fig. 211. Roehl³, 80. 25. Ribezzo, op. cit. 76 ff. Naples Mus.                      PL. 47

**5.** Bronze disk bearing an oracular text, probably from Kyme; early 6th c.? Maiuri, *Ausonia* vi (1911), 1 ff. Ribezzo, op. cit. 71 ff. *DGE* 789. Guarducci, *Bull. Comm. Arch. di Roma* lxxi (1946–8), 129 ff., fig. 1. Naples, Carafa d'Andria coll.

**6.** Graffito on a sherd found at Kyme; early 6th c.? Minervini, *Bull. Arch. Nap.* viii (1860), 25 ff. Guarducci, op. cit. 135, fig. 3. Lost?

**7.** Tomb-inscription of Lenos from Kyme; *c.* 525–500? *IG* xiv. 871. Roberts i. 177a. *SGDI* 5269 (3a). Roehl³, 80. 29. Gàbrici, op. cit. 572 f., fig. 213. Ribezzo, op. cit. 71 ff. *DGE* 791. Buck 11. Naples Mus. 115389.                                                                                                         PL. 47

**8.** Bronze lebes offered as a prize at the funeral games of Onomastos, from a grave in Kyme; *c.* 500? *IGA* 525. *IG* xiv. 862. Roberts i. 174. *BMC Bronzes*, 257. *SGDI* 5265. Roehl³, 80. 24. *DGE* 788. BM.                                                                                                                      PL. 47

**9.** Tomb-inscription of Democharis from Kyme; 6th–5th c.? *IGA* 528. *IG* xiv. 867. Roberts i. 177. *SGDI* 5266. Roehl³, 80. 26. Gàbrici, op. cit. 572 f., fig. 212. Ribezzo, op. cit. 71 ff. *DGE* 787. Naples Mus.                                                                                                                    PL. 48

**10.** Coinage of Kyme with legend Κυμε̄, Κυμαιον; *c.* 500–450. *HN²*, 36. B ii. 1. 1437 ff., pl. 69.

**11.** Graffito on an Attic kylix, property of Xenophantos, from a tomb; *c.* 500–450? Gàbrici, op. cit. 463, 572. Naples Mus.                                                                                      PL. 48

**12.** Tomb-inscription for a sepulchre for Bacchic initiates from Kyme; *c.* 450? Sogliano, *NS* 1905, 377 ff. *SGDI* iv. 851. Roehl³, 80. 28. Gàbrici, op. cit. 573 ff., fig. 214. Ribezzo, op. cit. 85. *DGE* 792. Naples Mus. 129874.                                                                                              PL. 48

**13.** Graffiti on an amphora from Kyme; *c.* 450? *IGA* 530. *IG* xiv. 866. Roberts i. 185a. *SGDI* 5268. Roehl³, 80. 27. *DGE* 790. Naples Mus.

**14.** Graffito on a bronze bowl from Kyme; *c.* 450? *IGA* 529. *IG* xiv. 864. Naples Mus.

**15.** Graffito on a plate from Kyme; *c.* 450? *IGA* 531. *IG* xiv. 863. Naples Mus.

**16.** Curse against Oporis and Astron on a leaden plaque from Kyme; *c.* 450–425? Paribeni, *NS* 1903, 171 f. *SGDI* 5270. Comparetti, *Rend. Linc.* xxvii (1918), 202 ff. *DGE* 792a. Arangio-Ruiz, 157 ff., no. 22. Naples Mus.

NEAPOLIS

**17.** Inscribed coinage; *c.* 450 onwards. *HN²*, 38.

NON-GREEK (ETRUSCAN)

**18.** Ivory school-tablet from a grave at Marsiliana d'Albegna; *c.* 700–650? Buonamici, *Epigrafia Etrusca* (1932), 101 ff., pl. 1. 1 (= Bu). Huls, *Ivoires d'Étrurie* (1957), 43f., pl. 12. 2. Florence, Mus. Arch.                                                                                                                   PL. 48

**19.** Bucchero bottle from the Regolini–Galassi tomb, Caere; *c.* 650–600? Bu, 104 ff., pl. 2. Rome, Mus. Etrusco Vaticano.                                                                                          PL. 48

**20.** Bucchero amphora from Formello; *c.* 650–600? Bu, 107 ff., pl. 3. Rome, Villa Giulia Mus.

PL. 48

**21.** Bucchero goblet from Narce; *c.* 650–600? Bu, 111 ff., pl. 4. 7. Rome, Villa Giulia Mus. 4879.

PL. 48

**22.** Bucchero bird-shaped bottle from Viterbo; *c.* 550–500? Bu, 103 ff., pl. 1. 2. Fiesel, *AJP* lvii (1936), 264 f. Richter, *Handbook Etr. Coll.* (1940), 13, figs. 46–48. New York, MM 24.97.21.   PL. 48

**23.** Abecedarium painted on the wall of a tomb at Siena, now lost; *c.* 500–450? Bu, 108 ff., pl. 4.

PL. 48

*Inscription attributed to Kyme*

**24.** Krater signed by Aristonothos, from Caere; *c.* 675–650? *MuZ* i. 110 f., fig. 65. Helbig, *Ö.Jh.* xii (1909), 59 f., fig. 42. Ducati, *Mél. d'art et d'histoire* xxxi (1911), 33 ff. Cultrera, *Ausonia* viii (1913), 137 f. Köster, *Das antike Seewesen* (1923), 152 ff., pl. 35. Kirk, *BSA* xliv (1949), 120 f. Courbin, *BCH* lxxix (1955), 21, n. 1, figs. 12–13. Schweitzer, *RM* lxii (1955), 78 ff. Rome, Conservatori Mus.

# THE EUBOIC COLONIES, SICILY (CHALKIDIC)

*Letter-forms*: see Euboia, pp. 79 f. and Fig. 27.

## NAXOS

Naxos was the oldest Greek colony in Sicily. Her oikistes was Thoukles of Chalkis, who settled there *c.* 734 with a band of emigrants from Chalkis (Thuc. vi. 3. 1) and probably from the island Naxos also.[1] Except for her own early colonizing activities she has left little trace of her existence in the history of Sicily until her capture by Hippokrates of Gela *c.* 494. The only inscriptions known as yet are those on the coinage (**1**), which is held by Cahn on stylistic grounds to have begun *c.* 550–530, in the generation of the painters Exekias and the Amasis painter at Athens, the earliest issue being dated *c.* 550.[2] Milne would prefer a slightly lower date, perhaps a decade later,[3] and the developed appearance of the lettering endorses this, even if allowance is made for the skill of the die-engraver. The legend on the earliest issues, Ναξιον retrograde or (rarely) left to right, shows that the alphabet was of the 'red' type, and so by inference Chalkidic. The series ends in the late archaic period, presumably when Hippokrates seized the town. The fine new series which begins *c.* 461, when the overthrow of all the tyrannies had freed the subjugated states, still has NAXION; but the latest issues, dated *c.* 430–403, show an Ionic *xi* (type 3, Fig. 15), which suggests that here, as in the towns of Magna Graecia, the change to Ionic script began before the last quarter of the fifth century.

---

[1] Hellanikos *ap.* Steph. Byz. s.v. Χαλκίς: Ephoros *ap.* Strabo 267. It is further confirmed by the resemblance between the coin-types of the two places; cf. Dunbabin, 8 f.; Cahn, *Die Münzen d. sizilischen Stadt Naxos* (1944), 13; Milne, *JHS* lxiv (1944), 107 f.; van Compernolle, *Bull. Inst. belg. Rome* xxvi (1950), 163 ff. The arguments against this view are given by Bérard[2], 79 f.

[2] Cahn, op. cit. 30 f.

[3] Op. cit. 108.

## LEONTINOI

Only five years after Naxos had been founded, Thoukles and a band of Naxians advanced down the coast and seized the site of Leontinoi and shortly afterwards that of Katane, thus securing for the Chalkidic colonists one of the most fertile areas in Sicily.[1] Katane has so far yielded no inscriptions of the fifth century or earlier, Leontinoi none before her capture by Hippokrates *c*. 494. To that period her earlier coins are ascribed (3); the obverse bears a charioteer, as on the Geloan series, the reverse a canting badge of a lion's head. The legend on the first issues reads Λεοντινον, retrograde or left to right, with non-Euboic *lambda*; possibly the first die-engravers were Geloans, for whom this would be the normal type (pp. 262 f.). It is not until the issue of the series bearing the head of Apollo *c*. 479 that the Euboic *lambda* appears, and continues through the second quarter of the century, the Ionic type reappearing in the course of the third quarter (*HN*², 149). There is little other epigraphic material to record. Pausanias saw a bronze Zeus at Olympia (v. 22. 7), dedicated by three Leontines Hippagoras, Phrynon, and Ainesidemos, and observed that in his opinion this was not the Ainesidemos who was tyrant of Leontinoi, and who is dated by modern scholars in the late archaic period;[2] so we cannot estimate the date of the offering. One further inscription has been connected with Leontinoi. On Monte San Mauro, lying inland between Leontinoi and Gela, the architectural remains of a small settlement were found, which produced, among other sixth-century Greek material which is apparently Geloan,[3] twelve burnt fragments from two (or more?) bronze plaques, inscribed on both sides in nearly all cases (2). The texts are *boustrophedon*, and owing to the bad state of the surface the copies are not certain in all details; but the Euboic *lambda* is clear, and Leontinoi is the nearest Euboic colony from which it could have come. It is especially tantalizing that the *mu* appears to be both five- and four-stroked: five-stroked in fr. 1 and perhaps in fr. 2, l. 1 (this may possibly be IM, from [- - - πολ]εμιον r. to l.), but four-stroked in the same fragment, l. 6, and twice (once inverted) in fr. 3; the letter is uncertain twice in fr. 10. I do not think therefore that these fragments can be used as definite evidence that the five-stroked *mu* was used at Leontinoi, and I leave the question open until further material is found. The date should not be later than the last quarter of the sixth century, and may be a little earlier; *qoppa* is still in use, *rho* is still tailless; *chi*, on the other hand, is no longer tailed. All that can be made out of the fragments as they stand are sums of money(?) which may be fines (τετραϙο[σι - - -], δυϜō ταλαν[τα - - - ⊦ι?]ερα εναι, τρια τα[λαντα]), the beginnings of clauses (ιαν δε—, ⊦οστις α[ν]—), probably the names of two deities ([το Απολō]νος: και τēς Αθēν[αιēς]?), and parts of various words evidently with the root φον-, which has caused the texts to be identified as part of a criminal code, and to be associated tentatively with the famous lawgiver Charondas, who legislated for Katane and other Chalkidic cities.[4]

---

[1] Thuc. vi. 3. 3; cf. Dunbabin, 10 f. and Bérard², 82 ff.

[2] Ainesidemos, son of Pataikos, was a contemporary of Gelon and a member of Hippokrates' bodyguard: Hdt. vii. 154. The father of Theron of Akragas was also called Ainesidemos, but his father's name was Emmenides, or Chalkiopieus.

[3] According to Dunbabin (115 ff.) the site was occupied by Sikels until the early 7th c., and thereafter by Greeks from Gela, whose earliest remains belong to the first part of the 6th c. and cease in ruin *c*. 500, perhaps in the course of the Sikel campaigns of Hippokrates.

[4] Orsi, *MA* xx (1910), 844 f.; cf. Dunbabin, 68, 129.

## ZANKLE

Zankle on the Straits was originally settled by a freebooting expedition from Kyme in Italy, under a man named Perieres; but she soon received an official colony sent out from Chalkis under Krataimenes, which contained elements from other parts of Euboia as well.[1] The date is held to have been a decade or so before the end of the eighth century, since Rhegion, *vis-à-vis* on the Italian side of the Straits, was colonized shortly after the start of the First Messenian War (p. 244).[2] The coins of Zankle (4) apparently begin *c.* 525, and E. S. G. Robinson has demonstrated[3] how the vicissitudes of her history during the next seventy-five years are reflected in the lettering of her coin-legends. Until *c.* 493 the legend was Δανκ or Δανκλ, in Chalkidic script; upon her occupation by Samian refugees, *c.* 493–489, the coinage carried Samian types and Samian numerals (Α, Β, (Γ?), Δ, Ε); when Anaxilas of Rhegion thereafter occupied the town and changed the name to Messene *c.* 489, the coinage adopted (with the Rhegine types of a lion's and a calf's head) the legend Μεσσενιον (σ3); in 480 the types were altered to celebrate Anaxilas' victory with the mule-car at Olympia and the *sigmas* inadvertently reversed; at the time of the expulsion of the Sicilian tyrants (*c.* 466–461) the Rhegine element in Zankle-Messene was evidently temporarily ousted, for a brief issue appeared bearing the old legend Δανκλαιον once more; then the Rhegine type prevailed again, with the legend Μεσσενιον or Μεσσανιον; and henceforward the Doric form only of the name was used. It is in this period, after the middle of the fifth century, that the local σ3 becomes four-stroked, and the first example of *omega* appears in the legend. The curved form of σ3 on the coins may be noted, for it recurs in Rhegine inscriptions (p. 244).

Two further relics of Zankle's history have been found at Olympia. The first (5) is a fragmentary bronze plaque inscribed *boustrophedon* with what seems to be part of a treaty against aggression between Zankle and an unknown state. *Epsilon* has little or no tail, *heta* is in the open form ⊢3, *nu* varies between ν1 and ν3; it is probably to be dated not long before the seizure of Zankle by the Samian refugees *c.* 493. The circular letters are made with a punch, occasionally twice over if the first attempt was badly centred. To the same period probably belonged the offering at Olympia by Euagoras 'of Zankle', seen by Pausanias (v. 25. 11; a group showing Herakles fighting a mounted Amazon). It was made by Aristokles of Kydonia, which would indicate as a *terminus post quem c.* 519, the date of Kydonia's Aiginetan settlement; for the Aiginetans were renowned bronze-workers, and Kresilas of Kydonia carried on the tradition in the fifth century. The offering also seen by Pausanias (v. 25. 4), which was made by 'the Messenians of the Strait' to commemorate the shipwreck of a chorus of boys and their trainers while crossing to compete at a festival in Rhegion (p. 245), may be of any date between *c.* 489 and the end of the century, when Hippias the sophist, Pausanias says, added an elegiac verse to the original inscription. The second relic of Zankle actually found at Olympia is part of a panoply: a bronze greave and a shield, both inscribed Δανκλαιοι Ρεγινον (6). The naturalistic

---

[1] Thuc. vi. 4. 5–6; cf. Dunbabin, 11 f.; Bérard², 92 ff.; Vallet, *Rhégion et Zancle* (1958), 59 ff.

[2] The date given by Eusebios for Zankle (757–756) is agreed to be too high; Bérard suggests, op. cit. 96,

that this may have been the date of the first prospecting there by the Kymean ships.

[3] *JHS* lxvi (1946), 13 ff., pl. 5.

treatment of the knee-cap of the greave does not suggest an early date, and Kunze ascribes it to the late archaic period not long before 493, pointing out that it cannot be attributed to the period of Rhegine domination, *c*. 489–461.[1]

## RHEGION

Though separated from the Sicilian Chalkidic colonies by the narrow Straits, Rhegion is here counted among them since her fortunes were so closely bound up with theirs. She was in a sense a colony of Zankle, in that Zankle had invited colonists to the site from Chalkis, and had provided Antimnestos as oikistes; but an important element of the Rhegine community was a body of Messenians who were in exile during the First Messenian War, i.e. near the end of the eighth century, and who had apparently been advised by the oracle at Delphi to join the Chalkidic colony then going out. From these Anaxilas of Rhegion was descended.[2] There are as yet no sixth-century inscriptions from Rhegion.[3] The earliest Rhegine coinage (*c*. 510–494) has the legend Ρϝγινον retrograde (7), which continues with little change (except that *c*. 461 appears a variant Ρϝγινος) until in the third quarter of the fifth century the Ionic *eta* and *gamma* appear (ΡΗΓΙΝΟΣ).[4] Four brief inscriptions have been found on the site: the lip of a bronze lebes (?) inscribed Ϝεℎρακλεος Ρϝγινυ (11), and three small clay pellets, each bearing an incised name, whose exact provenance could not be established: Κλεοφαντος Γλαυκιυ (12), Κλεομενϝες Εμμενιδευ (13), and Δϝεμο⟨φ⟩ανης Θραρυος (= Θρασυος) (14). All except 12 show the same curved σ3 as that on the coins of Zankle-Messene at about the same date (*c*. 475–450?); the local spelling of υ for the improper diphthong ου is interesting.[5] 14 has *eta* η, the earliest appearance of the Ionic form.

About 467 Mikythos 'of Rhegion and Messene' (as his dedications say), who had been steward to Anaxilas and regent for the latter's sons after his death in 476, was suspected of undue ambition, and retired to settle in Tegea (Hdt. vii. 170. 4; Diod. xi. 66). During his retirement he made an astonishing number of offerings at Olympia,[6] and parts of two bases have survived, apparently with duplicate inscriptions (8–10). 8 and 9 are the second blocks of these bases, and the fragments 10 belonged to the first block of one or the other. The best version of the dedication, restored from Pausanias' description of the monument,[7] is that made by Preuner with the help of previous suggestions.[8] The lettering of 8 shows the typical λ2 and σ3; 9 is the same in all respects, except that it has λ3. The

---

[1] The neat lettering would suit a date in the 460's, when the old name of Zankle was briefly restored; but Kunze observes that a date below 475 is impossible for the strata concerned; *Olympiabericht* v (1956), 38 and 176.

[2] Cf. Dunbabin, 12 f.; Bérard[2], 101; Vallet, op. cit. 66 ff.

[3] Recent studies, however, incline to the view that 'Chalkidic' ware was probably distributed, and possibly made, at Rhegion (p. 81); see Vallet, op. cit. 212 ff., 225 ff., 301; Boardman, *BSA* 52 (1957), 12 f.

[4] Robinson, op. cit. 19.

[5] Cf. Sestieri, *Epigraphica* ii (1940), 23 f.

[6] Pausanias (v. 26. 2–5) gives an incomplete list of four groups with a total of fifteen figures.

[7] v. 26. 5: τὰ δὲ ἐπὶ τοῖς ἀναθήμασιν ἐπιγράμματα καὶ πατέρα Μικύθῳ Χοῖρον καὶ Ἑλληνίδας αὐτῷ πόλεις Ῥήγιόν τε πατρίδα καὶ τὴν ἐπὶ τῷ πορθμῷ Μεσσήνην δίδωσιν· οἰκεῖν δὲ τὰ μὲν ἐπιγράμματα ἐν Τεγέᾳ φησὶν αὐτόν, τὰ δὲ ἀναθήματα ἀνέθηκεν ἐς Ὀλυμπίαν εὐχήν τινα ἐκτελῶν ἐπὶ σωτηρίᾳ παιδὸς νοσήσαντος νόσον φθινάδα.

[8] *JdI* xxxv (1920), 59 ff. See Transliteration of Plates. The underlined letters there are those preserved on fragments *a*–*c* of 10. As Preuner himself says (op. cit. 61), his restoration of ll. 3–4 cannot be quite accurate, for it does not allow for the surviving letters on fragments *d* and *e*: —γε—|—πε— and —ν—|ιδεπ̣—.

best explanation for this seems to be that suggested by Purgold,[1] that the inscribing was done by an Elean mason who, following an original draft of the text written in the Chalkidic script of Rhegion and Messene, on one occasion at least lapsed and cut his own form of *lambda*. *Heta* in the form ⱶ4 does not recur elsewhere in Rhegion or Elis, and may be another slip; the normal Rhegine at this time would be the open type (cf. **11**).[2]

A single block from a Rhegine dedication survives at Delphi (**15**): Ρ̣ε̄γινο̣ι [- - -]. The occasion is unknown, but the upright ν4 suggests that it should not be dated earlier than the middle of the fifth century; as Bourguet remarks,[3] it may commemorate some defeat of the natives—presumably some years after the disastrous defeat of the Tarantine and Rhegine forces by the Messapioi in 473 (Diod. xi. 52). The Ionic *eta* occurs on an inscription *c.* 450 (?) (**14**, p. 244); it first appears on the coinage of Rhegion (with Ionic *gamma*, γ4) during the third quarter of the fifth century (p. 244).[4] It is used also (with ε1, ν3, and ρ3) in the dedication of 'Glaukis son of Lykkides' at Olympia (**16**), a statue of Hermes carrying a kerykeion, made by Kalon of Elis (Paus. v. 27. 8). Kalon's only other known work is the dedication by Zankle-Messene for the chorus of boys lost in the Straits (p. 243); from **16** it would appear that he was active in the third quarter of the century, perhaps very soon after 450; for the *epsilon*, *nu*, and *rho* of the dedication are not yet standardized to E, N, and P. A date in the 440's would suit the Elean lettering of the sculptor's signature also.

## HIMERA

Himera was founded in 648 by a band of colonists from Zankle, strengthened by a Syracusan clan, the Myletidai, who had been exiled from Syracuse; for this reason, Thucydides says, her dialect was a mixture of Chalkidic (Ionic) and Doric, but in her institutions (νόμιμα) the Chalkidic element prevailed.[5] She was the only Greek settlement of any size on the north coast of Sicily, and it has been suggested that her importance lay mainly in serving as a Greek port of call on the route to Kyme and Etruria, and also in tapping the rich silver resources of Spain (Tartessos).[6] Her early silver coinage is abundant, and against the conservative date 'before 482' ascribed to it by Head and others, a date as early as 580 has been suggested by Milne, based mainly on grounds of general historical probability.[7] This is disturbing to the epigraphist, for the legend of the earliest coins is IH, and an open *heta* in the first quarter of the sixth century would be astonishing. The later types which show (*a*) a hen in the incuse square on the reverse (to balance the

---

[1] *Ol.* v. 267.

[2] The German excavators at Olympia report the discovery of a greave, probably part of a panoply, dedicated by the Rhegine people after a victory over Lokroi: [P]ε̄γινοι Λοκρōν (*BCH* lxxxi (1957), 568, fig. 5). The lettering (from the photograph) suggests a date in the first half of the fifth century.

[3] *FD* iii. 1. 328. It was to this dedication that Pomtow wrongly added the fragment Argos **35**: see p. 166.

[4] If Rhegion was consistently using the Ionic alphabet before 425, the gravestone in the Athenian Kerameikos *IG* ii². 5220, commemorating in Ionic

script the Rhegine Silenos son of Phokos (ambassador for the renewal of the Athenian–Rhegine treaty in 433/2, *GHI*² 58 and p. 263) may not be as late as 410–380, the date suggested by Peek, *Kerameikos* iii. 28; Silenos may have died before the embassy left Athens, and his colleagues drafted his epitaph.

[5] Thuc. vi. 5. 1; cf. Bérard², 240 ff.; Dunbabin, 300 f. There were three oikistai, Eukleides, Simos, and Sakon; the latter may have led the Myletidai, for the grave of a Sakon son of Mylos and his son has been found near Akragas; see p. 274.

[6] Milne, *Num. Chron.* xviii (1938), 36 ff.; Dunbabin, loc. cit.

[7] Milne, loc. cit.

cock on the obverse, the city's badge) and the legend τυ or λυ inverted (?), and (b) the legend λυ (?) or ⊢ι and the hen in an incuse circle, are dated by Milne (a) c. 540 and (b) after 510; but, granting that the earliest types and (a) may be earlier than 510, I should not like to set the open *heta* before the last quarter of the sixth century.

In 480 Anaxilas of Rhegion and Terillos of Himera, having called in the Carthaginians to drive off the encroaching power of Theron of Akragas, brought about the famous defeat of Hamilcar by Syracuse and Akragas at Himera, and thus set Himera in the power of Akragas and, ultimately, of Syracuse; about 476, after a massacre of the citizens by the governor, Theron's son Thrasydaios, Himera was practically refounded as a new colony by Theron, for not only Dorians but any others who wished were invited to emigrate thither. Ergoteles, the famous Cretan runner, was one who joined the settlers (see below). The weight and types of the city's coinage changed, the legends reading ⊢ιμερα or ⊢ιμε (c. 480–472?), and Ιμερα (retrograde), Ιμεραιον or (on the smaller denominations) ⊢ιμερα retrograde with ⊢2 (c. 472 onwards; *HN²*, 144 f.). The name is certainly in the Doric form now, and the alphabet is no longer Chalkidic; for the reverse of the coins inscribed Ιμερα retrograde shows Pelops spelt Πελοψ, with Ionic *lambda* and *psi*. The use of *psi* is noteworthy; it occurs also on Selinountine coins of about this period. The source of Selinous' alphabet is discussed on pp. 264, 270, where I have suggested that it may ultimately have been Syracuse; hence one might infer (a) that Himera's die-engravers at this time were either Selinountine, or of Syracusan stock, or (b) that Himera was by this time using the Ionic script. The only inscriptions found at Himera so far are the single letters—masons' marks—on the cornice of the temple, which was built during the first half of the fifth century:[1] A, B, Γ (or ‹ ?), Δ (or ▷ ?), E, Γ, Ι, H, ⊕. The masons cannot have been Selinountine (nor Syracusan?), for *beta* would then be in the form Ϻ (p. 262); they might have been from Akragas or Gela, or even from the surviving Chalkidic element in Himera. This helps us little; but there is also a fragmentary bronze plaque found at Olympia, which may be in Himeran script (**19**). It was once fastened to a stone base, and bears part of a metrical dedication made by the famous long-distance runner Ergoteles of Knossos, who was exiled from Crete during a time of civil strife, and made his home, with other Doric settlers, at Himera (Sch. *ad* Pind. *Ol.* xii, inscrr. a–b; P. Oxy. 222). Pausanias saw his statue at Olympia (vi. 4. 11), and gives us the sense of the inscription without quoting it. Ergoteles was twice periodonikes, and his victories have been assigned to the years between 478 and 464. The statue must have been set up after his retirement, for clearly the inscription which Pausanias saw mentioned them all. Did Ergoteles set up his statue immediately after his last victory, or some years later (pp. 112, 167)? The inscription is in the Ionic script, cut *stoichedon*, but showing the crossed *theta* and tailed *nu*. It is certainly not Cretan, certainly not Elean. We may guess then that Ionic appeared in the script of Himera about the middle of the fifth century, as elsewhere in the West (Rhegion, Taras, Thourioi, Selinous); this inscription is unlikely to be much, if at all, later than 450, because of the early forms of *theta* and *nu*. The general appearance of the inscription may be compared with that of Selinous **44**, the dedication of an Asklepiad; this also shows crossed *theta* with the Ionic forms.

[1] Marconi, *SMG* ii (1930), 194; Dunbabin, 429.

Lastly may be briefly mentioned two cups now in Palermo, from a collection made at Gela, which have long been identified as from a Chalkidic colony by their dialect and script. They were apparently offered by women to a local hero Pedios: Ͱιπποδρομɛ̄ς τοδε δο̄ρον Πεδιο̄ι and Αρ⟨ι⟩φυλε̄ς? (rather than Αρϙυλε̄ς, as given hitherto) τοδε δο̄ρον Πεδιο̄ι (**20, 21**). They may be *c.* 500 in date; *heta* is open, but one would expect tailed *rho* in the fifth century.[1] A bronze plaque found at Olympia (**22**) has nothing to show whether it comes from Euboia or her colonies; but it is perhaps more likely to be from one of the colonies than from Euboia herself, for the colonial patronage of Olympia needs no stressing. It bears fragments of a judicial text, and combines Ͱ2 and *qoppa* with the later forms ε4, θ3, ρ3, and χ3. The curved *sigma* may perhaps point to Rhegion, but this is very uncertain. I should place it in the first quarter of the fifth century.

The general characteristics of the letter-forms used by the Chalkidic colonies are included in the discussion of the script of Euboia herself, pp. 79 ff.

## CATALOGUE

### NAXOS

**1.** Coin series from the second half of the 6th c. onwards, with legend Ναξιον. Cahn, *Die Münzen d. sizilischen Stadt Naxos*, 1944.

### LEONTINOI

**2.** Fragments of opisthographic bronze plaques from Monte San Mauro, containing parts of a legal text on homicide(?); *c.* 525? Orsi and Comparetti, *MA* xx (1910), 739 ff., 830 ff. Arangio-Ruiz, 171 ff. *SEG* iv. 64. Syracuse Mus.

**3.** Coin series from the early 5th c. onwards, with legend Λεοντινον. B ii. 1. 1501 ff., pl. 73. *HN*[2], 148 ff.

### ZANKLE

**4.** Coin series from *c.* 525 onwards, with legend Δανκ, Δανκλ, Μεσσενιον, Μεσσανιον. E. S. G. Robinson, *JHS* lxvi (1946), 13 ff., pl. 5.

**5.** Fragment of a bronze plaque from Olympia, containing part of a treaty against aggression; *c.* 500–494? *Ol.* v. 24. *IGA* 518. Roehl[3], 78. 13. *SGDI* 5275. *SEG* xi. 1180. Olympia Mus. 328.     PL. 49

**6.** Greave and shield from a dedication by Zankle at Olympia for a victory over Rhegion; *c.* 500–490? Kunze and Schleif, *Olympiabericht* ii (1938), 69 f., fig. 43, pls. 41–42, and v (1956), 37 ff., 54, no. 23, fig. 18, pl. 22. Gàbrici, *Atti dell'Accad. Palermo* ix (1948), 253 ff. *SEG* xi. 1205. Olympia Mus.

PL. 49

### RHEGION

**7.** Coin series from *c.* 510 onwards, with legend Ρε̄γινον, Ρε̄γινος. E. S. G. Robinson, op. cit. 13 ff., pl. 5.

**8–10.** Block from the base of a dedication at Olympia by Mikythos of Rhegion and Messene (**8**), part of a duplicate block from a second base (**9**), and fragments of another block from one of these bases (**10**); *c.* 467–450? *Ol.* v. 267–9. *IGA* 532–3. Roberts i. 180. *SGDI* 5276. Roehl[3], 78 f., 17–18. *DGE* 794. Preuner, *JdI* xxxv (1920), 59 ff. Olympia Mus. 660, 303, 100, 501, 522 *a–b*, 498.     PL. 49

---

[1] Sir John Beazley warns me, however, that the inscriptions on these cups may be forgeries.

**11.** Fragment from the lip of a bronze lebes (?) dedicated to Herakles at Rhegion; *c.* 475–450? Sestieri, *Epigraphica* ii (1940), 21 ff., fig. 4. Naples Mus.　　　　　　　　　　PL. 49

**12–14.** Three clay pellets from Rhegion, inscribed with the names of Kleophantos, Kleomenes, and Demophanes; *c.* 475–450? Orsi, *NS* 1902, 44 ff. Roehl[3], 79. 19–21. *SGDI* 5278. Naples Mus.

　　　　　　　　　　　　　　　　　　　　　　　　　　　　　　　　　　　PL. 49

**15.** Block from the base of a dedication by Rhegion at Delphi; *c.* 450–440? Pomtow, *Klio* ix (1909), 174 f., fig. 7. *FD* iii. 1. no. 503. Delphi Mus. 3838.

**16.** Base for a statue of Hermes dedicated by Glaukias at Olympia; *c.* 450–440? *Ol.* v. 271. *IGA* 536. Roberts i. 182. *SGDI* 5277. Roehl[3], 79. 22. *DGE* 795. *SEG* xi. 1226. Olympia Mus. 401+1055.

　　　　　　　　　　　　　　　　　　　　　　　　　　　　　　　　　　　PL. 43

### HIMERA

**17.** Coin series of 6th c. with legend Ͱι, Τυ, Λυ(?), continuing in 5th c. with Ͱιμε, Ͱιμερα, etc. B ii. 1. 1561 ff., pl. 80. *HN*[2], 143 ff. Milne, *Num. Chron.* xviii (1938), 37 ff.

**18.** Masons' marks on the temple at Himera; *c.* 500–450. Marconi, *SMG* ii (1930), 95, fig. 44.

*Inscription attributed to Himera*

**19.** Bronze plaque with a dedication by Ergoteles of Himera at Olympia; *c.* 450? Kunze, *Kretika Chronika* vii (1953), 138 ff., pl. A, and *Olympiabericht* v (1956), 153 ff., figs. 61–62. Olympia Mus. B. 2488.　　　　　　　　　　　　　　　　　　　　　　　　　　　　　PL. 49

*Inscriptions of unidentified Chalkidic colonies*

**20–21.** Dedications to a hero Pedios (?) by Hippodrome and Ar(i)phyle (?) on two cups once in a collection at Gela; *c.* 500? *IGA* 519–20. *IG* xiv. 595–6. *SGDI* 5279–80. Roberts i. 183. Roehl[3], 78. 15–16. *DGE* 793. Pace, *Arte e Civiltà* iii (1945), 528 f., fig. 147. Palermo Mus.

**22.** Fragment of a bronze plaque from Olympia, with part of a judicial text; *c.* 500–475? *IGA* 374. Roberts i. 179. *SGDI* 5291. *Ol.* v. 25. Roehl[3], 81. 30. Olympia Mus. 460.

## THE ACHAIAN COLONIES

FIG. 42. Achaia and Colonies

*Notes on letter-forms*

α2 occurs occasionally at Kroton, Metapontion, Kaulonia. α3 is normal at Poseidonia (**3–7**), and frequent elsewhere.

The characteristic *gamma* in the colonies is the 'shorthand' γ1. It was apparently used on the mainland on occasion, for it occurs once in the word εγραψε on the LC pyxis by Chares (*NC* 164, no. 27 = p. 126, n. 5), though not again (as far as I know) in Corinthian. The coins of Αιγ— (Aigion?) in Achaia show γ2, the type normal in Corinth, Sikyon, Arkadia, Elis, Kephallenia. It is impossible to divine by what chance 1 was the type which perpetuated itself in the colonies.

ει is no longer used in **7** (early in the second quarter of the 5th c.?), nor in the three plaques **28, 29, 30**, which I take to be of about the same date.

Closed *heta* is not yet attested; either the Achaian script used ⊢2 remarkably early, or (more likely) the surviving inscriptions are not earlier than the late 6th c. (**3, 8, 15**).

The earliest examples of θ3 are apparently **8, 16** (late 6th c.?). The letter is sometimes cut rhomboid (cf. *omikron*), especially in the script of Poseidonia.

The three-stroked *iota* is one of the clearest hall-marks of the Achaian alphabet. It is still used on coins in the third quarter of the 5th c. (e.g. Pandosia, Terina, Metapontion), together with the *san*; but both letters appear to have been finally ousted during this period by the standard forms Ι and Σ.

λ3 appears on two 5th-c. inscriptions from Delphi, which I suspect to be in Phokian script (Phokis **22, 23**; see pp. 256, 258).

μ1 still occurs on the coins of Metapontion in the second quarter of the 5th c. (Noe, *Coinage of Metapontion* ii. 8 and pl. 24; for the date cf. Lehmann, *Statues on Coins*, 33 ff.).

ν1 likewise persists into the 5th c. (cf. **7, 25, 28–30**); the coins of Terina *c.* 475–450 still show it, although ν2 had also appeared before the end of the first quarter (cf. **25** (?) and the Metapontine coins inscribed Αχελōιο αεθλōν, p. 254).

The rhomboid ο2 is fairly common (cf. *theta*): e.g. **2, 3, 30, 31**.

As far as can be judged, *san* follows the course of the crooked *iota*, disappearing with it at some time during the third quarter of the 5th c., when *sigma* comes into fashion.

*Qoppa* is not found in inscriptions later than **8**, which suggests that its practical use had died by the beginning of the 5th c.; but it is retained in the legend Ϙρο on the coinage of Kroton until the third quarter of the century, or even later (cf. *HN²*, 96).

ρ1 is normal. ρ2, tailed *rho*, though current in the scripts of the Chalkidic, Spartan, and Lokrian colonies, is very rare in Achaian; I have noted only three possible instances: on an incuse coin of Kroton (*BMC Coins Italy*, 244), in the Metapontine inscription **14** (*BMC Coins*), and in a dedication of the Krotoniates at Delphi, which may well be in the Phokian script (p. 258, Phokis **22**).

Tailed *upsilon* is not yet attested. The late archaic υ2 is nearly always used; the exceptions are (*a*) the variant υ3 which appears on the axe **8**, in the legend Συ on some of the earliest incuse coins of Sybaris, and in the graffito **6**; (*b*) the form 4 apparently used in **18**, according to *SGDI* 1645, and possibly in **32**.

χ1 occurs in Achaia **7** and the colonial graffito **32**. χ2 appears *c.* 500 or slightly earlier (**16**); in **2**, an inscription which is probably earlier, the letter is damaged, but the surviving traces, compared with the bases of the other letters, suggest that this also was χ2. From the early 5th c. onwards the centre bar is prolonged upwards (χ3), a type common also to the Chalkidic script.

*Psi* is not yet certainly attested; ψ1 (attested in Lokris and Arcadia, pp. 105, 213 f.) may appear in the graffito **35** (p. 259); if this is so, we may perhaps conjecture that the form originated in Achaia as an elaboration of the Corinthian or Sikyonian Ψ.

*Punctuation*. 2 is used in the plaques **28** and **29**. Other Italian colonies which used this type were Taras (**1**) and Lokroi (**5**). 1 is used in the graffito **31**.

*Direction of the script*. The *boustrophedon* system seems to have been dying out in ordinary inscriptions by the end of the 6th c.; but on coins it was often still used in the 5th c. to achieve a symmetrical effect round the main design (p. 49). The latest example is on a coin of Kaulonia, in which the Ionic script is used (p. 258). A dedication could still be written retrograde *c.* 470 (**7**). The two 6th-c. inscriptions which are inscribed vertically *boustrophedon* both show this practice in a modified form; the first two lines of **14** are from left to right, and then the proper name, which was begun in l. 2, runs on *boustrophedon* in l. 3. In **16** the writer was obviously in difficulty with the vertical script, for in the hexameter he begins from left to right, continues *boustrophedon* for six retrograde letters, and then reverts to the forward script; in the pentameter his two lines are *boustrophedon* except for a relapse of five letters (δε Ϝ' ιν); in the single line of the signature he starts from right to left, and then alters to the other direction, perhaps to match the line immediately above. In fact this pyramid offers a good example of the pitfalls which vertical *boustrophedon* held for the inexpert writer.

The part played by the states of Achaia in the colonization of the West was not that of the trading pioneer, although they must have been encouraged by the example of their commercially-minded Doric neighbours. Achaia could hardly hope to rival the enterprise of Corinth; but other motives equally strong impelled her. The fertility of her narrow strip of coastal land encouraged an agricultural population, but there was land only for a limited number.[1] In southern Italy, however, there was room for all; and unlike the Corinthians, who had to establish bases for themselves among the peoples on the route, the Achaians had some such connexions already, for the Ionian islands Kephallenia, Ithake, and Zakynthos were peopled by their kindred, speaking the same north-west Greek dialect,[2] and in Ithake—when they became literate—using the Achaian script. Once beyond range of Ithake, the ships of Helike or Rhypes or Aigion had only to follow the Corinthian route up to Korkyra, make the crossing to the Iapygian peninsula, and deposit their emigrants at a favourable point on the fertile coast of the Gulf of Taranto. According to Antiochos (Strabo 262), Myskellos of Rhypes had the assistance of Archias the oikistes of Syracuse in choosing the site of Kroton; while Is of Helike, oikistes of Sybaris, shared the responsibility of settlement with a contingent of settlers from Troizen (Arist. *Pol.* 1303a; Strabo 263). Besides Sybaris and Kroton Kaulonia is the only Achaian colony which is known to have had an oikistes from a definite site in Achaia (Typhon of Aigion: Paus. vi. 3. 12), and this was evidently by the invitation and with the help of Kroton, for she is generally described as a Krotoniate colony.[3] As Kaulonia, under the aegis of Kroton, marked the southern limit of Achaian territory on this coast, so the northern limit was marked by Metapontion, which was said to have been founded under the aegis of Sybaris, if not directly from her;[4] and Sybaris and Kroton seem to have been responsible between them for all the other Achaian foundations in southern Italy, except for a few rather obscure places whose origins are hazy.[5]

All these colonies without exception used the same alphabet, which has been long recognized as that of their original source Achaia. It is possible that one colony learnt it from another; but we are not yet able to say which was responsible for introducing it. It may be argued that the colonists of Metapontion must have brought their alphabet with them, or they would have adopted the script of Taras, their nearest neighbour; and so

---

[1] Cf. Dunbabin, 32.

[2] Owing to the scarcity of examples it is not yet known whether the early dialect of the Ionian islands was in fact the same as the Achaian, or whether it was merely another branch of the same family, like Elean or Aitolian; cf. Thumb-Kieckers, *Handbuch* i². 227, 229.

[3] Ps.-Skymnos 318 ff.; Steph. Byz. s.v. Αὐλών;

Solinus ii. 10; cf. Bérard², 158 ff.

[4] Antiochos *ap.* Strabo 264; cf. Bérard², 175 ff.; Dunbabin, 32 f.

[5] Krimissa, Petelia, Brystakia, Skylletion; their founders were traditionally heroes of the epic period, and they came within the sphere of Krotoniate influence; Dunbabin, 159 ff.

must the Poseidoniates, or they would have adopted that of Kyme; whence it would follow that the alphabet existed already in Sybaris when these colonies of hers went out. This seems quite likely, for the Achaian alphabet was already established in Ithake in the early Orientalizing period (p. 230).

### SYBARIS

Sybaris, the first and most famous of the Achaian colonies, was founded in the last quarter of the eighth century.[1] The colonists were led by Is of Helike, and a contingent of Troizenians joined the venture, but were soon driven out by the stronger Achaian element in the newly founded colony (Arist. *Pol.* 1303a). It has been suggested that Poseidonia, which was settled not many years after Sybaris, and which was held by ancient authority generally to be a Sybarite colony, was in fact established by these same Troizenians;[2] if so, they must have been illiterate at the time, for the script of Poseidonia is good Achaian.

The Lindian chronicle (c. 26) preserves the description of a dedication by Amphinomos of Sybaris in the temple of Athena at Lindos; it was a wooden cow and calf inscribed:

Ἀμφίνομος καὶ παῖδες ἀπ᾽ εὐρυχόρου Συβάρειος
ναὸς σωθείσας τάνδ᾽ ἀνέθεν δεκάταν.

Traces have survived of the Sybarite Treasury at Olympia,[3] and records of inscribed offerings at Delphi, where there may have been a Treasury also;[4] but as yet the only extant inscriptions from Sybaris are those on her coins. Her coins also provide invaluable corroboration for the scattered statements of ancient authors concerning her renascence in various shapes after 510, the year when the great and wealthy city, whose citizens had boasted that they 'grew old on the bridges of their rivers' (Athen. 519e), vanished with her bridges beneath the river Krathis, diverted from its course by the armies of Kroton (Hdt. v. 45; Strabo 263). Her earliest coinage (**1**), which bears the incuse type of a bull looking back, and may be dated before the disaster of 510, has the legend Συ, or (on one example) the full title Συβαριτες—all retrograde, with *san*. The upper limit for the incuse coinage is generally set *c.* 550 by numismatists.[5] Its υ2 or 3 may be noted, for this is the late archaic type; *c.* 550 one would expect to see the tailed *upsilon*. The next Sybarite coin-series belongs properly to Kroton, being those coins which bear on the obverse a tripod and Ϙρο, and on the reverse, still in incuse, the Sybarite bull and Συ. They are dated in the first half of the fifth century, and confirm the conjecture drawn from the literary evidence that, besides the Sybarites who fled to their colonies Poseidonia, Laos, and Skidros, a remnant continued to live in the area of old Sybaris, under the rule of Kroton.[6] In 453 Sybaris was formally refounded, with assistance from Poseidonia, but

---

[1] The date is disputed, as between 720 and 709/8 (or 708/7); cf. Callaway, *Sybaris* (1950), 1 ff.

[2] Pais, *Storia della Sicilia e della Magna Grecia*, i. 246, 527 ff.; Bérard², 215 ff.; Sestieri, *Arch. Class.* ii (1950), 180 ff. and iv (1952), 77 ff.

[3] Paus. vi. 19. 10; cf. *Ol.* ii. 47 f. and Dyer, *JHS* xxv (1905), 299.

[4] Strabo 420; Theopomp. *ap.* Athen. 605a; cf. Callaway, op. cit. 97.

[5] E. S. G. Robinson advises me that in his view this date should be lowered; cf. the coinage of Poseidonia, p. 253, n. 3. For Sybarite coinage see also Addenda.

[6] Diod. xi. 48; Dunbabin, 365 f. For the coins cf. *HN²*, 95.

was destroyed again by Kroton in 448 (Diod. xi. 90; xii. 10); the coins attributed to these five years bear Poseidon on the obverse, and the Sybarite bull on the reverse, with the legends Συ, Συβ, Συβα (still with *san*). Lastly, during the brief period when the first mixed colony, settled on the site in 446/5, was known as Sybaris (later Thourioi), the coins show Athena's head on the obverse, and on the reverse the bull and legend Συβαρι (with *sigma*).[1] The coins of Sybaris, therefore, show the local alphabet in use until about the middle of the fifth century; the change of script thereafter may have occurred because the die-makers of Thourioi were Attic or Ionic; but the use of Ionic as well as local forms on other coins of the third quarter of the century (e.g. Terina, Kaulonia, Taras) suggests that at this time the Ionic script was beginning to exert a general influence over all the Achaian colonies.

## POSEIDONIA

Poseidonia, Sybaris' flourishing colony on the west coast of Italy, consists of two archaic sites: the first (dating apparently from the end of the eighth century) is at the mouth of the river Silaris, where stood a famous temple of Hera, recently excavated;[2] the second, farther down the coast, became the city proper, and has yielded some few inscriptions, in addition to her fine series of coins. The earliest inscription is a rough stone stele found (not *in situ*) near the sixth-century temple called the 'Basilica' (**2**). It reads from right to left Χιρōνος, and probably belongs to the second half of the sixth century. Professor Guarducci's suggestion that it comes from some precinct of Chiron may well be right, though it is just possible that it was a gravestone, since Χίρων is also attested as a proper name. A further find of great interest in the area of the temples at Poseidonia was a silver disk (diameter 0·093 m.). Its exact purpose is unknown; it bears a retrograde inscription to Hera: τας Ⱶερας Ⱶιαρον· Ϝρονθιτοξαμιν (**3**). The second part has been read: Ϝρōνθι τόξ' ἀμῖν ('fortifica a noi gli archi, o, in generale, le armi'). I have suggested elsewhere[3] that it may not be Greek at all, but Italic or 'prae-Italic' (p. 259). *Heta* is open, which indicates that it should not be dated before the second half of the sixth century. The silver plaque **4** was found in a grave and bears an inscription from left to right in a spiral: τας θεο τ⟨α⟩ς παιδος εμι;[4] it should also belong to the sixth century, for *theta* is still crossed, and from the evidence of other inscriptions (**8, 16**) it appears that in Achaian, as in the neighbouring alphabet of Sikyon, the dotted *theta* was already in use by about 500; cf. p. 138. An archaic graffito on a small black-figure amphoriskos (?) found in the Hypogeum (Nymphaion) has similar lettering; it reads τας νυνφας εμι Ⱶια[ρον] (**5** *bis*).[5] The bronze jug which has the name of its owner Δυμειαδα incised on the base (**6**) should also belong to the first years of the fifth century, if one may form a judgement from the drawing

---

[1] For the placing of the preliminary settlement in 446/5, before the full-scale colony was sent out in 444/3, see Ehrenberg, *AJP* lxix (1948), 153 ff.

[2] Zancani Montuoro and Zanotti-Bianco, *Heraion alla Foce del Sele* i–ii (1951–4).

[3] *BSA* l (1955), 78.

[4] The order of the words makes it clear that the deity is not 'the child of the goddess', but 'the goddess (known as) ἡ Παῖς'; whether this is Kore, as the provenance of the plaque might suggest, or Hera Παῖς (Paus. viii. 22. 2) is not certain; cf. Hoffmann, *SGDI* 1648; Tod, *JHS* lxix (1949), 103.

[5] Sir John Beazley advises me that, from the photograph, the vase should not be much later than the mid-6th c.

of the head on the handle.[1] Finally there is the dedication τἀθανα|ι Φιλλō | Χαρμυλι|δα δεκα|ταν written from right to left on the abacus of the Ionic capital which forms a plinth for a bronze statuette of a kanephoros (7); she has the dress and stance of a kore, but is later than most members of the famous series on the Athenian Akropolis; she is dated *c.* 470.[2] The dotted *theta* is used, with the full local alphabet. The statue of Poseidon which appears on the earliest coinage (*c.* 525–510; 5) wears his chlamys across his shoulders like a shawl, in a style which was evidently in high fashion on statuary of the last decade of the sixth century and the early years of the fifth.[3] The legend is Ποσ, with *san* and with *pi* sometimes the wrong way round, and some issues have also the legend Ϝιις (with *san*), which was the name both of a local river and of the oikistes of Poseidonia's mother city Sybaris. In the first half of the fifth century, when the coin-types with double reliefs were in use, the obverse bears, with Poseidon, the full title Ποσειδανιατας: the reverse, with Ποσειδ, the Sybarite bull; all the local letter-forms are used. But by the third quarter of the century some issues no longer show the local script, but the Ionic ΓΟΣΕΙΔ.[4]

## LESSER NEIGHBOURS

The incuse coins which bear a Sybarite bull and the legend Αμι have been tentatively assigned to Aminaia, the vine-growing area, and located near Poseidonia.[5] Those showing a boar at bay, with Παλ on obverse and Μολ on reverse, have not yet been identified, but their provisional assignment to settlements at Molpe and at Cape Palinuro, between Poseidonia and Laos, accords with what little is known of this area.[6] A few inscriptions have been found at various sites along the route which ran from Sybaris to Poseidonia, bridging the peninsula from the Ionian to the Tyrrhenian seas and bringing fabulous prosperity to sixth-century Sybaris. At S. Agata dell'Esaro, lying inland some way from Laos, was found a bronze votive axe (8), dedicated to Hera εν πεδιōι by a butcher[7] named Kyniskos, which bears a fine specimen of the archaic Achaian script. Four things indicate that it is not as early as appears at first glance: ⴕ2, θ3, υ3, and the fact that it is not written *boustrophedon*; for these reasons I should set it in the last quarter of the sixth century, not far from 500. *Qoppa* is still used; and we may note the first appearance of the Achaian γι. υ3 has already been noted on the incuse coins of Sybaris.

Laos itself was a colony of Sybaris which at the close of the sixth century was producing an incuse coinage whose type was a man-headed bull in the style of the Sybarite, with the

---

[1] Cf. the head on the coinage of Gela struck at about this time; Ashmole, *Greek Sculpture in Sicily and South Italy* (1934), 20, fig. 33.

[2] V. Poulsen, *Der strenge Stil*, 99.

[3] As examples may be cited the Ilissos kouros (Riemann, *Brunn-Bruckmann, Denkmäler* (1939), 781–2): Theseus on the pediment from Eretria (Richter[3], fig. 284): the male figure on the eastern pediment of the Alkmeonid temple at Delphi (*FD* iv, fig. 15 and hors-texte vi): for bronze statuettes cf. Richter, *MMNYC Bronzes*, 50: Martin, *BCH* lxviii–ix (1944–5), 375 ff. (esp. 378 ff. and references there cited), pls. 34–35. The date for the coinage is given by Richter, *AGA*, 183. See also Addenda.

[4] *HN*[2], 81; Seltman, *Greek Coins*, pl. 18. 2. E. S. G. Robinson kindly informs me that in his opinion the latter series (illustrated by Seltman) should be dated after the middle of the fifth century, thus attesting the spread of the Ionic script from Thourioi.

[5] Bérard[2], 397 ff. Cf. B, pl. 67. 13.

[6] B ii. 1. 1419, pl. 67. 14. For recent excavation on Cape Palinuro see Sestieri, *Arch. Class.* v (1953), 239 ff. The contents of the tombs suggest that the inhabitants were Greek-influenced natives, probably with some Greeks resident among them.

[7] He may have been the official slaughterer for the temple sacrifices.

legend (in local script) Λαϝινος in *boustrophedon*, Λαϝι (l. to r.) on the obverse and νος (r. to l.) on the reverse. In the following types with double relief, dated in the first half of the fifth century, the legend has become Λαι (r. to l.), still in local script, but with loss of the *vau*.

South of Laos lay the sites of Pyxous and Sirinos, places whose existence in the sixth century is known only from a series of incuse coins (**10**) which bear as type the Sybarite bull, with the joint legend Σιρινος / Πυξοες.[1] In the third quarter of the sixth century the Ionic colony Siris was destroyed by the Achaian combination Sybaris, Kroton, and Metapontion (pp. 286 f.); Sirinos and Pyxous, if they were her dependencies (as Sirinos' name suggests), will then have come under the control of the Achaian cities and begun their joint coinage, and Siris herself perhaps continued as an Achaian dependency.[2]

Temesa, which lay farther down the coast in a copper-mining area, may possibly have been originally a colony of Sybaris, but her coinage (**11**), bearing the legend Τεμ and dated in the beginning of the fifth century, shows by its badge that she was then a dependency of Kroton.[3] The same is true of Pandosia, a Hellenized Italic town on the route between Sybaris and Temesa, which in the third quarter of the fifth century produced a fine coinage inscribed (still in the local script) Πανδοσια and Κραθις (**12**).

## METAPONTION

Metapontion was said by Antiochos to be a colony from Sybaris, founded to prevent any expansion by the Lakonian colony Taras (Strabo 264–5); according to Ephoros it was a colony from Phokian Krisa, led by Krisa's tyrant Daulis (Strabo 265). Modern historians support Antiochos, though with the proviso that there were mixed elements in Metapontion,[4] and date the colony in the early seventh century. Her inscriptions are undoubtedly in the Achaian alphabet. Besides the coinage there are five inscriptions from the Metapontine area, one from Eleusis, and one (probably in the Phokian script) from Delphi (Phokis **23**). There is nothing as yet from Olympia, though the Metapontine Treasury there was apparently one of the earliest and richest.[5] The earliest coins (**13**), which bear (incuse) a head of barley and are generally dated throughout the second half of the sixth century and into the fifth, are inscribed Μετα l. to r., r. to l., or *boustrophedon*; one series has the fuller legend Μεταποντι, also *boustrophedon*, with ıı and ο2. The first series of double-relief types, which begins in the first quarter of the fifth century, bears on its reverse the river-god Acheloos with the legend Αχελōιο αεθλōν, the letters running down symmetrically from right to left and from left to right on either side of Acheloos' figure. The script is still Achaian, with crooked *iota*; we may note also χ3, θ2, and both *theta* and *omikron* in rhomboid shape (p. 249). The following two series, showing first Herakles and then an Apollo which is probably taken from the bronze statue seen by

---

[1] According to Diod. xi. 59. 4, Pyxous was founded in 471 by Mikythos of Rhegion; but a native settlement may have existed there previously. There are no archaeological remains at the site (Dunbabin, 153, n. 3). The separate existence of Sirinos was first pointed out by P. Zancani Montuoro (**10**, bibliography); see also J. Bérard, *Charites* (1957), 218 ff.

[2] Cf. p. 287 and Jeffery, *JHS* lxix (1949), 32 f.
[3] Dunbabin, 162 and 203.
[4] Bérard[2], 175 ff.; Dunbabin, 32 ff.
[5] Paus. vi. 19. 11 (ivory Endymion): Athen. 479b (golden phialai), 605c (golden laurel). Cf. Dyer, *JHS* xxvi (1906), 56 f. and Mayer, *JdI* xliv (1929), 299 ff.

Herodotos in Metapontion (Hdt. iv. 15), have only the legend Μετα, so that, as far as the coins are concerned, the evidence for the use of the local alphabet does not go beyond *c.* 470, the lower date generally assigned to the Acheloos series.

The two earliest inscriptions from Metapontion, brief though they are, have been of service in identifying the deities of the two early temples. In the larger of these temples, which lies about three miles outside the city and is usually called the 'Tempio delle Tavole Paladine' (built *c.* 525), among various votive objects dated between the late sixth and early fifth centuries was a fragment (15) from the rim of a terra-cotta basin, inscribed τας Ηε[ρας], thus vindicating Pliny's statement that at Metapontum was a temple of Juno (with vinewood columns; *NH* xiv. 9). The date might be shortly before or after 500; *heta* is open. The other inscription (14) was found near the temple called 'di Sansone', and is a stele, shaped in a rough curve at the top and inscribed vertically, partly *boustrophedon*: Απολõνος | λυκ εμι Θεα|γεος Βυρο(?) 'I am (the stone, or image?) of Apollo Lyk(ios), (property) of Theages (and) Byros(?).' I take this to be an example of a sacred stone of the kind seen by Pausanias at Pharai in Achaia, which he rightly recognized to be relics of the early tradition of aniconic stone-worship (vii. 22. 4): ἑστήκασι δὲ ἐγγύτατα τοῦ ἀγάλ-ματος [= Hermes] τετράγωνοι λίθοι τριάκοντα μάλιστα ἀριθμόν· τούτους σέβουσιν οἱ Φαρεῖς, ἑκάστῳ θεοῦ τινος ὄνομα ἐπιλέγοντες· τὰ δὲ ἔτι παλαιότερα καὶ τοῖς πᾶσιν Ἕλλησι τιμὰς θεῶν ἀντὶ ἀγαλμάτων εἶχον ἀργοὶ λίθοι. A good parallel is the series of stones from the precinct of Zeus Meilichios at Selinous (p. 270), on one of which the same grammatical construction is apparently used: το Διος το Μελιχιο εμι Προτα(?) Ευμενιδο το Πεδιαρχο. ει and θι in 14 suggest a date well before the end of the sixth century. The final name is uncertain; I suggest Βυρο instead of the alternative Ρυπο[ς] only because there seems to be no other example of the tailed *rho* in Metapontine inscriptions, though admittedly it was used at Taras not far away.

It is conceivable that the terra-cotta pyramid 39·5 cm. high on a moulded base (found near S. Mauro Forte), which was made and dedicated to Herakles by the potter Nikomachos (16), may also be a conventional representation of an original aniconic object, though this is very uncertain. It can hardly be a loom-weight, if we consider its size and its recipient. The inscription is written in four lines *boustrophedon* up and down the four faces of the pyramid; in l. 2 the writer has profited by the vertical direction of the lines to change from retrograde to forward script: χαιρε Ϝαναξ Η⟨ε⟩ρακλες | ο τοι κεραμευς μ' ανεθεκε· δος δε Ϝ' ιν ανθρōποις | δοξαν εχεν αγαθ⟨α⟩ν. The signature is added below l. 1: Νικομαχος μ' εποε: the letters have the characteristics of the late archaic Achaian script: Η2, θ3, υ2, χ2; medial *qoppa* is no longer used (Νικομαχος). Its date may be set conjecturally in the last quarter of the sixth century.

The Metapontine dedication at Eleusis (17) is on a pillar of black Eleusinian stone (now lost?), with a tenon at the top for the stone capital which bore the offering. It may belong to the first quarter of the fifth century—hardly earlier, for it is written *stoichedon*; but ει is used, according to the drawing: Αριστοδα[μος ανεθεκε?] | Μεταποντ[ιος]. It is fitting to find a Metapontine offering his tribute to Demeter at Eleusis, for Metapontion, with her παράσημον of a barley-ear, must surely have had a cult of Demeter too; at least the goddess's head appears on her coins of the fourth century and later (*HN²*, 76 ff.).

The squared stone inscribed ΛΥΚΟΜ (**18**) is known to me only from the type copies; if the isosceles *lambda* and tailed *upsilon* are accurate, it should not be earlier than the middle of the fifth century. The dedication of the Metapontines '— and Xenon', sons of Phayllos, at Delphi presents another problem. If it is indeed in the Metapontine script and earlier than the middle of the fifth century (as Pomtow suggested[1]), it would give a *terminus ante quem* for the loss of crooked *iota* and *san* in the Achaian alphabet. This would mean that all the coin-legends of the second quarter of the fifth century and later which use these letters are archaistic—as, indeed, they have been termed by Head (*HN²*, 97 and 105). It is true that in cases where part of a city's name is written on a coin the old letters may be retained because they have become a part of the badge whereby the city's coinage is identified (p. 65); but when the design for a die is especially drafted to bear a word describing some particular object or aspect of the city's life which it is desired to emphasize on the coinage—as Νίκα on the coins of Terina, οἰκιστάς on those of Kroton, Κρᾶθις on those of Pandosia—the case does not seem to me to be analogous. Why should they then desire to revert to lettering no longer in use? It seems more likely that the local script continued unchallenged until at least the middle of the fifth century, but that during the third quarter the straight *iota* and *sigma* began to oust the local forms, rapidly followed by the incursion of Ionic forms, perhaps from Thourioi (pp. 287 f.). Hence some coins of that period show the local letters still (Pandosia, Terina, Kroton), others the more advanced forms (Poseidonia). The Metapontine dedication at Delphi, like that of Kroton (p. 258), is not a good witness against this hypothesis, because the script of the dedication is identical with the local Phokian; I have therefore inferred that a Delphic mason not only made the base, but also drafted the inscription (Phokis **23**).

Important evidence for the duration of the local alphabet at Metapontion should be given by the abecedarium which was painted round the shoulder of a stamnos of local type, found in a grave outside the city (**19**). Unfortunately the stamnos itself is of a plain type not accurately datable; I am informed that its shape suggests the first half of the fifth century rather than the second.[2] *Gamma, delta, iota, san* are shown in their local forms; *vau* and *qoppa* are still in place, but the unused sign *sigma* is not represented. Its place in the line is taken by *san*. The complementary letters run: *upsilon, phi,* 'red' *chi,* and 'red' *xi* written twice. The repetition of this sign at the end has been variously explained, as a means of filling the vacant space,[3] or as an indication that the Metapontines were aware that a Χ with the value of *chi* existed as well as the Χ = ξ.[4]

With Metapontion ends the list of Sybarite foundations or connexions in Magna Graecia. Those remaining come within the sphere of Sybaris' great rival.

### KROTON AND LESSER NEIGHBOURS

Kroton was founded within a few years of Sybaris (*c.* 708?), the colonists being led by Myskellos of Rhypes on the advice of the oracle at Delphi (Diod. viii. 17). Her dominion extended—especially after the destruction of Sybaris—over the series of small towns which lay to her north and south along the coast and inland, in which the Greek settlers

[1] *Ph.W.* 1909, 251: *SIG³* 25.
[2] I owe this information to A. Cambitoglou.
[3] Kirchhoff⁴, 166; Roberts i. 306.
[4] Whatmough, *Prae-Italic Dialects* ii. 531, n. 4.

had mingled with the native element, so that most of them can hardly be said to have arisen as the result of any definite colonizing movement.[1] An exception is Kaulonia, founded by colonists under Typhon of Aigion perhaps in the seventh or early sixth century;[2] she struck fine incuse coins in the second half of the sixth century, which bear no Krotoniate badge of any kind to suggest dependence (p. 258, **24**); but undoubtedly she was counted within Kroton's sphere of influence, especially as her land marked the southern boundary of the Achaian expansion; beyond lay Lokrian and Chalkidic territory. Terina also produced an inscribed coinage in the fifth century (p. 258, **27**), and from Petelia and Krimissa have come two bronze plaques (**28**, **30**) with texts concerning the disposition of property, of a type which is, as yet, confined to this area (cf. also **29** and a fragment from Lokroi, p. 285, **3**).

The coinage of Kroton began, like others, in the second half of the sixth century, with an incuse series showing the Delphic tripod and the legend Ϙρο, Ϙροτ, or Ϙροτōν (*boustrophedon*). In the early fifth century began the series with double reliefs which, although interesting historically from the connexions which they record with other places (Kaul(onia), Da(nkle?), Te(-mesa or -rina), Pando(sia), Sy(baris); the last three on incuse coins), give little epigraphic information, except that the *qoppa* of the city's name was retained on the coinage until at least the middle of the fifth century, whereas in ordinary inscriptions it seems to have become obsolete at the start of that century (p. 249). In the second half of the century appears the series showing a seated Herakles, inscribed in the local script οικιστας, and on the reverse the tripod, with Apollo and the Python, and in the exergue Κροτōν. These coins have been dated *c.* 420, with a lower limit of 390 (*HN*[2], 96 f.). The Herakles has been tentatively identified as a later version of an original statue of *c.* 450–440;[3] in that case, one would conclude that the die-maker copied the lettering also from the original statue-base; for it is hard to believe that in the last quarter of the fifth century an archaistic revival of the old lettering would be contemplated, unless it were simply a deliberate copy of an actual, older inscription. The difficulty vanishes if we accept the coin-type as a commemorative issue, made when the statue was erected.[4]

Only three inscriptions in the local alphabet have yet been found at Kroton: a block inscribed from left to right Ϝερας | Ελευθερια⟨ς⟩ (**21**), which was built into the foundations of the fifth-century temple of Hera Lakinia; a pyramidal loom-weight with six letters painted on each side, known only from a hasty copy made (**23**); and a dedication to Zeus Meilichios (**22**). The inscription—almost a graffito—on the block is probably of the last quarter of the sixth century, judged by the direction of its lines and Ϝ2 combined with ε1, θ1. The loom-weight is hardly datable, but if the ν2, χ3 of the copy is correct, it should not be earlier than the fifth century. The dedication to Zeus Meilichios is interesting, for it was probably made by the great athlete Phayllos. It is an aniconic pillar like those found in the precinct of Meilichios at Selinous (pp. 270 f.), inscribed on two sides: το Διος | το Μελιχιο· | Φαϝλλος Ϝεθατο. The lettering is late archaic: Ϝ2, χ3. *Alpha* is crooked α3, a type frequent in the Achaian colonies (p. 248). The inscription may be dated *c.* 500, or

---

[1] Cf. Dunbabin, 159 ff.

[2] The date is uncertain; cf. Dunbabin, 28, 85; Bérard[2], 159 f.

[3] Lehmann, *Statues on Coins*, 43 ff.

[4] E. S. G. Robinson kindly informs me that he places this type in the third quarter of the century, not later than *c.* 430.

early in the fifth century. This would suit what we know about Phayllos from other sources. He was portrayed by Euthymides on a vase in the last decade of the sixth century as a young pentathlete practising with the diskos, and will therefore have been middle-aged when he fought at Salamis in 480; two Metapontines who may be his sons made an offering at Delphi *c.* 450 (Phokis **23**). He may have dedicated his aniconic Zeus at any time in his athletic career.

The circular base at Delphi inscribed Κροτō[ν]ιαται Ἀ[πο]λλōν[ι ανεθēκ- *or* δεκατ]αν (Phokis **22**) should perhaps be dated in the second quarter of the fifth century.[1] I believe this to be in the Phokian script, for in Phokian the tailed *rho* is normal, whereas at Kroton I have observed only one example, on a coin (p. 249).

The fine incuse coinage of Kaulonia (**24**) is inscribed Καυλ, Καυλō in either direction, with the *alpha* occasionally in the crooked form α2–3, which may occur likewise in the script of Kroton, Metapontion, and Taras, and particularly in that of Poseidonia. In the fifth century, with the appearance of coins with double reliefs, the legend is sometimes complete: Καυλōνιατας (local script); in one series (*c.* 450–440?), where the Ionic lettering is used, the *boustrophedon* system is retained for symmetry. This series, with those of Poseidonia inscribed Ποσειδ (p. 253) and the Tarantine 'horsemen' series with Ταραν-τινων ημι (*c.* 430?),[2] are perhaps the earliest examples of the influence of the Ionic script in these parts; cf. the coinage of Sybaris-Thourioi (pp. 251 f.), and the Ionic alphabet in Sicily (p. 267). See Addenda.

The temple at Kaulonia, which belongs to the early part of the fifth century,[3] has masons' marks on many of the stylobate blocks, some of them alphabetic (**25**). There is also a series of painted instruction-marks (**26**) on two sets of terra-cotta sima-fragments (the earlier dated in the last years of the sixth, the later in the first half of the fifth century),[4] which were found, with other architectural fragments, in a deposit on a hill some little distance from the site of Kaulonia. Some of these consist of numerals, in the acrophonic system;[5] judged by the similarity of the script in all the fragments, the two simae should be fairly close to each other in date.

The coinage of Terina (**27**), which begins in the first quarter of the fifth century (*c.* 480?) with a double-relief series showing the head of the nymph Terina, and a wingless Victory with a branch, carries the legends in local script Τēρινα (l. to r.) and Νικα (r. to l.). During the third quarter of the fifth century the local script disappeared and the legend became Τēριναιον; I infer that this change was not earlier, because the succeeding series dated *c.* 425–400 shows similar types, with the same legend (*HN*[2], 113).

Perhaps the most important inscriptions from Magna Graecia during this period are the three bronze plaques **28**, **29**, and **30**. Each bears a plain statement that so-and-so bestows his property upon so-and-so (in **29** and **30** the phrase 'in life and after death'

---

[1] Cf. *SIG*[3] 30. The first quarter of the century is suggested in *FD* iii. 1. 1; but this seems rather early for the neat, squared lettering, with *alpha* A and *nu* almost N.

[2] Evans, *Horsemen of Tarentum*, 31 f.

[3] Dunbabin, 86.

[4] Van Buren, *Archaic Fictile Revetments in Sicily and Magna Graecia* (1923) 10; Dunbabin, loc. cit.

[5] The surviving numbers are Γ, ΓΙ, ΓΙΙ, Ꝋ, ꝊΙ, ꝊΓΙΙΙΙ, ꝊꝊΙ, ꝊꝊΓΙΙΙΙ, ꝊꝊꝊꝊΙΙ; Ι = 1, Γ = 5, Ꝋ = 10. This last sign is perhaps a variant of D (= δεκα). The only parallel that I can find is the (much later) Ꝋ = 10 *staters* at Thespiai (Tod, *JHS* xxxiii (1913), 32 ff., and *BSA* xviii (1911–12), 109 f.).

(ζōος καὶ θανōν) is added), with the names of the demiourgos who was then in office, and of a number of witnesses (προξενϜοι). All come from a limited area, and are close in date: **28** is from Petelia, **29** was bought in the Rhegine district, and **30** was found near Krimissa. A contemporary fragment of some similar text comes from Lokroi Epizephyrioi (p. 285, **3**), and a text of the fourth century or later has been found at Terina.[1] As an approximate date for them I should suggest the years *c.* 475, comparing the lettering on Phillo's statuette **7**.

## NON-GREEK INSCRIPTIONS

None of the other Achaian colonies has yet produced any archaic inscriptions; but there are a few graffiti from southern Italy which are written in the archaic Achaian alphabet. In spite of some strenuous modern efforts to read them as Greek, they are evidently in one or other of the pre-Italic dialects. The first is on a late black-figure vase from southern Italy, once in the Hamilton collection, now lost (**31**): δισπεπυγιδοστοιοννυεπαμστοξεεν.[2] The second is on a small vase apparently of Apulian ware from the district between Bari and Taranto (**35**): αρκεσιλαϜος ) αλοϜε ) τυχαιος ) βοϜεον ) βλαμινι ) ταμπλερασκαιθοινϝυις; we may note α2, χ1 and punctuation 1, a form like the Lakonian (of Taras?). There is also a letter which appears to be ✶; it is transliterated tentatively as *kappa*, but just possibly it may be meant for *psi*, in the form which occurs also in Ozolian Lokris and in northern Arkadia (pp. 105, 213 f.). We have as yet no other example of *psi* in Achaian for comparison. It would be interesting to find this freak form in Achaia, geographically the bridge between Lokris and Arkadia; but to rely only on one colonial graffito is obviously unsafe. Three briefer inscriptions are **34**, on a vase found between Laos and Pyxous; **33**, on a stone block of uncertain provenance, now in Reggio Museum; and **32**, a nearly illegible graffito on a vase found in a native cemetery at Torre Galli north of Reggio. All these come probably or certainly from southern Italy, use the Achaian alphabet, are neither Greek nor Oscan, and should therefore be pre-Italic, possibly Messapic. In their company I should set the non-Greek part of the disk-inscription **3** from Poseidonia.

## CATALOGUE

### SYBARIS

**1.** Coinage from the second half of the 6th c. onwards, with legend Συ, Συβ, Συβα, Συβαριτες. B ii. 1. 1409 ff., pl. 67. *HN²*, 84 f. Kraay, *Schweizer Münzblätter* 7 (1957), 74 ff. and Welz, ibid. 77 ff.

### POSEIDONIA

**2.** Stele from a precinct of Chiron (?); *c.* 550–500? Guarducci, *NS* 1948, 185 ff., figs. 1–2. Paestum Mus.

PL. 50

---

[1] Arangio-Ruiz 21.

[2] Professor Whatmough comments (by letter): 'A puzzle, like most 18th cent. copies of inscriptions neither Greek nor Oscan. Not a forgery (no-one knew enough at that time to forge such a document). Mixed dialect (lingua 'Canusina'), perhaps: "I reft Dostas of his——; his bow and arrows were my prize" (??).'

**3.** Silver disk from a temple-deposit, Poseidonia; *c.* 550–500? Guarducci, *Arch. Class.* iv (1952), 145 ff., pl. 29. Jeffery, *BSA* l (1955), 78 ff. *SEG* xii. 412. Paestum Mus.

**4.** Silver plaque from a grave, Poseidonia; *c.* 550–500? *IG* xiv. 665. Roberts i. 303. *SGDI* 1648. Roehl³, 120. 10. *DGE* 435 (1). Friedlaender 178. Paestum Mus.

**5.** Coinage from the second half of the 6th c. onwards, with legends Ποσ, Ποσειδ, Ποσειδανιατας, Ϝιις, Σειλ. B ii. 1. 1427 ff., pl. 68. *HN*², 80 ff.

**5 *bis*.** BF amphoriskos (?) from the Hypogeum (Nymphaion) at Poseidonia; *c.* 550–525? Neutsch, τας νυνφας εμι Ϝιαρον (1957), 14, fig. 9.

**6.** Bronze jug, property of Dymeiadas, found near Salerno; *c.* 500–480? Minervini, *Bullettino Napolitano* iv (1856), 164, pl. 10. 1. *IG* xiv. 694. Roberts i. 305. *SGDI* 1649. Roehl³, 120. 12. Private coll.?

**7.** Bronze statuette of a kanephoros (part of a handle?), from Poseidonia; *c.* 470. *IG* xiv. 664. *SGDI* 1650. Roberts i. 304. Roehl³, 120. 11. *DGE* 435. 2. Neugebauer, *Ant. Bronzestat.* 64 ff., fig. 34. Studniczka, *JdI* xliii (1928), 203 ff., figs. 51, 57. V. Poulsen, *Der strenge Stil*, 99. Friedlaender 166. Berlin Mus. 7429.                                                                                    PL. 50

### S. AGATA DELL'ESARO

**8.** Bronze votive axe dedicated to Hera by Kyniskos; *c.* 525–500? *IG* xiv. 643. Roberts i. 306. *BMC Bronzes*, 252. Roehl³, 120. 13. *SGDI* 1653. *DGE* 437. Callaway, *Sybaris*, 49 f. BM.                    PL. 50

### LAOS

**9.** Coinage from end of the 6th c., with legend Λαϝινος, Λαι. B ii. 1. 1419 ff., pl. 68. *HN*², 73 f.

### SIRINOS AND PYXOUS

**10.** Coinage in last years of 6th c., with legend Σιρινος/Πυξοες. B ii. 1. 1407 ff., pl. 67. *HN*², 83 f. Zancani Montuoro, *Arch. Stor. Cal. Luc.* xviii (1949), 1 ff.

### TEMESA

**11.** Coinage of the early 5th c., with legend Τεμ. *HN*², 112.

### PANDOSIA

**12.** Coinage of the third quarter of the 5th c., with legend Πανδοσια/Κραθις. *HN*², 105. Lehmann, *Statues on Coins* (1946), 23 ff.

### METAPONTION

**13.** Coinage from the second half of the 6th c. with legend Μετα, Μεταποντι, Αχελοιο αεθλον. B ii. 1. 1395 ff., pl. 66. *HN*², 75 f. Noe, *Coinage of Metapontum* i (1927) and ii (1931). Lehmann, op. cit. 33 ff.

**14.** Stele of Apollo Lyk(eios), from temple 'di Sansone'; *c.* 550–525? Fiorelli, *NS* 1880, 190, pl. vi. 4. Roberts i. 302. *IG* xiv. 647. *SGDI* 1644. Roehl³, 119. 6. Bannier, *Ph.W.* xlvi (1926), 542 f. *SEG* iv. 78. Torremare Mus.                                                                                     PL. 50

**15.** Rim of a clay basin from temple 'delle Tavole Paladine'; *c.* 525? Galli, *SMG* 1926–7, 76, fig. 19. Sestieri, *NS* 1940, 51. Naples Mus.?

**16.** Clay pyramid dedicated to Herakles by Nikomachos, from S. Mauro Forte; *c.* 525–500? Fiorelli, *NS* 1882, 119 ff., pl. 11. *IG* xiv. 652. Roberts i. 304a. *SGDI* 1643. Roehl³, 119. 7. *DGE* 438. Rocco, *Epigraphica* i (1939), 322 ff., figs. 46–50 and vii (1945), 123 f. (Scarpat). Friedlaender 111. Naples Mus.

**17.** Pillar-base bearing a dedication by Aristode(mos), from Eleusis; *c.* 500–475? Roehl³, 120. 8. *IG* i². 814. Eleusis Mus.?

**18.** Block inscribed Λυκος, from Metapontion; *c.* 450–400? Fiorelli, *NS* 1883, 536. *SGDI* 1645. Torremare Mus.?

**19.** Stamnos with a painted abecedarium, from a grave near Metapontion; *c.* 475–450? Fiorelli, *NS* 1885, 607 f., fig. Roberts i. 306. *IG* xiv. 2420. 4. Roehl³, 120. 9. Whatmough, *Prae-Italic Dialects of Italy* ii. 531, n. 4. Private coll.?                                    PL. 50

### KROTON

**20.** Coinage from the second half of the 6th c. onwards, with legend Κρο, Κροτ, Κροτōν, οικιστας. B ii. 1. 1443 f., pls. 69–70. *HN*², 94 ff. Lehmann, op. cit. 43 ff.

**21.** Block from the temenos of Hera Lakinia at Kroton; *c.* 550–500? von Duhn, *NS* 1897, 346, fig. 3.

**22.** Cippus dedicated by Phayllos to Zeus Meilichios, near Kroton; *c.* 500–480? Iacopi, *NS* 1952, 167 ff., figs. 1–2. Reggio Mus.                                    PL. 50

**23.** Clay loom-weight with unintelligible inscription, from Kroton. von Duhn, op. cit. 355. Lost?

### KAULONIA

**24.** Coinage from the second half of the 6th c. onwards, with legend Καυλ, Καυλωνιατας. B ii. 1. 1459 ff., pls. 70–71. *HN*², 92 ff.

**25.** Masons' marks on blocks from the temple, Kaulonia; early 5th c. Orsi, *MA* xxiii (1915), 834, fig. 85.

**26.** Painted numerals, &c., on clay revetments found in a deposit near Kaulonia; early 5th c.? Orsi, *MA* xxix (1923), 448 ff., figs. 24–25.

### TERINA

**27.** Coinage from the early 5th c., with legend Τερινα/Νικα, Τεριναιον. Regling, *Terina* (1906). *HN*², 112 f.

### PETELIA, KRIMISSA, AND AREA

**28.** Bronze plaque with text concerning the property of Saotis, from Petelia; *c.* 475? *IG* xiv. 636. Roberts i. 307. *SGDI* 1639. *SIG*³ 1214. Comparetti, *Ann.* ii (1916), 230 ff. *DGE* 436 (1). Arangio-Ruiz 19. *SEG* iv. 74. Naples Mus.

**29.** Bronze plaque concerning the property of Simicho(s), bought in the Rhegine area; *c.* 475? Comparetti, op. cit. 224 ff. Arangio-Ruiz 20. *SEG* iv. 71. Naples Mus.                  PL. 50

**30.** Bronze plaque concerning the property of Philon, from Krimissa; *c.* 475? Comparetti, op. cit. 220 ff. *DGE* 436 (2). Arangio-Ruiz 18. *SEG* iv. 75. Private coll.?                  PL. 50

NON-GREEK

**31.** Graffito on a late BF lekythos 'from Magna Graecia', now lost; late 6th to early 5th c. *IGA* 550.
Roberts i. 307a. *SGDI* 1657. Jeffery, *BSA* l (1955), 80.                                         PL. 50

**32.** Graffito on a vase from a cemetery north of Rhegion; 6th c.? Orsi, *MA* xxxi (1926), 127 ff., fig. 123.
Dunbabin, 165. Jeffery, loc. cit. Reggio Mus.

**33.** Inscribed stone stele, provenance unknown; early 5th c.? Orsi, *Neapolis* i (1913), 165 ff., fig.
Ribezzo, *RIGI* vii (1923), 224. Jeffery, loc. cit. Reggio Mus.

**34.** Graffito on a vase found half-way between Laos and Pyxous; early 5th c.? Conway, *Italic Dialects*
ii (1897), 530, 41*. Vetter, *Handbuch d. italischen Dialekte* (1953), 186. Jeffery, loc. cit. Berlin Mus.

**35.** Graffito on a vase found allegedly on the Taranto–Bari road; early 5th c.? Kretschmer, *Glotta* lv
(1912), 200 f. Ribezzo, *RIGI* iv (1919–20), 237 ff. Whatmough, op. cit. 292, n. xxviii. F. P. Johnson,
*The Farwell Collection* (1953), 73 ff., figs. 88–90. Jeffery, op. cit. 78 ff. Chicago Univ., Classical Coll.

# THE DORIC COLONIES, SICILY

FIG. 43. The Doric Colonies in Sicily

*Notes on letter-forms*

Selinous uses β3 in the 5th c. (**39**); Akrai, Gela, and Geloan Kamarina β1–2 (**12, 18, 19**); elsewhere
it is not yet attested.

γ1–2 occurs in two inscriptions of the 6th c., from Syracuse (**3**) and Gela (**48**); otherwise γ3–4 is
the normal form everywhere, including that on the earliest coins of Akragas, which began *c.* 525.

δ1–2 is normal everywhere until the first quarter of the 5th c., when δ3 begins to replace it; an
exception is **33** (Selinous), which shows 3 in the late 6th c.

ε4–5 is used in two instances, one Geloan (**48**), the other possibly to be ascribed to Gela (**9**); but as
there are no other instances of this form in Geloan, I have sought to explain it on other grounds
(pp. 266 f.).

ϝ1 was still used in Geloan of the third quarter of the 6th c. (? **49**), but *c.* 500–480 ϝ2 was already in
use (**36**), as elsewhere among the western colonies.

In Syracuse and elsewhere, ⱶ1 was still used early in the second quarter of the 5th c. (**7, 54**); only at
Selinous it seems to have gone out of use before the end of the 6th c. (**33, 36**); at Himera ⱶ2 appears
on the coins apparently before the end of the same century (pp. 245 f.).

θ1–2 was still used in Syracuse *c.* 480 (**6**), and in a Selinountine inscription that can hardly be
earlier than *c.* 450 or the third quarter of the 5th c. (**44**); generally speaking, θ3 seems to have come in
round about the middle of the century, at least in the graffiti (**38**).

λ1–2 is used in the middle and second half of the 6th c. at Megara Hyblaia (**25**), Selinous (**31, 33**), and Gela (**48**); in a Syracusan inscription of perhaps the late 6th c. (**3**) it varies between 2 and 3. 3 is the regular form everywhere from the second quarter of the 5th c.

μι–2—tailless, or nearly so—is regular from the earliest example in the middle of the 6th c. (**25**).

ξ2 occurs at Selinous (not yet attested at Megara Hyblaia); it occurs also on a Syracusan gravestone in Athens, of about the mid-5th c. (**10**); I would suggest that it was in fact used in archaic Syracusan also. The 'red' ξι is attested at Gela in the first part of the fifth century (**54**); it is not yet attested at Akragas, but will presumably have been the same there as at Gela.

*Qoppa* had disappeared from the legend on Syracusan coins by *c.* 485, but was still used in a dedication *c.* 480 (**6**), and in the personal names in a Selinountine *defixio* of the second quarter of the 5th c. (?: **38***c*). It is no longer used in a Syracusan dedication made *c.* 474 (**7**), nor in a Selinountine formal inscription of *c.* 460–450 (**39**).

The earliest inscriptions show ρι (**25, 31, 33, 48, 49**); but ρ2 appears already on Syracusan coinage from *c.* 530 onwards, and by the 5th c. it is the normal form everywhere, with a few exceptions (**23, 62**).

σι is the regular form in three Geloan inscriptions of the 6th c. (**46, 48, 49**), on Syracusan coins *c.* 530–510, and on the first inscribed issue of Selinous; but apart from these instances, and one or two examples which may be later (**53, 27** ?), the common form everywhere is 2, in both the 6th and 5th c.

υι occurs in **4** (6th c.); all the other examples are υ2, **31** being perhaps the earliest inscription in which the letter is attested. 3 is occasionally used in the second quarter of the 5th c. (**9** (renewal), **62**, and cf. p. 265).

χ3–4 ('blue' *chi*) is regular in Selinountine, and attested at Akrai, Kasmenai(?), and Imachara; 2 ('red' *chi*) is regular at Gela and Akragas, attested at Akrai and Kasmenai (?). It is not yet known certainly which was the form used at Syracuse. 3 appears in an inscription from Gela *c.* 450? (**55**).

*Psi* is attested at Selinous on her coins of the 5th c. (**35**), and at Kasmenai(?) at the start of the century (**15**); there is no evidence yet from the colonies Gela and Akragas, nor from Syracuse.

*Punctuation* is rare. The earlier form is 2, used in examples from Megara Hyblaia (**25, 26**) and Syracuse (**3**) in the 6th c., and occasionally on Syracusan coins in the early 5th c. (p. 265). It is still rare in the 5th c.; ι occurs in Syracusan (**5**; it occurs also in the sculptor's signature of **6**, but this is apparently not in pure Syracusan), and 2 once in Selinountine about or after the middle of the 5th c. (**44**).

*Direction of the script*. The *boustrophedon* system is normally used until about the end of the 6th c., occasionally perhaps in the first years of the 5th (**36, 37**); as usual, it lasts later in some of the coin-legends (Akragas **60**). False *boustrophedon* is used on a tombstone at Akrai of the late archaic period (**13**), and in a *defixio* of about the middle of the 5th c. from Kamarina (**18**). The earliest example of an inscription written consistently from left to right seems to be the bronze plaque from Kasmenai(?), *c.* 500–490? (**15**). Judged by the surviving examples, the refinement of the *stoichedon* style does not appear to have penetrated to Doric Sicily until at least *c.* 450 (**44**).

The scripts of the three Doric elements in Sicily present a problem which is still unsolved. The alphabets of the districts whence the colonists came are known in all cases (Corinthian, Megarian, Cretan, Rhodian), but in no case does the colony appear to use all the characteristic letter-forms. The present views of their origins are that the Megarian colonies (Megara Hyblaia and Selinous) took their script from Megara Nisaia, because the Selinountine shows a freak *beta* and 'blue' *xi* and *chi*; and that the Cretan–Rhodian colonies (Gela and Akragas) took theirs from Rhodes, because of their 'red' *xi* and *chi*.[1]

[1] Cf. Roberts i, pp. 145, 158 f.; Wiedemann, *Klio* viii (1908), 525; *GHI²*, p. 73.

Syracuse, however, whose alphabet as we have it lacks all the peculiar characteristics of Corinthian, is held to have borrowed a 'red' script from some other source, such as Delphi or Lokroi Epizephyrioi.[1] But none of these theories is satisfactory. Syracuse and her colonies between them produce examples of both 'red' and 'blue' *xi* and *chi*, and we cannot yet say certainly which type was used in Syracuse herself; but the balance of the evidence appears to me to incline slightly towards the hypothesis (developed below) that Syracusan used the 'blue' letters, and that the Megarian colonial script, *beta* and all, was taken from the Syracusan.[2]

## 1. *Corinthian*

### SYRACUSE

Syracuse was founded *c.* 734, shortly after Chalkidic Naxos (Thuc. vi. 3. 2); the colonists came principally from the Corinthia (e.g. Tenea), under the oikistes Archias, but there were other unspecified Doric elements also (Strabo 270, 380).[3] The Syracusan alphabet, as we have it in coin-legends and at least one inscription of the sixth century (3), is not Corinthian, in that it has neither freak *epsilon*, crooked *iota*, nor *san*. In view of the early date of Syracuse's foundation, it has been claimed that this merely shows that, when Archias and his band left Corinth, the alphabet was still unknown in Greece; the first Syracusan colonists were illiterate, and when they did adopt a script, it was from another and a 'red' source; in all probability this source was Delphi, and so the Syracusan script is, properly speaking, Phokian.[4] I have already noted above the tentative conclusion that the script is in fact 'blue' rather than 'red'. Where it came from I cannot say, but it is at least possible that such a script may yet be found in the north-eastern Peloponnese. The famous Chigi vase[5] is certainly of Protocorinthian fabric, but the painter's script, as far as it goes, is like the Syracusan. I do not necessarily challenge the view that a settlement made before the end of the eighth century may well have been illiterate; I only maintain that the same could be said of Pithekoussai, Kyme, Taras, Sybaris, and Leontinoi, and yet all these places use the scripts of their mother-cities. There was presumably a certain amount of coming and going between a city and her colony after her founding, and so Syracuse might, equally with the rest, have got her alphabet thus from the next generation.

What then is the evidence that the Syracusan script is 'blue', but not actually Corinthian? For it must be remembered that the earliest datable inscription found there is in fact in the Corinthian alphabet. This is the graffito on a sherd from a Protocorinthian pyxis probably belonging to the first quarter of the seventh century, which was found in the lowest stratum in the precinct of Athena on Ortygia. (A larger sherd from the same stratum at Ortygia, of a plain ware which is probably local, bears five letters of an inscription which was painted and then incised (1); unfortunately they show nothing decisive.) I have discussed the pyxis-graffito among the Corinthian inscriptions (p. 125), regarding it as an import or else the work of someone actually from Corinth among the colonists;[6]

[1] Cf. *SGDI* 3227 (Delphi); Carpenter, *AJA* xlix (1945), 455 (Delphi); Guarducci, *Ann.* 1949–51, 103 ff. (Lokroi Epizephyrioi).

[2] Cf. also Carpenter, ibid.    [3] Bérard², 116 ff.

[4] Carpenter, loc. cit.

[5] *NC*, Cat. 39; Lejeune, *REA* xlvii (1945), 102, n. 5.

[6] M. N. Tod draws my attention to the fact that it is possible to read the letters -ανκλας on the sherd as [Δ]ανκλας; which would strongly suggest that the writer was himself familiar with Sicily.

for if we use it to establish the hypothesis that the original Syracusan script was in fact Corinthian, we are then faced with two problems instead of one: why did the Syracusans change their script during the seventh or early sixth century, and whence did their new script come?

The first securely-dated evidence for Syracuse's script is from the coinage (2); according to Boehringer's comprehensive classification,[1] the earliest group (c. 530–510) bears the legend Συραϙο|σιον (σι, ρ2) or Συρα, followed (c. 510–485) by Συρα and Συραϙοσιον retrograde (σ2), Συραϙοσιον (σ2) or Συρακοσιον (σ2), the last occasionally with punctuation 2. From c. 485 to 450 the legend is Συρακοσιον (σ2); in the series dated c. 474–450 *upsilon* is sometimes the curved form 3, and in the latest of this type, and during the period c. 450–425, *rho* becomes 5. According to the evidence of the coins, therefore, in the last quarter of the sixth century ϙ and the late archaic ρ2, σι were in use; in the first years of the fifth *qoppa* disappeared, and *sigma* changed to 2. The die-engravers, as Boehringer points out,[2] were apparently quicker than some other writers to abandon *qoppa*, for it is still used on the base of Gelon's tripod dedicated at Delphi c. 479 (6). It is also used (with σι and υι) on part of a base at Sparta, reading [- - -]αϙουσιον, which has been ascribed to Syracuse, and to the late sixth century (4).[3]

The temple of Apollo, or Artemis and Apollo, is usually dated in the first half of the sixth century;[4] but the inscription cut on the step of its eastern approach (3) appears to be later in date, perhaps in the third or even the last quarter of the century, for, though it has ⊢ι and ει, 2, or 3, it has also υ2, ρ2. Apart from its damaged letters, some of the rest are unexpected: λι and 3, γ2, and σ2 (as in the Megarian colonies in the sixth century), although on the coins σι was used until the fifth century. The full translation, which might provide the key to this, continues to elude scholars.[5]

---

[1] *Die Münzen von Syrakus* (1929), 110 ff.

[2] Op. cit. 93 f.

[3] The fragmentary block found at Olympia (*Ol.* iii. 16 f.) which reads -ϙυρ- and was tentatively ascribed to the remains of the 'Carthaginian' (= Syracusan) Treasury is, I think, too uncertain for inclusion among the Syracusan inscriptions. The Treasury was erected after 479, to commemorate the battle of Himera (Paus. vi. 19. 7; cf. Dyer, *JHS* xxv (1905), 303 f.), and the Syracusan inscriptions of this date show σι, not 2 as on the stone. Nor have I included the block at Delphi, inscribed -ρακϙσιϙ-, because there is nothing to show if it should be read: [Συ]ρακοσιο[ι] or [απο τὸν Συ]ρακοσιϙ[ν]: cf. *FD* iii. 3, 57 ff., no. 76; Guarducci, *Epigraphica* iv (1942), 204 ff.

[4] Cf. Robertson[2], 324; Guarducci, *Arch. Class.* i (1949), 9; but Cultrera (*MA* (1951), 701 ff.) holds that it cannot be dated closely by its style, for it is provincial work, and 'early' features are not necessarily early in date.

[5] The best attempt is that made by Guarducci, op. cit. 4 ff. She has rejected the elaborate reconstructions of previous editors in favour of a simpler and far more satisfactory rendering: Κλεο[. . .]ε̄ς εποιε̄σε τὸπελō̄νι ⊢ο Κνιδιε[ι]δα κ' Επικ[λ]ε̄ς ⟨σ⟩τυλεια καλα ϝεργα.

The worst crux is solved by reading a second name, Επικλε̄ς; one wonders whether to go farther still, reject ⟨σ⟩τυλεια, and read here a non-Greek patronymic of some kind instead, with the definite article omitted: e.g. Τυλετα? This leaves the reading καλα ϝεργα as direct object for εποιε̄σε; but as the stone has been recut after the last letter, the inscription may not have ended there, and an alternative reading might be possible: κατεϝεργα-[σατο]: i.e. 'Kleo(men)es (?) the son of Knidieidas (?) made (the temple) to Apollo, and Epikles son of Tyletas (?) finished it.' If such a meaning for κατα-ϝεργάζεσθαι is possible as an extension of its normal sense 'make, achieve, accomplish', this reading might explain why the inscription is apparently later in date than the temple. Guarducci's interpretation of the patronymic as Κνιδιε[ι]δας = 'son of the Knidian' (Κνιδιεύς being suggested as an alternative to the normal Κνίδιος) seems to me rather doubtful, not because of the awkwardness of the name—for, quite apart from any possible Knidian connexion, the Sikan and Sikel elements in Sicily resulted in some very un-Greek names in the Greek colonies; cf. **17, 20, 38c**—but because the marks read as [ι]δ (her plate 1, 2) might also be *upsilon*. Cultrera (op. cit.) thinks that the inscription may have been cut before the temple was finished.

For the fifth century, the literary and archaeological sources have between them pre-served seven offerings of the Deinomenid brothers Gelon, Hieron, and Polyzelos at Olympia and Delphi. Those of Gelon are: (1) a bronze chariot at Olympia, made by Glaukias of Aigina, for a victory in Ol. 73 (= 488), three years before he became tyrant of Syracuse (Paus. vi. 9. 4–5); one block of the base survives (**5**); (2) the Treasury at Olympia called 'τῶν Καρχηδονίων' to commemorate the battle of Himera; the founda-tions have survived;[1] (3) a golden tripod supported by a Victory, at Delphi, for the same occasion (Theopompos, *FGH* no. 115, F 193); the bell-shaped stone base survives (**6**), with its dedication presumably in the Syracusan alphabet (for it shows *qoppa*, which was not used in Phokian), and the signature of the maker, Bion of Miletos, in the Ionic dialect. Bion's letter-forms cannot be identified with those of any one state, but may be possibly a mixture of Ionic and Syracusan: that is, Ionic *gamma* and *delta*, the rest Syracusan. Bion himself may have been a craftsman who came west with other Ionic refugees after the fall of Miletos in 494. The surviving parts of two of Hieron's offerings—an Etruscan helmet at Olympia (**7**) and the base for a tripod at Delphi (**8**)—both show a more ad-vanced type of lettering: ε3, δ3, and no ϙ. **7** is certainly an offering after Kyme in 474, and so in all probability is **8**. Hieron's last offering, unfinished at his death and therefore actually dedicated by his son Deinomenes, was a group at Olympia, by Onatas of Aigina and Kalamis jointly, of a chariot and riding-horses (Paus. vi. 12. 1; viii. 42. 8–9).[2]

In none of these inscriptions was there occasion for *xi* or *chi*; but 'blue' *xi* is used in the original dedication (*c.* 475) on the base of the charioteer at Delphi (**9**), which, I would suggest, may be in Syracusan script. It will be recalled that the original epigram, cut in two lines, read:

[–ᴗᴗ–ᴗᴗ–ᴗ] Γελας ανεθεκε ϝανασσ[ον]
[–ᴗᴗ–ᴗᴗ–τ]ον αεξ' ευονυμ' Απολλ[ον],

but the first line was later erased and another line by a different hand superimposed:

[–ᴗᴗ–ᴗᴗ–ᴗΠ]ολυзαλος μ' ανεθηκ[ε].

The original dedicator has been identified as Polyzelos during his tenure of power at Gela, *c.* 478; the subsequent alteration was done most probably fifteen years or more afterwards, when the Geloans, like the other Sicilian states, were finally rid of tyranny, and might desire to erase this record of a 'prince of Gela', while retaining the fame of a Geloan's victory.[3] This latter possibility may derive some slight support from the lettering; it will be recalled that the renewal shows (as well as θ3, ν4, υ3) the Ionic H = η. This would be unusual for a Phokian mason; but perhaps less so for a Geloan. We do not know when Gela adopted the Ionic script; but it may have been as early as 450–440, as it was apparently used already then at Rhegion (p. 245). The Geloans in Kamarina were using Ionic letters (H, Ξ = ξ, X = χ) in the second half of the century (p. 269).

The first inscription on the Charioteer base has usually been called Geloan, on the strength of the peculiar four-barred ε5; but against this there is the use of 'blue' ξ, for *c.* 475 Gela still used the 'red' letters. The four-barred *epsilon* is also used in a name,

[1] Paus. vi. 19. 7. Cf. *Ol.* ii. 46; iii. 16 f., and above, p. 265, n. 3.

[2] A further possible, but very uncertain, attribution to Hieron is the fragmentary base at Delphi, ϙιαρου [- - -]: cf. *FD* iii. 1, no. 136, fig. 27.

[3] See Chamoux, *FD* iv. 5. 29 ff.

possibly that of a mason, inscribed on a block from the temple in the precinct of Athena Pronaia at Delphi: Μενεκ|λειδε, with Attic *delta* and *lambda*.[1] The temple is dated not later than 500 by the excavators, i.e. about twenty-five years earlier than Polyzelos' dedication, but it would not be chronologically impossible for the same man to have helped to build the temple, and to have cut Polyzelos' dedication. However that may be, I stress this point mainly to emphasize that the four-barred *epsilon* occurs spasmodically in several instances elsewhere than at Gela,[2] and no less spasmodically at Gela than anywhere else; for it only occurs in Geloan inscriptions in two of the six *epsilons* in a sixth-century dedication on bronze (48); in the rest of the dedication it is the normal ει, and normal again on all the fifth-century Geloan inscriptions yet found. Of the three possibilities for the script of Polyzelos' original dedication, therefore—Phokian, Geloan, or Syracusan— the last seems to me to be the least unlikely, with the proviso that the mason, while following his client's draft as a whole, cut his own species of *epsilon*.

The Ionic letters *eta* and *omega* appear on Syracusan coinage in the die-engravers' names, *c.* 430–420 (*HN*[2], 174 f.). Otherwise there is little to show when the Ionic script was finally adopted there. Two stone blocks from a grave-monument (24) found at Heloros near Syracuse, inscribed Λισσιας Νεμηνιου, show Ionic *eta*. The moulding of the upper edge appears to be fifth rather than fourth century.[3] There is also a shield dedicated at Olympia, inscribed Συρακοσ[- - -] Ακραγαντινων λαφυρα (11). Kunze has suggested that it may be read either Συρακοσ[ιοι ανεθηκαν απ'] Ακραγαντινων λαφυρα, referring to the Syracusan victory over Akragas at the river Himera *c.* 445 (Diod. xii. 8. 26); or it may read Συρακοσ[ιων και] κτλ, referring to their joint defeat by the Sikel leader Douketios at Motya in 452/1: the latter, he thinks, is perhaps the more likely, for we do not know what script the hellenized Sikels chose to adopt, and one would not expect to find Syracuse using the Ionic so early. The matter must remain open, but we have seen signs to imply that others of the western colonies changed to Ionic script *c.* 450 or early in the third quarter of the fifth century;[4] it may be that after all the shield belongs to the defeat of Akragas at the river Himera, and that Syracuse had adopted the Ionic script by the late 440's. We may note also the epitaph of Anaxagora on a tombstone found at Athens: Αναξαγορα Συρακοσια (10), with Ionic *gamma* and *xi*. The script suggests a date not much later than the mid-fifth century (cf. sloping ν3), and at that time the use of Ionic letters in the local Attic script was still fairly rare. Probably therefore this is the script of Anaxagora's own city.

One more inscription may be noted. The dedication at Olympia made by Praxiteles of Mantinea is thought by some authorities to be written in the Syracusan script; but there is nothing to show that it is not the Arkadian (pp. 160 f., 211). The puzzling inscription on this base is, rather, the joint signature of the sculptors Athenodoros the Achaian and Asopodoros of Argos—not Achaian, nor Argive (cf. *gamma*), nor Arkadian (Pl. 28, [19]). Can it have been inscribed for some reason by a Syracusan?

---

[1] *FD* ii. 3. 23, fig. 31.

[2] It appears once, by itself, among the graffiti names on the 'naiskos' tomb from Gela (56); see p. 273, n. 2. Other examples are: *IGA* 130, 152 (Tanagra); *IG* iv. 339 (Corinth)—all these on vases, graffiti or painted,

and probably therefore casual errors; cf. Keramopoullos, *AM* xxxiv (1909), 36 f.

[3] I owe this information to Miss Lucy T. Shoe.

[4] See pp. 241 (Naxos), 244 f. (Rhegion), 246 (Himera), 272 (Selinous), 282 (Taras), 288 f. (Thourioi).

## SYRACUSAN COLONIES AND LESSER NEIGHBOURS

Syracuse's first colony Akrai, founded *c.* 663,[1] has yielded three gravestones of the late archaic period, of which one (12) reads Βραχι|δα (or Βραχυ|λα) ειμι (*boustrophedon*), with χ2 and ΕΙ for the false diphthong, one [Λ]υσις ⱶο Χιμ|αρου (or Τιμ|αδου) with ⱶ1, 'blue' *chi* 4(?), and ου for the false diphthong (13), and one the feminine name Συϙōι (14). A fourth inscription (*IG* xiv. 218) is too mutilated for its subject-matter to be identified from the variant readings of three copies, and is therefore of little use. If 'Χιμ|αρου' is right, these examples show, surprisingly, both 'blue' and 'red' *chi* at Akrai. A more significant inscription is that on a fragment of a bronze plaque, bearing part of a decree mentioning the Gamoroi, which is said to have come from near Akrai (15). From the lettering (ε1, ⱶ1, ρ2, υ2) it should belong also to the late archaic period; it has been attributed to the near-by site at Monte Casale, and this site has been identified tentatively as Kasmenai, Syracuse's second colony, founded *c.* 644 (Thuc. vi. 5. 2); it was to Kasmenai that the Gamoroi, the Syracusan oligarchs, fled when the demos and the serf population, the Kyllyrioi, turned against them *c.* 490.[2] The identification seems very probable; but even if the plaque should not be from Kasmenai, the mention of the Gamoroi and the provenance suggest that it is from a Syracusan colony, and the alphabet shows the 'blue' *chi* and *psi*. On the other hand, Professor Guarducci reports an unpublished inscription from Monte Casale showing 'red' *chi* (as at Akrai, see above). She therefore suggests that the plaque 15 is in fact inscribed by exiles from Megara Hyblaia, who were given the rights of citizenship by Syracuse.[3] This is indeed a most attractive solution for the historical problem of the plaque; but it only takes the epigraphical problem a stage farther back. The script of Megara Hyblaia is not Megarian (p. 269); whence then did she get it, if not from Syracuse?

Kamarina, the third Syracusan colony (founded *c.* 599/8; Thuc. vi. 5. 3), received a fresh stock of Syracusan citizens after her unsuccessful revolt *c.* 552 (Thuc. vi. 5; cf. Dunbabin, 106 f.); but in 492 she was awarded to Gela, after the defeat of Syracuse by Hippokrates of Gela, who colonized her afresh, in the role of an oikistes (Hdt. vii. 156; Thuc. vi. 5). Her first coins, bearing the legend Καμαρι with ρ2 (16), are generally dated in this her first Geloan phase *c.* 492–485;[4] and I do not think that her earliest inscription, the gravestone of Choro and ?A(t)elos (17) can be earlier than the same period. ⱶ1 and θ1, used in 17, still occur at Syracuse and Gela in the first quarter of the fifth century (6, 7); ε is 3, and the first lines of the inscription are *stoichedon*. A date in the sixth century, as suggested,[5] seems most unlikely; it will not be Syracusan, therefore, but Geloan, and might even belong to the second Geloan occupation. For *c.* 485 Kamarina's population

---

[1] Thuc. vi. 5. 2: Bérard[2], 131 ff.

[2] Hdt. vii. 155: for the identification of the site and attribution of the plaque, cf. Dunbabin, 111 and 415.

[3] *Ann.* 1949–51, 111 ff.

[4] *HN*[2], 128; B ii. 1. 1533 ff., pl. 77. Thucydides says definitely that Hippokrates colonized Kamarina: αὐτὸς οἰκιστὴς γενόμενος κατῴκισε Καμάριναν (vi. 5. 3). I conclude from this that Geloans were introduced, but it has been suggested that the Syracusan population

remained, on the ground that the *defixio* 19 from Kamarina contains Doric forms (Pace, *Camarina*, 38 and 162; Dunbabin, 402). But (*a*) Doric forms are equally applicable to Geloan, and (*b*) the *defixio* is in any case to be dated after 461, not in 492–485, from the developed appearance of the letter-forms, so that it must be Geloan; see p. 273.

[5] Carratelli, *NS* 1942, 321 ff. For the later date, see now Peek i. 322.

was transported by Gelon to swell that of Syracuse (Hdt. vii. 156; Thuc. vi. 5); but *c.* 461, after the fall of tyranny in Sicily, she was again peopled by colonists from Gela (Thuc. vi. 5). The lettering on the three *defixiones* **18–20** should not be earlier than *c.* 450, although **18**, the longest, is written in false *boustrophedon*.[1] The lettering of all is neat, with θ3, v2, υ4; the 'blue' *chi* and *xi* are used, and in **18** H is twice used for η (Γηρυς, Ξηνιππος), although **19** still shows *heta* 1 = Ⱶ.

Two non-Greek sites, one from this area, may also be mentioned here, as they have yielded Greek inscriptions. In Hybla Heraia, to which Greek traders from Syracuse or Kamarina probably came,[2] were found two grave-inscriptions of the late archaic period: οιμ[οι] | Επαλυ[ϟ?]‖ο το Σαν‖ϙο (**21**) and Γοστιϙο (**22**). The names are perhaps Sikel, but the idiom is Greek; the use of οἴμοι in grave-inscriptions is not common, but examples occur at Selinous (**33**) and in Attica.[3] The other Greek inscription (**23**) is that on a bronze kerykeion of fifth-century type: Ιμαχαραιον δαμοσιον above another erased name. The site of Imachara is disputed; wherever it was, it is to be noted that the Imacharaioi had taken their script from an alphabet which contained the 'blue' *chi*.

## 2. *Megarian*

### MEGARA HYBLAIA

Megara Hyblaia was founded *c.* 727 (after previous unsuccessful attempts at Trotilon, Leontinoi, and Thapsos) by colonists from Megara Nisaia, under the oikistes Lamis.[4] Between her stronger neighbours Syracuse and Leontinoi she could not expand; a hundred years after her foundation, a band of her citizens departed to the other end of Sicily and founded a new colony, Selinous (Thuc. vi. 4; Strabo 267, 272). The colony flourished, but in 483/2 Megara Hyblaia herself was swept into the possession of Syracuse, her oligarchs endowed with Syracusan citizenship, her demos sold into slavery (Hdt. vii. 156; Thuc. vi. 94).

Few archaic inscriptions survive, all from her necropolis. Most of the details of her alphabet are known through the inscriptions of Selinous; and the joint evidence seems to indicate that, despite Selinountine freak *beta*, the current opinion is wrong in deriving the script from Megara Nisaia. The inscriptions of the latter are written in the local script even in the second half of the fifth century (p. 137); the earliest inscription from Megara Hyblaia is dated *c.* 550–540 (**25**), and the alphabet shows no sign of the characteristic *epsilon* or *rho*. It is unlikely that the colonists, having brought out the Nisaian form of script, would have altered several of its basic features so early. Both places used the 'blue' *xi*, *chi*, *psi*; both used an abnormal *beta*, though the Megarian type is not yet attested and may rather have been like the *beta* on Byzantion's coinage (see p. 132, Fig. 34); but Megara

---

[1] As it is a *defixio*, some sinister purpose probably underlay this. In the text itself, after the preamble [τοι]δε γεγραϐαται | επι δυσπραγι[αι] the following letters should be names heading the list: Κερδον Ελασ[.. | ..]ξε͎ο το Περκο (κτλ). The usual reading κερδον ελασ[ιο‖ς ] εξ Ⱶοτο περ κό (κτλ) makes no sense.

[2] Dunbabin, 107 f.

[3] *SEG* iii. 56: οιμοι Πεδιαρχο | το Ενπεδιōνος· | Πεδιαρχος αρχε τōσ|ε̄ματōν. I think that the gravestone

*IG* i². 1009 also should be restored: [οι]μοι, θανοσε̄ς εμι| [σε̄]μα Μυρινε̄ς instead of [λοι]μōι (κτλ), as read at present—a hypothetical plague which seems now to have become historical; cf., for example, Stuart Jones, *Ancient Writers on Greek Sculpture: Selections* (1895), 34, and *AAG*, 73, n. 4.

[4] For an alternative date (mid-8th c.), see Vallet and Villard, *BCH* 1952, 289 ff.

Nisaia used different types of *delta, epsilon,* and *rho* from those of her colonies. I have suggested above (p. 264) the possibility that this colonial script is the same as the Syracusan; for there is as yet no certainty whether Syracuse used the 'red' or the 'blue' letters, nor is there an example of her *beta* (unless at Akrai, **12**, p. 268). As far as they go, her few early inscriptions resemble those of Megara Hyblaia.

The earliest inscription from the Megarian necropolis is that inscribed retrograde on the right thigh of a kouros of Greek (?) marble, which was erected over a physician's grave: Σομροτιδα: το Ηιατρο: το Μανδροκλεος: (**25**). Even if we allow for some provincial conservatism of treatment, it should not be much later than *c*. 550.[1] The Doric capital **26**, though of archaic shape, is probably to be dated not very long before the capture of Megara (cf. ε3): Καλισ⟨τ⟩εος: ειμι. This should be true also of the last two monuments, a stone 'cippus' inscribed Κλεομεδεος (**27**), and a fresh, unweathered stele, evidently erected immediately before the necropolis suffered damage during the capture of the city:[2] τας Ηαγια θ|υγατρος ειμι | Καπρογονο (**28**). In all these examples, as in those of Selinous, the script is consistently non-Megarian. But two brief inscriptions have also been found in the area, which may be in Megarian. One is lightly written on a fragment of a stone moulding from the necropolis of Megara Hyblaia (**29**); it reads: ΙΟϐΛϰΙΟ, which may be either [- - -]οι Κλεοι[- - -] (retrograde) in Megarian script, or [- - -]οι Κυβοι[- - -] (left to right) in non-Megarian. The other is a graffito Η⟨ε⟩ρακλει on the base of a black-glazed skyphos found in the environs of Syracuse (**30**). It shows the freak *epsilon*, which could be either Megarian or Corinthian; *alpha* has its cross-bar tilted to the left, which is typical of Megarian. The first inscription is hardly datable; the second, from the general appearance of the letters, should not be very early in the fifth century. Did some of the oligarchs of Megara Hyblaia who were transported to Syracuse use the script of mainland Megara? Or was this dedication made by a Megarian visitor to Sicily, for whom the cult of Herakles had local associations (p. 136)? Further excavation perhaps will solve the problem.

### SELINOUS

The earliest[3] inscriptions of Selinous are those from the precinct of Zeus Meilichios, the consort of the Selinountine deity Demeter Malophoros. This precinct contained a series of stone stelai, the earlier roughly shaped, the later more carefully. They were erected over burnt deposits of small votive objects and animals' bones, and are evidently intended for aniconic images of the kind which Pausanias saw representing Zeus Meilichios at Sikyon.[4] The earliest is inscribed *boustrophedon* (**31**): το Διος το Μ|ελιχιο εμι | Προτα Ευμεν|ιδο το Πε|διαρχο;[5] it may perhaps be dated fairly late in the second half of the sixth

---

[1] Bernabò Brea, *Ann.* xxiv–vi (1946–8), 64.

[2] Orsi, *MA* 1892, 788.

[3] I note here the fragments of an amphora (7th c.?) from the precinct of Malophoros, which is of the type called Melian and bears the end of an artist's signature: –ς: εποιεσε: (Gàbrici, *MA* xxxii (1927), 303 ff., pls. 79–80). As far as it goes, the alphabet (which is not Melian) could be Selinountine; but vase-experts are agreed that the fabric of 'Melian' vases points to the Cyclades. See Boardman, *BSA* lii (1957), 18, n. 111 (a local western

imitation of an island ware?), and Addenda.

[4] Paus. ii. 9. 6: πυραμίδι δὲ ὁ Μειλίχιος, ἡ δὲ [Ἄρτεμις] κίονί ἐστιν εἰκασμένη. Cf. the stele of Apollo Lykeios at Metapontion (p. 255, Achaian colonies **14**).

[5] The alternative reading takes προτα not as a proper name (Προτᾶς) but as a noun πρώτη = ἀπαρχή: but this meaning seems to require a dative following it, not a genitive: ἀπαρχὴ τοῦ Διός (e.g.) would be a most unusual construction; and should it not be the Doric form πράτα?

century; cf. ε2, υ2 (but ρι). Others are briefer (**32**): ΛυκισϞο ε|μι Μιλιχιος (*boustrophedon*): Σοταιρ|ο ειμι (*boustrophedon*): Μελιχιος | τον Κλευλιδαν (l. to r.), and so on. A tombstone found at Delphi commemorates a Selinountine named Archedemos, who may have died there while representing Selinous on some embassy (**33**; p. 269): οιμοι ὀρχεδαμ|ε Ϝο Πυθεα Σε|λινοντιος and on the back ἑριον, perhaps to remind those wayfarers who came upon it from the rear that this stone was sacred. It is cut *boustrophedon*, with ει, ρι, Ϝ2, and δ3—the last a form which does not reappear in Selinountine until the second half of the fifth century (**44**). A small clay trapeza(?), found at Selinous and also of the late archaic period, is inscribed: Αρχεδαμο (**34**); it might be from a cenotaph for the same man, but this is very uncertain. Their date should be near that of a fragmentary bronze plaque from Olympia (**36**), which may be dated shortly before the capture of Megara Hyblaia *c.* 483, since it deals with the political status of certain exiles from Megara now attaching themselves to Selinous.[1] This also is cut *boustrophedon*, with Ϝ2, Ϝ2, ρ2—all forms of the late sixth century or later. Here also may belong the battered grave-stele **37**, rebuilt into a later structure.[2]

The earliest inscribed coinage of Selinous, once ascribed to the fifth century, has now been attributed to the years between *c.* 540 and 510 (**35**); the legend is Σελι (*boustrophedon* at first) with σι and then 2. The fine series begun during the second quarter of the fifth century (466?) has the full title Σελινοντιον and on the reverse, above the figure of the river Hypsas, is written Ϝυψας, with *psi* and sometimes with curved υ3 as on the Syracusan coins of the same period.

The precinct of Malophoros yielded several *defixiones*. The earliest appear to be **38a**, the circular leaden disk bearing curses against Timaso, Tyrrhana, Selinontios, and the 'ξενοι συνδιϞοι', and **38b**, the fragmentary curse directed against Sopatros and Phrynis; they are probably *c.* 500 or perhaps a little later, if one allows for the fact that the writer was not an expert; the large *defixio* **38c**, containing a good proportion of non-Greek names, should also be no later than the second quarter of the century. In all these *qoppa* is still used in the names (ΕϞοτις, ΦοινιϞος: **38c**), but *theta*, unattested in **38a**, is in *c* already 3. In the formal lettering of the large votive inscription from the Temple of Apollo (which refers to a Selinountine war against unknown opponents, who have been identified as the people of Egesta and Halikyai)[3] *theta* is still 2, but *qoppa* has gone (**39**). The squarely-proportioned lettering suits well the date proposed, between the years 460 and 450. The precinct of Malophoros has also yielded a few incomplete dedicatory graffiti on red-figure sherds (**40**), and two pillar-bases (**41–42**) which bore dedications, by an Arkadian Alexeas son of Xenon to Hekate, and by Th(e)yllos son of Pyrrhias to Malophoros; an altar-fragment(?) from the Apollonion, inscribed [Απολ]λονος Παιανος | [Αθ]αναιας is probably of the same date, i.e. the years round the middle of the fifth century (**43**). Alexeas' dedication is presumably in Selinountine script, since 'blue' *xi* was not used in Arkadian.

A certain number of brief inscriptions from Selinous show the use of Ionic *eta* and

---

[1] Cf. the detailed discussion of the date by Dunbabin, 417 f.

[2] The text appears to read: [- - - θαν]ατοιο φ|ιλἔσε μ[- - -|- - -]ιολασο|ρα (*boustrophedon*). The restora-tion suggested in *NS* 1917, 342 ff. is unacceptable: [- - -]λίῳ ᾧ φ|ίλησεν [γῆρας παιδὸς] Ἰόλας ὤ|ρα; but I cannot offer an alternative.

[3] Cf. the commentary in *GHI*² 37 and p. 261.

*omega*, but are not precisely datable, and may be later than the capture of the city in 409, though one fragment shows crossed θ2 still.[1] A longer inscription shows *eta* and *omega* combined with αι, θι, ν3—all forms which suggest a date not much, if at all, below 450. This is on the base of a dedication at Delphi by Φιλ- of Selinous, an Asklepiad (**44**). Since others of the western colonies appear to have adopted the Ionic script during the years *c.* 450–425, it is possible that Selinous did also.[2] The cuttings on top show that the bronzes (by Akron son of Proton, also of Selinous) represented a seated figure, with another standing in front; since an Asklepiad dedicated it, the figures may have been Asklepios and Hygieia his daughter, in the pose later made famous by the sculptor Demophon of Messene.[3]

Before leaving Selinous, we may recall briefly the inscriptions of Motya, one of the Phoenician trading ports at the western point of Sicily. By the fifth century, she contained a marked Greek element,[4] and this is well illustrated by three fragmentary gravestones of the sixth and fifth centuries found there, all apparently in Greek and in an alphabet which is presumably the Selinountine; one (**45**) is a metrical epitaph.[5] The fifth-century coinage of Elymian Segesta, on the other hand, with the legend Σεγεστα Ζιβ (with variant endings; *HN*², 164 f.), can hardly show Selinountine influence, for *beta* is not the freak form of Selinous; perhaps Himera or Akragas may be responsible.

### 3. *Rhodian–Cretan*

#### GELA

Gela, a fertile site on the south coast, was founded *c.* 688 by a mixed band of colonists from Lindos and Crete, led by Antiphemos of Lindos and Entimos of Crete; and from the start the Lindians were predominant, for the colony's earliest name was Lindioi (Hdt. vii. 153; Thuc. vi. 4). At some time in the archaic period, perhaps in the seventh century, the Geloans dedicated a large krater in the temple of Athena at Lindos, inscribed: Γελῶιοι τᾶ[ι] Ἀθαναίαι τᾶι πατρωίαι ἀκροθίνιον ἐξ Ἀριαίτου,[6] both the place Ariaitos (Ariaiton?) and the circumstances being now unknown. In 580 she founded a colony Akragas farther west along the coast towards Selinous (Thuc. vi. 4), and during the first half of the sixth century[7] a Geloan Treasury was built at Olympia (**46**). In the first years of the fifth century the energetic tyrant Hippokrates son of Pantares extended the Geloan power eastwards by acquiring control of Naxos, Leontinoi, and Zankle, defeating Syracuse at

---

[1] *NS* 1917, 345 f., 6–8 (gravestones); *DGE* 167a (3) (*defixio*).

[2] Bourguet suggests tentatively a date in the second quarter of the 4th c. (*FD* iii. 1. 330 f., no. 506), by identifying the dedicator with —χος of Selinous in an honorific text, op. cit., no. 391. He expresses some doubt, however, in view of the early letter-forms of **44**.

[3] Cf. Edelstein, *Asclepius* i (1945), T638–63, and ii. 216, for the popularity of this version; for Damophon's group in particular, Paus. vii. 23. 7, and Frazer, *Pausanias* iv. 161 f.

[4] Diod. xiv. 53. 2; cf. Whitaker, *Motya*, 133 f., 266 f.

[5] The other two are: (i) Gàbrici, *NS* 1917, 348, no. 11, fig. 11: 6th c.? (ii) Ibid., no. 9, fig. 9: too fragmentary for restoration: first half of 5th c.? **45** has been restored variously by past editors; my version (Transliteration of Plates) assumes that a hexameter is lost in the break, and we have the pentameter only, giving the dead man's name and some non-Greek patronymic.

[6] Lindian Chronicle, c. 25; cf. Dunbabin, 113.

[7] This date, ascribed to the revetments in *Ol.* ii. 56, has been re-affirmed in detail by Dunbabin, 272, and by Schleif and Süsserott in Kunze and Schleif, *Olympische Forschungen* i (1944), 109 ff.

the Heloros in 492, and receiving Kamarina as war-spoils. His successor Gelon shifted the centre of this small empire to Syracuse.

The alphabet of Gela and Akragas is not quite the same as that of Rhodes, and quite unlike that of Crete. Like Rhodian it uses the 'red' *chi* and *xi* (the only example of *xi*, **54**, is of the fifth century and shows Χ; Rhodian retained ΧΣ); but it uses δ1–2, only changing in the fifth century (like the other Doric colonies in Sicily) to δ3; and it has not the Rhodian use of *heta* for η as well as Ⱶ. Thus all the Doric colonies in Sicily use scripts which are alike, except that the Rhodian uses the 'red' forms of *xi* and *chi*, the Megarian the 'blue', Syracuse's colonies vary between the two, and Syracuse herself remains *sub judice*—a problem which only further epigraphic discoveries can solve.

The earliest Geloan inscriptions are painted letters of the makers on the terra-cotta revetments of the Treasury at Olympia (**46**). About half a century later Pantares, father of Kleandros and Hippokrates (whose tyrannies began in 505 and 498 respectively), made a dedication at Olympia. All that survives is part of a rectangular bronze plinth torn off a lost stone base, with one remaining hole set at an angle for the tenon of a bronze statuette which was probably in a striding stance (**48**): Πανταρȇς μ' ανεθȇκ[ε] Μενεκρατιος Διο[ς αθλον] το Γελοαιο.[1] The inscription is incised *boustrophedon*, and is probably of about the third quarter of the sixth century, if Pantares' son Kleandros was a grown man in 505. The alleged 'Geloan *epsilon*' has already been discussed above (pp. 266 f.). Pantares reappears among a series of graffiti owners' names and brief comments on pottery of the sixth and fifth centuries found on the north side of the Akropolis (**50**). A gravestone from Gela commemorating one Pasiades (**49**) is also written *boustrophedon*, and may be of about the same date as **48**: Πασιαδαϝο το | σαμα· Κρατȇς ε|ποιε. The coinage (**52**) with the legend Γελας (less often Γελοιον) probably begins *c.* 491, under the rule of Gelon (*HN*[2], 140); the bronze weight shaped like a knucklebone (**51**) may be a little earlier, cf. λι : τōι Γελōιōν εμι. Four more inscriptions may be briefly mentioned: a graffito dedication on a white-ground cup-foot from the heröon of the oikistes Antiphemos (**53**): the funeral stele of Philistides the καλοποιος (**54**): a fragmentary leaden *defixio* found in a grave which contained no datable pottery later than *c.* 470 (**57**): and a series of graffiti names on the raking cornices of a tomb in the form of a naiskos (**56**), with a straggling many-barred sigma like the Lakonian; all four might belong to the first half of the fifth century.[2] The Geloan script in Kamarina, and perhaps also on the base of the charioteer at Delphi, has already been discussed, and it has been suggested that the Ionic *eta*, *xi*, *omega* were beginning to appear in Geloan from *c.* 450 onwards.[3] I should also set *c.* 450 the inscription

---

[1] Previous editors restore this bronze as a plaque which was nailed like a label to a larger stone base; but the irregular setting of the tenon-hole, and, above all, the arrangement of the inscription round the edges of the bronze, indicate that it was inscribed round the feet of a lost statuette, which was fastened to this as its plinth. In this belief, I have restored the dedication as a hexameter with two extra feet, assuming that only a small piece of the plinth is missing; the previous restoration is: Πανταρȇς μ' ανεθȇκ[ε] Μενεκρατιος Διο[ς αθλον]|[Ⱶαρματι? νικασας, πεδο εκ κλε]το Γελοαιο.

[2] The tomb and graffiti were attributed to the 6th c. by Gentili, *Epigraphica* viii (1946), 11 ff., but this date seems too early for the letter-forms (δ3, λ3, v3). In any case, surely this is not the proper epitaph of the tomb, but only names, &c., scrawled on it at some later date? There are two oddities in the script: *alpha* with a dot for cross-bar, and a long *sigma* like the Lakonian. One solitary *epsilon* has four bars (p. 267, n. 2). The first names, read as: Τιναχσινος, Οιμτις?, should rather be: Τιναξ, Σινος, Οινιτις. Βιοτος should perhaps be read for Βιογος.

[3] Pp. 266 ff. We could then place the coins with

Λευκōν Χαιρεσιλεōι (**55**) on the top of a fluted marble pedestal which originally supported a marble basin.

Gela's colony Akragas, whose power grew rapidly under the able if unscrupulous direction of the tyrants Phalaris (*c.* 570–555) and Theron (488–472), has yielded little epigraphic material as yet. Only the record survives, in the Lindian Chronicle c. 27, of Phalaris' dedication to Athena at Lindos, a krater inscribed: Φάλαρις ἐξ 'Ακράγαντος τᾶι Λινδίαι 'Αθάναι, and bearing another inscription on the rim, by which presumably Phalaris sought to add an impressive touch of local colour to his gift: Δαίδαλος ἔδωκε ξείνιόν με Κωκάλωι. In the second half of the sixth century, perhaps in its last years,[1] Akragas seized Minoa, a Selinountine settlement which lay between herself and Selinous, and commemorated this also at Lindos, with a Palladion for Athena's temple inscribed: 'Ακραγαντῖνοι τᾶι 'Αθάναι τᾶι Λινδίαι ἀκροθίνιον ἐκ Μινωίας (Lindian Chronicle, c. 30).

The earliest inscription is that on a gravestone found at Ravanusa inland from the site of Akragas, which commemorates the deaths of a father and son(?), Mylos and Sakon (**58**). These are probably two members of that Syracusan family named the Myletidai, which, under an earlier Sakon, helped Zankle to found Himera on the north coast (Thuc. vi. 5). The inscription is written *boustrophedon*, and the letters suggest a date in the first years of the fifth century (ϙ, but ε3, ν3), which agrees with the suggestion[2] that these men may have settled near Akragas because of trouble with the tyrant Terillos at Himera; for anyone who was against Terillos would be sure of a welcome at Akragas. The gravestone of a woman, which may be of about the same date, shows ει but runs from left to right (**59**): [- - -]τος εμι τας | Ανχεμαχο. There are in addition a few single letters, builders' marks, on the sima of the temple of Demeter (*c.* 480–470: **61**), a bronze handle perhaps of the early fifth century inscribed Χρυσιπο (**62**), and a block from the base of a dedication at Delphi by an unknown [Ακρ]αγαντινος (**64**), in lettering of *c.* 475. There is also a second gravestone from Ravanusa, on which [- - -]αδα εμι remains legible (**63**). Apart from these, there are the legends of the coinage (**60**), which began in the latter part of the sixth century (*c.* 525?) with Ακραγας followed by Ακραγ|αντος *boustrophedon*. The latter system was still used *c.* 480 (B ii. 1. 1550, pl. 78. 6); on one example of about this time, the reverse also carries εξα retrograde (magistrate's name?).

Lastly, we may recall the dedication at Olympia which Pausanias says that the Akragantines made after defeating the Phoenicians of Motya (Paus. v. 25. 5); it represented some boys supplicating, and was said to be the work of Kalamis. Kalamis' *floruit* extended over the second quarter of the fifth century, and this victory may have been a sequel to the Phoenician defeat at Himera in 480.[3] See also Addenda.

---

ΓΕΛΩΙΟΝ, illustrated in *HN*², 141, fig. 74, in the third quarter of the 5th c. (as the style of the head surely suggests) rather than to the last decade before 405 (as Head, ibid.).

[1] The date is that suggested by Dunbabin, 353 f.
[2] Mingazzini *ap.* Dunbabin, 420, n. 7.
[3] Cf. Frazer, *Pausanias* iii. 641; Dunbabin, 430 f.

It can hardly have been before 472, however, for Pausanias says that the dedication was made by the Akragantines. Had it been in Theron's lifetime, it would surely have been offered in the name of Theron and the Akragantines—a point which Pausanias would not have omitted, if one judges by his care in the case of Ainesidemos of Leontinoi (v. 22. 7).

## CATALOGUE

### SYRACUSE

**1.** Fragment of a vase of local clay from the early stratum of the Athenaion; 7th c.? Orsi, *MA* xxv (1918), 607 f., fig. 202. Syracuse Mus.    PL. 51

**2.** Coinage with legend Συρα, Συραϙοσιον; *c.* 530 onwards. B ii. 1. 1511 ff., pls. 74–76. *HN²*, 171 ff. Boehringer, *Die Münzen von Syrakus* (1929).

**3.** Inscription on the step of the temple of Apollo (and Artemis?) at Syracuse; second half of 6th c.? *IG* xiv. 1. Roberts i. 110. *SGDI* 3227. Roehl³, 48. 34. *SEG* iv. 1. Drerup, *Mnemosyne* 1935, 1 ff. Guarducci, *Arch. Class.* i (1949), 4 ff., pl. 1. Cultrera, *MA* xli (1951), 701 ff. *SEG* xii. 406.   PL. 51

**4.** Fragment of a base with dedication (?) from Sparta; *c.* 500–480? Woodward, *BSA* xiv (1907–8), 137. *IG* v. 1. 217. Sparta Mus.

**5.** Block from the base of a chariot-group dedicated at Olympia by Gelon of Gela; *c.* 485. *IGA* 359. *Ol.* v. 143. Roehl³, 63. 6. *DGE* 115. 2. Olympia Mus. 382a–c. *SEG* xi. 1223. See Aigina **12**.    PL. 16

**6.** Base for a golden tripod and victory dedicated at Delphi by Gelon of Syracuse after Himera; *c.* 480–479. *SIG³* 34. Roehl³, 49. 35. *DGE* 144. *GHI²* 17 and p. 259. Marcadé i. 9, pl. 3. Delphi Mus. 1615.    PL. 51

**7.** Etruscan helmet dedicated at Olympia by Hieron of Syracuse after Kyme; *c.* 474. *IGA* 510. Roberts i. 111. *Ol.* v. 249. *SGDI* 3228. *SIG³* 35. *BMC Bronzes* 250. Roehl³, 49. 36. *DGE* 144 (2). *GHI²* 22 and p. 259. *SEG* xi. 1206. BM.    PL. 51

**8.** Base for a golden tripod dedicated at Delphi by Hieron of Syracuse; *c.* 474? *SIG³* 35. *FD* ii. 1. 249 ff., fig. 197. *GHI²*, p. 20. Guarducci, *Riv. Fil.* lxxv (1947), 250. Delphi Mus. 1617.

**9.** Block from the base of a bronze chariot-group dedicated at Delphi by Polyzelos of Gela; *c.* 478 and *c.* 460? Keramopoullos, *AM* xxxiv (1909), 33 ff. Wade-Gery, *JHS* liii (1933), 101 ff. La Coste-Messelière, *RA* 1934 (i), 254 f.; 1941 (ii), 150 f. Hampe, *Brunn-Bruckmann, Denkmäler* (1941), 786–90, 20 ff., fig. 19. Chamoux, *FD* iv. 5 (1955). Delphi Mus. 3517.    PL. 51

**10.** Gravestone of Anaxagora at Athens; *c.* 450? Conze 1488, pl. 307. *IGA* 511a. *SGDI* 3229. *IG* i². 1081. EM.    PL. 51

*Inscription attributed to Syracuse*

**11.** Shield from a trophy for a victory over the Akragantines (?); *c.* 445. Kunze, *Olympiabericht* v (1956), 38 ff., pls. 24–25. Olympia Mus. B2590.

### AKRAI

**12.** Part of stone cover of a tomb or cippus for Brachidas (or Brachyla) from Akrai; *c.* 525–500? Orsi, *NS* 1889, 387 f. *IG* xiv. 221a. Roehl³, 48. 31. Guarducci, *Ann.* xxvii–xxix (1949–51), 103 f. Brea, *Akrai* (1956), 160, pl. 36. Syracuse Mus. 6823.    PL. 51

**13.** Gravestone of (L)ysis, son of Timados (or Chimaros) from Akrai; *c.* 525–500? *IGA* 507. *IG* xiv. 227. Roberts i. 109a. *SGDI* 3237. Roehl³, 48. 32. *DGE* 146 (1). Guarducci, op. cit. 104. Brea, op. cit. 161. *SEG* xii. 408. Lost?    PL. 51

**14.** Gravestone of Syko from Akrai; *c.* 500? *IGA* 508. *IG* xiv. 228. Roberts i. 109b. *SGDI* 3238. Roehl³, 48. 33. *DGE* 146. 2. Brea, op. cit. 161. Lost?                                    PL. 51

### KASMENAI(?)

**15.** Fragment of a bronze plaque with text concerning a grant of citizenship; *c.* 490–480? Alexander, *Bull. Metr. Mus.* xx (1925), 270, fig. 2. *SEG* iv. 27. Dunbabin, 415. Guarducci, op. cit. 111 ff., fig. 5. *SEG* xii. 407. Brea, op. cit. 151 f., pl. 34 (to be attributed to Megara Hyblaia?). New York, MM. 25.97.19.                                    PL. 51

### KAMARINA

**16.** Coinage with legend Καμαρι; *c.* 492–485. *HN*², 128 f. B ii. 1. 1533 ff., pl. 77.

**17.** Gravestone of Choro and ?A(t)elos from Comiso; *c.* 485–450? Carratelli, *NS* 1942, 321 ff., fig. 1. Friedlaender 79a. Peek i. 322. Syracuse Mus.                                    PL. 51

**18.** Leaden plaque containing a curse, written in false *boustrophedon*; *c.* 450? Ribezzo, *RIGI* viii (1924), 86 ff. Pace, *Camarina* (1927), 162. *SEG* iv. 30. Dunbabin, 402. Jeffery, *BSA* l (1955), 74. Syracuse Mus. 24086.                                    PL. 52

**19.** Leaden plaque containing a curse; *c.* 450? Ribezzo, op. cit. 83 ff. Pace, op. cit. 161 f. *SEG* iv. 29. Jeffery, loc. cit. Syracuse Mus. 23963.

**20.** Fragmentary leaden plaque of same type, from Kamarina; *c.* 450? Pace, op. cit. 161, fig. 65. Jeffery, loc. cit. Syracuse Mus.

### NON-GREEK SITES: HYBLA HERAIA, IMACHARA, ELOROS

**21–22.** Two grave-inscriptions from Hybla Heraia; late 6th c.? Orsi, *NS* 1899, 410 ff., figs. 8–9. Syracuse Mus.                                    PL. 52

**23.** Herald's bronze staff from Imachara; *c.* 475–450? *IGA* 512. *SGDI* 5253. Crome, *AM* lxiii (1938), 117, pl. 17. 1. Palermo Mus.

**24.** Grave monument of Lissias from Eloros; *c.* 450–400? Orsi, *NS* 1933, 197 ff., fig. 3. Syracuse Mus.

### MEGARA HYBLAIA

**25.** Epitaph of Somrotides on a marble kouros from the necropolis; *c.* 550–540? Brea and Carratelli, *Ann.* xxiv–xxvi (1946–8), 59 ff., fig. 5 and pls. 7–9. *AGA*, 186, n. 150. *SEG* xiv. 599. Syracuse Mus.                                    PL. 52

**26.** Epitaph of Kalis(t)eus from the necropolis; *c.* 500? Orsi, *MA* i (1892), 786 f., pl. 4. *SGDI* 3043. Roehl³, 54. 10. Syracuse Mus.                                    PL. 52

**27.** Epitaph of Kleomedes from the necropolis; *c.* 500? Orsi, op. cit. 788 f. *SGDI* 5242. Roehl³, 54. 9. *DGE* 164 (1). Syracuse Mus.

**28.** Epitaph of Kaprogonon from the necropolis; *c.* 500–485? Orsi, op. cit. 787, pl. 4. *SGDI* 5242. Roehl³, 55. 8. *DGE* 164 (2). Peek i. 66. Syracuse Mus.

**29.** Inscribed fragment of stone from the necropolis; late 6th to early 5th c.? Calderone, *NS* 1949, 198 f., fig. 6. Syracuse Mus. 10869.

**30.** Graffito on the base of a skyphos, found near Syracuse; first half of 5th c.? Calderone and Agnello, *Epigraphica* x (1948), 143 ff. Guarducci, op. cit. 103, n. 2. Syracuse Mus.

## SELINOUS

**31.** Cippus of Zeus Meilichios from the sanctuary adjoining that of Malophoros; *c.* 525? Gàbrici, *MA* xxxii (1927), 381 ff., 403 ff., pl. 97. Palermo Mus.                                           PL. 52

**32.** Six similar cippi, descending in date into the 5th c. (ibid.). Palermo Mus.

**33.** Funeral stele of Archedemos, found at Delphi; *c.* 525–500? *SGDI* 3044. Roehl³, 54. 11. *SIG*³ 11. *DGE* 165. Friedlaender 175. Peek i. 1670. Delphi Mus.                                       PL. 52

**34.** Clay trapeza(?) of Archedemos, from Selinous; *c.* 525–500? Salinas, *NS* 1900, 112 f., figs. 1–2. *SGDI* 5214. Roehl³, 55. 13. Palermo Mus.?

**35.** Coinage with legends Σελι, Σελινοντιον, Ⱶυψας: latter part of 6th c. onwards. *HN*², 167 f. B ii. 1. 1551 ff., pl. 79. Milne, *Num. Chron.* xviii (1938), 43 ff. Lehmann, *Statues on Coins* (1946), 15 ff.

**36.** Fragmentary bronze plaque from Olympia, containing a legal text concerning exiles from Megara Hyblaia; *c.* 484? *Ol.* v. 22. *IGA* 514. Roberts i. 116. *SGDI* 3045. Roehl³, 53. 7. *DGE* 165g. Bérard², 245. *SEG* xi. 1179. Olympia Mus. 603+804+305+697+416+958+1074.

**37.** Fragmentary gravestone from Selinous; *c.* 500–475? Gàbrici, *NS* 1917, 341 ff., fig. 2. Palermo Mus.

**38a–c.** Curses on leaden plaques or scrolls from the precinct of Demeter Malophoros, Selinous. (*a*) On an opisthographic disk; *c.* 500–475? *DGE* 167a. Arangio-Ruiz 23. Gàbrici, *MA* xxxii (1927), 384 ff., fig. 180. *SEG* iv. 37–38. Jacobsthal, *Diskoi* (1933), 31. (*b*) On a fragmentary plaque; *c.* 500–475? Ferri, *NS* 1944–5, 174. (*c*) On a complete plaque; *c.* 475–450? Ferri, op. cit. 168 ff., figs. 1–2. (*a–c*) Jeffery, op. cit. 72 f. Palermo Mus.

**39.** Vow made by the Selinountines in war, inscribed in the temple of Apollo; *c.* 460–450? *IGA* 515. Roberts i. 117. *IG* xiv. 268. *SGDI* 3046. Roehl³, 55. 12. Hulot and Fougères, *Sélinonte* (1910), 101 ff. *SIG*³ 1122. *DGE* 166. *GHI*² 37 and p. 261. Buck 98. Palermo Mus.

**40.** Dedicatory graffiti on RF sherds from the precinct of Demeter Malophoros; *c.* 450–400? Gàbrici, op. cit. 340 ff., pl. 95. Palermo Mus.

**41.** Pillar-base with a dedication by Alexeas, an Arkadian, to Hekate; *c.* 450? *IGA* 517. Roberts i. 118b. *SGDI* 3048. Gàbrici, op. cit., pl. 96. Guarducci, *Parola del Passato* xxx (1953), 209 ff. *SEG* xiv. 594. Palermo Mus.

**42.** Pillar-base with a dedication by Th(e)yllos son of Pyrrhias to Malophoros; *c.* 450? Salinas, *NS* 1894, 209 f., fig. 9. *SGDI* 5213. Roehl³, 56. 14. *DGE* 167 (1). Gàbrici, op. cit. 380 f., pl. 96. *SEG* xii. 411. Palermo Mus.

**43.** Fragment of an altar(?) from the Apollonion; *c.* 450? *IGA* 516. Roberts i. 118a. *SGDI* 3048. Palermo Mus.

**44.** Base for a dedication at Delphi by Phil—, an Asklepiad, signed by Akron of Selinous; *c.* 450–425? Pomtow, *Klio* xv (1918), 303 f. *FD* iii. 1. 330 f., no. 506, fig. 49. Marcadé i. 2, pl. 1. 2. Delphi Mus. 3522.                                                                                          PL. 52

## NON-GREEK SITE: MOTYA

**45.** Metrical grave-epigram; *c.* 475–450? Gàbrici, *NS* 1917, 347 f., no. 10, fig. 10. Whitaker, *Motya* (1921), 286 f., fig. 67. *SEG* iv. 44. Dunbabin, 334.                                          PL. 52

## GELA

**46.** Painted letters on the revetments of the Geloan Treasury at Olympia; *c.* 600–550. *Ol.* v. 943. Kunze and others, *Olympische Forschungen* i. 83 ff. Dunbabin, 272.

**47.** Graffito on a vase dedicated to Hera, Gela; mid-6th c.? Orlandini, *Rend. Linc.* 1954, 454, fig. 1. Gela Mus.

**48.** Dedication of Pantares at Olympia; *c.* 525? *Ol.* v. 142. *IGA* 512a. Roberts i. 131e. Roehl³, 34. 11. *SGDI* 4248. *DGE* 304. Carpenter, *AJA* xlix (1945), 455. *SEG* xi. 1215. Olympia Mus. 521.   PL. 53

**49.** Gravestone of Pasiades, from area of Gela; *c.* 525? Salinas, *NS* 1896, 254 f. Roehl³, 34. 10. *SGDI* 4247. *DGE* 302. Friedlaender 163c. Palermo Mus.   PL. 53

**50.** Graffito of Pantares on a skyphos from Gela, late 6th c.? Orlandini, *RM* lxiii (1956), 140 ff., no. 6, pl. 60, 4. Gela Mus.   PL. 53

**51.** Weight in the form of a bronze knucklebone, ?from Gela; *c.* 500–490? *IGA* 513. *IG* xiv. 593. *SGDI* 4249. Kubitschek, *Ö.Jh.* x (1907), 127 f., pl. 6. *DGE* 305. Vienna, Kunsthist. Mus.   PL. 53

**52.** Coinage with legend Γελας, Γελōιον; *c.* 491 onwards. *HN²*, 140. B ii. 1. 1537 ff., pl. 77.

**53.** Graffito dedication to Antiphemos; *c.* 500–450? Orsi, *NS* 1900, 274 ff. and *MA* xvii (1906), 559, fig. 380. *SGDI* 5215. *DGE* 303. Guarducci, *Ann.* xxvii–xxix (1949–51), 107 ff., fig. 3. *SEG* xii. 409. Lost?

**54.** Funeral stele of Philistides; *c.* 500–450? Orsi, *NS* 1900, 281, fig. 4. *SGDI* 5216. Roehl³, 34. 12. Palermo Mus.?

**55.** Pedestal bearing a dedication by Leukon to Chairesileos; *c.* 450? Orsi, *Riv. di Storia ant.* v (1900), 50 f., n. 19. Pernice, *Die hellenist. Kunst in Pompeji* v. 41, pl. 24. 7. Guarducci, op. cit. 109 f., fig. 4. *SEG* xii. 410. Gela Mus.?

**56.** Graffiti names on the façade of a tomb at Gela; *c.* 475–450? Gentili, *Epigraphica* viii (1946), 11 ff., pl. 2. Guarducci, op. cit. 110 f. Syracuse Mus. 20087.

**57.** Leaden *defixio* found in a grave at Gela; *c.* 450? Orsi, *MA* xvii (1906), 472 ff., fig. 336. Jeffery, op. cit. 74.

## AKRAGAS

**58.** Gravestone of Sakon and Mylos, from Ravanusa; *c.* 500–490? Mingazzini, *MA* xxxvi (1937), 662 ff., fig. 23. Dunbabin, 420, n. 7. Girgenti Mus.   PL. 53

**59.** Gravestone of the daughter of Anchemachos, from Akragas; *c.* 500–490? Salinas, *NS* 1895, 239 f. *SGDI* 4253. Roehl³, 34. 15. Girgenti Mus.

**60.** Coinage of Akragas, with legend Ακρα, Ακραγας, Ακραγαντος; *c.* 525 onwards. *HN²*, 119 ff. B ii. 1. 1543 ff., pl. 78.

**61.** Builders' marks on the temple of Demeter; *c.* 480–470? Marconi, *NS* 1926, 134, fig. 27.

**62.** Bronze handle inscribed with name Chrysippos; *c.* 500–475? *IGA* 521. *IG* xiv. 263. Roberts i. 187. Roehl³, 34. 14. Girgenti Mus.

**63.** Gravestone from Ravanusa; *c.* 475? Mingazzini, op. cit. 662 ff., fig. 22. Girgenti Mus.

**64.** Block from the base of an Akragantine dedication at Delphi; *c.* 475? Daux, *BCH* lxi (1937), 60 f., pl. 7. Delphi Mus. 5098.

# THE DORIC COLONIES, ITALY

## TARAS, HERAKLEIA

*Letter-forms*: see Lakonia, pp. 183 f. and Fig. 39.

Taras was the only colony sent out from Sparta until the affair of Dorieus *c.* 514–510. Traditionally she was founded after the first Messenian War, at the end of the eighth century.[1] The marked influence of her mother-city, evident from the start in the Tarantine choice of a monarchy for her constitution and Lakonian deities for her religious cults, continued to show itself in her general culture, especially in the import of Lakonian pottery.[2] Although her nearest Greek neighbours were the long belt of Achaian colonies to the west—of which the nearest, Metapontion, was said to have been founded by Sybaris deliberately to check any Tarantine expansion westwards (Strabo 264–5)—no traces of Achaian influence are visible in her dialect, cults, political institutions, or art. Only her coinage—for which, incidentally, Sparta could supply no model—was originally based, in its fabric and weight (though not in its denomination), on that of the Achaian colonies.[3]

The Tarantine alphabet also illustrates this close adhesion to Sparta. Sharply distinct from that of her Achaian neighbours, it resembles the Lakonian, except for the absence as yet of the long *sigma*; an absence probably due to deficient evidence, for the letter is attested in the Messapic script. If the original settlers were literate, this provides an obvious *terminus ante quem* of *c.* 706 for the introduction of the alphabet to Lakonia; but it is also possible that it came later, at any time during the subsequent traffic between Taras and Lakonia which kept Lakonian influence conspicuous in the culture of the colony. Only one concession to local influence seems to have been made; punctuation, when it occurs, is the single dot used in the inscriptions of the Achaian colonies. The few Greek inscriptions of the fifth century which have been found at other sites on or near the Iapygian peninsula are likewise in a 'red' script which presumably must be traced to Taras; and it is almost certain that the Messapic alphabet is derived from the same source.[4] These Greek inscriptions are therefore listed here with those of Taras. They consist of two fibulae from near Bari (**11–12**), a kerykeion from Brentesion (**13**), another from Gnathia which may be fourth-century (**14**), and a helmet from Anxia which should probably be connected with her colony Herakleia rather than with Taras herself (**9**).

In addition to her famous coinage which bears the legend Ταρας, later Ταραντινος, Ταραντινων, the following inscribed objects have been found in or near Taras: an Attic eye-kylix (**1**), a cube-shaped die (**2**), a votive base (**8**) and capital (**4**), and a mould for

---

[1] The Eusebian date is 706; cf. Wuilleumier, *Tarente* (1939), 29 ff.; Dunbabin, 28 ff., and for Dorieus' expeditions 348 ff., 362 ff.; Bérard[2], 162 ff.

[2] Wuilleumier, op. cit. 43 ff.; Dunbabin, op. cit. 31, 89, 91 ff.

[3] The unit of the early coins of the Achaian colonies was the stater, divided into thirds (and sixths): that of Taras was the didrachm, divided into halves (and

fifths): *HN*[2], 53 f.; Vlasto, Ταρας οἰκιστής (1922), 211, n. 3; Wuilleumier, op. cit. 199.

[4] Kirchhoff[4], 156; Roberts i, pp. 271, 273 f.; Whatmough, *Prae-Italic Dialects of Italy* ii (1933), 537 f.; Wuilleumier, op. cit. 658. For a Messapic example of the long *sigma*, cf. the archaic funeral inscription *Archivio Storico Pugliese* v (1952), 69 ff.

a terra-cotta statuette (**5**). At Delphi there are the remains of two bases bearing dedications by the Tarantines for victories over the natives of the Iapygian peninsula (**6, 7**) and at Olympia three spear-butts from victories over Thourioi (**10a–c**). There is nothing earlier than the fourth century from her colony Herakleia, unless the helmet found at Anxia came from there; for the masons' marks on the stones of a building excavated near the site belong, in my opinion, to the fourth rather than to an earlier century, as was suggested in the publication.[1]

The earliest datable Tarantine inscription is the graffito on an Attic eye-kylix dated in the decade 540–530, which records that it is the prize won by Melousa for carding wool (or making roves?):[2] Μελοσας εμι νικατēριον· ξαινοσα τας κορας ενικε (**1**). The provenance is said to be Taras, and this is confirmed by the details of the inscription, which shows isosceles *mu* and no *qoppa* in κορας, indicating that Taras followed Lakonia in ignoring this letter in practice, though it kept its place in the abecedarium (p. 283). Only in one detail does the inscription show local influence; the single dot is used for punctuation, and this is characteristic of the Achaian colonies (p. 249), not of Lakonian, which shows a curved line like a bracket. The dot recurs in the Messapic abecedarium of Vaste (**15**). A terra-cotta die also from Taras (**2**) is inscribed κυ(βος) (ace), δυο, τρια, τετο(ρα), πεν(τε), ϝεξ. Here *rho* is the tailed form ρ2, *epsilon* is tailless, *qoppa* again missing, *upsilon* the late archaic V; the die may be somewhat later than **1**, but might still belong to the last years of the sixth century. The earliest coins of Taras (**3**), which were struck in the incuse style of the Achaian colonies, belong to the second half of the sixth century; the legend reads Ταρας retrograde, with tailed *rho*.[3] According to the present system of dating these coins,[4] the incuse types ceased *c*. 520, and were followed by those types which bear the same design on the obverse (hero on dolphin), but on the reverse a second relief. Those showing a wheel (*c*. 520–500?) read Ταρας still with tailed *rho*; those with a hippocamp (*c*. 500–473?) and those with the head of Satyra (*c*. 473–450?) have σ1, ρ both 2 and 3, and read in either direction. Those of the overlapping series which shows on the reverse the oikistes Taras seated, after the style of the heroized figures on Lakonian reliefs, at first show σ1, with ρ both tailed and tailless (*c*. 485–473?); in the next series (*c*. 473–460?), as well as varying *rho*, the four-stroked σ2 sometimes appears instead of σ1; in those after 460, *rho* still varies, but *sigma* remains four-stroked; and they continue thus in the famous series showing a horseman on the reverse, which began about the middle of the fifth century. On the evidence of the coinage, therefore, the four-stroked *sigma* first appeared in the second quarter of the fifth century, and had displaced the three-stroked by about the middle. *Rho* seems to have varied throughout the period under discussion, if the graffito on Melousa's kylix (**1**) and the earliest incuse coinage alike belong to the third quarter of the sixth century.

[1] Galli, *NS* 1934, 472.

[2] Haspels, *Bulletin . . . te 's-Gravenhage* 1954, 30.

[3] The retrograde direction on the obverse is invariable, as far as I know; on the reverse of some issues, the legend reads from left to right, presumably to represent the other side of the obverse legend: Vlasto, op. cit. 16 f. It must be noted here that whereas Vlasto's majuscule texts are accurate, the majuscule versions of this legend in the relevant pages of Babelon, Wuilleumier, Ravel, and the *BMC Coins* will be found on occasion to read P, Σ where the accompanying photograph shows R, Ϟ.

[4] *HN²*, 53 f.; Vlasto, op. cit., *passim*, esp. p. 22; Wuilleumier, 371 ff.; Ravel, *Cat. Coll. Vlasto* (1947), 10 ff.

If we accept this dating for the adoption of the four-stroked *sigma*, the base for a dedi-cation (**8**, illustrated only in majuscule type), which shows this *sigma*, might be attributed tentatively to the second quarter of the fifth century; moreover, it is printed as a text cut *stoichedon*: [- - -]εποιε ‖[- - -]ες ανεθēκε. A bronze plinth on a stone capital in Boston (**4**) bears a similar inscription: Πολυλος ανεθēκε. | Ευπιδας εποιε. The appearance of the letters suggests a date at the end of the sixth century, or a few years later. Another inscrip-tion, illustrated only in majuscule type, which is incised retrograde on a mould (un-published?) for a terra-cotta statuette of a seated goddess, I conclude from the comment by Wuilleumier[1] to be of the early fifth century (**5**); it reads Φιλοξενο εμι. Two more inscriptions are on two silver fibulae which were found in the necropolis at Valenzano, south-east of Bari (**11–12**). They are very neatly incised and read: Ραμια εδōκε and Μυρθō μ[ε εδōκε?]. Without prejudice to any dating of the fibulae themselves, I should be inclined to ascribe the inscriptions to about the middle of the fifth century; hardly earlier, as the dotted *theta* is used.

The two dedications by the Tarantines at Delphi were both described by Pausanias (x. 10. 6), who says that one (**7**), which is usually called the lower, from its position not far from the start of the Sacred Way at the foot of the slope, was dedicated by the Taran-tines ‘from the Messapians’ and made by Ageladas of Argos: [Ταραντ]ινο[ι ανεθεν απο τōν Μεσσαπιōν ͱελ]οντες [δεκαταν]: the parts underlined are supplied by the fourth-century re-dedication (see below). The other (**6**), the upper, of which part was found *in situ* adjoining the base of the golden tripod dedicated after Plataia (p. 102), was dedicated ‘from the Peuketians’, and made by Onatas of Aigina and a collaborator named Kalynthos (?; Paus. x. 13. 10). Both dedications were re-inscribed in the fourth century. The lettering of the upper is demonstrably the earlier of the two original inscriptions (e.g. tailed *epsilon*, sloping *nu*); nevertheless the excavators incline to the view that the lower base should be dated somewhere in the first quarter of the fifth century, before the great defeat of Taras and her ally Rhegion in 473, and the upper shortly after, *c.* 466(?), when Taras had become a democracy. The main grounds for this order are (*a*) that the *floruit* of the sculptor Ageladas is held to be earlier than that of Onatas, from the literary evidence, (*b*) that the lettering of the lower base was assigned on its discovery to the first quarter of the fifth century, and (*c*) that Amandry has shown[2] that, though certainty is not possible, the positions of the respective foundation-courses for the bases of the upper dedication and the tripod of Plataia suggest strongly that the tripod was erected before the Tarantine offering. A possible alternative, which would at least avoid the epigraphical difficulty, would be to date the upper base somewhere between 478 (erection of tripod) and 473 (defeat of Taras); this would fit Onatas’ period of activity, which seems to have been *c.* 500–460,[3] and would not be impossible for the forms of *epsilon* and *nu*; the retro-grade direction of the script was probably, as Amandry points out, because the monument lay on the right of the visitor climbing the Sacred Way from the entrance. The lower base, on the other hand, might be dated after the disaster of 473, as a victory scored over

---

[1] Op. cit. 394: ‘Une cinquantaine [de moules] . . . portent des inscriptions; quelques-unes datent du Ve siècle, la plupart des IVe–IIIe siècles. La plus ancienne et la plus explicite est gravée à rebours sur un moule archaïque de déesse assise: φιλοξένο εἰμί: elle désigne donc le possesseur, qui doit se confondre avec l’artiste.’

[2] *BCH* lxxiii (1949), 459 f.

[3] Cf. *DAA*, 521 f.

the Messapians at some later time by the democracy. A date in the second quarter of the fifth century would in any case suit better the lettering of this base; and as for Ageladas, it is true that he must have been active before the end of the sixth century, but he also made the Zeus Ithomates for the Messenians of Naupaktos, presumably shortly before the middle of the fifth century (Paus. iv. 33. 2).

The inscribed helmet of Corinthian type (**9**) which was found at Anxia has an undoubted connexion with Herakleia, because the name Δαзιμος Πυρρω occurs again in the Herakleian Tables, at the end of the fourth century (*DGE* 62; Buck 79); also, Anxia is nearer to Herakleia than to Taras. Either the helmet and inscription must be dated after 433, the date of the foundation of Herakleia, or it must be concluded that the helmet was among the possessions of the family when they settled there; the four-stroked *sigma* suggests a date after the first quarter of the fifth century. The three spear-butts from Olympia (**10***a–c*) are dated with reasonable assurance in the decade 443–433, because they are 'spoils from Thourioi', i.e. from the period when Taras and Thourioi struggled together for the site of Siris on which Herakleia was eventually founded. They show crossed *theta* still, and sometimes even a tailed *epsilon*; in fact, their general character has been described as archaizing;[1] but while the existing material is so scanty, it is impossible to be precise on this point. The first coins showing *omega* in their legend Ταραντινων are set tentatively by Vlasto in the period *c*. 460–443.[2] If this is correct, it is a further proof of the conservatism of the writing on the spear-butts; but the style of the coins might extend some years later than 443, and in fact it is hard to see whence Taras could have got the *omega* as early as *c*. 460; the introduction of the Ionic letters in these parts is generally attributed to the Ionic element among the emigrants who settled the colony of Thourioi, so that 443 should be the *terminus post quem* rather than *ante quem* for these coins.

### NON-GREEK PLACES

The Ionic script of Thourioi (pp. 287 f.) is well illustrated on a herald's staff found in the area of Brentesion (Brundisium), **13**. It is inscribed on one side in Ionic: δαμοσιον Θουριων, and on the other in what is presumably the Lakonian–Messapic script of a hellenized native: δαμοσιον Βρενδεσινōν (retrograde). The use of the Greek language shows how Greek culture had spread in Iapygia, though the sibilant letter may be a Messapic one (p. 40).[3] It has been rightly pointed out that the staff cannot have been re-used by one or other of the two states, because the second user would surely have cancelled the first inscription (as on the kerykeion of Imachara, Sicilian Doric colonies **23**); it was either jointly used by the heralds of Thourioi and Brentesion, or jointly dedicated in some sanctuary. A suitable time for this amity is the decade *c*. 440–430, when Thourioi, in her struggle against Taras, may well have called in the Messapians.[4] The kerykeion from Gnathia **14** is Greek in language and (Ionic) alphabet; but whether

---

[1] Lejeune, *RA* (1944), 10, n. 1.

[2] Τάρας οἰκιστής, 129 f., 136 ff. (types 22, 26–27, 33–34).

[3] Whatmough, *Prae-Italic Dialects* ii, lists four possible examples (none certain) in his Messapic nos. 358,

394, 438, 567, apart from the doubtful example in the alphabet of Vaste (see p. 283, and Arkadia, p. 213, n. 1).

[4] De Simone, *Arch. Class.* viii (1956), 15 ff. and x (1958), 102 ff.

the latter is taken from Thourioi also, or was written at a time when Ionic had become normal in these parts, it is impossible to say.

One of the most valuable witnesses for the Tarantine alphabet is the abecedarium copied by Cepolla at Vaste in 1805 (**15**). The abecedarium itself is Messapic,[1] but inasmuch as the Messapic alphabet is almost certainly derived from the Tarantine, we have in effect a reflection of the Tarantine alphabet. The punctuation mark of a dot evidently separated the letters, though Cepolla did not always observe it. Two letters are missing (θ, π), two (three?) badly copied (α, ε, Ϡ?). *Gamma*, not yet attested in Tarantine inscriptions, is the Lakonian form; *vau* is 2, not yet Ϝ; *heta* is open, but not the half-letter Ⱶ, first attested *c.* 400 (pp. 29, 183). *Qoppa*, though unused in Tarantine inscriptions, must have been preserved by convention in its place in the alphabet, for otherwise it could not appear thus in the Messapic abecedarium—and, further, in Messapic inscriptions, though rarely.[2] *San* also must have been fossilized in the Tarantine abecedarium, for it appears here in the form H, according to Cepolla, and may be the origin of the sibilant on the kerykeion of Brentesion, and in the other doubtful examples (p. 282, n. 3). The *rho*-like letter following *tau* has been variously explained;[3] I incline to think that it may be meant for ϛι, retained by convention in the Messapic alphabet, though the letter itself was not used.[4] The two final identical signs may be, as Whatmough has suggested,[5] the Messapic 'red' *chi* (from Tarantine), and a local Messapic letter developed from *tau*; or, again, the second letter might be the Greek φ, retained by convention.[6] In this Tarantine–Messapic alphabet the sibilants *xi* and *san* have shifted their positions, as they have in other abecedaria (pp. 117, 256), so that we read *nu, o, xi, qoppa, rho, san* instead of *nu, xi, o, san, qoppa, rho.* Was this the work of the Messapic writer, or did the alphabet of Taras normally follow this order? Lastly, we may speculate whether the Tarantine alphabet acquired its *qoppa* and *san* from the neighbouring script of the Achaian colonies—although it had no practical use for them—or whether in fact (as I should prefer to believe) they were retained by convention in the abecedarium of Lakonia (see p. 192), and so passed on to Taras.

## CATALOGUE

### TARAS

**1.** Graffito on an Attic eye-kylix won by Melousa; *c.* 540–530. Bloesch, *Formen attischer Schalen* (1940), 8. Milne, *Bull. Metr. Mus.* iii (1944), 110 ff. and *AJA* xlix (1945), 528 ff., figs. 1–3. *CVA* USA ii, 39 a–f, pls. 25–26. New York, MM 44.11.1.    PL. 53

**2.** Cube-shaped clay die, from Taras; *c.* 510–500? Wuilleumier, *Istros* i (1934), 14 ff. and *Tarente* (1939), 657, pl. 44, 6. Trieste Mus. 412.

[1] Cf. Whatmough, op. cit. 407 ff., no. 555; *CQ* xix (1925), 68 ff.

[2] Whatmough, op. cit. 536.

[3] See *CQ*, loc. cit. Whatmough believes it to be an error for X, i.e. the Ionic χ, which the Messapians incorporated into their alphabet in addition to the original Tarantine X = ξ; but the abecedarium shows the earlier forms of *gamma, delta, vau* and may therefore be of the 5th c., whereas the Ionic *chi* occurs, so far, only in inscriptions of the 4th c. and later, as listed by Whatmough, *Prae-Italic Dialects*, 533; cf. also 538.

[4] Op. cit. 595 f.    [5] *CQ*, loc. cit.

[6] Whatmough observes that *phi* is 'almost certainly altogether wanting' from Messapic: op. cit. 532 f.

**3.** Inscribed coinage, second half of 6th c. onwards. B ii. 1. 1379 ff., pl. 65. *HN²*, 53 ff. Vlasto, Τάρας οἰκιστής (1922), with bibliog. Wuilleumier, op. cit. 371 ff. with bibliog.

**4.** Capital for a dedication, bearing an inscribed bronze plinth, from Taras; *c.* 500–490. Wuilleumier, op. cit. 657, n. 1. Boston, MFA B12235.                                                        PL. 53

**5.** Mould for a clay seated kore, from Taras; *c.* 500–475? Mayer, *NS* 1896, 541. Roehl³, 105. 36. Wuilleumier, op. cit. 394.

**6.** Upper Tarantine dedication at Delphi, from a victory over the Peuketians; *c.* 478–473? Bourguet, *REG* xxv (1912), 15 f. *SIG³* 40a. Dunbabin, 149. *DAA*, 520 f. Amandry, *BCH* lxxiii (1949), 447 ff., figs. 1–4. Delphi Mus.

**7.** Lower Tarantine dedication at Delphi; *c.* 450? *FD* iii. 1. 73 ff., no. 126, fig. 26 and pl. 3, 3. La Coste-Messelière, *RA* 1948, 522 ff. Amandry, loc. cit. Delphi Mus.

**8.** Base for a dedication by ——es, Taras; *c.* 475–450? *IG* xiv. 669. Roehl³, 105. 38. Wuilleumier, *Istros* i (1934), 15.

**9.** Helmet from Anxia, inscribed; *c.* 450? *IGA* 547. *IG* xiv. 655. Roberts i. 269. Roehl³, 104. 35. *BMC Bronzes* 317. BM.                                                                            PL. 53

**10***a–c.* Three inscribed spear-butts from a victory of Taras over Thourioi, dedicated at Olympia; *c.* 443–433. *Ol.* v. 254–6. Roberts i. 270. Roehl³, 105. 37. Richter, *AJA* xliii (1939), 198. Lerat, *RA* 1944, 10, n. 1. Kunze, *Olympische Forschungen* i, pl. 63. *SEG* xi. 1209. Olympia Mus. 692, 906, 1076.                PL. 53

### NON-GREEK PLACES

**11–12.** Two inscribed silver fibulae from the necropolis at Valenzano near Bari; *c.* 450? Gervasio, *Bronzi e Ceramica di Bari* (1921), 87 f., pl. 12, 7 and fig. 49. Bari Mus.                          PL. 53

**13.** Kerykeion from Brentesion (Messapic); *c.* 443–433? *IG* xiv. 672. Kubitschek, *Ö.Jh.* x (1907), 129. Whatmough, *Prae-Italic Dialects of Italy* ii (1933), 514, 537. Crome, *AM* lxiii (1938), 118. Wuilleu-mier, *Tarente*, 198. De Simone, *Arch. Class.* viii (1956), 15 ff., pls. 7–8. Venice, Olvrado Lebreton Coll.                                                                                                        PL. 54

**14.** Kerykeion from Gnathia; 5th c.? *IG* xiv. 685. Kubitschek, loc. cit. Crome, op. cit. 117 f., pl. 17, 2. Whatmough, op. cit. 281. Berlin Mus. 1325.

**15.** Abecedarium at Vaste (Messapic, known only from a copy); 5th c.? *IG* xiv. 2420. 5. *IGA* 546. Roberts i. 268. Whatmough, *CQ* xix (1925), 68 ff., and op. cit., no. 555.                              PL. 53

# THE LOKRIAN COLONIES

*Letter-forms*: see Lokris, Ozolian and Opountian, pp. 104 f. and Fig. 31.

### LOKROI EPIZEPHYRIOI

About a generation after the first Achaian colonists had settled in southern Italy a band of Lokrian emigrants under the leadership of Euanthes founded the colony of Lokroi Epizephyrioi, between the territories of Achaian Kroton, on the one hand, and Chalkidic Rhegion, on the other (Strabo 259). The Eusebian date for the colony is 679/8 or 673/2.

There is no agreement among the ancient writers as to whether they came from Ozolian or from Opountian Lokris,[1] and no surviving tradition to tell us anything of the circumstances in which this solitary Lokrian contribution to the colonization of the West was made, except that they were aided by the Syracusans and (probably) the Tarantines.[2] The Ozolian Lokrians must have been familiar with the sight of ships from Corinth and Achaia making westwards past their own shores; the Opountians equally must have seen the ships from Euboia set off on the same journey. Both the mainland Lokrides used basically the same 'red' script, but the Ozolians used 'Ionic' *lambda* and four-stroked *sigma*, whereas the Opountians used mainly the Chalkidic–Boiotian form of *lambda* and three-stroked *sigma* (four-stroked in the earliest inscriptions; p. 105). The colony's alphabet, as far as is known, is like that of the Ozolians; which suggests an Ozolian origin. For what it is worth, we may note also one certain example of an Ozolian Lokrian who had to do with the route to the West: Menekrates, proxenos at Oianthea for Korkyra, who was buried with public honours in Korkyra (p. 232).

Not long after her foundation Lokroi produced her famous lawgiver Zaleukos, whom Ephoros maintained to be the author of the first written code of law (Strabo 259). The partial preservation of this code is due to the literary sources; no traces of it have yet been found in the excavations of the site. At some early date—possibly still in the seventh century—the colony expanded across the peninsula, as her Achaian neighbours were doing, and founded her daughter-colonies Hipponion, Medma, and Metauron(?);[3] and in the third quarter of the sixth century, after the fall of Siris (which Lokroi was said to have aided against the Achaian colonies' attack), Lokroi herself was attacked by Kroton, and won a resounding victory at the river Sagra *c.* 540–530.[4]

With one exception, the archaic inscriptions found at Lokroi all come from a precinct of Persephone. The exception is a piece of a bronze plaque (**3**), like those found near Kroton which deal with the disposition of property (pp. 258 f.). It is written between faint guide-lines, with a dot for punctuation as in the Achaian examples, and may belong to the early years of the fifth century (tailed *rho*, dotted *theta*). One inscription from the precinct of Persephone appears to be earlier, perhaps *c.* 525–500: a small fragment (**1**) from a bronze plaque (legal text?) written *boustrophedon*, with a dot for punctuation. Two dedications on helmets (**4–5**) may be of about the same date as **3**, *c.* 500–480? (crossed *theta*, tailed *rho*). A small bronze mirror given by Sir Arthur Evans to the Ashmolean Museum has been tentatively assigned to the precinct of Persephone at Lokroi (**8**). This cannot be certain, for it came from a Greek dealer who believed it to be from Olympia; but the case for Lokroi seems very strong on general grounds. The inscription is retrograde and may belong to the last years of the sixth century, or possibly a little later.

### HIPPONION, MEDMA

Hipponion and Medma, the two colonies established across the peninsula, were

---

[1] The fullest discussion of the sources is that of Bérard[2], 199 ff. Cf. also Lerat, *Les Locriens de l'ouest* ii (1952), 22 ff., who supports the Ozolian Lokrians on the grounds of general probability.

[2] Strabo, loc. cit. Ἄμα Ταραντίνοις is amended from †ἅμα γὰρ οὗτοι ἐν οἷς†.

[3] Thuc. v. 5; Strabo 256; Steph. Byz., s.v. Μάταυρος. Cf. Dunbabin, 163 ff.; Bérard[2], 210 ff.

[4] For the date see Dunbabin, 359.

probably founded in the seventh century, though no material earlier than the sixth century has yet been found.[1] They have left their record at Olympia, where were found two fragments from a trophy (2): a bronze appliqué for a shield-blazon, inscribed *en pointillé*: τοι Ϝειπ̄ονιες α̣[ν]ε̣θ[ε̄καν] | τ̄ον Ϙροτ̄ονια[ταν] | και Μεδμαιοι και Λ[οκροι], and a bronze strip: [- - -] και Λοκροι και [- - -]. It is tempting to identify this victory with that at Sagra, since Lokroi's colonies may well have helped her there; but these dedications can hardly be earlier than the last quarter of the sixth century (Ϙ still, but ε2, ρ2 and lines no longer written *boustrophedon*). Pausanias saw at Olympia a wooden Apollo (which sounds archaic) dedicated by Lokroi (vi. 19. 6), and this statue may also have been part of the spoils of the same campaign; for the sculptor was Patrokles of Kroton, and it is unlikely that any Krotoniate sculptor would have received a commission from Lokroi.

## CATALOGUE

**1.** Fragment of a bronze plaque from the sanctuary of Persephone at Lokroi; *c.* 525–500? Comparetti, *NS* 1911, suppl., 51, fig. 39. Reggio Mus.                   PL. 54

**2.** Parts of a trophy dedicated at Olympia by Hipponion, Medma, and Lokroi; *c.* 525–500? Kunze and Schleif, *JdI* lvi (1941), *Olympiabericht* iii, 77 ff., pls. 24–25. *SEG* xi. 1211. Olympia Mus.    PL. 54

**3.** Part of a bronze plaque from Lokroi (Carace), concerning disposition of property; *c.* 500–480? L. Robert, *Coll. Froehner* i. 127 f., no. 82, pl. 43. Paris, Bib. Nat.                   PL. 54

**4.** Helmet dedicated by Phrasiades to Persephone at Lokroi; *c.* 500–480? Toscanelli, *Le Origine Italiche*, fig. 157. R. Carpenter, *AJA* xlix (1945), 455, fig. 2. Private Coll.?            PL. 54

**5.** Helmet dedicated by Xenai(des?) to the same deity; *c.* 500–480? *IG* xiv. 631. *IGA* 538. Roberts i. 235. *SGDI* 1486. Naples Mus.

**6.** Stele bearing the dedication of Oiniades and others at Lokroi; *c.* 475–450? *IGA* 537. Roberts i. 234. *SGDI* 1485. Roehl³, 93. 5. Naples Mus.                   PL. 54

**7.** Dedication of Kaparon and Proxeno at Lokroi; *c.* 450–425? Orsi (?), *NS* 1913, suppl., 4, fig. 1. Naples Mus.

*Inscription attributed to Lokroi*

**8.** Bronze mirror dedicated by Xenodoke, said to be from Elis; *c.* 500? Tod, *JHS* l (1930), 32 ff., figs. 1–2. Oxford, Ashmolean Mus.

## THE IONIC COLONIES

*Letter-forms*: see the Ionic Dodekapolis, pp. 325 f. and Fig. 46.

### SIRIS

Siris in southern Italy was said to be an Ionic colony, founded in the first part of the seventh century by fugitives from Kolophon who had fled from the attack of Gyges of Lydia (Strabo 264; Athen. 523c). A loom-weight has been found on the site, inscribed in the Ionic alphabet of the early or middle sixth century (1); it reads: Ισοδικης εμι, with closed *eta*. In the third quarter of the sixth century the city was captured by the Achaian

---

[1] Dunbabin, 163 ff.; Bérard², 210 ff.

combination Sybaris, Kroton, and Metapontion, and this was the end of her existence as an independent Ionic settlement, though she may have continued as an Achaian dependency like Sirinos and Pyxous (p. 254. See also Addenda).

## MASSALIA AND COLONIES

Massalia in southern France was founded by Phokaia *c.* 600, a coastal settlement among the Ligures which was soon to dominate a great part of the western Mediterranean, flourishing on her trade with Spain and the interior of France, and defying with her fleet the jealous hostility of Carthage.[1] There was a Massaliote Treasury at Delphi (Diod. xiv. 93), and Pausanias mentions two of their offerings there: a bronze image to Athena Pronaia (x. 8. 6) and an Apollo dedicated from the spoils of a victory over the Carthaginian fleet (x. 18. 7). The Massaliotes used the Ionic script of their mother-city; there is a grave-stele at Delphi to one of their citizens, Apellis son of Demon, in rather straggling, ill-spaced Ionic lettering, perhaps of the early fifth century (**2**). No early inscriptions have been found as yet on the site of Massalia herself; perhaps it is not too much to hope that one day excavation may produce some parts of her famous Ionic law-code mentioned by Strabo (179), of which tantalizing glimpses are preserved in Valerius Maximus (*Facta Dictaque Memorabilia* ii. 6. 7–8), on the manumission of slaves, the conduct of funerals, the beheading of criminals (with a rusty sword barely equal to the task, *rubigine quidem exesus et vix sufficiens ministerio*), the banning of mimes, and so on. From Antipolis, one of the colonial offshoots which she planted round her for ἐπιτει-χίσματα against the natives (Strabo 180), there is a dedication by someone to Aphrodite (**3**), in Ionic lettering not earlier than the middle of the fifth century. Her main settlement in northern Spain, Emporion, was founded, according to the archaeological evidence,[2] in the next generation after Massalia herself. Several Ionic graffiti have been found there on sherds (mostly Attic imports) of the late sixth and the fifth century (**4**), and one fragmentary leaden scroll, presumably a *defixio*, written in large, careful letters which can hardly be later than the fifth century (**5**). See also Addenda.

## HYELE, THOURIOI

Hyele (Velia), founded in Oinotria *c.* 535 by those Phokaians who survived the Etruscan vengeance after the battle of Alalia (Hdt. i. 165–7), also used the Ionic script of her mother-city, for her earliest inscribed coinage (**6**; *c.* 490–480?) bears the legend Υελη; only her later series show F for Velia, the letter perhaps borrowed from her Lokrian neighbours.[3] Thourioi, the mixed colony founded *c.* 445–3 by Athens on the site of ancient Sybaris, shows from the start the Ionic script on her coins inscribed Θουριων (**7**); it has been suggested that this was because there was a strong Ionic contingent among the colonists—strong enough, certainly, to damp any hopes which Athens may have had that Thourioi would be a dutiful and valuable daughter-city to her in the west—and further that it was Thourioi which was mainly responsible for spreading the Ionic alphabet to

[1] Thuc. i. 13; Ps.-Skymnos 211 ff.; Strabo 179; Ol. 45 (600–596) in the Eusebian chronicle. Cf. Gomme, *Thucydides* i. 124 f.; Brunel, *REA* 1 (1948), 5 ff.

[2] Bosch-Gimpera, *CQ* 1944, 53 ff.

[3] The series showing *vau* has sometimes been wrongly classed as the earlier: *DGE* 705, *SGDI* 5631.

the other Italiote colonies.[1] The Ionic inscription **8** on a herald's staff found near Brindisi should belong to the decade *c.* 443–433 (p. 282, **13**); it may commemorate an anti-Tarantine alliance between Thourioi and the natives of Messapia, the perpetual enemies of Taras.

## CATALOGUE

### SIRIS

**1.** Clay loom-weight marked with the name Isodike, from Siris; *c.* 575–550? Orsi, *NS* 1912, suppl., 61, fig. 63. Blinkenberg, *Lindos* i. 145, n. 1. Jeffery, *JHS* lxix (1949), 32 f., fig. 9. J. Bérard, *Charites* (1957), 220 f. Lost?                                        PL. 54

### MASSALIA

**2.** Gravestone of Apellis, Delphi; *c.* 500–475? Perdrizet, *Rev. des Universités du Midi* iii (1897), 129 ff., fig. in text. *SIG*³ 12. Clerc, *Massalia* i (1927), 185, fig. 28. Delphi Mus. 2364.                        PL. 54

### ANTIPOLIS

**3.** Dedication to Aphrodite, from Antipolis; *c.* 450–425? *IGA* 551. Roehl³, 31. 52. Clerc, op. cit., 256, fig. 60. Friedlaender 40. Marseilles Mus.                        PL. 54

### EMPORION

**4.** Graffiti on sherds of the 6th and 5th c., Emporion. Almagro, *Las Inscripciones Ampuritanas griegas, ibéricas y latinas* (1952), 50 ff., nos. 37–40, 42–45, 48. Barcelona Arch. Mus., Ampurias Mus.   PL. 54

**5.** Leaden scroll bearing remains of a curse (?), from Emporion; 5th c.? Almagro, op. cit. 34 ff., no. 21, fig. in text. Ampurias Mus.

### HYELE (VELIA)

**6.** Coinage with legends Υελη, Ϝ; *c.* 490–480 onwards. B ii. 1. 1427, pl. 68. *HN*², 88 ff.

### THOURIOI

**7.** Coinage of Thourioi with legend Θουριων; *c.* 443 onwards. *HN*², 85 ff. Ehrenberg, *AJP* lxix (1948), 152.

**8.** Herald's staff of Thourioi, found near Brindisi; *c.* 443–433? For bibliography, see p. 284, Taras **13**.                        PL. 54

[1] *HN*², 85, 96, 106. This is the view of E. S. G. Robinson (see the Achaian colonies, p. 253, n. 4).

# THE AEGEAN ISLANDS

## THE IONIC ISLANDS (CENTRAL AND NORTHERN AEGEAN)

| | α | β | γ | δ | ε | F | 3 | η | ⊢ | θ | ι | κ | λ | μ | ν | ξ | ο | π | M | ϙ | ρ | σ | τ | υ | φ | χ | ψ | ω | P | |
|---|---|---|---|---|---|---|---|---|---|---|---|---|---|---|---|---|---|---|---|---|---|---|---|---|---|---|---|---|---|---|
| 1 | A, C | Λ | Δ | ⪢ | ⪦ | | | B | ⊗, I | κ | Γ | Μ | Ν | Xϛ, ο | Γ | ‒ | ϙ | P, | ⪦ | T | Γ | φ | X, | | ⊓ | : | | | | 1 |
| 2 | A | B | Γ | | ⪦ | ⊏ | | H | ⊕ | | κ | Λ | Μ | Ν | □ϛ⁺Ω^x | | | P | ϛ | | Y | Φ | + | ⊓ϛ | Ω | | | | 2 |
| 3 | Λ | | | | E | | | ⊔ | ⊙ | | | Λ | Μ | Ν | ‡ | | | R, | ⟨ | | V | V? | | Ω | | | | | 3 |
| 4 | A | | | | | | | | | | | Γ^x | | N | Ⅎ | | | R | | | Y | | | ⊓ | | | | | 4 |
| 5 | | | | | | | | | | | | | | | Ξ | | | | D | | | | | Ω | | | | | 5 |
| 6 | | | | | | | | | | | | | | | | | | | P | | | | | ⌒ | | | | | 6 |
| 7 | | | | | | | | | | | | | | | | | | | | | | | | o^x ⌒ | | | | | 7 |

X = Paros, Thasos    + = Naxos

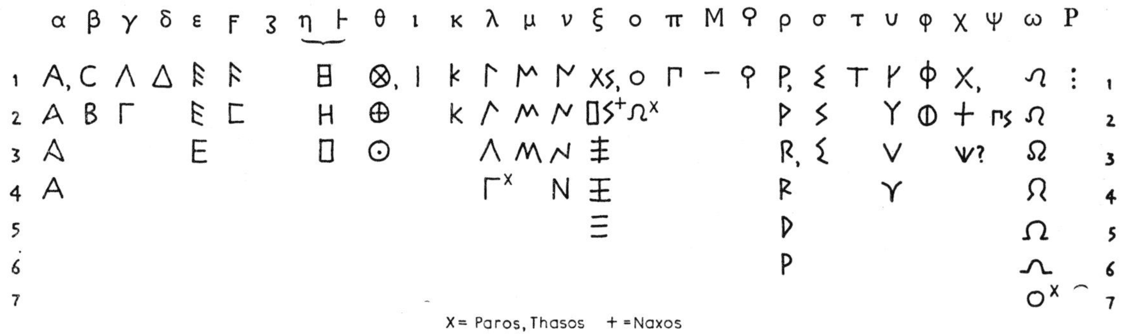

FIG. 44. Central and Northern Aegean Islands (Ionic)

### Notes on letter-forms

β1 (cf. the Theran and Argive types) is attested in Naxos, Paros, Thasos, Keos, Delos; and presumably it was used also in Siphnos. The earliest examples from Amorgos and Andros show β2 (**22**, **53**), but do not antedate the 5th c. β1 was still in use in Naxos c. 525–500 (**11**), and in Paros and Thasos c. 475–450 (**35**, **70**); both types occur on Delos in the late archaic period (**43c–d**).

γ1 is the more common form (e.g. Naxos, Paros, Delos), but γ2 occurs in early inscriptions of Amorgos (**15**, **17**), Samothrace (**56**), and in Tenos (**51**, 5th c.); the straight line in Amorgos **23** (5th c.) may be an error for γ2.

Naxos used E for η under certain circumstances (p. 291); Syros, Keos, and Delos show a confused system, H for ε and E for η with no proper consistency.

Although it was not used in the dialect of any of the islands, *vau* occurs once in an iambic line (αϝυτο) at Naxos (**10**); it is also attested in its 5th c. form ϝ2 in an abecedarium in Amorgos (**23**).

As in the Doric islands and Hexapolis, *heta* does duty for both aspirate and vowel. In Naxos, ⊢1–2 was used (*a*) for ⊢, (*b*) under certain circumstances for η (p. 291). The Naxians also used the doublet ⊢3 for the aspirated sound of their *xi*. By the early 5th c. they had dropped this ξ2 in favour of the more normal ξ1, and were using H for *eta* in all circumstances, as well as for the aspirate (**12**). Delos, Keos, and Syros show a confused use of ⊢1–2 (*a*) for aspirate, (*b*) for ε and sometimes for η. Paros used ⊢1–2 in the more common Ionic fashion for η, and occasionally also for the aspirate (p. 294). Siphnos used it for the aspirate (**40**); possibly for η (no examples as yet); not for ε (**40**). The earliest inscriptions to show the later form 2 appear to be Paros **28** and **29**, here conjecturally assigned to the middle and third quarter of the 6th c.; but the examples are too few for a more precise date to be suggested.

θ1–2 was still used in Naxos c. 525–500 (**11**), and in Paros in the early 5th c. (**35**); θ3 appears in Thasos c. 525–500 (**64**).

λ1 is still used in the early 5th c. (Naxos **12**), though the normal late archaic type is λ2. λ4 appears in Paros and Thasos in the first half of the 5th c., and is frequent thereafter to the end of the century (Paros **37**, Thasos **70–72**, **76**).

Paros (with Thasos) used ξ1 (cf. also Attic). Andros shows the full Ionic form 3–4 in the first half of the 5th c. (**53**), and Keos in the late 6th c. (**46**). ξ5 occurs in *IG* xii, suppl., p. 131, no. 279 (5th c.), an epitaph for a Naxian found on Andros.

Paros, Thasos, Siphnos show ω for the short vowel (o for the long); the earliest example appears to be in Paros **25** (end of 7th c.?).

*Qoppa* was used throughout these islands; the latest attested examples are dated *c.* 525–500 (Paros **32**, Thasos **63**).

ρ3–4 is attested in the late archaic period at Delos (**43** *b*, *e*, *f*) and Thasos (**64**); ρ5 occurs in Paros *c.* 500 (**34**). Naxos **3** shows ρ3 in Roehl³, 27. 30. I read ρ2 on stone and squeeze.

Naxos used σ2, Paros σ1, Thasos, Amorgos, and Delos both forms, Keos σ1.

υ2, a rare, early form, occurs in the early inscription Amorgos **15**.

Contrary to most of the archaic scripts, Naxos and Paros appear to have used φ2 instead of the more usual φ1 in the 7th and early 6th c. (cf. Naxos **1**, **2**, Paros **27**); and φ2 is the normal form thereafter, with an occasional φ1 as an exception (Paros **29**).

χ3 is very doubtful; see pp. 297 f.

*Psi* was probably φσ in most of these places, as in Attic; but the only example as yet shows πσ (Amorgos **17**). Paros, Thasos, Siphnos used o for *omega* and the form ω for *omikron* (q.v.); the rest show o for both long and short vowels, until the Ionic *omega* was adopted during the 5th c. (Naxos **14**). Amorgos used *omega* from an early period, because her script was influenced by Samian (p. 293).

*Punctuation* 1 is attested at Naxos *c.* 600 (**3**), but hardly ever occurs thereafter (cf. Thasos **63**). The *boustrophedon* system seems to have died out shortly after the middle of the 6th c. (cf. Paros **28–30**), though occasional examples are found thereafter (e.g. Paros **33**, which is both *boustrophedon* and *stoichedon*; Naxos **13**, which appears to be a sacred text of some kind). The true *stoichedon* style does not appear before the 5th c. (e.g. **37**, **41**, **53**, **68**, **72**), though a 6th c. graffito from Delos (**43**c) has a half-line written thus below the first line.

## A. CENTRAL AEGEAN

Cycladic pottery forms much of the eighth-century Greek material from Al Mina,[1] and it may be conjectured that some at least among the Cycladic Greeks became acquainted very early with the Greek alphabet from their trading along the Semitic coast. The script of the Cyclades may be divided basically into two types, the Naxian and the Parian, the chief points of difference being that Naxian had a curious by-form of closed *eta* which was used for the aspirate in the Naxian spelling of *xi* (p. 291); while Parian, in its turn, distinguished the long ō from the short by the use of two letter-forms, as the eastern Ionic did also. The curious *eta* is common to Knidos, while the distinction between *omikron* and *omega* is found also in Knidos and in Melos (the latter apparently not before the fifth century: p. 321). Against their differences, Naxian and Parian resemble each other in making no use of the letter Ξ = ξ until the fifth century, and in using the 'blue' *chi*, and a remarkable open form of *beta*, which seems to be kin to the variations used also in Argive, Theran, Cretan, Corinthian, and Melian (cf. further pp. 23, 114). The presence of the curious *eta* and of an *omega* in Knidian may be thought to prove some connexion between the Knidian and Cycladic scripts; but it must be stressed

---

[1] Cf. M. Robertson, *JHS* lx–lxi (1940–41), 2 ff. J. Boardman, however, suggests that much of the so-called Cycladic material may be in fact Euboic; *BSA* lii (1957), 1 ff.

that there may have been other, intermediate links, for the archaic script of many of the islands is still unknown. It was only a chance find of one archaic inscription in 1931 which proved that Sikinos was not in fact Ionic like her close neighbour Ios, but must be classed with the Doric islands Melos, Pholegandros, Thera and Anaphe (p. 322). The script of Naxos and Amorgos is attested as early as the seventh century, it is true, but there is nothing as yet earlier than the sixth from Paros, Keos, Syros, Tenos, or Ikaros, and nothing certainly before the fifth from Andros, Siphnos, or Ios. The archaic scripts of Oliaros, Gyaros, Kythnos, Seriphos, Mykonos, and Doric Astypalaia are still unknown. But at least it can be said that the inscriptions of Amorgos, Andros, and Keos show Naxian influence in varying degrees, and the earliest in Siphnos show Parian. At Delos, as might be expected from the early control of the island by Naxos, Naxian dedications are conspicuous; the local script of Delos, as far as it can be identified, seems to have been a mixture of Naxian and Parian.

### NAXOS

Before reviewing the early inscriptions of Naxos, we may recall briefly the two most distinctive features of the Naxian script, both of which apparently arose from the local pronunciation of certain sounds. Firstly, Naxian used *epsilon* to express also the original long *$\bar{e}$* (which became $\bar{e}$ in all Greek dialects), and *eta* only to express the original long *$\bar{a}$*; in most Ionic dialects this latter sound also became $\bar{e}$(η), but in Attic it remained $\bar{a}$ after vowels and *rho*, and in Naxian it evidently differed in pronunciation from $\bar{e}$ so markedly as to result in this distinction in the letters used for each.[1] The second Naxian peculiarity is the expression of *xi* by a sibilant, *sigma*, preceded by a letter which appears to be a variant of closed *heta/eta*; this same letter appears in Knidian as *ēta*, but in Naxian *xi* it will presumably be the aspirate, and implies therefore that the Naxian ξ was not pronounced as *ks*, but as something like *hs*.[2]

Practically all the features of archaic Naxian are admirably illustrated in the well-known dedication of the Naxian Nikandra (**2**), inscribed *boustrophedon* vertically up the left side of a 'Daedalic' female statue found on Delos, which belongs to about the middle of the seventh century. The inscription Αϕροδιτη on an amphora of Orientalizing style found in Naxos (**1**) was dated in the second quarter of the same century in the original publication, but the dating of Cycladic Orientalizing, as compared with Protoattic, is not yet certainly established, and it may be slightly later.[3] The inscription on the triangular base of a kouros which was made and dedicated on Delos by a Naxian sculptor Euthykartides towards the end of the seventh century shows the earliest use of punctuation in Cycladic inscriptions (**3**). A fragmentary inscription (**4**) painted on a ring-aryballos from the Artemision at Delos may also be Naxian, though the characteristic letters which would identify it securely as either Naxian or Parian chance to be absent. The inscription

[1] Buck, 19 f.; cf. Dittenberger, *Hermes* xv (1880), 229.

[2] Kalinka, *AM* xvii (1892), 116; Kretschmer, *AM* xxi (1896), 422. Buck suggests (p. 190) that the freak letter may itself be a special form of ⊥, thus giving a spelling Ναξσιος, &c.

[3] Karouzos, *JdI* lii (1937), 166 ff., and Brock, *BSA* xliv (1949), 76 ff. (second quarter of century); Buschor, *Griech. Vasen* (1940), 57 (about middle of century).

(painted *boustrophedon* in two lines, running from lower to upper line) is tall and narrow, suggesting a seventh-century date, and is not, I think, a dedicatory inscription to Apollo, but the record of a gift from some woman to a man, who presumably dedicated it later in the Artemision: [- - -]λη μ' εδōκεν [- - -]ιōνι.[1] A fragment of a clay relief-plaque from the same precinct, probably also of the seventh century, bears part of what seems to be a dedication, incised from right to left before firing (5): [- - -]αιδη[ϛ μ?]ε ͱισ[- - -]. Other Naxian fragments may also belong to the seventh or early sixth century: a flat tile of Naxian marble from the Akropolis at Athens, marked Βυ (7):[2] a fragmentary verse incised along a spiral guide-line on a flat marble stone from Delos, which seems to suggest some unofficial athletic record (8):[3] and the puzzling fragments of four lines on an unidentified piece of marble sculpture also from Delos, containing apparently part of a dedication and a sculptor's metrical signature (9).[4]

About the first quarter of the sixth century the Naxians dedicated on Delos the colossal Apollo of which scattered fragments still survive, the drilled holes for metal additions below its mutilated curls in front proving that it merited well the epithets χρύσεος, χρυσοκόμας, χρυσοχαίτης bestowed upon Apollo by the poets.[5] The upper edge of the base has been worn or chipped away to a depth of 0·16 m.; the surviving line of the inscription (10) starts immediately below this, and it is possible that this was in fact a second line, the actual dedication having been lost with the original edge. The verse itself reads: [τ]ο αϝυτο λιθο εμι ανδριας και το σϕελας. Since statue and base were quite obviously not made in one single piece, the meaning (as Guarducci has pointed out)[6] must be that the statue is monolithic, not jointed (i.e. at the neck or elbows, as such a colossus well might be), and that the base too is a monolith, not formed from several blocks as large bases normally were. The mere fact that the base is marble (not limestone) would hardly merit surprise in the Cyclades; but the transport of a monolithic block of marble 3·50 × 5·15 m. from Naxos to Delos deserved some admiration.

The late archaic bronze statuette dedicated to Apollo by Deinagoras (11) shows for the last quarter of the sixth century η2, but θ1 and β1 still in use. In the first quarter of the fifth century (c. 490–475?)[7] the signature of the Naxian sculptor Alxenor on a grave-stele in Boiotia shows that the Naxian *xi* 2 had now been replaced by the more normal type 1, and also that *ē̄* was now being spelt with *eta*, as in Ionic elsewhere (12): Αλχσηνōρ εποιησεν ͱο Ναχσιος· αλλ' εσιδε[σθε]. The lower part of the shaft of a column from Naxos,

---

[1] [Απο]λōνι has been suggested tentatively, but there is no sign of the crook of *lambda*. There follows what may be another letter, or part of the design; it was badly smeared before the paint had dried.

[2] It was identified as Naxian by Wiegand (*Poros-architektur* (1904), 180 f.), who connected it tentatively with Byzes of Naxos, the alleged inventor of marble roof-tiles; Paus. v. 10. 3.

[3] The inscription reads: πεντε̄ϙοντα π[οδας? . . . . .]σε μοι (ϛ εμοι?) ε⟨ν⟩θαδ[- - -], and recalls Phayllos' record (?hop, step, and) jump of 55 ft.; cf. Hyde, *AJP* lix (1938), 405 ff. and Peek, *Delische Gedichte*, 572. Whether this stone was inset in some wall by the jumping-pit (or perhaps in the floor of an adjoining portico) in order

c. 5

to record a jump—or possibly a throw—in the Delian Games is quite uncertain; but the wording suggests something of the kind. See further Peek, loc. cit.

[4] (a) [- - -]ης ποιησεν εριν ο[- - - | - - -?ε]μ ⟨β⟩ροτοισιν η(ͱ?) [- - -]. (b) [- - -]ει συ αναχ[ϛ - - - | - - -]λ̄ηος αει[- - -]. For a suggested restoration *exempli gratia* see Peek, op. cit. 570 ff., to whom the above readings are due.

[5] See Kallimachos, fr. 114 Pfeiffer, with commentary.

[6] *Epigraphica* iv (1942), 155 ff.

[7] The stele is of Boiotian marble, which suggests that Alxenor may have emigrated to Boiotia after the Persian expedition of 490; it can hardly be later than c. 475, from the style.

inscribed *boustrophedon* with a sacral text of some kind too worn to be deciphered, is perhaps to be dated shortly before the Persian destruction of the city in 490 (**13**); but this is very uncertain. The Ionic *omega* makes its first appearance (in the developed form ω6) in a retrograde graffito, which can hardly be earlier, despite its direction, than the third quarter of the fifth century (**14**).

## AMORGOS

The early inscriptions from the three towns of Amorgos (Arkesine, Minoa, Aigiale) bear out the tradition that the first Greeks who settled there were Naxians, followed by Samians.[1] The earliest example is undoubtedly the epitaph of Deidamas, carved from right to left on a rock at Aigiale (**15**): Δηιδαμανι, followed by: Πυγμας ο πατερ τονδ' οιϙ[ον - - -]. This lettering may be compared with that of the earliest inscriptions from Crete, Thera, Rhodes, Corinth, and Attica; the great height of the letter-forms, the curved lines of *alpha* and *delta* and the small *omikron*, all suggest a date not later than the first half of the seventh century. The spelling πατερ for πατηρ confirms it as Naxian, though the *gamma* is Samian (Ionic). The remaining inscriptions from Amorgos, considerably later in date, are sometimes in Naxian, sometimes in Samian; the earliest in the latter script is perhaps the graffito beginning Σατελης ποτε καλως from Arkesine (**16**), which apparently shows open η2.[2] Two more appear to be Naxian, the grave-stele of Demainete (**17**), inscribed *boustrophedon* Δημαινετης εμι μν|ημα της Λαμπσαγο|ρεο (η2; middle or second half of the sixth century?), and the later gravestone erected by Staphylis to his sister Alexo (**20**); it is no longer *boustrophedon*, but the *xi* appears to be written Hϟ—that is, the 'freak' closed *heta* has been replaced by the normal open form, but the spelling is not yet the χσ of the early fifth century (cf. **13**). Other Samian examples are the grave-stelai of Stesimachos and Xenokrite (**18**, **19**), both *boustrophedon* still, and **19** showing a sidelong *xi*.[3] The stone from Arkesine with the names of two archons (or one archon with patronymic) is perhaps in Samian also, from the use of *omega* (**21**): αρχοντες της πολεος | Σωνδρος, Πεισινο[ϟ?]. It may however be as late as the early fifth century, and if so might possibly be Naxian; for, though *omega* apparently was not used in Naxian *c.* 490–475 (**12**), it may have come in not very long afterwards; we have as yet no inscriptions from Naxos from the period *c.* 475–450, for comparison. The altar of Dionysos from Arkesine (**22**) is apparently in Naxian (H = Ͱ, E = η), but shows normal *beta* and *omega*, and should, from the script, be earlier than the mid-fifth century. Lastly, the start of an abecedarium scratched on a rock near Aigiale (**23**), fragmentary though it is, is of great interest because it shows *vau* (in the fifth-century form 2) still 'fossilized' in the row, though it was not used in Samian, and only poetically in Naxian (**10**), as in Attic (p. 66). The normal *beta* suggests that this graffito is Samian; but we do not know the exact date when the local form was given up in Naxian (p. 292), unless **22** provides any clue. See also Addenda.

---

[1] Cf. Hiller, *IG* xii. 7, p. vii, and references there given.

[2] The copies vary as given in *IG* xii. 7. 106.

[3] This *xi* is probably not deliberate, but merely cut thus in error because the whole inscription was to be read vertically on the stele.

## PAROS

Paros, Naxos' neighbour and perpetual enemy, had certain ties with Miletos in the archaic period. A Milesian embassy to Paros was shipwrecked in the straits between Paros and Naxos in the seventh century or earlier (Demeas, *FGH*, no. 502, F 1); Parian adjudicators were chosen to settle a political dispute in Miletos *c.* 525 (Hdt. v. 28–29); Miletos and Erythrai joined with Paros to found the colony Parion in the Propontis (Strabo 487, 588). Hence it has been suggested[1] that Miletos was the source whence Paros acquired her use of the letter Ω, which, as we have seen, archaic Naxian did not share. The form which Paros used was always the eastern Ionic Ω, not the Knidian type (p. 351); but it is significant that Paros and Knidos were alike in using a 'broken' form of o to indicate the short ŏ (whereas eastern Ionic used it for the long ō), and this, in my opinion, outweighs in importance the dissimilarity between the forms of the letter which each developed. It may be suggested as a hypothesis that, when this doublet of o, the broken circle, was evolved in the Ionic area during the seventh century or earlier, the Parians preferred the type with struts (as Ionic) rather than without them (as Knidian), because the latter form was too much like their own Parian *beta*. The use of *heta* for Ⱶ and η in the Doric inscriptions of Rhodes and Knidos seems to be reflected not only in the consistent Naxian use of *heta* for both Ⱶ and η<*ā*, but also in the intermittent use of *heta* for Ⱶ in Parian, in addition to its regular service there as η; cf. *IG* xii. 5. 148, and **36** (both of the early fifth century).

Three early Parian inscriptions written *boustrophedon* show the closed form of *eta* 1 still (**25, 26, 27**). If we may assume that Parian lettering achieved the same rate of development as eastern Ionic, this would give these inscriptions a *terminus ante quem* at latest of about the middle of the sixth century (cf. Miletos **27** and **29**; Naxos **8** and **11** span a stretch of nearly a century, and are therefore of little use for comparison here). **25** is painted on a fragment of a vase of advanced Orientalizing style from Delos: [- - -] νγεδειν [- - -]ηγω. I assign it here to a Parian hand because of the use of Ω.[2] Parians, like Naxians, made many dedications at Delos in the sixth century, and no small part of our evidence comes from the Delian sanctuaries.

**26**, part of a legal text on a column-fragment from Paros, shows *omega* still in the early form 1, before the start of the development to 2; **27**, probably a dedicatory stele,[3] has also the early υ2. The block inscribed by the septuagenarian builder Ason may be of about the middle of the sixth century; it shows open *eta*, *qoppa*, and *omega* varying between the earlier form 1 and the later 3 (**28**).[4] The well-known pillar-capital from Delos which bears the names of Mikkiades and Archermos can hardly be earlier than the third quarter of the century (**30**). I list it here, though doubtfully, among the inscriptions of Paros, because the other fragmentary dedication mentioning Mikkiades was found on Paros (**29**), and because the script used resembles the Parian in its o-vowels, though their use is inconsistent in σο[φ]ιεισιν and Μελανος, perhaps also in καλον. But if one follows the

---

[1] Hiller *ap.* Rubensohn, *RE*, s.v. Paros, 1804 f.

[2] Cf. Rubensohn, *DM* i (1948), 39, n. 6.

[3] The text suggests a dedication: [–◡–]ιτη|ς με ε[δōκ|εν] {ε} Ευπαλō|[ι χ]αριν φε[ρ|ō]ν. For other inter-

pretations cf. *IG* xii. 5. 219 and Bannier, *Ph.W.* 1927, 925.

[4] *Rho* here is not tailed, as Roehl's facsimile suggests; there is a crack in the stone at this point.

most straightforward restoration of the text—that of Peek and others—there seems no reason at all for the use of Parian:

Μικκια[δηι τωδ' αγα]λμα καλον (*sic*) τ[ετελεσμενων εργων?]
Αρχερμω σο[φ]ιἐισιν ηκηβω[λε δεχσαι Απωλλων]
τοι Χιοι, Μελανος πατροιων ασ[τυ νεμωντι].

This makes the dedicator Mikkiades a Chian (l. 3). We know from literary and epigraphical evidence that the sculptor Archermos was also a Chian. The script is not Chian; why should it be Parian? We might defeat the difficulty by holding that a local Delian mason cut the inscription; for in σο[φ]ιεισιν and perhaps also in ηκηβω[λε] there is some suggestion of the confusion of H = ε and E = η which appears to be characteristic of Delian in other examples (pp. 296 f.; **42**, **43** *a*, *b*, *c*, *e*); and occasionally the o-vowel inversion is found in Delian (**43** *b*, *e*).

The inscription is not written *boustrophedon*, but arranged carefully so that each line of verse shall begin at the left-hand edge of the main face of the stone; *eta* is open, and *omega* throughout has curled struts, as in the late archaic ω3. Archermos made a statue which was dedicated on the Athenian Akropolis in the last years of the sixth century (*IG* i². 487 = *DAA* 3), so that a date *c.* 550–530 will in any case fit better into his life, if it was of normal span, than *c.* 550 or earlier, the date usually assigned to the Delian dedication. Whether Mikkiades, its presumed dedicator, was in fact Archermos' father (as Pliny records, *HN* xxxvi. 5. 11) is a matter of dispute, as is also the question of the sculpture which originally adorned it.[1] The other surviving dedication by Mikkiades, on the fragment of a round capital which was found in the precinct of Apollo Pythios at Paros, appears to be slightly earlier in date and inscribed by a different hand (**29**).[2]

Somewhat later in date—i.e. not before 530—may be placed a large base bearing the dedication of Therseleides to Anios (**31**) on Delos, from a precinct whose little temple has been dated *c.* 530–500.[3] The column-capital **32**, which bears the socket for a plinth of a marble kouros, and is inscribed: Νιϙωλεος ανεθηκεν, has, like **31**, the lettering which seems characteristic of the late archaic period in the islands—tall, neat, and shallow. The dedication of Telestodike on a column (now lost) which was brought to Italy in the eighteenth century seems to have had similar lettering, and probably belonged also to the last quarter of the sixth century (*IG* xii. 5. 216); the same name appears on a second dedication, which should be some years after the first in date (**34**). The fragmentary stele **33** is *boustrophedon* but also partly *stoichedon*; it came from the Pythion, like **29**,

---

[1] The latest discussion (Rubensohn, op. cit. 21 ff.) maintains that the winged statue found not far from the inscription does belong to it, and represents a winged Artemis; Richter (*AGA*, 116 f.) inclines to the belief that they belong together, but calls the statue a Nike, and dates it about the middle of the 6th c. Lippold (*Griech. Plastik* (1950), 63) denies the connexion. If the statue could be dated as low as *c.* 550–540, the balance of the evidence would incline to the connexion: (*a*) statue and 'base' were found near each other. (*b*) As Raubitschek and others have shown, the 'base' is the top member of a high pillar-base, and the big letters suggest that the writing was above eye-level. Winged figures must be mounted high. (*c*) How did the tradition arise that Archermos had made the first winged Nike (Schol. Ar. *Av.* 573)? Could it be from this same dedicatory verse, from which the names of Melas and Mikkiades wrongly got into the literary record, and should we then restore: Μικκια[δηι τωδ' αγα]λμα καλὁν (*sic*), Ν[ικην πτερωεσσαν], κτλ?

[2] Klaffenbach, *ap.* Rubensohn, op. cit. 39, n. 1.

[3] Vallois, *L'Architecture hellénique et hellénistique à Délos jusqu'à 166 av. J.-C.* (1944), 109.

and bore some kind of prohibition: [?Μη - - -]ηστ[ο?] | εσο το|ν λιθ|ον [- - -]. The lettering is neat and well-spaced; *epsilon* has no tail, *eta* is open. It does not look earlier than *c.* 525, and the *boustrophedon* system may have been used from religious conservatism (p. 49).

The local script was still in normal use in the first half of the fifth century. The altar of Zeus Elasteros (**35**) may belong to the early years of this century; it has ε3, θ1, ω4, and *rho* tailed. The epitaph for the sister of Pythonax may be *c.* 475 (**36**); the script, though more developed, recalls that of **34**. It is perhaps rather earlier than the *stoichedon* law concerning the disposal of ἐκκαθάρματα (*c.* 475–450? **37**), or the sacral law forbidding Dorians or slaves to take part in the ritual to Persephone (**39**). All three show θ3, ρ6. *Xi* is still written χσ (**36**, **39**). Only **37** chances to show *lambda*, and twice it has the type λ4, which appears in Thasos also in the second quarter of this century (p. 302). If *IG* xii. 5. 109 (part of a treaty between Paros and Thasos, in Ionic script) is correctly assigned to the years 411/10–409/8, then the local script had ceased at least a decade before the end of the century.

SIPHNOS, IOS

The one certainly archaic[1] inscription from Siphnos (**40**) νυφεον Ηιερων (*c.* 500?) shows that Siphnian resembled Parian in the use of Ω and o, and in the use of the aspirate (whether regularly or only intermittently, as at Paros, is unknown). By 449 she had apparently adopted the eastern Ionic script, for it is used in the Siphnian copy of the Athenian currency decree (*ATL* ii, D 14). The early alphabet of Ios is not yet known, but a fragment of a decree which from its lettering should not be later than *c.* 450 (ν3, ω3) is in the eastern Ionic script (**41**).

DELOS, KEOS

We have already observed a number of dedications on Delos which from their script must be attributed to Naxos or Paros. But there was evidently a local Delian script, for archaic inscriptions have been found which, written neither in Naxian nor in Parian, yet have the general characteristics of the Cyclades. The alphabet resembles that of Keos (p. 297); that is to say, it shows confusion between the letters E = ε and H = η or Η. This confusion usually takes the form of a reversal, H for ε and Η, and E for η; but this is not done consistently, and the results suggest that Delos and Keos used the Naxian system of e-vowels, but without a proper comprehension of the rules. Admittedly, it is not possible to decide in many of the very fragmentary inscriptions of Delos whether they are Delian, or Naxian or Parian. I have taken as a touchstone for the identification of this local Delian script the dedication **42**: [οι - - -] . .ος παιδης το Δηλιο ανηθησαν Αθηναιει Πολιαδι. This shows H for ε and for *ā*, and E once for *ā*. More support comes from the graffiti on vases and a mask offered by women in the Heraion of Delos, which show the same uncertainty and confusion. The objects on which these graffiti appear extend in date

---

[1] A graffito on a sherd which might be of the 6th c. is published by Brock, *BSA* xliv (1949), 73 f., fig. 16. 5: –παριο–.

from the second quarter to the end of the sixth century; but of course they may not all have been new when they were dedicated. They are as follows: on a little clay female mask, *c.* 525: Μⱶηγαρις μ᾽ ανηθε|κεν ⱶερηι (**43a**);[1] on an Attic black-figure Siana cup, *c.* 560–550, by the Epignote Painter: Επιγνοτη μ᾽ ανηθεκην τηι ⱶερηι and [τ]ης ⱶερης εμι· ανηθεν (*sic*) δε Επιγνοτη (**43b**; here the inscription might well be appreciably later than the date of the vase); on an Attic late black-figure skyphos, *c.* 550–525: Αριστοτεθη (*sic*) ανεθεκεν Ηρει Βαικυλεο (**43c**; in this inscription, written *stoichedon*, the use of Β (β2) may be noted); on an Attic early red-figure cup by the Delos Painter (last quarter of the sixth century): Βολη [ⱶερ]ει αν[εθε]κε ερ[- - -] (**43d**; here the freak 'open' β1 is used). Two other graffiti show *omega*: one, on a late Corinthian kothon (*c.* 550–500) uses the Parian system: Πρωξηνη μ᾽ ανηθεκην (**43e**); the other, on a small black-figure lekythos, *c.* 525, has the normal Ionic type: Φανυλις ανεθεκ[ε]ν ⱶερηι θεω[ι] (**43f**).[2]

The fully-illustrated corpus of Delian fifth-century inscriptions is not yet available, and so the development of the script in this century cannot be discussed in detail here, nor the precise date when the full Ionic script was taken over. The capital dedicated by Eupolis (*ID* 17), which should belong to the first half of the century, shows Ε throughout for both ε and η; the text concerning the κρήνη Μινόη (*ID* 69; second half of the century?) still shows Ε occasionally for η.[3] It is possible that the full Ionic script had been adopted by 432 at latest, for *IG* i². 377 is written in that script. It is the Athenian copy of the accounts for 434–432 of the Attic Amphiktiones then administering the sanctuaries on Delos. In 432 the full Ionic script was still unusual for an Attic inscription; one would expect that both the Attic and Delian copies of these accounts were drafted and cut at the Delians' expense, and therefore probably in their own script. The Delian copies of the accounts for 410/9 and 408/7 are also in full Ionic,[4] and so is the addendum which the Delians inscribed below the Lakonian text (Lakonia **62**, p. 198), giving the names of those in office at Sparta and Delos in one of the years 403–399.

The earliest inscriptions attributed to Keos are the first issue of the coins of Koresia marked ϘΟ (sixth century? **45**), and the names painted on an amphora of Attic fabric to be dated *c.* 570 (**44**), depicting a Gigantomachy. It shows the characteristic Η = ε, Ε = η of Keos, but the normal *beta* should also be noted, for this is at variance with the open, curved *beta* in the earliest inscription from Keos itself, a verse dedication to Athena made by a sculptor (?) Alkidamas of Siphnos (**46**); the lettering suggests a date *c.* 525–500:

[–◡ Αθε]ναιες χρυσαιγιδ{ε}ος οββριμ[οπ]α[τρες] |
[–◡ ηποιε]σην Σιφνιος Αλκιδαμας |  c. 4
[———◡]η τ᾽ ηξηπον[ε]σ᾽ αναλοτα φυλα[. . . .] |
[- - -]νατ[- - -].

It may also be observed that here Ξ is used for *xi*; in a later inscription (**47**), σχ (for χσ) occurs, with the normal Ε for ε and Η for η (second half of fifth century?). A lost

---

[1] I would suggest this reading in preference to those previously given (Μνηλαρις or Μνηγαρις; *ID* 33, 1).

[2] A LC plate bears a faint painted inscription which has been read as: Ταμιαι Πυρος φε[·]ος Μολεω (*ID* 33, xv);

another possibility is: ταμιαι Πυρος Φεδ[ι]λος Μολες.

[3] For new readings added after *ID* 69, see Coupry, *BCH* lxxviii (1954), 293; *SEG* xiv. 495.

[4] Coupry, *BCH* lxi (1937), 364 ff.

inscription is reputed to have shown the 'red' *chi* (χ3), perhaps through Euboic influence (*IG* xii. 5. 648). The dedication of two treasurers ('deposit-collectors', ἐνθεμολογήσαντες) is in the eastern (full) Ionic script, and by its appearance should not be earlier than the second half of the fifth century (**48**).[1]

## SYROS, TENOS, ANDROS, IKAROS, SKYROS

It might be expected that Syros, lying between Delos and Keos, would use a similar alphabet. A solitary sixth-century graffito found there, which congratulates a dancer, supports this, for it shows σ2, and the *epsilon* is written both E and H (εϙολιαδη: **49**). The one archaic fragment from Tenos (**50**) is too mutilated to reveal anything significant except that it is apparently cut *boustrophedon*; but another inscription, which was found in a modern house near the site of the ancient city, shows the eastern Ionic alphabet, with open *eta*, and *omega* (**51**). It is an abusive inscription carved on a large block, in lettering which suggests the end of the sixth or first half of the fifth century: Πυριης Ακηστο|ρος | οιφολης· | Θρη⟨ι⟩σα καταπυγων.[2]

A fifth-century decree at Delphi, inscribed on two sides of a pillar, has been attributed with great likelihood to Andros (**53**). The lettering suggests the first quarter of the fifth century (αι, νι, ω3–4).[3] The traces of the Naxian vowel-system are plain, for *eta* is used once for ⱶ and fifteen times for *ā*; *epsilon* ten times for η<*ē*. Ikaros, lying on the route through the Cyclades to Samos, apparently used the full Ionic script, as Samos did. A fragmentary graffito on a sherd from the precinct of Artemis Tauropolos gives little help: [τα]υροπ[ολωι?];[4] but there is also an inscription cut in the upper right-hand corner of a relief-stele found in a necropolis at Kataphygion (**54**). It gives the names of those who erected the stele: Κοιρανος και Ευρυμη[δης] αδελφεοι Απολλων[ιη]ς. The relief is dated *c.* 470 by its style, and was the work of one Palion of Paros (**38**). A graffito on the rim of a hydria dedicated to Apollo, which was found in a small precinct excavated on Skyros (**55**), has been called Chalkidic, but there seems no good reason for regarding it as earlier than the Athenian occupation of the island *c.* 475; the use of the crossed *theta* can be cited in Attic graffito writing later than 475, and *delta* is the Attic, not the Euboic type.[5]

[1] The dedication made at Delphi by one Philon in a script resembling in some ways that of Keos remains a problem (*FD* iii. 4, nos. 187–8): ηυξαμηνος μη Φιλὸν δηκαταν ανηθηκη Λυκειδι | αυτο και παιδὸν· τυ δη δηξαι, Φοιβη Απολλον. The use of 'blue' *xi* and H for ε throughout suggests Keos; but *delta* is the rounded type, as in Phokian, and the dialect is not Ionic (δεκάταν, τύ). Lejeune points out (*REA* li (1949), 14 f.) that it could have been cut by a local Delphic mason, who either followed an Ionic client's draft but occasionally substituted his own idiom, or else for some reason himself confused the letters ε and η. Traces of three more inscribed lines on the side give no help.

[2] The editor reads tentatively: Πυριης Ακηστο|ρος | οιφολης | ⟨ε⟩θρησα, καταπυγων: but there is no break apparent before θρησα, which should therefore be a complete word.

[3] The date *c.* 425 suggested by Daux (*Hesperia* xviii (1949), 65) seems to me to be too late, in view of the letter-forms. He takes it for a Delphic copy of an Andrian draft, I for an Andrian original.

[4] Polites, *PAE* 1939, 137, fig. 11d.

[5] Plut., *Thes.* 36; cf. Gomme, *Thucydides* i. 281, 291. An ostrakon cast against Perikles (*Hesperia* x (1941), 2 f., fig. 2) shows crossed *theta* still.

## B. NORTHERN AEGEAN

### SAMOTHRACE

Samothrace, which a strong tradition declared to have been colonized by Samians,[1] has produced a fine example of eastern Ionic lettering *c.* 560–550, in the names Αγαμεμνων, Επε[ιος], Ταλθυβιος incised beside the figures of a marble relief (**56**). The excavations in the Sanctuary of the Great Gods have produced a series of brief graffiti dedications on vases, written in the original non-Greek language of the island (**57**). The earliest of these are ascribed to the sixth and fifth centuries by the excavator. The alphabet used may well be the eastern Ionic, as one would expect from its use in **56**; for the graffiti include the signs H, X, Ψ, and Ω—though naturally, since we do not know the meaning of the words, the values of X and Ψ cannot be considered certain. *Vau* also is represented;[2] we may recall its appearance in the abecedarium of Amorgos, and it need not surprise us that the Samothracian language should have found a practical use for it, though the east Greek dialect had none. One graffito, whose letter-forms suggest a fifth-century date, has for its seventh letter, as the excavator points out, an odd shape resembling the *beta* used in Thera (Pl. 57). The only other *beta* in the texts from the Sanctuary is on a stele of the late fifth or early fourth century;[3] here the shape is normal, as it is also in the Greek inscription **56**. The nearest 'freak' *beta*, geographically speaking, is the open *beta* used in Thasos and on the mainland opposite (pp. 300 ff.); and it does not resemble this graffito example. It is probable that the graffito-writer merely meant to write *epsilon* and his point slipped on the central bar, as it apparently did also on the following *epsilon*.

### LEMNOS, IMBROS

The Pelasgian inhabitants of Lemnos used a script similar to the Phrygian, with which we are not here concerned.[4] The island became a possession of Athens when Miltiades the younger, using the Chersonese as his base, occupied it on behalf of Athens in the decade either before or after 500. The theory of Eduard Meyer that there had been an earlier occupation of Lemnos by Miltiades the elder was revived by Segre[5] in connexion with a boundary-stone found at Myrrhina, inscribed in Attic letters Ϝορος | τω τεμ|ενως τε̄|ς Αρτε|μιδος (**58**). This was dated by Segre in the middle of the sixth century, but it should belong rather to the years *c.* 500–480; *omega* for ου also appears at about that time in an Attic inscription on the Athenian Akropolis.[6] The lettering may be compared for date with that of the casualty-list on a pillar found at Hephaistia, inscribed with names under the headings of the Kleisthenic tribes (**59**), which is generally assigned to the first years of the fifth century. The pillar is apparently of local stone (grey calcareous), but the

---

[1] See the discussion by Jacoby, *FGH*, no. 548, F 5 and commentary.

[2] Lehmann, *Hesperia* xxii (1953), 7 and xxiv (1955), 99, no. 34.

[3] Ibid. xxiv. 100, no. 40, pl. 40; probably (not certainly) from the Sanctuary. The right edge is the only one preserved. The face carries the broken ends of 10 lines of varying lengths. The editor suggests that it might be poetry; or could it be a list of names, some with patronymic added?

[4] See Buonamici, *Epigrafia Etrusca* (1932), 88 ff. (Lemnian stele); Della Seta, *Scritti . . . B. Nogara* (1937), 119 ff. (inscribed pottery); Falkner, *Frühgeschichte u. Sprachwissenschaft* (1948), 91 ff.

[5] *Ann.* xv–xvi (1932–3), 294 ff.

[6] *DAA*, 110; further Attic examples are there cited.

lettering resembles that of the mason who inscribed the 'Hekatompedon' inscriptions and others at Athens.[1] If the Lemnian stone is indeed his work, it would mean that these are not the names of Miltiades' own Attic settlers from the Chersonese, but of Athenians from the mother-city, who died on a campaign on Lemnos. With this may be connected the helmet-fragment from Olympia inscribed Αθεναιοι τον εγ Λεμν[ο] and the similar fragment from the Athenian Acropolis inscribed: [- - -?ανεθεσ]αν εγ Λε[μνο?], which Kunze has shown to be examples of a type common in the last third of the sixth century. He has connected these victory-offerings with the seizure of Lemnos by Miltiades, and ascribed it tentatively to the period of the Ionic Revolt, c. 500–495.[2] These dedications are not likely to be those of the Chersonesian settlers, for surely they would not have described themselves as Athenians without further qualification; they did not do this in their dedication at Olympia described by Pausanias (vi. 19. 6):

Ζηνί μ' ἄγαλμ' ἀνέθηκαν 'Ολυμπίῳ ἐκ Χερρονήσου
τεῖχος ἑλόντες Ἀράτου· ἐπῆρχε δὲ Μιλτιάδης σφίν.

It may be, therefore, that, when Miltiades swooped on Lemnos and seized it in the manner described by Herodotos (vi. 140), he was aided by a detachment of troops from Athens, who shared in the spoils and whose dead were buried on the island, with a funeral stele cut by an Attic mason.

It seems that after the middle of the fifth century the Greek settlers on Lemnos adopted the eastern Ionic alphabet; for this is used on a horos-stone c. 450–425, and in an epitaph c. 425–400.[3]

On Imbros also a gravestone has been found bearing the remains of an epitaph in Attic script of the first half of the fifth century (**60**).

### THASOS

Thasos was colonized from Paros at the end of the eighth or beginning of the seventh century,[4] and her colonists brought the Parian alphabet with them; it is used in all the archaic inscriptions of Thasos, and was passed thence to the opposite mainland, to appear on the late archaic coinage of the Bisaltai (p. 364). Thasian relations with Paros were from the start close and continuous, and, as far as can be judged, the two scripts kept pace with one another in their development. The archaic inscriptions of Thasos have been the subject of an exhaustive study by J. Pouilloux,[5] and so need be only briefly discussed here. Many of the early ones are on plain grave-stelai with only the letter-forms to suggest a date; but there are a few valuable exceptions, which provide historical or sculptural clues on which to base the dating of the Thasian script. The first is the *boustrophedon* inscription on a stepped structure, apparently an altar, in the Agora at Thasos (**61**). It is the μνῆμα

---

[1] Picard, *BCH* xxxvi (1912), 337 f.; Wilhelm, *Anz. Ak. Wien* (1934), 111.

[2] *Festschrift Carl Weickert* (1955), 7 ff.

[3] Segre, op. cit. 297 f., no. 5 (horos stone), 299 ff., no. 7 (= *IG* xii, suppl., p. 147, no. 338), the gravestone of Nausikydes, killed in action, perhaps during the Peloponnesian War.

[4] *C.* 720–700? Jacoby, *CQ* xxxv (1941), 102; the higher date (720) is still advocated by Launey, *Études thasiennes* i (1944), 210 f., n. 4. For a general view of the problem, see Pouilloux, *Recherches sur l'histoire et les cultes de Thasos* i (1954), 22 ff.

[5] Op. cit.

erected by the 'sons of Brentes' to Glaukos son of Leptines, to whom Archilochos addressed some of his poems. We may note the archaic forms of ηι, λι, ωι. The letters have not the tall, spidery look of many seventh-century inscriptions from the mainland, and indeed from some of the Aegean islands also (e.g. Naxos **1–2**); they may be compared rather with the squat and straggling *ductus* of the early eastern Ionic (pp. 327, 341 ff., **4, 22–23**). One would hardly venture to date this long before the end of the seventh century, but Glaukos may well have lived on until *c.* 625, and in any case we are not bound to assume that the sons of Brentes, whoever they were, erected this monument immediately after his death. A μνῆμα in the Agora savours of the honours instituted for the oikistai of colonies, often many years after their deaths.

The second inscription which appears to offer a clue to its date from its content is the dedication to Herakles by Akeratos, inscribed on a large base from the precinct of Herakles (**64**). The verses say that Akeratos held the office of archon in both Paros and Thasos; and Pouilloux has shown that this is probably the Akeratos son of Phrasiarides whose name appears on one of the Thasian archon-lists in a context which suggests that he was archon *c.* 520.[1] The lettering is neat and very shallow with θ3 and tailed *rho*; the mason has produced a symmetrical *omega* (always an awkward letter to cut) by describing a complete circle and then adding the struts at the base. If Akeratos made this dedication immediately or fairly soon after his archonship in Thasos, it should not be far in date from **63**. This inscription, built into the city wall beside the southern gate, belonged originally to two large reliefs depicting Herakles and Dionysos, sons of Zeus and twin guardians of the city, which adorned the defences at this point: Ζηνως και Σεμελης και Αλκμηνης τανυπεπλω : εστασιν παιδες τησδε πωλεος φυλαϙωι. The one relief which survives has been dated by its style in the last quarter of the sixth century; it shows Herakles the archer, kneeling in his lion-skin with an arrow poised for shot. The inscription shows a drooping *epsilon*, *qoppa*, and *omega* 3 with curled ends; *rho* and *theta* are not used, but the hand is clearly different from that which cut the inscription of Akeratos. An inscription which might be called the connecting link, and dated also in this quarter-century, is the epitaph of Thrasykles (**65**), cut in lettering which tends to droop like the *epsilon* of **63**, but shows *theta* and *rho* in the same late archaic forms as those of **64**. This mason has confused occasionally the values of *epsilon* and *eta*: [Θ]ρασυκληως τω | [Π]ανταγαθω | [μ]ετερ τωδε | [σε]μ' επωηεσε. (Cf. another Thasian inscription, *IG* xii. 8. 360: Πειθος | ιηρον.) Another gravestone, **66**, shows ρι and θι, but otherwise looks like a member of this group, and is probably of about the same date.

The next series of inscriptions, while retaining the archaic λι, is otherwise slightly more advanced in all its letter-forms: ε2, ρ3, ω4. The head of this group is the μνῆμα of Akeratos son of Phrasiarides, a verse inscribed on blocks of an ancient circular tower at the north-east end of the bay of Potamia (**67**):

[Α]κηρατω εμι μνημα τω Φ[ρασι]ηριδο·
κειμαι δε επ' ακρω ναυσ[τ]α[θ]|μω σοτηρ[ι]ων
νηυσιν τε κα[ι] ναυτησιν· αλλα χαιρετε̣.

The memorial (μνῆμα) of some honourable detail in a person's life may be erected in his

[1] Op. cit. 269 f., no. 31.

own lifetime, but the μνῆμα of the person himself must be posthumous, whether it is raised over his actual grave or not. In this memorial of Akeratos the letters are clearly later than those of his dedication **64**. If we set his death tentatively some twenty years after his last tenure of the archonship—i.e. *c.* 500 or a little later—we should ascribe to about the same date the gravestone of Learete (**68**), which is in similar lettering. Two graffiti inscriptions, **69***a–b*, may also be set with this group. The first is the name of Herakles, cut twice on a seaside rock near the city. The second is the name of one Parmenon cut, with others, on a block of the city wall; he may have been one of the masons who worked to raise the wall between 494 and 491, the year when it was pulled down at the order of the Persians (Hdt. vi. 47–48).

Hereafter the inscriptions of Thasos through the fifth century reveal a high standard of lettering. The most obvious epigraphic change which differentiates the inscriptions reviewed above from those which follow is the curious Thasian λ4 which now appears. It is identical with the normal Ionic *gamma* in its fifth-century form, but, as Thasian *gamma* was the near-isosceles type, no confusion resulted. The two most important inscriptions of this next series are the sacral laws **70** and the wine-law **71**. **70** is cut on a set of reliefs (now in the Louvre) showing on one side Apollo Nymphegetes with the Nymphs acclaiming him, and on the other Hermes with the Graces. The reliefs had been set in a passage apparently leading[1] to the Prytaneion. The date originally proposed for the sculpture, *c.* 490–480, was disturbing to epigraphists, for it implied that Thasian lettering had already reached a stage of development only reached by other states— Athens, for example—some twenty years later. Subsequently a date was proposed *c.* 485– 470 for the reliefs and *c.* 475–450 for the inscriptions, with the observation that, if they are contemporary, they may be set in the 'common zone' *c.* 475–470, but that we need not assume that the laws must have been inscribed when the reliefs were made.[2] If the date of the sculpture can be brought down yet further, *c.* 465,[3] that would suit well the lettering.

In general the script of **70** is not unlike that of the wine-law **71**, but it has earlier forms: ν3, υ3, ω5–6. **71** has ν3, υ4, ω6; it also shows an unusual curved σ3. It is *boustrophedon*, which might be held to imply an earlier date than **70**; but this system of writing is in any case abnormal for the fifth century. The other known examples at this date are mainly legal texts, and it is possible that they are in fact faithful copies of earlier texts, or (if they are sacral laws) new texts written in the old style through religious conservatism (pp. 49, 296). **71** is inscribed on a long block of marble trimmed very like that of **76** (411/10), with a frame projecting slightly round the inscribed surface. The text concerns the penalty for corrupt practices in the manufacture and sale of wine and vinegar; since part is missing, we do not know exactly what was the crime here referred to. Among the many points of interest fully discussed by the editor J. Pouilloux, two only concern us directly: that a penal law of assault must already have existed, for the informer (prosecutor) is directed to follow the same procedure as that for cases of this kind (κατάπερ τῶν βιαίων); and that the informer is to deposit his security with the Three Hundred, which indicates that at the time Thasos was presumably under oligarchic rule (cf. **74**, in which this body is again

---

[1] But see R. Martin, *REG* 1959, 315 f.     [2] Daux, *RA* 1948, 244 ff.     [3] Dr. Jacobsthal (by letter).

mentioned). Strictly speaking, if **70** is dated somewhere *c.* 465, then **71** should be rather later, after the Thasian Revolt. This is possible, since there is no reason to think that Thasos changed to a democratic constitution as the immediate result of her defeat.[1]

The brief law concerning the cult of Herakles from the Herakleion (**72**) is like **71** in its script, except for its normal *sigma*. The two should be fairly close in date, the wine-law being perhaps the earlier. If this law is set tentatively *c.* 460–450, **72** should be somewhere about 440.

Pouilloux has pointed out that the first datable monument to show the loss of the local script is the sculptured stele of Philis (**73**), Φιλις Κλεομηδεος, which has been dated *c.* 430.[2] Other inscriptions in the normal Ionic alphabet which have been assigned on their letter-forms to the years *c.* 425–410 are the first of the two commercial laws *IG* xii, suppl., p. 150, no. 347 (I) (*c.* 425–415),[3] and the list of men whose property was confiscated for Apollo ʻκατὰ τὸν ἄδον τῶν τριηκοσίωνʼ (**74**). The assignment of this list to the years of the oligarchy 411–408 is confirmed by the Athenian decree *IG* ii². 6 (*c.* 403 or not long after), in which is mentioned an earlier proxenia conferred by the demos on the sons of Apemantos the Thasian; for Apemantos son of Philon is among those proscribed in **74**.[4] Furthermore, a gravestone found on Thasos records in Ionic script the names of two Corinthians: Λοκριων | τοξοτας | Κορινθιος. | Λυσιστρατος | Ευκλεος | Κορινθιος (**75**). As has long been recognized, these men must have been in the Peloponnesian squadron commanded by Timolaos of Corinth, which touched off the Thasian revolt (*Hell. Ox.* ii. 4; see also Pouilloux, op. cit. 136, nos. 16–17). But another document, which appears also to be the product of the new oligarchy in 411/10, still shows the local script (**76**). This is the finely-cut pair of laws on a long block like an orthostate (cf. **71**) from the Agora. The internal evidence for dating these laws in the first year of the revolt has been convincingly marshalled by Pouilloux;[5] they concern the rewards to be offered for information laid against those who plotted ἐπὶ Θάσῳ (not ἐπὶ τῷ δήμῳ τῶν Θασίων), or against the colonies of her peraia, the Three Hundred acting as judges. The developed letter-forms can hardly be earlier than the last decade of the fifth century; and we can only conclude, as Pouilloux suggests, that the oligarchic party returned to the local Thasian script in a burst of patriotic insularity.

## SELECT CATALOGUE

### A. Central Aegean[6]

#### NAXOS

**1.** Inscribed amphora, Orientalizing style; *c.* 675–650? Karouzos, *JdI* lii (1937), 166 ff., figs. 1–12. Buschor, *Griech. Vasen* (1940), 57. Brock, *BSA* xliv (1949), 74 ff. *AGA*, 27. NM.

**2.** Statue dedicated by Nikandra on Delos; *c.* 650? *IG* xii. 5. 2, p. xxiv. Roberts i. 25. *SGDI* 5423. Roehl³, 65. 2. *DGE* 758. *AGA*, 27. *ID* 2. Peek, *Delische Gedichte* (Wiss. z. Univ. Halle, Ges. Sprachw. vi, 1956–7), 570, 16. NM 1.

PL. 55

---

[1] See *ATL* iii. 259.

[2] Op. cit. 87. Cf. *IG* xii, suppl., p. 159, no. 380, also in Ionic script. [3] Pouilloux, op. cit., 130.

[4] Cf. *GHI* ii. 98 and Pouilloux, op. cit. 195 f.

[5] Op. cit. 139 ff; but cf. Chamoux, *REG* 1959, 351 ff.

[6] For **2–4, 10, 30, 42**, see also Addenda.

**3.** Base for a kouros dedicated by Euthykartides on Delos; *c.* 620–600? *IG* xii. 5. 2, p. xxiv. *SGDI* 5419. Roehl³, 65. 1. Kern, pl. 6. *DGE* 757. *AGA*, 27 f. *ID* 1. Delos Mus. A728. PL. 55

**4.** Inscribed ring-aryballos from Delos; 7th c. *Délos* xvii. 124, pl. 65. *ID* 32b. Delos Mus. PL. 55

**5.** Inscribed clay plaque from Delos; 7th–6th c. *Délos* xvii. 117, pl. 67. *ID* 31b. Delos Mus.

**6.** Fragment of an Ionic capital from Delos, inscribed retrograde; 7th–6th c. *ID* 7. Delos Mus. A4213.

**7.** Naxian marble tile, from Athens; 7th c.? Sauer, *AM* xvii (1892), 41. Wiegand, *Die archaische Poros-architektur d. Akropolis* (1904), 180 f., fig. 188. Athens, Acrop. Mus.

**8.** Spiral inscription on a flat marble stone from Delos; 7th c.? *ID* 5. Peek, op. cit. 572, 18. Delos Mus. Γ 256.

**9.** Unidentified inscribed marble fragment from Delos; 7th c.? *ID* 3. Peek, op. cit. 570 ff., 17, fig. 3. Delos Mus. A2464.

**10.** Inscribed base of a colossus dedicated by the Naxians on Delos; *c.* 600–575. *IG* xii. 5. 2, p. xxv. Roberts i. 27. *SGDI* 5421. Roehl³, 66. 4. *DGE* 760. *ID* 4. *Kouroi*, no. 13. Homann-Wedeking, *Die Anfänge*, 56. Guarducci, *Epigraphica* iv (1942), 155 ff. Delos, E200. PL. 55

**11.** Bronze statuette dedicated to Apollo by Deinagoras; *c.* 525–500. *IG* xii. 5. 42. Roberts i. 26a. *SGDI* 5420. Roehl³, 65. 3. *DGE* 759. Neugebauer, *Kat. Bronz. Berlin* i (1931), 90 ff., no. 192, fig. 30 and pl. 31. Friedlaender 14b. Buschor, *Frühgriech. Jünglinge* (1950), 118 f. Berlin Mus. 7383. PL. 55

**12.** Stele made by Alxenor of Naxos, from Boiotia; *c.* 490–475? *IG* vii. 3225. Roberts i. 28. *SGDI* 5422. Roehl³, 66. 5. *DGE* 761. Richter³, 132, fig. 425. NM 39. PL. 55

**13.** Part of a column bearing a sacral text, built into a church at Roudies, Naxos; *c.* 500–490? *IG* xii. 5. 40. *SGDI* 5418. Naxos Mus.

**14.** Graffito on a rock, Naxos; *c.* 450–425? *IG* xii. 5. 97. Roehl³, 66. 6. PL. 55

### AMORGOS

**15.** Epitaph of Deidamas on a rock at Aigiale; *c.* 700–650? *IG* xii. 7. 442. *SGDI* 5351. Roehl³, 27. 30. Peek i. 1413. PL. 56

**16.** Graffito of Sateles on a rock at Arkesine; *c.* 550–500? *IG* xii. 7. 106. *SGDI* 5353. Peek i. 2041.

**17.** Grave-stele of Demainete, from Arkesine; *c.* 550? *IG* xii. 7. 141. *SGDI* 5352. Roehl³, 28. 33. *DGE* 751 (4). EM. PL. 56

**18.** Grave-stele of Stesimachos, from Arkesine; *c.* 550–500? *IG* xii. 7. 140. *SGDI* iv, p. 854. *DGE* 751 (6). Syra Mus.?

**19.** Grave-stele of Xenokrite, from Arkesine; *c.* 550–500? *IG* xii. 7. 139. *SGDI* 5357. Roehl³, 27. 32. Syra Mus.

**20.** Grave-stele of Alexo, from Arkesine; *c.* 525–500? *IG* xii. 7. 142. *SGDI* 5358. Roehl³, 29. 39. *DGE* 751 (5). Syra Mus. PL. 56

**21.** Stele bearing the names of two archons, from Arkesine; *c.* 500–475? *IG* xii. 7. 103. Roberts i. 160c. *SGDI* 5354. Roehl³, 28. 37. *DGE* 750 (2). Syra Mus.?

**22.** Altar of Dionysos, from Arkesine; *c.* 500–450? *IG* xii. 7. 78. Roberts i. 160b. *SGDI* 5349. Roehl³, 28. 36. *DGE* 750 (1). Kastri village? PL. 56

**23.** Part of an abecedarium cut on a rock near Aigiale; *c.* 450? *IG* xii. 7. 413. Roberts i. 159b. Roehl³, 28. 34. PL. 56

**24.** Gravestone of Polyidos, Arkesine; *c.* 450–425? *IG* xii. 7. 107. *SGDI* 5379. Peek i. 889. Broutsi village.

## PAROS

**25.** Fragmentary inscribed vase, Orientalizing style, from Delos; 7th c. *Délos* xvii. 17, pl. 10. Picard, *RA* 1942–3 (ii), 88 ff. Rubensohn, *DM* i (1948), 39, n. 6. *ID* 32a. Delos Mus.

**26.** Fragment of a column bearing a legal text, from Paros; *c.* 600–550? *IG* xii. 5. 105. Roehl³, 59. 1. Paros Mus. 73.                                                                        PL. 56

**27.** Stele dedicated to a deity, from Paros; *c.* 600–550? *IG* xii. 5. 219. Roehl³, 59. 2. *IG* xii, suppl., p. 107. Paros Mus. 58.

**28.** Inscription of the builder Ason; *c.* 550? *IG* xii. 5. 252. Roberts i. 16. *SGDI* 5432. Roehl³, 59. 3. Kern, pl. 6. *DGE* 770. Paros Mus.                                                    PL. 56

**29.** Fragment of base for a dedication by Mikkiades from Paros; *c.* 550–530? *IG* xii. 5. 147. Roehl³, 61. 9. Rubensohn, op. cit. 38 f., n. 1. EM.

**30.** Capital for a dedication (winged Nike?) of Mikkiades, made by Archermos, from Delos; *c.* 550–530? *IG* xii. 5. 147. *IGB* 1. Petersen, *AM* xi (1886), 384 ff. Sauer, *AM* xvi (1891), 182 ff. Roehl³, 64. Kern, pl. 7. Gotsmich, *Probleme d. frühgriech. Plastik*, 112 f. Raubitschek, *Bull. Bulgare* xii (1938), 148, n. 5, 161. Rubensohn, op. cit. 38 ff. Friedlaender 47. Peek, op. cit. 572 ff., 19, fig. *ID* 9. Marcadé ii, 21 f., pl. 29, 1. NM 21a. (Possibly Delian.)                                              PL. 56

**31.** Dedication of Therseleides, from Delos; *c.* 530–500. *ID* 10. J. and L. Robert, *REG* lxvi (1953), Bull. epig. no. 143. Delos Mus. A3043.

**32.** Capital for a statue dedicated by Nikoleos, Paros; *c.* 525–500. *IG* xii. 5. 260. Kontoleon, *A. Delt* xiv (1931–2), parart., 49. Paros Mus.

**33.** Part of a stele bearing a prohibition, Paros; *c.* 525–500? *IG* xii. 5. 150. Roehl³, 60. 4. Paros Mus. 46.

**34.** Base for a statue dedicated by Demokydes and Telestodike, Paros; *c.* 500? *IG* xii. 5. 215. Roberts i. 17. Roehl³, 61. 10. *DGE* 771. *SGDI* 5430. Karouzos, op. cit. 558, 575. Church of St. John the Theologian.                                                                                     PL. 56

**35.** Altar of Zeus Elasteros, Paros; *c.* 500–480? *IG* xii. 5. 1027. *SGDI* iv, p. 857. Roehl³, 60. 7. *DGE* 772. Kontoleon, *AE* 1948–9, 2 ff. Paros Mus.                                       PL. 56

**36.** Gravestone of the sister of Pythonax, Paros; *c.* 475? *IG* xii. 5. 298. Roehl³, 61. 12. Pcck i. 166. Paros Mus.

**37.** Stele bearing a text on ἐκκαθάρματα; *c.* 475–450? *IG* xii. 5. 107. *SGDI* iv, p. 856. Roehl³, 62. 14. *IG* xii, suppl., p. 105. Paros Mus.

**38.** Relief stele from a necropolis at Kataphygion on Ikaros, signed by a Parian sculptor Palion; *c.* 470. *BCH* lxxx (1956), Chron. fouilles, 334, fig. 13. See also **54** (Ikaros).

**39.** Sacral law on the ritual to Persephone, Paros; *c.* 450? *IG* xii. 5. 225. *SGDI* 5427. *DGE* 773. *IG* xii, suppl., p. 107. Paros Mus.                                                    PL. 56

## SIPHNOS

**40.** Inscription in the rock by a cave dedicated to the nymphs at Korakies, Siphnos; *c.* 500? *IG* xii. 5. 483. Roberts i. 20. *SGDI* 5490. Roehl³, 64. *DGE* 781.                           PL. 57

## IOS

**41.** Part of a stele with a decree on pasturage, Ios; *c.* 450? *IG* xii. 5. 1. Private Coll., Ios?

### DELOS

**42.** Column bearing a dedication to Athena, Delos; *c.* 525–500? *ID* 15. Delos Mus. E357.    PL. 57

**43a–f.** Graffiti dedications on (*a*) a mask and (*b–f*) vases from Delos; *c.* 550–500. (*a*) mask: *Délos* xi. 177 f., fig. 146, xxiii. 74 f. pl. 12. (*b*) Attic BF Siana cup: *Délos* xi. 180 f., fig. 149. *ABF* 75. (*c*) Attic BF skyphos: *Délos* xi. 179, fig. 147. (*d*) Attic RF cup: op. cit. 182 f., fig. 151. *ARV* 58. (*e*) LC II kothon: *Délos* xi. 182, fig. 152. *NC*, cat. 1521. (*f*) Attic BF lekythos: *Délos* xi. 179 f., fig. 148. *ID* 33, i, iv, ii, x, xiv, iii. Delos Mus. A 3525, B 6107, B 6138, B 6109, B 6174, B 6136.    PL. 57

### KEOS

**44.** BF amphora, names in Keian (?) script; *c.* 570. Pottier, *Vas. ant. Louvre* ii. 68 ff., E732, pl. 54. Kretschmer, *Griech. Vaseninschriften* 59. Gotsmich, *AA* 1941, 872, fig. 8. Paris, Louvre E732 (cleaned).

**45.** Inscribed coinage of Koresia, 6th c. *HN²*, 483 f. B ii. 1. 1289 ff., pl. 61.

**46.** Dedication of a sculptor (?) Alkidamas, from Keos; *c.* 525–500? *IG* xii. 5. 611. Roberts i. 32. Roehl³, 57. 2. *IG* xii, suppl., p. 116. Friedlaender 148. Lost?    PL. 57

**47.** Graffiti names on the town wall, Karthaia; *c.* 475–450? *IG* xii. 5. 566. Roberts i. 31b. *SGDI* iv, p. 855. Roehl³, 57. 3. *DGE* 764.    PL. 57

**48.** Dedication by Diophanes and Diodoros, Poiessa; *c.* 430–400? Dunant and Thomopoulos, *BCH* lxxviii (1954), 346 ff., no. 17, figs. 21-22. *SEG* xiv. 547. Poiessa, in terrace wall of church.

### SYROS

**49.** Graffito of Smikon on a rock; *c.* 525–500? Peek, *AM* lix (1934), 64 ff., no. 21, Beil. 5. *IG* xii. suppl., p. 118, 244. Latte, *Glotta* xxxii (1952), 39 f.    PL. 57

### TENOS

**50.** Fragmentary stele (?) apparently inscribed *boustrophedon*, from Tenos; 6th c. *IG* xii. 5. 959. Tenos Mus.

**51.** Abusive inscription on a stone block, Tenos; *c.* 500–450? Kontoleon, *PAE* 1949, 133 f., fig. 19.

**52.** Fragments of inscribed 6th-c. sherds and a bronze strip of the 5th c. inscribed [- - -]μνηστος, Tenos. *BCH* lxxx (1956), Chron. fouilles, 332.

### ANDROS

**53.** Decree concerning the preparation of a θεωρία, from Delphi; *c.* 500–475? Daux, *Hesperia* xviii (1949), 58 ff., pl. 1. Buck 7. Delphi Mus. 3410.

### IKAROS

**54.** Relief stele inscribed with names of donors (?), from the necropolis at Kataphygion; *c.* 470. *BCH* lxxx, op. cit. 334. See also **38**.

### SKYROS

**55.** Graffito in Attic (?) script on a sherd from a temple-precinct, Skyros; *c.* 475–450? Philadelpheus, *A. Delt.* iv (1918), parart. 38, fig. 6. *SEG* i. 408.

## B. *Northern Aegean*

### SAMOTHRACE

56. Names incised by the figures on a marble relief from Samothrace; *c.* 560–550. *IG* xii. 8. 226. Roberts i. 162. Louvre, *Encycl. phot. de l'Art* iii. 135. Bousquet, *RA* 1948 (*Mél. Picard*) i. 112 ff., fig. 1. *AGA*, 96. Paris, Louvre. PL. 57

57. Graffiti of the late 6th and 5th c. from the sanctuary of the Great Gods, Samothrace. Lehmann, *Hesperia* xxiv (1955), 93 ff., pls. 39–40. PL. 57

### LEMNOS

58. Boundary-stone in Attic script from Myrrhina; *c.* 500–480? Segre, *Ann.* xv–xvi (1932–3), 294 ff., fig. 6. PL. 57

59. Stele bearing Attic names in Attic script from Hephaistia; *c.* 500–490? Picard, *BCH* xxxvi (1912), 329 ff., figs. 15–17. Wilhelm, *Anz. Ak. Wien* (1934), 111. *IG* xii, suppl., p. 147, 337.

### IMBROS

60. Gravestone with Attic script and epitaph: *c.* 500–450? *IG* xii. 8. 90. Peek i. 916.

### THASOS

61. Memorial erected to Glaukos by the sons of Brentes in the Agora at Thasos; *c.* 625–600? Pouilloux, *BCH* lxxix (1955), 77 ff., pl. 3. *SEG* xiv. 565. Peek i. 51a. Thasos Mus. 1355. PL. 58

62. Graffito on a handle from the precinct of Herakles, Thasos; *c.* 550–500? Launey, *Études thasiennes* i (1944), 91, no. 1, fig. 74. Thasos Mus.

63. Inscription under reliefs of Herakles and Dionysos by the southern city gate, Thasos; *c.* 525–500. *IG* xii. 8. 356. *SGDI* 5455a. Deonna, *RA* 1908, 15 ff. Roehl[3], 63. 3. Launey, op. cit. 126. Friedlaender 118. Pouilloux, *Recherches sur l'histoire et les cultes de Thasos* i (1954), 439. *In situ*. PL. 58

64. Base for a dedication to Herakles by Akeratos; *c.* 525–500? Launey, *BCH* lviii (1934), 173 ff., pl. 3. *IG* xii. suppl., p. 163, 412. Launey, *Études*, 91, no. 2. Friedlaender 143. Pouilloux, op. cit. 439, pl. 6. 2–4. Thasos Mus.

65. Gravestone of Thrasykles, Thasos; *c.* 525–500? *IG* xii. 8. 395. Friedlaender 157. Pouilloux, op. cit. 439, pl. 5. 4. Peek i. 142. Thasos Mus. 320. PL. 58

66. Gravestone of Anaxipolis, Thasos; *c.* 525–500? *IG* xii. 8. 397. Roehl[3], 63. 2. Friedlaender 90. Peek i. 1636. Thasos, built into a house.

67. Memorial of Akeratos at Potamia Bay, Thasos; *c.* 500–490? Tod, *JHS* xxix (1909), 95 ff. Launey, *BCH* lviii (1934), 180 f. *IG* xii. 8. 683. *IG* xii, suppl., p. 163, 412, n. Friedlaender 168. Pouilloux, op. cit. 439. *In situ*.

68. Gravestone of Learete, Thasos; *c.* 500–490? *IG* xii. 8. 398. *SGDI* 5457. Roehl[3], 63. 7. Friedlaender 60. Pouilloux, op. cit. 439. Peek i. 164. Thasos Mus. PL. 58

69a–b. (*a*) graffito on rock near Thasos town; *c.* 500–490? Picard, *BCH* xlvii (1923), 259, fig. 1. (*b*) graffiti on blocks of the city walls; *c.* 491? *IG* xii. 8. 390. Roehl[3], 63. 1. Pouilloux, op. cit. 439, pl. 5. 1.

**70.** Inscriptions on reliefs of Apollo, Hermes, Nymphs, and Graces, from the passage to the Prytaneion, Thasos; *c.* 475–465? *IG* xii. 8. 358. Roberts i. 22. *SGDI* 5455. *SIG*³ 1033. Roehl³, 63. 6. *DGE* 777. Louvre, *Encycl. phot. de l'Art* iii. 148–9. Daux, *RA* 1948 (i), 244 f. Pouilloux, op. cit. 59 ff. and 440. Paris, Louvre.                                                                                                                        PL. 58

**71.** Wine-law inscribed *boustrophedon*, from the Agora, Thasos; *c.* 460–450? Pouilloux, op. cit. 37 ff., no. 7, pl. 5. 3. Thasos Mus. 895.

**72.** Stele with text concerning the cult of Herakles, Thasos; *c.* 450–440? Picard, *BCH* xlvii (1923), 241 ff., pl. 4. *IG* xii, suppl., pp. 163, 414. Launey, op. cit. 126. Daux, op. cit. 243 f., fig. 2. Pouilloux, op. cit. 85 ff. and 440, pl. 11. 3.

**73.** Relief stele of Philis, from Thasos; *c.* 430. *IG* xii. 8. 401. Devambez, *BCH* lv (1931), 413 ff., pl. 21. Pouilloux, op. cit. 87 and 440, pl. 10. Paris, Louvre.

**74.** Stele with a list of proscriptions from the precinct of Apollo Pythios, Thasos; *c.* 411–408? *IG* xii. 8. 263. Pouilloux, op. cit. 138, pl. 13, 4. Thasos Mus. 643.

**75.** Gravestone of the Corinthians Lokrion and Lysistratos, Thasos; *c.* 411? *IG* xii. 8. 402. Pouilloux, op. cit. 136, pl. 14, 2. Paris, Louvre M 2706.                                                                                 PL. 58

**76.** Laws concerning treason to the oligarchy, from the Agora, Thasos; *c.* 411–410. Pouilloux, op. cit. 139 ff., no. 18, pl. 13, 1. Thasos Mus. 753.                                                                                                        PL. 58

# THE DORIC ISLANDS (SOUTHERN AEGEAN)

FIG. 45. Southern Aegean Islands (Doric)

*Notes on letter-forms* (Cretan cities in italics)

β1 occurs with β2 at *Gortyn*, from the earliest examples to the 5th c.; Guarducci has also identified this form in the letter resembling *pi* on coins of *Sybrita* in the 5th c. (cf. *IC* ii, p. 290). Thera uses β3, developing to 4 in the 6th c. Melos uses 5 (cf. also Selinous, p. 269).

γ1 is used by those Cretan places which show λ1 (*Dreros, Knossos, Praisos, Eltynia*); elsewhere in Crete γ2 is used, presumably to avoid confusion with the more common λ2. Thera shows γ1, becoming γ3 in the late archaic period (Thera **14**); the reversed γ4 is Melian.

*Eltynia* shows a shorthand form, δ2 (*IC* i. x. 2; early 5th c.?).

*Eleutherna* shows a shorthand form ε4 in the late archaic period (*c.* 525–500?).

ϝ1–2 occurs at *Gortyn* in the earliest inscriptions, apparently illustrating the development of the original Phoenician *wāw* into the Greek doublet form. ϝ5, which looks like a broken-down version of the Gortynian, is used at *Prinias, Axos,* and *Eleutherna*.

In Crete *zeta* was used apparently for -σσ-: *Dreros* 1*e* (οϡʼ = οσσ(α)?); *Gortyn* 2, nos. 4–5 (αναδα-ϡαθαι, οϡοι = αναδασσασθαι, οσσοι: cf. Buck, 70 f.).

At *Dreros* η1–3 are all used; elsewhere 1 is normal, becoming 5 in the 5th c. (?); only *Eleutherna* uses 3–4 regularly in the late archaic period (cf. *epsilon*). *Eta* is not employed in the Gortyn Code, *c.* 450?, which shows *epsilon* throughout for ε and η; the reason for this is not certain (p. 28, n. 2).

11 is the normal early form in Crete; later (*c.* 525?), an angled form 2 appears (*Axos* **21** and **22**). In the 5th c. 11 becomes common again (*Gortyn* **7**).

For λ1, see *gamma* above. *Axos*, *Afrati*, and the coins of *Lyttos* show λ3 in the early 5th c. (**17, 24, 25**).

μ1–2 is normal for Crete, Melos, Sikinos; μ4 is attested in a copy of a 5th c. (?) text from *Axos* (**24**).

In Crete ξ2–3 is attested in the Eteocretan of *Praisos*, *c.* 550–525? (**19**), also once at *Lyttos*, *c.* 500? (**16**); the latter may be an error for *zeta*. The normal spelling of the sound was ξ1. In Thera, ξ2–3 is used for the initial Z in Zeus (p. 317); ξ4 appears in the 6th–5th c. (Thera **15**, Melos **25***c*).

o2 occurs at *Lyttos*, and o4 (with θ3) at *Eleutherna*. o5 is Melian (see *omega* below, and Knidos, p. 351).

π1–2 (*Dreros*, *Prinias*, *Axos*, *Gortyn*) apparently developed thence to π3 at *Gortyn*, and so to π4; 4 is attested elsewhere in the 6th and 5th c. (*Lyttos*, *Afrati*), but 5 was also used (*Axos* **22, 23**, *Eleutherna* **26**).

*Qoppa* is not used in the early inscriptions from *Dreros*, nor, apparently, in those from *Praisos* (see *phi*). It appears to be normal elsewhere: ϙ1 (*Gortyn*, *Lyttos*), which becomes 3 (*Prinias*) or 2 (*Gortyn* **3**, late archaic). It was apparently disused by the 5th c.

ρ3 occurs in a few inscriptions of the late archaic period (*Chersonesos*, *Axos*), and in the coin-legends of *Eleutherna* (**28**). ρ4 occurs in Thera from the late archaic period onwards (**13, 15**).

In the early period we find both υ2 (*Dreros*, *Prinias* **10**) and υ1 (*Gortyn* **2**, *Lyttos* **15**, *Chersonesos*); 3 appears to have superseded these forms in Crete, as elsewhere, during the late archaic period (*c.* 525–500?).

The psilotic dialect of Crete used *pi* for *phi*. φ2 is attested in Eteocretan at *Praisos* (**19**): the letter might be *qoppa*, but cf. κο (not ϙο) in the other fragment of this inscription. φ3 first appears in Greek Cretan in a graffito from *Itanos* (*Samonion*), *c.* 525? (*IC* iii. vii. 2).

ω1 is attested for Thera (cf. Buck, 305), but the examples are not all certain, and it may possibly be merely *omikron*, cut with a compass or not dotted at all. ω2 is used in Melian (see *omikron* above).

For *ligatures* and curled letters in Theran, see p. 319.

*Punctuation* 1 occurs in Crete, and occasionally in Thera (Thera **4**). P2 or 3 occurs once at *Dreros* (**1***a*), at *Lyttos* (**16**, *IC*, no. 5), and at *Gortyn* (**7**, col. ix, ll. 24, 43). 4 occurs in solitary examples at *Gortyn* (**3**) and *Eleutherna* (**26**), 5 at *Afrati* (**25**); painted leaves, &c., are used between paragraphs in *Gortyn* **7**. Guide-lines are used at *Lyttos*, *Gortyn*, *Praisos*, *Prinias*, *Afrati*, *Eleutherna*. The *boustrophedon* system lasted at *Gortyn* until the 4th c., and perhaps elsewhere also. The paragraphing system will be further described (p. 311; cf. p. 44); it appears to have died out before the 5th c., although the convention of beginning a text from right to left persisted rather longer (*Gortyn* **7**).

The letter-form here called doubtfully χ2 is attested in the Eteocretan inscriptions of *Dreros* and *Praisos*, and at Sikinos; see also pp. 39 f., 322.

CRETE

The archaic inscriptions of Crete have been fully edited and illustrated in the great corpus *Inscriptiones Creticae* i–iv (1935–50) by Professor Guarducci; the only additions of importance which have been discovered since these volumes were issued are the legal fragments from Dreros, also published in detail (**1**). The following discussion will therefore have nothing to contribute to the actual texts themselves, but will merely touch upon certain aspects of the Cretan script as a whole, referring for all examples to the material as presented in *IC* i–iv and in the French publications of Dreros.

It has long been agreed that Crete was, if not the birthplace, at least one of the earliest receivers of the Greek alphabet. Her relations in the eighth century with Cyprus, Rhodes, Corinth, and some at least of the Cyclades have been emphasized by archaeologists,[1] and epigraphists have observed that her script is the nearest of all to the Phoenician—that is, if a selection is made from all the letter-forms used throughout Crete; for Crete is a large island, and there are certain minor differences in the script used in different places (see notes above). The forms which correspond most closely with their Phoenician equivalents are β1 (Gortyn), ϝ1–2 (Gortyn), ι1–2 (*passim*), λ1 (Dreros, Knossos, Eltynia, Praisos), μ1–2; ξ2 was known, though used (as far as the present evidence goes) only in inscriptions in the Eteocretan language at Praisos (**19**); π1–3 (becoming 4 in many places) again recalls the Phoenician. φ2 is attested doubtfully in Eteocretan, and in one graffito at Itanos (p. 309); Χ and Ψ do not appear. It has been generally concluded that their absence in inscriptions means that they had not yet been invented when the alphabet came to Crete, the graffito at Itanos being then an example of later contamination. This may well be so, but as the Cretan dialect apparently had no aspirate in any case, either initial or medial,[2] only the discovery of an early abecedarium will prove conclusively whether these letters were totally unknown in Crete, or whether they were merely ignored for practical purposes from the start, yet handed on in the abecedarium, e.g. to Samos or Corinth (pp. 42, 116 ff.). Two further (incidental?) likenesses to Phoenician may be mentioned: the Cretan punctuation ı, which is also common in North Semitic inscriptions, but not normal elsewhere in Greece; and the persistent tradition, which lasted into the fifth century, that every inscription should begin from right to left (cf. Gortyn **7**). The same type of alphabet was used also in the Doric islands north of Crete (Thera, Melos, Sikinos, Anaphe), and is undoubtedly kin to the Corinthian and Argive.

The Cretan script is illustrated chiefly by the fragments surviving from legal codes in eight of her ninety cities, which amply confirm the literary tradition[3] that the Cretans were pioneers among the Greeks in the establishment of legal systems, a practice perhaps inherited by the Doric incomers from the native Eteocretans with their traditions of the lawgiver Minos and the judge Rhadamanthys in the Minoan period. The most complete and therefore the best known of these systems is the great fifth-century Code at Gortyn (**7**). Fifth-century fragments remain from Eltynia (*IC* i. x. 2), Gortyn (**4–5**), and Lyttos (**16**). At Eleutherna and Axos large portions survive which may be of the late sixth century (**22–23, 27**). Parts of still earlier codes have appeared at Gortyn (**2**), Prinias (**11–12**), Lyttos (**15**) and Knossos (**13**), and (perhaps earliest of all) at Dreros (**1**). In nearly all cases the codes were inscribed on walls, either of temples or of other public buildings, and their survival is mainly due to this, since old wall-blocks were always useful for later rebuilding. Apart from the laws, the Cretan material consists of graffiti on rocks at Itanos (*IC* iii. vii. 3–4), Olous (*IC* i. xxii. 64) and (on a stone) at Gortyn

---

[1] Cf. Kirsten, *Das Insel Kreta im v. u. iv. Jdt.* (1936); Demargne, *La Crète dédalique* (1947), esp. 119 ff., 329 f., 331 ff., 335 ff., 340 ff.

[2] Buck, 53.

[3] Arist., *Pol.* 1271b, 1274a; Plato, *Laws* i, *passim*; Ephoros *ap.* Strabo 260, 480–2; Plut. *Lycurg.* 4.

(*IC* iv. 50); coin-legends, none of which is earlier than the fifth century (**6, 9, 14, 17, 28** and *IC* ii. xxvi (Sybrita)); one inscribed clay figurine (**18**); plain funeral bases or stelai (**20, 29**); a dedication on a plain block (**25**); and a few very brief or illegible fragments, omitted here. There are as yet no inscribed vases or sculpture, and so any attempt at precise dating of Cretan inscriptions before the fifth century is most uncertain, for we have only the letter-forms themselves on which to form a judgement, qualified by the knowledge (derived from the fifth-century material) that the Cretan alphabet was distinctly conservative in its retention of old forms and methods.

The fragments at Dreros (**1**) consist of eight inscriptions cut on long roughly-trimmed blocks of grey schist from a plundered wall of the temple of Apollo Delphinios, which was built apparently in the Late Geometric period, and continued in use until at least the third century B.C.[1] The lettering varies somewhat; probably new clauses were added as occasion arose, each starting with the formula: αδε εϝαδε πολι, or simply εϝαδε. It is noteworthy that part of at least one clause appears to be in the Eteocretan language (**1***b*). The lettering of the longest surviving law (**1***a*), which appears also to be among the earliest, bears a marked resemblance to that on Nikandra's statue at Delos, *c.* 650 (p. 291, **2**) in its general appearance; i.e. a small *omikron* and tall, thin, long-tailed, straggling letters; it may be placed very tentatively in the middle or second half of the seventh century. It also shows the earliest example of the Cretan system of paragraphing; and this point needs amplification, for it is of importance in the restoration and dating of fragmentary texts such as the early laws from Gortyn (**2**). Though it occurs elsewhere (see p. 50), paragraphing is especially characteristic of archaic Cretan wall-inscriptions. The Cretan mason began his text from right to left, and proceeded along the wall with his line; if the clause ended before the space did, he did not continue in the same line with the next clause, but, leaving a *vacat*, returned to the right-hand edge and began the next paragraph under the first. Thus, where several paragraphs have been written in this way across several blocks of a wall, one surviving block from any point may give the impression that it belongs to a single inscription written in continuous retrograde. If, on the other hand, there was not space enough to finish the clause in a single line, he wrote it *boustrophedon* in the normal way. In this Drerian law **1***a* the mason cut the first paragraph *boustrophedon* in three lines, and then, leaving a *vacat* at the end of l. 3, he began his new paragraph (concerning the oaths to be taken) from right to left again, marking it with the punctuation-sign 2.

The most archaic inscriptions from Gortyn are the series inscribed on the walls and steps of the temple of Apollo Pythios (**2**). It is generally agreed that they must extend over a considerable period, because of the minor differences in the lettering; but the date of the earliest examples has been disputed, some scholars assigning them to the middle of the seventh century,[2] others to the sixth.[3] As far as can be judged from the lettering, it can only be observed here that (*a*) it appears to be distinctly later than the Drerian, in that none of it has the very thin, long-tailed, straggling look of extreme archaism, but

[1] Marinatos, *BCH* lx (1936), 268.  iv, pp. 5, 40 ff.

[2] Comparetti, *MA* iii (1893), 367 ff.; Roberts i, [3] De Sanctis, *MA* xviii (1907), 297 ff.; Kirsten, op. p. 54; Guarducci, *Riv. Fil.* lxvi (1938), 272 ff. and *IC* cit. 46 ff.; Demargne, op. cit. 348.

that (*b*) it may belong to the end of the seventh century, if the Drerian does in fact extend through the period *c.* 650–600. But when one considers the four points on which the dating of the Gortynian fragments has depended—namely, the age of the temple itself, the direction of the script on the wall-blocks, the letter-forms, and the content of the text—none appears to offer any positive argument for a date in the seventh century. The temple itself, it is true, has been assigned tentatively by architectural experts to the seventh century,[1] but this conclusion rests in part at least on the previous assumption that the inscriptions are of that date; Weickert noted particularly that the 'Quadertechnik' of the blocks was remarkably developed for so early a building, and this point seems to me of some significance, although it has not been cited by the advocates of the sixth century. Nor has the internal chronology evolved by Comparetti[2] from the direction of the script been challenged by them; yet his argument may be said to approach the problem from the wrong angle. Starting with the principle that all retrograde inscriptions should be earlier than those written *boustrophedon*, he therefore separated the extant blocks into two periods: (i) all those containing one or more retrograde lines, and (ii) all those written *boustrophedon*; and, since some of the latter are very archaic, he assumed that the retrograde examples, being yet earlier, could not be later than the seventh century. It will be recalled that the inscriptions are written on (*a*) the orthostates, or lowest blocks of the walls, *c.* 1·20 m. high, (*b*) the 'headers' (*c.* 0·50–0·65 m. high), and (*c*) the 'stretchers' (*c.* 0·30 m. high), which, in alternating layers, formed the wall above the orthostates. In all three types, some blocks (the majority) are inscribed retrograde, and others *boustrophedon*; indeed, some of the orthostates and 'headers' show both methods on the same block, and in some cases the lettering of the *boustrophedon* examples appears more archaic than that of the retrograde; nor has the very great size of the letters in some of the single lines on some 'stretchers' been taken into account. The true explanation seems to me to lie in the two points (i) that the inscriptions did not form a continuous code like that of the fifth century, but were cut at different times as occasion arose, and fitted in by the masons as space allowed, and (ii) that the paragraphing system, described on p. 311 above, was used. Thus a whole clause might run in one long retrograde line over any number of blocks, followed by another clause below it (so that an isolated surviving block may now suggest wrongly a shorter inscription written in two lines retrograde); or, if the available wall-space happened to be limited, or the mason remembered his client's convenience, the inscription might be cut *boustrophedon* in much shorter lines. As the walls became more closely covered, and the masons had to cut the texts well above eye-level, the size of the letters would have to be increased; so that the 'stretchers' which carry single retrograde lines of letters almost as tall as the block itself should be counted among the latest rather than the earliest of the series. In short, the division into a 'first and second period' ('antiquiores tituli sinistrorsum, recentiores βουστροφηδόν decurrunt'[3]) is unreal. As for the third argument (based on the individual letter-forms), it cannot be denied that the forms β1, ϝ1–2, ϙ1, υ1 which the texts exhibit are very close to the Phoenician, but their usage alone will not prove the inscriptions to be of the seventh century, for they are used

[1] Weickert, *Typen d. archaischen Architektur*, 62; Robertson[2], 57, 323.
[2] Op. cit. 331 ff.          [3] *IC* iv, p. 41

from beginning to end of the period covered by the texts, and β1 at least survived into the fifth century (4). As for the general appearance of the letters, it can only be said that some of the texts show ε3, which might suggest a date later than the middle of the sixth century, while others, showing ε1–2, may be earlier; but this criterion is of small value until we have some external factor (as those provided by sculpture, pottery, architecture) to help in dating Cretan inscriptions within the sixth century. The last argument for an early date maintains that the references in the text to the tripod, lebes, and obelos as units of currency indicate the seventh rather than the sixth century, even though it is granted that by 'tripod' and the rest is meant a lump of metal equivalent in value to the utensil itself; but de Sanctis has pointed out[1] that an inscription of the third century B.C. from Knossos (*IC* i. viii. 5) refers to lebetes, staters, and obols as units of currency, and therefore, whatever were the actual objects[2] to which the Cretans gave these names, their occurrence in a text will not of itself prove that the text is particularly early. Indeed, since coinage was not introduced among the Greeks before the end of the seventh century, it is probable that the Cretans continued the system of barter through the sixth century (apart from the odd Aiginetan 'turtle'), merely using the old units of value, the tripods &c., as a standard of reckoning; their own cities' coinages begin with the fifth century.

The archaic system of paragraphing apparently died out before the end of the sixth century, for the lines run *boustrophedon* continuously in the series of inscriptions which follow the Pythion texts. In the great Code (7), which may be dated not earlier than *c.* 450,[3] the breaks between paragraphs are marked by a *vacat* of one or two letters, filled with a stylized leaf or flower in red paint. In the series of those which, according to the lettering, are to be placed between the Pythion texts and the great Code, those showing α1, ε1, ϝ3, and ϙ3 would appear to be earliest (3; end of sixth century?), followed by the numerous blocks from the 'north and east' walls in the Agora (4), which differ little in appearance from the Code itself, except that β1 and η5 are still used. The *boustrophedon* system was still in use in the fourth century, for the latest examples show Ionic lettering (*IC* iv. 141–59), which is hardly likely to have taken root in Crete earlier than that century.

Little remains to be said of the archaic inscriptions from the rest of Crete, apart from the discussion of their individual letter-forms; I call attention here only to a few points of interest. At Prinias (ancient Rhizenia?) the middle part of a stout pillar was found, inscribed vertically with a legal text of some kind on all sides (12); its large, awkward lettering, which allowed only four lines to the surviving wide face, resembles the early fragments from Gortyn (2). The mutilated lines evidently ran continuously from one face to the next, and the end was marked off from the start by a guide-line drawn between two of the lines on the wide face. At Lyttos, the earliest of many fragments of Lyttian legal codes (15) shows a style of lettering different from those of Dreros, Gortyn, and Prinias already mentioned; it shows vertical lines and sharp angles (except for 1), and has a general air of competence; if the earliest from Gortyn and the Prinias pillar are to be

---

[1] *MA* xviii (1907), 302 ff.

[2] De Sanctis suggested (loc. cit.) that the 'lebetes' stood for Aiginetan drachmai.

[3] 'c. 480–460', Guarducci (*IC* iv, p. 126); second half of 5th c., Shoe (*Profiles* i. 18, pl. 8. 5), Carpenter (*AJA* xxxvii (1933), 24), Kirsten (op. cit. 44 ff.).

dated in the first half of the sixth century, the Lyttos fragment should fall in the period *c.* 550–525. Similar lettering, also between guide-lines, occurs on the two Eteocretan fragments from Praisos (**19**), and on the base of a statue from Chersonesos, inscribed with an epitaph for a woman named Timo (**20**); but in the latter *iota* is also 12, and *rho* is ρ3. The same *iota* and *rho* appear in the numerous fragments of a long legal code from Axos (**22**), and here we are apparently in the late archaic period, for it also shows ε3 and υ3, and the old paragraphing system is no longer in use. The latest piece from Axos should be the lost block copied by Barrozzi and Spratt (**24**), which apparently showed (with a remarkable shorthand μ4, not otherwise attested) η5 and λ3, the latter form being used also on a dedication from Afrati (**25**), which shows η1 combined with the neat squared lettering of the fifth-century texts from Gortyn. At Eleutherna inscriptions apparently contemporary with the main series from Axos (**27**, *c.* 525–500?) show a peculiar local shorthand for *epsilon* (ε4) and *eta* (η3–4), which is not used on an earlier fragment (**26**), or on her coins (**28**); one fragment (**26**) shows paragraphing from left to right, a reversal of the normal Cretan practice. Last, but not least, there is the local script of Kydonia (**29**), which, as a colony of Aigina, stood apart from the rest of Crete in using the script of her mother-city, even to the Aiginetan 'reversed' α2 (p. 109). Three tomb-stones found there are in Aiginetan script of the early fifth century (**29**). Like the true Cretans, the Kydoniate colonists sometimes turned mercenaries, especially in the service of Egypt. The funeral temple of Seti I at Abydos (which the Greeks wrongly took to be the Palace of Memnon: Strabo 813) bears innumerable Greek graffiti. The earliest, Ionic of the sixth century, were presumably made by mercenaries; as at Abou Simbel, they occur with similar scrawls in Carian and Phoenician. Among the fifth-century examples is one by a Kydoniate, Onesandros, who was one of the mercenaries serving under Amyrtaios (**30**a). The script might be as early as *c.* 460, when the prince Amyrtaios revolted against the Pharaoh (Thuc. i. 110). More probably, we should assign it to the revolt of Amyrtaios the Saïte, *c.* 400; a mercenary might still use the local script at that late date. Two Doric names incised together in a script which might be Aiginetan of the early fifth century may also be those of Kydoniates (**30**b). Elsewhere in Crete at this time the 'primitive' script was still in use, but for one possible exception. At Phaistos two sherds were recently found in the dump made during the excavation of the Minoan palace in 1900–1.[1] They bear the names Ϝέρακλἔς | Γόρτυς and Σαστ϶κ? | Θεμιστοκλἔς in script like the Kydoniate, and apparently of the sixth to fifth centuries. The archaic script of Phaistos, as attested on the coinage (**9**) is, as one would expect, the usual 'primitive' Cretan, like that of Gortyn. The graffiti appear to have been arranged to fit onto the sherds—that is, not to be part of any original inscription made on the pottery before it was broken—and one can only speculate whether they were written casually by Kydoniates on a visit.[2]

---

[1] Guarducci, *Ann.* 1952–4, 167 ff., figs. 1–3. As she points out, the aspirate in the first name is unparalleled in Crete, and the sign doubtfully read as ω is in fact the punctuation-sign 3.

[2] One might even suspect them of being modern works, in view of their divers oddities—either small forgeries 'planted' on the dump by the hopeful perpetrator, or simply jokes dating from the dig of 1900–1, thrown on the dump when the joke was over. (See now Mastrokostas, *AE* 1955, 90, who reads Κάστωρ for Σαστ϶κ).

## SELECT CATALOGUE[1]

### DREROS

**1a–h.** Eight fragments of laws inscribed on the walls of the temple of Apollo Delphinios; middle and second half of 7th c.? (*a*) Van Effenterre, *BCH* lxi (1937), 333 ff.; lxii. 194 f. Guarducci, *Riv. Fil.* lxvii (1939), 20 ff. Ehrenberg, *CQ* xxxvii (1943), 14 ff. (*b*) (bilingual): Van Effenterre, *Rev. Phil.* xx (1946), 131 ff. Georgiev, *Rev. Phil.* xxi (1947), 132 ff. Lejeune, *REA* xlix (1947), 274 ff. Jeffery (*K. Ch.*) iii (1949), 143 ff. (*c*) Van Effenterre, *BCH* lxx (1946), 588 ff., no. 1. (*d*) Op. cit., no. 2. (*e*) Op. cit., no. 3. (*f*) Op. cit., no. 4. (*g*) Op. cit., no. 5. McDonald, *Hesperia* xxv (1956), 69 ff., pl. 27. (*h*) Op. cit., no. 6. Dreros (Neapolis) Mus.     PL. 59

### GORTYN

**2.** Inscribed wall-blocks and steps from the temple of Apollo Pythios; *c.* 600–525? *IC* iv. 1–40. Heraklion Mus., and on site.     PL. 59

**3.** Inscribed blocks from various parts of the site at Gortyn; *c.* 525–500? Op. cit. 62–64. Heraklion Mus.     PL. 59

**4.** Inscribed blocks from 'north and east walls'; *c.* 500–450? Op. cit. 41–51. Heraklion Mus. and on site.

**5.** Inscribed blocks from the 'Odeion' and elsewhere; *c.* 500–450? Op. cit. 52–61, 65–71. Heraklion Mus. and on site.     PL. 59

**6.** Coins inscribed Γορτυνος το παιμα right to left; *c.* 480–450? *HN*², 465. B ii. 3. 961 ff., pl. 252.

**7.** Great Code; mid-5th c.? *IC* iv. 72. On site.     PL. 59

**8.** Inscribed blocks similar to Great Code; *c.* 450–400? Op. cit. 73–140. On site.

### PHAISTOS

**9.** Coins inscribed Παιστιōν το παιμα right to left; *c.* 480–450? *HN*², 472. B ii. 3. 979 ff., pl. 255.

### PRINIAS (RHIZENIA?)

**10.** Graffito of several men's names (?); 7th c.? *IC* i. xxviii. 1. On site.

**11.** Legal fragments; early 6th c.? Op. cit. 2–6, 8–15. Heraklion Mus.

**12.** Legal code inscribed on a pillar; early 6th c.? Op. cit. 7. Heraklion Mus.     PL. 59

### KNOSSOS

**13.** Fragments of a legal code; mid-6th c.? *IC* i. viii. 2. Jeffery, *JHS* lxix (1949), 36 f. Heraklion Mus.

**14.** Coins inscribed Κνōσ, Κνōσιο right to left; *c.* 480–450? *HN*², 460. B ii. 3. 937 ff., pl. 249.

### LYTTOS

**15.** Fragment of a code; *c.* 550–525? *IC* i. xviii. 1. Lost?     PL. 60

**16.** Fragments of later codes; *c.* 500? Op. cit. 2–7. Heraklion Mus.

**17.** Coins inscribed Λυκτιον; 5th c. *HN*², 471. B ii. 3. 926 ff., pl. 247.

[1] Since so many cities within the island are concerned, I have listed the Cretan inscriptions as a separate catalogue from those of the other Doric islands (pp. 322 ff. below).

## PRAISOS

**18.** Graffito on a 'Daedalic' terra-cotta figure; 7th c. *IC* iii. viii. 1: there ascribed to Setaia; cf. Dohan, *MM Studies* iii (1931), 216, fig. 15. New York, MM. 53.5.24. PL. 60

**19a–b.** Two fragments of an Eteocretan code(?); *c.* 550–525? *IC* iii. vi. 1, 4. Jeffery, *K.Ch.* iii (1949), 146 f. (*a*) Heraklion Mus. 99. (*b*) Lost? PL. 60

## CHERSONESOS

**20.** Gravestone of Timo; *c.* 525? Petrou-Mesogeites, Ἑλληνικά x (1938), 204 ff., fig. 7. Private Coll., Koutoulouphari. PL. 60

## AXOS

**21.** Fragments of a legal code(?); early 6th c. *IC* ii. v. 12–14. Heraklion Mus. 97, 98.

**22.** Fragments of a later code; *c.* 525–500? Op. cit. 1–8, 11. Heraklion Mus. PL. 60

**23.** Fragment of another code; *c.* 525–500? Jeffery, *JHS* lxix (1949), 34 ff. Rhethymno Mus.

**24.** Fragment concerning sacrifices; early 5th c.? *IC* ii. v. 9. Lost.

## AFRATI

**25.** Part of a dedication; early 5th c.? *IC* i. v. 4. Built into a house.

## ELEUTHERNA

**26.** Fragment of a legal code(?); early 6th c.? *IC* ii. xii. 1. Rhethymno Mus. 33.

**27.** Fragments of legal codes; *c.* 525–500? Op. cit. 2–19. Rhethymno Mus. PL. 60

**28.** Coinage inscribed Ελευθερ right to left; 5th c. *HN*², 464. B ii. 3, 1001 ff., pl. 258.

## KYDONIA

**29a–c.** Grave-stelai in Aiginetan script; early 5th c. *IC* ii. x. 7, 10, 13. Theophaneides, *AE* 1948–9, Arch. Chron. 18, figs. 29–30. Canea Mus. PL. 60

**30a–b.** Graffiti by Kydoniate mercenaries in Abydos, Egypt; 5th c. Perdrizet and Lefebvre, *Les Graffites grecs du Memnonion d'Abydos* (1919), nos. 405, 445. PL. 60

## THERA (WITH KYRENE)

The island of Thera had connexions with Crete in the Bronze Age, as the pottery found there shows;[1] she was later colonized by Doric Greeks from Lakonia (according to the tradition, led by one Theras) in the general emigration eastward which planted Doric settlements on a bridge of islands across the southern Aegean as far as the coast of Asia Minor. The further tradition that the Lakonian emigrants under Theras found a Phoenician colony already settled there (Hdt. iv. 147 ff.) was not confirmed by the excavators of the main site, who reported a total lack of any signs of Phoenician settlement.[2] The archaic script of Thera and the small Doric islands round her is obviously

---

[1] Hiller von Gaertringen, *Thera* iii. 44 ff. and *RE*, s.v. Thera, 2277 ff.  [2] *Thera* i. 142; ii. 235.

much more closely connected with that of Crete than with that of her other neighbours, the Ionic Cyclades; and since one island must have passed it to the other within this Doric nucleus, it seems more likely that the seafaring Cretans were the first of the nucleus who learnt the alphabet (from its original source?) and passed it on to the rest, than that the Therans were the pioneers. In certain details, however, Theran differs from Cretan (see pp. 308 f., β, μ). *Vau* is not used in any Theran inscriptions, which suggests that the dialect may have been influenced in this by the neighbouring Ionic (cf. also Rhodian); but the letter may have existed nevertheless in her abecedarium. *Zeta* also is missing from the inscriptions; but only one occasion for it has occurred as yet, in Ζευς, which is written Ξευς (see on *xi* below): *heta* has both values, Ⱶ and η, which suggests either that Crete passed it on in the abecedarium with its full value (though her dialect was psilotic) or that here also the script of the Ionic Cyclades influenced Thera. *Xi* is used consistently for the initial letter of Ζευς (see *zeta* above), which may possibly reflect some dialectal oddity, since we have no warrant for assuming that all Greek dialects gave to the Ξ precisely the same sound-value as did the Ionic. The complementary letters φ, χ, which replace the earlier Theran πⱵ, κⱵ probably in the late sixth century, may have come from the Cycladic alphabet: Ψ, when it appears in Theran in the late sixth to fifth centuries, has the value of *xi*, as in Melian of the same period.

To suggest an absolute chronology for the development of the Theran alphabet is as hazardous as in the case of the Cretan, for here also, as in Crete, the controls of sculpture and pottery are very rare. Much of the Theran evidence consists of names on gravestones chiefly from the cemetery outside the archaic town, on the south-west side of the near-by ridge called the Sellada (saddle), which divides the high ridge of Prophet Elias from that of Mesavouno, on which the town stood. The cemetery extended over the north side of the saddle as well; only the south grave-field has been excavated, but some few of the inscribed stones were casual finds from the north side. Some of the stones are rough stelai, with the names written vertically downwards; others are slabs, either laid flat on the ground, or furnished with three feet to make a funeral τράπεζα. Of a hundred and five graves excavated by Dragendorff on the Sellada, not one had an inscribed stone still *in situ*, although the site contained many such markers, either lying uprooted on the ground or rebuilt into much later graves. The burials were dated from the Geometric period (which in Thera apparently lasted through the seventh century)[1] to the end of the sixth century.[2] The gravestones can be divided into an earlier and a later series, the former (**3**) being written in tall, long-tailed lettering on roughly-trimmed narrow stelai, the latter (**12**) on flat slabs and trapezai in a more developed script which eventually shows χ3, ξ4; but the two types of monument must have overlapped for a long time, for we find rough stelai showing χ3 (*IG* xii. 3. 785, **12**) and the later β4 (*IG* xii. 3. 772, **12**; 775, 778), and a block or trapeza (*IG* xii. 3. 783, **3**) whose lettering looks as early as any on the stelai. A stele such as *IG* xii. 3. 771 might, from its lettering, belong to the first half of the seventh century, and the slabs 811 (= **15**) and 812 can hardly be earlier than the fifth.

The most famous of the gravestones from Thera is the one found by Ross below the Sellada, which bears certainly nine, possibly ten names (**5**). It is a large flat slab of

[1] *MuZ* i. 84; Buschor, *Griech. Vasen* (1940), 53 f.  [2] Cf. *Thera* ii. 236.

volcanic stone, with three words occupying the centre of the upper face: Ρ̄εκσανο̄ρ |
ΑρκͰαγετας | Προκλης. Two more names are crowded in near the edge of this face, and
five more on three of the low vertical sides of the slab. It has been suggested that Ἀρχαγέτας may not be a proper name but a title belonging to either Rhexanor or Prokles,
signifying King, or, possibly, Leader of a group of Orgeones or the like, who had the right
to be all buried in this plot of ground.[1] Several of the graves on the Sellada contained
a number of separate burials; Dragendorff's no. 17, for example, showed five surviving,
and an unknown number in a part of the grave which had been destroyed.[2] It is impossible
to say with certainty whether the names on **5** were all cut at the same time or not. There
are small variations in the shapes of the letters, but none of any marked significance; all
are well and carefully cut. The date might be anywhere within the second half of the
seventh century and the first half of the sixth. The only point on which we can be sure is
that three names, or two names and a title, were cut first and largest on the stone, and the
rest then added. If they were added at the same time, these men must have been acknow-
ledged subordinates; if they were added later, the smaller letters and the crowding may
mean only that the mason had no space to do better.

A little help comes from the scanty inscribed material found within the graves; it
included a plain amphora bearing the graffito Δαμαινις, which contained a little cup of
Subgeometric type (**2**), and a plain skyphos from the fill of Dragendorff's grave no. 17,
with the graffito Τερπσια ημι (**9**), which might belong to the first half of the sixth century.
Three amphorae not of Theran make, containing children's bones, bear very brief graffiti,
which might be in the script either of Thera or of some Ionic exporting state; (1) με, (2) λη,
η, πε, (3) αγλ.[3] In another cemetery, just outside the city wall on the Mesavouno, a grave
was found with the gravestone lying face downwards over the 'Opfergrube' outside; the
stone bears the names of two children whose bones were found in the grave (**6**): Νανος,
Νιϙοκας (= Νικοκράτης), and on the Ionic amphora which held the bones of one child is
the graffito Ͱιπο (**7**). The 'Opfergrube' held the remains of a Corinthian oinochoe, and
the Ionic amphora is dated tentatively in the beginning of the sixth century.[4] The name
of a child in the next grave was written on the rock: Υπερας (= Ὑπερίδας: **8**); but it
contained seven children in all, with pottery from both the seventh and the early sixth
centuries.[5] From the above, therefore, we gather the scanty information that in the early
sixth century (*a*) the open *eta* was already used in graffiti (**9**) and (*b*) the formal stone
inscriptions still retained all the characteristics of great archaism.

Everywhere on the rocky plateau of the ancient town there are casual graffiti. Their
value, great as it is, would be doubled if any had something other than the bare letter-
forms to suggest an absolute date. The personal names and remarks incised in the area
near the later gymnasium contain some inscriptions whose appearance is earlier than any
of the epitaphs (**1a**; cf. also *IG* xii. 3. 536–44); but there are no external circumstances
to offer more precise evidence for their date, and it can only be said that they may well

---

[1] For a discussion of the various views, see the
bibliography to **5**; Hiller von Gaertringen holds
that it is Prokles, ἀρχηγέτης of the royal house of
Thera, and Vollgraff that Prokles was leader of a
religious band, on the analogy of the title ἀρχαγέτας

used in Argive and other inscriptions of a later period.

[2] *Thera* ii. 28 ff.; *IG* xii. 3. 984, 987–8.

[3] *Thera* ii. 62 ff.

[4] Pfuhl, *AM* xxviii (1903), 87.

[5] Op. cit. 89 f.

be as early as the graffiti on the sherds from Hymettos (p. 69, Attica **3**). Nor are there any certain aids for dating the names of deities incised beside small cuttings for offerings in the so-called 'holy area', the plateau between the later temple of Karneios and the great retaining wall built at the southern edge of this plateau (**1***b*; cf. *IG* xii. 3. 350–63); it is true that some of the graffiti are written under the presumed floor-level of a small building with polygonal walls whose foundations still remain on the plateau, and are therefore, by inference, older than the building; but as the latter itself is undated within the archaic period,[1] this is of very little help. The numerous personal names written (often in pairs, enclosed within an incised frame) on the face of the rock or on stones all over the site illustrate two particular characteristics of the archaic Theran script: the habit of making a kind of ligature with *mu* or *nu* and a following vowel, and of elaborately curling the ends of *iota* and *kappa* (**1***a*; *IG* xii. 3. 548, 552, 582, suppl. 1435, 1448, 1463). These inscriptions all bear a general resemblance to each other, and may therefore all fall within a comparatively short period, illustrating a passing fashion. Ligatures appear also in **10** (μα) and **3** (*IG* xii. 3. 781: λη).

The Theran script, unlike that of more distant Crete, had lost all its peculiar characteristics before the middle of the fifth century, according to the *stoichedon* inscription of Agloteles (**16**), which by its general appearance can hardly be earlier than *c.* 480–450; indeed, it had apparently lost them earlier than *c.* 480, according to the lettering of the sacral law inscribed *boustrophedon* on a fluted column from the Agora (**14**). The surface of the flutes is so badly damaged that many of the letter-forms are uncertain, but it is evidently earlier than **16**, using ρι and punctuation 5. It might be set tentatively *c.* 500; the use of *boustrophedon* here may be due to religious conservatism (see Attica **44**), but we have no evidence to show exactly how long its normal usage lasted in Thera, since the earlier inscriptions rarely have occasion for a proper second line. Nor can we trace with any precision the development of individual letters. χ3 and φ3 appeared comparatively early, while the archaic script was still in full force otherwise (**10**, **11**); ρ4 occurs with *san* on a stone weight (**13**), whereas ρι and *sigma* appear together in **14**; γ3 first appears in **14**, and (with ξ4 and ρ4) on the gravestone of Alexagoras (**15**), which is perhaps of about the same date as **16**; ⸀5 occurs with the local *iota* and *san* on a gravestone (*IG* xii. 3. 768; Peek i. 1529).

The inscriptions cut inside a cave near Vari in Attica by Archedemos of Thera (**17**) are dated tentatively in the second half of the fifth century. They are not in Attic, and therefore presumably are in Archedemos' native script; but it is no longer the 'primitive' alphabet. ξ3 is used, and both tailed and tailless *rho*.

Kyrene in Libya was founded from Thera *c.* 630, perhaps with Lakonian settlers also; a later renewal in the sixth century brought additional settlers from the Aegean islands, notably from Lindos in Rhodes.[2] Her script is attested by a few graffiti on vases, and two inscriptions on stone; and from these it is almost certain that she used the script of Thera. The earliest example is the fragmentary block from Olympia inscribed Ϙυρα— (**18**). This may be connected with some dedication in the archaic treasury of Kyrene (Paus. vi. 19. 10). It cannot be ascribed to the treasury itself, for, according to the excavators, it is

---

[1] *Thera* i. 283 f.          [2] Hdt. iv. 145 ff.; cf. Paus. iii. 14. 3 and the Lindian Chronicle, c. 17.

not an architectural block. The next example, from the Apollonion at Kyrene, is a graffito of the early sixth century incised on a painted clay plate: το Απολλōνος εμι (**19**), showing the archaic Theran *iota* and *san*. The next, a dedication on a stele in the Apollonion by Aiglanor son of Antipatros (**20**), resembles the Theran sacral text **14** in general appearance, but shows γι, and *eta* as ε3: Αιγλανōρ μ' ανεθε̄κε | ┣όντιπατρο δεκαταν. Several graffiti on fragments of pottery dedicated to Apollo appear to be of about the same date (**21**): το Απολλōνος, and the like.

The inscribed coinage of Kyrene (**22**) starts in the late archaic period, with the silphion plant always prominent and, on one series, *kappa* on the reverse. During the fifth century the legend expands to Κυρα. Evidently the letter *qoppa* was already obsolete when the inscribed series began. See also Addenda.

### MELOS

The script of Melos presents several interesting features. As would be expected, it is clearly of the same general type as Cretan and Theran, showing (in contrast with its Ionic neighbours) ι2, μι–2, *san*, ξι, and π┣, κ┣ for *phi, chi*. All these are illustrated in the earliest inscription from Melos (**23**), the dedication on a fluted marble column-shaft now in Berlin, which was found somewhere on the island in the eighteenth century. The deity, called the child of Zeus, is thought to be Athena, since other, later inscriptions attest a cult of her on Melos (*IG* xii. 3. 1077, 1081). The dedicator should be Ekphantos, on whose behalf she is asked to receive the acceptable offering; then follows: σοι γαρ επευκ┣ομενος τουτ' ετελεσσε Γροπ┣ōν, 'for Grophon (?) made this vow to you and fulfilled it'. Perhaps Ekphantos began the work on the dedication, but died before he could complete it, and Grophon thereupon vowed to finish it in his name. Other explanations have been offered, but none is satisfactory. The simplest would be to take εκφαντōι as a vocative epithet, and Grophon as dedicator and perhaps maker, according to the interpretation of ἐτέλεσσε; but the name or epithet 'Εκφαντώ is otherwise unknown. Another theory takes Ekphantos as maker and dedicator, who accomplished it γρόφων (γράφων). But γράφειν should mean only to paint, write, or incise, and the lost capital of the column must have held sculpture of some kind: γράφων could refer only to the cutting of the inscription, which seems unlikely. Moreover, the word appears again in an inscription of about the same date from Olympia, which also concerns Melians (**29**); and here it is hard indeed not to accept it as a sculptor's name: Θρασυμαχο παιδες το Μαλιο [- - -]μ̣ε α̣[νεθεν - - -] | τōι Δι, Δαιαλκος και [- - -?νικασαντ]ες *vac.* | Γροφōν εποιε Μαλιος κἀγ[- - -].[1] The script of this dedication is not Melian, nor Elean. It corresponds to that used in Thera in the late archaic period, after the loss of the local script (e.g. **16**). Again we are reduced to conjecture. Can Grophon and the sons of Thrasymachos have gone from the one Doric island to the other, and adopted the script of their new home?

The date of **23** should not be earlier than the last quarter of the sixth century, from the forms of η5 and υ3. The typical Melian β5 and reversed γ4 may also be noted. This is as yet the only Melian inscription which shows crooked *iota* and the lack of the

---

[1] In this restoration I have moved the floater (with the lines [- - -]μ̣ε α̣[- - - | - - -]ες *vacat*) one flute upwards, to continue ll. 1 and 2 instead of ll. 2 and 3.

complementary signs after *upsilon*. Nearly all the rest of the evidence comes from the well-known series of Melian gravestones. Most of these were found at various times in the grave-fields at Trypete and Klimatovouni, not far from the ancient town. They are all small, narrow stelai of the local reddish trachyte, the top cut to form an obtuse angle like a pediment, with the name (in the nominative) and patronymic of the dead below. Nearly all were found built into houses in the village of Trypete, and only one was connected with the contents of any particular grave. This was **25g**, said by the owners to have come from a family cave-tomb, which also contained the red-figured neck-amphora *ARV* 852, no. 6 (Suessula painter, late years of fifth century to early fourth). Since it was a family tomb, there may be a good many years between the stele and the vase. But probably none of these stelai antedates the fifth century. They all show large, neat, squared letters between deep guide-lines (from two to five letters in each line, usually *stoichedon*). There is a steady development in the letter-forms used, which may be plotted in their relative sequence despite the lack of absolute dates. All show straight *iota* and tailless *epsilon*; for *xi* the earlier have ξ4 (as at Thera), the later ξ3; for *chi* and *phi* all have the normal Ionic forms. Both η1 (*IG* xii. 3. 1183) and η5 occur (*IG* xii. 3. 1076, a dedication). The most distinctive feature, which persists through the series, is the use of a half-circle for *omikron* and full circle for *omega*, forms used also in Knidos (pp. 346, 351). The dedication of Ekphantos (**23**) does not show this difference. Melos had a colony Kryassos in Caria, not too far from the Knidian peninsula; but we know nothing of this colony's script.

According to the usual criteria, the earliest of the series should be those showing α1–2, μ1, ξ4; e.g. **25** *a, b, c*, which show also ρ1–2 and 4. Ionic ξ2–3 came in while *san* was still in use (**25d**), and *san* presumably changed to *sigma* when *mu* lost its fifth stroke. **25e** shows μ3 with the local forms of *beta* and *gamma*. ο5 remains throughout. It is usually held that this series ended in 416, when the Athenians sacked the city and killed or exiled the population. The surviving Melians returned after 403, and then—presumably—began the series of gravestones of this type in Ionic script, e.g. *IG* xii. 3. 1177, 1185.

The earliest inscribed coins of Melos (amphora/cross in incuse) have been dated in the second quarter of the fifth century, being followed closely by the first of the series with the canting device of an apple for obverse (*c.* 470?).[1] The amphora-series has the legend Μαλι with ι3, λ2, μ1. The latest of the series with apple/cross in incuse is dated tentatively *c.* 450, and on one die at least of this series *mu* is now 3. The subsequent remarkable series of Melian coins, nearly all known only from a single hoard and showing thirty-one different reverse types, has not yet been satisfactorily dated. The legends are Μαλιον (μ2 or 3, ν2, ο5), Μαλιων (μ3, ω2). Numismatists suggest that all were struck within a fairly short period, for the total number of different dies used for the apple obverse is surprisingly small.[2] Coins sharing the same obverse die show on their reverses now μ2, now μ3: α1 and 3: both Μαλιον and Μαλιων. If all the coins are indeed close in date, then

---

[1] I owe these dates, and much helpful information on the coin-series, to E. S. G. Robinson.

[2] I owe all my information on the die-sequences here to C. M. Kraay. I have not followed the view of Milne (*Num. Notes and Monographs*, 1934), who would set the whole series in the last quarter of the 5th c., not long before the fall of Melos in 416; a date so late, and within so very short a span, seems to me incompatible with the appearance of the letters, and of some of the types.

the series should belong to the transitional period of the Melian alphabet. The only reverse clearly datable by style (head of youth wearing a pilos, legend ΜΑΛΙΟΝ) has been set *c.* 440,[1] which gives a rough estimate of about ten years (*c.* 450–440) for the whole series. If this date is right, it is difficult not to connect this great activity of the Melian mint with the Athenian Coinage Decree *c.* 449/8; perhaps in forbidding the Allies to coin in silver any more, it gave Melos a chance to exploit her independence.

One other inscription which is not in Melian script may be noted here. This is on an intaglio gem of the seventh century showing the suicide of Ajax, which (Miss Richter has suggested)[2] may be of Melian make, as other similar gems are known to be. The retrograde legend ⱶαⱶιϝας (= Αιϝας) is certainly not in Melian script—nor Corinthian, though the gem is said to have been found at Perachora. Open *heta* with sloping bar is typical of the Etruscan script, at least from the late archaic period onwards, and the abnormal version of the name also looks Etruscan—though why it should have been added to the gem so much later, I do not know; but certainly open *heta* would be remarkable in the seventh century. (See also Addenda.)

## ANAPHE, SIKINOS

The archaic script of Anaphe is attested by one very early gravestone, a flat slab (gravetable?) bearing the inscription on one of its vertical sides (**26**): Αγϙυλιōν τονδε τον θōϙον εποιε[- - -]; whence it is plain that her script was like the Theran. The dialect and script of Sikinos were both unknown until 1931, when an archaic epitaph (**27**) was found, written retrograde round the vertical sides of a flat, broken tombstone. The dialect is Doric, and the script, which has the wavering *ductus* of the seventh century, corresponds closely with Cretan:

Αντιδο[τος μεν τυμβον εχō|σ' αυτο]ς και παιδες
Πα|σιδιϙōι· το δε σαμ' Ευνο||[ο]ς εστασ[ε] καλōν κεχαρ|ισμενον εργōν.

The fifth line continues *boustrophedon* from the fourth, on the last face of the stone, and the most notable letter is the χ2, written for *chi* in κεχαρισμενον; it will be recalled that a similar letter occurs twice in Crete, in the Eteocretan inscriptions of Praisos and Dreros. The letter does not belong to the Greek alphabet, and I have suggested elsewhere that it may be the same as the very similar one in the non-Greek script of Phrygia and Lemnos, though the latter is usually transliterated as *z*.[3] A second inscription found on Sikinos is evidently later, for it is cut in two lines from left to right, with η5 (**28**): [ὁ δεῖνα λυκ?]ηιον επο[ιε?] | [- - -]ησαν.[4]

[1] Jacobsthal, *Die melischen Reliefs* (1931), 154, fig. 32.

[2] *AGA*, 31; *MMNYC Engraved Gems* (1956), no. 13, pl. 3.

[3] *Kretika Chronika* iii (1949), 143 ff.; cf. pp. 39 f.

[4] The restoration [λυκ]ηιον is suggested as a possible alternative spelling for the normal form λύκειον (cf. *Milet* i. 7. 282, Λυκηος for Λυκειος). For other examples of dedications of λύκεια (at Thera and Delphi), cf. *IG* xii. 3. 389 and xii, suppl., p. 86.

## SELECT CATALOGUE

### THERA

**1.** (*a*) Graffiti names and remarks incised on a rock plateau near the later gymnasium; end of 8th c. onwards? *IG* xii. 3. 536–7, 540, 543, 573, 767. Roehl³, 2. 6–7. *DGE* 214 (1, 2, 4). Buck 109.
(*b*) Graffiti names of deities beside niches in the plateau between the temple of Apollo Karneios and the Retaining Wall; same date? *IG* xii. 3. 350, 357, suppl., 1313. PL. 61

**2.** Graffito on an amphora from a child's burial; *c.* 700–650? *IG* xii. 3. 986. Blegen, *AJA* xxxviii (1934), 27, n. 6. Thera Mus. PL. 61

**3.** Rough stelai from Sellada cemetery; 7th c.? *IG* xii. 3. 765, 771, 781, 802. Roehl³, 1. 3. *DGE* 215 (4). *IG* xii. 3. 783 (table). Thera Mus. PL. 61

**4.** Grave-stele of Praxilas; end of 7th c.? *IG* xii. 3. 763. Roehl³, 3. 11. *DGE* 215 (2). *SEG* ii. 499. *IG* xii, suppl., p. 89, no. 763. Thera Mus.

**5.** Gravestone of Rhexanor and others, from the Sellada; *c.* 600? *IG* xii. 3. 762. Roehl³, 1. 1. *DGE* 215 (1). Hiller von Gaertringen, *JdI* xlvii (1932), 127 ff., fig. 1. *IG* xii, suppl., pp. 89, 762. Vollgraff, *L'Inhumation en terre sacrée* (1941), 18 f. *SEG* xiv. 522. Buck 110. EM. PL. 61

**6.** Gravestone of Nikokas and Nanos from Mesavouno cemetery; early 6th c. Pfuhl, *AM* xxviii (1903), 86 f., fig. 15. *IG* xii. 3, suppl. 1609. Thera Mus. PL. 61

**7.** Graffito Ϝιπο on an amphora from same grave; early 6th c. Pfuhl, op. cit., Beil. 23. 6. Thera Mus.

**8.** Grave of Hyperas and others from same cemetery; early 6th c. Pfuhl, op. cit. 87 f., fig. 16. *IG* xii. 3, suppl. 1610. Thera Mus.

**9.** Graffito of Terpsias on Ionic cup, Sellada cemetery; first half of 6th c.? *IG* xii. 3. 990. Roehl³, 5. 27. Thera Mus. PL. 61

**10.** Stone lifted by Eumastas, from S. side of Prophet Elias; 6th c.? *IG* xii. 3. 449. Roehl³, 5. 26. *SGDI* 4735. *DGE* 217. Friedlaender 56. Thera Mus.

**11.** Gravestone of Philotima, found near Perissa; *c.* 550? *IG* xii. 3. 805. Roehl³, 5. 25. Thera Mus.

**12.** Flat gravestones and tables from the Sellada; *c.* 550–500? *IG* xii. 3. 772, 776–7, 779, 780, 789, 807. Roehl³, 1 ff. 2, 5, 17, 22, 24. *DGE* 215 (1–2). *IG* xii. 3. 785 (stele). Thera Mus. PL. 61

**13.** Stone weight; end of 6th c.? *IG* xii. 3, suppl. 1638. *SGDI* iv, p. 798. *DGE* 218. Thera Mus.

**14.** Shaft of Doric column bearing remains of a sacral text from the Agora; *c.* 500? *IG* xii. 3. 450. Prott-Ziehen, *Leges Graecae Sacrae* i (1896), 19. *SGDI* 4736. Herzog, *Heilige Gesetze*, 9. *IG* xii, suppl., pp. 87, 450. Once in Megalochorio; lost?

**15.** Gravestone of Alexagoras, from the Sellada; *c.* 480–450? *IG* xii. 3. 811. Roehl³, 5. 21. Thera Mus. PL. 62

**16.** Inscription of Agloteles concerning the Karneia, cut in the rock; *c.* 480–450? *IG* xii. 3, suppl. 1324. Roehl³, 6. 29. *SGDI* iv, p. 794. *DGE* 219. Friedlaender 176. Buck 111. PL. 62

**17.** Inscriptions by Archedemos in a cave near Vari (Attica); *c.* 450–400? Thallon and Hill, *AJA* vii (1903), 289 ff. *IG* i². 778, 784–8.

## KYRENE

**18.** Dedication on a block at Olympia; 6th c.? *Ol.* v. 246. *IGA* 506a. Roberts i, p. 321. *SGDI* 4838. Roehl³, 7. 30. *DGE* 229. Chamoux, *Cyrène* (1953), 379. Olympia Mus. 853.       PL. 62

**19.** Dedication to Apollo on a Rhodian (?) clay plate from Kyrene; early 6th c. Oliverio, *Cirenaica* ii (1936), 267, fig. 106. *SEG* ix. 313. Kyrene Mus.       PL. 62

**20.** Dedication of Aiglanor on a stele from Kyrene; early 5th c. Oliverio, *Africa Italiana* i (1927), 156 f., fig. 24. *SEG* ix. 78. Chamoux, op. cit. 264, n. 1. Kyrene Mus.       PL. 62

**21.** Graffiti to Apollo on pottery fragments from Kyrene; first half of 5th c. Oliverio, op. cit. iii (1930), 220 ff., figs. 81–90 and *Cirenaica* ii. 267, fig. 107. *SEG* ix. 302–15. Chamoux, loc. cit. Kyrene Mus.

**22.** Inscribed coinage with K, Κυρα; end of 6th c. onwards. *HN*², 866 f. B ii. 3. 1058 ff., pl. 263.

## MELOS

**23.** Dedication of Ekphantos on an Ionic column-shaft from Melos; late 6th c. *IGA* 412. *IGB* 5. *IG* xii. 3. 1075. Roberts i. 7. *SGDI* 4871. Roehl³, 14. 1. Kern, pl. 4. *DGE* 207. *SEG* iii. 738. Pontani, *Riv. Fil.* lxv (1937), 50 ff. *IG* xii, suppl., pp. 91, 211. Harder, *Neue Beiträge zur klass. Alt.* (ed. Lullies, 1954), 198 ff., pl. 44. Friedlaender 114. Buck 114. *SEG* xiv. 523. Berlin Mus. 1485.       PL. 62

**24.** Inscribed coinage of Melos; c. 475–416? *HN*², 486, 492. B ii. 1, 1317 ff., pl. 62. Milne, *Num. Notes and Monographs* 1934.

**25.** Melian gravestones; *c.* 480–416? (*a*) J. M. Cook, *JHS* lxvi (1946), 116, fig. 6. (*b*) *IG* xii. 3. 1139. (*c*) Ibid. 3. 1149. (*d*) Ibid. 3. 1151. (*e*) Ibid. 3. 1153. (*f*) Ibid. 3. 1143. (*g*) Ibid. 3. 1147. Cf. also *SGDI* 4889, *DGE* 210 (1).       PL. 62

## ANAPHE

**26.** Gravestone erected by Ankylion; early 7th c.? *IG* xii. 3. 255. Roehl³, 7. *DGE* 238.? In church of Christ, village of Ant. Sigalas.       PL. 62

## SIKINOS

**27.** Gravestone erected for Pasidikos; 7th c.? Keramopoullos, Πρακτ. Ἀκαδ. Ἀθην. 1931, 457 ff., figs. 1–5; 1932, 84 f. Hiller von Gaertringen, *Ph.W.* 1932, 1021 ff. *IG* xii, suppl., p. 100, 178. Friedlaender 162. Peek i. 1739. Schoolhouse Coll.       PL. 62

**28.** Inscribed fragment; late 6th c.? *IG* xii. 5. 25. Hiller von Gaertringen, loc. cit. *IG* xii, suppl., *ad* 178. Schoolhouse Coll.

*Inscription attributed to Thera or Melos*

**29.** Dedication of Daialkos and others at Olympia; *c.* 525–500? *IGA* 12. *Ol.* v. 272. *SGDI* 4872. Roehl³, 122. 3. *DGE* 209. Olympia Mus. 405+978.       PL. 62

# THE EASTERN GREEKS

## THE IONIC DODEKAPOLIS

| α | β | γ | δ | ε | F | ʒ | η | ⊦ | θ | ι | κ | λ | μ | ν | ξ | ο | π | Μ | ϙ | ρ | σ | τ | υ | φ | χ | ψ | ω | | P |
|---|---|---|---|---|---|---|---|---|---|---|---|---|---|---|---|---|---|---|---|---|---|---|---|---|---|---|---|---|---|
| 1 A, B, Γ Δ Ɛ – I B – ⊗, I Κ Γ Μ Ν Ξ Ο Γ – ϙ Ρ ₹ Τ Φ Χ Ψ ꔷ Ⲧ : 1 |
| 2 A B ( Λ H ⊕ Κ Λ Μ, Ν Ξ Ρ ₴ V Φ + Ψ ꔷ : 2 |
| 3 A Ɛ ⊙ Λ Μ Ν Ρ ₴ Υ Φ Ω ⸭ 3 |
| 4 E Μ Ν Ρ Υ Ω ∴ 4 |
| 5 Ω 5 |
| 6 Ω 6 |

FIG. 46. The Ionic Dodekapolis

*Notes on letter-forms*

γ2 occurs once, *c.* 550–540 (Samos **7**).

Tilted ε2 is common in early Ionic (**4, 23, 53**); ε3 is already in use *c.* 550 (**27**), ε4 by the early 5th c.

η2 was in use at Samos *c.* 570–560 (**4**), and at Ephesos by the middle of the 6th c. (**53**); η1 seems to have lasted till *c.* 550 at Miletos (η1 **27**, η2 **29**). η2 is already used in a Teian's graffito *c.* 591 (**58**).

θ3 occurs on stone in Aiakes' dedication **13**, *c.* 525–520? and in Milesian at about the same time or a little later (**33**); it was evidently regular by the 5th c. It was used rather earlier (*c.* 540–525?) in the painted vase-inscription **63**.

λ2, and even λ3 occasionally, is used in 'cursive' lettering before 550 (**4–6, 41**); the earliest λ3 in a well-cut stone inscription seems to be **13**.

μι is attested occasionally in the 6th c. (**7**), and allegedly in the 5th c. (Teos **62**); but the normal archaic type is the sprawling, almost tailless μ2–3 (**4**). μ4 is normal by *c.* 480 (**17**), and in graffito writing considerably earlier.

ν1 occurs in the 7th c. (**1**) and rarely in the 6th c. (**53**), ν2 is the normal form through the 6th c. ν4, used in Attica after the middle of the 5th c., appears in Ionic some years earlier (**21, 46, 48**).

ξ2 is attested in various cities in the 6th (rarely) and 5th c.: Samos (**20**), Teos (**59**), Chios (**48**), Miletos (**26**); and also in the Ionic of the Aegean and elsewhere, pp. 290, 346, 369.

*Qoppa* was apparently used in Ionic until about the middle of the 6th c., possibly later (Miletos **31**; Ephesos **53**).

ρ2 is frequent in the 6th c. (**4, 23, 41**). ρ4 is attested only on **54** (Ephesos, mid-6th c.?).

σ1 is normal; but σ2 occurs also in the early inscriptions: Kolophon (**56**), Teos (**58**), both from Abou Simbel. The untidy, curved σ3 is fairly common in the 7th–6th c. (**1, 22, 34, 53**).

υ2 appears already in the second quarter of the 6th c. (**4, 41**); υ3, common in the 5th c., occurs in the 6th c. at Ephesos (**53**), Samos (**10**), Miletos (**33**). υ4 occurs in the 5th c. (**19**, *c.* 470).

φ1 is 7th c. (**1**), and occurs throughout the 6th c., though φ2 is also used. φ3, with flattened circle, appears before the middle of the 5th c. (**19, 21, 48**).

ω is normal in Ionic, but for some reason lacking in the earliest inscription from Kolophon, **56** (see p. 340). The earliest examples are tilted (**2, 22, 41**); the curled ω4, starting in graffiti as early as the 7th c. (**69**), descends into the 5th c. (**17, 46**). ω5 occurs on **48**, and is normal in the second half of the 5th c. For the 'flattened' ω6, see (e.g.) pp. 302–3, **71, 74–76**, and p. 371, **33**.

The '*sampi*' Ⲧ occurs in the 6th and 5th c., at Ephesos (**53**), Erythrai (**52**), Teos (**62**), but not as yet at Miletos, although her colonies evidently used it (cf. pp. 38 f., 368).

*Punctuation* 1–2 occurs on **41** (*c*. 575–550?), and 1 and 3 on the plaque from Ephesos, *c*. 550 (**53**); followed by an even greater elaboration 4 (with 1) in the calendar of sacrifices at Miletos, *c*. 525–500 (**33**). 1 is fairly common in the 6th and 5th c.; 2 is less common, but is found on several of the graffiti from Naukratis, and in Milesian dedications of the second half of the 6th c. and early 5th c. (**37**).

The *boustrophedon* system does not appear to have continued beyond the middle of the 6th c. at Samos; but in Miletos it was still used in the early 5th c., at least for religious texts (**37**). The technique of inscribing both *boustrophedon* and *stoichedon* is attested at Samos (**10**) and Miletos (**34, 39**). The first example of *stoichedon* writing from l. to r. is the Samian dedication of Aiakes (**13**).

Across the Aegean from the Saronic Gulf, at the end of a route threading past the islands Tenos, Mykonos, and Ikaros to Samos, lay the twelve states which combined to celebrate the religious festival of the Panionia to Poseidon Helikonios, and claimed the common title of Ionians (Hdt. i. 142). According to their tradition they were composed of elements from Athens herself, Euboia, Boiotia (Thebes and Orchomenos), Phokis, Epidauros, Arkadia, the Achaian coast, and Dryopia (Hdt. i. 145; Strabo 632 ff.; Paus. vii. 2–3).[1] More excavation is needed in Asia Minor before it is possible to establish the dates of this great settlement and the corresponding immigrations of Aiolic peoples on the north, and Doric on the south. The work at Smyrna has shown that the Greeks were there already in the Late Protogeometric period.[2] It is obvious that these emigrations happened before the introduction of the alphabet to Greece, for none of the settlers brought any local scripts with them. Miletos did not use the alphabet of Attica, nor Chios that of Euboia, nor Kolophon, Priene, and Teos that of Boiotia, nor Phokaia that of Phokis, nor Samos that of Epidauros; all used the common alphabet which has been termed the eastern Ionic, whose peculiar hall-mark is the use of Ω for ō, and lesser characteristics the use of Ξ for ξ, X for χ, Ψ for ψ and H for η only.

It is usually assumed[3] that Ionia, or at least Miletos, was acquainted with this alphabet at least as early as the eighth century. If we accept the hypothesis that the Greek alphabet was born somewhere on the north Syrian coast in a settlement like that at Al Mina, Ionia may well have been one of the earliest places to receive the new art. But it is not justifiable to cite the presence of *vau* in the Ionic abecedarium as a proof of this high antiquity, on the grounds that, if F occurs in the abecedarium, it must have still been a living sound in the Ionic dialect when the alphabet was first brought to Ionia.[4] I have already argued (pp. 1 ff.) that it is not natural for illiterates, learning from an outside source an automatic mnemonic recitative and a row of letters, to reject at once the name and letter for which their dialect has no use—though they may not use the letter in practice. The dialects of Naxos and Attica normally had no use for *vau*; but the letter appears in inscriptions in Naxos (p. 289, **10**), and in Athens (p. 66, **7, 23**); and we know that it existed in the abecedarium of Amorgos also (p. 293, **23**). It is possible that

---

[1] Cf. Bilabel, *Die ionische Kolonisation* (1920), 2 f.; Roebuck, *CP* 1 (1955), 31 ff., and Addenda.

[2] J. M. Cook, *JHS* lxxii (1952), 104 ff.

[3] Larfeld[3], 241, 294; Schwyzer, 146; Bilabel, op. cit. 134. R. M. Cook sounds a note of warning (*JHS* lxvi (1946), 89): 'there must be very few specimens [of writing] from Ionia as early as the earliest from Old Greece, but this may be due to the little excavation there has been of early strata at Ionian sites.'

[4] Larfeld[3], 295.

this rare use of *vau*, perhaps confined to verse, was not unknown in Ionia also, even as late as the sixth century, and so may have provided some faint shadow of justification for the retention of the letter in the abecedarium, until it was fixed there firmly once and for all by the establishment of the so-called 'Milesian' alphabetic numeral system. Here again, as Keil has pointed out,[1] there is no evidence for assigning the invention of this system also to the eighth century, as Larfeld does. It has not been found on any pottery earlier than the second half of the sixth century,[2] and is not used *c.* 550 for the numbers quoted on the silver plaque from Ephesos (**53**). If I may repeat in part here what was said above on the letter-forms (pp. 25, 35 ff., 42), a tentative reconstruction of the early history of the Ionic alphabet is as follows. Before the end of the eighth century, southern Ionia, like Rhodes, had received an alphabet consisting of the Phoenician letters (plus *upsilon*, the doublet of *vau*). In this alphabet the *san* was never used, and so it finally dropped even from the abecedarium before the middle of the sixth century—i.e. before the invention of the 'Milesian' numeral system; but *vau* kept its seat (and so won a place in the numeral system) possibly because, though equally useless for practical purposes, it had once had a limited use in poetry. *Heta* at once became '*eta* in the psilotic speech of Ionia, and so acquired the value of *ē*. The alien signs Φ = *ph*, X = *ch* (*kh*?), Ψ = *kh* (*ch*?), Ψ = *ps*, belonging to some other writing system, attached themselves, in part or in whole, to the scripts of Ionia, Rhodes and (for all we know) the early Greek colonies in Pamphylia and Cilicia, and even Posideion (Al Mina?) herself. The doublet ◠ from ○ was evolved in Ionia; and the last alien sign, the sibilant ⊓, had been adopted into some at least of the eastern Ionic scripts by the middle of the sixth century, and so won its place (as '*sampi*') at the end of the alphabet and thus at the end of the numeral system also.

Herodotos divides the twelve states into four groups, according to the differences in dialect (i. 142); he does not tell us what these differences were, and they are not very obvious in the extant inscriptions. Perhaps the speech of the first group (Miletos, Myous, Priene) was tinged with a flavour of Carian; that of the second group (Ephesos, Kolophon, Lebedos, Teos, Klazomenai, Phokaia) with Lydian; that of the third (Chios, Erythrai) with the Aiolic Greek of their northern neighbours;[3] the purest Ionic being then that of the fourth, the island Samos.

Before discussing the various inscriptions, we may recall once more the general characteristics of eastern Ionic writing of the early sixth century, noted above (p. 57). It differs from the contemporary script of the rest of Greece, being smaller and more carelessly formed (e.g. *epsilon* and *mu*, Fig. 46). This suggests that the Ionians were familiar at an earlier period than the other Greeks with the practice of writing on leather (and later papyrus) rolls: that is, that they had developed a 'book hand' which was already influencing their inscriptions on stone in the early sixth century. It will be recalled further that Ionians were the pioneers of early prose writing, as is indeed evident in their use of prose for dedications and epitaphs during the sixth century.[4]

---

[1] *Hermes* xxix (1894), 266.
[2] The examples listed by Hackl (*Merkantile Inschriften auf attischen Vasen*, 79 ff., nos. 546–66) are all later than 550. Cf. also Amyx, *An Amphora with a Price Inscription* (1941), 190 and *Hesperia* xxvii (1958), 287 ff.
[3] Buck, 143.
[4] Cf. Rudberg, *Eranos* xl (1942), 128 ff.; Friedlaender, 8 f.

## SAMOS

We may begin with Samos for two reasons: firstly because one of the earliest existing eastern Ionic inscriptions was found in the Samian Heraion, and secondly because the sequence of archaic inscribed statues which were dedicated there has already been carefully studied and dated, whereas that of the similar Milesian series still awaits a comprehensive publication. (See now Addenda.)

The earliest Samian inscription is the fragment of a metrical dedication, or record of a private gift, incised on a sherd from the rim of a dinos described as 'Rhodian', of seventh-century type, found at the Heraion (**1**):[1] [- - - με]γαλης αντι φιλημ[οσυνης]; we may note the tall, carefully-written letters of the seventh century, which in the first half of the sixth century are replaced by a smaller, hastier, more cursive style. The earliest Samian inscription on stone should be, from its appearance, the epitaph cut *boustrophedon* on a small marble grave-stele (**2**): Δημανδρο το | Πρωτοχαριος. It begins retrograde, and has the only other example of closed *eta* in Samian,[2] and the earliest form of *omega*, the tilted type 1 (p. 38); it should therefore belong to the first quarter of the sixth century at the latest, for by the second quarter the open *eta* was already in use (**3–6**). The inscription was discovered in the necropolis at Myli and, as far as I know, has not been found again since its first publication in facsimile by Roehl, *IGA* 383; it is interpreted by Buschor[3] as cut horizontally, and so to be read from the lower line upwards (as **8**); it is possible also, though less likely, that it was meant to be read vertically.

Some very fragmentary sherds (**3a**) were found at Naukratis bearing graffiti dedications to Hera, which must be from the separate precinct which the Pharaoh Amasis (569–526) allotted to the Samians for a Heraion (Hdt. ii. 178); all show the open *eta* and *rho* varying between 1 and 2. The legless ρ2 is characteristic of Samian, and occurs with increasing frequency on stone from the second quarter of the sixth century onwards. It may be noted in the graffito: Ροιϙος μ' ανεθηκε τη[ι Αφρ]οδιτηι on a double eye-bowl from a precinct of Aphrodite at Naukratis (**3b**), which has been assigned[4] to a Samian donor because of the name Rhoikos, famous in the history of Samian craftsmen. The date of the bowl may be in the first quarter of the sixth century.[5]

The most famous of the statues from the Heraion, the veiled Hera dedicated by Cheramyes, may be dated in the decade 570–560[6] (**4**): Χηραμυης μ' ανεθηκεν τηρηι αγαλμα. This is an excellent example of the cursive Ionic script on stone; we may note ε2, ν2, ρ2, and the hasty, indifferent use of αι–2 and μ2–3. The inscription is written up the side of the veil; for it was evidently a characteristic Ionic practice to cut the inscription on the statue itself rather than on the base—a sharp contrast with the Attic habit, in which it is very rare indeed to find the dedication anywhere but on the base.[7]

---

[1] I have not included in the catalogue the inscribed fragments *AM* liv. 64, no. 3 (fragment of a Rhodian plate, not yet fully published) and no. 4 (two very fragmentary sherds); lviii. 106, fig. 46b (part of a 7th-c. dinos, with nonsense-inscription).

[2] I am excluding that on the grave-stele **18**, which is of the early 5th c.; see p. 330.

[3] *AM* lviii (1933), 24.

[4] Prinz, *Funde von Naukratis* (1908), 118.

[5] I owe this information to R. M. Cook. Except for Samian, Chian and Teian, the graffiti in Ionic to Aphrodite cannot be assigned to definite states (*Naukratis* ii, pl. 22).

[6] Cf. Buschor, *Altsamische Standbilder*, 25 f.; *AGA*, 103: 'perhaps about 570'.

[7] The only exception of which I know is the dedication on the leg of a kouros found at Sounion (p. 73, Attica **27**).

A second offering at the Heraion by Cheramyes, once in the Berlin Museum, is now known only by record. It was a standing woman like the Louvre statue, but later in date, perhaps *c.* 550; a hexametric dedication (unpublished) was cut on the hem of the veil.[1] Fragments of a colossal kouros offered by the same man *c.* 540 were also found in the Heraion; see **7** below.

The kouros dedicated by Leukios to Apollo, from an unknown Samian sanctuary which may be that mentioned by Pausanias (ii. 31. 6), is also dated *c.* 575–550,[2] and it is significant that the two lines of the dedication run from left to right (**5**); the *boustrophedon* system is already waning. A third dedication, somewhat later than the Hera of Cheramyes but still within the first half of the sixth century, is the group—or, to be more accurate, the line of figures—made by Geneleos in the Heraion. The long base, which still survives, lay along the right-hand side of the path leading to the temple, and carried at one end a seated female figure, at the other a recumbent one, and between them four standing figures, only one of which now survives. The dedication[3] (cut on the mattress beneath the recumbent figure) and the sculptor's signature (in two lines on the cloak or veil of the seated figure) are both written retrograde, which was natural in view of the position of the group beside the path; while the names of Phileia and Philippe (seated and standing) read from left to right and retrograde respectively (**6**). We may note the doubled consonant in Φιλιππη, which was not used in **5** (Απολωνι). The lettering of **6** moreover is slightly neater and taller, showing the start of a change for the better in the Ionic style of lettering which develops slowly through the second half of the sixth century, and which is exemplified by **7**: [Χηρα]μυης μ' ανεθη[κε θεηι περικαλλ]ες αγαλμα on the leg of a colossal kouros from the Heraion, dated in the third quarter of the century, *c.* 540.[4]

At this point the dating of the remaining archaic material becomes more difficult. Among the numerous grave-stelai of the sixth and fifth centuries which were studied as a series by Buschor,[5] several were inscribed, usually only with the name of the dead person (**8–12, 14, 18**); of these, **10** was dated by Buschor in the first half of the sixth century chiefly because the text is *boustrophedon*, **9, 11, 12, 14** in the third quarter, **8** tentatively in the late archaic period without a closer dating, and **18** in the early fifth century. **10** (of which the shaft only survives) cannot, I think, be equated epigraphically with **3–5**. Its tall, neat letters have more in common with **6**; its *upsilon* is υ3, which is, generally speaking, a later development than υ2; and it is *stoichedon* as well as *boustrophedon*, like the altar of Hekate at Miletos (**34**), which certainly is not earlier than the late sixth century. I should not therefore set **10** earlier than the third quarter of the century, at the highest. The lettering of **9** and **11**, which still possess each its crowning anthemion, fits well with Buschor's dating of the latter decorations in the time of Polykrates, but **14** (again a shaft only) looks remarkably advanced for a date in the same period, as Buschor

---

[1] Buschor, *Neue Beiträge* (ed. Lullies, 1954), 97 f.
[2] Buschor, *Altsam. Standbilder*, 17 f.; *AGA*, 105.
[3] This inscription, which is barely legible, was read by the excavators as [· ·]οχη ειμι [:η] κ' ανεθηκε τηι Ηρηι (Buschor, op. cit. 28 and fig. 101). I studied it in 1947 in Tigani Museum, and read it as: [· · ·]ναρχη ημεας

ανεθηκε τηι Ηρηι. The group is dated *c.* 560 by Richter, *AGA*, 104.
[4] Karouzos, *Epitumbion Tsounta* (1941), 539; Buschor, op. cit. 12 and *Neue Beiträge*, 97 ff.
[5] *AM* lviii (1933), 22 ff.

has suggested. **8**, on the other hand, which reads *boustrophedon* from bottom line to top, has more the small, straggling appearance of the earlier inscriptions.[1] It will be recalled that none of these can be certainly assigned to any particular grave, so that, in cases where the crowning anthemion has been lost, the chief criterion must be the letter-forms. **18**, as Buschor observes, must belong to the early fifth century; that is to say, perhaps to the second quarter rather than the first, if we compare the lettering with that of Euthymos' dedication at Olympia (**19**); the anomalous η1 which occurs in the second line of **18**, just before η2, is perhaps an *epsilon* corrected to η2.

The period *c.* 500–475 is represented by the base at Delphi inscribed Σαμιοι τὠπόλλωνι (**17**). It has been ascribed to the year 500/499,[2] but might equally well be an offering after the battle of Mykale, *c.* 479; the curled ω4 may be compared with that on the coins of Kos in the first quarter of the fifth century (p. 352). Here should belong also the fine base **16**, which originally held the marble grave-statue of a Samian, Aischros son of Zoilos, in the Kerameikos at Athens; destroyed by the Persians in 480–479, it was among those bases and fragments used by Themistokles in the rebuilding of the near-by stretch of the city wall, across the modern Odos Erysichthonos. The base was still in excellent condition when it went into the wall, and probably belongs to the decade 490–480. At the upper end of the period, *c.* 500, is the little bronze hare dedicated to Apollo Prie(n)eus by Hephaistion (**15**). Though it was bought in Samos, this bronze may well have come from Priene, in view of the dedication; πριηληι (*sic*) is almost certainly an error for πριηνηι, with the last chisel-stroke of *nu* omitted. *Omega* has not yet settled into the schematized ω3, but *theta* is already 3. The same *theta* is used in a more famous dedication, the *stoichedon* inscription on the seated statue of Hera offered by Aeakes (*sic*) son of Brychon (Bryson?) during his office as ἐπιστάτης of Hera's property (**13**). The inscription has been dated by most authorities *c.* 540, in the belief that this was the father of Polykrates;[3] but others, notably Schede and Pomtow, have sought to lower the date to *c.* 500–490, and attributed it to an otherwise unknown cousin of Aiakes II, son of Syloson, or even to Aiakes II himself.[4] If it belongs to Polykrates' family at all, the dates to which it can be assigned are necessarily limited, owing to the intermittent nature of their power. Aiakes the father could hardly have held the office of ἐπιστάτης after his son's assassination *c.* 520, even were he alive then; and in my own view the nearest connexion epigraphically with Aiakes' inscription is the round altar at Miletos (**34**), which has been dated by its moulding not long before 494 (p. 335). Yet to suggest, as Pomtow did, that Aiakes II made this dedication anew in his grandfather's name is very lame, and Buschor's authority in setting the date of the statue *c.* 540 cannot be lightly dismissed. I should like to think myself that it does belong to Aiakes I, but that it was dedicated during the years of Polykrates' tyranny, perhaps *c.* 525–520 (since the date of Aiakes' death is not actually known); for, clumsy though the figure is, the naturalistic treatment of the legs shown through the fine linen chiton recalls the latest of the seated figures from Didyma,

---

[1] The text reads apparently: Γορδιαμο τ[ο] Νηλω (*sic*) εμι; when I studied it at Tigani in 1947, the initial *gamma* was visible, but I could make very little of the three letters between *tau* and *lambda*.

[2] Pomtow, *SIG*³ 20.

[3] Dittenberger, *SIG*³ 10; Buschor, *Altsam. Standbilder*, 40; cf. Austin, *Stoichedon Style*, 13 f., and Tod, *GHI*² 7 and p. 258.

[4] Pomtow, *SIG*³ 20; Schede, *Abh. Ak. Berlin* 1929, no. 3, 22. Cf. Lippold, *Griech. Plastik* (1950), 58.

which is generally set in the last quarter of the sixth century.[1] But such rearrangement of the existing opinions without fresh evidence is of little use, and we must await the publication of the unpublished material from Samos and Miletos, which should give more comparative material for the period. The dedication of the boxer Euthymos at Olympia (**19**), whose third victory in 472 supplies the *terminus post quem* for the inscription, offers a timely warning against the infallibility of letter-forms alone as a basis for absolute dating, for in this instance a correction to the first inscription, which was made *in rasura* over the first by a different cutter, is actually earlier in appearance than the original (cf. *epsilon, nu* in the first and in the second); the difference in age and outlook between two masons at work in one particular generation is an incalculable factor.

The reason for the alteration on this base must remain conjectural. It is clear that in the original inscription Euthymos himself did not dedicate the statue: Ευθυμος Λοκρος Αστυκλεος τρις Ολυμπι' ενικων· | εικονα δ' εστησεν—◡◡—◡◡—. | Ευθυμος Λοκρος απο Ζεφυριο. | Πυθαγορας Σαμιος εποιησεν. For some reason the original donor (the father Astykles, or the state?) did not in the end make the dedication, so Euthymos himself did; and thus another mason had to re-cut over the original donor's name the stock ending τηνδε βροτοις εσοραν in the second line, and add ανεθηκε after Euthymos' name in line 3; he forgot, however, to alter ενικων to ενικα, and so the verb εστησεν was left apparently without a subject.

A contemporary of Euthymos' dedication is the fragmentary list of names on a base-block in the Heraion (**20**), which probably recorded those Samians who were prominent in the battle of the Eurymedon. The block was re-inscribed in the Hellenistic period, and the second inscription certainly commemorates that battle, giving the chief glory to the general Maiandrios. A like memorial (**21**) was set up some years later to the Samians in the Allied fleet which captured Memphis in the opening stages of the Egyptian campaign of 460–454 (Thuc. i. 104). A series of private gravestones, bearing only the name and patronymic of the dead, extends over the fifth century, but offers few clues for any closer dating.

The above examples of the archaic Samian script show that it varied in quality, the standard on the whole being low. It was well observed by Boehlau, and emphasized by Buschor, that the inscriptions on the grave-stelai in almost all cases were so hasty and shallow that they resembled graffiti rather than formal inscriptions, in sharp contrast with the finely-worked anthemia; was it possible in some instances that the relatives of the dead had purchased a blank stele from the mason's yard, and themselves scratched the inscription?[2] Yet under Polykrates the fine arts were in high favour at Samos as well as engineering and shipbuilding, and Polykrates himself is said to have founded some kind of a library (Athen. 4)—an undertaking certainly easier for a tyrant to conceive in Samos, where commercial contact with the source of papyrus was close, than in mainland Greece or the west. But in the fifth century the standard of formal lettering was evidently high (**16–21**).

[1] Cf. Pryce, *BMC Sculpture* i. 111 f., pl. 15; Langlotz, *FGB* 105, pl. 58a. If Chares' dedication at Miletos (**29**) is correctly dated (*c.* 550–540; p. 334), Aiakes' should surely be 15–25 years later, from the difference in style.

[2] Boehlau, op. cit. 154; Buschor, *AM* lviii (1933), 25.

## MILETOS, THEBAE AD MYCALEN

Miletos was by tradition the oldest of the Ionic cities; it is actually the only one as yet which has yielded what may be a Mycenean settlement. The Mycenean sherds lay under the Hellenistic town on the peninsula, in the quarter near the temple of Athena, which was built after 494; the archaic bronzes and sherds excavated in this area were unfortunately lost or destroyed before full publication. A small Geometric settlement lay on the hill Kalabaktepe to the south, but so far the site of the archaic town itself has not been excavated.[1] For early inscriptions therefore we depend on the archaic dedications from Didyma, some scattered fragments from the area of the temple of Athena and the later bouleuterion and Delphinion, and the graffiti from the precinct of Apollo Milesios at Naukratis (**28**).[2]

Herodotos records (ii. 159) that Necho, Pharaoh of Egypt, dedicated his corslet to Apollo at Didyma after the defeat of Josiah of Judah at Megiddo *c.* 608; and it was probably from the great temple precincts of Egypt that the Ionic Greeks adopted the impressive practice of lining the Sacred Way up to the temple with a long row of dedicated statues on either side, of the same pattern if possible, like the repeated columns of a colonnade. Traces of the practice remain in the surviving fragments of kouroi and korai at the Samian Heraion, in the seated lions at Delos, and perhaps in the many kouroi, colossal or life-size, from the precinct of Poseidon at Sounion. But the seated statues and kouroi of Didyma provide our clearest picture, and it is interesting to note from the inscriptions that many of the dedications consisted not of single statues but of groups, like the six statues by Geneleos at Samos (**6**). They may be listed for convenience as follows:

**22.** Group dedicated by the sons of Orion (or Python), of which one lion survives, with an inscription on its back beginning: τα αγαλματα ταδε ανεθεσαν, κτλ.

**23.** Group dedicated by the sons of Anaximandros and made by Terpsikles, of which only part of the base survives; its length (2·1 m.) makes it certain that Terpsikles' work must have consisted of more than one figure.

**24.** Lost group dedicated by Hermesianax, of which one seated statue was seen by Gell, inscribed on the side of the chair: [Ερ]μησιαναξ ημ|εας ανεθηκεν | ο Αιγιδεω τώπ|ολλωνι.

**25.** Group by an unknown dedicator, from which remain the shoulders, hips, and a drawing of one thigh of a colossal kouros, the inscription on the thigh beginning: τοϙδε τος ανδριαντ[ας - - -] (pp. 333 f.).

**29.** Group dedicated by Chares, ruler of Teichioussa. Only the seated figure of Chares himself survives; but the *lex Molporum* of the fifth century decreed that, in their procession, the Molpoi were to pause and sing their paean παρα Χαρεω ανδριασιν among other landmarks.[3]

The other inscribed figures are that signed by Eudemos (**27**), the fragment of a

---

[1] Von Gerkan and Weickert, *Bericht ü. d. vi. Internat. Kongress Berlin* (1940), 323 ff., esp. 325 ff.; Hanfmann, *HSCP* lxi (1953), 4 f., 7 f. See also Weickert, *Istanb. Mitt.* vii (1957), 102 ff.

[2] None of these seems to be earlier than *c.* 569, from Petrie's copies.

[3] *Sb. Ak. Berlin* 1904, 619 (phot.); *SGDI* 5495; *SIG*³ 57; Milet i. 3, no. 133.

dedication by Histiaios (**32**), and a lost seated figure (**38**).[1] There is also a large bronze knucklebone which was carried off to Susa by Dareios with other spoils after the sack of Miletos, and retrieved by de Morgan in 1900 (**30**).

A good starting-point for discussion of the dedications at Didyma is the statue by Eudemos (**27**). It is apparently later in date than the seated figure of Phileia at Samos (**6**; *c.* 560); the himation is stacked in a zigzag fold, the cushion bulges between the chair-arm and seat; if the figure were standing, it might be a slightly earlier brother of the standing clothed kouros of Cape Phoneas, which came almost certainly from the Asian mainland, dated by Buschor *c.* 550–540.[2] If **27** is then dated tentatively *c.* 560–550, we may note ηι still in use then, and ε2–3; the lettering is inclined still to be small and hasty. This is of some interest, because the occurrence of the ηι in **22** was one of the factors which caused the lion of **22** to be dated in the first years of the sixth or even in the seventh century.[3] The type of this lion, which was clearly borrowed from an Egyptian model,[4] has nothing in common with the formal, stylized lions of seventh-century Greece (derived from late Hittite sources), which in their turn gave way to the ferocious chequer-maned lions of Assyrian art.[5] The Milesian lion is one of the finest examples of naturalism to be found in early Greek art, couching in meditation with front paws crossed and the weight of the relaxed body resting on one haunch, the pads of the hind foot just appearing. **22** is plainly the earliest of the Milesian series, with massive paws and raised head; the most developed example, the lion in Berlin whose head lies on his front paws, is now dated late in the sixth century.[6] The lettering of the dedication is a hasty, untidy cursive, like that on the base **23** by Terpsikles; *epsilon* droops slightly but not noticeably, *omega* is inclined to tilt (as far as can be seen), and in **23** *rho* is the legless type 2. Apart from the closed *eta*, which Miletos evidently retained longer than Samos, I see no reason to place **22** and **23** any earlier than the first quarter of the sixth century. The seated statue in a lost group dedicated by Hermesianax (**24**) cannot be dated closely from the copies of the inscription; but as it included closed *eta*, it is here dated *c.* 575 *exempli gratia*.

The colossal kouros whose fragments survive (**25**) may perhaps be dated *c.* 575–550; there is little enough detail surviving, but the treatment of the hair in pointed ends recalls that of Leukios' kouros at Samos (**5**). The start of the *boustrophedon* dedication remains on the extant hip, the rest is known only from a hasty and imperfect copy by Lord Aberdeen. The tentative restoration offered by Roehl in *IGA* 487 and followed by subsequent editors seems unnecessarily elaborate: 'τους αν[δ]ριαντ[ας - - - Λα]τμιοι αν[εθε]σα[ν νεας τρεις Κερ]αμιας Δω[ρι]εων σ[υλησαντ]ε[ς], vel simile quid'; it is probably a straightforward dedication of the usual kind: τοσδε τος ανδριαντ[ας οι - - - | - - - ]τ[ο] υιοι αν[εθε]σαν παντας, Δωμεων (?), Σ[- - - | - - - τὠπολωνι δεκατ]ην. The closed *eta* is not likely to have persisted long after 550; the latest occurrence seems to be that on

[1] See now Addenda.

[2] *Altsam. Standbilder*, 46; dated earlier, before the mid-6th c., by *AGA*, 105.

[3] *SGDI* 5504; *DGE* 723; *BMC Sculpture* i. 112 f.

[4] Loewy, *Ö.Jh.* xiv (1911), 1 ff. I cannot agree with Schröder (in *Brunn-Bruckmann*, *Denkmäler*, pls. 641–5, text p. 11) that a Milesian artist developed the type independently.

[5] Payne, *NC*, 67 ff.

[6] Wiegand, *Berliner Museen* xlviii (1927), 61 ff. (dated there as early 6th c.; for the more recent dating late in the 6th c., cf. Richter, *Animals in Greek Sculpture*, 5 f., 48 and *AGA*, 170; Gerke, *Griech. Plastik* (1938), 214; Weickert, *Griech. Plastik* (1946), 29 f.).

a marble disk from Miletos (**35**), which, from its developed ε5, ν3, should be fairly late in the century. Another attribution to the second quarter of the sixth century is the inscription on the fragmentary female statue **26** found near the bouleuterion of the Hellenistic town; its original position is unknown, but it was perhaps one of a group which had the names incised on the figures, as in Geneleos' group **6**. ξ2, though common in graffiti in the sixth century, is rare on stone at that date (p. 325). Anaximandros was a fairly common name in Ionia, so that we cannot be sure that this donor was either the man whose sons made the dedication **23**, or the philosopher of that name.[1]

Apart from a dedication to Athena, possibly early but only published as yet in a preliminary report,[2] the first inscription to show open *eta* (with tilted *omega*) is the dedication of Chares (**29**). The treatment of the drapery here shows some advance on that of Eudemos' statue, and Chares' has been placed in the second half of the sixth century, *c.* 550–540.[3] The doubled consonant is now used (Απολλωνι); but λ is still 1; the '*sampi*' is not used in Τειχιοσης (p. 325). The bronze knucklebone-weight from Susa (**30**) was apparently one of a set, according to the opening words of the dedication: ταδε τἀγαλματ' απο λειο Αριστολοχ[ος, . . . . | . .], Θρασων ανεθεσαν τ[ὡ]|πολλωνι δεκατην· εχε[ε] δ' αυτα Ιτσικλης (*sic*) ο Κυδιμανδ[ρο]. It has been dated in the last years of the sixth century,[4] but, though the faint and careless lettering makes judgement uncertain, I think that it belongs rather to the earlier period, *c.* 550–525: it shows tailed *epsilon* throughout, ω is 1 or 2.

The lost fragment of a dedication by Histiaios (**32**) is generally assigned to the Milesian tyrant of that name, and, as far as can be deduced from Newton's copy, it shows an advance in the style of lettering from those inscriptions previously discussed: λ2, ω2. A date in the last quarter of the sixth century would suit the career of Histiaios, perhaps before his enforced sojourn with Dareios at Susa.

There follows a group of archaic texts from the Hellenistic town, with a few more from Didyma which seem to be of the same period. The former were rebuilt into structures in and round the area of the post-Persian Delphinion, or came from the archaic stratum discovered in 1904 under the later town, in the area of the temple of Athena (itself also post-Persian).[5] The natural assumption is therefore that they are all from sacred buildings which were destroyed by the Persians in 494, but there is no certain proof of this, and one at least (**39**) suggests a date after 494 rather than before it.

The best known is the magnificent calendar of offerings, originally inscribed in columns on the wall of a building, of which two long blocks and an anta-block survive (**33**).[6] Though the cutting is shallow, like that of so many Ionic inscriptions, the actual lettering is far superior to anything else of this kind produced in Ionia, and has been well compared

---

[1] The statue used to be dated in the 7th c. and called male (Wiegand, *Milet* i. 2. 112; Karo, *Greek personality in archaic sculpture*, 323, n. 44); but I have not found parallels for ξ2 before 575–550, and those of this date are incised on pottery, written by Ionic Greeks in Naukratis (Payne and Beazley, *JHS* xlix (1929), 261, no. 29; Teos **59**). Darsow now argues convincingly that it is female, and to be dated *c.* 560 (*JdI* lxix (1954), 101 ff.).

[2] See now Addenda.

[3] Pryce, op. cit. 104 f.; Richter, *AGA*, 108 f. suggests a date *c.* 575–550.

[4] Perdrizet, *REG* xxxiv (1921), 64 ff.

[5] Von Gerkan, *Bericht ü. d. vi. Kongress* (1940), 323.

[6] The two main blocks were built into the south wall of the portico of the Hellenistic Delphinion, the anta-block into a medieval Turkish building. The structure to which they originally belonged has been identified tentatively as a propylon (*Milet* i. 3. 134, 162 ff., 397 f., 401 ff.).

with that of the famous 'Hekatompedon' inscriptions from the Akropolis at Athens.[1] Though generally agreed to be earlier than 494, it is not an easy inscription to date precisely, because of the combination of archaic and advanced elements: ε3, λ2, but θ3, υ3, ω4. *Kappa* shows curves; υ3 was used in Ephesos **53**, and also on the Samian gravestone **10**, written *boustrophedon* and *stoichedon*, but does not appear in the lettering of mainland Greece (Athens) and the western colonies (e.g. on the coins of Syracuse and Selinous) until the second quarter of the fifth century. On the whole, I think it safest to set this inscription early in the last quarter of the sixth century, and assume that the mason used the dotted *theta* of the vase-painters. Certainly the inscription differs widely from that of the dedication to Hekate on a round base or altar (found, like **33**, in the later Delphinion), which has been dated *c.* 500–494 from the style of its moulding at the base (**34**):[2] [*c.* 11 Λ]|εοθρασ[. . . . . .| . .] Λεωδαμας | Οναξο πρυτ[α]|νευοντες α|νεθεσαν τῆ|κατηι. *Theta* and *omega* are still archaic and, though the inscription is neatly planned in a comparatively narrow column of script cut *boustrophedon* and *stoichedon*, it has none of the finished precision of **33**.

Another block from the same building as **33** carries part of a text (unillustrated) of one of those oracular replies given to supplicants in ἐπιφάνειαι during dreams, such as that of Apollo recorded in the Lindian Chronicle during the priesthood of Pythannas son of Archipolis.[3] A similar text may perhaps be identified on the fragment, copied by Newton and others, which was once built into the wall of a modern house near the Sacred Way at Didyma (**36**; a squeeze was made by Haussoullier): [ . . . . . ]σοι[σι] | ληιστοι· θε[ο|ς] δε επεν· δικ|αιον ποιεν | ως πατερες. It appears to refer to something which the god said, and some instruction to do something ὡς πατέρες, i.e. κατὰ τὰ πάτρια. According to the squeeze the lettering should not be earlier than the late archaic period, and may perhaps be compared with that of **39**, a stele rebuilt into the Delphinion, which bears what is apparently our latest example of a *boustrophedon* text from Miletos. It contains instructions given by the god (cf. θεος επεν in l. 2) concerning ritual in the cult of Herakles, and is inscribed not only on the face and back, but vertically up and down the surviving narrow side, and even across the top. If **34** belongs to the years shortly before 494, this inscription must be later in the first quarter of the fifth century; there is, indeed, no strict necessity to set it in the years before the fall of Miletos, for the list of eponymous stephanephoroi continues unbroken through the subsequent years,[4] showing that here at least, in spite of the disaster to the city and her population, there was no wholesale evacuation of the site.

A fragmentary inscription (**37**) now in the museum at Smyrna may be mentioned here; the provenance is not known certainly, but believed to be Miletos, for other material from that area, both published and unpublished, is collected here. In appearance it

---

[1] Rehm, *Handbuch d. Archäologie* i (1939), 217 f.

[2] Shoe, *Profiles of Greek Mouldings* (1936), 18 and 151.

[3] *Milet* i. 3. 397 f., no. 178; Lind. Chron., D, ll. 60 ff.

[4] Rehm observes (*Milet* i. 3. 242, no. 122) that there may in fact have been an actual gap in the list, between Charopinos, eponymous for 479/8, and his immediate

precursor Semagnes, the latter belonging then to 495/4, not 480/79; but it is hard to believe that any blank years would not have been registered no less than the rest, inasmuch as the record was primarily annalistic, like the Athenian archon-list, whose point as a chronological system failed entirely if gaps were not noted as well. Cf. Jacoby, *Atthis* (1949), 357, n. 25.

resembles so closely the texts discussed above that I think there can be no doubt that it belongs to the same series, though not identical with either **33** or **39**; stylistically it lies between the two, showing ε4, λ2, punctuation 1. It is both *boustrophedon* and *stoichedon*; the few surviving words indicate that it contained religious instructions of some kind: [- - - φ]ερε[τω δε] | οσον αν θ[εληι? - - - | - - - οσον α]ν θεληι ⋮ ε|[κ]α̣στη ⋮ τ[- - -].

From these texts it is clear that the *boustrophedon* system continued at Miletos throughout the second half of the sixth century and even into the fifth, at least in religious documents. A similar survival is attested for Athens, in the fragments of sacral instructions from the Eleusinion, which can hardly be earlier than 500 B.C. (pp. 75 f., **44**); but whereas in Athens the system had long been disused for dedications and secular decrees, in Miletos it apparently persisted on occasion in dedications (**38**; see Addenda). Nor is there yet any evidence as to when it ceased to be used in secular texts; we only know that it had certainly ceased by the middle of the fifth century, when the decree was passed concerning the punishment of the sons of Nympharetos and Stratonax for attempted tyranny.[1]

There are as yet no archaic inscriptions from Priene[2] or Myous; the only one from the promontory of Mykale is the grave-stele **40** found by the excavators of Priene on the site of Thebae ad Mycalen, inscribed *boustrophedon* in irregular lettering of perhaps the same period as Chares' dedication **29**: [Παμφ?]αιεω ειμι σ[ημ|α] το Δεινεω.

## CHIOS, ERYTHRAI

The archaic inscriptions of Chios are very scanty compared with the numbers from Samos and Miletos, though recent excavation at Emporio on the S.E. coast has slightly increased their number. They consist of the famous 'rhetra' (see p. 53), painted inscriptions on the delicate white-slipped 'Naukratite' ware now attributed to Chios, one dedication, and various graffiti by Chians on Chian and other ware from Naukratis; there are also several inscriptions apparently belonging to the first half of the fifth century.[3]

The text of the 'rhetra' (**41**), one of the most important early constitutional documents which we possess, has been discussed in detail elsewhere;[4] I therefore confine myself here to those points which concern us at present in our survey of the archaic Greek alphabet. The stone, which has sometimes been given the misleading title of 'kurbis', is a well-cut stele with no perceptible taper in its wide faces, and only a very slight one (0·17–0·16 m.) in its narrow. On top is a square mortise, still containing a leaden filling, for the tenon of a lost crowning member. As already observed by the previous editors, the lettering of sides A–B differs from that of C–D. That of C–D is deeply cut, squat, and straggling, of the kind familiar to us already from the Samian and Milesian inscriptions;

---

[1] *Milet* i. 6. 100 ff., no. 187, fig. 98 (*SIG*³ 58; *GHI*² 35; *ATL* iii. 256, there dated tentatively in the year 452; Earp, *The Phoenix* 1954, 142 ff.; *SEG* xiv. 740).

[2] I have not included the stelai *AM* xvi (1891), 291 (= *SGDI* 5586), which are evidently of the 5th c., but illustrated in type only. For a bronze hare perhaps from Priene, see Samos **15**.

[3] They are: *DGE* 689, 690; Haussoullier, *BCH* iii (1879), 230 ff.; Plassart and Picard, *BCH* xxxvii (1913), 224 f. The full corpus of Chian inscriptions is to be published by W. G. Forrest.

[4] *BSA* li (1956), 157 ff.

the circles are made by a series of punch-points joined together,[1] *epsilon, lambda,* and *omega* are sometimes tilted, and there is no punctuation. The lettering of A–B has greater height and keeps a straighter line on the stone, though its shallow cutting detracts from its appearance; the circles are cut freehand with the chisel, the tilt of the letters is less marked, and punctuation 1–2 is used. Both types show open η2, ρ2 as in Samian and Milesian, υ2; C also shows *qoppa* (not required on A, B or D). Wilamowitz dated the stone *c.* 600,[2] and this is possible, since we have nothing else of this date from Chios with which to compare it, and very little from elsewhere in Ionia; but I can see no palaeographic reason for considering it to be earlier than the Samian dedications **4–6**, which are dated with reasonable security by the sculptures on which they are cut in the years *c.* 575–550. If we were to compare it with Milesian work, the nearest parallel would be Chares' dedication **29** (*c.* 550–540?); but it seems more reasonable to equate it with Samian, and to regard the mainland's development as slightly slower than that of the islands. At all events, the Chian who framed the instructions was not necessarily a forerunner of Solon, as Wilamowitz suggested. If we bear in mind (*a*) the difference in the scripts of A–B and C–D, and (*b*) the fact that the text as a whole had to be intelligible to the reader, who could hardly be expected to follow it unless it were consecutive from one face to the next, the sequence may be restored as shown in Pl. 65. In C–D the reader began at the top of C, and read down it horizontally; the last line ran from left to right, and continued vertically up the narrow face D adjoining on the right. D carries the last line of this paragraph (whose whole concerns the composition of a βουλή δημοσίη), and a following, much shorter paragraph (concerning oath-taking) which begins afresh from left to right, to mark the break in the text (p. 50). D ends with a *vacat*; therefore the text on the adjacent wide face A cannot follow on as part of D, but must start with a fresh text (cf. the different lettering, possibly by another hand). This wide face reads vertically, perhaps to emphasize to the reader that this was not part of the same text as C–D. A appears to deal with fines prescribed for malpractices committed by state officials; its last line (partly preserved) runs from left to right, and continues directly over in false *boustrophedon* on to B, which carries the final three lines, read from bottom to top. This seems to me to be the easiest arrangement for a reader to follow, and in addition it may be noted that whereas B's lowest line keeps close to the edge (following the custom of the first lines of archaic inscriptions generally, though here it is the lower edge instead of the upper), the top line starts with a wide *vacat* between it and the edge, as though the mason had found on arrival there that he had more room than he needed. It is also possible that the text of C does not begin independently with εκκαλεσθω,[3] but is a continuation from the lost ending of B: ην δε αδικηται : παρ[α] | δημαρχωι : στατηρ[ας? - - -]; we should then read ABCD, and speculate as we choose on the reason why the style of lettering was changed half-way through the work. Despite the many gaps in the text, it appears to establish a Council of the People in Chios, and also, in cases of wrong judgements by the magistrates, a right of appeal either to this Council, or *via* it to the Assembly.

---

[1] This technique has been described in detail by Casson, *AJA* xxxix (1935), 514 ff.

[2] *Nordionische Steine*, 65.

[3] '(A person) should appeal.' For a similar abrupt opening, cf. the Lokrian plaque p. 106, 4*a*: Τον ξενον με Ϝαγεν, κτλ: perhaps also the Eretrian law (Euboia **9**), the Gortyn code (Crete **7**), and the Thessalian law (Thessaly **1**).

There are several fragmentary graffiti by Chians at Naukratis (**43**), mainly from the precinct of Aphrodite; none of them appears to be earlier than *c.* 570. The painted dedications on the inscribed fragments of white-slipped chalices found in Naukratis, Aigina, and Chios (**42**) also suggest the second quarter of the sixth century for their date; η is open in all the examples, θ3 more often than 1–2, ω has the curled ends which seem to have been copied in due course by masons also for formal inscriptions (p. 38). In a detailed study of the inscriptions on this Chian ware[1] it has been observed that the inscribed chalices seem to have been all produced within a fairly short time, and by a limited number of writers: also that the dedicators' names recur often (e.g., Zoilos, Aristophanes, Mikis). These men may have been Chian traders, who brought their wares to the markets of Naukratis and Aigina, and on their safe arrival there dedicated the special inscribed vases which they had ordered in Chios as εὐχωλαί for a safe journey; or they may have been traders of Naukratis and Aigina, who came to Chios for cargoes of wine and pottery, and included in their orders there some inscribed chalices, as εὐχωλαί against their safe return. A fine example of a potter's signature painted on a Chian chalice was found in Chios at the temple of Athena at Emporio (**42e**): Νικησερμος την[δε] την Ϙυλικα εποιησε: we may note σ1–2 (reversed), η2, Ϙ, and no tails to *mu*, *nu*, or *epsilon*. (See Addenda.)

The dedication to Apollo **44**, written in a spiral from below upwards on the pedestal of a louterion (?), should belong to the third or fourth quarter of the sixth century; λ is not geminated in Απολωνι, but the type is λ3. Also of the late sixth century is the fluted column-shaft found near Tholopotami (whence came also **41**), inscribed in neat letters with a dedication by one Lykaithos (**45**). The altar dedicated by the Chians at Delphi (**46**), mentioned by Herodotos (ii. 135), has been attributed to the first half of the fifth century, perhaps to the period shortly after the battle of Mykale, when Chios was free once more from the Persians.[2] The forms ν4, ω4 may be noticed; the former apparently becomes frequent in non-Ionic inscriptions only after the middle of the fifth century. Very similar lettering occurs on the gravestone of Heropythos (**47**) and on the boundary-stone **48**, in the part which defines the rights of those who bought land in Lophitis (sides B, C, D of the stone). The lettering of the fourth side (A) differs in its η, ν, and ω5; all show Ionic ξ2. ν3 is still used in the list of slaves who won their freedom in the late years of the Peloponnesian War.[3]

At Erythrai a dedication and two epitaphs have been found. The first epitaph, if the copy is correct, may be dated in the last quarter of the sixth century (**49**). The dedication **50**, cut *stoichedon* on a pedestal-base crowned with an ovolo moulding, records a vow paid to Apollo Delphinios and should belong to the last years of the sixth century. The second epitaph, to Hekataia wife of Aristokles, is also cut *stoichedon*, and belongs perhaps to the first quarter of the fifth (**51**). The fragmentary legal text **52** shows that 'sampi' was used at Erythrai, though there are no examples yet from Chios.

---

[1] R. M. Cook and A. G. Woodhead, *BSA* xlvii (1952), 159 ff. See also Boardman, *BSA* li (1956), 55 ff.

[2] Homolle, *BCH* xx (1896), 617; cf. Daux, *FD* iii. 3. 173 f.

[3] L. Robert, *Études épigr. et philol.* (1938), 118 ff.

## EPHESOS

The excavations of the temple of Artemis at Ephesos produced a disappointingly small number of archaic inscriptions. The finest example, the opisthographic silver plaque **53**, was found in fragments beside the eastern foundations of the 'Kroisos' temple, in a pocket of earth containing also 160 elektron stars originally attached to some vanished material. None of the fragments was found either under the foundations, or in the deposit inside the central basis, which contained objects from the earlier structures which preceded the 'Kroisos' temple.[1] The plaque bears a record of the amount of gold and silver collected from various sources, and Hogarth's interpretation is attractive: that it is an account of the funds which were raised to build the temple itself. From a small quantity of the silver, the temple treasurers had this plaque made for a commemorative dedication in the building, just as the treasurers of Athena dedicated a small bronze plaque on the Akropolis at about the same time, recording the collection and dedication of certain bronze objects (p. 72, Attica **21**). The temple itself is held to have been begun about the middle of the sixth century, though it was still in building long after the death of its chief benefactor, Kroisos tyrant of Lydia, who gave 'the golden oxen and most of the columns' (Hdt. i. 92). The plaque should thus belong to the years round 550, and this suits well the lettering, if it is compared on the one hand with the Samian dedications **4–6** (*c.* 575–550) and on the other with the Milesian **29** (*c.* 550–540?). The plaque shows the archaic ε2, ϙ, a straggling σ3, and a curled *omega* of varying size and shape. η is 2, υ 3 as on the later wall-inscription from Miletos **33**, and the elaborate punctuation, varying between 1 and 3, also recalls that of **33**. The plaque also shows the earliest example yet of the '*sampi*', the side-strokes noticeably longer than in later examples.

Little can be said of the fragmentary dedications, attributed to Kroisos, which were inscribed on the astragals of at least two column-drums whose sculptured parts are lost (**54**); the tailed ρ4 is remarkable, for it is not normal in Ionic (p. 325). A more certain trace of Kroisos' dedications is the fragmentary inscription in Lydian on part of a plain drum.[2]

The names Οδιος, Αια[ς], Νεστωρ, in Ionic script on a 'Caeretan' hydria of the third quarter of the sixth century have been tentatively ascribed to an Ephesian potter:[3] but this is uncertain. In a recent study of these hydriai it is suggested that they are all the work of two men, eastern Greeks, who made them in Etruria for the Etruscan market.[4]

The fifth-century material from Ephesos is likewise very scanty, and mention need be made only of two blocks from what was evidently an extensive wall-inscription, cut *stoichedon* in columns of twenty-one letters' width, which were separated from each other by vertical lines, with short horizontal lines separating sections of the text within the columns (**55**). The two surviving blocks deal with different subjects: augury, and the ritual of oath-taking for a witness before the dikastai. They may be dated provisionally

[1] Hogarth, *Excavations at Ephesus* (1908), 45 f., 120 ff. I have followed the chronology set forth by Gjerstad, *Liverpool Annals* xxiv (1937), 15 ff., who supports (with important modifications) Hogarth's original reconstruction of three successive early periods (A–C) before the building of the large archaic temple D (the

'Kroisos' temple) *c.* 550. A is probably early 6th c.; see Jacobsthal and E. S. G. Robinson, *JHS* lxxi (1951), 85 ff., 156 ff.

[2] *BMC Sculpture* i (1928), 62, fig. 69.
[3] Devambez, *Mon. Piot* xli (1946), 60.
[4] Hemelrijk, *De Caeretaanse Hydriae* (1956), 60, 120.

in the first quarter of the fifth century; *nu* is not yet ν4, nor *omega* ω5. Punctuation 1 is copiously employed. (See further p. 353, Addenda.)

### KOLOPHON, TEOS, KLAZOMENAI, PHOKAIA, SMYRNA

The other Ionic cities of the Lydian area have very little as yet to contribute. Kolophon is represented by the graffito signature Πα⟨μ⟩βις ο Ϙολοφōνιος συν Ψαμματα⟨ι⟩ at Abou Simbel (**56**); we may note that the three-stroked σ2 is used consistently, instead of the four-stroked σ1 normal in Ionic, and also that *omega* is not used. It is unlikely, however, that this was because *omega* had not yet reached Kolophon; for it has been recently attested in a graffito from Smyrna which antedates the sack of Smyrna *c.* 585 (**69**). It is possible therefore that Ϙολοφōνιος here is merely a mis-spelling. Apart from this signature there are only the legends of the coinage, which in the period *c.* 525–490 shows ημ or τε in monogrammatic forms, and in some issues Κολο (retrograde, but *qoppa* now apparently obsolete), while in the following period *c.* 490–400 the full legend Κολοφωνιον (retrograde) is used. Her script is attested indirectly at Smyrna (see below); on a solitary loom-weight from the site of her western colony Siris, which was destroyed by the Achaian colonies in the third quarter of the sixth century (pp. 286 f.); and also on a kouros of early fifth-century type found in the precinct of Apollo at Klaros, an oracular shrine near Kolophon which was evidently under her control.[1]

Lebedos is unrepresented, as far as I know, except very doubtfully by a retrograde inscription, apparently of the first half of the fifth century, on the rim of a bronze hydria found there; it is perhaps an import, for it shows the 'red' *chi* and tailed ρ4, abnormal in Ionic, in combination with ου for the false diphthong.[2] The nearest source for a 'red' letter would appear to be Rhodes.

Teos is a little better represented; there is one signature by a Teian mercenary at Abou Simbel, Ελεσιβιος ο Τηιος (**58**), showing σ2 (as at Kolophon), and η2. A fragmentary graffito on a sherd from Naukratis of the first quarter of the sixth century reads: [ὁ δεῖνα ανεθη]κεν : τἀφρο[διτηι - - -]ο ο Τηιος, another: Ερμαγορης μ' ανεθηκε ο Τ[ηιος] τὠπολλωνι, in letters recalling those of the years round 560 mentioned above (p. 338), and a third, with later lettering: [- - -]χιδεω [τἀ]φροδιτηι ο Τηιος (**59**). In all these *rho* is legless ρ2, as in Samos and Miletos. The inscribed coinage, beginning *c.* 545 (**60**), bears the legends Τηιον, Τη, Τ. A late archaic gravestone of a Teian (**61**) was found south of Athens, in the same area as Attica **28** (p. 74). No close date can be given from the type copies of the most famous inscription from Teos, the lost 'Dirae Teiae' (**62**), except that it should not be later than the middle of the fifth century in view of the punctuation 2 and the early μ1, a type which in any event is somewhat surprising in an Ionic inscription of this century. Teos' Thracian colony Abdera also used the Ionic script, as the fine series of Abderan coins testifies (pp. 364 f.).

From Klazomenai there are: a dedication to Hermes on the lip of a Klazomenian pyxis, perhaps *c.* 540–525 (**63**); a graffito [- - -]ο Κ[λ]αзομ[ενιος?] (**64**) on two insignificant sherds from Naukratis; a mutilated legend [Κ]λαз (retrograde) on a coin of the late sixth

---

[1] L. Robert, *Fouilles de Claros* (1954), 8.
[2] Reinach, *REG* ii (1889), 177 f. Once in the collection of Van Lennep, Smyrna.

century (?), and the fifth-century series K, Κλα (**65**); and a gravestone of the second quarter or middle of the fifth century (**66**). Nor is there better material from Phokaia; her coinage (beginning in the sixth century) shows a possible θο (**67**),[1] and a single east Greek sherd from Naukratis is inscribed [- - - ανεθηκ]εν ο Φωκαι[ευς] (**68**), and may belong to the first half of the sixth century. Her script is better attested in her colonies Massalia, Hyele (Velia), and Lampsakos (pp. 287 f., 367).

In the recent Anglo-Turkish excavations at Smyrna a cup of seventh-century type was found, with an incised inscription on the foot: Δολιωνος εμι Ϙυλιχνη (**69**), showing ηι, Ϙ, ω4. A sherd (unpublished; E. Greek, c. 650) has long *sigma*, as in Lakonian (p. 34).

## SELECT CATALOGUE
### SAMOS

**1.** Graffito on the rim of a dinos from the Heraion; *c.* 650–600? Technau, *AM* liv (1929), 64. Eilmann, *AM* lviii (1933), 109 f. Friedlaender 94. Samos, Tigani Mus.     PL. 63

**2.** Gravestone of Demandros from the necropolis at Myli, Samos; *c.* 600–575? *IGA* 383. Roberts i. 151. *SGDI* 5718. Roehl[3], 23. 20. *DGE* 713. Buschor, *AM* lviii (1933), 24 f. Lost?     PL. 63

**3a–b.** (*a*) Samian graffiti from the precinct of Hera at Naukratis; *c.* 600–550? Petrie, *Naukratis* ii. 60 ff., nos. 841–8, pls. 10 and 22. Prinz, *Funde auf Naukratis* (1908), 118: (*b*) dedication of Rhoikos on a bowl from Naukratis. Petrie, op. cit. 66, no. 778, pl. 7.

**4.** Statue dedicated by Cheramyes in the Heraion; *c.* 570–560. *IGA* 384. Roberts i. 152. *SGDI* 5710. Roehl[3], 24. 21. *DGE* 715. Buschor, *Altsamische Standbilder* (1934), 25 f., 29 f., figs. 86–89, 107. Bloesch, *Agalma* (1943) 18. *AGA*, 103 f. Paris, Louvre 686.     PL. 63

**5.** Kouros dedicated by Leukios in a precinct of Apollo near Glyphada, Samos; *c.* 575–550. *SGDI* 5705. Roehl[3], 25. 22. *DGE* 715 (1). Buschor, op. cit. 17 f., figs. 20, 57, 59–60. *Kouroi*, 143, figs. 201–3. Buschor, *Frühgriechische Jünglinge* (1950), 77 f. Samos, Vathy Mus.     PL. 63

**6.** Dedication of six statues signed by the sculptor Geneleos in the Heraion; *c.* 560. Buschor, op. cit. (1934), 26 ff., figs. 90–101. Raubitschek, *Bull. Bulgare* xii (1938), 140 f. *AGA*, 104 f. Vathy Mus.

**7.** Leg of a colossal kouros from the Heraion, dedicated by Cheramyes; *c.* 540. Buschor, op. cit. 12, figs. 17–18. Karouzos, *Epitumbion Tsounta* (1941), 539. Bloesch, op. cit. 17. Buschor, *Neue Beiträge* (ed. Lullies, 1954), 97 ff. Vathy Mus.

**8.** Grave-stele of (G)ordiamos; *c.* 550–540? Buschor, *AM* lviii (1933), 26, no. 1, fig. 2. Tigani Mus.     PL. 63

**9.** Grave-stele of Diagoras; *c.* 540–520? Boehlau, *Aus ionischen u. italischen Nekropolen* (1898), 41, 153 f., pl. 1. Buschor, op. cit. 31 f., no. 1, Beil. xi. Johansen, *The Attic Grave Reliefs* (1951), 75, fig. 32. Vathy Mus.

**10.** Grave-stele of Aris-; *c.* 540–520? Boehlau, op. cit. 31 f., 40, 154, pl. 1. Buschor, op. cit. 24, no. 2. Vathy Mus.

**11.** Grave-stele of (An?)themis; *c.* 540–520? Buschor, op. cit. 30, Beil. x. Tigani Mus.

**12.** Grave-stele of Protodikos; *c.* 540–520? Curtius *AM* xxxi (1906), 185. Roehl[3], 26. 27. Buschor, op. cit. 24 f., no. 3. Vathy Mus.

---

[1] Babelon suggests (ii. 1. 99 f.) that the two circles on either side of the seal (the canting badge of Phokaia) which appear on a hekte are the letters θο = φο-. If this is correct, it would show that at that time *omega* was not used in the Phokaian alphabet; but the identification is very uncertain.

**13.** Statue dedicated to Hera by Aiakes; *c.* 525–520? Curtius, op. cit. 151 ff. Roehl³, 26. 26. Kern, pl. 7. *SIG*³ 10. *DGE* 714. Evangelides and Theophanides, *AE* 1924, 64. Schede, *Abh. Ak. Berlin* 1929, no. 3, 22. Buschor, *Altsam. Standbilder* (1934), 40 f., figs. 141–3. Austin, *Stoichedon Style*, 3, 13 f. *GHI*² 7 and p. 258. H. R. W. Smith, *The Hearst Hydria* (1944), 264, n. 184. Klaffenbach, *DM* vi (1953), 16 f., n. 5. Lippold, *Griech. Plastik* (1950), 58, pl. 13, 4. *SEG* xiv. 556. Tigani Mus.　　PL. 63

**14.** Grave-stele of Konche; *c.* 520–500? Boehlau, op. cit. 35. 154, pl. 1. Buschor, *AM* lviii. 25, no. 5. Vathy Mus.

**15.** Bronze hare dedicated to Apollo Prie(n)eus by Hephaistion; *c.* 500? *IGA* 385. Kirchhoff⁴, 31. Roberts i. 153. *BMC Bronzes*, 237. Roehl³, 26. 23. *DGE* 715, 2. BM.

**16.** Base for the grave-statue of Aischros, from the Kerameikos at Athens (reused in the city wall); *c.* 490–480. Threpsiades, *PAE* 1953, 70 f., figs. 8–9. Kerameikos Mus.　　PL. 63

**17.** Base of a bronze statue dedicated to Apollo at Delphi by the Samians; *c.* 479? Pomtow, *Klio* xv (1918), 60 f., no. 87, fig. 3. *SIG*³ 20. Delphi Mus. 1790.　　PL. 63

**18.** Grave-stele of Technandros(?); *c.* 475? Buschor, *AM* lviii (1933), 25, no. 7, fig. 1. Vathy Mus.
PL. 63

**19.** Dedication of Euthymos at Olympia, made by the sculptor Pythagoras of Samos; *c.* 470. *IGA* 388. *Ol.* v. 144. Roberts i. 156. Roehl³, 27. 28. *SEG* xiv. 354. Moretti 13. Olympia Mus. 357.　　PL. 63

**20.** Fragment of a list of Samians who fell in the battle of the Eurymedon, from the Heraion; *c.* 469–465. Klaffenbach, *AM* li (1926), 26 ff., 155. Buschor, *Philologus* lxxxvi (1930–1), 424 ff. Wade-Gery, *JHS* liii (1933), 97 ff. Wilhelm, *Anz. Ak. Wien* 1934, 117 ff. Tigani Mus.

**21.** Fragmentary dedication for the Egyptian campaign, probably from the Heraion; *c.* 459–454. Peek, *Klio* xxxii (1939), 289 ff. Tigani Mus.　　PL. 63

### MILETOS (See Addenda)

**22.** Dedication by the sons of Python(?) at Didyma; *c.* 600–575? *IGA* 483. Roberts i. 133. *BMI* 930. Roehl³, 19. 2. *SGDI* 5504. *SIG*³ 3. *DGE* 723 (1). Pryce, *BMC Sculpt.* i (1928), 112 f., pl. 16. Bloesch, op. cit. 20. *AGA*, 42, fig. 69. BM B 281.

**23.** Dedication by the sons of Anaximandros; *c.* 600–575? *IGA* 484. *IGB* 2. Roberts i. 134. *BMI* 931. Roehl³, 19. 3. *SGDI* 5505. Raubitschek, *Bull. Bulgare* xii (1938), 141, n. 1. BM.　　PL. 64

**24.** Dedication by Hermesianax; *c.* 575? *IGA* 486. Roberts i. 136. *SGDI* 5508. Woodward, *BSA* xxviii (1926–7), 108, 119. Lost.

**25.** Dedication of a colossal kouros; *c.* 575–550? (*a*) *IGA* 487. Roberts i. 137. (*b*) Pontremoli and Haussoullier, *Didymes*, 202 ff. Déonna, *Les Apollons archaïques* (1909), 231 f. Haussoullier, *Mémoires de la Délégation en Perse* vii (1905), 163 f. Jeffery, *BSA* l (1955), 84.

**26.** Fragmentary statue dedicated by Anaximandros, found by the Bouleuterion, Miletos; *c.* 575–550? *Milet* i. 2, 112, no. 8, fig. 103. Rehm, *Handbuch d. Archäologie* i (1939), 217. Darsow, *JdI* lxix (1954), 101 ff., figs. 1–5. *SEG* xiv. 746. Berlin Mus. 1599.　　PL. 64

**27.** Dedication of a statue by the sculptor Eudemos at Didyma; *c.* 560–550. *IGA* 485. *IGB* 3. Roberts i. 135. *BMI* 932. *SGDI* 5506. Roehl³, 20. 4. *DGE* 723 (2). Pryce, op. cit. 107 f., pl. 8. BM B 273.
PL. 64

**28.** Graffiti dedications from precinct of Apollo Milesios at Naukratis; from *c.* 575 onwards. Petrie, *Naukratis* i, pls. 32–33. Roberts i. 132. Prinz, op. cit. 17 f. BM.

**29.** Dedication by Chares at Didyma; *c.* 550–540? *IGA* 488. Roberts i. 138. *BMI* 933. *SGDI* 5507. Roehl[3], 20. 5. *DGE* 723 (3). Pryce, op. cit. 110 f., pl. 13. Richter[3], 36. Bloesch, op. cit. 20. BM B 278.
PL. 64

**30.** Dedication of bronze weights (one surviving) at Didyma, carried off to Susa; *c.* 550–525? *SGDI* iv. 860 f., 34. Pontremoli and Haussoullier, op. cit. 188. Haussoullier, op. cit. 155 ff., pl. 29. *SIG*[3] 3g. Perdrizet, *REG* xxxiv (1921), 64 ff. Pézard and Pottier, *Cat. Antiq. de la Susiane*[2] (1926), 107, no. 234. *SEG* vii. 9. Paris, Louvre.

**31.** Graffito dedication at Naukratis by Phanes son of Glaukos; *c.* 525? Petrie, *Naukratis* i, pl. 33, 218. Roberts i. 132 *ter* and p. 165. BM.

**32.** Dedication by Histiaios at Didyma; *c.* 525–500? *IGA* 490. Roberts i. 140. *SGDI* 5509. *SIG*[3] 3f. *GHI*[2] 9 and p. 258. Lost.

**33.** Part of a calendar of offerings on blocks of a wall rebuilt into the later Delphinion at Miletos; *c.* 525–500? Rehm, *Milet* i. 3. 134, 162 ff., 401 ff., nos. 31a–c, figs. 51, 99. Kern, pl. 8. *DGE* 725. Rehm, *Handbuch d. Archäologie* i. 217 f., pl. 28, 1. Sokolowski, *Lois sacrées de l'Asie Mineure* (1955), 41. Berlin Mus. 851, 1471.
PL. 64

**34.** Round base or altar dedicated to Hekate, from the later Delphinion; *c.* 500–494. Rehm, *Milet* i. 3. 153 f., 275 f., no. 129, figs. 41, 71. *DGE* 724. Shoe, *Profiles* (1936), 18, 151, pls. 8 and 70. Rehm, *Handbuch* i. 217, pl. 27. 1. Miletos.
PL. 64

**35.** Fragment of a marble disk from Didyma; *c.* 525–500? Jacobsthal, *Diskoi*, 23, fig. 13. Private Coll.?

**36.** Fragment of an oracular text from Didyma; *c.* 500? *IGA* 489. Roberts i. 139. Lost.

**37.** Fragment of a sacral text; *c.* 520–494? Jeffery, *BSA* l (1955), 83, pl. 9. Izmir, Arch. Mus.

**38.** Fragment of a statue dedicated at Didyma; *c.* 500–494? Pontremoli and Haussoullier, op. cit. 202. Lost.

**39.** Part of a stele from the Delphinion concerning sacrifices to Herakles; *c.* 500–480? Rehm, *Milet* i. 3, 276 f., no. 132. Sokolowski, op. cit., 42. Berlin Mus. 675.
PL. 64

### THEBAE AD MYCALEN

**40.** Gravestone; *c.* 550–540? Hiller v. Gaertringen, *Inschriften v. Priene* (1906), no. 369. *SGDI* 5724. Roehl[3], 20. 7. Berlin Mus. 104.
PL. 65

### CHIOS

**41.** Legal text inscribed on four sides of a stele; *c.* 575–550? Wilamowitz and Jacobsthal, *Nordionische Steine* (1909), 64 ff., figs. 7–8, pl. 2. *SGDI* iv, pp. 873 ff. *DGE* 687. *GHI*[2] 1 and p. 257. Jeffery, *BSA* li (1956), 157 ff., pl. 43. Istanbul Arch. Mus. 1907.
PL. 65

**42a–e.** Painted inscriptions on Chian chalices; *c.* 600–550? (*a*) Kourouniotes, *A. Delt.* ii (1916–17), 199, fig. 16. (*b*) Lamb, *BSA* xxxv (1934–5), 161, fig. 12. (*c*) *CVA* Cambridge, 2, 32 ff., pl. 17. (*d*) *CVA* Oxford, 2, 82, pl. 5. (*e*) *JHS* lxxv (1955), Arch. Suppl., 22, pl. 2, e. Cook and Woodhead, *BSA* xlvii (1952), 159 ff., pls. 34–35.
PL. 65

**43.** Graffiti dedications on sherds from Naukratis; *c.* 570 onwards. *Naukratis* ii. 63 f., pl. 21. Edgar, *BSA* v (1898–9), 55, nos. 51, 60, pls. 4–5. *CVA* Brussels, 3, 20, pl. 28.

**44.** Pedestal of a louterion (?), *c.* 550–500? Kontoleon, Ἑλληνικά iv (1931), 425 ff. Chios Mus.

**45.** Column-shaft with a dedication by Lykaithos; *c.* 525–500? Kontoleon, *PAE* 1952, 528 ff., figs. 11–12. Chios Mus.

**46.** Altar dedicated by the Chians at Delphi; *c.* 479? *SIG*³ 19. *FD* ii. 119 ff., fig. 97; iii. 3. 173 f., no. 212, pl. 5. Delphi Mus. 940. PL. 65

**47.** Gravestone of Heropythos; *c.* 475? *SGDI* 5656. *DGE* 690. Wade-Gery, *The Poet of the Iliad* Chios Mus. (1952), 8 f., fig. 1. Church of H. Paraskevi. PL. 65

**48.** Boundary stone of the area Lophitis; *c.* 475–450? Roberts i. 149. *SGDI* 5653. Roehl³, 24 f., 18. *DGE* 688. Chios Mus.

### ERYTHRAI

**49.** Gravestone erected by Phanokrite; *c.* 525–500? *IGA* 495. Roberts i. 141. Roehl³, 20. 10. Peek i. 151. Izmir, Arch. Mus. Lost?

**50.** Dedication on a pedestal base with a cutting on top for the plinth of a marble statue; *c.* 510–500? Wilamowitz and Jacobsthal, op. cit. 15 f. *SGDI* iv, p. 879. *DGE* 699. Istanbul, Arch. Mus. PL. 65

**51.** Gravestone of Hekataia; *c.* 500–475? Judeich, *AM* xv (1890), 339, fig. in text. *SGDI* 5694. Roehl³, 22. 16. *DGE* 709, 1. Schoolhouse Mus., Erythrai (Ritri). PL. 66

**52.** Law concerning δικασταί; *c.* 465? Wilhelm, *Ö.Jh.* xii (1909), 126 ff. *SGDI* iv. 879 ff. *DGE* 701. Chios Mus.

### EPHESOS

**53.** Silver plaque recording contributions of gold and silver, from the Artemision; *c.* 550? Hogarth, *Excavations at Ephesus* (1908), 45 f., 120 ff., fig. 29, pl. 13. *SGDI* iv. 870 ff. *DGE* 707. Löwy, *Sb. Ak. Wien* (1932), 27 f. Istanbul, Arch. Mus. PL. 66

**54.** Fragments of dedicatory inscriptions of Kroisos on lower column-drums; *c.* 550? Hogarth, op. cit. 293 f. *SIG*³ 6. Roehl³, 20. 8. Pryce, *BMC Sculpture* i. 38 f. *GHI*² 6 and p. 258. BM B 16.

**55a–b.** Two blocks dealing with (*a*) augury and (*b*) oath-taking, from a series of sacrificial instructions inscribed on a wall; *c.* 500–475? (*a*) *IGA* 499. Roberts i. 144. *BMI* 678. *SGDI* 5600. *SIG*³ 1167. Roehl³, 22. 13. *DGE* 708. (*b*) Heberdey, *Ö.Jh.* ii (1899), Beibl. 48 ff. *SGDI* 5598. Roehl³, 20. 11. *DGE* 708 add., p. 462. Sokolowski, op. cit. 30. (*a*) BM. (*b*) Vienna, Kunsthist. Mus.

### KOLOPHON

**56.** Mercenary's signature at Abou Simbel; *c.* 591 (Bernand and Masson, *REG* 1957, 19 f., 6 *bis*; see p. 358, **48**). PL. 66

**57.** Inscribed coinage from *c.* 525 onwards, with legend ημ-, τε-, Κολο-, Κολοφωνιον. *HN*², 569 f. B ii. 2. 1109 ff., pl. 153. Milne, *Kolophon and its coinage* (1941), 10 ff.

### TEOS

**58.** Mercenary's signature at Abou Simbel; *c.* 591 (Bernand and Masson, op. cit. 15 f., 3; see p. 358, **48**). PL. 66

**59.** Graffiti dedications to Aphrodite and Apollo at Naukratis; *c.* 600–550? Petrie, *Naukratis* i, pl. 6. 5 and pl. 35. 700; ii, pl. 20. 876 and pl. 21. 779. *SGDI* 5637–8.

**60.** Inscribed coinage beginning *c.* 545. *HN*², 595. B ii. 1. 318, pl. 13.

**61.** Gravestone of a Teian in Athens; late 6th c.? *IG* ii². 10444. Harrison, *Hesperia* xxv (1956), 38 ff., pl. 11. EM 416.                                                                    PL. 66

**62.** Stele bearing the official curses of Teos (Dirae Teiae); *c.* 475–450? Roehl³, 21. 22. *SGDI* 5632. *SIG³* 37–38. *DGE* 710. *SEG* iv. 616. *GHI²* 23 and p. 259. Buck 3. Lost.

### KLAZOMENAI

**63.** Dedication to Hermes on a bowl; *c.* 540–525? Zahn, *AM* xxiii (1898), 62 f., fig. 1. *SGDI* 5608. R. M. Cook, *BSA* xlvii (1952), 139. *SEG* xii. 479. Bonn Mus. 2042.                        PL. 66

**64.** Fragmentary graffiti from Naukratis; *c.* 550? Edgar, *BSA* v (1898–9), 55, no. 55a–b, pl. 4.

**65.** Coin of late 6th c. (?) with legend [K]λαз, and 5th c. series. *HN²*, 567. B ii. 1. 310 ff., pl. 12; ii. 2. 1143 ff., pl. 155.

**66.** Gravestone of [Hes]ychia; *c.* 475–450. Judeich, *AM* xv (1890), 338 f., fig. in text. *SGDI* 5609. Roehl³, 22. 17. Berlin Mus.                                                              PL. 66

### PHOKAIA

**67.** Coinage beginning in the 6th c., with doubtful lettering. *HN²*, 587 f. B ii. 1. 95 ff., pl. 4.

**68.** Graffito from Naukratis; *c.* 575–550? Petrie, *Naukratis* i, pl. 35, 666. *SGDI* 5622.

### SMYRNA

**69.** Graffito on foot of a cup; end 7th c.? J. M. Cook, *JHS* lxxi (1951), 250, fig. 9. *SEG* xii. 480. Izmir, Arch. Mus.                                                                         PL. 66

## THE DORIC HEXAPOLIS AND NEIGHBOURS

FIG. 47. The Doric Hexapolis

### Notes on letter-forms

The earliest form of *gamma*, γ1, is indistinguishable from *lambda* (**4**); the classical Ionic γ2, λ3 are first attested in the third quarter of the 6th c. (**15**); γ3 appears only twice, in graffiti (**17**, **18**); see p. 325, Samos **7**. Knidian sometimes shows a γ not unlike γ3 (**33**, **36**).

δ1 is normal; δ2 occurs only in a graffito (**55**).

Rhodian uses Ⱶ1–2 for both Ⱶ and η; the letter-form is usually tall and narrow. Ⱶ2 appears in a graffito of the early 6th c.? (**8**), and in formal lettering on a dedication of *c.* 550–525? (**16**). Ⱶ1 occurs in **25** at the ? end of the 6th c. Knidian uses, as well as the aspirate, a doublet η3 for η (cf. the similar

Naxian letter, p. 289); η3 was apparently abandoned at some time in the late archaic period, according to the evidence of the coinage (p. 352).

θ3 first appears *c.* 550–525 (?) in **15**, but θ1–2 still occurs frequently at least to the end of the 6th c.: cf. *DGE* 277 (= Blinkenberg, *Lindos* ii. 2, no. 580).

μ1 is used very early (**1**), but the more cursive μ2 appears before the end of the 7th c. (**2**), and μ3 is normal thereafter, except (rarely) in well-written inscriptions (**11**, **16**).

ν1, the early form, has developed to ν2 by *c.* 550–540 in **33**.

ξ1 is used in Rhodian **4**, **15**, **27**, and has therefore been restored tentatively in **1**. The Ionic ξ2 occurs in **56** (possibly not Rhodian?) before the end of the 6th c., and ξ3 in **25** (end of 6th c.?). Knidian uses the interesting ξ4, as in Pamphylian; see also below, p. 348, n. 3.

o2 is Knidian (cf. Melos, p. 321). This may also have been the form used in Kos (p. 352).

*Qoppa* occurs still in graffiti of the third quarter of the 6th c. (**18**, **20**), but has disappeared in **27**, *c.* 490. It is not yet attested in Knidian (cf. **31**, Διοσκοροισι, *c.* 590–570?).

ρ3 appears in Rhodian graffiti of the third and fourth quarters of the 6th c. (**20**, **23**) and once on stone *c.* 500? (**25**); an early instance of ρ3 in a formal inscription is the inscription on the Knidian Treasury, **33**. For ρ3 in Ionic, cf. p. 325. ρ4 makes a doubtful appearance on a gravestone [- - -] ημι σαμα το Αριστι- (*IG* xii. 1. 898 = Roehl³, 33. 7) and in a graffito Ροδιος Κλετηας on an Attic plate (*IG* xii. 1. 728); the former is not closely datable within the late archaic period, the plate is described as of 5th-c. fabric.

σ1 is used at Ialysos (**2**, **4** and on a signet-ring inscribed *boustrophedon* Ελεφαντι|δος εμι (*Clara Rhodos* iii. 60, fig. 51), once at Kamiros (p. 348, n. 4); otherwise σ2 is the form in general use.

υ2 appears in an inscription *c.* 550? (**11**), but is rare; υ3 in a graffito of the early 6th c.? (**8**), and on stone by about the mid-6th c. (**15**, **33**); the early υ1 reappears later in a graffito which has other abnormalities, as δ2, and 'blue' Χ, Ψ (**55**, p. 350).

χ1–2, the 'red' type, is used by Rhodes; χ3–4, the 'blue', by Knidos, Kos(?), Halikarnassos, Kalymna and the Doric mercenaries who wrote **48** at Abou Simbel.

ω1–2 first occurs in Rhodian in the late archaic period, probably as part of a wholesale adoption of the eastern Ionic alphabet. Knidos and Kos used ω4; the coins of Kos show that there ω1 had replaced it in the first quarter of the 5th c.

The diphthong ει is normally spelt with *eta* in Rhodian, being pronounced as an open vowel in the Doric dialect; but *epsilon* is occasionally found instead, cf. **23** and the signet-ring noted above under *sigma*, both examples from Ialysos.

*Punctuation* 1 is used in the Knidian graffito **32a** (*c.* 550), and in the 5th-c. Halikarnassian inscription **41**.

*Direction of the script.* Only the very early graffito **1** is retrograde; thereafter all begin from left to right. The dedication of (S)myrdes is the earliest example of an inscription written consistently from left to right, and is the only example showing the use of guide-lines (**11**: *c.* 550?). In the last quarter of the 6th c. a half-line ending is written *boustrophedon*, but with the letters facing from left to right (**23**).

## RHODES (LINDOS, KAMIROS, IALYSOS)

The island of Rhodes occupied a vital position on the trade-route between Greece and the East; for she lay in the path of all Greek ships which came either down the coast of Asia Minor or across from the Peloponnese through the Doric islands of the southern Aegean. Such shipping passed Kamiros or Ialysos or Vroulia; while on the eastern coast

Lindos offered harbour to all vessels, Greek or foreign, making for Greek ports from Cyprus or the Syrian coast or, farther still, from Egypt.

It is likely therefore that Rhodes was one of the first places to receive the Greek alphabet when it started to spread beyond the confines of its birthplace. The Rhodian historians Ergias and Polyzelos (*FGH* nos. 513, F1, and 521, F1) maintained that Ialysos had actually been settled by Phoenicians under one Phalanthos, until the Greeks under Iphiklos drove them out by a trick, and they left much Phoenician treasure behind, both captured and buried; a third, Zenon (*FGH* no. 523, F 1), recorded that Kadmos, searching for Europa, had put in and founded a precinct of Poseidon at Ialysos, and the Phoenicians whom he left there, marrying among the Ialysians, had provided a hereditary clan of priests for the temple. Kadmos had also left his mark at Lindos, by dedicating in the temple of Athena Lindia a large bronze lebes, bearing an inscription φοινικικοῖς γράμμασιν (Zenon, ibid., and Polyzelos, Lindian Chronicle, c. 3). But the excavations at Lindos have produced no traces of Phoenician settlement; only such small portable objects as might have come from Cyprus or Egypt.[1] The same appears to be true of Kamiros, according to the material from the site,[2] and of Ialysos, whose necropolis has been published, although the material from her temple of Athena Polias still awaits full publication.[3]

The same alphabet was used by the three cities.[4] Its salient features are the lack of *vau*, although the people were Doric (as at Thera); the use of *heta* for both ⊦ and η (as at Naxos, and perhaps also at Corinth, if the 'freak' *epsilon* there is a doublet from closed *heta*), and of Ψ for *chi* and ΧΣ for *xi*. The Ionic Ξ and Ω are attested from the late archaic period onwards, but not earlier.

Rhodes has provided one of our earliest examples of Greek writing. I do not mean by this the little aryballos of the early seventh century from Ialysos, with a band of Orientalizing animals and a few signs scattered in the field as filling-ornament, for it is not certain that they are actually meant for proper letters, although admittedly they might have been done by an illiterate potter who had seen someone else writing.[5] But the graffito **1** on part of a cup of Subgeometric type which was bought in Rhodes is, by its appearance, as early as any inscription which we have, except the Dipylon oinochoe (p. 68, Attica **1**). It reads (from right to left) Ϙοραϙο ημι ϙυλιχϛ, with ϙι, a very small *omikron*, and tall, long-tailed letters. The letter in the break following χ may be an untidy attempt at *sigma*, since other Rhodian inscriptions show ΧΣ for ξ. It has already been said (pp. 10, 14, 40 f.) that, if this cup is as early as the eighth century, and yet shows no crooked *iota* like those of the 'primitive' scripts of the southern Aegean, or Corinthian, or the Dipylon oinochoe, it does suggest that the alphabet which took root in Rhodes and the neighbouring mainland (perhaps spreading thence to the non-Doric islands of the Aegean and much of the mainland) was never identical with the 'primitive', but that from the start Rhodes used

[1] Blinkenberg, *Lindos* i. 42 f.

[2] Jacopi, *Clara Rhodos* iv (1931); vi–vii (1932–3).

[3] Op. cit. i (1928); iii (1929), viii (1936). The precinct of Athena Polias is described briefly in i. 74 ff.

[4] At Vroulia in the south, where extensive excavation was done by Kinch, only three inscribed fragments were found, too small to be of any value: a mason's mark (?) on a stone block, parts of two letters on a sherd of an amphora, and a possible monogram on another; Kinch, *Fouilles de Vroulia* (1914), 109, 159, fig. 29 and pl. 28. 5–6.

[5] Jacopi, *Clara Rhodos* iii. 38 f., figs. 22–23; Carpenter, *AJA* xxxvii (1933), 24.

such letters in the abecedarium as suited her dialect, with an *iota* simplified to Ι to avoid confusion with *sigma*, and a *mu* which had been altered in transmission from five to four strokes.

A graffito of the same type (but written from left to right) on a sherd from Ialysos was found in a cremation-area with bird-bowls and Protocorinthian aryballoi, the latest of which belong to the second half of the seventh century: [- - -]νος ημι (**2**). Two more graffiti are from graves at Kamiros, and from their lettering should not be later than the end of the seventh century (**3**): αιρχε (for χαιρε?) on a little Rhodian (?) bird-bowl, found with Corinthian Transitional vases of the third quarter of the seventh century (**3a**); and ευ επιον on the lid of a pithos (**3b**). This graffito looks very archaic (cf. ει, υι); but the pithos to which the lid apparently belongs is of sixth-century type, and the other grave-furniture appears to be later than the mid-sixth century. Either the writer had a very archaic style, or the lid is older than the rest of the material in the grave.[1]

For the first quarter of the sixth century we have at least one landmark, the signatures of the mercenaries Telephos[2] and Anaxenor of Ialysos at Abou Simbel, between the years 594 and 589 (**4**); the early υι and φι, with μ2 (as in **2**) may be noted.[3] The three-stroked σι continues in Ialysian inscriptions; but at Lindos and Kamiros we find only σ2.[4] The stone of Idameneus near Kamiros (**5**) may be of about the same age as **4**, from the letter-forms.[5] It is generally assumed to be a gravestone, but it may possibly be a marker erected for some other purpose. The name of a deceased person can only be restored if we take Ιδαμενευς as being a very early instance of the genitive ending -ευς for -εος (cf. **19** and Buck, 40); and σᾶμα . . . ἵνα κλέος εἴη recalls the dedication on one of the archaic plaques recorded in the Lindian Chronicle (c. 15), dedicated by the tribe which won some contest at the local festival: Νίκας τόδ' ἐστὶ σᾶμα· τῶν Αὐτοχθόνων | φυλὰ κρατήσασ' ἀγλάι⟨ξ⟩ε τὰν θεόν. Ἵνα κλέος εἴη, or a similar phrase, is common among dedications rather than epitaphs; cf. Phokis **1**; p. 255, Achaian colonies **16**.

Ϝι is still used in the graffiti Ϝεκατιος and Βηρετις (twice), on stone statuettes of Cypriot appearance found at Lindos (**6, 7**). They have the deceptively primitive look characteristic of such sculpture, and might be of any date in the first half of the sixth century. A fragment of a black basalt seated statuette (Egyptian?) from the temple of Athena at Kamiros (**10**) may be slightly later, perhaps *c.* 550 (ε3): [- - -]δης με ανε[θηκε - - -].

---

[1] A cup of East Greek fabric, dated *c.* 625–600, was found at Corinth, inscribed [- - -]ομενος εμι which might be either Rhodian or Ionic; for εμι occurs twice in inscriptions from Ialysos, though ημι is normal Rhodian; *Corinth* vii. 1 (1943), no. 307, pl. 37.

[2] Telephos the mercenary reminds one of the phiale once on show in the temple of Athena Lindia as an offering of the hero Telephos: Τήλεφος Ἀθάναι ἱλατήριον, ὡς ὁ Λύκιος Ἀπόλλων εἶπε (Lind. Chron., c. 8). One might speculate whether the original dedication was simply Τηλεφος Αθαναι, to which the priests added the rest, to further their claim that the great Telephos had offered it.

[3] Anaxenor's name (Αναχσανōρ) was identified by Bernand and Masson (**4**, bibliography). They note that the lines across top and bottom of the X are casual

scratches; otherwise one might compare the Knidian *xi*. The 'blue' *chi* and *psi* in the name Psammetichos which follows is odd for Rhodian; possibly both this and the name Amasis (see transliteration of **4**b) were added by another hand.

[4] An exception is σι on a graffito Εργιας on a pithos of local type from a grave in Kamiros, 6th c.? Jacopi, *Clara Rhodos* iv (1931), 333; Segre and Carratelli, *Ann.* xxvii–ix (1949–51), 270, no. 175.

[5] The variation between δ and ʒ in this inscription has often been commented on; it suggests to me a confusion between *delta* and *zeta* (*sd*) made by the cutter. Instead of Δευʒε (= Δευς δε, for Ζευς in the Rhodian dialect; cf. **30**) and τοδιδα- (= τοδ' ιδα-), he cut Ζευδε and τοʒιδα-.

Another dedication, which might conceivably be by the same man, is on a stone from the precinct of Zeus Atabyrios at Kamiros (**11**): [Σ]μυρδης με | ανηθηκην ⊢ο Συνδο. This inscription, written from left to right between guide-lines, shows η1 still (in error twice for ε), but the later form of υ3. υ3 and η2 occur already on the graffito Αστυοχιδα ημι (**8**) on an Early Corinthian aryballos (625–600) from Kamiros; but the date of an imported vase gives only a *terminus post quem*, strictly speaking, and little help can be given from the other object in the grave, which is said to have been a red-figure hydria. If Telephos of Ialysos, the mercenary at Abou Simbel, wrote in the current script of his day, Astyochidas' graffito should be later than 589. A plastic vase of Middle Corinthian type (seated komast) from Kamiros bears a graffito (**9**): χεȝει οϙου ναμα ιχεται (?). The vase appears to be of local Rhodian make, perhaps about the middle of the sixth century; if it was made in Corinth, it would belong to the years 600–575.[1]

Rhodian inscriptions from the end of the archaic period show that here, as elsewhere, *gamma* and *lambda* changed from the ambiguous γ1, λ1 to the classical Ionic forms γ2 and λ3. The earliest inscription to show this change is the epigram on the λέσχη of Euthytides (**15**), which runs throughout from left to right, showing (like **11**) ⊢1 still for ⊢, η, but θ3, υ3 and the late archaic χ2. A dedication on the rim of a marble louterion from Lindos: Κλετολαος μ' ανεθηκε τάθαναιαι (**16**) shows the archaic λ1 and small *omikron*, but η2. Neither of these inscriptions (**15–16**) provides any external clue for an absolute date, and I can only suggest 'third quarter of the sixth century' with all reserve; they may even belong to the fourth quarter, but I do not think the upper limit should be raised. Probably the dedication from Kamiros **14**, partly *boustrophedon*, should be of the same period. The fragment -χος μ' ανεθηκε, inscribed on the flank of a broken stone kouros statuette from Kamiros (**12**), may well be as early as *c.* 550, at all events not later than 525; cf. η1, θ1. The badly-spelt dedication on a miniature chariot-wheel also from Kamiros, by the non-Doric bronze-worker Onesos (**13**) may also be *c.* 550–525; cf. η1, θ1, ϙ, χ2.

A series of owners' names incised on vases appear to belong to varying dates throughout the sixth century: Αγης (*sic*) ⟨η⟩μι on a jug described as of 'altattischer Fabrik' in Berlin, with γ3, an abnormal form for Rhodian (**17**); the same *gamma* was apparently used (with λ2) on an amphora: ϙοσμια ημι · αγε δε με Κλιτομιας (**18**); a jug (**21**) has Διυλλο ημι. Two black-figure cups are also inscribed: one of the third quarter of the century, Ισαμενηος ημι (**19**), and one *c.* 490, Φιλτος ημι τας καλας α κυλιχς α ποικιλα (**27**). Between them should come the black-glazed skyphos **23** from Ialysos; the first owner's name, Τ̣[ελεστο]δικο εμι has been partially erased, and Τελεσιγεροντ|ος εμι added, the ending being *boustrophedon* but with letters reversed; in addition to γ2 and λ2, the absence of *qoppa* may be noted.

The exact date of the introduction of the Ionic letters ξ2–3, χ3–4, ψ, and ω is uncertain. All except *psi* occur on a gravestone found in a Hellenistic necropolis in the area of the city of Rhodes (**25**): Χαρω|νιδα|ς Ξην|οτιμω. With ρ3 and ω1 (late archaic), and η1, it should not be later than the sixth century; as Maiuri suggests,[2] either it was brought

[1] The reading in *Clara Rhodos* vi–vii. 90 is ψήχη ὅϙου νᾶμα ἵψεται, the graffito being described as Corinthian; but this is impossible. Payne dates these Corinthian vases about the first quarter of the sixth century; the 'analogous Rhodian terracottas' mainly to the middle and later years of the century (*NC*, 175 f., 180).

[2] *Ann.* ii (1916), 150 f.

there from elsewhere (Ialysos?), or there was some earlier settlement on the site of Rhodes before 408. This gives at least a *terminus ante quem*; it is perhaps supported by the vase **30**, which bears a painted inscription on either side: καλλιστα γας ⊢α Βρασια | ⊢ως εμιν δοκει, and Δευς ⊢ερμας Αρταμις Αθαναια. Though Shear dated the vase at the end of the fifth century from the shape,[1] I do not think that υ3 and ω1–2 should be set later than *c.* 450. On the other hand, it should be noted that Philto's cup **27** (*c.* 490–470) does not yet show *omega* in the Doric genitive (Φιλτῶς), nor ⊟ for ξ; nor does the plain bronze mirror **28** from Ialysos (which from the other contents of the grave may belong to the second quarter of the fifth century) show *omega*: Μελανθιος μ' εδōκε. The earliest examples of *omega* seem to be in **25** and **24**, the latter the flat gravestone of a woman whose name is evidently Carian, from Lindos: Ιμασαωλας ημι τας Απολωμιδα. The letter is in its late archaic form ω1, with λ3. The earliest example of 'blue' *chi* and *psi* is in the graffito νικασα Υψεχιδας on a vase-rim found at Kamiros (**55**). This should belong to the sixth century (ε2, υ1), but its rounded *delta* is not Rhodian, so that this may be the script of some other state. In the same way, 'blue' *xi* occurs on a skyphos from Lindos (**56**): Ξενοφανēς Αθαναιαι, in lettering not later than the first quarter of the fifth century; but the un-Rhodian E for η here makes it also uncertain. I do not think that we can say more than that ω was certainly, the rest probably, in general if not universal use by the fifth century. Certainly the Ionic script was well established by the last quarter of the century; cf. the dedication of Dorieus the Rhodian at Olympia (*Ol.* v. 153).

Before leaving Rhodes, we may recall briefly the earliest inscribed coinage. The Ialysian (**26**), which shows Ιελυσιον, later Ιαλυσιον, might be earlier than the fifth century with its ε3, though *lambda* is 3, which would support Head's date for these, the early fifth century (*HN*², 636 f.). The Kamiran (**29**), inscribed Καμι|ρεων, should not, from its ω3, be earlier than the second quarter of the fifth century (cf. *HN*², 636). The Lindian coin-legends appear to be late archaic, like the Ialysian: Λινδι (retrograde), Λινδι, Λινδ|ιον (**22**). Cahn sets them in the last quarter of the sixth century, Λινδ|ιον being the latest, *c.* 500.[2]

## KNIDOS

Within the common circle of the Doric Hexapolis (or Pentapolis, after the ejection of Halikarnassos; Hdt. i. 144), the fortunes of Knidos in the sixth century were linked especially with those of the three Rhodian cities. All four were traders with Cyprus and Egypt, being among the commercial cities to which Amasis gave Naukratis *c.* 569 (p. 355); and Knidos and Rhodes made a joint venture in Ol. 50 (582–578), when they sent colonists to settle at Lilybaion in the western corner of Sicily beyond Selinous, in the middle of Phoenician and Elymian territory.[3] Lilybaion was a disastrous failure, but the survivors settled in Lipara, the largest of the Aeolian islands, and here they flourished, and at least on two occasions in the fifth century they caught and defeated Etruscan squadrons in

---

[1] *AJP* xxix (1908), 461 ff. The suggestion of Tarbell (*CP* (1917), 190 f.) that ⊢αβρασια is a hetaira's name is doubtful; the further suggestion that vase and inscription are Boiotian is impossible.

[2] *Charites* (1957), 23 f. The earliest Lindian issue,

which he dates *c.* 550, appears to have a solitary *lambda* in the incuse on the reverse (19 f.).

[3] Diod. v. 9; Paus. x. 11. 3. The Rhodian element is recorded by Diodoros; but Lipara was known generally as a Knidian colony.

their waters, and from the spoils made two large dedications of bronze statues at Delphi. Fragments from the bases have been recovered, and as far as can be judged, the lettering appears to be of the second quarter of the fifth century, and may be Phokian script; it shows tailed *rho*, normal in Phokian but abnormal in any East Greek local script.[1]

Though its letter-forms are not yet all known, the Knidian alphabet has already shown itself to be one of the most distinctive of all the local scripts. Broadly viewed, it belongs to the Ionic family, but has its own forms *eta* 3, *xi* 4, *omikron* 2. The Knidians apparently took from the eastern Ionic the device of creating a doublet from O by breaking the circle; but in Knidian, as in Parian, the broken letter was used for the short vowel, the full circle for the long; and the Knidian letter, following its own course, by the sixth century (the date of our earliest examples) had developed not into the strutted type, but into a half-circle, o2, a form used also by Melos (see p. 321). Secondly, in the Doric dialect of Knidos the aspirate was sounded, as in Rhodian; but whereas Rhodian used *heta* for both Ͱ and η, Knidian appears to have formed a doublet again; for η it used 3, reserving the normal H for the aspirate. The evidence for the latter is in a Knidian graffito from Lindos (**34**). (It will be recalled that in Naxian also the doublet η1 and η3 was used, the former for the long *ā which became ē in Ionic, the latter for the guttural aspirate in the combination ξ, which in archaic Naxian was spelt -Ͱσ-.) Lastly, a Knidian inscription of the late archaic period (**36**) shows that, although Knidian followed Ionic in using X for χ, for ξ it used not ☲, but the form ξ4. This is the letter which was used in the Pamphylian alphabet also for *xi*; were there perhaps Knidians among the Doric peoples who settled in Pamphylia and established a form of the Doric dialect there?[2] The Pamphylian *xi* has been variously traced to an original 'blue' ☲ or 'red' χ.[3] The latter is perhaps the more likely from its appearance; it might be postulated that Knidos originally used, like Rhodes, the combination χσ for ξ, and then, by elaborating the X to distinguish it from Knidian *chi*, was enabled to drop the redundant *sigma*.

The dedication by Euarchos to the Dioskouroi found on Knidos (**31**) has been assigned to the period *c.* 590–570,[4] from the style of the feet of the little limestone kouros, which is all that remains of the offering; we may note the archaic ε2, υ1, and the *boustrophedon* ending. The latter is used also in the dedication on a step of the Treasury erected by the Knidians at Delphi (**33**): [Κνιδιοι] τον θησαυρον τονδε και τἀγαλμα[τα Απολλωνι?] Πυθιωι [ανεθεν] δεκατ[αν απο των πολεμι]ων. The date for this monument should be earlier than *c.* 540, since it is unlikely that the Knidians achieved this military success

---

[1] (*a*) Blocks of limestone from one base were found near the Temple of Apollo, inscribed [Κνιδιοι τοι ε]λλιπαραι τοδ[ε - - - α]πο Τυρσαν[ὀν], with a 4th-c. re-dedication added below; *FD* ii. 1 (1927), 142 ff., figs. 107–13. (*b*) Blocks of marble from another base were found scattered over the site, inscribed -αραιοι, -ϙσ-, [φ]οιβ-, Ͱικατι π-, -θ-. Here also there was a 4th-c. renewal below, and, according to Bousquet, the letters αραιοι are also 4th-c., the others *c.* 475: *REA* xlv (1943), 40 ff., fig. 1. Pausanias at Delphi saw two offerings, one near the Temple, with twenty statues (x. 16. 7), which, from the Ͱικατι (= Ϝίκατι, Ionic εἴκοσι) must be (*b*); and one lower down, near the Treasuries

(x. 11. 3), which should be (*a*), except that (*a*) was found near the Temple. As Bousquet says, the problem must remain unsolved for the present, unless we are to accuse Pausanias of confusion. I do not think the lettering of either can be earlier than 475–450.

[2] Our main information on the Doric element in Pamphylia is that Aspendos was traditionally an Argive colony (Strabo 667), that at Sillyon a Doric dialect was spoken (*SGDI* 1266–7), and that the name Πάμφυλοι might be from the Doric tribe of that name. Cf. further Bossert, *Parola del Passato* v (1950), 32 ff. (Side).

[3] Cf. Roberts i, pp. 316 f.

[4] *Kouroi*, 120, fig. 114.

after their subjugation to Cyrus of Persia; on the other hand, the style of the surviving sculpture suggests a date not much earlier, if at all, than the middle of the sixth century.[1] In the inscription we see σι instead of the normal Knidian σ2, and the later υ3. The dedication of Mikos son of Magnes (**34**) on the foot of a kylix from the precinct of Athena at Lindos shows the difference, noted above, between the aspirate and the long vowel η; the foot may be from an Attic Little Master cup, and, if so, should be of the third quarter of the sixth century.[2]

Among the Milesian graffiti dedications in the precinct of Apollo Milesios at Naukratis there are three Knidian (**32**): (*a*) Χαροφνης : με ανε[θηκε] ṭἀπολ[λωνι τωι Μ]ịλασιωι, (*b*) Θ[εο]θεμιος ημι κ[υλιξ?], (*c*) Δαμο. They are all on sherds from brown-glazed kylikes, and can only be set tentatively *c*. mid-sixth century.

Knidian coins begin during the second half of the sixth century (**35**). H. A. Cahn considers the earliest to be the issue bearing abbreviated names of magistrates (r. to l.), Επη- and Ευφρ-. These he would date by their style *c*. 530–525; if this is right, it would indicate that already by this time Knidian had ceased to use its local *eta*, in favour of the normal Ionic H. The series (retrograde) Κνιδιον or Κνι Cahn would set *c*. 515, and those with Κνι (l. to r.) to the fifth century, before the Athenian Coinage Decree in 449/8 (?) stopped the Allies from coining silver. Those which bear the legend Κνιδιων in standard eastern Ionic belong to the last years of the fifth century, when Knidos again was free.[3]

It is hard to date the fragment of an elegiac verse found at Kumyer on the Knidian peninsula (**36**). It can hardly be earlier than the late archaic period, for the letters are tall and neat, and *boustrophedon* is not used; it shows γ2 and ξ4. The text seems to offer a cordial invitation to passers-by to visit an ἐργαστήριον near by. I should date it *c*. 500. Another fragment, found at Kızlan (**37**), has only part of a name, on what looks like a grave-stele: -κρατ-. A gravestone from Marion in Cyprus bears a name in Cypriot and also Knidian script (Κασιγνητας, with η3), perhaps of the end of the sixth century.[4]

### KOS

Very little is known of the archaic alphabet of Kos, the fifth member of the Pentapolis, and such evidence as exists at present[5] is mainly that of the coinage; but it is at least clear that the script was not originally the eastern Ionic, in that it did not use the Ω, for the earliest inscribed coinage (which is of Attic weight and bears a frontal discus-thrower of the type seen also on reliefs of the first quarter of the fifth century[6]) has the legend Κος (**38**), which may mean either that Kos did not distinguish between ο and ω in her early alphabet, or that she used the same letters as Knidos, with O for ω. Soon after this issue, still in the first quarter of the century, the legend becomes Κωιον (ω1). It will be recalled that the Rhodian cities also appear to have adopted the Ω by this time.

The only other published inscription from Kos earlier than the fourth century is the

[1] *AGA*, 120.

[2] I owe the identification to T. J. Dunbabin.

[3] H. A. Cahn, who is preparing a comprehensive study of the coinage of Knidos, kindly supplied me with information on the inscribed coins.

[4] P. Dikaios, *A Guide to the Cyprus Museum*² (1953), 187, pl. 34, 3.

[5] An epigram from the end of the 6th c. is reported in *Clara Rhodos* ix (1938), 177 (cf. *ATL* i. 509). As far as I know, it is still unpublished. See Addenda.

[6] Cf. the relief fragments, p. 195 (Lakonia **51**), and p. 368 (**60**, Olbia).

horos marked Αποⲗ|ⲗωνο|ς Πυθιο (**39**), which from its θ3, υ4 and slightly curled *omega* may be of about the middle of the fifth century.

### HALIKARNASSOS

By tradition Halikarnassos was colonized from Troizen, and was the sixth member of the Doric Hexapolis until her expulsion therefrom (Hdt. i. 144; vii. 99). The earliest certain examples of her script belong to the second quarter of the fifth century (**40, 41**) and are in the eastern Ionic, with H, Ξ, and Ω. As we have seen, Kos and perhaps the Rhodian cities were also using the eastern Ionic by this time, so that these inscriptions do not necessarily prove that the Halikarnassian script was originally Ionic like that of her nearest Ionic neighbour Miletos. But it must be recalled also that Halikarnassos, unlike the other cities of this group, used the Ionic dialect as well as the script, and this is significant, for the only thing which could change a city's dialect so radically as this would be, obviously, a change of population. If Halikarnassos really was Doric originally, as Herodotos says, her population must have changed at some time in the archaic period; in other words, she may not have been ejected from the Hexapolis solely because one of her athletes refused to give up his prize for dedication at the Triopia, as Herodotos narrates the tale. Furthermore, if the well-known elektron coin stamped with the badge of an official named Phanes (?) (Φαενος εμι σημα) was in fact found at Halikarnassos (Budrun), as claimed, it would be evidence that she was already Ionic in dialect in the seventh century.[1] (See now Addenda.)

One of her inscriptions needs little comment; this is the famous decree of her σύλλογος concerning claims to real property (**42**), which (since the tyrant Lygdamis is active in it), should antedate 454, when she belonged to the Athenian Empire, but should not, from the letter-forms, be much earlier than the middle of the century (cf. ν4, υ4, ω3). The second inscription may from its letters be nearer to 475 (ν3, υ2); it records (in verse) a dedication to Apollo by Panamyes son of Kasbollis (**40**), who is cited as one of the μνήμονες in the decree **42**. A third Halikarnassian inscription was found at Amathous in Cyprus (**41**). It is the gravestone of Idagygos son of Aristokles, 'servant of Ares'. The lettering is eastern Ionic, not the local syllabic script of Cyprus. Some of the letters are earlier than those of **40** and **42** (ν2, υ3); but the inscription is not by a very skilled hand, and so should perhaps be dated beside **40** rather than before it.

### KALYMNA

The early inscriptions on sherds from Kalymna have already been briefly described on p. 154. Here the temple-dumps in the precinct of Apollo yielded two fragments from a vase, apparently of 'Rhodian geometric' style of the early seventh century (**45**). They

---

[1] Cf. Head, *BM Guide to the Principal Coins of the Greeks*, 2 f., pl. 1. The inscribed coinage of Carian Termera may also show the Halikarnassian script. It was first struck during the rule of a Tymnes who will be either the father or the son of Histiaios of Termera who joined in the Ionic Revolt (Hdt. v. 37; vii. 98).

The letters of the legend suggest perhaps the early 5th c. rather than the 6th c.: Τυμνο and Τερμερικον (B ii. 1. 415 ff., pl. 18; *HN²*, 627; *BMC Caria*, lxxvii); but this is very uncertain. Halikarnassos is the nearest place whence Termera would get a Greek alphabet.

bear parts of the name ?Αλκιδαμ[ος] with other indistinct letters, and the alphabet appears to be that of Argos. Were Argive workmen then resident here, painting in the local style but retaining their native script? One would not have expected the local script of Kalymna to differ so much from those of her Doric neighbours Kos, Knidos, and Rhodes. The other inscriptions consist of the following: (*a*) graffiti inscribed on both sides of a sherd described as 'geometric' (**43**). They might be Greek letters, written singly for practice; or, as the editor suggests, they might be Carian graffiti. (*b*) a fragmentary graffito neatly written on another sherd also described as 'geometric' (**44**); for the reading the editor suggests that it runs right to left, showing *san*: [- - - Σ]ατυρος τ[- - -], with *rho* inverted. *San* is certainly right; I read the central letter as Argive *lambda* rather than an inverted *rho*, and think that the graffito reads left to right, in Carian or with some mis-spelling: -ιτσολυτι-. (*c*) a fragment of a white marble ring-shaped object, with part of a dedication in Ionic letters of *c.* 550–500: [- - -]με ανεθηκεν[- - -] (**46**). Is (*b*) or (*c*) more likely to show the local Kalymnian script? The problem must await further excavation. We can only say that Kalymna has produced sherds ranking among the earliest Greek inscriptions which we have; and these sherds *may* show that the Argive local script came not from the same source as the Corinthian, but from Kalymna or else some other, unidentified place whence Kalymna and Argos both took their writing. At all events, I have listed the Euphorbos plate (pp. 153 f.) among these Kalymnian inscriptions (**47**), since there is no longer any reason to ascribe its inscriptions directly to an Argive source. It is quite likely that Argive emigrants settled on Kalymna in the early period.[1]

## GREEKS IN EGYPT

Here may conveniently be mentioned the few early Greek inscriptions which have been found in Egypt. Psammetichos I made a permanent settlement of his Greek and Carian mercenaries at 'The Camps' (τὰ στρατόπεδα) on the Pelusiac branch of the Delta; Amasis moved the settlement to Memphis (Hdt. ii. 154).[2] Psammetichos also set a frontier garrison of mercenaries (?) at Daphnai (Hdt. ii. 30), which may well be the site occupied by Greeks which has been excavated at Tell Defenneh.[3] Herodotos calls the Greek mercenaries in Egypt Ionians, but the Abou Simbel inscriptions (**4** and below, **48**) show that there must have been Dorians too, Rhodians and others from the area of the Hexapolis. Besides the military settlements, there was the great Greek trading port of Naukratis on the Canobic branch of the Delta. Greeks had been in this part since the end of the seventh century,[4] presumably mostly Greek merchants bringing in to their fellow-countrymen decent wine, table-pottery of decorative and familiar types, and olive-oil to replace the rank-smelling oil produced in Egypt (Hdt. ii. 94). By the time of Amasis fourteen Greek cities had trading interests there—six Ionic (Samos, Miletos, Chios, Teos, Phokaia, Klazomenai), seven Doric (Aigina, Phaselis, Halikarnassos, Knidos, and the three cities

[1] Cf. Blinkenberg, *Lindos* ii (1941), 1013, and Segre, *Ann.* xxii–xxiii (1944–5), 4 f. Schiering ascribes **47** to some common centre in the Doric Hexapolis area, most probably in Rhodes (see **47**, bibliography).

[2] For Greek pottery at Memphis see Clairmont,

*Bérytus* xi (1955), 88, 98 ff.

[3] See R. M. Cook, *JHS* lvii (1937), 227 ff. He leaves the question open; but the likeness between the two names is persuasive.

[4] Cook, op. cit.; Roebuck, *CP* 1951, 212 ff.

of Rhodes) and one Aiolic (Mytilene); and Amasis gave Naukratis formally to these
traders, to be the Greek city which thenceforth was to handle all Greek trade coming to
the Delta (Hdt. ii. 178–9). By this diplomatic act he pleased both the Greeks, who gained
a valuable monopoly, and the Egyptians, who might now hope that these unclean foreigners
would henceforth be channelled into one specific zone. The majority of the Naukratite
Greeks were probably Ionic (the Samians and Milesians had special precincts to their
patron deities, and Miletos regarded herself as the metropolis of Naukratis), and many
of the Ionic graffiti without ethnics found in the temple precincts of the city may be those
of local residents (cf. *SGDI* 5756, 5758–69). A gravestone showing a Grecized Egyptian
name and fifth-century lettering reads: Τεαω (*sic*) εμι | σημα (**53**).[1] There are also traces
of the Greek garrison at Memphis. A bronze sheath for the base of an Egyptian statuette,
said to be from Memphis, bears a dedication in Ionic letters of the sixth century by one
Melanthios to the Zeus of Egyptian Thebes (**49**). A fifth-century graffito in the 'Memnonion' at Abydos is by Chariandros son of Straton, Μεμφίτης (**54**). One Timarchos of
Daphnai has also signed at Abydos (**51**): Τιμαρχος ο Δαφναιτες. Two more inscriptions
are from unknown places; they may equally be by mercenaries or by resident merchants.
One is on a bronze statuette of Isis and the child Horus, now in Cairo Museum (**50**),
dedicated by Pythermos; the lettering is Ionic, and suggests the late archaic period. The
other is on a bronze statuette of an Apis-bull now in the British Museum, in Doric
dialect and a script (early fifth-century?) that uses *eta* but not *omega* (**52**): τōι Πανεπι μ'
ανεστασε | Σōϙυ|[δι]δης (?). In this connexion we may recall that the main inscription
carved by Greek mercenaries on the leg of one of the colossi outside the temple at Abou
Simbel in Ethiopia is in a Doric dialect (**48a**). The alphabet has 'blue' χ and ψ, η for both
aspirate and long vowel, and no *omega*; it differs from the scripts of the Doric cities of the
Hexapolis discussed above. The Pharaoh Psammetichos II (594–589) directed an expedition against Ethiopia *c.* 591 (Hdt. ii. 161), sending forward from the frontier garrison of
Elephantine a force of Egyptians and foreign mercenaries, including Carians and Greeks,
up the Nile as far as the Second Cataract. This inscription describing the journey was cut
by Archon son of Amoibichos and Pelekos son of Eudemos (Eudamos). Elsewhere are
the signatures and comments of other Greeks: Elesibios of Teos (p. 340), Telephos and
Anaxenor of Ialysos (p. 348), Python son of Amoibichos (**48b**) and, one supposes, brother
of Archon, Pa(m)bis of Kolophon (p. 340), and a joint signature (**48c**) by one Krithis and
others whose names are now illegible.[2] Archon, Pelekos, Python—possibly also Krithis
and his friends—may have come from elsewhere in the area of the Hexapolis. Or does
their omission of an ethnic mean that they, like Psammetichos son of Theokles who went
with them, were the second generation of Greek mercenaries in Egypt, from 'The Camps'
in the eastern Delta? As was said above, Herodotos calls these Greeks Ionians (ii. 153),
but there may well have been Dorians from the Hexapolis among them; whence a mixed
script might result.

---

[1] Another found at Naukratis is that of a Milesian,
not a Naukratite: *SGDI* 5513.

[2] The most recent readings of the names are those by
Bernand and Masson (see **4** and **48**, bibliography).

## SELECT CATALOGUE

### RHODES (LINDOS, KAMIROS, IALYSOS)

**1.** Graffito of Korakos on a cup, exact provenance unknown; 8th c.? Blinkenberg, *Lindos* ii. 2. 1003 ff., no. 710. Copenhagen, Nat. Mus.?       PL. 67

**2.** Graffito -νος ημι on a sherd from a cup (?), from Ialysos; *c.* 650–600? Jacopi, *Clara Rhodos* iii (1929), 66 f., fig. 56. Rhodes Mus. 11459.       PL. 67

**3a–b.** Graffiti on a lid and an East Greek bowl, from Kamiros; 7th c.? Jacopi, op. cit. iv (1931), 269 f., 333; vi–vii (1932–3), 56 and fig. 66. Rhodes Mus.       PL. 67

**4a–b.** Graffiti of Telephos and Anaxenor of Ialysos at Abou Simbel; *c.* 591. *IGA* 482. Roberts i. 130. *SGDI* 4109. Roehl³, 18. 1. *SIG³* 1. *DGE* 301. *GHI²* 4 and pp. 257 f. Bernand and Masson, *REG* 1957, 10 ff., 16 ff., 2, 4. See also **48**.       PL. 67

**5.** Monument of Idameneus, from Kamiros; *c.* 600–575? *IG* xii. 1. 737. *SGDI* 4140. Roehl³, 32. 1. *DGE* 272. Friedlaender 33. Rhodes Mus.       PL. 67

**6.** Statuette inscribed Ϝεκατιος, from Lindos; *c.* 600–550? Blinkenberg, *Lindos* i. 435 f., fig. 54. Rhodes Mus.       PL. 67

**7.** Statuette inscribed Βηρετις (twice), from Lindos; *c.* 600–550? Blinkenberg, op. cit. 422 f., fig. 52. Rhodes Mus.

**8.** Aryballos of Astyochides, from Kamiros; *c.* 600–550? C. Smith, *JHS* vi (1885), 375 f. Roberts i. 131d. *IG* xii. 1. 720. *SGDI* 4132. Roehl³, 33. 6. *NC*, 289, no. 555. Segre and Carratelli, *Ann.* xxvii–ix (1949–51), 271, no. 180. BM 85.12.13.32.       PL. 67

**9.** Corinthian plastic vase (seated komast), from Kamiros; *c.* 550? Jacopi, op. cit. vi–vii (1932–3), 90, figs. 97–100, pl. 4. Segre and Carratelli, op. cit. 271, no. 177. Rhodes Mus. 13809.       PL. 67

**10.** Fragment of black basalt statuette, from Kamiros; *c.* 550? Jacopi, op. cit. 288, fig. 11. Rhodes Mus. 14341.       PL. 67

**11.** Stone fragment dedicated by (S)myrdes son of Syndes, Kamiros; *c.* 550? Jacopi, op. cit. ii (1932), 236 f. Rhodes Mus.       PL. 67

**12.** Fragment of a kouros statuette, Kamiros; *c.* 550? Jacopi, op. cit. vi–vii. 282, fig. 3. Kontes, *Ann.* xxvii–xxix (1949–51), 348 f., fig. 2. *SEG* xii. 365. Rhodes Mus. 14335.

**13.** Bronze wheel dedicated by Onesos, Kamiros; *c.* 550–525? Kontes, op. cit. 347 f., fig. 1. *SEG* xii. 364. Rhodes Mus. 14464.       PL. 67

**14.** Part of a dedication on a stele, Kamiros; *c.* 550–525? Segre and Carratelli, op. cit. 243, no. 113, fig. 86. Kamiros Mus. 24.

**15.** Gravestone of Euthytides, from Kamiros; *c.* 550–525? *IG* xii. 1. 709. *SGDI* 4127. Roehl³, 32. 2. Kern, pl. 10. *DGE* 273. Segre and Carratelli, op. cit. 266, no. 160. Berlin Mus.

**16.** Part of a louterion dedicated by Kleitolaos, from Lindos; *c.* 525? Blinkenberg, op. cit. ii. 201 f., no. 4. Copenhagen, Mus. Nat.

**17.** Jug inscribed Αγης ⟨η⟩μι, said to be from Kamiros; 6th c. *IG* xii. 1. 722. Segre and Carratelli, op. cit. 271 f., no. 182. Berlin Mus.       PL. 68

**18.** Amphora of Kosmias, from Kamiros; 6th c. *IGA* 473. Roberts i. 131a. *IG* xii. 1. 718. *SGDI* 4130. Roehl³, 32. 3. *DGE* 274. Segre and Carratelli, op. cit. 271, no. 178. Lost?

**19.** BF kylix of Idameneus, from Ixia; *c.* 550–525. C. Smith, op. cit. 374. Roberts i. 131c. *IG* xii. 1. 904. *SGDI* 4230. Roehl³, 32. 5. BM B 451.

**20.** BF cup given by Akratetos as a gift, from Kamiros; *c.* 550–525. Jacopi, op. cit. iv. 169 f., figs. 175–6. Segre and Carratelli, op. cit. 269, no. 170. Rhodes Mus. 12894.

**21.** Jug of Diyllos, from Kamiros; 6th c. Jacopi, op. cit. 246, fig. 275. Segre and Carratelli, op. cit. 270, no. 171. Rhodes Mus. 13179.

**22.** Inscribed coinage of Lindos; late 6th c. onwards. B ii. 1. 473 ff., pl. 20. *HN²*, 637. Cahn, *Charites* (1957), 18 ff., pl. 3.

**23.** Skyphos of Telesigeron, from Ialysos; end of 6th c.? Jacopi, op. cit. iii. 222 ff., fig. 219. Rhodes Mus. 11760. PL. 68

**24.** Gravestone of Imasaolla, from Lindos; end of 6th c.? *IG* xii. 1. 887. *SGDI* 4223. Roehl³, 33. 8. *DGE* 276. Rhodes Mus.

**25.** Gravestone of Charonidas, from a necropolis in the city of Rhodes; end of the 6th c.? Maiuri, *Ann.* ii (1916), 150 f. *DGE* 277a. Rhodes Mus. PL. 68

**26.** Inscribed coinage of Ialysos; late 6th c. onwards. B ii. 1, 467 ff., pl. 20. *HN²*, 636.

**27.** Late BF kylix of Philto, from Kamiros; *c.* 490–470. Smith, op. cit. 372 ff. *IG* xii. 1. 719. Roberts i. 131b. *SGDI* 4131. Roehl³, 32. 4. *DGE* 275. Friedlaender 177. Segre and Carratelli, op. cit. 271, no. 179. BM B 450.

**28.** Bronze mirror, gift of Melanthios, from Ialysos; *c.* 475–450? Jacopi, op. cit. iii. 238, fig. 235. Rhodes Mus. 11887.

**29.** Inscribed coinage of Kamiros; *c.* 475–450? B ii. 1, 463 ff., pl. 20. *HN²*, 636.

**30.** Inscribed vase from Rhodes, exact provenance unknown; *c.* 450? Shear, *AJP* xxix (1908), 461 ff. *DGE* 276a. Richter, *MMNY Handbook to Gk. Collection* (1953), 104, n. 110, pl. 84c. New York, MM. 06. 1116. PL. 68

### KNIDOS

**31.** Plinth and feet of a limestone statuette dedicated by Euarchos to the Dioskouroi, from Knidos; *c.* 590–570? Roehl³, 17. 1. Pryce, *BMC Sculpt.* i (1928), 151, fig. 190. *Kouroi*, 120, fig. 114. *AGA*, 50. Friedlaender 18. Bean and Cook, *BSA* xlvii (1952), 175. BM B 321. PL. 68

**32a–c.** Graffiti on three fragmentary cups from the precinct of Apollo Milesios at Naukratis; mid-6th c.? Petrie, *Naukratis* i² (1888), 60, pl. 33, nos. 237, 239, 354. Prinz, *Funde auf Naukratis* (1908), 83, 118. BM. PL. 68

**33.** Dedication on step of Knidian Treasury at Delphi; *c.* 550–540? Roehl³, 17. 2. *FD* iii. 1. 150 ff., pl. 5. *AGA*, 120 f. Delphi. PL. 68

**34.** Graffito dedication on the foot of a Little Master cup (?) from Lindos; *c.* 550–525? Blinkenberg, op. cit. i. 666 and 757 f., no. 2806, pl. 132. Lost. PL. 68

**35.** Coinage from second half of 6th c. onwards, with legends Επη, Ευφρ, Κνι, Κνιδιον. *HN²*, 614 f. B ii. 1. 425 ff., ii. 2. 979 ff., pls. 18 and 145.

**36.** Part of an elegiac poem mentioning an ἐργαστήριον, Kumyer (Knidos); *c.* 500? Cook and Bean, op. cit. 193 f., pl. 40a. *SEG* xii. 436. Schoolhouse?

**37.** Fragment of an epitaph, Kıslan (Knidos); 6th–5th c.? Cook and Bean, op. cit. 185. 1, pl. 38b. Schoolhouse, Reşadiye.

## KOS

**38.** Coinage with legend Κος, Κως, Κωιον; *c.* 500 onwards. *HN*², 632. B ii. 2. 1031 ff., pl. 148.

**39.** Horos from the precinct of Apollo Pythios; *c.* 450? Herzog, *Koische Forschungen* (1899), no. 36, pl. 2. Roehl³, 29. 42. *DGE* 248. *ATL* i. 509.                                                          PL. 69

## HALIKARNASSOS

**40.** Base of a bronze statue dedicated to Apollo by Panamyes, built into the later city wall; *c.* 475? Karo, *AM* xlv (1920), 157 ff., pl. 4. Maiuri, *Ann.* iv–v (1921–3), 461 f. Budrun Mus.

**41.** Gravestone of Idagygos, from Amathous, Cyprus; *c.* 475? *BMI* iv. 971. Peek i. 324. BM.   PL. 69

**42.** Decree concerning claims to property, mentioning Lygdamis; *c.* 475–454? *SGDI* 5726. Roehl³, 23. 14. *SIG*³ 45. *DGE* 744. *GHI*² 25. BM.

## KALYMNA

**43.** Graffiti on both sides of a sherd of Geometric type from the precinct of Apollo; 8th c.? Segre, *Ann.* xxii–xxiii (1944–5, 1952) 217, nos. 245a–b, pl. 125. Rhodes Mus.                                    PL. 69

**44.** Graffito on a similar sherd from the precinct; 8th c.? Segre, op. cit. 217, no. 246, pl. 126. Rhodes Mus.                                                                                                       PL. 69

**45.** Inscriptions painted on sherds of an E. Greek krater from the precinct; early 7th c. Segre, op. cit. 218, no. 247, pl. 126. Rhodes Mus.                                                                         PL. 69

**46.** Fragmentary dedication on a marble object from the precinct; *c.* 550–500? Segre, op. cit. 145, no. 98, pl. 64.

*Inscription attributed to Kalymna*

**47.** E. Greek plate with painted names, from Rhodes; *c.* 600? *MuZ* i. 139, fig. 117. Buschor, *Griech. Vasen* (1940), 51 ff., fig. 62. Schiering, *Werkstätten orientalisierender Keramik auf Rhodos* (1957), 11. 64. BM.                                                                                                       PL. 69

## GREEKS IN EGYPT

**48a–c.** Main inscription (Doric dialect) and some of the names cut by Greek mercenaries at Abou Simbel; *c.* 591. Roehl³, 18 f. 1. *GHI*² 4, and pp. 257 f. Bernand and Masson, op. cit. 1 ff., 1, 5, 6. Abou Simbel.                                                                                                       PL. 69

**49.** Dedication by Melanthios on the base-sheath of a statuette, said to be from Memphis; *c.* 550–525? Smith and Griffiths, *CR* v (1891), 77 ff., fig. Private coll.                                              PL. 70

**50.** Dedication by Pythermos on a statuette found in Egypt; *c.* 500? Edgar, *JHS* xxiv (1904), 337. *SGDI* 5771. *DGE* 749. Cairo Mus.                                                                              PL. 70

**51.** Graffito by Timarchos of Daphnai at Abydos; *c.* 500–450? Perdrizet and Lefebvre, *Les Graffites grecs du Memnonion d'Abydos* (1919), no. 614.                                                              PL. 70

**52.** Dedication by Sokydides(?) on a bronze Apis-bull statuette, from Egypt; *c.* 500–450? *BMC Bronzes*, 3208. Roscher, *Lexikon* iii. 1. 1532. BM.

**53.** Gravestone found allegedly in the temenos of the Dioskouroi, Naukratis; *c.* 500–450? Petrie and Gardner, *Naukratis* i. 62 f., pl. 30. 1.

**54.** Graffito by Chariandros of Memphis at Abydos; *c.* 450? Perdrizet and Lefebvre, op. cit., no. 536.

*Inscriptions probably not Rhodian*

**55.** Graffito of Hypsechides on a vase-fragment from Kamiros; end of 6th c.? Jacopi, op. cit. vi–vii. 103, fig. 115. Segre and Carratelli, op. cit. 270 f., no. 176. Rhodes Mus. 1346–8.

**56.** Skyphos dedicated by Xenophanes, from Lindos; *c.* 500–475? Blinkenberg, op. cit. i. 667, no. 2826, pl. 132. Rhodes Mus.


# THE AIOLIC AREA

Of the twelve cities of southern Aiolis mentioned by Herodotos (i. 149)—Kyme, Larisa, Neon Teichos, Temnos, Killa, Notion, Aigiroessa, Pitane, Aigaiai, Myrina, Gryneia, and Smyrna—only Larisa, Temnos, and Smyrna have yet produced any archaic inscriptions; and Smyrna early became Ionic (cf. Ionic Dodekapolis **69**). There are two from Pergamon in Mysia, and isolated examples have been found in the Troad at Sigeion,[1] Neandria, Kebrene, Thymbra, Assos, and Skepsis. Very little has been found on Lesbos, and nothing from Tenedos but her coinage. Nevertheless, these scattered fragments between them reveal an alphabet which is of considerable interest, for it is not identical with the Ionic, nor can it be precisely identified with the script of the Aiolic states of mainland Greece. As the material is very scanty, I propose to discuss the letter-forms with the inscriptions, with no separate table of letter-forms.


### AIOLIS

Fragments of two archaic inscriptions (unpublished) were found by the French at Temnos.[2] At Larisa were found several graffiti, a painted dedication on bucchero sherds, and a painted fragment in the temple of Athena on the Akropolis (**1***a–i*). The graffiti are all on the inner rims of large amphorae, which have been dated by their profiles from about the middle of the seventh century into the sixth.[3] The appearance of the letters of *a*, *b*, and *c*, which are the earliest fragments according to this system, does not suggest the seventh century (cf. the open *eta*), though *a–b* is written retrograde; but they show two interesting usages. First, as Hiller pointed out,[4] *eta* (whose value as an aspirate had no place in the psilotic dialect of Aiolis) is here employed to express not η but the *e*-vowel which in Aiolic was sounded instead of ι in a diphthong (dative Αθηναηαη; cf. Buck, 30). The sherds from Larisa and the Magnesian graffito **2** provide the only examples as yet of the letter H in Aiolic, for η is expressed elsewhere by E; only in *f–g*, which are the latest of the graffiti (according to the profiles of the rims and also the look of the letter-forms), H is used for ε (Θηοδōρος) in *f*, and for η (εποη-) in *g*. Larisa lay near Ionic Phokaia, and it is possible that she borrowed thence the letter H, and gradually extended its usage. The second point of interest is that *a* and *f* both show rounded *delta*; in

---

[1] I have discussed Sigeion among the northern Colonies, her more natural companions; see pp. 366 f.

[2] L. Robert, *REG* lii (1939), 497, no. 330.

[3] Boehlau and Schefold, *Larisa am Hermos* iii (1942), 123 f., 183 f.

[4] *AA* 1938, 372.

other Aiolic examples of the letter (which happen to be later in date than *b* and *g*) it is Δ. *Sigma* varies between Σ (*f*) and a curved letter like English S.

No archaic inscriptions have yet been found at Magnesia ad Sipylum; but a Magnesian mercenary named Kaikos scratched a record of his presence at Egyptian Abydos in the so-called Memnonion (the funeral temple of Seti I); closed *eta* is used, and the graffito probably belongs to the sixth century (**2**).

In Lesbos, the earliest inscription is a brief graffito from Mytilene: [- - -]ϙστετιλμεν-[- - -], upside down on a figured sherd probably of the late seventh century (**3**). Then follow several dedicatory graffiti on Lesbian bucchero from the precinct of Aphrodite at Naukratis, which may be dated from *c.* 569 onwards through the sixth century (**4**); and one of them, inscribed Νεαρχος με και Σα[- - -] shows that the Aiolic alphabet used the 'blue' χ for *chi*. This is confirmed by the two solitary graffiti from Antissa, Ευμαχος on the shoulder of a late archaic kantharos, and -χος on a sherd (**5**). The fine coins of Methymna, which begin *c.* 530[1] with the legend Μαθυμναιον, add nothing that is epigraphically new (**6**); nor do the sixth-century coins of Tenedos (**7**), which in the late archaic period bear the legend (r. to l.) Τενε, Τε|νε, followed in the early fifth century (?) by TE|NE|ΔION.

### TROAS, MYSIA

The earliest Aiolic inscription from Troas is on the fragment of a doorpost found at Neandria, which refers to a dedication, and mentions an ἐπιστάτης (or two?) (**8**): [- - ο]νε-θēκα[ν] | το επιστα|τα οκαικε|μεν[- - -]. It is cut *boustrophedon*, with four-stroked *sigma*, and cannot be later than the sixth century, though the awkward lettering makes a more precise dating impossible. A second inscription from Neandria (**9**) was found on a statue-base for a marble kouros, whose shattered fragments (unpublished, as far as I know) lay beside the base. The lettering, partly *stoichedon*, indicates a date in the first years of the fifth century (cf. the appearance of tailed *rho*): τονδε τον ανδ[ριαντα Απο]λλōνα ονεθē|κε Ερμεας αρα[σαμενο] το παιδος | ὁγεμαχ[ιος]. At Assos in the necropolis was found the lower part of a Doric (?) column, with the inscription cut *boustrophedon* up and down two of the flutes (**10**): Αριστανδρει κ[αι? - - -]ικιος. The tailed forms of *epsilon* and *nu* suggest an early date, perhaps not long after 550; it may be noted that here three-stroked *sigma* is used. Another grave-inscription, from Kebrene, is evidently later in date, perhaps of the early fifth century (**11**; cf. dotted *theta*): σ[ταλλ]α 'πι Σθενειαι εμμι τō Νικιαιōι το Γαυκιο. A third from Thymbra, apparently cut *stoichedon*, may be nearer to the middle of the century (**12**): the curious letter in it is generally taken for a form of *phi*. At Pergamon in Mysia was found a base for a bronze statue dedicated to Poseidon, inscribed *stoichedon* in letters suggesting a date *c.* 475–450 (**13**): [Π]οτοιδανι ꞉ Ανδρομēδες | [Π?]ολειο. An unpublished[2] bronze signet-ring in the Museum bears the legend Διφι|λου written *boustrophedon* in raised letters which cannot be earlier than the fifth century (**14**); for the prolongation of the *boustrophedon* technique in the legends of coins, see p. 49. At Troy a sherd of local grey ware which might be of the sixth century has a graffito τροα,

---

[1] Cahn, *Monnaies grecques archaïques* (1947), 11, 28.

[2] I have to thank Ogan Bey of the Museum at Pergamon for permission to photograph the signet and describe it here.

with tailed *rho*.[1] Lastly, the coins of Skepsis testify to the usage of the Ionic *psi* in the first half of the fifth century (**15**).

The characteristics of the Aiolic script as far as it is known may therefore be summed up briefly as follows.[2] It used the 'blue' *chi* and *psi*; it used neither *eta* (except in S. Aiolis at Larisa and Magnesia, perhaps through the influence of Ionic Phokaia), nor *omega*; *delta*, normally Δ, is written D in the early inscriptions of Larisa (seventh (?) to sixth century); both three- and four-stroked *sigma* are used; punctuation is expressed by either two dots (sixth and fifth century) or three (fifth century). It has been suggested[3] that the Aiolic alphabet, like certain of the Ionic scripts, included the non-Greek letter '*sampi*', the argument being that Aiolic did not possess the letter Ψ = ψ, and therefore the letter used by Sappho to spell her own initial letter may really have been the '*sampi*', corrupted by later copyists. But Aiolic certainly possessed the *psi* in the fifth century (**15**), and this argument is therefore doubtful.

## CATALOGUE

### AIOLIS

**1a–i.** Graffiti on sherds from the temple of Athena at Larisa; (*a–e*) 7th c. (?), (*f–i*) 6th c. Hiller von Gaertringen, *AA* 1938, 371 ff., fig. 1. Boehlau and Schefold, *Larisa am Hermos* iii (1942), 123 f., 183 f.
PL. 70

**2.** Graffito of a mercenary Kaikos from Magnesia ad Sipylum in the 'Memnonion' at Abydos in Egypt; 6th c.? Perdrizet and Lefebvre, *Les Graffites grecs du Memnonion d'Abydos* (1919), no. 427.
PL. 70

**3.** Graffito on sherd of East Greek style at Mytilene; end of 7th c.? Schefold, *AA* 1933, 154 f., fig. 12. *IG* xii, suppl., p. 23, 64. Mytilene Mus.

**4.** Graffiti by Mytilenians on sherds from the precincts of Aphrodite and Apollo (?) at Naukratis; *c.* 569 onwards? Petrie, *Naukratis* i, pl. 32, 185; ii. 656, pl. 21, 786–93. Roehl³, 35. 2–3. *DGE* 647a.

**5.** Graffiti on vases from Antissa; 6th to 5th c. Lamb, *BSA* xxxi (1930–1), 178, pl. 28; xxxii, 56, pl. 22. *IG* xii, suppl., p. 32. Mytilene Mus.

**6.** Coinage beginning *c.* 530 at Methymna, with legend Μαθυμναιον. *HN*², 560 f. B ii. 1. 361 ff., pl. 15. Cahn, *Monnaies grecques archaïques* (1947), 11, 28, fig. 10.

**7.** Inscribed coinage of Tenedos beginning in last years of 6th c., with legend Τενε, Τενεδιον. *HN*², 550 f. B ii. 1. 365 ff., pl. 16.

### TROAS, MYSIA

**8.** Part of a dedication (?) on a door-post at Neandria; second half of 6th c.? Koldewey, *Neandria* (1893), 12, fig. 10. *DGE ad* 731.
PL. 70

---

[1] Blegen, Caskey, and Rawson, *Troy* iii. 1 (1953), 129 f. As the date of sherd and graffito is uncertain, I have not included it in the Catalogue.

[2] See now Addenda for *omega* and *delta* (Troy).

[3] Zuntz, *Museum Helveticum* viii (1951), 16 ff. See further pp. 38 f., n. 2.

**9.** Base for a marble kouros dedicated by Hermeas at Neandria; *c.* 500–475? Koldewey, op. cit. 27 f., figs. 56–57. Wilhelm, 7. Roehl³, 35. 1. *DGE* 639. Pergamon Mus.

**10.** Grave-inscription on a column at Assos; third quarter of 6th c.? Clarke, *AJA* ii (1886), 267 f., fig. 33. Roberts i. 166a. Mendel, *Cat. Sculpt. Constantinople* ii (1914), 24 f. Istanbul Mus.　　PL. 70

**11.** Grave-inscription from Kebrene; first quarter of 5th c.? *IGA* 503. Roberts i. 166b. *SGDI* 307. Roehl³, 35. 4. *DGE* 638. Buck 24.

**12.** Grave-inscription from Thymbra; second quarter of 5th c.? *IGA* 504. Roberts i. 166c. *SGDI* 308. Roehl³, 35. 5. *DGE* 637.

**13.** Base for a statue dedicated to Poseidon at Pergamon (Mysia); second quarter of 5th c.? Hepding, *AM* xxxii (1907), 303 f., fig. 2. *DGE* 642. Pergamon Mus.

**14.** Bronze signet-ring of Diphilos from Pergamon; second quarter of 5th c.? (unpublished). Pergamon Mus.

**15.** Inscribed coinage of Skepsis (Σκαψιον, Σκηψιον), beginning in first quarter of 5th c.? *HN²*, 548 f. B ii. 2. 1285 ff., pl. 165.

# THE NORTHERN COLONIAL AREA

THE material from the northern colonies is still very meagre, and much of it inadequately published. This section consists of little more than a brief list of those places which have yielded any relevant inscriptions, within the following groups: Chalkidike; Macedonia and southern Thrace (as far as the Chersonese); the Hellespont and Propontis; and the Euxine. The alphabet concerned is in nearly every case the eastern Ionic (Fig. 46); exceptions are discussed as they occur.

## CHALKIDIKE

The Greeks who settled on this peninsula in the early period were, according to the tradition, from Chalkis and Eretria, Andros, and Corinth. One city—Aineia—claimed by her name to be of Trojan origin. Potidaia certainly used the script of her mother-city Corinth; Stageira, Akanthos, and Sane may have used the Andrian. Nothing demonstrably in Euboic letters has been found as yet among the rest, and such fifth-century material as we have is in the east Ionic script.

Aineia, traditionally founded by Aineias, shows on her coinage, dated at the end of the sixth century, the legend Αινεας in a script which might be identified equally well with that of Macedonia, or that of the Ionic members of the Chalkidike (**1**). The coins of the Eretrian colonies Dikaia and Mende in the first half of the fifth century show Δικα (**2**) and Μινδαον (**3**); it may be guessed that this (which might be either Eretrian of the fifth century, when the characteristic five-stroked *mu* had disappeared, or else Ionic) is in fact Eretrian, for Skione, probably also of Euboic origin, shows on her earliest coins at the end of the sixth century the non-Ionic Σκιο (**4**). On the other hand, at Sermyle (Euboic?) the coins of about the same period show Σερμυλικον, Σερμυλιαιον with non-Euboic *lambda* (**5**). Chalkidic Torone shows Τε on her coins, *c.* 500–480 (**6**). The grave-stele of a Toronaian who was buried in Athens is in the eastern Ionic script (**7**): Μικκος | Καλλικλειδο | Τορωναιος. The lettering suggests a date before the middle of the fifth century, when the use of Ionic in Athens would still be abnormal; probably therefore this is the local script of Torone. A second grave-stele of a Toronaian in Athens, also in eastern Ionic, belongs probably to the second half of the fifth century (**8**).[1] Andrian Akanthos shows Ακαν on her coins *c.* 480 (**9**). Potidaia, founded *c.* 600 by the Kypselid dynasty of Corinth, used the Corinthian script; a base at Delphi bears the dedication of one Theugenes of Potidaia (**10**) in lettering of the early fifth century, showing Corinthian *epsilon* and *san*. Her coinage, begun *c.* 550 or later, shows only Γο or Γ (**11**) in imitation of Corinthian Ϙ. She passed the Corinthian alphabet on to Olynthos, her neighbour to the north, which was inhabited by the half-Greek Bottiaioi until 480/79, when it fell into the possession of Chalkidic Torone.[2] Two gravestones have been found in pre-Chalkidic Olynthos; both bear women's names in the genitive case, and are probably to be dated in the first years of the fifth century: Πολυξενας (**12**) and Νευμους (**13**), both showing the

[1] A third (not in Conze) appears from the publication to be 5th-c. also: *IG* i². 1074.
[2] Cf. Gomme, *Thucydides* i. 203 ff.

late archaic tailless *upsilon*. A gravestone of an Olynthian in Athens belongs to the middle or third quarter of the fifth century; it shows the Ionic script, as we see it at Torone (**14**). I have not included here the two tetrobols inscribed with 'red' *chi*, which some scholars ascribe to the mint of Olynthos and others to that of Chalkis in Euboia; see pp. 82 f. above. Of Aphytis south of Potidaia we know only that she was evidently using the eastern Ionic script *c.* 449/8, for her copy of the Athenian Coinage Decree is in that script (**15**).[1]

### MACEDONIA AND SOUTHERN THRACE

The Bisaltai used mostly the Thasian alphabet, having presumably learnt the art of coining itself from Thasos; their early coins (*c.* 500–480?) show Βισαλτικον or Βισαλτικος, with Thasian *beta* and ο or ω used confusedly (**16**). Those of Mosses show the same confusion (**17**), and so sometimes does the coinage of Getas of the Edonoi (**18**). But non-Thasian forms too were used, as *beta* B on Getas' coins and occasionally in the legend Βισαλτικον; the coins of the Derrones also show non-Thasian *omikron*, Δερρōνικος (**19**). The coins of the Orreskioi likewise show uncertainty in the use of ο or ω, and of *epsilon* or *eta* (**20**). The Thasian colony Neapolis has yielded only two graffiti on sherds from a precinct of the Parthenos, both of the sixth century: παρθ[ενōι?] and -ς μ' ανεθε[σαν?] (**22**). The royal coinage of the kings of Macedonia, started by Alexandros I (498–454) on the model of the coinage of the Bisaltai, shows the Ionic *xi* (Αλεξανδρο, **27**); but the earlier coinage of Ichnai (*c.* 500–480) shows [I]χναι[ον?] with both 'blue' and 'red' *chi* (**23**), the latter perhaps taken from some Euboic source in Chalkidike. Aigai, the old capital, whose early coins are of about the same date, has only δε in ligature, λα, or dotted *theta* (**24**). Lete, whose abundant coinage begins at the end of the sixth century, shows the legend (r. to l.) Λετ̄αιον (**25**). Tragilos produces coins with Τραι, Τραιλιον (*sic*) *c.* 450–400 (**26**); and lastly, various issues by unidentified states or rulers show Τυντενον, Δοκι, Ζαιελεων, and (retrograde) Διονυ- or -ναιω (**21**). Thus the Thasian, the Chalkidic (?) and an eastern Ionic script with Ξ and Ω = ω all make their appearance in different parts of Macedonia; and, judging by the coins of Alexandros I, we may infer that it was the Ionic which, in the first half of the fifth century, became the official Macedonian alphabet.

Beyond the river Nestos, we follow the Greek colonies strung along the coast of southern Thrace. Abdera, colonized by Teos *c.* 540 after an unsuccessful colony from Klazomenai had occupied the site (Hdt. i. 168; Strabo 644), shows a fine series of coins inscribed in the eastern Ionic of her mother-city (**28**). They are distinct from other early Greek coinage in that from the start each issue records the name of the eponymous priest of Apollo in whose year of office they were struck. It is not certain that the series began immediately upon the foundation of Abdera, although the type (a seated griffin) is modelled directly upon that of Teos; for the standard is not the Teian,[2] and the lettering on the earliest series, tentatively dated *c.* 540–512, looks surprisingly advanced in some respects for any date before 525 (e.g. A, E). The coins continue through the fifth century; at first the names are still abbreviated on the obverse, as in the earlier issues; later they

---

[1] Cf. also the Aphytis–Potidaia decree of 428/7, *ATL* ii. 75, D 21. This is not the place to discuss the problems of the Coinage Decree, but the lettering of D 14 (**15**) looks advanced for a date *c.* 449; possibly it is from a republication of the decree some years later.

[2] *HN*[2], 253 f.

are moved to the reverse (as on the coinage of Alexandros I), with the full phrase (επι Μανδρωνακτος, &c.); the struts of *omega* alter gradually from curled to straight, and *upsilon* from V to Y. The only other Abderite inscription of this period is the dedication of Python (made by Euphron of Paros) from the Peiraieus at Athens (**29**); Euphron's *floruit* appears to have been *c.* 475.[1] Dikaia-by-Abdera shows Δικ (r. to l.) or Δικαι on her earliest coins (**30**; *c.* 500–480?), and Maroneia, colonized from Chios, has the Ionic legend Μαρ, Μαρω, Μαρωνος (r. to l.); in the second quarter of the fifth century, επ' Αρχεμβροτο appears on the obverse, apparently in imitation of Abdera, and thereafter officials' names become the regular reverse type (**31**). Ainos, founded by the Aiolic cities Mytilene and Kyme, bears on its coinage *c.* 450 the legend Αινιον, Αινι (**32**). The sculptor Paionios of Mende, a small place inland from Ainos, used the eastern Ionic script on the base of his statue of Nike which was dedicated by the Messenians of Naupaktos at Olympia, and on the similar base at Delphi (**33**). See also Addenda.

### HELLESPONT AND PROPONTIS

#### A. *Northern side*

No archaic inscriptions, Attic or other, have yet been found in any of the towns on the Chersonese, except for the coins inscribed Χερ (in Attic script?), which are attributed to *c.* 515–493, during the rule of the second Miltiades[2] (**34**). At Perinthos, colonized *c.* 600 by Samians (Strabo 331, fr. 56), was found the shaft and broken anthemion of a grave-stele of Samian type, inscribed Ηγησιπολιος | το Φαναγορε|ω in Samian script (**36**); cf. the typical legless *rho* (p. 328). The lettering should belong to the period *c.* 525.[3] A dedicatory stele, erected in the Heraion at Samos (**35**), records in typical Samian lettering the gifts of certain Perinthians, (Me?)niskos and Demi(s), to Hera: 'a golden γοργυρή (Gorgon?), a silver male Siren, a silver phiale, a bronze lamp-stand, the value of the whole being 212 Samian staters, including the marble stele'. The lettering suggests a date after the middle of the sixth century: crossed *theta* and tailed *epsilon* are archaic features, but *lambda* is isosceles, *omega* shows no sign of the archaic tilt (p. 325), and there is an occasional attempt at *stoichedon* order. This would mean that the phrase οικηι{ηι}οι means not 'the settlers' (i.e. original colonists), but simply 'the colonists'.[4] Perinthos was heavily defeated by the Persians under Megabyzos *c.* 512 (Hdt. v. 1 ff.), and some time before that, according to Herodotos, it had suffered a reverse from the Paionians. The Paionian incident is altogether mysterious, but Perinthos could hardly have made this rich dedication

---

[1] *DAA*, 500 f. A gravestone of an Athenian named Thaliarchos has also been found at Abdera. The illustration appears to show Attic script, perhaps *c.* 450–425: Lazarides, *PAE* 1952 (1955), 277, no. 4, fig. 25.

[2] For his dedication of a helmet to Zeus at Olympia, see Kunze, *Olympiabericht* v (1956), 69 ff.; the lettering is Attic.

[3] Dr. Richter suggests the third quarter of the 6th c., from the decoration (*AAG*, 85).

[4] Klaffenbach and Guarducci (see bibliography to

**35**) both agree that the sense is 'original settlers', i.e. the generation of those who settled Perinthos *c.* 600. Klaffenbach explains the word itself as οικηιοι with dittography (as printed here); Guarducci proposes a conjectural form οικητηιοι. L. Robert (by letter to Klaffenbach) suggests the other meaning of οικεῖοι, 'kindred'. Is it possible that (Me?)niskos and Demi(s) were οικηιοι in the sense of Perinthian officials responsible for the gifts stored in a Perinthian οἶκος or Treasury in the Samian Heraion, like the οἶκοι at Delphi and Olympia? (See now Robert, *REG* 1959, 225, no. 320.)

after 512, nor does the lettering suggest it; though we cannot tell whether the cutter was a Samian or a Perinthian, crossed *theta* savours of a date not later than 525.

The coins of Selymbria, a Megarian foundation, carry Σα, Σαλυ (**37**), which could be either Ionic or Megarian: they are dated shortly before the middle of the fifth century. The verse epitaph of Pythagoras, a Selymbrian proxenos who was buried in the Athenian Kerameikos about the middle of the fifth century (**38**), is in the eastern Ionic; so is the memorial of another Selymbrian of this century buried in Athens (**39**), whose ethnic is given mainly in the Doric, Σηλυμβριανά. We may then conjecture that by the middle of the fifth century, if not earlier (cf. Kalchedon, below), this Doric colony used the Ionic script.

No early inscriptions have yet been found at Byzantion, the most famous colony founded by Megara, but her silver coinage (**40**), begun *c.* 416, bears the legend Βυ, with a freak *beta* (see p. 132, Fig. 34), which, as Kirchhoff pointed out,[1] must be the Megarian *beta*. It is unlikely that Megara herself or Byzantion still used this archaic form *c.* 416, but, as Byzantion's local iron coinage had begun earlier,[2] the local *beta* may have been in normal use when the legend was first devised, and retained as part of the badge, like Corinthian *qoppa* and Sikyonian *san*.

## B. *Southern side*

Byzantion, then, evidently used the alphabet of Megara; but at Kalchedon on the opposite shore of the Bosporos a relief of about the middle of the sixth century has been found, bearing an inscription in the Ionic script (**41**): [· ·]ικος [*c.* 16–18] εμε κατεθηκε. The clumsy sculpture was once thought to show the Birth of Athena, but the wording of the inscription and the mourning gestures of the figures alike reveal it to be a grave-stele. Kalchedon presumably received this alphabet from the Milesian colonies round her; she may have passed it on further to the Euxine colony Mesambria (p. 368). Her coinage (*c.* 450–400) reads Καλχ (**42**).

There are as yet no inscriptions in the Aiolic alphabet from Sigeion. Attention may be drawn to a possible memorial of the Attic colony there, namely, a large Middle Corinthian aryballos, which was found somewhere in the Troad[3] and bears on its rim an Attic graffito: τενδι σοι Θοδεμος διδōσι ⫶ (**75**). As far as can be seen from its bad condition, the vase itself appears to belong to the first quarter of the sixth century, and this is confirmed by the lettering of the graffito, which at the lowest should not be later than *c.* 550. I have already discussed the lettering of the Attic inscription on the famous stele of Phanodikos found at Sigeion (**44**), and assigned it tentatively to the period *c.* 575–550 (p. 72).[4] The upper inscription, in the eastern Ionic script and dialect, is to be assigned to Phanodikos' native island Prokonnesos (**43**); the stele itself may have come from the famous marble

---

[1] Kirchhoff[4], 113.

[2] E. S. G. Robinson, *Hesperia*, suppl. viii (1949), 333.

[3] It was once thought to have come from Ophryneion, but P. Corbett informs me that there is no mention of this in the British Museum register, which describes it simply as 'discovered by Mr. Frank Calvert in the Troad'.

[4] Richter classes it with her earliest group of Attic stelai, *c.* 600–575, but without insisting on a fixed date (*AAG*, 21 f.); this would indeed be hardly possible, since the crowning member has gone and only the plain shaft survives.

quarries there. The lettering shows open *eta*, no *qoppa*, and geminated *nu*; the double-dot punctuation occurs occasionally in Ionic graffiti from Naukratis, and in the constitutional text from Chios (p. 337, **41**). The second (Attic) inscription (**44**) may have been ordered by the Attic colonists Haisopos and his brothers, when the stone was set up in Sigeion, simply because the shallow Ionic lettering was not easy to read after a short exposure to the weather.[1] A Prokonnesian named Melpothemis was buried at Athens (Conze 1504a, pl. 312); the script might be of the fifth century, or, equally possibly, of the early fourth.

Milesian Abydos has the Ionic Αβυδηνον on her coins (**45**) *c.* 480–450; the grave-stele of Simos of Abydos, buried in Athens, should also be of the fifth century (**46**; cf. sloping *nu*). Phokaian Lampsakos shows her Ionic script on a bronze hydria (**47**) found at Notion near Kolophon, inscribed as a prize from the games at Lampsakos: αθλον εγ Λαμψακο επι Λεωφαντο ⟨το?⟩ Λαμπρο. The lettering is perhaps to be dated *c.* 450.[2] The gravestone of Alexileos, buried in Athens, should not be later than *c.* 450–425, on the lettering (**48**). Two soldiers from Parion share a grave-stele in Athens, inscribed in Ionic and dated in the last decade of the fifth century (**49**). A fine Ionic inscription has been found in this area at Sidene, near the modern Biga on the Granikos,[3] commemorating two benefactors of a temple (**50**); the dedication is inscribed **boustrophedon** on one of two Ionic columns, and according to the lettering should not be earlier than the last quarter of the sixth century; it may be compared with similar lettering on inscriptions from Miletos (**32–34, 37**), and with the only archaic inscription yet found at Kyzikos, another Milesian colony. This is the broken stele which bears a copy (made in the first century B.C.) of a decree passed by the city in the year of Maiandrios (επι Μαιανδριου), the last two lines of the original being visible in the break (**51**); they correspond closely with those on the column from Biga (cf. *epsilon, nu, omega*), are also **boustrophedon**, and may also be dated *c.* 525–500; the 'sampi' of the early Ionic has been copied in the late script (p. 39). The gravestone of Mandron (**52**), found on the island Halone opposite Kyzikos, is palpably earlier (*c.* 550?); *epsilon* is still tailed, *omega* tilted.

## EUXINE

A considerable number of gravestones, said to be all of the fifth century, has been found at Apollonia, Miletos' colony founded *c.* 610 (Strabo 319; Ps.-Skymnos 730 ff.); but

[1] Professor Wade-Gery drew my attention to a full-sized copy of this inscription now in the Bodleian at Oxford (Gough Maps 44, p. 121, no. 218), made by Bernard Mould on the morning of 10 June 1722 during a voyage from Smyrna to Constantinople. It was then in the church of 'a poor village called Gaurkioï'. The left edge of his paper is torn away, with the description of the stele itself. He apparently copied the upper (Ionic) inscription carefully, the lower (Attic) in more of a hurry, and so had some scruples over the points where his copy disagreed with the printed text of Chishull. On the upper, he read the archaic upright vi throughout, *rho* with slightly varying loops, and *omega* with curled struts as ω4 in Fig. 46, p. 325. On the lower he read the normal Attic *gamma* in κἀγō, and κ|δōκα

wrongly for ε|δōκα in ll. 5–6. He adds a note: 'I had forgot to observe that the sculpture of the inscription is very mean & poor, a thin, shallow stroke. Especially the upper one, wch. looks more like scratching than engraving. Tho' the under one be something more even, & bold than the upper, yet neither of them is any argument for the skill of those times, or at le(a)st for the art of those engravers.'

[2] The letters include a flattened *phi*, which normally suggests a date after 450, and *omega* with curled struts, which should be rather earlier; the hydria itself is ascribed to the 4th c. in the *Führer d. Antiquarium* (Berlin) i. 99, but I do not think that the inscription can be so late.

[3] The site was identified by Professor G. E. Bean.

only two are of interest here. One is the funeral stele of Anaxandros (**54**); the style of the relief belongs to the first years of the fifth century, and the epigram is an excellent example of good Ionic script of the first quarter of the century. The second, written *boustrophedon* upwards (cf. the Samian stelai **1** and **8**) is probably considerably earlier (**53**). There are no early inscriptions from Mesambria, a joint colony of Kalchedon and Megara, but her coins dated *c.* 450–350 show the legend ΜΕΤΑ (**56**); it has been suggested that her script, with this unmistakable Ionic '*sampi*', may have come from Apollonia, but, as we have seen, the Ionic alphabet was used at Kalchedon, and Mesambria's script may well have come thence (p. 366). Two inscribed grave-stelai are reported, one said to be *c.* 420–410, the other possibly of the fourth century.[1] The excavations of V. Pârvan and others at Istria, founded by Miletos probably in the second half of the seventh century,[2] have yielded two statue-bases inscribed in good Ionic letters of the second half of the fifth century (**57**).[3] The bases held bronze statues of Leto and Apollo ἰητρός; and both are dated by the name of the eponymous priest of Apollo, επι Ιππολοχο | το Θεοδοτο ιερεω. At Olbia, one of the greatest of Miletos' northern settlements, large numbers of vases and other small objects inscribed with graffiti (mostly brief or fragmentary) have been found, showing the Ionic script of the mother-city; judged by the published illustrations, none is earlier than the sixth century. Some are in the museum at Odessa (**59**), others in the Hermitage, Leningrad (**58**). A fine double-relief grave-stele from Olbia, bearing up its side the epitaph of one Leoxos (**60**), is dated by its style to the first quarter of the fifth century, perhaps *c.* 490. Many graffiti on vases and other small objects have been found also in the flourishing settlement on the island at the mouth of the Borysthenes, a few dated in the sixth century (**61**). A fragmentary graffito on a sherd from Chersonesos is dated to the fifth century (**62**); and several from Nymphaion are apparently earlier (**63**). A graffito on a kylix from Theodosia should belong to the first half of the fifth century, according to the type copy of some of the letters (**64**). At Pantikapaion the grave-stelai of Neomenis(?) (**65**) and Eualkides (**66**) may (according to the copies) belong to the first half of the fifth century; that of Tychon (**67**) can hardly be earlier than the second half (cf. the flattened *omega*, as Fig. 46, ω6), although the third line was apparently written in false *boustrophedon*.[4] The coins of Pantikapaion ascribed to the fifth century show Παντ (**69**). There are also many brief graffiti on vases and sherds of the fifth century from this site, all in the Ionic script (**68**); and some few, of the same style and date, from Taman (**70**).

Little can be said of the inscription on a sculptured relief, 'mightily impaired by Time', found somewhere between the Tanais and Phanagoreia by La Motraye in the early eighteenth century (**71**); since it showed crossed *theta*, it probably belonged to the archaic period. The published drawing of the relief is hopelessly overlaid with eighteenth-century taste. A silver phiale mesomphalos from Phasis is said to be not later in date than the early fifth century, but the dedication to Apollo inscribed on it (illustrated in type only) is assigned to the years *c.* 420–400: Απολλωνος ηγεμονος ειμι τὸμ Φασι. The coins of Sinope, Miletos' great colony on the southern coast of the Euxine, probably belong to

---

[1] Mihailov i. 330–1.

[2] See V. Pârvan, *Dacia* (1928), 82 ff.

[3] Pârvan published another Istrian inscription as 5th c. (*Dacia* ii (1925), 199. 1); but from his illustration the letters suggest rather the 4th c.

[4] Watzinger no. 37, pl. 1, is also perhaps of the 5th c., judged by the photograph.

the mid-fifth century or shortly after; *omega* has not yet the flattened shape of the later examples (**74**). A sculptured grave-stele, chiselled by a provincial hand in the style of the second quarter of the century, bears the name of Gaga, wife of Anaximbrotos (**73**). The lettering is the normal eastern Ionic, with the 'spineless' ξ for *xi*. A solid young Bithynian, Gaga sits on a chair with her maid standing by. Plainly the picture is copied straight from some earlier Greek prototype of Hegeso's stele in the Athenian Kerameikos. It serves to remind the viewer how seldom other nations, when presented with a Greek model, could work on it such alchemy as that which transmuted their own gifts to the Greeks.

## SELECT CATALOGUE (B = Babelon ii. 1.)

### CHALKIDIKE

*Aineia*

**1.** Coinage inscribed Αινειας; 6th c. end, onwards. B 1111 ff., pl. 49. *HN²*, 214.

*Dikaia*

**2.** Coinage inscribed Δικα; *c.* 500–450. B 1125 ff., pl. 51. *HN²*, 213.

*Mende*

**3.** Coinage inscribed Μινδαον; *c.* 500–450. B 1129 ff., pl. 51. *HN²*, 211.

*Skione*

**4.** Coinage inscribed Σκιο; 6th c. end, onwards. B 1145 ff., pl. 52. *HN²*, 210.

*Sermyle*

**5.** Coinage inscribed Σερμυλικον, &c.; 6th c. end. B 1163 ff., pl. 53. *HN²*, 207.

*Torone*

**6.** Coinage inscribed Τε; *c.* 500–480. B 1159 ff., pl. 52. *HN²*, 206 f.

**7.** Gravestone of Mikkos, buried in Athens; *c.* 475–450? Conze 1325, pl. 280. *IG* i². 1044. EM?

**8.** Gravestone of Nautes, buried in Athens; *c.* 450–400? Conze 1328a. *IG* i². 1043.

*Akanthos*

**9.** Coinage inscribed Ακαν; *c.* 480. B 1165, pl. 53. *HN²*, 204.

*Potidaia*

**10.** Dedication of Theugenes at Delphi; *c.* 475? *SIG³* 15. Roehl³, 44. 6. Marcadé i. 29, pl. 5. 3. Delphi Mus. 2254+3080. PL. 70

**11.** Coinage inscribed Πο, Π; 6th c. B 1147 ff., pl. 52. *HN²*, 212.

*Olynthos*

**12.** Gravestone of Polyxena from Olynthos; *c.* 500–480. D. M. Robinson, *TAPA* lxii (1931), 40 f. PL. 70

**13.** Gravestone of Neumo from Olynthos; *c.* 500–480. D. M. Robinson, *TAPA* lxix (1938), 43 f., pl. 1. PL. 70

**14.** Gravestone of Antiphilos, buried in Athens; *c.* 450–425. Conze 928, pl. 184. PL. 71

*Aphytis*

**15.** Copy of Athenian Coinage Decree; *c.* 449/8? *ATL* ii. 63 f., D 14.


### MACEDONIA AND SOUTHERN THRACE

**16.** Coinage inscribed Βισαλτικον, &c.; *c.* 500–480. B 1071 ff., pl. 45. *HN*², 199.

**17.** Coinage inscribed Μοσσεω; *c.* 500–480. B 1069 ff., pl. 46. *HN*², 200.

**18.** Coinage inscribed Γετα, &c.; *c.* 500–480. B 1049 ff., pl. 45. *HN*², 201.

**19.** Coinage inscribed Δερρονικος; *c.* 500–480. B 1039 ff., pl. 44. *HN*², 201.

**20.** Coinage inscribed Ωρησκιων, &c.; *c.* 500–480. B 1057 ff., pls. 45–46. *HN*², 194.

**21.** Coinage inscribed Τυντενον, Δοκι, Ζαιελεων, Διονυ-, -ναιω; *c.* 500–480. B 1107 f., 1067 f., 1065 ff., pl. 46. *HN*², 195, 199.

*Neapolis*

**22.** Graffiti on 'Ionian' cups from the precinct of the Parthenos; 6th c. Bakalakes, *AE* 1938, 112 f.

*Ichnai*

**23.** Coinage inscribed [I]χναι[ον]; *c.* 500–480. B 1103 ff., pl. 49. *HN*², 199.

*Aigai*

**24.** Coinage inscribed δε, λα, θ; *c.* 500–480. B 1095 ff., pl. 49. *HN*², 198 f.

*Lete*

**25.** Coinage inscribed Λεταιον; 6th c. end. B 1113 ff., pl. 50. *HN*², 197.

*Tragilos*

**26.** Coinage inscribed Τραι, &c.; *c.* 450–400. *HN*², 217.

*Kingdom of Macedon*

**27.** Coinage inscribed Αλεξανδρο; *c.* 480–454. B 1077 ff., pls. 47–48. *HN*², 218.

*Abdera*

**28.** Coinage with names of eponymoi; late 6th c. onwards. B 1203 ff., pl. 56. *HN*², 253.

**29.** Dedication of Python at the Peiraieus, Athens; *c.* 475–450? Roehl³, 30. 44. *IG* i². 826. *DAA* 500. Peiraieus Mus.

*Dikaia-by-Abdera*

**30.** Coinage inscribed Δικ, Δικαι; *c.* 500–480? B 1209 ff., pl. 56. *HN*², 252.

*Maroneia*

**31.** Coinage inscribed Μαρω, &c., *c.* 500–480; magistrates' names, *c.* 475 onwards. B 1215 ff., pl. 57. *HN*², 248.

*Ainos*

**32.** Coinage inscribed Αινιον, &c.; *c.* 450. *HN*², 246.

*Mende in Thrace*

**33.** Dedicatory inscriptions and signature, drafted by the sculptor Paionios, for the Nike of the Naupactian Messenians at Olympia and Delphi; *c.* 425. *Ol.* v. 259. Roehl³, 30. 45. *SIG³* 80–81. *GHI²* 65. Harder, *JdI* 1943, 128 f., fig. 34; *Neue Beiträge* (ed. Lullies, 1954), 192 ff. *SEG* xiv. 352. Olympia Mus. 5. PL. 71

### HELLESPONT AND PROPONTIS

*Chersonesos*

**34.** Coinage inscribed in Attic script Χερ; *c.* 515–493? B 1223 ff., pl. 57. *HN²*, 257.

*Perinthos*

**35.** Stele recording Perinthian gifts to the Heraion at Samos; *c.* 525? Klaffenbach, *DM* vi (1953), 15 ff., pl. 3. *SEG* xii. 391. Guarducci, *Studi di storia e antichità gr. e rom.* i (1956), 23 ff. Vathy Mus. PL. 71

**36.** Gravestone of Hegesipolis from Perinthos; *c.* 525? *SGDI* 5722. Roehl³, 30. 46. *AAG*, 85, fig. 17. PL. 71

*Selymbria*

**37.** Coinage inscribed Σα, Σαλυ; *c.* 475–450. B 1221 ff., pl. 56. *HN²*, 271.

**38.** Gravestone of Pythagoras, buried in Athens; *c.* 450. *SGDI* 5781. Conze 1440a, pl. 293a. *IG* i². 1034. Peek i. 45. Kerameikos.

**39.** Gravestone of Xeno, buried in Athens; 5th c. Conze 1330. Lost?

*Byzantion*

**40.** Coinage inscribed Βυ; *c.* 416. B ii. 4, 973 ff., pl. 347. *HN²*, 266.

*Kalchedon*

**41.** Gravestone of -iko (?) from Kalchedon; mid-6th c.? Mendel, *Cat. Sculpt. Constantinople* ii (1914), 524. Jeffery, *BSA* l (1955), 81 f., pl. 10. Istanbul Mus. 1136. PL. 71

**42.** Coinage inscribed Καλχ; mid-5th c. onwards. B ii. 2. 1491 ff., pl. 181. *HN²*, 511.

*Prokonnesos*

**43.** Gravestone of Phanodikos from Sigeion, upper part inscribed at Prokonnesos; mid-6th c.? Roberts i. 42. *BMI* 1002. *SGDI* 5531. *SIG³* 2. *DGE* 731. *SEG* iv. 667. Brouwers, *REG* 1928, 107 ff. Berve, *Miltiades* (1937), 26 ff. Guarducci, *Ann.* iii (1941–2), 135 ff. *AAG*, 21 f. Buck 1. BM. PL. 71

*Sigeion*

**44.** Lower inscription on gravestone of Phanodikos from Sigeion; mid-6th c.? See **43.**

*Abydos*

**45.** Coinage inscribed Αβυδηνον; *c.* 480–450. B ii. 2. 1321 ff., pl. 167. *HN²*, 538.

**46.** Gravestone of Simos of Abydos, Athens; 5th c.? *IG* i². 1076.

*Lampsakos*

**47.** Bronze prize hydria from Notion; *c.* 450? Fölzer, *Die Hydria* (1906), 88, pl. 9. Neugebauer, *Führer d. das Antiquarium* i (1924), 199. Richter in *Antike Plastik* (1928), 189. Berlin Antiquarium 30636.

**48.** Gravestone of Alexileos, buried in Athens; *c.* 450–425? Conze 1327, pl. 280. *IG* i². 1049. EM.

PL. 71

*Parion*

**49.** Gravestone of two soldiers buried in Athens; *c.* 410–400. *BMI* 1107. Peek i. 218. BM.

*Sidene*

**50.** Dedication of a temple; *c.* 525–500. L. Robert, *Hellenica* ix (1950), 78 ff., pl. 10. Istanbul Mus. 4933.

PL. 71

*Kyzikos*

**51.** Fragment of an honorific decree; *c.* 525–500? Roehl³, 20. 6. *DGE* 732. Vollgraff, *Mnemosyne* l (1922), 37 ff. Istanbul Mus.

PL. 72

*Halone*

**52.** Gravestone of Mandron; *c.* 550? Wilamowitz and Jacobsthal, *Nordionische Steine* (1909), 63 f., fig. 6. Istanbul Mus.

PL. 72

EUXINE

*Apollonia Pontica*

**53.** Gravestone of Aspasia; 6th c. Papaioannides, *Thrakika* ii (1929), 294. 3. Mihailov i. 404. Odessa Mus. II. 930.

**54.** Gravestone of Anaxandros; *c.* 500–475. *AA* 1896, 136 ff. Langlotz, *FGB*, 138. 17. Apostolides, *Thrakika* ix (1938), 9. 20. Friedlaender 78. Johansen, *The Attic Grave Reliefs* (1951), 127. Peek i. 326. Mihailov i. 405. Sofia, NM 727.

PL. 72

**55.** Gravestones from Apollonia; 5th c. *SGDI* 5536–8. Roehl³, 30. 47. Apostolides, op. cit. 1 ff. Mihailov, *Mus. Nat. Bulg.* ii (1948), 59 ff. (known to me only from *REG* 1950, 174). Mihailov i. 406–49. Sofia, NM.

*Mesambria*

**56.** Inscribed coinage; *c.* 450 onwards. B ii. 4. 1031 ff., pl. 352. *HN²*, 278.

*Istria*

**57.** Dedications on two statue-bases of Leto and Apollo; *c.* 450–400. Lambrino, *Dacia* iii–iv (1927–32), 391 ff., figs. 8–10.

*Olbia*

**58.** Graffiti on vases of the 6th and 5th c. I. Tolstoi, *Grecheskie Graffiti* (1953), nos. 5, 10, 18–19, 39–41, 59 (6th c.), 1–2, 6, 11–15, 20–29, 42–49, 70–72 (5th c.). Leningrad, Hermitage.

PL. 72

**59.** Graffiti on vases of the 5th c. Von Stern, *Philologus* lxxii (1913), 547. Kočevalov, *Würzb. Jahrbücher* 1948, 265. Odessa Mus.

**60.** Gravestone of Leoxos; *c.* 500–475. Wilhelm, 205 ff. *IAOSPE* i² (1916), 270. *SEG* iii. 594. Langlotz, *FGB* 127, 130, pl. 76. Bakalakes, Ἑλληνικὰ Ἀμφίγλυφα (1946), 46 ff. Johansen, op. cit. 127 f. Peek i. 1172. Cherson Mus.

PL. 72

*Borysthenes island*

**61.** Graffiti on (*a*) small vase, 6th c. Von Stern, loc. cit. (*b*) lamp, 6th or early 5th c.? Von Stern, loc. cit. (*c*) sherds, Tolstoi, op. cit. 76–77 (6th c.), 75, 78–79 (5th c.). Leningrad, Hermitage.

PL. 72

*Chersonesos*

**62.** Graffito on sherd; 5th c. Tolstoi, op. cit. 87. Leningrad, Hermitage.

*Nymphaion*

**63.** Graffiti on sherds and vases; 6th to 5th c. Tolstoi, op. cit. 97, 106, 129 (6th c.), 98–103, 107–21, 127–8, 130–9, 142, 144 (5th c.). Leningrad, Hermitage.              PL. 72

*Theodosia*

**64.** Graffito on a kylix; *c.* 500–450? *SGDI* 5579. Leningrad, Hermitage.

*Pantikapaion*

**65.** Gravestone of Neomenis; *c.* 500–450? Watzinger, *Griech. Grabreliefs aus Südrussland* (1909), 3, pl. 1. *IAOSPE* iv. 328. Kertch Mus.

**66.** Gravestone of Eualkides; *c.* 500–450? Watzinger, op. cit. 102, pl. 5. Kertch Mus.

**67.** Gravestone of Tychon; *c.* 450–400? Watzinger, op. cit. 1. *SEG* iii. 608. Peek i. 325. Kertch Mus.

**68.** Graffiti on vases and sherds; 6th–5th c. Tolstoi, op. cit. 165, 185 (6th c.), 159–61, 163–4, 166–72, 186–204, 206, 209–15, 238–41, 244 (5th c.). Leningrad, Hermitage.

**69.** Coinage inscribed Παν, Παντ, Παντι; 5th c. B 410. *HN*², 280.

*Taman*

**70.** Graffiti on vases and sherds; 5th c. Tolstoi, op. cit. 246–9, 251, 254. Leningrad, Hermitage.

*Phanagoreia* (?)

**71.** Inscribed relief found by La Motraye between Tanais and Phanagoreia; late archaic? A. de la Motraye, *Voyages en Europe, Asie, Afrique* ii (1727), 73 ff., pl. 4. 11–12 (English ed. (1732), 50 ff., pl. 27. 11–12). *CIG* 2133. *IGA* 350. Guarducci, *L'Istituzione della Fratria* i (1937), 76 f. Lost.

*Phasis*

**72.** Silver phiale mesomphalos from the river Kuban; 5th c. V. Kieseritzky, *AA* 1901, 56.

*Sinope*

**73.** Gravestone of Gaga; *c.* 450? Akurgal, *Zwei Grabstelen vorklassischer Zeit aus Sinope* (1955), 5 ff., figs. 5–7. Akurgal and Budde, *Vorläuf. Bericht ü. d. Ausgrab. in Sinope* (1956), 19 ff., pl. 7. *SEG* xvi. 751. Kastamonu Mus.              PL. 72

**74.** Coinage inscribed Σινω; *c.* 450–400. B ii. 2. 1521 ff., pl. 184.

*Inscription attributed to Sigeion*

**75.** Attic graffito on a MC aryballos from the Troad; *c.* 600–575? *IGA* 2. Roehl³, 72. 16. BM. PL. 72

# ADDENDA AND CORRIGENDA

*P. 6, n. 2.* See now R. M. Cook and A. G. Woodhead, *AJA* lxiii (1959), 175 ff., on the diffusion of the Greek alphabet. In their view the local differences may be due to the fact that in Al Mina, and perhaps other such coastal settlements in the area, individual Greeks chanced to learn different forms of letters; 'so a multiplicity of personal alphabets arose, and it was mostly chance which (and how many) of these personal adaptations were brought by returning traders to any Greek city' (p. 178). They admit, however, that all these varieties had certain common characteristics (the five vowels, the style of the letters, the alteration of certain consonantal values, and the invention of new letters). Thus their observations would seem to differ more in emphasis than in substance from those advanced in Part I of this book, where it is suggested that a nucleus of bilingual Greeks in Al Mina, or in that general area, adopted the Semitic script, producing in their alphabet the characteristics noted above, and that the variations in shape of certain letters (as, e.g., in *iota* or in *mu*) came chiefly by chance or error in the transmission thence to other Greek centres.

*P. 21.* See now R. S. Young, *AJA* lxii (1958), 139 ff., for Phrygian graffiti on bronze and clay vessels in a tomb at Gordion, tentatively dated in the late 8th c. B.C. The Phrygian, Lydian, Lycian, and Carian alphabets are usually held to be derived mainly from the Greek, but because none of the examples of these scripts known hitherto could be dated with any confidence as earlier than the 6th c. B.C., I have not used these as evidence for the date of the earliest Greek alphabet. The suggested date for this tomb rests chiefly on the radio-carbon analysis of the wood and textiles, and on the style of the fibulae and certain of the vessels.

*P. 50, n. 1.* I. Zinn suggests that this style, which he calls 'Schlangenschrift' or 'Ur-Boustrophedon', was the original whence developed the true *boustrophedon* style (*AA* 1950, 1 ff.).

*P. 70.* **10d** was wrongly described by me as 'from Naukratis' in *BSA* l (1955), 69.

*P. 83, n. 2.* Another inscription assigned to Euboia by dialect and alphabet is the signature Συριἒς εποιἒσε on a late archaic gem in the British Museum, to which Sir John Beazley drew my attention (Beazley, *The Lewes House Collection of Ancient Gems* (1920), 18 ff.).

*P. 95,* **11.** *Add:* Papagiannopoulos-Palaios, *Polemon* vi (1956–7), 3 ff., fig. 1.

*P. 98.* M. Sordi (*Riv. Fil.* 1958, 59 ff.) dates **10**, the bronze plaque from Thetonion, shortly after 457, following the eviction of Orestes of Pharsalos, *tagos* of Thessaly (Thuc. i. 111).

Part of a grave-inscription apparently of about the middle of the 5th c., found near Larisa, is published by P. Frank, *AA* 1956, 19 f.

*P. 102, n. 6, and p. 104.* See now G. Daux, *BCH* lxxxii (1958), 329 ff., pl. 23, for a base at Delphi which once bore the bronze statue of a horse. He restores the inscription: Θεσσαλοι τον ⱶιππον ανεθεν τὀπολλōνι δεκαταν τον α[π]ο Ταναγ[ραιōν or -ρας], | πολεμαρχεοντōν τōνδε· | Αμυντα | Αρχαγορο | και{ς} | Προτεας | Ευκρατιδας |Μεννēς | ⱶυβριλαος | Πολυδαμας. I have no doubt that Daux is right in assigning this offering to one of the Athenian battles in Boiotia *c.* 458, either Tanagra (i.e. the Thessalians shared in the spoils), or Oinophyta (if the Thessalians rejoined the Athenian side); as he says, there are many gaps in our knowledge of the shifts of Thessalian policy at this time. The dialect is Phokian, and so is the script, which appears to me to be that of the mason who cut **17**. Another Phokian 5th-c. inscription: Bousquet, *BCH* lxxxiii (1959), 146 f., fig. 1.

*Pp. 107 f.,* **17**. See also Bousquet, *BCH* lxxx (1956), 591 ff., for the same view as Wade-Gery, loc. cit.

*P. 112.* For examples of athletes whose dedications were made some time after their victories, see P. Amandry, *Charites* (1957), 63 ff.

*P. 119.* Inscriptions in the local script have now been found by Dr. O. Broneer in his excavation of the temple of Poseidon on the Isthmus: a Panathenaic amphora of the 6th c., with a graffito in Corinthian, Δαμōν ανεθēκε (*BCH* lxxxi (1957), 531, fig. 11); a stone haltēr also of the 6th c., inscribed on both sides *boustrophedon*: [- - -]ε πεντα϶ε|θλεον νικα and [- - -]αιον δ' Ϝιν|[ο]ιδ'(?) ευχομενο[- - -] (*Hesperia* xxviii (1959), 322 f., fig. 4, pl. 73*a*); and a very fragmentary metrical inscription (early 5th c.?) on a damaged poros base, probably from a grave, which appears to include the phrase πασι και εσομε[νοις] (op. cit. 323, pl. 65*a*). Single letters mark some of the blocks of the *diolkos* across the Isthmus, excavated by N. Verdeles; they are described as early 6th c. (Verdeles, *AM* lxxi (1956), 51 ff., Beil. 37–38), but, from the photographs, need not be earlier than the 5th c.

*P. 127, n. 3.* For an explanation of the animals on the roots of the palm-tree, see P. Jacobsthal, *Greek Pins* (1956), 59. I owe this reference to Sir John Beazley.

*P. 157, n. 1.* G. Huxley returns to a date for Pheidon in the second half of the 8th c. (*BCH* lxxxii (1958), 588 ff.).

*P. 192, n. 1.* C. Rolley (*BCH* lxxxii (1958), 168 ff., figs. 1–3) denies that the letters on the Vix krater are typical Lakonian; but cf. my comments on p. 192. The letter in the place of *rho*, as R. rightly notes, is not like Lakonian *rho*. I think that in fact it is *qoppa;* it should not immediately precede *sigma* in the abecedarium, but here the letters μ, ν, ο, π, M are omitted as well as ρ. He claims that the 'Lakonian *sigma*' on the neck is a four-stroked one badly written, but I should call it a five-stroked one badly written (see my remarks on the Lakonian *sigma* on pp. 186 f.).

*P. 251, n. 5.* For a detailed study of the coins of Sybarite type and their distribution among the successive settlements of the later Sybarites, including the final Sybaris V on the Traeis, see now C. M. Kraay, *Num. Chron.* xviii (1958), 13 ff., pls. 3–4. In particular he makes the interesting suggestion that the settlers of Sybaris V may possibly have struck an archaizing stater which returned to the incuse style and the local script.

*P. 253, n. 3.* Dr. Kraay has drawn my attention to S. P. Noe, *Am. Num. Soc. Museum Notes V*, 9 ff., pls. 5–6. A series of Poseidoniate coins of the latter part of the 5th c. ('*c.* 430–10', Noe) shows die-sequences lettered consecutively with the Ionic alphabet α–ι, with the legends still in the local script; and in some cases the same coin has one die with legend in the local script, the other with legend in Ionic.

*P. 255.* For '*NH* xiv. 9', read '*NH* xiv. 2. 9'.

*P. 258.* Dr. Kraay kindly sends me the following information on the coinage of Kaulonia: 'Preceding the regular use of Ionic forms there is a period going back to *c.* 425, in which both local and Ionic forms are used within the same groups of coins. Earlier than this the local forms are invariable. These conclusions are based on (1) the date of destruction of Kaulonia, and presumed end of her coinage, in 389, and (2) the fact that coin groups using only Ionic forms amount only to 16 obverse dies, so cannot be spread over a very long period.'

*P. 263, line 21.* For '2' read '1–2'.

*P. 270, n. 3.* See also Vallet and Villard, *BCH* lxxxii (1958), 21 f., fig. 6. Republishing this vase, they observe that the technique is Sikeliot, the clay and paint being typical of large vases from Megara Hyblaia, and point out that the script used corresponds with the earliest scripts of Syracuse and Megara Hyblaia. For the kouros **25**, see also Schefold, *Meisterwerke griechischer Kunst*, 173, no. 111a (reference from Sir John Beazley).

*P. 274.* See also Bousquet, *BCH* lxxxiii (1959), 149 ff., fig. 4, for the base of a dedication at Delphi, *c.* 475–450?: Ακραγαντινοι τ[οῖ Απολ]λōνι.

*P. 287.* Siris: M. Guarducci has published (*Atti e Memorie della Società Magna Grecia*, 1958, 51 ff., pl. 14) an inscription on a bronze plaque, found near Metapontion: θεος : χρēματα : τας θεο επι | Σιρι επι δρομōι. | κραδεσμα : αργυρεα : τεзερα | χαλκιον : ι (private collection of the Barone Gioachino Malfatti). The script is Achaian; I should set it in the first half of the 5th c., *c.* 475 (?); for the resettlement of Siris with Achaians after her defeat by her Achaian neighbours in the late 6th c., see *JHS* lxix (1949), 32 f. Miss Guarducci dates the plaque in the second half of the 6th c., and thinks that the original Sirites remained, but were compelled to adopt the dialect and alphabet of their conquerors (p. 58). Massalia: in *BCH* lxxxii (1958), 360 ff., figs. 1–2, Daux republishes with photograph and drawing the fragment (Inv. no. 5844) from the architecture of the Massaliote Treasury at Delphi inscribed —σσαλ—, the second *sigma* apparently added afterwards. The Treasury itself is plausibly identified with the Aiolic building in the Marmaria, dated by its style to the latter years of the 6th c. Daux holds the inscription to be of the end of the 5th or start of the 4th c. In view of the advanced, if sometimes untidy, look of much Ionic script compared with the contemporary lettering of other states, this inscription might possibly belong to the end of the 6th c., the $-\sigma\sigma-$ being spelt by a single *sigma*, until later (as Daux suggests) another mason added the second.

*P. 289. Zeta*, omitted from Fig. 44, is attested in the early 5th c. (**34**).

*P. 293.* L. Polites publishes in *AE* 1953–4 ii (1958), 24 ff., figs. 1–2, an inscribed stele-base found in the region of Aigiale, and now in the archaeological collection at Katapola. The inscription, in good lettering, may be c. 450:

αντι γυναικος εγω Παριο λιθο ενθαδε κειμαι
μνημοσυνον Βιττης, μητρι δακρυτον αχος.

*P. 303, n. 6.* See now H. Gallet de Santerre, *Délos primitive et archaïque* (1958), for references to **2** (253 f., 290 f.), **3** (242 f.), **4** (323), **10** (242), **30** (254 f., 290 f.), **42** (264).

*P. 320.* A fine silver coin of Kyrene, now in the British Museum, shows (obverse) head of Zeus Ammon to r., (reverse) in square incuse a silphion plant, a bridled horse's protome to r., and legend KYP (Jenkins, *Num. Chron.* 1955, 150 ff., pl. 13). Jenkins suggests (loc. cit.) a date shortly after 480; E. S. G. Robinson (ibid., n. 39) prefers 462 or 460, recalling the chariot-victories of Arkesilas IV. Since *qoppa* is gone and *upsilon* is in the developed form, the later date may be preferred by epigraphists.

*P. 322.* I have not seen the article by Kontoleon, Ἐπιστημ. ἐπετηρὶς τῆς φιλοσ. σχολῆς Πανεπ. Ἀθηνῶν, 1957–8, 218 ff. (reported by J. and L. Robert, *REG* 1959 (Bull. Épig.), 220, no. 294): he suggests that the Grophon of **29** was a descendant of Grophon of **23** (for which he retains the early 6th-c. date), and also (p. 233) describes a newly found base, not later than the beginning of the 5th c., Φειδον ανεθηκεν.

*P. 326, n. 1.* See now also M. B. Sakellariou, *La Migration grecque en Ionie* (1958), and Roebuck, *Ionian Trade and Colonization* (1959).

*Pp. 328, 333 n. 1, 334 n. 2, 336, 342 f.* The archaic inscriptions of Didyma have now been fully published (Harder, *Didyma* ii, 1958), and I add the following references: (i) *Pp. 333 n. 1, 336.* **38.** Fragment from the left-hand side of the chair of a seated figure, bearing 10 lines *boustrophedon* (now lost, but known from a squeeze). Apollo and ?Hekate are mentioned. The lettering, neat and square like that of **39**, can hardly be earlier than *c.* 500. Op. cit., no. 16, fig. 21. (ii) *P. 334, n. 2.* Dedication by one Timandros, cut *boustrophedon* on a broken twelve-sided pillar-base; letters small and straggling, as in Samos **4**; *c.* 575–550? Ibid., no. 4, fig 4. (iii) *Pp. 342 f.* Add new references: **22**, ibid., no. 1, fig. 1. **23**, ibid., no. 2, fig. 2. **24**, ibid., no. 9, figs. 12–14. **25**, ibid., nos. 12–13, figs. 17–18. **27**, ibid., no. 5, figs. 5–6. **29**, ibid., no. 6, figs. 7–9. **30**, ibid., no. 7, fig. 10. **32**, ibid., no. 14, fig. 19. **36**, ibid., no. 11, fig. 16.

*P. 338,* **42e.** J. Boardman informs me that this cup almost certainly belongs, on the evidence of style and stratigraphy, to the end of the 7th c. (that is, to the Early Corinthian period as at present dated).

*P. 341, line 9.* For 'ω 4' read 'υ 4, ω 4'.

*P. 343,* **41**. See now also J. H. Oliver, *AJP* 1959, 296 ff.

*P. 352, n. 5.* J. Cook and G. Bean refer briefly to this epigram, *BSA* lii (1957), 121, 123. *SGDI* 5773 is an inscription from Astypalaia, apparently of the late 6th or early 5th c., in Ionic script and dialect: Κλεταγορηι και Ξειναγο[ρηι]. The Ionic dialect indicates that the inscription was not the work of a Koan.

*P. 353.* The British Museum has now acquired an electrum *trite* inscribed r. to l. Φανεος, i.e. an unusual genitive form of Phanes. E. S. G. Robinson observes that in the 'Halikarnassian' coin's legend the die-cutter probably cut Φαενος in error, and then erased *epsilon*: and that the series was probably struck at Ephesos, because a small-change coin bearing a deer-protome of like style has been found at Ephesos, and small coins travel less than large ones (*Am. Num. Soc. Centenary Vol.* (1958), 586 ff., pl. 39, 3).

*P. 361, n. 2.* In *Troy, Settlements VIIa, VIIb, and VIII,* iv. 1 (1958), 266, Professor Blegen and others publish a few more pre-4th-c. graffiti from the archaic site of Troy VIII: e.g. p. 266, fig. 293. 4,—οσμηω (6th c.?); 280, fig. 316, Απολλōνιδαιαι : εμμι : [το]ι Ιπποκλειοι (late 5th c.? see Blegen ad loc.). The use of curved *delta* D in Aiolic is here confirmed, and *omega* is attested.

*P. 365.* In Τὸ Ἔργον τῆς Ἀρχαιολογικῆς Ἑταιρείας *1959*, 42 f., fig. 41, Dr. Lazarides publishes a marble stele from a small shrine in the area of Amphipolis, inscribed: Ευμητις | Ηγησιστρατο | Κλεοι | ανεθηκεν. The script is Ionic, and suggests a date in the 5th c., perhaps not later than the third quarter.

# INDEX I. EPIGRAPHICAL

## A. PERSONS

## B. PLACES, ETHNICS, ETC.

## C. DEITIES, HEROES, ETC.

## D. PRINCIPAL WORDS

# INDEX II. INSCRIPTIONS NOT IN THE CATALOGUES

# INDEX III. ANCIENT AUTHORS

# INDEX IV. GENERAL

Reference to a catalogue is made here only if an inscription included there has not been mentioned elsewhere in the text. insc. = inscribed, p. = pot-painter, s. = son, sc. = sculptor.

Abdera 60, 340, 364 f.; Abderites in Athens 365

abecedaria, general 4, 21, 26 ff., 48, 326 f.; examples of: Greek 44, 69, 94, 116 f., 125, 183, 190 n. 4, 192, 236 f., 256, 280, 283, 293; Etruscan 4, 48, 236 f.; Messapic 283

Abou Simbel, Greek inscriptions at 38, 48, 314, 338, 340, 348, 355

Abydos (Egypt) 314, 355, 360; (Hellespont) 367; Abydenes in Athens 367

Achaia 213 f., 221 ff.; western colonies of 248 ff.; Achaians in Aitolia 225 f., Akarnania 227, Delphi (?) 223, Ithake 230, Olympia 221

Acheloos 213, 254

Achilles 71, 141, 159, 226

Admetos 159

Adrastos 156, 159

Aetos (Ithake) 230 f.

Afrati 314

Agamemnon, heröon of 173

Agariste of Sikyon 157, 225

Agatha(rchos?) 141

Agathon 93

Ageladas, sc. 160 f., 281 f.

Agemo 209 f.

Agesilaos of Sparta 55

Agloteles 319

agreements, written 106, 218 f.; see also arbitration, treaties

Aiakes (Aeakes) s. of Brychon (Bryson?) 330; Aiakes I 330

Aigai (Macedon) 364

Aigiale (Amorgos) 293 and Addenda

Aigina 109 ff., 338; Aiginetans in Athens 110, Eretria 86, Kydonia 314, Naukratis 110, Olympia 112

Aigion (Achaia) 222

Aiglanor s. of Antipatros 320

Aigletes 192

Aineia 363

Aineias (Arkadia) 210; (hero) 363

Ainesidemos of Leontinoi 242

Aineta 121, 125 f., 126

Ainetos 195, 197

Ainia (Amazon) 71

Ainis 96

Ainos 365

Aiolis 359 f.

Aischron 172 n. 2

Aischros s. of Zoilos 330

Aischyllos s. of Theops 162

Aitolia 105, 225 ff.

Ajax, suicide of 159, 322

Akanthos 363

Akarnania 227 ff.

Akeratos s. of Phrasiarides 301 f.

Akmatides 191

Akousilaos of Argos 55 f.

Akragas 272, 274; defeat of by Syracuse 267; Akragantines at Delphi 274 and Addenda

Akrai 262 f., 268

Akraiphia 60, 93

Akron s. of Proton 272

Aleuadai of Larisa 97

Alexagoras 319

Alexandros I of Macedon 171 n. 2, 364

Alexeas s. of Xenon 271

Alexias s. of Lyon 178 f.

Alexileos 367

Alexo 293

Alkibiades I 75

Alkidamas, sc. (?) 297

Alkmeonides 73; Alkmeonidai 73

Al Mina (Posideion?) 11 f., 16, 21, 68, 326

*alpha* (general) 15, 21, 23

alphabet, Greek, general: introduction of to Greece 5 ff., 12 ff., 22; transmission of 21 ff., 40 ff.; changes in 6 f., 13 ff.; 'cursive' letters in 6 f., 18, 28 f., 33, 48, 57, 64, 188, 327 f.; order of letters in 25 ff., 37; vowels in 2; sibilants, alterations in 5, 7, 25 ff.; supplementary letters of 4 f., 35 ff.; adapted by non-Greek speakers: Carians 39, 314, 354; Eteocretans 311, 314; Etruscans 2, 4, 35, 117 n. 1, 236 f.; Italic people? (unidentified) 252, 259; Messapians 40, 183 f., 279 n. 4, 282 f.; Pamphylians 351; Romans 4; Samothracians 299; Sicilians 271; see also abecedaria, inscriptions, Greek, and Addenda to pp. 6, 21

alphabet, Phoenician 2, 5 ff., 17 ff., 114 n. 2, 310

Alpheios 193

altars, insc. 71, 75 f., 86, 112, 122 f., 146 f., 180, 271, 293, 296, 300 f., 329 f., 335, 338

Alxenor, sc. 107, 292

Amasis (of Egypt) 102, 328, 350, 354 f.; (Abou Simbel) 348 n. 3

Amasis Painter 74

coinage, archaistic lettering on 65, 116, 142, 228, 256 f., 366; *boustrophedon* legends on 49, 249, 254, 258, 274; early (general) 65, 84, 97, 123, 313; insc.: Abdera 60, 340, 364, Abydos 367, Aigai 364, Aigion (?) 222, Aineia 363, Ainos 365, Akanthos 363, Akragas 274, Aminaia (?) 253, Anaktorion 228, Argos 151, Arkadia 207, 210, Athens 68, Bisaltai 300, 364, Boiotia 93, Byzantion 133 ff., 269, 366, Chalkidike 83, 363 f., Chalkis 82 f., 364, Chersonese 365, Corinth 116, 129 f., Crete 311, 313 ff., Delphi 102, Derrones 364, Dikaia by Abdera 365, by Mende 363, Egesta *see* Segesta, Eretria 84, Gela 273, Getas 364, Halikarnassos (?) 353, Heraia 210, Himera 245 f., Hyele (Velia) 287, Ialysos 350, Ichnai 364, Kalchedon 366, Kamarina 268, Kamiros 350, Karystos 87, Kaulonia 257 f., Klazomenai 340 f., Knidos 352, Kolophon 340, Koresia 297, Koronea 89, Kos 330, 352, Kranion 232, Kroton 257, Kyme 80, 238 f., Kyrene 320, Laos 253 f., Leontinoi 242, Lete 364, Leukas 227 f., Lindos 350, Macedonia 364 f., Mantinea 210, 213, Maroneia 365, Melos 321 f., Mende 363, Mesambria 368, Metapontion 254 ff., Methymna 360, Molpe (?) 253, Mosses 364, Naxos (Sicily) 241, Neapolis (Italy) 239, Olympia 219, Olynthos 364, Pale 232, Palinurus (?) 253, Pandosia 254, Pantikapaion 368, Phaistos 314, Phleious 145 ff., 147, Phokaia 341 n. 1, Phokis 102, Poseidonia 253, Potidaia 363, Psophis 207, 212 f., Pyxous 254, Rhegion 244 f., Segesta 272, Selinous 39 n. 2, 271, Selymbria 366, Sermyle 363, Sikyon 142, 181 n. 1, Sinope 368 f., Sirinos 254, Skepsis 361, Skione 363, Sybaris 251 f., Syracuse 265, Taras 183 f., 279 f., 282, Temesa 254, Tenedos 360, Teos 340, Terina 258, Termera 353 n. 1, Thaliadai (?) 207, Thessaly 97 f., Thourioi 287, Thrace 364 f., Torone 363, Tragilos 364, Troizen 177, Zankle-Messana 205, 243

Coinage Decree, Athenian 296, 322, 352 f., 364

colonies, scripts of: 13, 18 f.; Achaian 248 ff., Corinthian 130, 134, 232, 262 ff., Euboic 235 ff., Ionic 286 f., 363 ff., Lakonian 279 ff., Lokrian 284 f., Megarian 263 f., 269 ff., 366, Syracusan 268 f.

columns, insc. 55, 60, 93, 128 n. 4, 159, 176 f., 214, 292 f., 294 f., 319 f., 338 f., 360, 367; *see also* capitals

Corinth 114 ff.; battle with Megara 135; Corinthians in: Aitolia 225 f., Akarnania and Epeiros 227 ff., Delphi 102, Ithake 230, Korkyra 232, Thasos 303, Thessaly 98; W. colonies of 263 ff.

counters (?), clay, insc. 213 f.

cows, dedicated at Hermion 178

craftsmen, literacy of 62

Crete 9, 195 f., 308 ff.; laws of 47, 53 f., 310; W. colony of 263 f., 272 ff.

cult-images, aniconic 255, 257 f., 270 f.

curses, see *defixiones*

Cyclades, script of 290 f.

Cyprus, script of 7 f., 352 f.; insc. bowls from 18, 34

Daidalos 62

Daiochos, ephor 197

Daiton 86

Damonon 60, 185, 196 f.

Daphnai 354 f.

Dareios of Persia 333 f.

Daulis of Krisa 254

decrees, insc. 198, 353, 367; *see also* laws

*defixiones* (curses) 56, 86, 239, 268 n. 4, 269, 271, 273, 287; official curses 158, 340

Deidamas 293

Deinagoras 292

Deinias 107, 127

Deinomenes 266; Deinomenids in Sicily 266

Delion, battle of 93 f.

Delos 289 ff., 296 f.; Lakonians at 198, 297; Naxians at 291 f.; Parians at 294 f.

Delos Painter 297

Delphi, general 100 ff.; head of statuette from 90; Kypselid offerings at 127 n. 3; lebes from 92; visited by citizens of: Achaia (?) 223, Akragas 274, Andros 298, Argos 101, 162 f., 167, Arkadia (Gortys) 211 f., Chios 338, Corinth 102, Hermion 178, Knidos 351 f., Korkyra 112, 233, Kroton 102, 258, Lakonia 101, 185, 190, Lipara 350 f., Massalia 287, Metapontion 102, 256, Naupaktos (Messenians) 205, 365, Paros 101, Phaselis 103, Pieria (?) 102, Potidaia 363, Rhegion 245, Samos 330, Selinous 271 f., Sikyon 140, Sybaris 251, Syracuse 265 f., Taras 281 f.; *see also* oracles, treasuries

*delta* (general) 24

Demainete 293

Demeter 175, 178, 209, 255, 274; Chthonia 166, 178; Malophoros 270 f.; Thesmophoros 208 f.

Demetrias (Thessaly) 97 f.

demiourgoi 59 f., 106, 156 ff., 259

Demi(s) 365

Demokedes 222

Demokratides of Argos 157 n. 1

Demon 287

Demophon, sc. 272

Demotimos s. of Amphidame 176

Derketos 165

Dermys 92, 155

Derrones 364

Despoina 210

Dexippos 190

Didyma 332 ff.

die, insc. 280

Dikaia by Abdera 365; by Mende 363

Diodoros, archon 100

Psophis 212 f.
Psoriani (Aitolia) 105
Ptoiodoros 85
Ptoion (Boiotia) 73, 75, 92 f.
Pylos 205, 425
pyramid, clay, insc. 255
Pyrrhiadas 98
Pyrrhias (Corinth) 172 n. 2; (Selinous) 271
Pythagoras of Selymbria 366
Pythannas s. of Archipolis 335
Pythermos 355
Pythias of Akraiphia 93
Pythioi 185
Pythokles (Elis) 166 f.
Python (Abdera) 365; s. of Amoibichos 355
Pythonax, sister of 296
Pyxous 254

*qoppa* (general) 33 f.

Ravanusa 274
Regolini–Galassi tomb 237
relief-strips, bronze, insc. 158 f.
revetments, insc. 273; (simae) 226, 258, 274
Rhadamanthys 310
Rhegion 243 ff.; Rhegines at Delphi 245, Olympia 244 f.
rhetrai 53, 216 ff., 336
Rhexanor 318
Rhion, narrows of 225
Rhipis(?) 220
Rhizenia, *see* Prinias
*rho* (general) 34, 160
Rhodes 9, 346 ff.; W. colony of 263 f., 272 ff.
Rhodopis 102, 124
Rhoikos 328
(Rh?)onbos s. of (P?)alos 72
Romans, script of 4

Sagra, battle of 285 f.
Sakon s. of Mylos 245 n. 5, 274
Salamis, battle of 118 ff., 127, 129; dispute over in 6th c. 135
sale, record of 16
Samaria, insc. sherds from 18, 25
Samos 325 ff.; sculptors of 48, 73; colonies of 365 ff.; Spartans at 185; Samians at Eurymedon 331, in Amorgos 293, Athens 330, Delphi 330, Egypt 331, Naukratis 328, Samothrace 299, Zankle 243
Samothrace 299
'*sampi*' 38 f., 327, 338 f., 361, 367 f.
*san* (general) 26 f., 33, 100 f.
Sappho 39 n. 2, 102, 361
sculpture, insc.: *stelai* (painted) 94, 127, (relief) 71, 74 f., 93, 98, 107, 167 f., 185 f., 192 f., 195 ff., 280, 292, 298 f., 301 ff., 352, 366, 368 f.; *statues*: korai

72 f., 92, 291, 328 f., 334; kouroi 72 f., 92 f., 154 ff., 270, 292, 329, 332 ff., 340, 351, 360; seated figures 209 f., 329, 332 ff.; statue-pillar (?) 196; lion 332 f.; *statuettes*: (bronze), animals 114 n. 3, 141, 194, 207, 330, 355 (Egyptian); deities, male 46 f., 130, 133, 136, 210 f., female 191, 355 (Egyptian); herdsmen 210 f.; hoplites 194, 202,; korai 191, 253; kouroi 156, 210 f., 228, 292, 349; (clay) 311; (stone) 348 (Cypriot, Egyptian?), 349, 351
seats, insc. (Corinth) 130; (Sparta) 190
Segesta 272
Selinountios 271
Selinous 246, 255, 262 f., 269 ff.; Arkadians at 271; Selinountines at Delphi 271 f.
Sellada ('Thera), cemetery on 317 ff.
Selymbria 366; Selymbrians at Athens 366
Sepeia, battle of 141, 149, 164, 171
Seriphos 291
Sermyle 363
Seti I 314
sheath for statuette-base (Egyptian), insc. 355
shields, insc. 93, 129 n. 3, 135, 159, 162, 243, 267; shield-signs 142 n. 2, 286; *see also* greaves, helmets, panoplies, spear-butts
sibilants, Greek confusion of 5, 25 ff.
Sidene 367
Siena, abecedarium of 237
Sigeion 72, 359, 366 f.
*sigma* (general) 26 f., 34, 184 ff., 341
signatures, artists', 62 f., 74 f., 92 f., 98, 102 n. 1, 111 f., 137, 141, 155, 160, 165 ff., 173, 178 f., 189 f., 195, 205, 211 n. 3, 219, 222, 266 f., 270 n. 3, 292, 297, 329, 332, 365
signet-rings, insc. 113, 346, 360; *see also* gems
Sikels 269
Sikinos 309, 322
Sikyon 138 ff., 148 n. 1, 225 f.; Sikyonians in Corinthian potteries 139 f.; in north-west Greece 140, 225, Delphi 140, Olympia 139 f., Perachora 141
Silaris 252
Silenos s. of Phokos 245 n. 4
simae, *see* revetments
Simos 367
Sinope 368 f.; hydria from 164
Siphnos 289 ff., 296
Sirinos 254
Siris 254, 286 f. and Addenda to 287
Skepsis 361
Skillous 218 f.
Skione 363
*skutale*, use of 57 f.
Skyllis, sc. 140
Skyros 298
slaves, manumission of 197; Argive revolt of 149, 163
Smyrna 326, 340 f.

# TRANSLITERATION OF PLATES

An inscription marked * contains some new reading or emendation, suggested in the text of Part III *ad loc.* Punctuation ׃ is used here to represent varieties of multiple-dot type, as well as triple-dot.

## ATTICA

### Plate 1

**1\*.** ϳος νυν ορχεστον παντον αταλοτατα παιϳει, τοτοδεκλλμιν (το τοδε κλ{μ}μ{ν}ν ?).

**2\*.** [- - -]ενκεκαλ[υπται ? - - - | - - - α]νϥτοεροιν (*sic*) ε̣[- - -].

**3a.** [- - -]εμ᾿ α⟨ν⟩δρο[ς μ?]α̣[λισ]τα φιλει τε̣[- - -]. (*A few letters scratched below.*) *b.* Νι̣[ϙο]δεμος (Μ[ενε]δε̄μος?) Φ[ιλ]α̣ι̣δε̄ς καταπυγον. Λεο̄[φρα]δε̄ς ερι[*erased*]. *c.* αβγ.

**4.** Θαριο ειμι ποτεριον.

**6a.** Ϝε̄ρακλε̄ς. Νετος. *b.* Αθε̄ναια. Περευς. Αρεπυια.

### Plate 2

**7.** [- - -]ν αϥυτ[αρ ? - - - δ]εκα[τ]|εν [׃?] τ̣α̣θ̣[ε̄ναι ? - - - αν]εθε̄κε- - -]. (*Traces of two letters, οι(?), cut vertically on left side.*)

**8.** Ενιαλο θυγατρ[ος Σποδιδ]ο̣ | Κεραμος στε̄λε̄.

**9c.** Ἐγεστρατος | Ϝα⟨ι⟩σιμιο̄νι. *e.* Πισισ⟨τ⟩ρατος.

**10a.** Ϙλο̄πετιο̄ν⟨ο⟩ς. *c.* Μυρμε̄ρος. *f.* Περαδο ειμι.

**13.** Φυ[- - - γλ]α̣υ̣ϙοπιδι ϙ[ορει].

**14a.** Σοφιλος εγραφσεν. Ϝεστια. Χαριϙλο̄.

**17.** [Ρ̣ϝ]ονβος Ξ ανεθε̄κεν ׃ ϳο Ͳαλο ([Β]ονβος, Ι̣ταλο ?).

### Plate 3

**18.** [το]ν δρομον [׃ εποιε̄σαν ׃ *c.* 11 | *c.* 9 | Κρ]ατε̄ς [׃ Θρασ]υκλε̄ς ׃ Α[ρ]ι̣σ̣|το̣δ̣ιϙος ׃ Βρ[υσο̄ν ׃] Αντε̣[νο̄ρ *c.* 7 | Ϝιροποιοι τον α̣γο̄[να θεσ]αν προ̄το̣[ι] γλ|α̣υ̣-[ϙ]ο̄πιδι ׃ ϙορ[ε̄ι].

**19.** [ειτ᾿ αστο]ς τ̣ι̣ς ανε̄ρ ειτε χσενος | αλοθεν ελθο̄ν ׃ Τετιχον οικτιρα|ς̣ ανδρ᾿ αγαθον παριτο̄ ׃ εν πολεμο̄ι | φθιμενον, νεαραν ϳε̄βεν ολεσαν|τα ׃ ταυτ᾿ αποδυραμενοι νεσθε επ|ι πραγμ᾿ αγαθον.

**20.** Χαιρεδε̄μο Ξ τοδε σε̄μα Ξ πατε̄ρ εστε̣[σε | θ]ανον-τος Ξ
Ανφιχαρ⟨ε̄⟩ς Ξ αγαθον παιδα ο|λοφυρομενο[ς].
Φαιδιμος εποιε.

### Plate 5

**2.** Ευφε̄μος ανεθε̄|κεν.

### Plate 4 (right column, heading)

**21.** ϳοι ταμιαι ׃ ταδε χαλκια ׃ [- - - χ]|συνλεχσαντες ׃ Διος κρατερ[οφρονι παιδι - - -׃]| Αναχσιον και Ευδιϙος και Σ[- - -]| και Ανδοκιδε̄ς ׃ και Λυσιμαχ[ος - - -].

**24.** Ϝε̄φα⟨ι⟩στος. Νεαρχος μ᾿ ε|γραφσεν κα̣[νεθε̄κεν ?].

**25.** [Αναχσιλε]ο̄ς ? ׃ καλκμεο[νι]δε̄ς ׃ π̣ε̣ν̣τ̣[ε ׃ ϳιπ]ιον τε ν[ικ]ε̄σαντε ανεθετε̄ν].

**28.** [- - -]ε̣ς | [- - -]ς | [- - -]ε̄ς | [- - -] | Τλε̣[σιας ?] | Κλε̣[- - -] | Λα̣[- - -] | [- - -].

**29.** σε̄μα Φρασικλειας᾿ | κορε̄ κεκλε̄σομαι | αιει, αντι γαμο | παρα θεο̄ν τουτο | λαχοσ᾿ ονομα.

### Plate 4

**31.** τοδ᾿ Αρχιο ᾿στι σε̄μα ׃ κα̣|δελφε̄ς φιλε̄ς ׃ Ευκο|σμιδε̄ς ׃ δε τουτ᾿ εποι|ε̄σεν καλον ׃ στε̄λε̄|ν ׃ δ᾿ επ᾿ αυτο̄ι θε̄κε Φ|αιδιμο⟨ς⟩ σοφος.

**32.** μνε̄μα φιλο̄ι με[◡ – ◡]| πατε̄ρ επεθε̄κε θανοντ[ι], χσυν δε φιλε̄ με̄τε̄ρ ׃ | [– ◡ ◡ – ◡ ◡ –].

**33.** Ϝερμε̄ι | μ᾿ αγαλμα *vac.*

**34.** Αντιγενει ׃ Παναισχε̄ς επ|εθε̄κεν.

**36.** Ευμαρ[ε̄ς - - -].

**37.** μνε̄μα τοδε ϳε̄ς αρχε̄ς Πεισιστ̣[ρατος Ϝιππιο ϳ]υιος
θε̄κεν Απολλο̄νος Πυθ[ι]ο εν τεμενε[ι].

**40.** [ενθα]δε Φι[ *c.* 12 ]ιος κα̣τεθε̣|κε θανοσαν ׃ Λ[αμπι]το̄ αιδοιε̄ν γες απ|ο πατροιε̄ς. ׃ Ενδοιος εποιε̄σεν.

**43.** [δεσμο̄ι εν αχνυθεντι σιδε̄ρεο̄ι εσβεσαν ϳυβ]ριν ׃ παιδε[ς Αθε̄ναιον, εργμασιν εμ πολεμο]| [εθνεα Βοιοτο̄ν και Χαλκιδεο̄ν δαμασαντες] ׃ τον̄ ϳιππος δ[εκατε̄ν Παλλαδι τασδ᾿ εθεσαν].

**44.** [- - - ?χριθο̄ν ϳε̄μ]ιεκτεα ϳ[ε]πτα, ׃ ο[ινο χ|οες ϳεχ]ς ׃ κα[ι ϳε̄μιχου, [- - - | - - - ϳεκ]τευς, ׃ με[λ]ιτος κο[τυλα|ι οκτο̄,: ελαιο[:] ϳε̄μιχο[- - - | - - - ϳε̄μ]ιτε-ταρ[τ]εον, [:] τυρο[: τρ|ις] τ̣ε̣τα[ρ]τ̣α̣ι, ׃ [κ]υαμο̄[ν ?λευκο̄ν τ]ρις χο[ινικες,:] μελ[α]νο̄ν τρις χοι]νικε̣[ς, - - - | - - - δ]υο [- - - | - - -]υ[- - -].

## EUBOIA

**3.** Επικυδειδε̄ς.

**6.** Σε̄μονιδε̄ς μ᾿ ανεθε̄κεν.

7. Ξανθος. Ϙρōπιος. Γλαυρος. Δēμοδοϙος. Ͱιππο-
λυτē. Περιφας. Αχιλλευς. Αθēναιē. Ͱēρακλēς. Γαρυ-
ϙονēς. Αντιοχος. Ϙαχυς.
9*Α1. δικēν ⠶ επεαν ⠶ κατομοσει ⠶ τιν[υ]|σθα⟨ι⟩ ⠶
τριτēι ͱēμε[ρ]ēι ⠼ χρēματα | δοκιμα ⠼ κἀ[ντ]υπα ⟨⠼⟩ ιαν ⠼
μē τεισ|ει (rasura). Α2. επι Γολο ⠼ αρχ[οντος - - - |
- - -]ιν τēͰ ͱυστερēι ⠼ δυϜε | [- - - | - - -] ιαν μē τεισει, ⠼
αρχος απο ρētōν ⠼ ποιεν. | ͱοστις αν ⠼ μē ποιēι, ⠼
αυτον οφελεν | [- - -].
10. [- - -]δρος τōι Ͱēρακλει π|οιϜ[ēσας].
11. [- - - ] τοδε ⠶ σēμα | τετυκται.

## BOIOTIA

*Plate 7*

1. Μαντικλος μ' ανεθēκε ϝεκαβολōι αργυροτοχσōι
   τας {δ}δε|κατας· τυ δε Φοιβε διδοι χαριϝετταν
   αμοιϝ[αν].
2a. επι Εκπροπōι.  b. ͱιαρον το Πυθιο Ϝισϝοδιϙος
   ανεθēκε.  c. τōν επ vac.
3*a. [- - -]ε[·· ·]αιͱυ[ c. 4 ]εϝ[- - - ?Αρχε]μοριδι και
   Χιχιδαι κα[ι - - -].  b. τōν επ[ι] Δ⟨α⟩μ⟨α⟩σιδαι
   α[ιθλōν εμι?].  [- - -] τ' εθ⟨ē⟩κεν (τεθ⟨ē⟩κεν?).  c. τōν
   επι Γελαν[ορι? - - -]οπιδες || ειμι.  [- - -]οιραχσιαδ[ας
   με εδōκε? ε]π' Ͱυπεδοσθενιδαι.  d. [- - -]α αιθλον με
   [εδōκε?].  e. [- - -]αδα[ς με ?] εδōκε επ[ι] | Δαμαλαι.
4. [- - -]ϙōν ανεθēκε τōι Απολ|ōνι τōι Πτōιει.|[- - -]οτος
   εποιϝēσε.
5. Δēμοθερēς (Euboia 23, Plate 6). | ͱιαρον Απολōνος
   Καρυκēϝιο.

*Plate 8*

6*. [ͱιαρον ε]μͱι το Ελιϙōν[ιο - - -].
7. ͱιαρον το Καρυκēϝιο Φλοϙαϙος απαρχοντος
   λεϙτοι{ς} Θēβαιοι{ς} ανεθεαν.
11. Ερχομενιοι ανεθειαυ τōι Δι τōι Ολυ⟨ν⟩πιōι Ϙορō-
   νειᾳ[θεν].
12. Ταναγραιοι τōν [- - -].

*Plate 6*

13. επι Μενε|φρονι ειμι.
17. Σπαρτα μεν πατρις εστιν, εν ευρυχ|οροισι
   Αθαναις
   εθραφθε· θανατο | δε ενθαδε μοιρ' εχιχε. | Πλειστιας.
19. Φιλēσιος εποιε. | Ερετριες τōι Δι.
22. Πυρος μ' εποιēσεν Αγασιλēϝο.
(23. Δēμοθερēς. *See* Plate 7, 5.)
24. Χαριδ|εμο.
26. Αισχυλιōν. Λοφαξ. Ζευξις. Ͱεσχατιōν.

13. Σιμōνιδα αρχοντος τōι Ͱēρōι τōι Πτōιōι Ακριφιες
   ανεθεαν.
14. μναμ' επ' Αγαθōνι | κἀριστοκρατει.

*Plate 9*

15. Πυθιας ὁκραιϝ[ιευς] | και Α⟨ι⟩σχριōν ανε[θεταν ?].
   φιλ[- - -] | Πτōι[- - - αργ]υροτοχσōι.
16. τōν Θēβαις αιθλōν.
17. [Ε]πιδδαλος τōπο[λλōνι] | Βοιοτιος Ξ εχς Ερχ[ο-
   μενο]. | [Ͱ]υπατοδōρος Ξ Αρισστ[ογειτōν] | εποēσαταν
   Ξ Θēβαιō.
18. Μογεα διδōτι ται γυναι|κι δōρον Ευχαρι |
   τεύτρετιφαντο κο|τυλον ὁς χ' αδαν πιē.

*Plate 10*

19a. Ευφατας | Αρχελαος | Λεσχōν | Λεβερος |
   Δραπυς | Κοκκυφς.  b. Κοερανος | Αφροδιτος |
   Σαλυθινιδας | Σαυγενēς | Ευκλιδας | Δαμοξενος |
   Χαρōνδας | Καφισοφαōν | Καλλικρατēς | Ϝισοκλεēς.
20. α β γ δ ε ϝ з ͱ θ ι κ λ μ | ν ο π ρ σ τ υ ξ φ χ ψ ω.
   α β γ δ ε ϝ з ͱ θ ι κ λ | μ ν ο π ρ σ τ υ ξ φ χ.
21. Ρυνχōν.
22. ͱēμιτριτον Π{ο}τōιοδōρο.

## THESSALY

*Plate 11*

1*. αι κε αφελēται το δα[- - - | - - -]εχς ē προχος· αι
   κε το|ν αραχον αφελēται, α[πισαι? - - - | - - - ? και
   αρα]χον διαδυμεν. αι κε μē θ|ελē, απισαι πεντεϙοντα
   [- - -].
2*. Ανδροϙυδēς εϙρουσε. | Ϙολουρος δικαστορευϝōν
   | ετευξε ο Παισιαδας το τεγος.
3*. [- - -?θ]αυ|ατōι, Να|υκιδαι|ōνιε, στ|αλα.
4. μναμ' εμι Πυριαδα, ͱος ουκ επͺι|στατο φευγεν,
   αλ' αυθε περ γας | τασδε πολον αριστευōν εθανε.
7. Πολυξεναια ⠶ εμμι.

8. 'σφιξ, ͱαιδ[α]ο κυον, τιν ε[χοσα·· ·] | οπͺιδ[··
   φυ]λασεις:
   ͱεμεν[α εν φ]|ρο[ραι κα]δο[ς] αποφθιμ[ενο;'] |
   'ξε[νε, - - -'].
10. (2nd line) Θētōνιοι εδōκαν Σōταιρōι τōι Κ|οριν-
   θιōι κ' αυτōι και γενει και ϝοικιαταις και χρēμασιν
   ασυλια|ν κ' ατελειαν· κ' ευϝεργεταν ε|ποιēσαν κ' εν
   ταγ⟨ι⟩α⟨ι⟩ κ' εν αταγ|ιαι. αι τις ταυτα παρβαινοι,
   το|ν ταγον τον επεστακοντα ε|ξξανακαδεν. τα χρυσια
   και τα | αργυρια τēς Βελφαιο απολ|ομενα εσōσε,
   Ορεσταο Φερεκρατ| (top line) ε⟨ο⟩ς ͱυλōρεοντος Φιλο-
   νικο ͱυιος.
14. Κινεα ⠶ και ⠶ Φρασιμηδας.

## PHOKIS, LOKRIDES

*Plate 12*

**1.** (*reading upwards*) τασδε γ᾿ Αθαναιαι δραϝεος
Φα[·]ε|αριστος εθε̄κε,
ⱶε̄ραι τε, ⱶο̄ς και κ|ενος εχοι κλεϝος απθιτον αιϝει.
(δραχμας *Raubitschek*, Φαϝαριστος *Friedlaender*.)

**2.** Χαριμε̄δε̄ς.

**3.** μναμα Χιο̄νος.

**4.** τοι Χαροπινο παιδες ανεθεσαν το Παριο.

**5.** Δαιϝος. Σαϝοβικος. Σαμος. Δεξις. Πολυτιμιδας.

**7.** [- - - ανεθε̄]κε Ροδ[ο̄πις].

*Plate 13*

**11.** χαιρε Χαρο̄ν, | ουδ⟨ε⟩ις τυ κακο̄ς | λεγει ουδε
θα|νοντα,
πολος | ανθρο̄πο̄ν λυ|σαμενος | καματο.

**15.** Μυκανες | Κειοι | Μαλιοι | Τε̄νιοι | Ναξιοι |
Ερετριες | Χαλκιδες | Στυρες | Γαλειοι | Ποτειδαιαται |
Λευκαδιοι | Ϝανακτοριες | Κυθνιοι | Σιφνιοι | Αμπρα-
κιο̄ται | Λεπρεαται.

**17.** τον ϝοινον με̄ φαρεν ες του δρ|ομου· αι δε κα
φαρε̄ι, ⱶιλαξασθο̄ | τον θεον ⱶο̄ι κα κεραιε̄ται, και |
μεταθυσατο̄ κἀποτεισατο̄ πεν|τε δραχμας· τουτου δε
το̄ι κατα|γορε̄σαντι το ⱶε̄μισσον.

**21.** Κοριν[θιοι - - -].

**23.** [*c.* 5 ανεθε̄]|κε και Ξενο|ν Φαυλλο ⱶυ|ιοι δεκαταν |
Μεταποντιν|οι.

*Plate 14*

**1.** Χαριλαος.

**2Α.** (*obverse*) τεθμος οδε περι τας γας βεβαιος εστο̄
κατ τον | ανδαιθμον πλακος Ὑλιας και Λισκαριας και
το̄ν α|ποτομο̄ν και το̄ν δαμοσιο̄ν. επινομια δ᾿ εστο̄
γο|νευσιν και παιδι· αι δε με̄ παις ειε̄, κοραι· αι δε με̄
κορα ειε̄, | αδελφεο̄ι· αι δε με̄ αδελφεομ (*sic*) ειε̄,
ανχιστε̄δαν επινεμεσθο̄ κα⟨τ⟩ το | δικαιον· αι δε με̄
τοι επινομοι (*then follows* οιι...ν *in rasura.* ?*Insert
here the top line on reverse of plaque, marked C on
plate, as follows*) κομιζοιεν, αξιοδοτας εστο̄ ταν
αυτο δ̄ιτινι χρε̄ιζοι. ⱶο τι δε κα φυτευσεται, | ασυλος
ε{ι}στο̄. αι με̄ πολεμο̄ι ανανκαζομενοις δοξξαι αν|δρα-
σιν ⱶενι κ᾿ εκατον αριστινδαν το̄ι πλε̄θει ανδρας
δια|κατιος μειστον αξξιομαχος επιϝοικος εφαγεσθαι,
ⱶοστ|ις δε δαιθμον ενφεροι ε̄ ψαφον διαφεροι εν
πρειγαι ε̄ ᾿ν πολι ε̄ | ᾿ν αποκλε̄σαι ε̄ στασιν ποιεοι
περι γαδαισιας, αυτος με|ν ϝερρετο̄ και γενεα αματα
παντα, χρε̄ματα δε δαμευοσθο̄ν | και ϝοικια κατα-
σκαπτεσθο̄ κατ τον ανδρεφονικον τετθμο|ν. οδε τετ-
θμος ιαρος εστο̄ το Απολλο̄νος το Πυθιο και το̄ν
συνν|[αο̄ν· εμεν δε το̄ι τα]υτα παρβαινοντι εξξο̄λειαν
αυτο̄ι και γενεαι και πα|ματεσιν, το̄ι δ᾿ ευσεβεοντι
ⱶιλαος εστο̄. α δε γ[α το μεν ε̄μισον] | (*reverse*) το̄ν
υπαπροσθιδιο̄ν εστο̄, το δ᾿ ε̄μισον το̄ν επιϝοικο̄ν
εσ|το̄. | τος δε κοιλος μορος διαδοντο̄ : αλλαγα δε
βεβαιο|ς εστο̄, αλαζεσθο̄ δε αντι το αρχο. B (*reverse,
inverted*) [αι δε τοι] δαμιοργοι κερδαινοιεν αλλο | τον
γεγραμενο̄ν, ⱶιαρον το Απολλο̄|νος : εχετο̄ αγαλμα
δι᾿ εννεα ϝετ|εο̄ν και με̄ ποτιγραψαι κερδος.

**5.** Ευφαμος : και τοι συν|δαμιοργοι : ανεθε̄καν | το̄ι
ⱶε̄ρο̄ι.

**8.** Ϝασιο̄ν μ᾿ ανεθε̄κε ⫶ Διακριος μ᾿ εποιϝε̄σα.

*Plate 15*

**4Α.** (*obverse*) ⫶ τον ξενον με̄ ⱶαγεν ⫶ ε τας Χαλειδος ⫶
τον Οιανθεα, μ|ε̄δε τον Χαλειεα ⫶ ε τας Οιανθιδος, ⫶
με̄δε χρε̄ματα αι τι⟨ς⟩ συ|λοι, ⫶ τον δε συλο̄ντα
ανατο̄⟨ς⟩ συλεν. τα ξενικα ε θαλασας ⱶαγεν ⫶ |
ασυλον ⫶ πλαν ε λιμενος ⫶ το κατα πολιν. ⫶ αι κ᾿
αδικο̄⟨ς⟩ συλοι, τε|τορες δραχμαι. ⫶ αι δε πλεον δεκ᾿
αμαραν εχοι το συλον, ⱶε̄|μιολιον οφλετο̄ ϝοτι
συλασαι. ⫶ αι μεταϝοικεοι πλεον με̄νος ε̄ | ο Χαλειευς εν
Οιανθεαι ε Οιανθευς εν Χαλειδι, ται επιδαμιαι δικαι
χ|ρε̄στο̄. ⫶ B. τον προξενον : αι ψευδεα προξενεοι :
διπλ|ειδι θο̄ιεστο̄. | (*reverse*) αι κ᾿ ανδιχαζο̄ντι τοι
ξενοδικαι, : επο̄μοτας ⫶ ⱶελεσ|το̄ : ο ξενος : ὀπαγο̄ν :
ταν δικαν : εχθος προξενο | και ϝιδιο ξενο : αριστιν-
δαν, : επι μεν ταις μναια|ιαις : και πλεον : πεντε και
δεκ᾿ ανδρας, : επι ταις | μειονοις : εννε᾿ ανδρας. : αι
κ᾿ ο ϝαστος ποι τον ϝαστον δικαζεται κα⟨τ⟩ τας
συνβολας, : δαμιοργος | ⱶελεσται : τος ⱶορκομοτας
αριστινδαν ταν πε|ντορκιαν ομοσαντας. : τος ⱶορκο̄-
μοτας τον αυτο|ν ⱶορκον ομνυεν, : πλε̄θυν δε νικεν.

**10.** καλο Παντελεος ⱶα ποτε̄ρια καλα.

**17.** Φαλας πεδιαρχειο̄ν ανεθε̄κε τὀπολο̄νι.

## AIGINA

*Plate 16*

**1\*.** [– ◡ ◡ – Λυ?]σο̄νος Επιστ[αμο̄ν ανεθε̄κε?].

**2.** Μενελας.

**3.** ⱶε̄ρακλεος.

**4.** [?επι Κλ]εοιτα ⫶ ιαρεος εοντος ⫶ τἀφαιαι ⱶο|ιρος |
[- - -]ε̄θε ⫶ χὀ βο̄μος ⫶ χὀλεφας ⫶ ποτεποιε̄θε | [- - -]ς
π̣ερι[ε]ποιε̄θε.

**5.** Θαλε̄ς | μ[ε] αν[εθε̄]κεν | [*c.* 4 ?] | Θε̄βας⟨σ⟩ιμαχο̄ι.

**11.** [Ονατας? ε]ποιε ⋮ Αιγιναι.

**12.** [Γελōν ο Δεινομενε]ος ⋮ ανεθēκε. | Γλαυκιας ⋮ Αιγινατας ⋮ ε|[π]οιε̄σε.

**13.** [τοι Κερκυραιοι] τō̂πολλōνι ανεθεν. | [Θ]εοπροπος ⋮ εποιε ⋮ Αιγινατας.

*Plate 17*

**16.** Πλαθōν ⋮ Εκεσθενē̄ς ⋮ ανεθεν ⋮ ͰϜιοι ⋮ Προκλεος ⋮ Ͱελλανιōι ⋮ Διι.

**18*.** Ͱερμαιο | σαμα |⋮ τοδε | το |⋮ Αγριτα | το Κυδονικο.

**19.** χαιρετε οι παριο|ντες· εγō δε Αντιστα|τē̄ς ͱυος Αταρβο
κειμαι | τε̄ιδε θανōν, πατριδα | γε̄ν προλιπōν. Αντιστατē̄ς | Αθε̄ναιος.

**21.** [– ∪ ∪ – ∪ ∪ – ∪]υμειαι, ͱυιε Χαρε̄τ[ος]
[– ∪ ∪ – ∪ ∪ – || – ∪ ∪]λαν Φεριας.

# CORINTH

*Plate 18*

**1.** A. [– – –] τοι Μαλε̄φο ⋮ και Σ[– – – | – – –]υιδας ⋮ Αμυντας [– – – | – – –]αυϜιος ⋮ Σōκλε̄ς ⋮ [– – – | – – –]κεας ⋮ Ανγαριος ⋮ [– – – | – – –? Μ]ελαντας ⋮ Χαι[– – –]. B. [– – –] Χαιρια[– – – | – – –]αλος ⋮ Χ[– – – | – – –]τελεσ[– – –]. C. [? Προκ]λεος [– – –].

**2.** β γ δ Ϝ ͱ(?) ʒ | α β γ δ ε Ϝ ͱ(?) ʒ (Kyme **2**, Plate 47).

**3.** [– – –]παρε[– – – | – – –]ανκλασε[– – –].

**4.** (base) [– – –]ξε[– – –]. [– – –]δεια[– – –]. (side) Θοας. Δ[ιας]. Τελε[σ]τροφος. [– – –]μαιναφ[ο?– – –].

**5.** Λυγōνος.

**6.** ΔϜεινια τοδε [σαμα] τον ōλεσε πο|ντος αναι[δε̄ς].

**7*.** [– – –ε]υμενεοι|σα ͱυποδ[εξαι? – – –].

*Plate 19*

**8.** [Π]οτειδα[ν]. Σιμιōν μ' ανεθ⟨ε̄⟩κε ΠοτειδαϜōν[ι Ϝα]νακτι.

**9.** Μενεας | Θε̄ρōν | Μυρμιδας | Ευδιφος | Λυσανδριδας | Χαρικλιδας | Δεξιλος | Ξενϝōν | Φρυξ. | Αινε̄τα | ειμι.

**10.** (*NC* 482) Ͱιπποστροφος. Ͱιπποβατας.

**11.** (*AD* ii, pl. 39, 1 a) Α⟨ν⟩φιτρειταν. Ϝιο[– – –].

**12*.** [– – –] Ορσιας(?) ποταγοντο θεαι λευϝōλενōι | [Ͱε̄]ρα[ι].

**13.** Ϙυψελιδαι ανεθεν εξ Ε̄ρακλειας.

**14b.** Λορδιος. Ϝͱαδε̄σιος. Παιχνιος.

**15.** (*AD* i, pl. 8, 15) a. [– – –] ανεθε̄κε τōι Ποτειδανι. | b. Τιμōνιδα[ς] | εγραψε Βια.

*Plate 20*

**16.** [α β γ δ] ε ι Ϝ ʒ ͱ θ ι κ λ μ ν ο π ξ ϙ ρ σ τ [υ φ χ ψ ε ?].

**17*.** δραχμα εγō Ͱε̄ρα λευϝ[ōλενε ταιδε ανακειμαι?] [– – –]λαι.

**18.** Φοινι[κ – – – | – – – τετο]ρες χοι|ρο[ι – – –]. [– – –]ς αι κ|ε μ[– – – | – – –]ͱ|[– – –].

**19.** (*NC* 1474) Ξανθος. Δαιφονος. Πολυξενα.

**20.** (*Hoppin*, *Handbook Bf* 10 f.) Μιλōνιδας εγραψε κἀνεθēκε.

**23.** Πατροκλεος ⟨ε⟩ιμι.

**24.** (*AD* ii, pl. 29, 22) [Π]οτειδαϜōνος αφοιτις.

**25.** (*AD* i, pl. 7, 25) Α⟨ν⟩φιτρι[τα]. Ποτειδαν.

**26.** [– – –]ς αγγειλας· τυ δε δο[ς χα]ριεσαν αμοιϝαν.

**28.** Ανθεσιλας.

*Plate 21*

**29.** [ō ξεν', ευͱυδρ]ον ποκ' εναιομες αστυ Ϙορινθο, [νυν δ' αμε Αια]υτο[ς νασος εχει Σαλαμις.] (*The letters above and below l. 1 are modern; the illustration omits the traces of l. 2.*)

**35.** τας Αφροδιτας ειμι.

**37.** [ͱορος | ͱαρος, ασ]υλος· | με̄ κατα|βιβασσκ|ετō· ʒαμι|α Ι Ι Ι Ι Ι Ι Ι Ι .

**38.** [ναϝος μεν φιαλαν χρυσεα]ν εχει· εγ δε [Ταναγρας] [τοι Λακεδαιμονιοι συν]μαχια τ' αν[εθεν] [δōρον απ' Αργειōν και Αθα]ναιōν και [ͱανōν], [ταν δεκαταν νικας ͱειν]εκα του πο[λεμου]. [– – –] Κορ[ινθιο]ι [– – – | – – –]ρ[– – –].

**39.** ⋮ κορϝαν.

**40.** Καφισοδōρος | Αισχλαβιōι.

# MEGARA

*Plate 22*

**1.** [– – –] ⋮ καθες ⋮ ͱυπο τōι ͱοδōι ⋮ τας θυρ[ας τ]ας το καπο ⋮ πριον[α].

**2.** Αθαναιας ⋮ ιαρα ⋮ τας Μͱεγαρōι.

**3.** [– – – | ∙ ∙ ∙ ∙ ∙]οιπαλ[∙ ∙ ∙ ∙ | ∙ ∙] [Ευ(?)]κλειτον Προκ|λεος· ται δ' ενπιδε|ς αι τε κα αλει ⋮
και κ|αλει θαψειν τειδε τρ|οπōι πολ[ιο]ς.

4. Ναυστολο | Νεōριδος | Λιμενοτο | Ͱαλιροθιο |
Ανχιαλο | Ευρυαλο.

5. Αθαναδας : Θεονικο :

6. Ͱε̄ρακ⟨λ⟩εας.

7. Απολōνος Λυκε̄ιο.

8. [τ]οιδε απο λα[ι]|σταν δεκατα[ν] | ανεθε̄καν Αθα|-
ναι.

## SIKYON

*Plate 23*

2. Σερυϝο̄νιιος.

3. [- - -]ταθος τ̣α̣ριστερον πυρριτο[- - -]·

4. Αχιλευς. Μεμνο̄ν.

8. τουτōνδε κοινα εστō το εστιατοριον και τα ορε̄
και Ͱο χαλκιōν | και τᾶλα ϝοικεουσιν γα και τα τελε̄
φερουσιν· ⟨με̄⟩ πōλειν δε | με̄δε συναλαζεσθαι εξεστō.
(73 *names follow*.)

11. [- - -]πισθυι[- - -].

12. Σεκυōνι⟨οι ?⟩.

13a. Αγαθα[ρχος ? ανεθε̄κε - - -] | Πυθοι | Ισθμοι |
Νεμεα[ι] | Ισθμοι | Σεκυō[νι] | Αθαν[αις] | [- - -]. b.
[- - -]οις.

16. Διōν | Καλλιō[ν ?] | Μουσος | Αρμοδιο[ς] | Ερασιπ-
π[ος] | Αισχινα[ς] | Αριστοκ[λε̄ς ?].

21. [Διο]ς Ολυμπιου.

## PHLEIOUS (1), KLEONAI WITH NEMEA (5–7), TIRYNS (8–11)

*Plate 24*

1*a: [Ͱιππōνα ?]ξ και Ͱιπποκρατ[ε̄] d: ς εθ[εταν ?
- - -]. b: [- - -Ͱ]ορϙος ενδετō αι λωι τον το[- - -] g: αι
τ’ Ͱορϙον οτια οφελ[- - -] f: δεξεται τον Ͱορϙον [- - -]
e: τō τοις Ͱορϙιο[ις ? - - -]|| δεκατας αιτε κ[- - -] c:
[- - -]ς και Λαστρατος αρχε[ταν ?].

5. Αριστις με ανεθ|ε̄κε Δι Ϙρονιōνι ϝα|νακτι
πανκρατιο|ν νιϙον τετρακις | εν Νεμεαι,
Φειδō|νος ϝͱιος το Κλεō|ναιο.

*Plate 25*

6a: [- - -]τα τὸλατηριο|ν : αποβαμα ξε[νϝος ? - - - |
- - -]ος ειμεν : αινητ|ον ϝρεξαντα : α[- - - | - - -] μη

μιαρ[ο]ν [ε]ιμε[ν ?] b: α[ι] ανθρōπον Ͱα[- - - | - - -]αντα
χρημα μηθ|εν : μιαρον ειμεν [- - - | - - - χρημ]ατōν
μηθεν Ͱ[ιλασ] c: μον ειμεν : αι [- - - | - - - ανθ]ρōπōι
μιαρōι : κα|θαρσιν δε ειμεν Ͱ[- - - | - - - α]ποθανοι
καθαρα|μενον : κατα νομ[ον - - - | - - -] Ͱιαρο δαμο |
τε[- - -].

7. [- - - τα ?]ι Εφοδιαι.

8*a: [- - -]αρχ[α]ι [- - - | - - -] αρχεν :[- - - | - - -]καν :
υη[- - - | - - -]ε | ανοιγο[ντō ? - - - | - - -]ν καθ[- - - |
- - -? μηδ]ε Ͱα[- - - | - - -] b: αγοι[- - - | - - -]ξα και
τ[- - - | - - -]στō : Ͱο λαχō[ν - - - | - - - ε]πιθετας
κα[- - - | - - -] εγ δαμο [- - - | - - -].

11*. χος {η}εμι.

## ARGOS

*Plate 26*

2. τὸνυϝαλιο ιαρα.

3. Χαλϙοδαμανς με ανεθε̄κε θιιοιν περικαλλες αγαλμα.

4A. [- - -]τον : τ[ c. 5 ? ]τ[·]ρα ? B. a: [Πολυ ?]με̄δες
εποιϝε Ͱαργειος. b: ε αγαγοντοιδυιοι :

5. Πολυκρατε̄ς ανεθε̄κε.

6. τὸν ϝαναϙōν : τοι Νιραχα : ανεθεν.

7. [?τοιδε]ν ενν[εϝα δ]αμιοργοι εϝ|ανασσαντο· Ποτα-
μος | και Σθενελας Ͱο̣χεδαμιδα | και Ͱπομεδōν | και
Χαρōν Ͱο Αρχεσιλα | και Αδραστος | και ϝορθαγορας
| και Κτετος Ͱο Μιντōνος | και Αριστομαχος | και
Ιχōνιδας.

*Plate 27*

9*. [αι τιστις τα γ]ραθματα :: ταδεν :: Ͱ⟨ε̄⟩ αγνο[ι, ::
Ͱε̄ αφανε|ας ποιεοι, ::] Ͱε̄ συνχεοι, :: τας αρας :: τας

[Ͱε̄ρας c. 7 :: και τρε̄τō εκ] γας :: τας Αργειας, :: τα
δε παμα[τα :: δαμοσ|ια εστō. :: α]ι κα [θ]ανατον :: Ͱε̄
αλλο τι καϙον : Ͱε̄ [c. 10 | c. 9 Ͱε̄ ε]πιτεχνοιτο :: ⟨Ͱ⟩ε̄ ϝοι
ϝισϙειε :: το [c. 8 | c. 7 τ]ος :: προγρο[φ]ος :: εξπριιασ-
[θōν c. 8 | c. 7 α?]ι δε με̄ δαμιιο[ρ]γοι τις :: Ͱōι σ[- - - |
- - -]ς Αργειας :: και Ͱōι ϝοι επ[ c. 15 | c. 15 εστ]ō. ::
τοι Ͱυλες :: αποδομ[ c. 8 | c. 8 ] γας Αργειας γα ::
κα⟨τ⟩ τα κ[ειμενα ? c. 9 | c. 11 νε̄ποι]νον ϝοι εστō ::
ποι τας Ͱ[ε̄ρας].

14. τας Ͱε̄ρας.

16. a. [- - - εν ?] Νεμεαι Τεγεαι τε [- - -]
[- - - Κλ]ετορι Πελλαναι [- - -].
b. Τιμοκλε̄ς μ’ εθε̄κε.

17*. [?βōμον νικασας ϝαν]|αϙōν ανεθε̄κε [βα|σι]ν τε
Αισχυλλο[ς] | Θιοπος τοις δαμ|οσιοις εν αε-
θλο|ις ·

τετρακι τε σ|παδιον νικε κα[ι] | τρις τον
οπλιτα[ν].

**18.** τᾰργ[ει]οι ανεθεν τοι Διϝι τον Ϙορινθοθεν.

*Plate 28*

**[19].** ξυνον ⦂ Αθανοδōρο τε | και Ασōποδōρο τοδε
Ϝεργον, |
χὸ μεν Αχαιος ⦂ ⊢ο δ᾽ εξ Αργεος | ευρυχορο.

**19.** Ατōτος ⦂ εποιϝε̄ε ⦂ Αργειος | κᾰργειαδας ⦂
⊢ᾰγελαιδα ⦂ τᾰργειο.

**21\*.** τοι ιαρομναμονες τōν [εκ] το ⊢ιπϙ|δρομο ανεθεν ⦂
Κριθυλο[ς ⦂ Α?]ϝακτο[ς ⦂] | Φιλεας ⦂ Γναθις ⦂

**23** Αργειοι ανεθεν τᾰπολλōνι.

*Plate 29*

**26.** παρ ⊢ε̄ρας Ξ Αργειας Ξ ⊢αϝεθλον.

**30.** Αργε[ιōν τοι]δ᾽ εθ[ανον Ταν]αγραι Λακ[εδαιμο|-
νιōν ⊢υπο χερσ]ι,
πενθο[ς δ᾽ ετλασα|ν γας πε]ρι μαρναμ[ενοι].
Col. I: ⊢υλεες | [Π]ολλιχος | [Αλ]κισθενε̄ς | [ 7 ]ος |
[- - -] | [ 4 ]μα[- - -] | [ 3 ]θισ[- - -] | [⊢ι]ππος[θενε̄ς] |
[Νι]κεας | [Α]ριστοβι[ος] | Τελεστας | Αιθε̄ρ | Φιλο-

κρατε̄ς | Στιλπōν | Ἐπιτιμος | [- - -]. Col. II: [ 2 ]τριος
| [Α]ριστιōν | [Σ]φενδονιōν | [Λ]υκινος | [Ϝ]αναξιλας |
[Δ]ερκετος | [Εχ]εμενε̄ς | [ 5 ]ις | [- - -]. Col. III:
[- - -]ος | [- - -] | [- - -]ος | [- - -] | [- - -]ς | [- - -]. Col.
IV: Αντ[- - -] | Θε[- - -] | Ε[ 5 ]ς | Φοινιξ | [Φ]ιλεας |
[Β]ραχας | Τελεσστας | Δαμοφανε̄ς | Θυμαρε̄ς |
Δαικλε̄ς | Συλιχος | Δερκετος | Λυϙοδορκας | Κλεōν |
Κρατιαδας | [Α]ισχυλος | [Ευα]ρχι[δ]ας | [- - -].

*Plate 30*

**31.** Col. I: [- - -]ς | [- - -] | [- - -]ς | [- - -] | [- - -]ε̄ς |
[- - -]ς | [- - -]. Col. II: [- - -] | Ευ[- - -] | Ξενο[- - -] |
Βουτα[- - -] | Φιλλο[- - -] | Θιοκρι[τος] | Θερσαν[δρος]
| Δερκετ[ος] | Σōστρατος | Σ[- - - | - - -].

**42.** [- - -]γραφōν [- - - | - - -]μιστε ·· [- - - | - - -]οιαν
τον [- - - | - - -]ανς τανς τ[- - - | - - -]⊢ιαι οφλετ[ō
- - - | - - -]ορευοντō [- - - | - - -]ον αλλον [- - - | - - -]
τοτο ⊢ε̄μ[- - - | - - -]εντ[- - -].

**45a.** Πυθοκλ[ε̄ς - - -].  *b.* Πολυκλετος [- - -].

**46.** [- - -] | ⊢υβριλας | ανεθεταν.

**47.** [Αργειοι τᾰπολλōνι ?] απο Λακεδαιμονος δεκαταν.

**48.** Αργειοι [- - -].

**49.** Πολυστρατα ανεθη|κε.

# MYCENAE

*Plate 31*

**1.** αι με̄ δαμιοργια ειε̄, τος ιαρομναμονας τος ες
Περσε̄ το⟨ι⟩σι γονευσι κριτε̄ρας εμεν κα⟨τ⟩ τα ϝεϝρε̄-
μενα.

**2.** Φρα⊢ιαριδας ⦂ Μυ|κανεαθεν ⦂ παρ᾽ Α|θαναιας ⦂ ες
πολιος | ⦂ ικετας ⦂ εγεντο ⦂ | επ᾽ Αντια ⦂ και Πυρ|ϝια ⦂
ειεν δε ⦂ Αντι|ας ⦂ και Κιθιος ⦂ καιˆσ|χρōν.

**3.** [c. 14 ?] τοι ιαρομναμονες | [c. 14 ?]εας Σϙοραδευς
ασσ|[πιδα, ϙυνιαν, αϙο]ντιον· Βυτιος ?Ασ[·· | c. 4 ?
ασπιδα, ϙυ]νιαν, αϙοντιον· [·· | c. 7 ? ασπιδα,
ϙυ]νιαν, αϙοντιο[ν· | c. 9 ? ασπι]δα, ϙυνιαν, αϙο|-
[ντιον· c. 10 ? ]ος ασπιδα, ϙυν|[ιαν, αϙοντιον· - - -].

**5.** Πενπυλος.

**6.** το ⊢ε̄ρōος Ɔ εμ[ι].

# EASTERN ARGOLID: METHANA AND TROIZEN (1–6), HERMION (7–9), EPIDAUROS (10–17)

*Plate 32*

**1.** Ευμαρε̄ς με πατε̄ρ Ανδροκ|λεος ενταδε σαμα
πο|ιϝε̄σανς καταεθε̄κε | φιλο μναμα ⊢υιεος εμ|εν.

**2.** Δαμοτιμōι ⦂ τοδε σαμα ⦂ φιλα ϝεργασατο ματε̄ρ
Αμφιδαμα ⦂ ου γαρ παιδες ενι μεγαροις εγενοντο· |
και τριπος ⊢ον Θε̄βασσι θεōν ε̄νικε ⦂ ασ̣τ[οισιν]
[θαυμ᾽ ανακειτ]α[ι] δευρ᾽ απαθε̄ς ⦂ επεθε̄κε δε παιδι.

**3.** Πραξιτελει τοδε μναμα Ϝισōν ποιϝε̄σε θανο[ντι],
[τ]ουτο δ᾽ εταιροι | σαμα χεαν βαρεα στεναχοντες
ϝεργον αντ᾽ αγ[α]θōν, κε̄παμερον | εξετελεσα[ν].

*Plate 33*

**4.** Μεθανιοι απο Λακεδαιμονιōν.

*Plate 34*

**10.** τōι Αισκλαπιōι ανεθε̄κε Μικυλος.

**6.** Ευθυμιδας | ανεθε̄κε· | ⊢α κα πωιων | πωι των
θεον | ιωιει λωυσαμε|νως δαηναι χρε̄|[ι]ζōν. θυσαμεν
| ⊢ε̄ρακλει αλιω[ι] | ιδωντα [ε]πιαλε̄ | ωιωνων.

**7.** Φερσεφονα. | ⊢ερμιονες ανεθ[ε̄καν τᾰπολλōνι ?].

**8.** Αλεξιας ⦂ Λυϙνος ⦂ αν[εθ]ε̄[κε] | ται Δαματρι ⦂ ται
Χθονια[ι] | ⊢ερμιονευς. | Κρε̄σιλας ⦂ εποιε̄σε ⦂ Κυδωνια-
τ[ας].

**9.** Αριστ[ο]μενε̄ς αν[ε]ε̄θε̄κε Αλεξια | ται Δαματρι
τα̣[ι] Χθονιαι | ⊢ερμιονευς. | Δōροθεος εϝεργασατο
Αργειος.

12\*. ⱶεπροροε (= ⱶιροποιοι ?) ανεθ̄εκαν | ανφοξυν (= ανφοιυν ?).

14. Φιλισκος | ⱶὁρμιαδας ( ?) | παρεδōκε.

16. Καλλιστρα|τος ανεθ̄εκ|ε τōι Ασκλαπι|[ō]ι ⱶο μαγιρος.

17. [- - -]|[· ·]ασυλια|ν Καλλιφ|ανεος θυ|γατρι Μ|νασōνο|ς γυναικ|[ι] αυται κ|[αι] γενει.

## LAKONIA

### Plate 35

1. Ϝορθαια.
2a. Ϝριθισα | α[νε]θικε | ⱶιρον.
3a. [- - -] ται Ϝορθα[ιαι]. b\*. Αυ̣ταρετος (?).
5. Δορκōνιδα (Δορκοιλιδα ?) | Απελōνι.
6. Θιοκορμιδας. Χισιμιδας.
7. Τελεσστας.
8. Αρκεσιλας. Σοφορτος. Σλιφομαχος. 'ορυξο'. Μαεν.
9. [- - - τōι Α]μυκλαιō[ι].
11. [– ◡ ◡]δας με ⱶο Δεξιπο Πυθōδ' ανεθ̄εκ[εν].
16a. Ανιοχιδας. Αρχιλοχιδας. Δενομαχ|ος. Συνις.

### Plate 36

15. Γοργος | Λακεδαιμονι|ος προξενος | Ϝαλειōν.
19. [– ◡ ◡ – ανεθ̄ε̣]κε Ευρυστρατιδας ) ταδε τα ⱶοπλα )
τ̣[ο Λακεδ]αιμονιο ) τυ δε τōι χαριν αιες ⱶ[υπαρ-χοις ?].
22. Αιγλατας τōι Καρνειō[ι | τ]οδ' αγαλμ' ανεθ̄εκε πε|νπακι νικα̣σας τον | μ[ακ]ρον, και ποτεθ̄ε̣|[κε] [τ]ον δολιχον τρι|ακις Αθαναιοις ε[ν αγō|σιν ?], [ⱶ]α̣ιπερ συρμαια| [- - -].
24. Πλεστιαδας μ' α[νεθ̄εκε] | Διος κοροισιν α[γαλ-μα],| Τινδα̣ριδαν δ[ιδυμōν] | μανιν οπιδομ̣[ενος].
25\*. Κορας | Σōτιας.
27. Ϝαναξιβιος.

### Plate 37

29\*. Κορōι Θιοκλενα μ' [ανεθ̄εκεν ?].
30. Ετεοι[τας] | ανεθ̄ε̣[κε τ]|α̣θανα[ιαι].
31\*. [Γ]λαυκατ[ιας ?νι|κας το] μναμα | καλας [ανε-θ̄ε̣κ|ε ?]
[Πραξ]ο̣ιδα ⱶυι|υς ) παι[δι Διος μ|εγαλο].
32. Τεχναρχος.
43\*. Δαμαρ[ετος μ' αν]ε̣θ̄εκε. | [κυρανας, modern graffito ?]. Κυραναιος | δε μ' επο[ιϝε ?].

44. [- - -] | [·] το[- - -] | Κασ[- - -] | Σαμōν | ⱶιππιαδα | Παρφ[- - -] | Ζουμι[ς] | Δαμοξενιδα | Αλκιπος.
46. [· ·]λεōν | Αϝαναξ | Τεϝυκιος | Αμιτας | Αμυλος | Αϝαναξ.
49. [δεξ]ο Ϝαν[α]ξ Κρον[ι]δα{ι} Δευ Ολυνπιε καλον αγαλμα
ⱶιλε̄ϝō[ι θυ]μōι τοι(λ) Λακεδαιμονιο[ις].

### Plate 38

52. (facsimile) Δαμōνōν | ανεθ̄εκε Αθαναια(ι) | Πολιαχōι
νικαϝας | ταυτα ⱶατ' ουδες | πēποκα τōν νυν. |
ταδε ενικαϝε Δαμ[ōνōν] | τōι αυτō(ι) τεθριππō(ι) | αυτος ανιοχιōν· | εν Γαιαϝοχο τετρακι | και Αθαναια τετ[ρακι] | (κτλ.) (photograph) ⱶυπο δε Αριστε̄ εφορον | ταδε ενικε̄ Δαμōνōν· | εν Γαιαϝοχο ενⱶε̄βοαις | [ⱶ]ιπποις αυτος ανιοχιōν | και ⱶο κελε̄ξ μιας αμερας· | ⱶαμα ενικε̄ και ⱶο ⱶυιος | σταδιον και διαυλον και | δολιχον μιας αμερας | ενικōν παντες ⱶαμα. | ⱶυπο δε Εχεμενε̄ εφορον | ταδε ενικε̄ Δαμōνōν | εν Γαιαϝοχο ενⱶε̄βοαι[ς] | ⱶιπποις αυτος ανιοχιōν | κα̣ι ⱶο ⱶυιος σταδιον κα̣[ι | διαυλον και δολιχον μιας | αμερας ⱶαμα ενικε̄].
53. ανεθ̄ε̣[κε] | τōι Ποⱶοιδα[νι] | Θεαρε̄ς | Κ̣λεογενε̄. | [ε]φορος | Δαιοχος. | επακο̣(ō) Αριō(ν), Λυōν.
54. ανεθ̄εκε | Εκεφυλος | Νεαρεταν | τōι Ποⱶοιδανι. | εφορος | Αριστευς. | επακοω | Αριστοτελε̄ς, | Δαμοφōν.
60. Ευαλκε̄ς | εν πολεμōι | εν Μαντινεαι.
62. [- - - | ·]ν και θι[ō]|ν και ναϝō|ν και τōν χ|ρε̄ματōν τ|ōν το θιο. | εβασιλευον | Αγις, Παυσανιας. | εφοροι ⱶσαν | Θυιωνιδας, | Αριστογενιδας, | Αρχιστας, | Σολογας, | Φεδιλας. | εν Δηλωι ⱶρχε̣ν | [Α]ν̣δ̣[ρο-δικ ?]ος.

### Plate 39

63. Κοιρις.
64. το Διος Ολυνπιο.
66. α β γ δ ε ϝ з ⱶ θ ι κ — ϙ σ τ ξ χ (repeated).
67. Χιμαριδας ται Δαιδαλ|αι.

## MESSENIA

3\*. Μεθαν[ιοι] | ανεθε[ν απ' ?] | Αθαναι[ōν τας ?] | λαιδο[ς].
6. ⱶιαρος | Χαροπ(ι)νος. | ⱶιαρ[ος] | Αρισστοδαμος.

8. (below) [Απολλōνι ?] Πυ[θιōι] ανεθεν [Μεσ]σανιοι. (above, 2nd c. B.C.) [Μεσσαν]ιο[ι Απο]λλω[νι Πυ]θιωι.
10. Απελλōνος ⱶιαρον.

## ARKADIA

### Plate 40

**1\*.** Ϙōμαδας υνεθēκε.

**2.** [ει γυ]να ϝεσ̄τοι ϡτ̄ραιον λōπος, | [ιερο]ν εναι ται Δαματρι ται Θεσμοφορōι. | [ει δε] μ̄ υνιερōσει, δυμενε̄ς εασα επε ϝεργο | [c. 4 ]ϟ ϡ’ εϟολοιτυ, κα οϡις τοτε δαμιοϝοργ̄ε | [αφαε]ϡται δαρχμας τριακοντα. ει δε με αφαετοι, | [οφλεν] ταν ασεβειαν. εχ̄ε οδε κυρος δεκο ϝετεα. ενα[ι | c. 5] τοδε.

**3.** [ι]ερα τ⟨α⟩ι Αρταμ⟨ι⟩τι.

**5.** [- - -]ιος Ͱαλεαι μ’ ανε[θ̄κε - - - | - - -] αϝεθλ[ον] και τ̄επιοντα λ[αβεν ?].

**6.** Αγεμō.

**11.** ιερος Τυνδαριδαιυς απ’ Ἐ̄ραεōν.

**38.** [- - - γ]ενεσται ϝο[ι ? - - - | - - -] χρ̄εματα : ος ιε[- - - | - - -]ο τοδε : τελλο[- - - | - - -] τον πινακα : [- - - | - - -] ολοισθαν : Ͱος [- - - | - - -]ν : αι δ’ αλλος τ[- - - | - - -]ν[- - - | - - -]ι[- - -].

### Plate 41

**12.** Καμō υνεθυσε ται Κορϝαι.

**20.** Πραξιτελε̄ς ανεθ̄κε Συρακοσιος τοδ’ αγαλμα | και Καμαριναιος· προσθα δε Μαντινεαι | Κρινιος Ͱυιος εναιεν εν Αρκαδιαι πολυμε̄λō⟨ι⟩, | Ͱεσλος εōν, και ϝοι μναμα τοδ’ εστ’ αρετας.

**27.** Ϡουθιαι παρκαθ̄κα τōι Φιλαχα|ιο ϡετρακατιαι μναι αργυριο. ει μ|εν κα ϡō̄ε, αυτος ανελεσθō· αι δε κ|α μ̄ε ϡō̄ε, τοι υιοι ανελōσθō τοι γν̄ε|σιοι επει κα ̄εβασōντι πεντε ϝετε|α. ει δε κα μ̄ε ϡōντι, ται θυγα-τερες | ανελōσθō ται γν̄εσιαι· ει δε κα μ̄ | [ϡō]ντι, τοι νοθοι ανελōσθō· ει δε κα | μ̄ε νοθοι ϡōντι, τοι{ς} ασιστα ποθικ|ες ανελōσθō· ει δε κ’ ανφιλεγōντ⟨ι⟩, | οι Τεγεαται διαγνοντō κα⟨τ⟩ τον | θεθμον.

**32.** [- - -] Απολλōνι | και συνμαχōν δεκοταν.

**37.** Ϝριϡιδας | Ερατιαυ. | Ϝισϝοδαμος | Πανθιος. | Διαιθōν.

**39.** Ͱυβρισϡτας | εποιεσε.

## ELIS

### Plate 42

**1.** Ϙοιος μ’ αποēσεν.

**2.** [- - -]φερο[·]α[- - - | - - -ι]αρομαοι αι μα πεν[- - - | - - -] αι τιρ μαιτο χρēεστ[αι - - - | - - -]θαι Ολυνπιαι αι ϡα[- - - | - - -]ον αι τιρ ταυτα πα[ρβαινοι - - - | - - -]ρ ορ τιρ τοκα θεοκολ[εοι - - - | - - -τōι] Ζι Ολυνπιōι λατραι[ōμεν - - - | - - - τōι ] Ζι Ολυνπιοι τοι ϡ[- - -].

**4.** [- - -]ο δε κα ξενος επει μ⟨ο⟩λοι εν τ|α[ρον ? - - - | - - -? ϝαρ]ιϙος κα θυσας επι τōι βōμōι τα π[- - - | - - -]ι αποδος ενēβεο[ι] ο ξενος· αι δ[ε ? - - - | - - - δα]ρχμας αποτινοι τōι Δι Ολυν[πιōι - - - | - - -]οα δōōν ταδε-κυαιυσεβοικα[- - - | - - -] κατ τα πατρια.

**5.** [- - -] {κα} κα θεαρος ειē. αι δε βενεοι εν τ|αρōι, βοῖ κα θοαδοι και κοθαρσι τελειαι και τον θεαρον εν τ|αυται. αι δε τις παρ το γραφος δικαδοι, ατελēς κ’ ειē α δικα, α δε κα ϝρατρα α δαμοσια τελεια ειε̄ δικαδοσα. τōν δε κα γραφεōν, ο τι δοκεοι καλιτερōς εχεν πο⟨τ⟩ τον θεον εξαγρεōν κ’ αλ⟨λ⟩’ ε|νποιōν συν βολαι πεντακατιōν αϝλανεōς και δαμōι πλ̄εθυοντι δινακοι. κοι δε κα εν τριτ|ον, αι τι ενποιοι αιτ’ εξαγρεοι.

**6.** α ϝρατρα τοιρ Ϝαλειοις : και τοις Ἐ̄ρ|ϝαōιοις. : συνμαχια κ’ εα εκατον ϝετεα, : | αρχοι δε κα τοῖ. : αι δε τι δεοι : αιτε ϝεπος αιτε ϝαργον, : συνεαν κ’ αλαλοις : τα τ’ αλ⟨α⟩ και πα|ρ πολεμο. : αι δε μα συνεαν : ταλαντον κ’| αργυρο : αποτινοιαν : τōι Δι Ολυνπιōι : τοι κα|δαλ̄εμενοι : λατρειōμενον. : αι δε τιρ τα γ|ραφεα : ταῖ καδαλεοιτο : αιτε ϝετας αιτε τ|ελεστα : αιτε δαμος : εν τ̄επιαρōι κ’ ενεχ|οιτο τōι ’νταυτ’ εγραμενōι.

### Plate 43

**15.** α ϝρατρα τοις Ϝαλειοις. Πατριαν θαρρεν και γενεαν και ταυτο· | αι ϡε τις κατιαραυσειε, ϝαρρεν ōρ Ϝαλειο. αι ϡε μ̄επιθειαν τα ϡι|καια ορ μεγιστον τελος εχοι και τοι βασιλαες, ϡεκα μναις κα | αποτινοι ϝεκαστος τōν μ̄επιποεοντōν κα⟨τ⟩θυταις τōι Ζι Ολυν|πιōι, επενποι ϡε κ’ Ελλανοϡικας, και τ’ αλλα ϡικαια επενπ|ετō α ϡαμιοργια· αι δε μ̄εντοι, ϡιφυιον αποτινετō εν μαστρα|αι. αι ϡε τις τον αιτιαθεντα ϡικαιōν ιμασκοι, εν ται ϡεκαμναιαι κ̄ε|νεχο[ιτ]ο, αι ϝειϡōς ιμασκοι. και Πατριας ο γροφευς ταυτα κα πασκοι, | [αι τ]ιν’ [αϡ]ικεοι. ο π[ι]ναϟ ιαρος Ολυνπιαι.

**16.** Ριπιρ | εγō | Ϟεν|ϝαρε|[ορ].

**18.** [Ζ]ευξιαι κα⟨τ⟩ τον π[ολεμον ? - - - τεσ|σα]ρα-κοντα κ̄εκατ[ον - - -]. | Ζευξιαι κα⟨τ⟩ τον π[ολεμον ? - - -τ]ρες μνας και ϝ[- - -].

**19.** [Γλαυκι]αι με Καλōν γενε[αι ϝ]αλει[ο]ρ εποιē. | [Γλ]αυκιēς ο Λυκκιδεō | [τō]ι Ερμηι Ρ[η]γινος.

**21.** μναματ’ Απολλōνιας α[νακειμεθα ταν ενι ποντōι] | [Ι]ōνιōι Φοιβος ϝοι[κισ’ ακερσεκομας], | [Ͱοι γ]α[ς τε]ρμαθ’ [Ͱελοντες Αβαντιδος ενθαδε ταυτα] | [εστασαν συν θεοις εκ Θρονιο δεκαταν].

## ACHAIA

*Plate 44*

**3.** [- - -]θεος.

**5.** Μιριϙυθος.

**6.** Ζενος Ολυνπιο.

**7.** το Διος εμι.

## AITOLIA

**1.** Προμαθο τοδε σαμα φιλοξενο ανδρος.

**2.** Χελιδϝον. Χαριτες. ϝιϙις.

**4.** μια επι ϝικατι πο εσπερας.

**9.** [Αρτε]μιδος ꜧιαρος.

## AKARNANIA, EPEIROS

**1.** Ευφραιος μ' ανεθεκε τἀθαναι.

**2.** [- - -]δας : ταϙ[··]τον αθυμ[- - - | - - -]σεν εμαις τον οπα[- - - | - - -]ρεοι ꜧ[···]εκαπιϙδο[- - - | - - -]ο Θεμιστιο[- - - | - - -]ομενος δυ[- - - | - - -]ατ[··]πλαθ- [- - - | - - -]ο αιτιον [- - - | - - -] αμα[·]ιπ[- - - | - - -]σ [- - - | - - -].

**8.** Προκλειδας τοδε σαμα κεκλ|εσεται ενγυς οδοιο, | ꜧος περι τας αυτο γας | θανε βαρναμενος.

**13.** ꜧερμον τινα | κα θεον ποτθεμ|ενος γενεα ϝ|οι γενοιτο εκ Κ|ρεταιας Ονα|σιμος ποτ ται ε|ασσαι.

## IONIAN ISLANDS: ITHAKE (1–4), KEPHALLENIA (5), KORKYRA (8–16)

*Plate 45*

**1.** *a (above)* [- - -] μαλιστα ꜧον [- - -] *(below)* [- - -]π [- - -] *b–c (above)* [- ⏑ ⏑ - ξ]ενϝος τε φιλος και π[ιστο]ς εταιρος [- - -] *(below)* [- - - φ ?]ιλα εν π[ *c.* 14 ]οι τ' εν ατ[- - -].

**2.** Καλικλεας ποιασε.

**3\*.** [- - - τας Α]θανας {τας} | τας Πολ[ιαδ|ος] κα[ι τ]ας ꜧερ|ας τας Τελ[ει|ας] τοι [π]εριπολ|[ο]ι (?) με ε[πο]ιεσ- [αν··| *c.* 7 ]πι[- - -].

**4.** ꜧιαρος.

**5.** Εχσοιδα μ' ανεθεκε Διϝος ϙοροιν μεγαλοιο : χαλκεον ꜧοι νικασε Κεφαλανας μεγαθυμος.

**8.** [σταλα Σ]ιμου ματρος εγο ꜧεστακ' | επι τυμοι Πολυνοϝας· σ[τοναχα | δ' υιοι κατελει]πετο ματρ[ος].

**10.** Λοφιος μ' ανεθεκε.

**11.** σαμα τοδε Αρνιαδα· χαροπος τονδ' ολε|σεν Αρες βαρναμενον παρα ναυσ|ιν επ' Αραθθοιο ροϝαισι, πολλο|ν αριστευ{τ}οντα κατα στονοϝεσαν αϝυταν.

**13.** σταλα Ξενϝαρεος του Μϝειξιος ειμ' επι τυ|μοι.

**14.** Ϙυνισκ⟨ο⟩ς.

**15.** *(below)* Ϙ[ορϙ]υραιοι το͂πελ[λο͂νι]. *(above, later)* [Κερκυρ]αιοι.

**16.** Λεξειατας.

## EUBOIC COLONIES, ITALY: PITHEKOUSSAI (1), KYME (2–12)

*Plate 47*

**1.** Νεστορος : ε[ιμ]ι : ευποτ[ον] : ποτεριο[ν :] | ꜧος δ' α⟨ν⟩ τοδε π[ιε]σι : ποτεριο : αυτικα κενον {νε} | ꜧιμερ[ος] : ꜧαιρ]εσει : καλλιστε[φα]νο : Αφροδιτες.

**2.** α β γ δ ε ϝ ꜧ (?) ʒ. (*See* Corinth 2, Plate 18.)

**3.** Ταταιες εμι λεϙυθος· ꜧος δ' αν με κλεφσει θυφλος εσται.

**4.** Κριτοβ|ολες.

**7.** ꜧυπυ τει κλινει τουτει Λενος ꜧυπυ.

**8.** επι τοις Ονομαστο το Φειδιλεο αθλοις εθεθεν.

*Plate 48*

**9.** Δεμοχ|αριδος | εμι το | [- - -].

**11.** Ξενοφαντο εμι.

**12.** ου θεμις εν|τουθα κεισθ|αι ι με τον βε|βαχχευ- με|νον.

## ETRURIA

18. α β γ δ ε ϝ ʒ ⱶ θ ι κ λ μ ν ξ ο π Μ ϙ ρ σ τ υ χ φ ψ.

19. α β γ δ ε ϝ ʒ ⱶ θ ι κ λ μ ν ξ ο π Μ ϙ ρ σ τ υ χ φ ψ.

20. α β γ δ ϝ ε ʒ ⱶ θ ι κ λ μ ν ξ ο π Μ ϙ ρ σ τ υ χ φ ψ.
(*repeated below, with* ε *and* ϝ *correctly placed.*)

21. α β γ δ ε ϝ ʒ ⱶ θ ι κ.

22. α β γ δ ε ϝ ʒ ⱶ θ ι κ λ μ ν ξ ο π Μ ϙ ρ σ τ υ σ φ ψ.

23. α β γ δ ε ϝ ʒ ⱶ θ ι κ λ μ ν ̣ ξ ο. (γ *and* ϝ *are perhaps transposed.*)

## EUBOIC COLONIES, SICILY:
### ZANKLE (5–6), RHEGION (8–14), HIMERA (19)

*Plate 49*

5. [- - -]ι ⱶελοντο̄|ν γαν τας [- - - | - - - ει δε βια?]-
ʒομενος | νικε̄θε⟨ι⟩ε̄ [- - - | - - - πο]λεμιος βλ|ε̄θε̄ναι
[- - - | - - - Δα]νκλε̄ν κ[α|ι] τον Δα[νκλαιον - - - | - - -]ς
συνμα|[χ]ις ⱶος [- - - | - - -].

6. Δανκλαιοι [Ρ]ε̄γιν̣ο̄ν.

8. [Μικυθος ⱶο Χοιρο Ρε̄γινος και Μεσσε̄]νιος ϝοικε̄ν
εν Τεγεε̄ι | [τἀγαλματα ταδε θεοις ανεθε̄κε πασι]ν και
θεαις πασαις· | [παιδος εκ νοσο φθιναδος σο̄θεντος
κ]αι χρε̄ματο̄ν ⱶοσσα ϝοι πλειστα εγεν|[ετο δεκατε̄ν
απερξαμε̄ν, ες Ολυνπιε̄ν] ελθο̄ν, επειτα ε̄υξαμε̄ν.

11. Ⱶε̄ρακλεος Ρε̄γινυ.

12. Κλεοφαντος | Γλαυκιυ.

13. Κλεομενε̄ς | Εμμενιδευ.

14. Δε̄μοφανης | Θραρυος.

19. Εργοτελης μ' ανεθηκ[ε Φιλανορος αγλαος ⱶυιος?],
Ελλανας νικων Πυθι[α δις δολιχον?]
και δυ' Ολυμπιαδας δ[υο δ' Ισθμια και Νεμεαι
δις?],
Ιμεραι αθανατον μν[αμα πορων αρετας?].

## ACHAIAN COLONIES: POSEIDONIA (2–7), UNKNOWN (8),
### METAPONTION (14–19),
### KROTON (22), PETELIA (29), KRIMISSA (30); NON-GREEK (31)

*Plate 50*

2. Χιρο̄νος.

7. τἀθανα|ι Φιλλο̄ | Χαρμυλι|δα δεκα|ταν.

8. τας Ⱶε̄ρας ⱶιαρος | εμι τας εν πεδι|οι· Ϙυνισκο|ς
με ανεθε̄|κε ὀρταμο|ς ϝεργο̄ν | δεκαταν.

14*. Απολο̄νος | Λυκ εμι Θεα|γεος, Βυρο̣(?).

19. α β γ δ ε ϝ ʒ ⱶ θ ι κ λ (*handle*) μ ν ο π ϙ ρ Μ τ υ
φ χ ξ ψ (?; *handle*).

22. το Διος | το Μελιχιο · | Φαϝλλος |ⱶεʒατο.

29*. [c. 9 ]πε Ονατα δαμ|[ιοργεοντο]ς · | Διαιτε̄ς ·
ⱶα · | [c. 9 ]λονα · Σιμιχο | [c. 10 ]ο · ταὐτο · παν|[τα?
και ʒο̄ος] · και θανο̄ν | [c. 8 πρ]οξενοι · δυ · δ|[c. 9 ]ν ·
Φιλιππος | [c. 9 ]ς · ξαν · Δορκευ|[ς c. 9 ] · ις · *vac.*

30. θεος τυχα. Καλλιφαο|ντος δαμιοργεοντος |
Φιλο̄ν διδο̄τι ταὐτ[ο] | παντα και ʒο̄ος κ[αι θ]|ανο̄ν ται
γυν[αικι · · | · ·]τα ο[· ·]υχ[- - -].

31. δισπεπυγιδοστοιοννυεπαματοξεεν.

## DORIC COLONIES, SICILY: SYRACUSE (1–10), AKRAI (12–14),
### KASMENAI? (15), KAMARINA (17–18), HYBLA HERAIA (21–22),
### MEGARA HYBLAIA (25–26), SELINOUS (31–44), MOTYA (45),
### GELA (48–51), AKRAGAS (58)

*Plate 51*

1. [- - -]ν[- - - | - - -]αε[- - - | - - -]ϙο[- - -].

3*. Κλεομ[εν?]ε̄ς : εποιε̄σε το̄πελο̄νι : ⱶο Κνιδιε[ι]δα :
κἐπ̣ικλε̄ς ⟨σ⟩τυλεια καλα ϝεργα (*or* Τ̣υλετα (?) :
κα[τ]εϝεργα̣[σατο ?]).

6. Γελο̄ν ο Δεινομεν[εος] | ανεθε̄κε το̄πολλο̄νι | Συρα-
ϙοσιος. | τον τριποδα : και τε̄ν : Νικε̄ν : εργασατο |
Βιο̄ν : Διοδο̄ρο : υιος : Μιλε̄σιος.

7. Ⱶιαρο̄ν ο Δεινομενεος | και τοι Συρακοσιοι | το̄ι
Δι Τυραν' απο Κυμας.

9. ⟨⟨[μναμα Πολυʒαλος με] Γελας ανε[θε̄κ]ε[ν] αϙασσ[ο̄ν]
*first line, erased*⟩⟩
[νικασας ⱶιπποισι (?) Π]ολυʒαλος μ' ανεθηκ[εν] (*in
rasura*)
[ⱶυιος Δεινομενεος, τ]ον αεξ' ευο̄νυμ' Απολλ[ον].

10. Αναξαγορα | Συρακοσια.

12. Βραχι|δα (Βραχυ|λα?) ειμι.

13. [Λ]υσις Ϝο Τιμ|αϟου (Χιμ|αρου?).

14. Συϟοι.

15. [τοι - - -]οι εψαφισαν|[το - - - προξενϝιαν και ατ]ελειαν και εν|[κτασιν γας - - - ϝομα]λικα γαμορōν | [- - -] αρχαν πεδειμ|[εν ?πλαν - - - και] Ϝιπαρχου και | [- - -].

17. τειδε Χορōι κα[τ]|ελος (or κα[ι] | Ελος?) κει⟨ν⟩ται θα[ν]|ατοιο λαχοντε|ς· ανφοτερος δ|ε καλōς Ϝυιος ε|θαπσε φιλος.

*Plate 52*

18*. [τοι]δε γεγραβαται | επι δυσπραγι[αι]· | Κερδōν Ελασ[··|··]ξε(?)ο το Περκο, | Πυθōν Διοκλ[- - -].

21*. οιμ[οι] | Επαλυ[ϙ?]|ο το Σαν|ϙο.

22. Γοστιϙο.

25. Σομροτιδα : το Ϝιατρο : το Μανδροκλεος :

26. Καλιϟτεος ⋮ ειμι.

31*. το Διος το Μ|ελιχιο εμι Προτα(?) Ευμε|νιδο το Πε|διαρχο.

33. οιμοι ὀρχεδαμ|ε Ϝο Πυθεα Σε|λινοντιος.

44. Φι[c. 11 ]ος | ανεθηκε [Σε]λινοντιος | Ασκλαπιαδας. | Ακρων Πρατωνος | εποιε : Σελιν[οντιος].

45*. [- - - | ··] Αϙτυ[λο]|ν Τιμετο(?) [α]|νδρα θαϟ[ο]|ντ' αγα[θον].

*Plate 53*

48*. Πανταρēς μ' ανε|θēκ[ε] | Μενεκρατιος Διο[ς αθλον?] το Γελοαιο.

49. Πασιαδαϝο το σ|αμα· Κρατēς ε|ποιε.

50. Πανταρεος ειμι | κα⟨ι⟩ τōν φιλōν ϙοινα ειμι.

51. τōν Γελōιōν ειμι.

58. Μυλο εμ⟨ι⟩ τϙ Σαϟονος | και Σαϟονος το Μυλο εμι.

# DORIC COLONIES, ITALY: TARAS (1–10), NON-GREEK (11–15)

1. Μελοσας · εμι · νικατēριον · ξαινοσα · τας κορας · ενικē.

4. Πολυλος ανεθ|ēκ⟨ε⟩ν. | Ευπιδας εποιε.

9. Δασιμος Πυρρο.

10. σκυλα απο Θουριōν Ταραν|τινοι ανεθēκαν Διι Ολυ|μπιōι δεκαταν.

11. Ραμια εδōκε.

15. α · β · γ[·]δ · ε[·]ϝ[·]ϡ · Ϝ · ι · κ[·]λ · μ[·]ν[·]ο[·]ξ · ϙ · ρ[·]Μ[·]σ·τ[·]υ[·]φ[·]χ·

# ITALY: LOKROI EPIZEPHYRIOI

*Plate 54*

1. [- - - | - - -]αμα[- - - | - - -]δε αν[- - - | - - -]ος διαλ-[- - - | - - -]μος · με[- - - | - - -]· παντōν [- - - | - - -]υτο · συ[- - - | - - -]ετο · ξ[- - - | - - -]οι γαν[- - - | - - -]ν · [- - -].

2. τοι Ϝειπōνιες ανεθ[ēκαν απο] | τōν Ϙροτōνια[ταν] | και Μεδμαιοι και Λ[οϙροι].

3. θεος · καθ[- - -]|αν · προξε[νϝοι? - - -]|αν · Κρατιπ-[πος? - - -]|νον · δυο τα[λαντα? - - -]|λα · σταθμ[ος - - -]|ος · νεον ο[- - -].

4. Φρασιαδας ανεθēκε ται θεōι.

6. Οινιαδας | και Ευκε|λαδος | και Χειμ|αρος | ανεθēκ|αν ται θ|εōι.

# IONIC COLONIES (WEST): SIRIS (1), MASSALIA (2–3), EMPORION (4), THOURIOI (8)

1.⋮ Ισο|δικ|ης ε|μι.

2. Απελλι|ος το Δη|μωνος Μ|ασσαλι|ητεο.

3. Τερπων ειμι θεας θεραπων | σεμνης Αφροδιτης·

τοις δε καταστησασι Κυπρις | χαριν ανταποδοιη.

4. Σανης διζησθαι [- - -] | Ερμης ων.

8. δαμοϟιον Βρενδεσινōν. | δαμοσιον Θουριων.

# AEGEAN ISLANDS, CENTRAL AND NORTH: NAXOS (2–14), AMORGOS (15–23), PAROS (26–39), SIPHNOS (40), DELOS (42–43), KEOS (46–47), SYROS (49), SAMOTHRACE (56–57), LEMNOS (58), THASOS (61–76)

*Plate 55*

2. Νικανδρη μ' ανεθēκεν Ϝ⟨ε⟩κηβολōι ιοχεαιρηι, ϙορη Δεινο|δικηο το Ναϟσιο, εϟσοχος αληōν,

Δεινομενεος δε κασιγνēτη, | Φϝραϟο δ' αλοχος ν⟨υν?⟩.

**3.** Ευθυκαρτιδης : | μ᾽ α{⋮}νεθēκε : ⊢ο | ΝαϞσιος : πο|ιēσας.

**4.** [- - -]λη μ᾽ εδōκεν [- - - | - - -]ιōνι.

**10.** [τ]ο αϝυτο λιθο εμι ανδριας και το σφελας.

**11.** Δειναγο|ρης μ᾽ ανεθēκεν ε|κηβολōι Α|πολλōνι δεκατ[ην].

**12.** Αλχσηνōρ εποιησεν ⊢ο Ναχσιος· αλλ᾽ εσιδε[σθε].

**14.** Δωροθεα κα⟨ι⟩ | Καριων | οιφολης.

## Plate 56

**15.** Δηιδαμανι | Πυγμας ο πατēρ [τ]ονδ᾽ οιϙ[ον ετευϞσεν?].

**17.** Δημαινετης εμι μν|ημα της Λαμπσαγο|ρεο.

**20.** Σταφυλις μνημα | εστησεν αδελ|φηι ΑλεϞσōι.

**22.** βωμον Διενυσω | ⊢ιποκρατēς, ⊢ιποκλēς.

**23.** α β γ δ ε ϝ ζ ⊦ θ.

**26.** [- - -]τωσω[- - - | - - -]ο η γης Π[αριης? - - - | - - -]ι κατασ[- - - | - - -]ν ||| ον[- - - | - - -]ωιας δē[- - - | - - -] νηπ[ϟ]οινει τεθνατο? - - - | - - -]ροτ[- - -].

**28.** Ασον τεσε|ρα και εβδω|ϙωντωτης εο|ν τας ϝοικιας ε|χσεπωιησεν.

**30\*.** Μικκιạ[δηι τωδ᾽ αγα]λμα καλον̣ (sic) Ṇ[ικην πτερωεσσαν?]

Ạρχερμω σο[φ]ιēισιν ηκηβω[λε δεχσαι Απωλ-λων]

[τ]οι Χιοι, Μελα̣νος πατροιοι ασ[τυ νεμωντι].

**34.** Δημωκυδης τωδ᾽ αγαλμα Τε|λεστωδικη τ᾽ απω κωινον |

ευχσαμενωι στησαν παρ|θενοι Αρτεμιδι |

σεμνοι ενι ϟαπεδοι κω|ρηι Διως αιγιωχωιω, |

τον γενεην βιωτων τ᾽ α|υχσ᾽ εν απημωσυνηι.

**35.** βομως Διως Ε̣[λαστε]|ρω τον απω Μ[α]ν̣δρω]-θεμιως· μελιτι | σπενδεται.

**39.** χσενοι Δοριηι ων θεμι[ς - - -] | ων[δ]ε δ[ωλ]οι α Κωρηι Αστοι ε[ρδεται].

## Plate 57

**40.** νυ⟨ν⟩φεον ⊢ιερων.

**42.** [- - -]ος παιδης το Δηλιο ανηθησαν Ạθηναιει Πολιαδ[ι].

**43a\*.** Μϟηγαρις μ᾽ ανεθε|κεν ⊢ερηι. *b.* Επιγνοτη μ᾽ ανηθεκην τηι ⊢ερηι.

**46\*.** [‒ ∪ Αθε]ναιες χρυσαιγιδεος οβριμ[οπ]ạ[τρες] |

[‒ ∪ ηποιε]σην Σιφνιος Αλκιδαμας |

[‒ ‒ ‒ ∪]η τ᾽ ηξηπον[ε]σ̣᾽ αγ̣αλοτα φυλα[ c. 4] |

[‒ ‒ ‒]νατ̣[- - -].

**47.** Δραλιος | Ενκαιρος | Σχενηρετος (= Χσενηρετος) | Ευδημος.

**49.** Σμ(ι)ϙ̣ρ̄ν τον ο|⊢πλοφορον κ|αλιστα εϙολι|αδη.

**56.** Αγαμεμνων. Ταλθυβιος. Επε[ιος].

**57.** [- - -]επποτεψενευσαντοκαε[- - -].

**58.** ⊢οϙος | τω τεμ|ενως τē|ς Αρτε|μιδος.

## Plate 58

**61.** Γλαυϙω ειμι μνη|μα τω Λεπτινεο · ε|θεσαν δε με ωι βρεντ|εο παιδες.

**63.** Ζηνος και Σεμελης και Αλκμηνης τανυπεπλω: εστασιν παιδες τησδε πωλεος φυλαϙωι.

**65.** [Θ]ρασυκληως τω | [Π]ανταγαθω | [μ]ẹ̄τēρ τωδε | [σē]μ᾽ επωηεσε.

**68.** η καλων τω μνημα [πα]|τηρ εστησε θανωσ[ηι] | Λεαρετη· ων γαρ [ετ]|ι ϟοσαν εσωφϟωμ[εθα].

**70.** Νυμφηισιν κἀπωλλωνι Νυμφηγετηι θηλυ και αρσ|εν αμ βωληι πρωσερδεν. ϙιν ωυ θεμις ωυδε χωιρων. | ωυ παιονιζεται. | Χαρισιν αιγα ωυ θεμις ωυδε χωιρων.

**75.** Λοκριων | τοξοτας | Κορινθιος. | Λυσιστρατος | Ευκλεος | Κορινθιος.

**76.** ως αν επαναστασιν βωλευωμενην επι Θασοι κατειπηι και φανηι εωντα αληθεα, χιλιως στατηρ|ας εκ της πωλεος ισχετο· ην δε δωλως κατειπηι, και ελευθερως εστω· ημ πλεως η εις κατειποσι, | τριηκωσιωι κρινοντων δικην δικασαντες· ην δε τις τον μετεχωντον κατειπηι, τω τε αργυριων | ισχετο και κατομωτως κατ᾽ αυτω μη εστω μηδε δικη μηδεμια μητε ιρη μητε βεβηλη περι τωτον | μηδε εν τηι επαρηι εστω πλην ενως το πρωτω βωλευσαντως· αρχει εινατη απιωντως Απατωρι|ονως επι Ακρυπτω Αλεξιμαχω Δεξιαδεο αρχωντον.

ως αν εν τηις απωικιηισιν επαναστασιν βωλευω-μενην κατειπηι η πρωδιδωντα τημ πωλιν Θασιον | τινα η τον απωικον και φανηι εωντα αληθεα, διηκω-σιως στατηρας εκ της πωλεος ισχετο· ην δε τα | χρηματα ηι τω επανισταμενω πλευνως αξια διηκω-σιον στατηρον, τετρακωσιως στατηρας εκ της πωλεος | ισχετο· αν (sic) δε δωλως κατειπηι, τω τε χρημα ισχετο και ελευθερως εστω· ημ πλεως η εις κατειποσι, τριηκωσιωι | κρινοντων δικην δικασαντες· ην δε τις τομ μετεχωντον κατειπηι, τω τε αργυριων ισχετο και κατομωτως | κατ᾽ αυτω μη εστω μηδε δικη μηδε-μια μητε ιρη μητε βεβηλη περι τωτον μηδ᾽ εν τηι επαρηι εστω πλην ενως τω | πρωτω βωλευσαντως· αρχει τηι ρητρηι τριτη ισταμενω Γαλαξιονος επι Φανωδικω Αντιφανεως Κτησιππω | αρχωντον.

## Plate 59

**1a.** θιος ο λδιον. | αδ' εϝαδε | πολι· | επει κα κοσμηϲει, | δεκα ϝετιον | τον α|ϝτον | μη κοσμεν· | αι δε κοσμηϲιε, | οπε δικακϲιε | αϝτον | οπηλεν | διπλει | κἀϝτο|ν ακρηστον | ημεν | ας δδοι | κοτι κοσμηϲιε | μηδεν | ημεν. | 𝔛 ομοται δε | κοσμος | κοἰ δαμιοι | κοἰ ικατι | οι τας πολ[ιος].

**2.** (ϙοσμος ο επισ)τας | αι μη εστεισαιτο, αϝτ([ον ο]-πηλεν | και τον τιταν | αι μη 'στεισαιτο τ[- - -]. τρι[ο])ν ϝετιον τον αϝτον μη ϙοσ(μεν, | δεκα μεν γνδμονας, | πεντε [δε κσ]ενιος.) *(IC iv. 14. The illustration omits the parts shown here in curved brackets.)*

**3.** [- - -]νασ[- - - | - - -τ]οι Γο[ρτυνιοι? - - - | - - -ελε]-ϝθερος [- - - | - - -] τις δολ[- - - | - - - ϙοσ]μιδν : ε α[- - - | - - - λ]αγαιεν α[- - - | - - -] τα θινα : ευ[- - - | - - -]ι : αι δε με λε[οι - - - | - - -]οι : πινεν : τ[- - -]. *(IC iv. 62.)*

**5.** [θι]οι. | τδι Ζενι τδι [- - - | - - -] οιις θελεια λευκα, το δε κο[- - - | - - - α]μμνα, τα{τα}νδ|ε βοιαν ο ιαρε[υς - - - | - - -] κριον τδι Αλ|δι οιιν ερσεν[α - - - | - - -]α ταδε παρθυμ|αται περιϝοι[- - - | - - -]τε τριινς κάμ|ναν, τδν δ' αλδ[ν - - - | - - -] μεδιμνιαια | και τυρο εμιπ[- - -]. *(IC iv. 65.)*

**12. Α.** [- - - παν]σεϝδι αποϝει[π - - -]. | [- - -]κα ϝεκτος | α[- - - | - - -] περηται | πσεϝ?[- - - | - - -]εν | επει ταδε [- - - | (Β) - - -]ι | τρις ϝε[- - - | - - -]···νο [- - -].

## Plate 60

**15.** [- - -]στα[···]οзοι ανοθεν | γα[- - -]. | [- - -]ε

[π]ροϝειπεμεν | η αυτον | η [- - - | - - -]ν αμευσονται | αμποτερο[- - -].

**18.** Δοϙϙ[- - -].

**19a.** [- - -]νκαλμχ(?)τκυ|ος | βαρξε | α[··] | ο[- - - | - - -]αρκ[· ?]αχ(?)σετ | μεγγ|αρκρκοκλες | γεϙ[- - - | - - -]ασεχ(?)γναυχ(?)τ.

**20.** Τιμος ημι. | Ευαγρος μ' εστ|ασε.

**22.** [- - -]ϝκος | ιναντι (τδν ει[- - - | - - -]ιν δοκεν ακ)σια ημεν τας τ([ροπας] | και τας ατ)ελειας α τεκνα το ([τ]ινυμε[νο - - - | - - -] κατ') αμεραν зαμιομεν. | (αι δ' επελ|θοιεν ιν ταισ)ι πεντε αι μη λεοι [- - - | - - -]ν | τανδ' αμεραν | πεντ' α(μερας ϝεργακσα|[μενο]ς τα[ι πολι α)μιστδς. το δε μισ[το - - - | - - - τα]ς ιν αντρηιδι διαλ(σιος· ι δια[ c. 4 | c. 5 ]λοι επι) σποϝδδαν | εκσοαι [- - - | - - - α]ϝτος | ϝεκαστος μη ινθε(μεν | ται πο[λ]ι. π)ερι δε το μιστο | αι πον[ιο - - - | - - - τα]δε δε τελιοντι· ιος τε τ(αν εκατονβαν | ταν μεγαλα)ν | και το θυμα | και [··]δ[ c. 4 ]ν[- - - | - - - ?αντ]ρηιον δι-δομεν· τδν δ' αλδ(ν παντδν | ατελεια)ν και τροπαν ιν αντρηιδι ϙα[- - -]. *(IC ii. v. 1. The illustration omits the parts shown here in curved brackets.)*

**27.** [- - - | - - -]δοι τοις αλλοπολ[ιαταις - - - | - - -] κόρκον τιθεμεν τον [- - - | - - - τδι δε ορκ]δι ταν αραν ινημε[ν - - - | - - -]πινυμεν μητε θηριον [- - - | - - -]τα απατον ημεν οϝτο[- - - | - - -]ν, αι δε μη [···] βαλοι επο[- - - | - - -]πομε [c. 8 ]ϙο[- - -]. *(IC ii. xii. 3.)*

**29a.** Αυτομε|δεος εμι. *(IC ii. x. 7.)*

**30a.** επ' Αμυρταιο επικορο[ι] | Κρετες. τυχᾱγα[θ]ας *(sic)* | Ονασανδρ[ος] Κυδδ[ν]|ιατας. b. Θαρυσθενες. | Θιοκριτος | ο φιλο[ς] Θαρ[υσθενευς?].

# AEGEAN ISLANDS, SOUTH: THERA (1–16) AND KYRENE (18–20), MELOS (23–25, 29), ANAPHE (26), SIKINOS (27)

## Plate 61

**1a** (i). ναι τον Δελπhινιον ε Κριμδν | τεδε διπhε παιδα, Βαθυκλεος αδελπhεο[ν] *(IG xii. 3. 357)*. (ii). Θαρης | Ανασικλης *(IG xii. 3. 573)*. b (i). Ζευς *(IG xii. 3. s. p. 1313)*.(ii). Βορεαιος *(IG xii. 3. 357)*.

**2.** Δαμαινις.

**3.** (i). ⊢αδιμα *(IG xii. 3. 771)*. (ii). Ετεοκληια *(IG xii. 3. 781)*. (iii). Ευανιο *(IG xii. 3. 783)*.

**5.** Ρεκσανδρ | Αρκhαγετας | Προκλης | Κλεαγορας | Περαιευς.

**6.** Νιϙοκας | Νανος.

**9.** Τερπσια ημι.

**12.** (i). Εχετιμ⟨ος⟩ *(IG xii. 3. 785)*. (ii). Ανακσιβια *(IG xii. 3. 772)*. (iii). Εριπδν *(IG xii. 3. 779)*.

## Plate 62

**15.** Αλεξα|γορα.

**16.** Αγλδτελης πρατισ|τος αγοραν ⊢ικαδι | Καρνηια θεον δει|πνιξεν ⊢ον[ι]παντιδα | και Λακαρτος.

**18.** Ϙυρα[- - -].

**19.** το Απολλδνος εμι.

**20.** Αιγλανδρ μ' ανεθεκε | ⊢οντιπατρο δεκαταν.

**23.** παι Διος, Εκπhαντδι δεκσαι τοδ' αμεντhες αγαλμα, σοι γαρ επευκhομενος τουτ' ετελεσσε Γροπhδν.

**25.** b. Σμι|θδν | Ανδ|ραπο|μπο. c. Πραξ|ικυδ|εος [- - -]. e. Δαμ|αγο|ρα Τ|εμβ|ρια|ο. f. [- - -]υλε|σθε|τος.

**26.** Αγϙυλιδν τονδε τον θδρον εποιε.

**27.** Αντιδο[τος μεν τυμβον εχο|σ' αυτο]ς και παιδες
Πα|σιδιδοι· το δε σαμ' Ευνο|[ο]ς εστασε καλον
κεχαρ|ισμενον εργον.

**29\*.** Θρασυμαχο παιδες το Μαλιο [- - -] με α[νεθεν?
- - -] | τοι Δι Δαιαλκος και [- - - νικασαντ?]ες. |
Γροφον εποιε Μαλιος καγ[- - -].

# IONIC DODEKAPOLIS: SAMOS (1–21), MILETOS (23–39), THEBAE AD MYCALEN (40), CHIOS (41–47), ERYTHRAI (50–51), EPHESOS (53), KOLOPHON (56), TEOS (58–61), KLAZOMENAI (63–66), SMYRNA (69)

## Plate 63

**1.** [- - - με]γαλης αντι φιλημ[οσυνης].

**2.** Δημανδρο το | Πρωτοχαριος.

**4.** Χηραμυης μ' ανεθηκεν τηρηι αγαλμα.

**5.** Λευκιος ανεθηκε | τωι Απολωνι.

**8\*.** Γορδιαμο τ|ο (?):[· ·]λω εμι.

**13.** Αεακης ανεθηκεν | ο Βρυσωνος ⫶ ος τηι | Ηρηι ⫶
την συλην ⫶ ε|πρησεν ⫶ κατα την | επιστασιν.

**16.** Αισχρο ⫶ το Ζωιλο | Σαμιο.

**17.** Σαμιοι | τωπολλωνι.

**18\*.** [Τ]εχνανδρο. [ὁ δεῖνα εποιησ?]ε Κρης.

**19.** Ευθυμος Λοκρος Αστυκλεος τρις Ολυμπι' ενικων,
εικονα δ' εστησεν τηνδε βροτοις εσοραν.
Ευθυμος Λοκρος απο Ζεφυριο ανεθηκε. | Πυθαγορας
Σαμιος εποιησεν.

**21.** [τοδ'] εργο πολλοι παρα [μαρτ]υρε[ς, ευτ' επι
Νειλωι]
[Μεμ]φιος αμφ' ερατης νηυσιν εθηκ[ε μαχην]
[θου]ρος Αρης Μηδων τε και Ελλην[ων, Σαμιοι δε]
[νη]ας Φοινικων πεντε τε και δ[εκ' ελον·]
[αλλ'] Ηγησαγορην Ζωιλοτο και [◡ ◡ – ◡]
[- - -].

## Plate 64

**23.** οι Αναξιμανδρο παιδες το Μανδρομαχ[ο ?τωπο-
λωνι | ημεας ανε]θεσαν. εποιησε δε Τερψικλης.

**26.** [Αν]αξιμανδρο.

**27.** Ευδημος με εποιεν.

**29.** Χαρης ειμι ο Κλεσιος Τειχιοσης αρχος· | αγαλμα
το Απολλωνος.

**33.** (Ηρηι Ανθεηι ⫶ οις λευκη ⫶) εγκυαρ ⫶ λευκωι
αν|αβεβαμενη ⫶ χους (τηι ιερηι διδοται ⫶ και ξυλων ⫶
ο[- - - | - - - η]μιεκτο ⫶ ες το ιερεως ⫶ διδοται χο)υς
ξυλα ⫶ καπι βωμο|ν ⫶ αμφορευς οινο (⫶ τετραδι επι
δεκα ⫶ Δι Νοσιωι ⫶ [c. 10 ]ι ⫶ οις αρσην ⫶ εκτευς πυρων ⫶
εκτε)υς κριθεων ⫶ εκτη οι|νο ⫶ ξυλα ⫶ μελι ⫶ αλε(ιφα ⫶
Λευκωι ⫶ οις αρσην ⫶ Αργηι [- - - | - - - εκ?]τηι ιστα-
μενο ⫶ εορτη κηρυσσεται ⫶) Απολλωνος Δελφιν|[ιο
- - -]. (*The illustration omits the parts shown in curved
brackets.*)

**34.** [c. 9 ?Λ]|εοθρ[ασ c. 4|··] Λεωδαμας | Οναξο
πρυτ[α]|νευοντες α|νεθεσαν τη|κατηι.

**39.** [- - -]ες [:] ες μελα[ c. 5 | - - -] μηροι καιωνται,
π[α|ρ]α τοισι μηριοις[ι - - - | - - - πα]ρατιθεναι· ερδεν
ο|[ι]μ μελαιναν ολ[- - - | - - -] παρ τομ βον ε[π|ι]πεσ-
σεν : ηδε [- - - | - - -]ο : και εσσ[ c. 2 | - - -].

## Plate 65

**40.** [Παμφ?]αιεο ειμι σ[ημ|α] το Δεινεω.

**41.** (A) [- - -]κα : της Ιστιης δημο | ρητρας ⫶ φυλασ-
σω[ν? - - - | - - -]ον : ηρει : ημ μεν δημαρ|χων: η
βασιλευων : δεκασ[θηι? - - - | - - -?τη]ς Ιστιης απο-
δοτω : δημα|ρχεων ⫶ εξπρηξαι : τον ε[ξεταστην?
- - - | - - -]εν δημο κεκλημενο· | αλοιαι τιμη διπλησ[ιη
- - - | - - -]ν οσην παραλοιω[· ] (B) [c. 3] ην δ' ηκκλη-
τος δι[κη? - - - | - - -] ην δε αδικηται : παρα |
δημαρχωι : στατηρ[α - - -]| (C) εκκαλεσθω ες | βολην
την δημοσιην· τηι τριτηι | εξ Εβδομαιων | βολη
αγερεσθ|ω η δημοσιη ε|πιθωιος λεκτ|η πεντηκοντ'
απ|ο φυλης· τα τ' αλ[λ|α] πρησσετω τα δη|μο και
δικα[ς ο|φο]σαι αν εκκλ|ητοι γενωγ[τ|αι] το μηνος
π|ασας επι|κρι|νετω? · · · | c. 4] σερ [c. 3 | - - -]
(D) [- - - Α]ρτεμισιωνος. | [- - -]ων ορκια επι|τα-
μνετω φω[μνυτω? - - - | - - - β]ασιλευσιν.

**42e.** Νικησερμος την[δε] την φυλικα εποιησε[ν].

**46.** Χιοι Απολλωνι τον βωμον.

**47.** Ηροπυθο | το Φιλαιο | το Μικκυλο | το Μανδρο-
κεος | το Αυτοσθενεος | το Μανδραγορεω | το Ερασιω
| το Ιπποτιωνος | το Εκαιδεω | το Ιπποσθενος | το
Ορσικλεος | το Ιπποτιωνος | το Εκαο | το Ελδιο | το
Κυπριο.

**50.** Απολλωνι Δελφ|ινιωι ⫶ Φανοδικ|ος ο Φιλητεω
α|[νε]θηκεν ⫶ ευχω|[λην υ]περ εαυτο | [και γενεης?].

## Plate 66

**51.** Αριστοκλεος | γυναικος | το Τηλεφανεος | Εκα-
ταιης της | Δεονυδος.

**53.** [c. 9 ?] τεπαραφοντα μνεαι ⫶ το πρω[τον] εστα-
θ[ησ]αν ⫶ ⫶ εκ ττων δω[ρ|ων] χρυσο ⫶ εκ πολεως
ηνειχ[τθ]ησαν ⫶ ⫶ αργυραι πεντε ⫶ και ειρος(ι)
μν[ε|α]ι ⫶ ειν τωι πρωτωι χρυσωι ηνειχτησαν ⫶ ⫶
εκ ττο δορατος εξς μνεαι | εσταθ[ησαν] ⫶ δεκα δε σι
ενθενδε εσταθησαν μνεαι | χρυσο ⫶ αργυρο τρες
κα[ι] τριηφοντα μν[ε]αι ενθαδ' εσταθησαν ⫶ αργυραι

ε[κ ττο] ναυτι[ϙο *c. 6 ?* | *c. 7 ?*]υτο εβδομηϙοντα μνεαι
: καθα[ *c. 8* ]νο[ *c. 8 ?* ] | δεκα εκ ττο αλος :

**56.** Πα⟨μ⟩βις ο Ϙολοϕόνιος | συν Ψαμματ|α⟨ι⟩.

**58.** Ελεσιβιος ο Τηιιος.

**61.** [Ευ]ξενο ειμι | το Καλητορος | το Τηιιο.

**63.** Αθηναγορη : Ερμηι : ηθ[εκεν = εθηκεν ?].

**66.** στηλη | [Ησ]υχιης της | Λεωνος | γυναικος.

**69.** Δολιωνος εμι ϙυλιχνη.

# DORIC HEXAPOLIS AND NEIGHBOURS: RHODES (1–30), KNIDOS (31–34), KOS (39), HALIKARNASSOS (41), KALYMNA (43–47), GREEKS IN EGYPT (48–51)

## Plate 67

**1.** Ϙοραϙο ημι ϙυλιχϛ.

**2.** [- - -]νος ημι.

**3.** *a*: αιρχε (= χαιρε). *b*: ευ επιον.

**4.** *a*: Τηλεϕος μ' εγραϕε ɧο Ιαλυσιος. *b*: Αναχϛανδρ ε[γραϕε ?] ɧο Ιαλυσιος ɧοκα βασιλ|ευς ɧἔλασε τον στρατον το πρατον. Αμασις ɧαμα (?), Ψαματιχος.

**5.** σαμα τοϛ' Ιδα|μενευς ποιη|σα ɧινα κλεος | ειη, | Ζευ⟨ς⟩ δε νιν οστις | πημαινοι λειδ|λη θειἔ.

**6.** ɧεκατιος.

**8.** Αστυοχιδα ημι.

**9\*.** χεϛει οϙου ναμα ιχεται (?).

**10.** [Σμυρ ?]δης με ανε[θηκε - - -].

**11.** [Σ]μυρδης με | ανηθηκην | ɧο Συνδο.

**13.** Ονησος : με ανηθεκη : τὀπολōνι : ο χαλχοτυπος : τροϙον αρματο|ς :

## Plate 68

**17.** Αγης ⟨η⟩μι.

**23.** Τελεσιγεροντ | ος εμι. (Τ)[- - -]ικο εμι. (Τ *not shown in illustration.*)

**25.** Χαρω|νιδα|ς Ζην|οτιμω.

**30.** καλλιστα γας ɧα Βρασια | ως εμιν δοκει. Δευς ɧερμας | Αρταμις Αθαναια.

**31.** Ευαρχος με ανεθ|ηκε τοισι Διος|κοροισιν.

**32a.** Χαροϕνης : με ανε[θηκε] τὀπολ[ōνι τōι Μ]ιλασιδι.

**33.** τον θησαυρον τ[ο]νδε και τἀγαλμα[τα Κνιδιοι ανεθεν τωι] Πυθιωι δεκατ[αν απο τω|μ πολεμι]ων.

**34.** ɧο Μικος ɧο Μ[αγν]ητος τἀθαναιαι μ' α[νεθηκε].

## Plate 69

**39.** Απολ|λωνο|ς Πυθιο.

**41.** ενθαδε : μο|ιραν : εχων | Αλικαρνη|σσευς : Ιδα|γυγος : κει|ται : Αριστο|κλεος : πα|ις, : Αρεος | θεραπω|ν.

**43.** *Various letters* (ε, ϛ, ɧ, θ, λ, ο, ρ, ψ, *others perhaps not Greek*).

**44.** [- - -]τσολυτ ?[- - -].

**45.** Αλκιδαμ[ος ? - - -].

**47.** Μενελας. Ευϕορβος. Εκτōρ.

**48.** *a.* βασιλεος ελθοντος ες Ελεϕαντιναν Ψαματιχο | ταυτα εγραψαν τοι συν Ψαμματιχōι τōι Θεοκλος | επλεον · ηλθον δε Κερκιος κατυπερθε υις ο ποταμος | ανιη· αλογλōσος δ' ηγε Ποτασιμτō, Αιγυπτιος δε Αμασις. | εγραϕε δ' αμε Αρχōν Αμοιβιχο και Πελεϙος οὐδαμο. | *b.* και Χ[- - -] | Κριθις εγρα⟨ψ⟩αμες ? *c.* Πυθōν Αμοιβιχου.

## Plate 70

**49.** Μελανθιος με ανεθηκε τωι Ζηνι Θηβαιωι ακαλμα.

**50.** Πυθερμ|ος με ο | Νελων|ος ελυσ|ατο τ|ης Εσιο|ς αγαλμ|α.

**51.** Τιμαρχος | ο Δαϕναι|τἔς.

# AIOLIC AREA: LARISA (1), MAGNESIA AD SIPYLUM (2), NEANDRIA (8), ASSOS (10)

**1.** *a–b.* τανδε τα[ν - - - Αθαν]αηαη. *f.* Θηοδōρος ο Τιμ[- - -].

**2.** [Μαγν]ης ηλθ' [ε]νθαδε Καικος.

**8.** [- - -]νεθἔκα[ν] | το επιστα|τα ο και κε|μεγ[- - -].

**10.** Αριστανδρει κ[- - - | - - -]κιος.

# NORTHERN COLONIAL AREA: CHALKIDIKE (10–14), THRACE (33), HELLESPONT AND PROPONTIS (35–52, 75) EUXINE (54–73)

**10.** Θευγενἔς Πυθοκλεο[ς ανε]|θἔκε τὀπελλōνι Ποτει- δα[νιατας]. | Ρ(?)ōμις εποι[ε].

**13.** Νευμους.

## Plate 71

**14.** Αντιφιλος | Ολινθιος.

**33.** Μεσσανιοι και Ναυπακτιοι ανεθεν Δ‍ιι | Ολυμπιωι δεκαταν απο τωμ πολεμιων. | Παιωνιος εποιησε Μενδαιος | και τἀκρωτηρια ποιων επι τον ναον ενικα.

**35.** [Με]νισκος Ξ̣[εν|ο]δοκο, Δημι[ς | Π]υθοκλεος ο̣|[ι]κηιηιοι (sic) Περ[ι]|νθιοι τηι Ηρ|ηι ανεθεσαν | δεκατην ερ|δοντες γορ|γυρην χρυση|ν, σερηνα αργ|υρεον, φιαλη|ν αργυρην, λυ|χνιην χαλκι|νον, ονονημενα | συνπαντα δ|ιηκοσιων δυ|ωδεκων στα‌τ|ηρων Σαμιω|ν συν τωι λιθωι.

**36.** Ηγησιπολιος | το Φαναγορε|ω.

**41.** [Ελ ?]ικος [ε]μ[ι σημα ? c. 11]ε με (εμε ?) κατεθηκε[ν ?].

**43–44.** Φανοδικο | εμι τὀρμοκ|ρατεος το | Προκον‌νη|σιο· κρητηρ|α δε : και υποκ|ρητηριον : κ|αι ηθμον : ες π|ρυτανηιον | εδωκεν: Συκε|ευσιν.

    Φανοδικο : ειμι : το ┣ερμοκρατος : το Προκο|ν‌ēσιο : κἀγō ᛭ κρατε̄ρα | κἀπιστατον : και ┣ēθμ|ον : ες πρυτανειον ᛭ ε|δōκα ᛭ μνε̄μα ᛭ Σιγευ|ευσι ᛭ εαν δε τι πασχ|ō, μελεδαινεν ᛭ με ō ᛭ Σιγειες ᛭ και μ' επο|εισεν (sic) ᛭ ┣αισōπος : και | ┣ἀδελφοι.

**48.** Αλεξιλεως | Προκλειδο | Λαμψακηνος.

**50.** [- - -]ηνο τη⟨ν⟩ στεγην εποιησεν κοὶ ξυνεωνες απο των τεμε|νεωγ και των δερματων. | [- - -]ο Λευκιππο τον νεων εξεποιησεν αυτοχεριηι.

## Plate 72

**51.** [επι Μαιανδριου. | πολις (Μανη εδωκε τωι) Μηδικεω και τοισιν Αισηπου παισιν | και τοισιν εκγονοισιν ατελειην και πρυτανειον. δεδοται παρεξ ναυⲦο | και το ταλαντο και ιππωνιης και | της τεταρτης και ανδραποδωνιης· | των δε αλλων παν‌των ατελε̄ς· και επι τουτοισιν δημος ορκιον εταμον, την δε στ]ηλην τηνδε πολις Μ|ανη εδωκε τωι Με̄δικ[εω]. (( ) = words omitted in later copy.)

**52.** Μανδρωγ[ος το|δε σ]ημα το Μη|ησιπτολε[μο· μ|αχο ?]μενος δε | απεθαν[εν].

**54.** [ενθαδ' Α]ναξανδ[ρ]ο Δειν̣η|[ς δ]οκιμωτατος αστωγ
    κε|[τ]αι αμωμητος τερμα λα|[χ]ων θανατο.

**58.** Ηραγορεω. [τηι Αφ]ροδιτηι Συριηι Μητρω[- - -].

**60.** [– ∪ ∪ – εστ]ηκα· λεγω δ' οτι τηλε πολε[ως που ?] | [– ∪ ∪ – κεται Λεωξος ο Μολπαγορε[ω].

**61.** [- - -]ητρο ειμι. θα.

**63.** Ευθυμιης ειμι κυλιξ. [- - -]εω κυλιξ ε[μι].

**73.** Γαγας της Αναξιμ|βροτο.

**75.** τε̄νδι σοι Θοδε̄μος διδōσι ᛭

1. Graffito on jug, *c.* 725? (*rings mark scratches possibly unconnected with letters*). 2. Graffito on stone, 8th c.? 3 *a–c*. Graffiti on pottery, 7th c.?
4. Graffito on skyphos, *c.* 650. 6 *a–b*. Painted names on early BF ware, *c.* 625–600 (*not shown in position*).

PLATE 2                    ATTICA

**7.** Frr. of marble pillar-base (?), *c.* 625–600? **8.** Stone grave-stele, *c.* 625–600? **9 *c*, *e*.** Graffiti on ostraka, 7th c. ? **10 *a*, *c*, *f*.** Graffiti on amphorae, late 7th to mid-6th c. **13.** Limestone capital, *c.* 600–575? **14 *a*.** Painted inscrr. on BF ware, *c.* 570–550 (*not shown in position*). **17.** Limestone base, *c.* 570–560.

18

19

20

21

28

HEΦΑSTOS

ΛΡΑΦSΕΝΚΑ

ΝΕΑΡΧΟSΜΕ

24

25

ΣΕΜΑΦΡΑSΙΚΛΕΙΑΣ
ΚΟΡΕΚΕΚΛΕΣΟΜΑΙ
ΑΙΕΙΑΝΤΙΛΑΜΟ
ΓΑΡΑΘΕΟΝΤΟΥΤΟ
ΛΑΧΟΣΟΝΟΜΑ

29

18. Limestone stele, Panathenaia 566? 19. Marble base for grave, *c.* 560? 20. Limestone base for grave, *c.* 560–550? 21. Bronze plaque, *c.* 550? 24. Painted inscrr. on BF ware, *c.* 550 (*not shown in position*). 25. Limestone capital, *c.* 550? 28. Limestone name-list, *c.* 550? 29. Marble pillar-capital for grave, *c.* 540.

PLATE 4                    ATTICA

**31.** Marble grave-stele, *c.* 540.  **32.** Marble base of grave-stele, *c.* 540.  **33.** Graffito on sherd, *c.* 550–525.  **34.** Marble base of grave-stele, *c.* 510.  **36.** Fr. of marble pillar-base (?), *c.* 525?  **37.** Marble altar-top, *c.* 520–510?  **40.** Marble base for grave-stele, *c.* 525–500.  **43.** Marble base-block, *c.* 506.  **44.** Part of inscribed marble altar (?), *c.* 500–480.

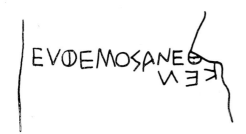

2

3

6

7

9 A 1

9 A 2

10

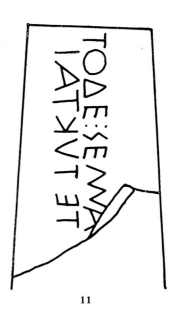

11

Chalkis: **2.** Stone stele, *c.* 500? **3.** Stone grave-stele, *c.* 500–450? **6.** Graffito on alabastron, *c.* 550? **7.** Painted names on 'Chalkidic' ware, *c.* 550–510 (*not shown in position*). Eretria: **9 A 1–2.** Laws on stone wall-blocks, *c.* 550–525? **10.** Graffito on clay vase, *c.* 550? **11.** Marble grave-stele, *c.* 525–500?

PLATE 6                    EUBOIA

ΦΙΛΕΣΙΟΣΕΠΟΙΕ
ΕΡΕΤΡΙΕΣΤΟΙΔΙ

19

24

22

AISϟVΛΙΟΝ          ΛΟΦΑ+

ΙΕVΤΙϟ            ΗΕϟVΑΤΙΟΝ

17              26

Eretria: **13.** Stone grave-stele, *c.* 500–480? **17.** Stone grave-pillar, *c.* 500–475? **19.** Stone base-block, *c.* 480? **22.** Painted aryballos (imitation Protocorinthian), *c.* 650? **24.** Seal-impression, *c.* 550–525? Styra: **26.** Graffiti names on leaden strips, *c.* 475?

1

3 a

3 b

3 c

3 d

3 e

2 a

2 b

2 c

DE M O ⊕ E ꟼ E Σ

Ξ I A ꟼ O ꟼ A Γ O L O Γ O Σ K A ꟼ Y K E F I O

5

4

1. Bronze statuette, *c.* 700–675? **2 a–c.** Bronze lebes-fr., *c.* 700–675? **3 a–e.** Bronze lebetes-frr., *c.* 700–600? **4.** Limestone statue, *c.* 650–625?
**5.** Bronze lebes-fr., *c.* 625–600?

PLATE 8 BOIOTIA

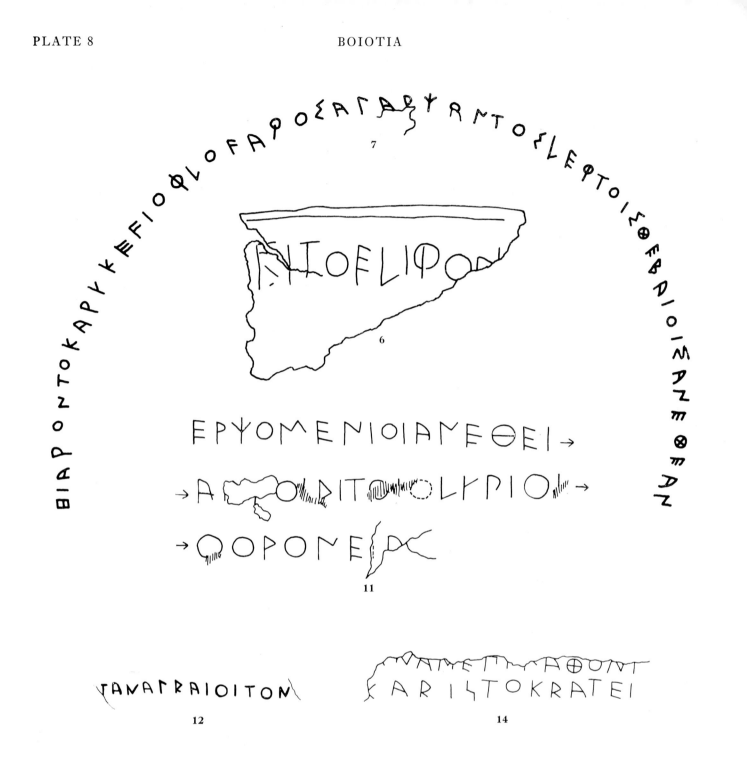

6. Bronze lebes-fr., *c.* 625–600? 7. Bronze phiale, *c.* 610–550? 11. Helmet (*single line*), *c.* 550–525? 12. Shield, *c.* 525–500?
13. Marble column, *c.* 525–500? 14. Marble grave-relief, *c.* 510–500.

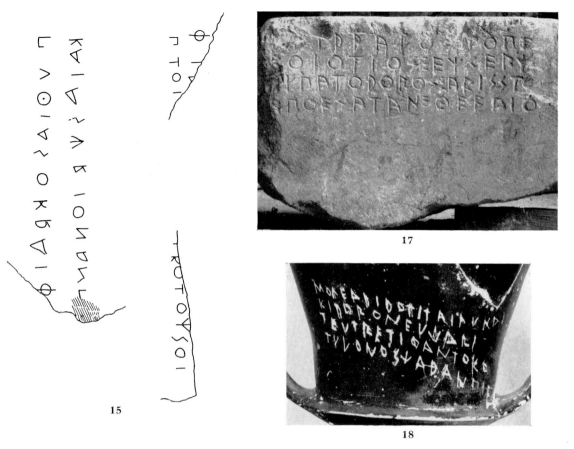

15

17

18

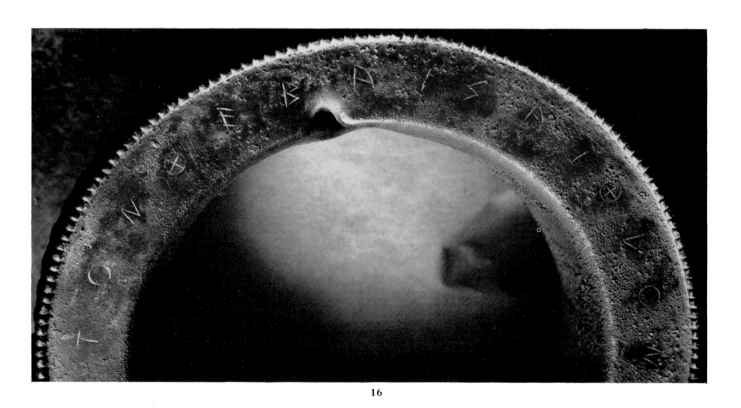

16

15. Marble statue, *c.* 500. 16. Bronze hydria, *c.* 470. 17. Marble base, *c.* 475–450? 18. Graffito on kantharos, *c.* 450–430.

PLATE 10 BOIOTIA

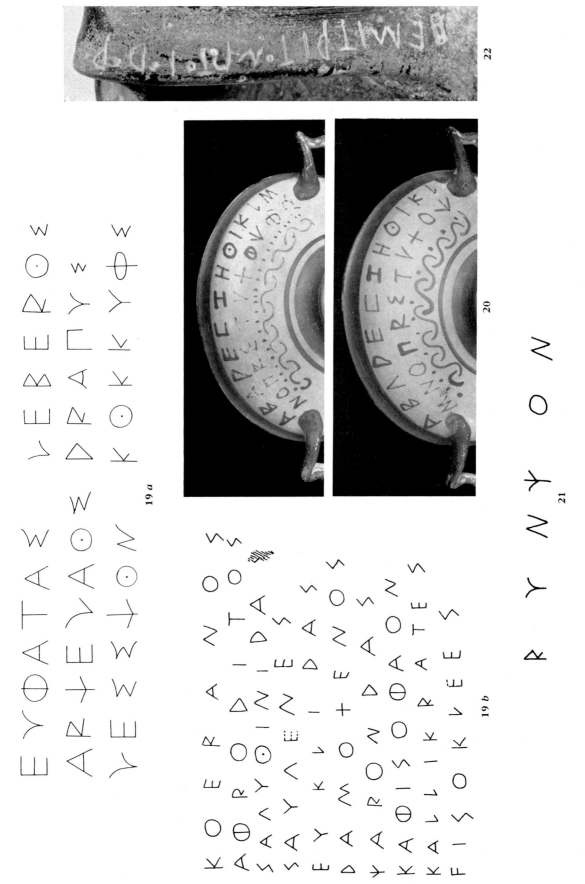

19 *a–b*. Grave-stelai, *a* marble, *b* limestone, *c.* 424 (*parts only*). **20.** Painted abecedaria on cup, *c.* 420. **21.** Marble grave-stele, *c.* 425–400. **22.** Graffito on oinochoe-handle, mid-6th c.?

2 (detail)

10

2

4

3

1

8

ΠΟΛΥ+ΕΝΑΙΑ: ΕΜΜΙ
7

ΚΙΝΕΑ: ΚΑΙ: ΘΡΑΣΙΜ Η ΔΑϞ
14

**1.** Stone stele, c. 550? **2.** Stone bearing a building record, c. 550? **3.** Stone grave-stele (?), c. 525–500? **4.** Stone base for a grave, c. 500–480?
**7.** Marble grave-stele, c. 460–450? **8.** Marble base for a grave-column, c. 450? **10.** Bronze plaque, c. 450–425? **14.** Marble grave-stele, c. 440–430.

PLATE 12    PHOKIS

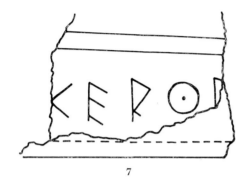

1

ΥΑΡΙΜΕΔΕΣ

2

3

7

5

4

**1.** Stone with dedication, *c.* 600–550? **2–3.** Gravestones, *c.* 550–540? **4.** Marble base and plinth of statue, *c.* 550–540. **5.** Names incised on
tufa blocks, *c.* 550–500? (*not in position*). **7.** Marble spit-holder, *c.* 530?

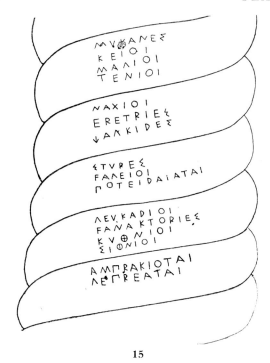

ΝΑΙΡΕΝΑΡΟΝ
ΟΥΔΙΣΤΥΚΑΚΟΣ
ΛΕΣΕΙΟΥΔΕΘΑ
ΝΟΝΤΑΠΟΛΟΣ
ΑΝΘΡΟΠΟΝΛΥ
ΣΑΜΕΝΟΣ
ΚΑΜΑΤΟ

11

17

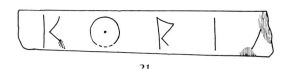

21

23

11. Gravestone, *c.* 500? 15. Bronze snake-column, *c.* 479 (*part only*). 17. Law on stone wall-block, *c.* 470–450? 21. Stone block from Treasury (?), 6th c.? 23. Stone base, *c.* 450?

PLATE 14          LOKRIS, OZOLIAN AND OPOUNTIAN

ΨΑΡΙΛΑΟΣ

1

A

2 (obv.)

C —

A

B

2 (rev.)

ΕΥΦΑΜΟΣΞΚΑΙΤΟΙΣΥΝ
ΔΑΜΙΟΡΓΟΙ:ΑΝΕΘΕΚΑΝ
ΤΟΙΗΕΡΟΙ

5

ϜΑΞΙΟΝΜΑΝΕΘΕ░░ΔΙΑΚΡΙΟΣΜΕΓΟΙϜΕΞΑ

8

1. Gravestone, c. 525?  2. Bronze plaque, c. 525–500?  5. Bronze handle, c. 450?  8. Stone capital for a dedication, c. 550–540?

4 (obv.)

4 (rev.)

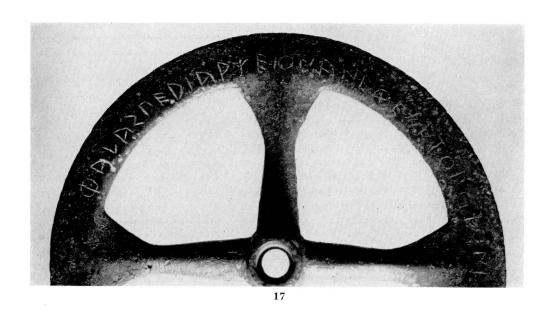

10

17

4. Bronze plaque, c. 475–450?  **10.** Graffito on skyphos, c. 500–475?  **17.** Miniature bronze wheel, c. 550–525?

PLATE 16 AIGINA

1

2

3

4 (detail)

4

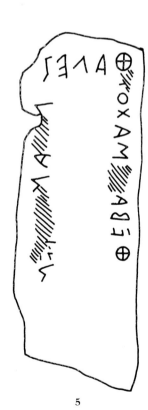

ΠΟΙΕ:ΑΙΓΙΝΑΙ

11

ΟΞ:ΑΝΕΘΕΚΕ

ΓΛΑΥΚΙΑΣ:ΑΙΓΙΝΑΤΑΣ:ΕΠΟΙΕΣΕ

12

ΤΟΠΟΛΛΟΝΙ ΑΝΕΘΕ
ΕΟΠΡΟΠΟΣ:ΕΠΟΙΕ:ΑΙΓΙΝΑΤΑΣ

5                                          13

1. Painted inscription on sherd, c. 710–700? 2. Name painted on vase, c. 650. 3. Boundary stone, 7th c.? 4. Building record on wall (?)-block, c. 550? 5. Stone pillar, c. 550–525? 11. Stone base, c. 500–480? 12. Stone base, c. 485? 13. Stone base, c. 480.

16

18

19

21

**16.** Bronze hydria, *c.* 470. **18.** Gravestone, *c.* 475–450? **19.** Gravestone, *c.* 450? **21.** Bronze plaque, *c.* 450?

PLATE 18 CORINTH

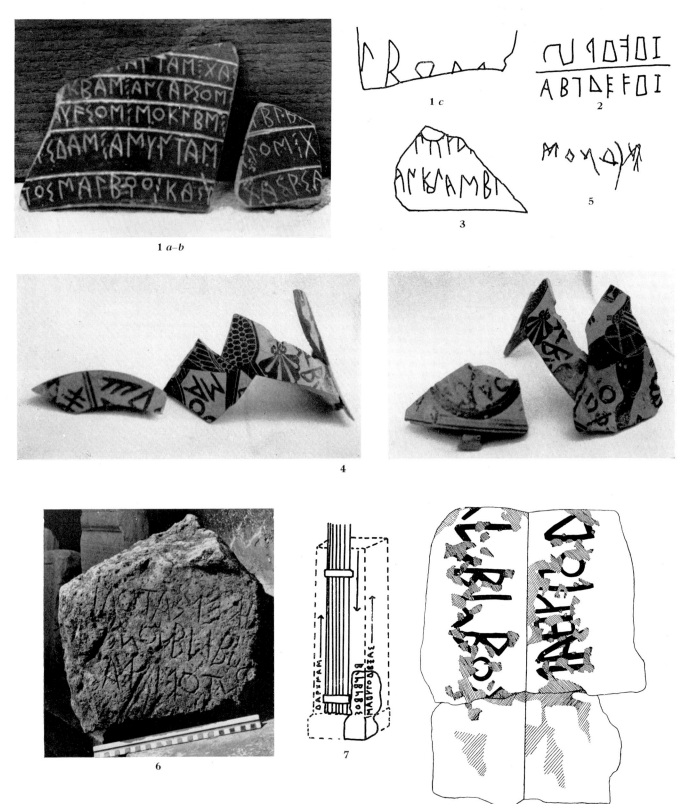

1 *a–c.* Graffiti on sherds, *c.* 700? **2.** Graffito on conical oinochoe, *c.* 700–675? **3.** Graffito on sherd, *c.* 700–675? **4.** Painted names on pyxis, *c.* 675–650 (*part only*). **5.** Graffito on sherd, *c.* 675? **6.** Stone grave-stele, *c.* 650? **7.** Inscribed spit-holder, *c.* 650?

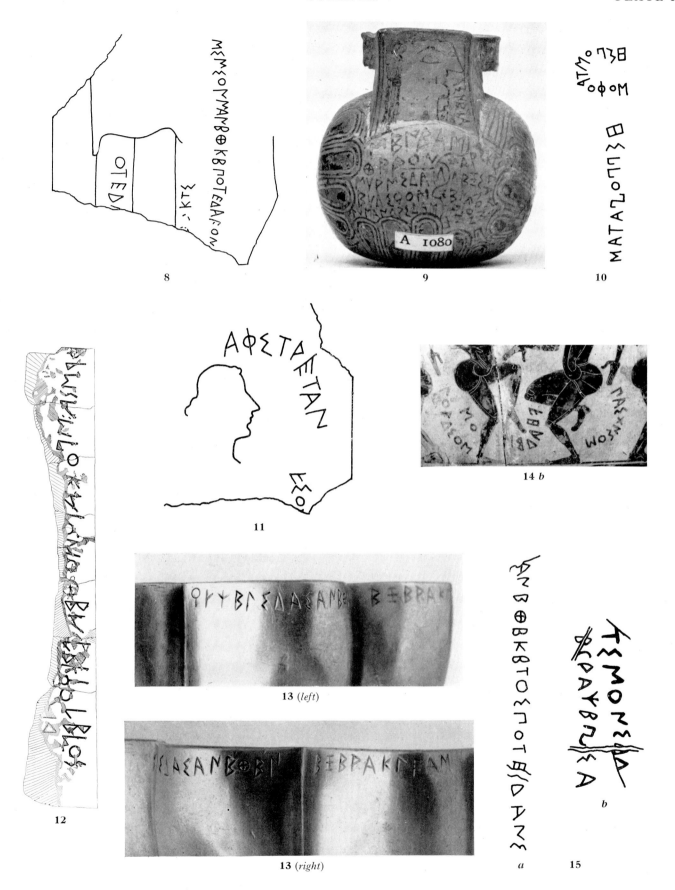

8. Painted clay plaque, 650–625. 9. Names painted on vase, *c.* 625. 10. Names painted on vase, *c.* 625–600 (*not in position*). 11. Painted clay plaque, *c.* 625–600. 12. Stone spit-holder, *c.* 625–575? 13. Gold phiale, *c.* 625–550? 14 *b*. Names painted on vase, *c.* 600–575. 15. Painted plaque, *c.* 600–575 (*a* graffito; *b* painted; *not in position*).

PLATE 20    CORINTH

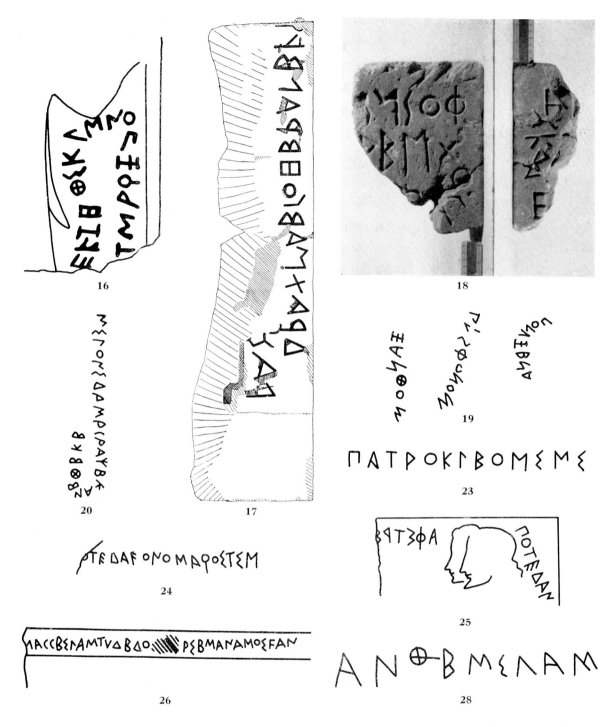

16. Painted clay plaque, *c.* 600–550.  17. Stone spit-holder, *c.* 600–550?  18. Stone pillar bearing a sacral law, *c.* 575–550?  19. Painted vase, *c.* 575–550 (*not in position*).  20. Painted clay plaque, *c.* 575–550.  23. Stone trapeza for a grave, 6th c.  24. Painted clay plaque, *c.* 550–525 (*not in position*).  25. Painted clay plaque, *c.* 525?  26. Graffito on clay plaque, *c.* 510–500.  28. Graffito on vase, *c.* 510–500.

29

35

37

38

ΚΑΦΙϟΟΔΟΡΟϟ
ΑΙϟΧΥΛΙΟΙ

40

{ ΚΟΡϜΑΝ }

39

**29.** Marble gravestone, *c.* 480 (*part only*). **35.** Bronze bowl, *c.* 500–475? **37.** Boundary stone, *c.* 475–450? **38.** Stone stele, *c.* 458. **39.** Stone theatre-seat, *c.* 400? **40.** Bronze statuette, *c.* 450–425?

PLATE 22 MEGARA

3

2

ΑΘΑΝΑΙΑΣ : ΙΑΡΑ : ΤΑΣ ΜΗΒΣΑΡΟΙ

2

ΑΘΑΝΑΔΑΣ : ΘΒΟΝΙ+Ο

5

4

ΔΠΟΛΟΝΟΣ
ΛΥΚΒΙΟ

7

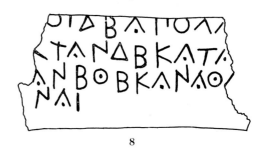

8

6

1. Graffito on sherd, *c.* 550–540? 2. Silver phiale, *c.* 500? 3. Stone grave-stele, *c.* 500? 4. Stone stele, *c.* 500–475? 5. Gravestone, *c.* 500–475? 6. Bronze statuette, *c.* 490–480. 7. Boundary stone, *c.* 475–450? 8. Bronze plaque, *c.* 450–440?

2. Graffito on stone block, 7th c.? **3.** Bronze strip, *c.* 600–550? **4.** Vase, *c.* 575–550? **8.** Bronze plaque, *c.* 500? (*part only*). **11.** Marble slab, *c.* 500–475? **12.** Bronze spear-butt, *c.* 500–475? **13** *a*–*b*. Front and back of stone stele, *c.* 500–475? **16.** Stone stele, *c.* 450? **21.** Bronze spear-butt, *c.* 500–475?

PLATE 24       PHLEIOUS, KLEONAI (WITH NEMEA)

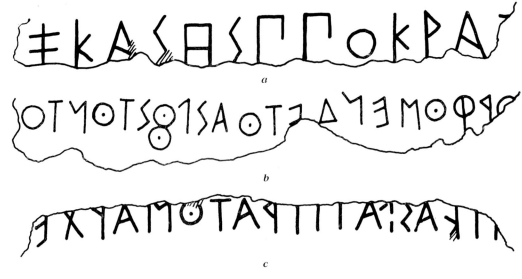

*a*

*b*

*c*

*d*

*e*

*f*

*g*

**1**

**5**

**5**

Phleious: **1.** Stone altar (?)-blocks, *c.* 600–550?  Kleonai: **5.** Stone stele, *c.* 560?

*a*          *b*          *c*

6

7

11

*a*          *b*

8

Kleonai: **6.** Stone stele with sacral law, *c.* 575–550?  **7.** Stone stele, 6th–5th c.?  Tiryns: **8.** Stone stele with sacral law,
*c.* 600–550?  **11.** Graffito on clay cup, *c.* 700–675?

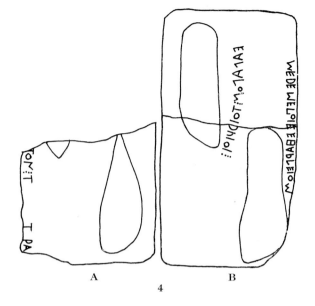

**2.** Bronze label, 7th c.?   **3.** Bronze aryballos, late 7th c.?   **4.** Marble plinths of statues (*uncertain letters omitted*).
**5.** Plinth of bronze statuette, *c.* 590–570.   **6.** Plinth of bronze statuette, *c.* 590–570?   **7.** Stone stele, *c.* 575–550?

**9**

**17**

**16 a**

**14**

**16 b**

**18**

9. Bronze plaque, *c.* 575–550? **14.** Silver pin, 7th– early 6th c.; inscription *c.* 550–525? **16 a.** Stone capital;
*b.* Column (*not in position*), *c.* 525–500? **17.** Stone stele, *c.* 500–480? **18.** Bronze helmet, *c.* 500–480?

PLATE 28 ARGOS

19

[19]

[19]

23

21

Stone base; [19] left-hand, 19 right-hand side, *c.* 480–475? 21. Stone base, *c.* 480–475? 23. Stone base, *c.* 480–460?

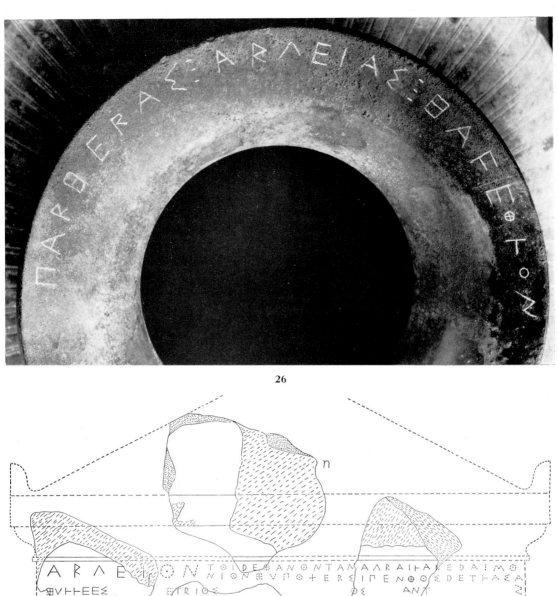

**26.** Bronze hydria, *c.* 470–460.  **30.** Marble gravestone, *c.* 458–457 (*part only*).

PLATE 30                    ARGOS

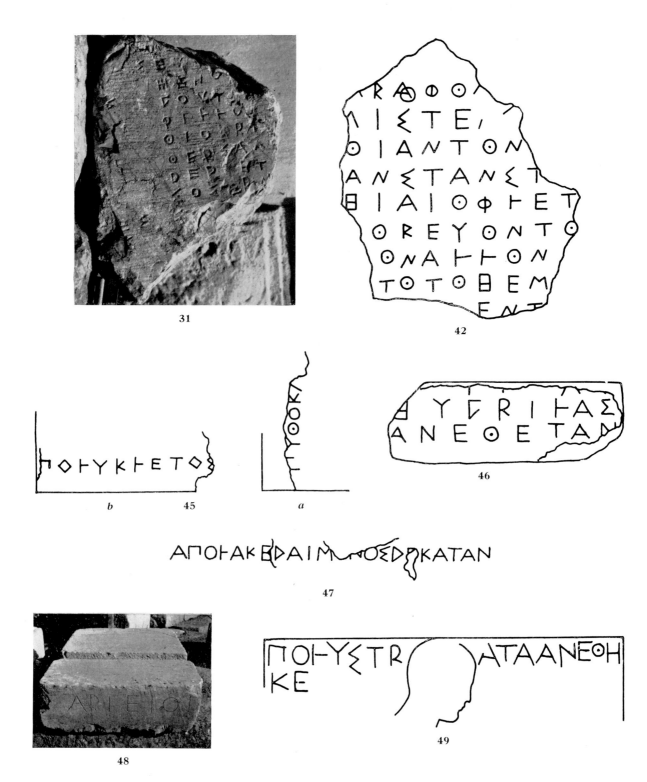

31. Stone stele, *c.* 460–450? **42.** Stone stele, *c.* 450–425? **45.** Stone base, *c.* 450–425? **46.** Stone base, *c.* 450–425? **47.** Stone base, *c.* 414. **48.** Stone base-block, *c.* 415–400? **49.** Marble stele, *c.* 415–400?

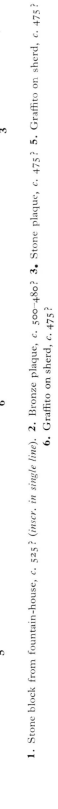

1. Stone block from fountain-house, *c.* 525? (*inscr. in single line*). 2. Bronze plaque, *c.* 500–480? 3. Stone plaque, *c.* 475? 5. Graffito on sherd, *c.* 475?
6. Graffito on sherd, *c.* 475?

PLATE 32　　　　　　　METHANA, TROIZEN

1

3 (top)

2

2

2

3

Methana: **1.** Gravestone, *c.* 600?　Troizen: **2.** Stone pillar for a grave, *c.* 550–525?　**3.** Stone pillar for a grave, *c.* 500?

ΜΕΘΑΝΙΟΙΑΠΟΛΑΚΕΔΑΙΜΟΝΙΟΝ

4

ΕΥΘΥΜΙΔΑΣ
ΑΝΕΘΕΚΕ
ΗΑΚΑΓΛΙΩΝ
ΠΛΙΤΩΝΘΕΟΝ
ΙΛΙΕΙΛΩΥΣΑΜΕ
ΩΣΕΡΑΘΝΑΙΟΡ
ΛΝΘΥΣΑΜΕΝ
ΘΕΡΑΚΛΕΙΑΝΙΩ
ΙΛΛΝΤΑΓΙΝΕ
ΛΙΛΩΝ

6

ΦΕΡΣΕΘΟΝΑ
ΗΕΡΜΙΟΝΕΣΑΝΕΘ

7

ΑΛΕΧΙΑΣ:ΛΥΟΝΟΣ:ΑΝ     Ε
ΤΑΙΔΑΜΑΤΡΙ:ΤΑΙΧΘΟΝΙΑ
ΗΕΡΜΙΟΝΕΥΣ

ΚΡΕΣΙΛΑΣ:ΕΠΟΙΕΣΕ:ΚΥΔΟΝΙΑΤ

8

ΑΡΙΣΙ   ΜΕΛ     Ε   ΕΑΛΕΤΙΑ
ΤΑΙΔΑΜΑΤΡΙ   ΧΘΟΝΙΑΙ
ΗΕΡΜΙΟΝΕΥΣ

ΔΟΡΟΘΕΟΣΕFΕΡΛΑΣΑΤΟΑΡΛΕΙΟΣ

9

Methana: **4.** Bronze spear-butt, *c.* 500–475? Troizen: **6.** Stone stele, *c.* 450–425? Hermion: **7.** Stone statue-base, *c.* 480–475?
**8.** Stone statue-base, *c.* 460–450? **9.** Stone statue-base, *c.* 460–450?

PLATE 34 EPIDAUROS

10. Bronze phiale (?), c. 500–475? 12. Bronze base for statuette, c. 500–475? 14. Bronze handle (?), c. 475–450?
16. Bronze plaque, c. 450? 17. Stone stele, c.  0–425?

1. Graffito on ivory plaque, *c.* 650–625? **2 *a*.** Painted inscription on clay plate, late 7th to early 6th c. **3 *a–b*.** Graffiti on bone flutes, late 7th to early 6th c.? **5.** Bronze handle, late 7th to early 6th c.? **6.** Stone plaques, *c.* 600–550. **7.** Bronze hydria-rim, *c.* 600–575? (*not in position*). **8.** Painted inscriptions on vase, *c.* 570–560 (*part only, not in position*). **9.** Helmet-fragment, *c.* 600–550? **11.** Bronze lebes-rim, *c.* 600–550? **16 *a*.** Painted names on vase, *c.* 560–550.

PLATE 36 LAKONIA

15

19

22

24

25

27

15. Marble seat, *c.* 600–550? **19.** Bronze strip, *c.* 550–525? **22.** Marble stele, *c.* 530–500? **24.** Marble relief-stele, *c.* 525? (*not in position*). **25.** Stone relief-stele, *c.* 525? **27.** Stone relief-stele, *c.* 525–500?

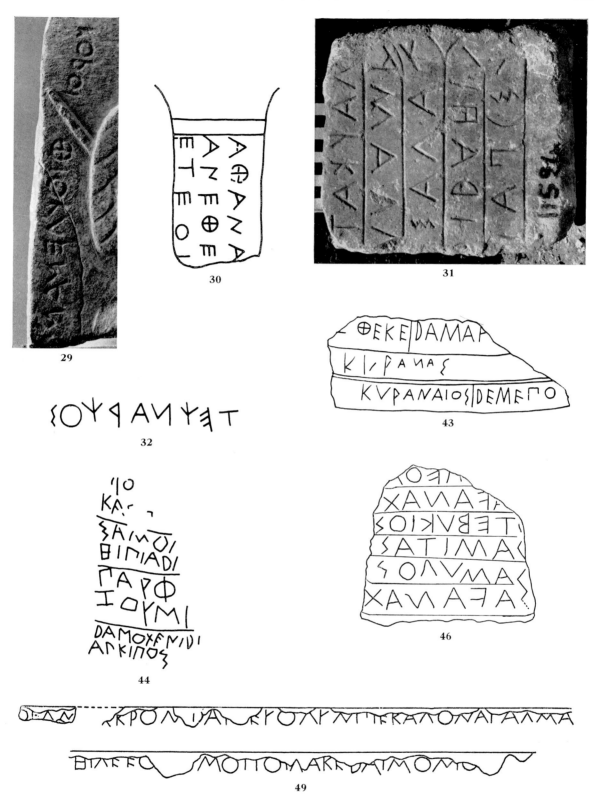

29

30

31

32

43

44

46

49

29. Marble relief-stele, c. 510–500. 30. Marble stele, c. 510–500? 31. Stone stele, c. 510–500? 32. Graffito on stone block, c. 510–500. 43. Fragment (lost) of perirrhanterion-base (?), c. 500–480? 44. Stone fragment, c. 500? 46. Stone stele, c. 500? 49. Stone dedication-base, c. 490? (single line).

PLATE 38 LAKONIA

52

54

52

60

62

53

**52.** Stone dedicatory stele, *c.* 450–431? (*parts only*). **53.** Stone manumission stele, *c.* 450–430? **54.** Similar stele, *c.* 440–430? **60.** Stone base for a grave-stele, *c.* 418. **62.** Marble stele, *c.* 403–399 (*lower half only*).

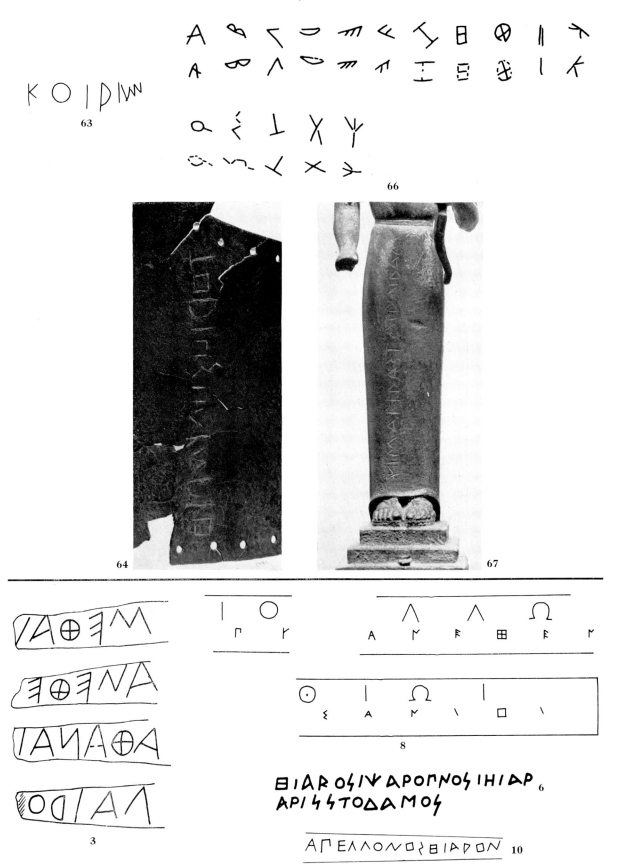

Lakonia: **63.** Graffito on stone jumping-weight, 6th c. **64.** Bronze helmet, 6th c. **66.** Graffiti on bronze krater, c. 530–525? **67.** Bronze statuette, c. 550–525? Messenia: **3.** Bronze spear-butt, c. 500–475? **6.** Gravestone (18th-c. copy), c. 500–475? **8.** Stone base, re-inscribed from a 5th-c. original (single line). **10.** Bronze spear-butt, c. 450?

PLATE 40      ARKADIA

1. Bronze apple, *c.* 550–525? 2. Bronze plaque, *c.* 525? 3. Bronze lebes-rim, *c.* 525? 5. Stone stele, *c.* 525–500? 6. Stone statue, *c.* 525? 11. Bronze spear-butt, *c.* 500–480? 38. Bronze plaque, early 5th c.?

12

20                                                    20 (detail)

27

32

ΕΡΙΧΙΔΑΣ          ΕΙΣΕΟΔΑ͜Σ
ΕΡΑΤΙΑΝ          ΠΑΝΘΙΟΣ

37

39

12. Bronze phiale, *c.* 500–480? 20. Stone base, *c.* 480–475? 27. Bronze plaque, *c.* 450? 32. Stone base, *c.* 422? 37. Painted clay counters, *c.* 450–400. 39. Bronze statuette, *c.* 480–470?

PLATE 42　　　　　　　　ELIS

1. Bronze helmet-aryballos, c. 550–525 (detail). 2. Bronze plaque, c. 525? 4. Bronze plaque, c. 500? 5. Bronze plaque, c. 500? 6. Bronze plaque, c. 500? 8. Bronze plaque, c. 500–475?

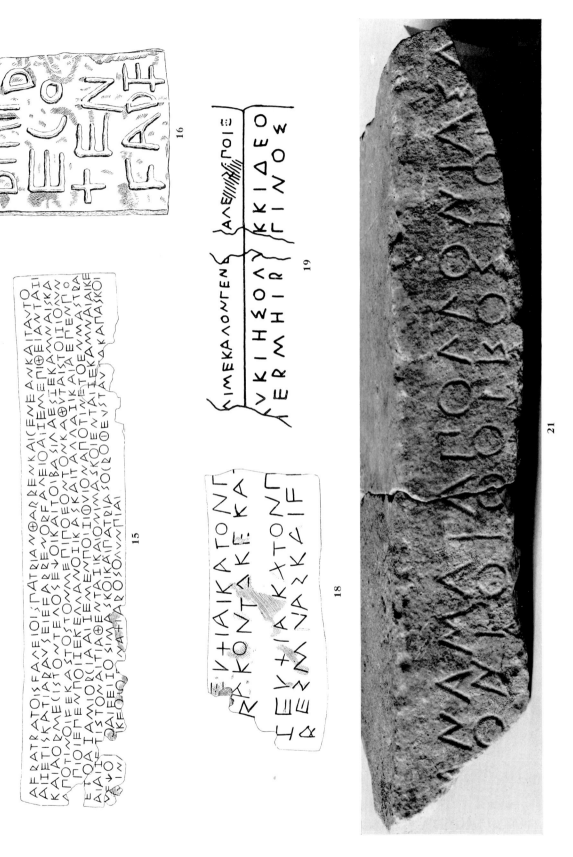

**15.** Bronze plaque, *c.* 475–450?    **16.** Gravestone, *c.* 475–450?    **18.** Bronze plaque, *c.* 475–450?    **19.** Stone base, *c.* 450–425?    **21.** Marble base, *c.* 475–450?

PLATE 44                    ACHAIA AND NORTH-WESTERN GREECE

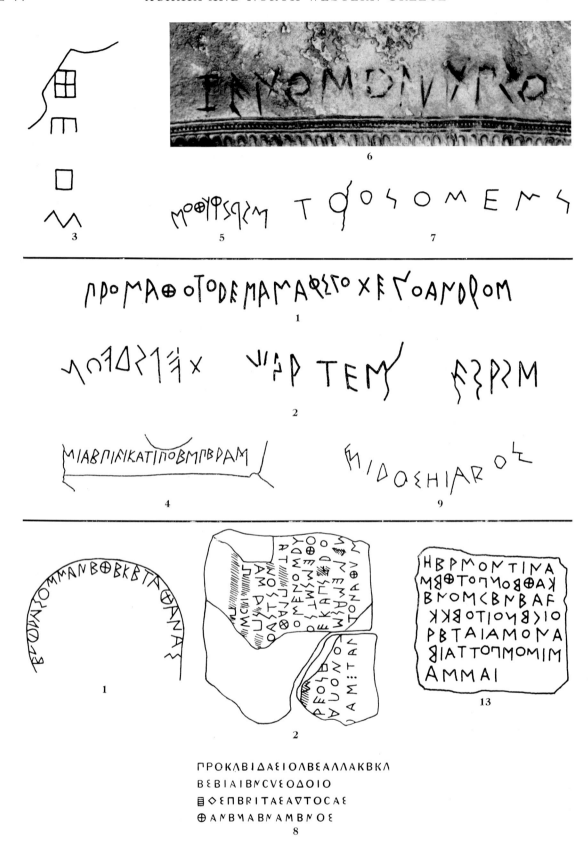

Achaia: **3.** Stone pillar, *c.* 450? **5.** Graffito on clay bobbin, 7th c.? **6.** Bronze helmet, *c.* 525–500. **7.** Bronze helmet, *c.* 510–475? Aitolia: **1.** Grave-stele, 7th c.? **2.** Painted inscriptions on clay metopes, *c.* 625? (*not in position*). **4.** Incised directions on clay sima, *c.* 600–575? **9.** Graffito on krater-rim, *c.* 450? Akarnania: **1.** Miniature bronze helmet-crest, 6th c. **2.** Gravestone (?), 6th c. **8.** Gravestone (*lost*), *c.* 475–450? Epeiros: **13.** Leaden plaque, *c.* 525–500?

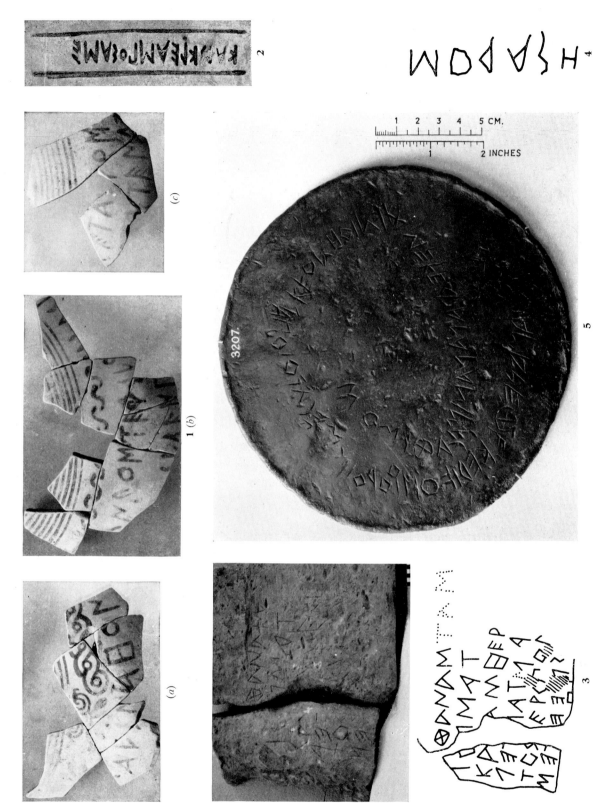

Ithake:  **1.** Painted inscription on vase (*part only*), *c.* 700?  **2.** Painted inscription on vase, *c.* 675–650?  **3.** Stone stele, *c.* 550?  **4.** Graffito on flute, *c.* 500?
Kephallenia:  **5.** Bronze disk, *c.* 550–525?

PLATE 46                    KORKYRA

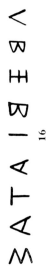

11

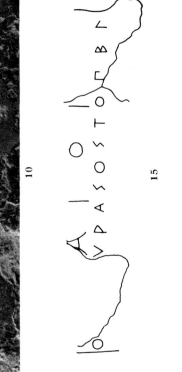

10

ΥΡΑSΟSΤΟΓΒΓ

15

ΣΑΤΑΒΙΑΣ

16

13

14

8

8. Grave-stele, c. 650–600? (lost).   10. Bronze label, early 6th c.?   11. Grave-stele, early 6th c.?   13. Grave-column (Doric capital), c. 575–550?   14. Graffito on sherd, c. 500–475?   15. Stone base, c. 525–500?   16. Grave-column (?), c. 475?   16. Grave-column (?), c. 475? (not in position).

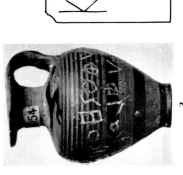

Pithekoussai: **1.** Graffito on clay skyphos, *c.* 700? Kyme: **3.** Graffito on clay aryballos, *c.* 675–650? (*single line*). **4.** Gravestone, *c.* 525–500? **7.** Gravestone, early 6th c.? **8.** Bronze bowl, *c.* 500? (*single line*).

PLATE 48                                    KYME, ETRURIA

9

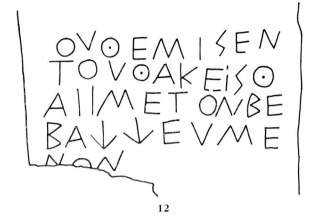

12

XENOOANTOEMI

11

18

A B C D F F I ⊞ Θ ⊙ I K L M M ⊞ O P M P E T Y X Φ Y

A B C D E F I ⊞ Θ I K L M N ⊞ Θ O M q P 3 T Y ✝ Φ Y

20

A B C D F F I ⊞ Θ I K L M M ⊞ O P M P E T Y ✝ Φ Y

19

A B C D F F I ⊞ Θ I K

21

A B C D E F I B Θ I K L M M Γ ⊞ O P M P P S T L S Φ V

22

A B C D E C I ⊞ Θ I K L M M N ⊞ O -----

23

22

Kyme: **9.** Tombstone, 6th–5th c.? **11.** Graffito on kylix, *c.* 500–450? **12.** Tombstone, *c.* 450? Etruria: **18.** Ivory school-tablet, *c.* 700–650? **19.** Bucchero bottle, incised, *c.* 650–600? **20.** Bucchero amphora, incised, *c.* 650–600? **21.** Bucchero goblet, incised, *c.* 650–600? **22.** Bucchero bottle, incised, *c.* 550–500? **23.** Painted inscription (*lost*), *c.* 500–450?

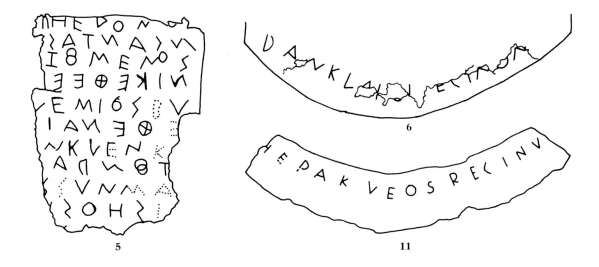

5

6

11

8

KVEOΘANTOS
SVAVKIV
12

KVEOMENES
EMMENIDEY
13

ΘEMΘANHN
ΘRARVOS
14

19

Zankle: **5.** Bronze plaque, *c.* 500–494? **6.** Bronze greave, *c.* 500–490? Rhegion: **8.** Stone base-block, *c.* 467–450? **11.** Bronze vase-rim, *c.* 475–450? **12–14.** Clay pellets, *c.* 475–450? Himera (?): **19.** Bronze plaque, *c.* 450?

PLATE 50     THE ACHAIAN COLONIES

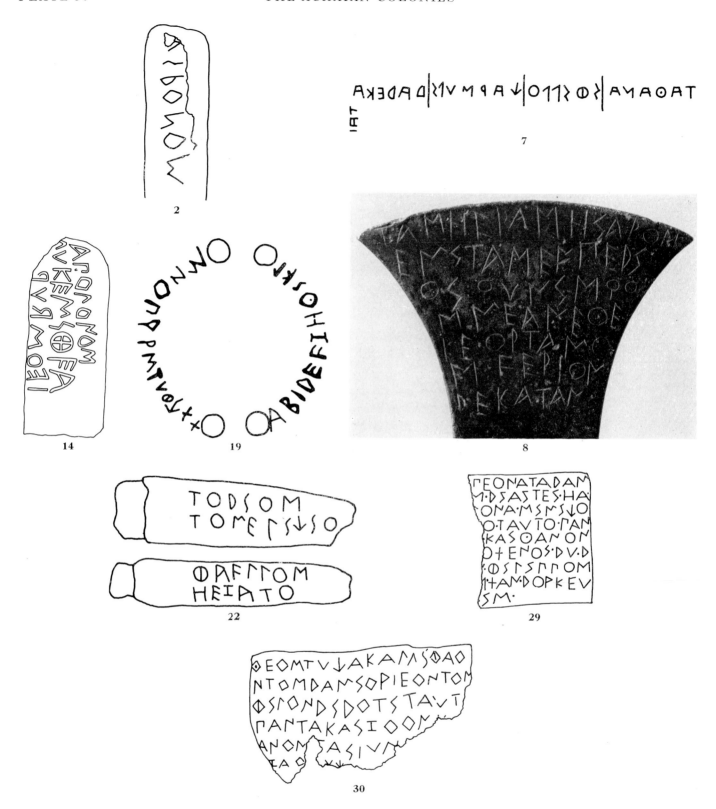

Poseidonia: **2.** Stone stele, *c.* 550–500? **7.** Bronze handle (?), *c.* 470. S. Agata dell'Esaro: **8.** Bronze axe, *c.* 525–500? Metapontion: **14.** Stone stele, *c.* 550–525? **19.** Painted inscription on clay stamnos, *c.* 475–450? Kroton: **22.** Stone cippus (*not in position*), *c.* 500–480? Petelia: **29.** Bronze plaque, *c.* 475? Krimissa: **30.** Bronze plaque, *c.* 475? Non-Greek: **31.** Graffito on BF vase (*lost*), late 6th to early 5th c.

ΚΛΕΟ΄  ΕΞΕΠΟΙΕΣΕ

ΤΟΠΕΓΟΝΙ:ΒΟΚΝΙΔΙΕΙΔΑ:

ΚΕΠΙΚΛΕΣΤΥΛΕΙΑ:ΚΑΛΛΑΡΕΡΛΑ

3

ΣΕΛΟΝΟΔΕΙΝΟΜΕΝ
ΑΝΕΘΕΚΕΤΟΠΟΛΛΟΝΙ
ΣΥΡΑϘΟΣΙΟΣ

ΤΟΝΤΡΙΓΟΔΑ:ΚΑΙΤΕΝ:ΝΙΚΕΝ:ΕΡΓΑΣΑΤΟ
ΒΙΟΝ:ΔΙΟΔΟΡΟ:ΥΙΟΣ:ΜΙΛΕΣΙΟΣ

6

7

9

ΑΝ ΑΞΑΓΟΡΑ

ΣΥΡΑΚΟΣΙΑ

10

12

13

14

15

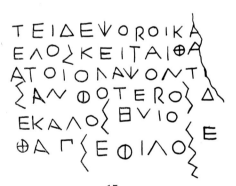

17

Syracuse: **1.** Graffito (*on painted lines*), clay sherd, 7th c.? **3.** Inscription on temple steps (*single line*), 2nd half of 6th c.?
**6.** Stone base, c. 480–479. **7.** Bronze helmet, c. 474. **9.** Stone base, inscriptions, c. 478 and c. 460? **10.** Gravestone, c. 450?
Akrai: **12–14.** Gravestones, c. 525–500? Kasmenai (?): **15.** Bronze plaque, c. 490–480? Kamarina: **17.** Gravestone, c. 485–450?

PLATE 52          THE DORIC COLONIES, SICILY

Kamarina: **18.** Leaden plaque, *c.* 450? Hybla Heraia: **21–22.** Gravestones, late 6th c.? Megara Hyblaia: **25.** Marble kouros, *c.* 550–540? **26.** Stone column-capital, *c.* 500? Selinous: **31.** Stone cippus, *c.* 525? **33.** Stone grave-stele, *c.* 525–500? **44.** Stone statue-base, *c.* 450–425? Motya: **45.** Gravestone, *c.* 475–450?

48

50

49

51

58

1

4

ΟRRΥ7ƷΟΜΙƷΑ△

9

ΡΑΜΙΑΕ△ΟΚΕ

11

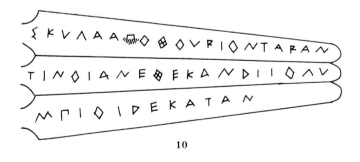

10

Λ.Β.Γ△.FFI.H.I.ΚΛ.Μ
ΝΟΧ.Ϙ.ΡΗS.ΤΡΨΨ.

15

Gela: **48.** Bronze statuette-plinth (?), *c.* 525? **49.** Gravestone, *c.* 525? **50.** Graffito on vase, late 6th c.? **51.** Bronze weight, *c.* 500–490? Akragas: **58.** Gravestone, *c.* 500–490? Taras: **1.** Graffito on BF vase, *c.* 540–530. **4.** Bronze statuette-plinth, *c.* 500–490? **9.** Helmet, *c.* 450? **10.** Bronze spear-butt, *c.* 443–433. Non-Greek: **11.** Silver fibula, *c.* 450? **15.** Abecedarium (*lost*), 5th c.?

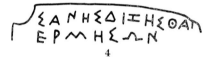

Lokroi Epizephyrioi: **1.** Bronze plaque, *c.* 525–500? **2.** Bronze shield-emblem (*inscription en pointellé*), *c.* 525–500? **3.** Bronze plaque, *c.* 500–480? **4.** Helmet, *c.* 500–480? **5.** Stone stele, *c.* 475–450? Siris: **1.** Painted inscription on clay loom-weight, *c.* 575–550? Massalia: **2.** Gravestone, *c.* 500–475? *Antipolis:* **3.** Stone dedication, *c.* 450–425? Emporion: **4.** Graffito on sherd, 5th c.? Thourioi: **8.** Bronze kerykeion, *c.* 443–433?

2. Marble statue, *c.* 650?   3. Marble statue-base, *c.* 620–600?   4. Ring-aryballos, 7th c.   10. Marble statue-base, *c.* 600–575.   11. Bronze statuette, *c.* 525–500.   12. Marble grave-stele, *c.* 490–475.   14. Graffito on rock, *c.* 450–425?

PLATE 56          THE AEGEAN ISLANDS (IONIC)

15

17

20

22

23

26

30

28

ΔΗΜ Ω ΚΥΔΗΣ ΤΩ ΔΑΛΑΓΜΑΤΕ
ΓΕ ΣΤΩ ΔΙΚΗ ΤΑ ΓΩ ΚΩ Ι ΝΟΝ
ΕΥ ΧΣΑΜΕ Ν Γ ΙΣ ΤΗ ΣΑ ΝΓΑΙ
ΘΕ Ν ΟΙ ΑΡΤΕ ΜΙ ΔΙ
ΣΕ Μ Ν ΟΙ Ε Ν Ι ΣΑ Γ Ε Δ ΟΙ Κ Ω
Ρ Η Ι ΔΙ Ω Σ ΑΙ Λ Ι Ω Χ ΟΙ Ω
Τ ΟΝ Λ Ε ΝΕ Η Ν C Ι Ω Τ Ω Ν ΤΑ
Υ Χ Σ Ε Ν Α Γ Η Μ Ω Σ Υ Ν Η Ι

34

35

ΧΣ Ε Ν ΟΙ ΔΟΡΙ Η Ι Δ Ν Υ ΘΕ Μ Ι
Δ Ν  Ε Δ    ΟΙ ΑΚ Δ Ρ Η Ι Α ΣΤΟΙ Ε

39

Amorgos: **15.** Inscription on rock, *c.* 700–650? **17.** Grave-stele, *c.* 550? **20.** Grave-stele, *c.* 525–500? **22.** Stone altar, *c.* 500–450?
**23.** Abecedarium cut on rock, *c.* 450? Paros: **26.** Inscribed marble column, *c.* 600–550? **28.** Marble building-block, *c.* 550?
**30.** Marble capital for statue, *c.* 550–530? **34.** Marble statue-base, *c.* 500? **35.** Marble altar, *c.* 500–480? **39.** Marble block, *c.* 450?

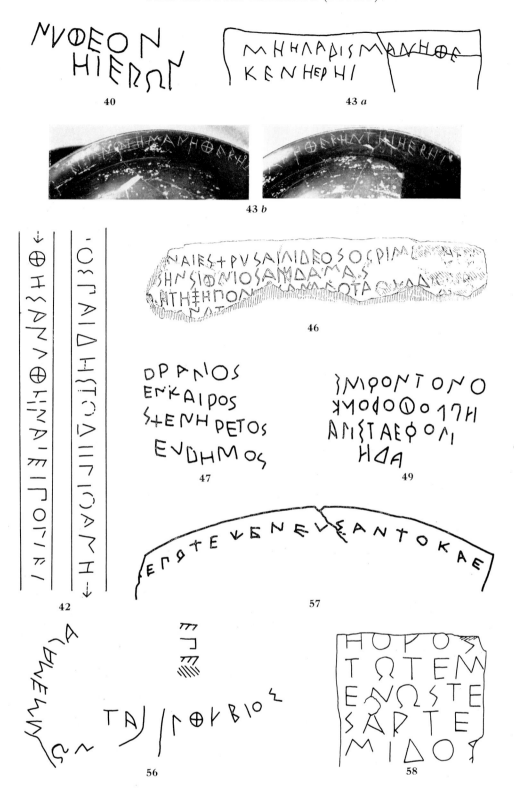

61

65

ΙΗΝΩΣΚΑΙΣΕΜΕΣΗΣΚΑΙΑΓΚΜΗΝΗΣΤΑΛΥΠΕΠΓΩ:
ΕΣΤΑΣΙΝΓΑΙΛΑΕΣΤΗΣΔΓΓΙΩΣΕΟΣΦΥΣΑϘΩΙ

63

ΝΥΜΦΗΙΣΙΝΚΑΓΛΓΓΟΝΙΝΥΜΦΗΛΕΤΗΙΟΗΓΥΚΑΙΑΡΣ
ΕΝΑΜΣΛΓΗΙΓΡΛΣΕΡΔΕΝΛΙΝΛΝΘΕΜΙΣΛΥΔΕΧΛΙΡΛΝ
ΛΥΓΑΙΟΝΙΣΕΤΑΙ

ΧΑΡΙΣΙΝΑΙΛΑΛΝΘΕΜΙΣΛΥΔΕΧΛΙ

70

ΗΚΑΓΩΝΤΩΜΝΗΜΑ
ΤΗΡΙΣΤΗΣΕΘΑΝΩΣ
ΓΕΑΡΕΤΗΙΩΥΛΑΡ
ΙΙΟΣΑΝΕΣΩΦΕΩΜ

68

ΛΟΚΡΙΛΝΛΥΣΙΣΤΡΑΤΟΣ
ΤΟΞΟΤΑΣΕΥΚΛΕΟΣ
ΚΟΡΙΝΘΙΟΣΚΟΡΙΝΘΙΟΣ

75

76

61. Marble block, *c.* 625–600? 63. Inscription under marble reliefs (*single line*), *c.* 525–500. 65. Marble grave-stele, *c.* 525–500?
68. Marble grave-stele, *c.* 500–490? 70. Inscriptions on marble reliefs (*not in position*), *c.* 475–465? 75. Marble gravestone, *c.* 411?
76. Marble block, *c.* 411–410.

1 a

1 a (detail)

2

3

5

7

A        12

B

Laws on stone. Dreros: **1 *a*.** Wall-block, middle or 2nd half of 7th c.? Gortyn: **2.** Wall-block, *c.* 600–525? **3.** Wall-block, *c.* 525–500?
**5.** Wall-block, *c.* 500–450? **7.** Law-code (*part only*), mid-5th c.? Prinias: **12.** Stone pillar with laws, early 6th c.?

PLATE 60 CRETE

**18**

**15**

**19 a**

**22**

**20**

**27**

**29 a**

ΕΠΑΜΥΡΤΑΙΟΕΠΙΚΟΡΟΑ⸢
ΚΡΕΤΕ⸢ ΤΥΥΑΠΑ⸢Α⸢
ΟΝΑ⸢ΑΝΑΡ   ΚΥΔΙ
ΙΑΤΑ⸢

**30 a**

ΘΑΡΥ⸢ΘΕΝΕ⸢
ΘΙΟΚΡΙΤΟ⸢
⸤ΦΙΛΟ ΘΑΓ

**30 b**

Lyttos: **15.** Law-fragment on wall-block, *c.* 550–525? Praisos: **18.** Graffito on clay figure, 7th c. **19 a.** Eteocretan law (?) on wall-block, *c.* 550–525? Chersonesos: **20.** Base for a grave-statue, *c.* 525? Axos: **22.** Law on wall-block (*cast*), *c.* 525–500? Eleutherna: **27.** Law on wall-block, *c.* 525–500? Kydonia: **29 a.** Gravestone, early 5th c. **30 a–b.** Graffiti at Abydos in Egypt, 5th c.

1 *a*-*b*. Graffiti on rocks, end of 8th c. onwards? **2.** Graffito on amphora, *c.* 700–650? **3.** Stone grave-stelai, 7th c.?
**5.** Flat gravestone (*top only*), *c.* 600? **6.** Flat (?) gravestone, early 6th c. **9.** Graffito on cup, *c.* 600–550? **12.** Grave-
stele (i) and flat gravestones (ii–iii), *c.* 550–500?

PLATE 62      AEGEAN ISLANDS (DORIC), AND KYRENE

Thera: **15.** Gravestone, *c.* 480–450? **16.** Inscription on rock, *c.* 480–450? Kyrene: **18.** Stone block, 6th c.? **19.** Graffito on plate, early 6th c. **20.** Marble stele, early 5th c. Melos: **23.** Marble column, late 6th c. **25.** Grave-stelai, *c.* 480–416? Anaphe: **26.** Gravestone, early 7th c.? Sikinos: **27.** Gravestone, 7th c.? Thera or Melos (?): **29.** Marble column, *c.* 525–500?

1. Graffito on vase, *c.* 650–600? **2.** Gravestone (*lost*), *c.* 600–575? **4–5.** Marble statues (**4** *not in position*), *c.* 575–550. **8.** Marble grave-stele, *c.* 550–540? **13.** Marble statue, *c.* 525–520? **16.** Marble statue-base, *c.* 490–480. **17.** Stone statue-base, *c.* 479? **18.** Marble grave-stele, *c.* 475? **19.** Stone statue-base, *c.* 470. **21.** Marble base, *c.* 459–454.

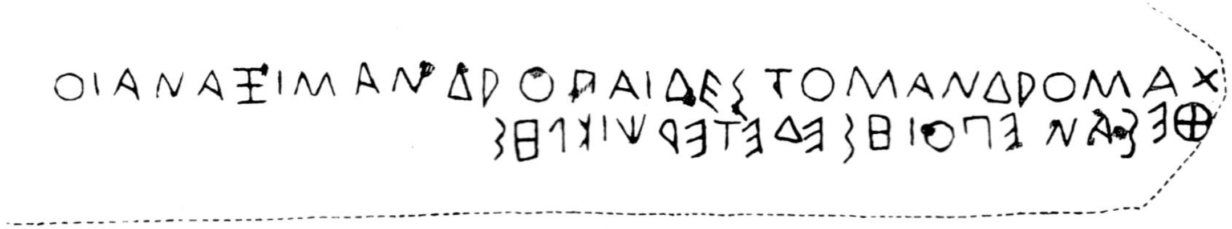

PLATE 64                    IONIC DODEKAPOLIS: MILETOS

26

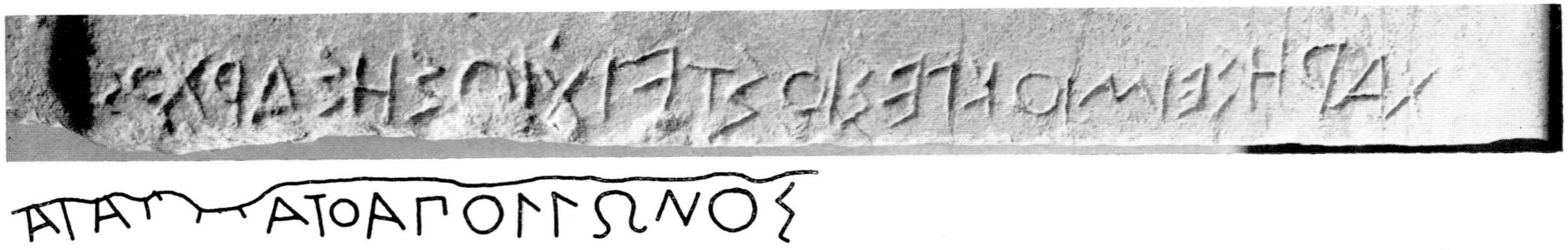

23

27

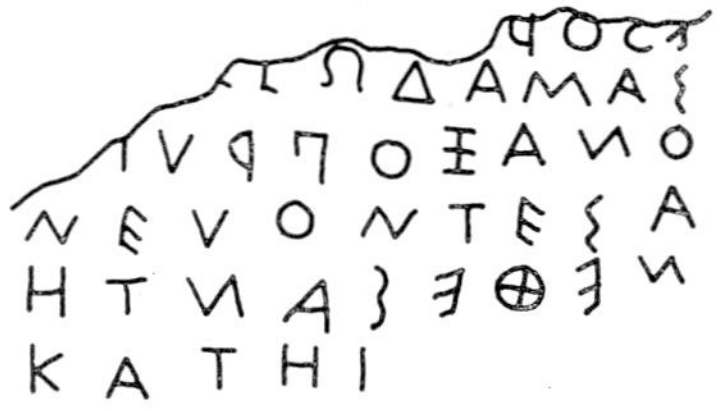

34

39

29

33

23. Stone base, c. 600–575?   26. Marble statue, c. 575–550?   27. Marble statue, c. 560–550?   29. Marble statue, c. 550–540 (*not in position*).   33. Marble wall-block (*part only*), c. 525–500?   34. Marble base (?), c. 500–494.   39. Marble stele (*part only*), c. 500–480?

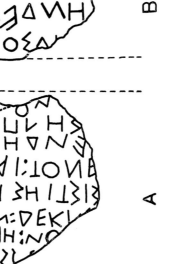

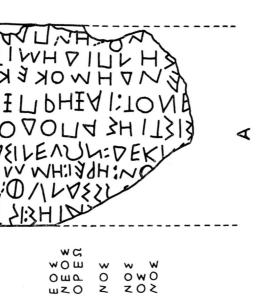

D

C

B

A

50

41

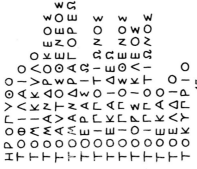

42 e

46

40

47

Thebae ad Mycalen: **40.** Gravestone, *c.* 550–540? Chios: **41.** Stone stele, *c.* 575–550? **42 e.** Painted inscription on vase, *c.* 600? **46.** Marble altar, *c.* 479? **47.** Marble gravestone, *c.* 475? Erythrai: **50.** Marble pedestal-base, *c.* 510–500?

PLATE 66                    IONIC DODEKAPOLIS

ΤΕ ΠΑΡΑΦΟΝΤ ΑΜΝ Ε ΑΙΤΟ ΠΡΣ    ΕΣΤΑΘ  ΑΜ ΕΚΤΤΩΝΔΟ
ΜΣΟΦΟΙ ΔΙΑΧ : ΙΤ Μ Ε Ι ΔΑ Υ ΤΟ Α Μ Μ ΑΖΗ   ΧΙΕ ΜΗ Σ Ω ΕΤΟΠΙ ΟΣΥΟΧ
ΕΙ Ν ΤΣΙ ΠΡΟΤΟ ΙΧΡΥΣΕΣ ΝΕΙΧ ΘΗ ΝΑ ΕΚΤΤΟΔΟΡΑΤΟΣ ΕΤ ΜΝΕΑΙ
ΔΕΚΑΚΑΧΙΕ ΜΟΘΑΜ ΜΥ ΑΙΧ Υ Ε Ο ΠΑΛ ΥΡΟΤ ΕΕ ΚΑ
ΤΔΙΗΘΟΝΤΑΜΝ ΑΙΕΝΘΑΔ ΕΣΤΑΘΗΣΑΝ ΑΡΓ ΝΑ Υ ΤΙ
ΥΤΟ ΕΒΔΟΜΗΘΟΝΤΑ ΜΝΕΑΙ ΚΑΘΑ
ΔΕΚΑ Ε ΚΤΤΟ ΑΛΟΣ

**53**

ΑΡΙΣΤΟΚΛΕΟΣ
ΓΥΝΑΙΚΟΣ
ΤΟΤΗΛΕΦΑΝΕΟΣ
ΕΚΑΤΑΙΗΣΤΗΣ
ΔΕΟΝΥΔΟΣ

**51**

ΓΛΒΙΣ ΟΡΟΛΟ ΦΟΝΙΟΣ
ΣΥΝΥΛΑΜΜΑΤ

**56**

ΓΓΕΣΙΒΙΟΣ ΟΤΗΙΟΣ

**58**

**61**

**63**

**69**

ΣΤΗΛΗ
ΥΧΙΗΣΤΗΣ
ΛΕΩΝΟΣ
ΓΥΝΑΙΚΟΣ

**66**

Erythrai: **51.** Gravestone, *c.* 500–475? Ephesos: **53.** Silver plaque (*obverse only*), *c.* 550? Kolophon: **56.** Graffito at Abou Simbel, *c.* 591. Teos: **58.** Graffito at Abou Simbel, *c.* 591. **61.** Marble grave-stele, late 6th c.? Klazomenai: **63.** Painted inscription on vase, *c.* 540–525? **66.** Gravestone, *c.* 475–450? Smyrna: **69.** Graffito on vase, end of 7th c.?

**1**

**2**

**3a**

**3b**

**4a**

ANAXZANOPEP

ΣΟΧΙΤΑΜΑΨ //////////// .... ........ ΝΟΤΑΡΠΟΤ

ΘΟΙΛΛΥΣΙΟΣΘΟΚΑΒΑΖΙΛ
ΖΒΕΛΑΣΕΣΤΟΝΣΤΡΑΤΟΝ

**4b**

**5**

**8**

**6**

**9**

**10**

**11**

**13**

Graffiti on pottery: **1.** 8th c.?; **2.** *c.* 650–600?; **3 a–b.** 7th c.? **4 a–b.** Inscriptions at Abou Simbel, *c.* 591. **5.** Gravestone (?) (*front and back*) *c.* 600–575? **6.** Inscription cut on statuette, *c.* 600–550? **8.** Graffito on vase, *c.* 600–550? **9.** Graffito on plastic vase, *c.* 550? **10.** Basalt statuette *c.* 550? **11.** Stone fragment, *c.* 550? **13.** Miniature bronze wheel, *c.* 550–525?

PLATE 68                    DORIC HEXAPOLIS

ΑΠΟΛ
ΛΩΝΟ
ΣΠΥΟΙΟ
**39**

**44**        **45**        **43**

**41**

**47**

ΒΑΣΙΛΕΟΣΕΛΘΟΝΤΟΣΕΣΕΛΕΦΑΝΤΙΝΑΝΨΑΜΑΤΙΧΟ
ΝΑΥΤΑΕΓΡΑΨΑΝΤΟΙΣΙΝΨΑΜΜΑΤΙΧΟΙΤΟΙΘΕΟΚΛΟΣ
ΕΠΛΕΟΝΑΛΘΟΝΔΕΚΕΡΚΙΟΣΚΑΤΥΠΕΘΘΕΙΥΙΣΟΠΟΤΑΜΟΣ
ΑΝΙΕΛΟΓΛΟΣΟΣΟΘΕ ΠΟΤΑΣΙΜΤΟΔΙΓΥΠΤΙΟΣΔΕΡΜΑΣΙΣ
ΕΓΡΑΦΕΔΑΜΕΑΡΧΟΝΑΜΟΙΒΙΧΟΚΑΙΠΕΛΕΦΟΣΟΥΔΑΜΟ
*a*

ΚΑΙΞ
ΚΡΙΘΙΣΕΓΡΑΔΕΜ          ΓΥΘΟΝΑΜΟΙΒΙΧΟΥ
*b*                    **48**              *c*

Kos: **39.** Boundary stone, *c.* 450? Halikarnassos: **41.** Gravestone, *c.* 475? Kalymna: **43–44.** Graffiti on sherds, 8th c.?
**45.** Painted inscription on sherd, early 7th c. **47.** Painted inscriptions on plate, *c.* 600? Egypt: **48 *a–c.*** Graffiti at Abou
Simbel, *c.* 591.

ΜΕΛΑΝΘΙΟΣΜΕΑΝΕΦΗΚΕΤΩΙΗΘΝΙΘΗΒΔΙΩΙΑΚΑΛΜΑ

49

51

| ΠΥΘΕΡΜΟΣΜΕΟΝΕΛΛΝΟΣΕΛΥΣ |
|---|
| ΑΤΟΤ ΗΣΕΣΙΟΣΑΓΑΛΜΑ |

50

---

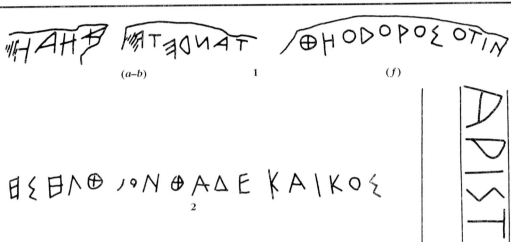

(a–b)     1     (f)

ΘΣΒΛΘ ΙΟΝΘΑΔΕ ΚΑΙΚΟΣ

2

8

ΑΡΙΣΤΑΜΡΕΙΚ
ΣΟΙΚ

10

10

ΝΒΥΜΟΜΜ

13

Egypt: **49.** Bronze sheathing, *c.* 550–525? **50.** Bronze statuette, *c.* 500? **51.** Graffito at Abydos, *c.* 500–450?
Aiolis: **1.** Graffiti on sherds, (*a–b*) 7th c.?, (*f*) 6th c. **2.** Graffito at Abydos, 6th c.? **8.** Inscribed stone door-
post (?), *c.* 550–500? **10.** Marble grave-column, *c.* 550–525? Potidaia: **10.** Stone base, *c.* 475? Olynthos:
**13.** Gravestone, *c.* 500–480.

Olynthos: **14.** Grave-stele, *c.* 450–425. Mende: **33.** Statue-base, *c.* 450–425. Perinthos: **35.** Marble stele, *c.* 525? **36.** Marble grave-stele, *c.* 525? Kalchedon: **41.** Marble grave-stele, mid-6th c.? Prokonnesos and Sigeion: **43–44.** Marble grave-stele, mid-6th c.? Lampsakos: **48.** Marble grave-stele, *c.* 450–425? Sidene: **50.** Marble column, *c.* 525–500 (*squeeze*).

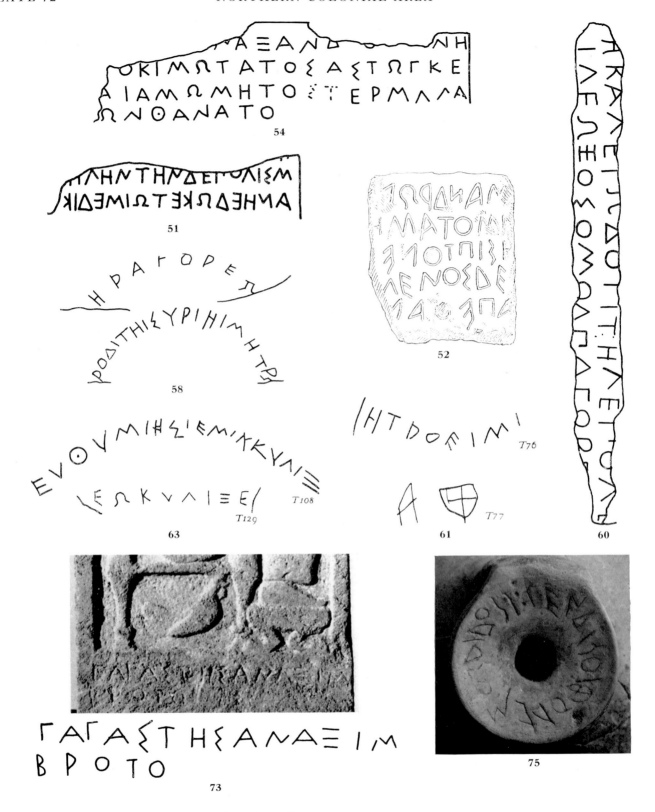

54

51

52

58

T76

ΗΡΑΓΟΡΕ

ΡΟΔΙΤΗΣΕΥΡΙΗΙΜΗΤΡΗ

ΕΥΟΥΜΙΗΣΙΕΜΙΚΚΥΛΙΞ

ΙΕΛΚΥΛΙΞΕΙ  T108

T129

63

61  T77

60

ΓΑΓΑΣΤΗΣΑΝΑΞΙΜ
ΒΡΟΤΟ

73

75

Kyzikos: **51.** Marble stele, *c.* 525–500?  Halone: **52.** Gravestone, *c.* 550?  Apollonia: **54.** Marble stele-base, *c.* 500–475. Olbia: **58.** Graffiti on sherds, 6th–5th c. (T41 & 25*). **60.** Marble grave-relief, *c.* 500–475. Borysthenes: **61*.** Graffiti on sherds, 6th c. Nymphaion: **63*.** Graffiti on sherds, 5th c. Sinope: **73.** Marble grave-relief, *c.* 450? Sigeion (?): **75.** Graffito on aryballos, *c.* 600–575? (*T = Tolstoi.)

# TABLE OF LETTERS

# TABLE OF LETTERS

| | N. Semitic | Attica, Sigeion | Euboia | Boiotia | Thessaly | Phokis | Lokrides and colonies | Aigina, Kydonia | Corinth, Korkyra | Megara, Byzantion | Sikyon | Phleious, Kleonai, Tiryns | Argos, Mycenae | Eastern Argolid | Lakonia, Messenia, Taras | Arkadia |
|---|---|---|---|---|---|---|---|---|---|---|---|---|---|---|---|---|
| Alpha | ⱅ | A | A | A | A | A,A | A,A | A | A,A | A | A | A | A | A | A | A |
| Beta | 9 | B | B | B | B | B | B | B | ⊔Γ | ᔓ | B | ㇄ | Ϲ | B | B | B |
| Gamma | ˥ | Λ ΓϹ | ΓϹ | Γ | Ϲ | Ϲ,Γ | Γ | ΓϹ | Ϲ | Ϲ | Γ | Γ | Γ | Γ | Ϲ |
| Delta | ◁ | Δ | Δ,D | D | D | D | D | Δ | Δ | Δ | Δ | Δ | D | D,Δ | D | D |
| Epsilon | ㇌ | Ϝ | Ϝ | Ϝ | Ϝ | Ϝ | Ϝ | Ϝ | B,Ϝ | B,E | ⴼ,Ϝ | Ϝ | Ϝ | Ϝ | Ϝ |
| Vau | Y,Ч | Ϝ | ϜϹ | ϜϹ | ϜϹ | ϜϹ | ϜϜ | ϜϜ | — | ϜϜ | Ϝ | Ϝ | ϜϜ | ϜϜ | ϜϜ | ϜϹ? |
| Zeta | ⊥ | I | I | I | I | I | I | I | I | | I | | I | I | I |
| Eta | — | — | — | — | — | — | — | — | — | — | ß | — | — | — |
| Heta | ᛃ | 日 | 日 | 日 | 日 | 日 | 日 | 日 | 日 | 日 | H | 日 | 日 | 日 | 日 |
| Theta | ⊕ | ⊕ | ⊕ | ⊕ | ⊕ | ⊕ | ⊕ | ⊕ | ⊕ | ⊕ | ⊕ | ⊕ | ⊕ | ⊕ | ⊕ |
| Iota | ㇉ | I | I | I | I | I | I | I | Ϟ,Ϛ | I | Ϛ,I | I | I | I | I,Ϛ |
| Kappa | Ϟ | K | K | K | K | K | K | K | K | K | K | K | K | K | K |
| Lambda | ㇄ | L | L | L | ᒋ | ᒋ | Γ,L | ᒋ | Γ | Λ | ᒋ | ᒋ | ᒋ | Γ | Λ | Λ |
| Mu | ㋲ | Μ | Μ,Μ | Μ | Μ | Μ | Μ | Μ | Μ | Μ | Μ | Μ | Μ | Μ | Μ | Μ,) |
| Nu | Ч | Ν | Ν | Ν | Ν | Ν | Ν | Ν | Ν | Ν | Ν | Ν | Ν | Ν | Ν |
| Xi | Ŧ | ΧϹ | ⊞ | ΧϚ | + | + | + | ΧϚ | 王 | 王 | 王 | 王 | ŦHH | + | Χ | Χ |
| Omikron | O | O | O | O | O | O | O | O | O | O | O | O | O | O | O | O |
| Pi | ㇝ | Γ | Γ | Γ | Γ | Γ | Γ | Γ | Γ | Γ | Γ | Γ | Γ | Γ | Γ | Γ |
| San | ㇏ | — | [Μ] | — | — | Μ? | — | — | Μ | — | Μ | Μ | Μ | ? | [Μ] | — |
| Qoppa | Ϙ | Ϙ | Ϙ | Ϙ | Ϙ | Ϙ | Ϙ | Ϙ | Ϙ | | Ϙ | Ϙ | Ϙ | | [Ϙ] | Ϙ |
| Rho | ㇂ | P | PR | PR | PR | PR | PR | P | P | DⱯ | PD | P | PR | PR | PR | PR |
| Sigma | w | Ϛ | Ϛ | Ϛ,Ϛ | Ϛ | Ϟ | Ϛ,Ϛ | Ϛ,Ϛ | — | Ϛ | — | — | Ϛ | Ϛ,Ϛ | Ϛ,Ϛ | Ϛ |
| Tau | Χ,† | Τ | Τ | Τ | Τ | Τ | Τ | Τ | Τ | Τ | Τ | Τ | Τ | Τ | Τ | Τ |
| Upsilon | — | Υ | Υ | Υ | Υ | V | Υ | V | Υ | V | Υ | Υ | Υ | Υ | Υ |
| Phi | — | Φ | Φ | Φ | Φ | Φ | Φ | Φ | Φ | Φ | Φ | Φ | Φ | Φ | Φ |
| Chi | — | Χ | Ψↆ | Ψↆ | Ψↆ | Ψↆ | Ψↆ | Χ | Χ | Χ | Χ | Χ | Χ | Χ,ↆ | Ψↆ | Ψↆ |
| Psi | — | Φϛ | Φϛ | Φϛ | Φϛ | Φϛ | * | Φϛ | Ψↆ | ↆ | | ↆ | | Φϛ | * |
| Omega | — | — | — | — | — | — | — | — | — | — | 8? | — | — | — | — |
| Punct. | ꞏ | ⠆ | ⠆ | | ⠆ | | ⠆ | ⠆ | ⠆ | ꞏ | ꞏ | ⠆ | ⠆ | ⠆ | ) | ⠆ |

Key: X + (e.g.) = earlier and later form. X, + = both forms attested, one not necessarily earlier than the other. [X] = letter attested only in abece-daria. — = letter not used. A blank = letter not yet attested. This table gives only typical forms for the identification of a script; for all details, see the text-figures.

Row labels (left column, bottom to top):

- Aiolis
- Knidos
- Rhodes, Gela, Akragas
- Ionic Dodekapolis and colonies
- Melos, Sikinos, Anaphe
- Thera, Kyrene
- Crete
- Delos, Keos, Syros
- Paros, Thasos
- Naxos, Amorgos
- Megara Hyblaia, Selinous
- Syracuse and colonies
- Euboic W. colonies
- Ithake, Kephallenia
- Aitolia, Epeiros
- Achaïa and colonies
- Elis